THE BOOK LOVER'S GUIDE TO FLORIDA

EDITED BY KEVIN M. MCCARTHY

Pineapple Press, Inc.
Sarasota, Florida

Copyright © 1992 by Kevin M. McCarthy

Inquiries should be addressed to:
Pineapple Press, Inc.
P.O. Drawer 16008
Southside Station
Sarasota, Florida 34239

LIBRARY OF CONGRESS
CATALOGING-IN-PUBLICATION DATA

The book lover's guide to Florida : authors, books, and literary sites / Kevin M. McCarthy, editor. — 1st ed.
p.   cm.
Includes bibliographical references and index.
ISBN 1-56164-012-3 : $27.95. — ISBN 1-56164-021-2 (pbk.) : $18.95
1. American literature — Florida—History and criticism. 2. Authors, American — Homes and haunts — Florida. 3. Authors, American — Florida — Biography. 4. Literary landmarks — Florida. 5. Florida — Intellectual life. 6. Florida in literature. 7. Florida — Bibliography. 8. Florida — Guidebooks. I. McCarthy, Kevin.
PS266.F6B66   1992
810.9'9759—dc20   92-20483
                                                          CIP

First edition
10 9 8 7 6 5 4 3 2 1

Design and composition by Millicent Hampton-Shepherd
Printed and bound by Edwards Brothers, Ann Arbor, Michigan

ACKNOWLEDGMENTS

For their assistance in various ways we would like to thank the following: Elizabeth Alexander, Bobbie Amo, Ed Baatz, Elizabeth Baker, Ken Barrett, Jr., Virginia Barrett, Norton Baskin, Denny R. Bowden, Margaret "Maggie" Bowman, Eileen Hubbard Butts, Angelica Carpenter, Bruce Chappell, Bill Coker, Carol Collins, Joan Crawford, Melanie Davis, Nan Dennison, Gina Dickson, Jennifer DeBolt, Judy DeBolt, Rodney Dillon, Hampton Dunn, Frances Eubank, Jeanie Fitzpatrick, Doreen Wildman Gauthier, Lillian Dillard Gibson, J.T. Glisson, Rosalie Gordon-Mills, John Griffin, Shirley Grubbs, George Hallam, George Hamilton, Gayle Harmon, Carol Harris, Karelisa Hartigan, John Hillis, Suzanne Harmon Hough, Ann Hyman, Rosemary Jones, Donald Justice, Stetson Kennedy, Katrina King, Sims D. Kline, Gertrude F. LaFramboise, Pearl Lancaster, Tina Marchese, Ellen Marcus, Karen Marlin, Martha Marth, Patricia Stone Martin, Philip May, Jr., Lea Michaelov, Asher Milbauer, Jack M. Moore, Marjorie Niblack, Joseph and Virginia Nolan, Sudie and Hamilton Nolan, Bob Perdue, Olive Peterson, Ann Peyton, Jolie Pond, Justine Postal, Bob Plunket, Kate Reich, Carol Rigolot, Joanne Runkel, Marjorie Schuck, James A. Servies, Becky Smith, Mary Elizabeth Streeter, Leilani Tillis, Jean Trebbi, Katherine and Henry Twine, Diane Vosatka, Vicki Webber, Ann Wilder, Lois Wolfe, John Wollinka, and Arnold Wood.

Also the following organizations: St. Augustine Historical Society, the Halifax Historical Society, and public libraries throughout the state.

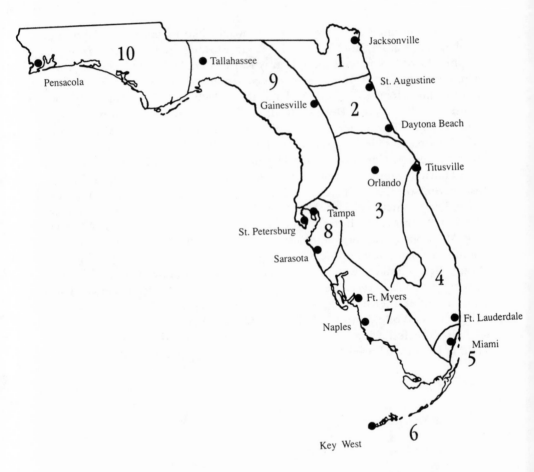

10

Pensacola

Tallahassee

9

Gainesville

Jacksonville

1

St. Augustine

2

Daytona Beach

Titusville

Orlando

Tampa

St. Petersburg

8

3

Sarasota

4

Ft. Myers

Naples

7

Ft. Lauderdale

Miami

5

Key West

6

CONTENTS

INTRODUCTION

Florida has attracted countless millions over the past five hundred years. Native Americans seeking better fishing grounds, Spanish conquistadors looking for a fountain of youth, French Huguenots hoping to establish a religious colony, developers looking for land on which to build high-rises, and Cuban refugees seeking political freedom: the Sunshine State has welcomed all. Including writers. Some of the latter have chosen to come for all or part of the year to write about other places, but even their choice of Florida for their residence tells us something about a land conducive to writers, if only in terms of a beautiful climate. Some have chosen to live here and write about their new home in fiction and nonfiction, in poetry and drama, in essays and editorials.

That symbiotic relationship of writer to land has been rocky. Some writers have concentrated on the mosquitoes and swamps and hurricanes and race riots and drug traffic; others have highlighted the voluminous springs and majestic panthers and moon-launch sites. Florida is all of those elements, and more. In fact, the state can easily surprise the unsuspecting in its length (the distance from Key West to Pensacola by road is longer than that between Jacksonville and Washington, D.C.), its ethnic groups (Hispanics, Afro-Americans, Czechs, Greeks, Italians, Minorcans), and its history (more Spanish than English or French). This work is no provincial effusion, no claim that Florida is the Athens of the South. Rather, the nine writers here contend that this state has much more to offer in cultural terms than theme parks, beaches, and football teams.

The origin of this book can be traced back to the summer of 1977 when I began camping my way around the state, determined to find out what literary sites it had. I spent much time in libraries and bookstores, asking knowledgeable residents about the writers, movies made or set in locales, literature set in each part, histories of the sites, even where the place name came from. As a young know-it-all Yankee in the early 1970s, I thought that I had found the formula for all of Florida fiction: an exotic setting (the Everglades, sea-swept island in the Keys, Spanish Pensacola), a natural disaster (hurricane, tidal wave, conflagration), villain (land developer, flim-flam artist, saboteur), maybe even a menacing animal (alligator, panther, wild boar); such a combination exists in many Florida novels, but in only a small percentage of them. Instead I found the same themes and characters found in good fiction from around the world; what I did not find in non-Florida literature was the particular touch this state exerts on writers in terms of climate, history, and mind-set. If place profoundly influences our lives and culture, then surely Florida has a place in journeys of literary America.

In the 1980s I came to know the other eight writers featured here, scholars who felt as I did, that residents and visitors to our state should know what literary culture Florida offers. The nine writers here have written or edited 30 books and numerous articles about Florida; they live in the area they write about or have frequently visited the area and are therefore more knowledgeable than a literary carpetbagger from elsewhere.

What we have tried to do is to describe many sites in the state from a literary point of view: what authors lived in or wrote about the place, which books and important articles describe the places, what important movies were made there, even literary trivia that we feel visitors might want to know to better grasp this sense of place. We have not tried to list every author who ever came to the state or who wrote about it. Our general criterion was that in order to be included an author had to have two significant books published. We have tried to give exact locations for as many authors as we could, but in general we have not listed street addresses of those still living here; writers intensely guard their privacy, and we would not intrude. We have concentrated on those authors who have lived here and who wrote about the state, while mentioning those who have lived here but written about other locales. If we have left out authors that should have been included, we invite readers to send in their suggested names to the editor whose address is below.

We have in general emphasized those books published since 1950 because books published before then are difficult for readers to obtain; those wishing to know more fiction titles should consult Janette C. Gardner's *An Annotated Bibliography of Florida Fiction 1801-1980* (St. Petersburg: Little Bayou Press, 1983) with its chronological, title, subject, and locale index.

Instead of a gazetteer arrangement, simply listing in alphabetical order the important sites associated with authors, we have chosen to divide the state into ten parts and to proceed along the main highways. We include information not often found in such guides, namely the origin of place names and a listing of further reading, both fiction and nonfiction, for each place. For the former we are indebted to *Florida Place Names* by Allen Morris (Univ. of Miami Press, 1974) and *Places in the Sun* by Bertha E. Bloodworth and Alton C. Morris (Univ. Presses of Florida, 1978); for the latter we thank the countless librarians and bookstore friends who have supplied us with much information. Sources of quotations in the text can be found at the end of the book.

Our hope is that some (many?) of the 12,000,000 residents living here now or the 900-plus who arrive every day or the 44,000,000 annual visitors would like to know more about this marvelous state than where the best surfing is or what theme parks are in a particular city or when the next shuttle launch is. And maybe the book will inspire a would-be author to write a novel about some neglected personage or slighted battle or disparaged place mentioned here. Good traveling and reading!

Kevin M. McCarthy
Department of English
University of Florida
Gainesville, FL 32611

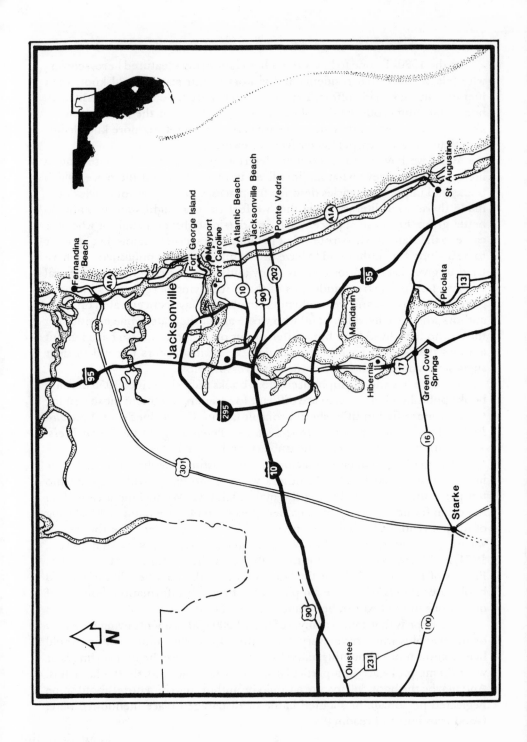

1 FERNANDINA BEACH TO PICOLATA & OLUSTEE

GARY L. HARMON

After the journey undertaken in this book, one thing at least is clear: authors, literature and lore, and history itself have distinguished and dramatized if not, on occasion, reinvented this area. Northeast Florida's songs and stories, authors and history offer a time-travel adventure from the legendary past of early settlements amid a mix of mud, swamp-marsh miasma, lazy rivers, and pine forests, through the era of Cracker towns, to the present of sprawling suburbs, rural communities, and downtown Jacksonville's few shining towers. Our book lover's tour of Florida begins in this northeast section, aptly renamed Florida's First Coast, as indeed it is, historically.

A sort of mythic parallel to our tour exists: we begin this exploration of Florida in the same northeast region the first Europeans settled in the sixteenth century, the region **William Bartram**, the late-eighteenth century naturalist, described in 1773, early in his four-year expedition through the Southeast to collect and classify exotic flora and fauna. As he skirted the shores of the "golden isles," including Amelia, the southernmost, he recorded in his *Travels* vivid first impressions we might wish to experience today, more than two hundred years later.

> ...we landed on the main. It was a promontory of high land, covered with orange-trees, and projecting into the sound, forming a convenient port. We pitched our tent under the shelter of a forest of Live Oaks, Palms, and Sweet Bays; and having, in the course of the day, procured plenty of sea fowl, such as curlews, willets, snipes, sand birds, and others, we had them dressed for supper and seasoned with excellent oysters, which lay in heaps in the water, close to our landing place.

Bartram is not the last to record awed emotions while spending the first day or night among the green groves and blue waters of *La Florida*, as the Spanish named it.

Previously called the Florida Crown, this northeast region seems to "crown" the state's peninsular landmass. But the regal connotations of this name link the area to the history of European crowns who made land grants to early settlers here. By the turn of the twentieth century, the area had earned the name Gateway to Florida. Soon, Henry Flagler extended his railway along the coast, reaching Key West by 1913; by so doing, he connected this northeast Florida sector to northern civilization and introduced the signs of industrial progress to a basically rural southern backwater. If New York was the gateway to America for masses of Europeans, and St. Louis was the gateway to the West for the pioneers, then northeast Florida was the gateway to the land of sandy shores and sunshine for commercial travel and successive waves of tourists.

All trains traveling to Miami, Tampa, or Fort Myers had to pass through Jacksonville and this Gateway area, bringing with them commerce, money, people, and — for our purposes — the connections and culture that would form the inspiration for the songs and stories emanating from Florida. In that era **Stephen Crane**, perhaps cruising by steamer along the coast — or riding Henry Flagler's new train tracks, arrived to visit Cora Taylor and create the legend of their famous romance centered in Jacksonville's then-red-light district.

Before the gradually increasing movement of late-nineteenth-century travelers, however, explorers and visionaries such as **William Bartram** (1739-1823) and **John Muir** (1838-1914) had passed through the region, recording their impressions and creating lenses through which strangers to the area would come to understand the nature of the place. In 1867, while passing from Amelia through Jacksonville to Cedar Key during the Florida portion of his 1000-mile trek from Louisville, Muir gained the definitive insight guiding the rest of his life: that the world was not made for mankind. His goal thereafter, he wrote, was to save humans for the wilderness, and the wilderness for humans. [See note.]

In 1867, **Ledyard Bill** wrote one of the earliest travel guides that begins in this region. His book *A Winter in Florida* is a narrative, a travel story, in which he observes that, though settlement, wars, destruction, and rebirth have occurred, yet "now the original wilderness everywhere covers the state, and as nearly primeval as in the time of Adam." As he enters the St. Johns River, he transforms the literal landscape into an Edenic vision: "It is undoubtedly the gate, as it were, to that tropical land where perpetual summer reigns. . . . On the north-western side of the city [Jacksonville] is a beautiful bluff, covered with attractive residences, shaded with stately trees, and bearing the pleasant name of 'La Villa.'" Travel literature of the late nineteenth century characteristically transforms the region into such idyllic visions.

Our tour winds through Nassau, Duval and — downriver — St. Johns and Clay counties. We progress from Fernandina on Amelia Island south along the coast to Ponte Vedra Beach, westward through Jacksonville and then southward on the St. Johns River to Picolata on the east bank and back north to the Buckman bridge and across the river to the west bank, moving southward through Orange Park and Hibernia, then leaving the river to travel westward toward Starke (and the state correctional institution at Raiford) and then Olustee.

FERNANDINA BEACH TO PONTE VEDRA BEACH

Fernandina Beach

At Florida's northeastern tip, at the Florida-Georgia border, Amelia Island and its two chief towns of Fernandina and Fernandina Beach offer a tranquility and peace unique to north Florida. Hundreds of acres of pine forests and marshes, fronted on the east side by the Atlantic Ocean and on the west by the inland waterway, offer a haven with the aura of a more serene time and place.

First named Santa Maria Island, after the Spanish mission here in the seventeenth century, this pleasant retreat became Amelia Island in 1736 when General Oglethorpe renamed it after the daughter of England's George II. The village, originally called Old Town, became Fernandina in 1811 when the Spanish governor pronounced that the island would take the name of King Ferdinand VII of Spain. The Spanish fort San Fernando, also named for the king, was built in 1686 at the island's north end, then moved to the south end, serving as the original inspiration for the name Fernandina. Another, competing story, probably apocryphal, connects the name Fernandina to a local eighteenth-century landholder, Don Domingo Fernandez. The village claims to be the second-oldest settlement in the United States, after St. Augustine to the south. Today, Fernandina calls itself The Ocean City because of its geography, history, and present reliance on the sea for a livelihood.

The surrounding county of Nassau commemorates with its name the Bahamians who immigrated here in large numbers during the British occupation of northeastern Florida (1763-1783). The area attracted many colonists loyal to England during the American Revolutionary War, including some from England's 13 colonies north of Florida. Spain's control of Florida for several centuries isolated the Florida peninsula from its neighbors to the north and slowed its eventual integration into the new American republic.

One side-street tour of Fernandina's houses with their gingerbread designs, towers, and porches can convince a traveler that Florida offers much more than golden beaches and high-rise condominiums. The state's oldest saloon, The Palace, built in 1878 in Fernandina, offers hand-painted murals, large cuspidors, and beveled-glass windows in walls seven bricks thick. Apart from a time when it served as an ice-cream parlor, The Palace has quenched the thirst of countless travelers and still deserves an appreciative stop from the contemporary visitor.

Despite Amelia Island's relative isolation from Interstate 95, its rich pirate lore, and a history involving some of Florida's most colorful characters, relatively few novelists have taken advantage of this rich source for dramatic stories. **Velda Johnston's** suspense novel, *The White Pavilion* (New York: Dodd, Mead, 1973), weaves its mystery around a young New York woman who reluctantly returns to her family home, on a north Florida island resembling Amelia, to catalogue family possessions she will inherit. **Lace Kendall's** *Rain Boat* (New York: Coward McCann, 1965) features the fictional town of Spanish

Fort at a time when England controlled Florida. **Baynard Kendrick's** *The Flames of Time* (New York: Scribner's Sons, 1948) also takes place on Amelia between 1787 and 1812. **Sam S. Slate** placed his *Satan's Back Yard* (New York: Doubleday, 1974) on Amelia to tell the story, set in the early 1800s, of a few American patriots who attempted to liberate Florida from the Spaniards. Georgians called Florida "Satan's Back Yard" at that time because of grief and bloodshed over the struggle between Americans and Spanish for the land. **Frank G. Slaughter's** *The Golden Isle* (Garden City, NY: Doubleday, 1947) realistically portrays the life of a doctor practicing medicine in the early 1800s on Amelia Island; Slaughter, a Jacksonville author/doctor, wrote several novels about historical episodes and medical situations set in Florida.

Georgia poet **Sidney Lanier** recognized the area's riches. While he also traveled down the St. Johns, his impressive poem, "The Marshes of Glynn," captures the aura of the vast marsh at the Florida-Georgia border. The poem reveals his gift for expressing the charm and morally uplifting beauty of what others often see as commonplace in this wild yet inspiring place:

> Inward and outward to northward and southward the beach lines
>   linger and curl
> As a silver wrought garment that clings to and follows the firm
>   sweet limbs of a girl.

This talented, neglected poet offers an internal, emotional tour of this still vast north Florida marshland, supplementing our physical tour.

Newspapers also play a role in the history of northeast Florida. While St. Augustine can rightly claim Florida's first newspaper, *The East Florida Gazette* (1783-1784), Amelia Island can claim its second: *El Telegrafo de las Floridas*, a Spanish weekly established in 1817. Its editor, **Vicente Pazos**, formerly editor of *La Cronica Argentina* in Buenos Aires, announced that the newspaper would record the events on Amelia Island and also extract articles of interest from North American and foreign papers. The first issue announced a meeting of the representatives of the Floridas and their plans to organize a new island government that would secede from Spanish control and set up a Republic of Florida. The newspaper soon ceased publishing because in December 1817 American war vessels quickly quashed the attempted establishment of a new government. For more about that early attempt at newspapering see **Charles H. Bowman, Jr.**, "Vicente Pazos and the Amelia Island Affair, 1817," *Florida Historical Quarterly* 53 (1975), p. 291 and **T. Frederick Davis**, "MacGregor's Invasion of Florida, 1817," *Florida Historical Society Quarterly* 7 (1928), p. 48.

The Intracoastal Waterway entering Florida at Fernandina Beach and gliding along the east coast plays an important part in a number of Florida stories, as well as the state's history and culture. Boats of all sizes cruise this liquid highway from New Jersey to southern Florida, and stories of yachts, smuggling, and battles romanticize this intracoastal path. For more about the waterway, especially for boaters heading south, see **Fessenden S. Blanchard's** *A Cruising Guide to the Inland Waterway and Florida* (New York: Dodd, Mead, 1958).

Joseph Burkholder Smith's *The Plot to Steal Florida* (New York: Arbor House, 1983) tells the nonfiction story of the Patriot Army of George Mathews that captured Fernandina in 1811, the same event featured in Slate's novel *Satan's Back Yard* (mentioned earlier). Mathews and his men planned to capture Amelia Island and then offer it to the United States. They managed to capture the island and first ran up their patriot flag for a day, substituting the United States flag the next day. But when Great Britain protested the patriots' year-long plundering of Florida plantations, the United States disassociated itself from Mathews and his soldiers.

In 1817 a Scottish adventurer named Gregor MacGregor captured Fernandina for several South American governments. An anonymous witness to this episode, known as the Amelia Island Affair, wrote *Narrative of a Voyage to the Spanish Main in the Ship "Two Friends"* (1819; reprinted by the University Presses of Florida, 1978). This Affair and Andrew Jackson's invasion of West Florida in 1818 prompted the United States to take control of Florida. Another book, *The Illustrated History of Florida Paper Money* (Jacksonville: Cassidy, 1980) by **Daniel G. Cassidy** describes the kinds of paper money used in the Florida of this era, including the dollars Gregor MacGregor printed in Fernandina in 1817.

The Union blockade of Florida during the Civil War prevented Fernandina Beach from becoming a major port on the Atlantic, despite the heavy traffic of smuggled goods entering the state. Florida's first senator, David L. Yulee, built a railroad from Fernandina to Cedar Key on Florida's west coast, connecting the Atlantic Ocean with the Gulf of Mexico; developers dreamed this Florida Railroad would spur profitable commerce in much of north Florida. Finished just as the Civil War started in 1861, the railroad never recovered from the war. *Adventurers in Florida History* (Pensacola: Town and Country Books, 1974) by **W.B. "Woody" Skinner** and **W. George Gaines** tells the story of Yulee and other history makers in the state.

Among the significant African-Americans who grew up in Fernandina was Richard Samuel Roberts (1880-1936), a commercial photographer who worked as a stevedore and then as a fireman-laborer in the Fernandina post office. He established and ran The Gem Studio in Fernandina, taking photographs of the local community and perfecting the photography skills he had taught himself. In 1920 he and his family moved to Columbia, South Carolina, where he continued taking photographs of the black community. Many years after he died, researchers discovered more than 3,000 of his glass photographic plates and published a selection in *A True Likeness: The Black South of Richard Samuel Roberts, 1920-1936* edited by **Thomas L. Johnson** and **Phillip C. Dunn** (Columbia, SC: Bruccoli Clark, 1986).

Nonfiction books recording Amelia Island's history and lore include *Florida: A Guide to the Southernmost State* (1939, directed by **Carita Doggett Corse**; reprinted New York: Pantheon Books, as *The WPA Guide to Florida: The Federal Writers Project Guide to 1930s Florida*, 1984) with a 13-page section on Fernandina; this book provides an older, but rich account of the island, along with 22 tours of other representative Florida locations. *Yesterday's Reflections*

(1976; revised, Callahan, FL: T.O. Richardson, 1984) by **Jan H. Johannes, Sr.** contains numerous historic photographs and vignettes of the county. **Helen Gordon Litrico**'s three works reflect close-up views: *Centre St. Fernandina: A Walking Tour of the Historic District* (Fernandina Beach, FL: Amelia Island Fernandina Restoration Foundation, 1976) describes preservation work in the historic district of Fernandina; *Amelia Island Explored* (Amelia Island, FL: Amelia Island Plantation, 1973) offers more history and photographs of the island; and *The Best of Amelia Now* (Litrico, available from Mickler's Floridiana in Chuluota, 1991) provides a wide range of history, facts, lore, and recent information. A more technical book explaining the early Indian and Spanish settlements on the island is *Excavations on Amelia Island in Northeast Florida* (Gainesville: Florida State Museum Publications, 1973) by **E. Thomas Hemmings** and **Kathleen A. Deagan**. *Florida Lighthouses* (Gainesville: The University of Florida Press, 1990) by **Kevin McCarthy** with paintings by **William L. Trotter** explains the background for the lighthouse on Amelia, along with lighthouses throughout Florida. *Victorian Florida: America's Last Frontier* by **Floyd** and **Marion Rinhart** (Atlanta: Peachtree Publishers, 1986) includes some early scenes of Fernandina as well as other parts of the state. "Fort San Carlos" in *Notes in Anthropology*, Volume 14 (Tallahassee: Florida State University, 1971) by **Hale G. Smith** and **Ripley P. Bullen** describes the fort's history and function.

In addition, a few self-published books of poetry about the island circulate in the area: *Fernandina* (1981), *Amelia* (1982), *Cottage Pudding Dreams* (1984), and *Before Angels* (1988) by **Nola Perez**; *The Crow Calls* (1991) by **John T. Everly**; *Ballads of the Dorion Dig* (1990) by **Denny Smith**; and *Landfall* (1988) by Nassau County Writers and Poets.

Amelia Island's most notable literary figure was novelist and editor **T. Howard Kelly**, born on the island in 1895 and author of several popular novels, mainly with World War I themes: *What Outfit, Buddy* (1920); *The Unknown Soldier* (1929); *Roll Call From on High* (1936); and others. His many feature articles concentrated on World War I and several Florida treasure hunts; Kelly also served in various editorial posts with *McClure's, Smart Set, Cosmopolitan*, and several Hearst magazines. He summered for many years in Fernandina Beach at 4250 Fletcher Avenue, until his death there in 1967.

Fort George Island

This island, south of Amelia Island on the so-called Buccaneer Trail (State Road A1A), figures prominently in **Eugenia Price**'s *Don Juan McQueen* (Philadelphia: Lippincott, 1974), a novel dramatizing the history of Spanish East Florida between 1791 and 1807. Price portrays a bankrupt American from Georgia, John McQueen, who moves to this section of Florida to escape debtors' prison. Her novel *Lighthouse* (Philadelphia: Lippincott, 1971), while set mostly off the coast of Georgia, continues the depiction of historic Spanish East Florida and the larger-than-life character of Don Juan McQueen.

On Fort George Island the traveler can visit the Kingsley Plantation House, built around 1800 and thus the oldest plantation house in Florida. **Zephaniah Kingsley** (1765-1843), a Scot who married an African Senegalese princess named Anna Madgigiane Jai and first lived with her near Doctor's Inlet on the St. Johns, imported hundreds of African slaves in his own ships and trained his human cargo for various skilled trades. Anna Jai was the first of four African women Kingsley married, establishing each on separate plantations along the St. Johns. See **Carita Doggett Corse**, *The Key to the Golden Islands* (Chapel Hill, NC: University of North Carolina, 1931) for more about Kingsley and life on the other islands in this area. Clay County, southwest of Jacksonville, commemorates him with Kingsley Lake and the town of Kingsley near Starke. In *A Treatise on the Patriarchal System of Society*, Kingsley argued that

> under a just and prudent system of management, negroes are safe, permanent, productive and growing property, and easily governed; that they are not naturally desirous of change but are sober, discreet, honest and obliging, are less troublesome, and possess a much better moral character than the ordinary class of corrupted whites of similar condition.

His views, like those of modern-day practitioners of patriarchy, surely derive from his experience and the cultural setting in which he lived. He would have

Home of Zephaniah Kingsley, located on Fort George Island in Kingsley Plantation State Park. Photo taken in 1886.

Descendants of slaves, pictured in the 1870s or 1880s in the field by their coquina houses. Remains of the houses still exist on the Kingsley Plantation grounds.

had great difficulty rising above them, given the comfort he must have experienced with the racial and gender "system" of his time.

After Kingsley died in 1843, his niece, Mrs. Anna McNeill Whistler, the mother of the American painter James McNeill Whistler and the subject of the famous painting known as "Whistler's Mother," challenged Kingsley's will in which he had written:

> ...whereas I have an African wife, and believe that the amalgama-
> tion of the white and colored races is to the best interests of
> America, and whereas I know that what I am about to do is going
> to bring down tremendous criticism, but I don't give a damn.

Kingsley's niece objected to his having left his land and possessions to his African wife and to their sons and to two other wives and the offspring "I acknowledge are mine." She argued that the Senegalese princess was merely a slave and therefore unable to claim these possessions, especially because Florida's miscegenation laws prohibited her marriage to Kingsley. Mrs. Whistler eventually lost that legal battle in the Duval County Court. Marjorie Kinnan Rawlings had thoughts of writing a novel about Kingsley, but abandoned that idea in 1940 and wrote *Cross Creek* instead.

Even so, **Edith Pope** (1905-1961), another novelist, then living in St. Augustine, wrote the novel *Colcorton* (New York: Scribner, 1944; reprinted New York: Plume, 1990), based on the story of the enigmatic Kingsley, her only book so far to earn lasting literary importance. Inspired by Rawlings's example and use of Florida for her work, Pope drew accurate portraits of 1940s Florida, creating the once-proud house of Colcorton and its inhabitants; Abby Clanghearne, a backwoods woman and mistress of the house, keeps secret from her family her descent from the fabled old slave-trader Clanghearne and his African-princess wife. Unmarried, Abby has reared a younger brother, Jared, and sent him through the University of Florida Law School.

At the novel's opening, Jared returns to Colcorton with his bride, Beth, sets up his law practice, and then accidentally discovers his mixed ancestry. While Abby has lived ably with this fact, Jared loses control of his life as a result of his identity confusion and is eventually murdered in a gambling fight. But his wife Beth is pregnant. And so the story goes, ending in Abby's retreat and her arranging for Beth and her son to move away from Colcorton to grow up free from the effects of the mixed heritage. Pope is best at portraying strong heroines who triumph over powerful histories, such as that left by Kingsley and his African wife.

The winding Fort George Island road leading from the main highway into Kingsley Plantation transports us from the twentieth century into the nineteenth, from the clamor and tension of modern life into an earlier era of political intrigue, dreams of commercial empires, and the mixing of African and American cultures. The plantation house, tabby house, and slave cabins are built from coquina, which consists of fractured and compressed sea shells. The plantation buildings provide a record, a real-life exhibit of how Floridians, both slaves and masters, lived under the Spanish before Florida became a state.

The calm setting on the scenic river evokes a way of life far different from our own, a quiet experience the traveler may enjoy by picnicking under the live oaks on the plantation grounds.

Music of Florida Historic Sites (Tallahassee: Florida State University, 1983) by **Deane L. Root** describes the music associated with Fort Clinch in Fernandina Beach and this Kingsley Plantation.

On the way to the Kingsley Plantation from the main highway, the traveler can find the site of the Mission San Juan Del Puerto, the mission of St. John of the Port, founded in the late 1500s by Franciscan missionaries and operated for over 100 years. Here, a Catholic missionary, Father Martinez, became one of the first religious martyrs in the New World. The St. Johns River takes its name from this mission. (Notice that no apostrophe appears in the name of this river; the Federal Board on Geographic Names discourages the use of the apostrophe.)

The St. Johns plays a part in **Jane Sheridan**'s fictional *Damaris* (New York: St. Martin's Press, 1978). Nonfiction works about the river include several journals and histories. **Charles E. Bennett**'s *Twelve on the River St. Johns* (Jacksonville: University of North Florida Press, 1989) portrays those who have played a major role in the history of the river — for example, William Bartram, Zephaniah Kingsley, Jean Ribault, and Eartha White. "Each story," writes Bennett, "speaks of both the individual's spiritual life and the blossoming of American idealism." **Edmund Berkeley** and **Dorothy Smith Berkeley**'s *The Life and Travels of John Bartram from Lake Ontario to the River St. John* (Tallahassee: University Presses of Florida, 1982) describes the adventures of one of Florida's most famous visitors to the river. **James Branch Cabell** and **A.J. Hanna**'s classic, *The St. Johns, A Parade of Diversities* (New York: Farrar & Rinehart, 1943), mentions that British poets such as Wordsworth, Coleridge, and Southey described the river in their own works. **Edward A. Mueller**'s *St. Johns River Steamboats* (Jacksonville: Mueller, 1986) relates the history of steamboat transportation that brought people and goods to Florida before the railroad.

A Description of the English Province of Carolana, By the Spaniards Call'd Florida, And by the French La Louisiane (1722; reprinted, Gainesville: University Presses of Florida, 1976) by **Daniel Coxe**, one of the first of many Florida promotions over the years, tried to lure Europeans to the land north of the St. Johns to Albemarle Sound. (The Picolata section, later in this chapter, provides more information about the St. Johns River as featured in British literature.)

Outside Kingsley Plantation and near State Road 105, a plaque on the right side of the road marks the site of the first Protestant prayer in North America, offered by the French explorer Jean Ribault (*Ribaut* is the old spelling) in 1562. This prayer preceded the English landing at Plymouth, Massachusetts, by about 60 years.

Several miles west on State Road 105 is Yellow Bluff Fort, designed by General Robert E. Lee and built by Confederate forces in 1862 to command the St. Johns River. Union forces took over the fort to protect their gunboats on the river.

Mayport

Across the St. Johns from Fort George Island lies Mayport, which claims to be the oldest fishing community in the United States. The town's name honors the sixteenth-century French who named the St. Johns River the *Riviere de Mai* or the May River because they discovered it on May 1, 1562.

In a more romantic view of nineteenth-century Mayport, **Robert Wilder** (1901-1974), a Daytona Beach novelist of popular historical romances from the 1940s to the 1960s, described the approach of General Burgoyne to the mouth of the St. Johns in *God Has a Long Face*, re-creating a scene many later travelers have experienced. Burgoyne's account is comparable to **Marjorie Kinnan Rawlings's** account of her first sight of the mouth of the St. Johns as she and her husband arrived by steamer. Burgoyne writes,

> ...the morning brought them their first sight of Florida. The early sun was a hot copper plate in an opal-flecked sky as the ship made the mouth of the St. Johns River and began beating his way up the tortuous channel which twisted and writhed through the marsh and sandy flats to the town twenty miles upstream. The Burgoynes stood forward, openly excited, taking in every detail of the scene from the sleek porpoise breaking the water ahead to the lazy, swooping flight of a fishing pelican.

Though cranes, bridges, and Mayport and its ships now line the same "tortuous channel," the sights still remain filled with such splendor as mythic portrayals of the river have wrought.

Mayport's U.S. Naval Station, established during World War I, is now the second-largest Navy carrier base on the eastern seaboard. *River In the Sun* (New York: Thomas Bouregy, 1958) by **Elizabeth Beatty (Teresa Holloway)** is her novel recounting the Navy's taking over Mayport for a carrier base. **Ed Smith's** *Them Good Old Days in Mayport and the Beaches* (Neptune Beach, FL: Smith, 1974) is a collection of stories and anecdotes dramatizing the Mayport area.

Governor Napoleon Bonaparte Broward (1857-1910) was born in Mayport and, among many jobs he held, was deckhand — and eventually captain — on a St. Johns River steamboat. His term of office as governor of Florida (1905-1909) spanned the initial draining of the Everglades, the establishment of the Choctawhatchee National Forest, and the amalgamation of the state-subsidized institutions of higher learning into three: The University of Florida, Florida State College for Women (later Florida State University), and Florida Agricultural and Mechanical College for Negroes (later Florida Agricultural and Mechanical University). Broward died soon after his nomination to the United States Senate. For more about him see **Samuel Proctor's** *Napoleon Bonaparte Broward: Florida's Fighting Democrat* (Gainesville: University of Florida Press, 1950).

Fort Caroline

To reach Fort Caroline, after crossing the St. Johns River by ferry, we turn right on State Road 10, then right on Girvin Road. The traveler will come to a reconstruction of Fort Caroline and a museum that describes the sixteenth-century conflict between the French, who built the fort in 1564, and the Spanish, who destroyed it in 1565. Nearby is the Ribault Memorial to the landing of French explorer Jean Ribault (or Ribaut) in 1562. The present column, erected at this site in 1924, resembles the one Ribault built at the mouth of the St. Johns on May 1, 1562, when he claimed the territory for the king of France. Passing ships can easily see the column, which the City of Jacksonville calls the Southern Plymouth Rock.

In his 23-page work, translated as *The whole & true discouerye of Terra Florida* (1563; Gainesville: University of Florida Press, 1964), one of the earliest descriptions of the state, Ribault described the coastline, geography, and Indians the French explorers met before they sailed back to France. Ribault's second-in-command, Rene de Laudonniere, returned to this area in 1564 accompanied by 300 would-be settlers and established Fort Caroline. With him was the artist Jacques Le Moyne, who made sketches of the Indians, their villages, and Ribault's monument, which the Indians were worshipping. When the Spanish destroyed Fort Caroline in 1565, Laudonniere managed to escape

Fort Caroline in 1568, showing the massacre of the French Huguenots being avenged by Dominique de Gourgues. The French and their Timucua Indian allies are attacking the fort, then called San Mateo. Remnants of the fort are visible on the grounds of the Fort Caroline National Memorial, which preserves the area on the St. Johns River just off Fort Caroline Road. This 1706 etching originally appeared among a group of such illustrations in a book by Pieter Vander Aa, and is based on an earlier painting by Jacques le Moyne.

19

and return to France. He then retired from public life and wrote *L'Histoire notable de la Floride,* which **Charles E. Bennett** translated as *Three Voyages* (Gainesville: University Presses of Florida, 1975).

Fort Caroline served as the first, though only temporary, place Protestants settled in the present-day continental United States. Historian **T. Frederick Davis** called this area the "cradle of United States history," for "the first white women and children landed in the territory now the United States in the first really substantial attempt at permanent colonization," though the actual first settlement was in Pensacola in 1559. The battle at Fort Caroline between the Spaniards and French was also the first between European nations on land within the present-day boundaries of the United States. Several novels describe the founding and settlement of the fort: **Edward Secomb Fox**'s *Massacre Inlet* (Garden City, NY: Doubleday, 1965); **Richard Parker**'s *The Three Pebbles* (New York: David McKay, 1956); and **Margaret Price**'s *Miracle, A Novel of the First Florida Colonies* (New York: Library Publishers, 1955).

For more about the fort and the historically important battle, see **Charles E. Bennett**'s *Laudonniere & Fort Caroline* (Gainesville: University of Florida Press, 1964) and *Fort Caroline and Its Leader* (Gainesville: University Presses of Florida, 1976). Bennett also wrote about an abortive French-inspired invasion of Spanish East Florida from 1793 to 1795 in *Florida's "French" Revolution, 1793-1795* (Gainesville: University Presses of Florida, 1982). Selections from Ribault's work are available to the armchair traveler in one of the best collections of Florida readings: *The Florida Reader: Visions of Paradise From 1530 to the Present* edited by **Maurice O'Sullivan, Jr.** and **Jack C. Lane** (Sarasota: Pineapple Press, 1991).

Atlantic Beach

South along the coast is the town of Atlantic Beach, the primary residence of author **Pat Frank** and his wife Josephine after he left the military service in 1946. Between 1946 and 1950, the couple lived at 659 Beach Avenue in Atlantic Beach; in 1950-51, they lived in Mandarin on Loretto Road; in 1952-53 they lived at 644 Beach Avenue; and in 1953-54 they lived on South Twenty-sixth Avenue in Jacksonville Beach. After that, records are not available to locate his residence, though he moved to Atlantic Beach. Frank's first book, *Mr. Adam* (1946), was a brilliant satire which sold over two million copies. He then wrote *An Affair of State* (1948), followed by *Hold Back the Night* (1952) and *The Long Way Round* (1954), a book of nonfiction. Successful with apocalyptic disaster fiction, he also wrote *Seven Days to Never* (1957) and *How to Survive the H-Bomb and Why* (1962), his final book.

Frank is probably best-known as the author of *Alas, Babylon* (Philadelphia: Lippincott, 1959), a Florida novel about a nuclear attack on the United States. Randy Bragg, an ordinary, even lazy man living in central Florida after a nuclear bomb just missed the people in a small town nearby, courageously takes responsibility for the lives of all those he cares for: "Lib, the girl with the most beautiful legs in Florida, for his brother's wife and children, for his friends, and eventually for the whole town of Fort Repose." Unhurt, but threatened on all sides, they must use their ingenuity to start life again from scratch. The genius and appeal of this book arise from its absorbing combination of danger, adventure, humor, and romance.

Born in 1907 in Chicago, Illinois, Frank, whose real name was Harry Bart Frank, studied at the University of Florida and then worked as a journalist for *The Jacksonville Journal* from 1927 to 1929. From there he moved to New York to work as a reporter on the *New York Journal* for three years, and then for five years on the *Washington Herald*. From 1938 to the war's end, he served in the Overseas News Agency (war correspondent in Italy, Austria, Germany, Turkey, and Hungary). After the war, while writing his best-sellers from Atlantic Beach, he also worked successively with the U.S. Navy, the United Nations (as a member of the mission to Korea), the Democratic National Committee, and as a consultant to the National Aeronautics and Space Council, and the Department of Defense. In addition, he wrote numerous magazine articles while authoring his eight books. Frank died in Atlantic Beach on October 12, 1964.

Jacksonville Beach

South of Atlantic Beach is Neptune Beach, named after the Roman god of the sea. Farther south is Jacksonville Beach, formerly known as Pablo Beach and memorialized in an 1898 poem by **Maley Crist** entitled "Revery," which begins

> The green sea dimples in the glowing sun,
> And at my feet soft casts its snowy foam,
> As dreamily I gaze far oceanward,
> Nor check my fancies which so idly roam.

Today's touring beachgoer may enjoy this romantic verse, though beachfront hotels, ocean flotsam, fashionable bikinis, and Walkman radios may inspire the contemporary muse to less airy reveries.

Two poets residing in different parts of Jacksonville Beach are professors at the University of North Florida. **Mary Baron**, born in Providence, Rhode Island, in 1944, came to the University from Alaska in 1987, settling a few blocks from the ocean north of Beach Boulevard. Having earned her academic degrees successively at Brandeis, Michigan, and Illinois universities, she specializes as a professor in creative writing and the English Renaissance. Her books of poetry include *Letters for the New England Dead* (Boston: David R. Godine, Publisher, 1974) and *Wheat Among Bones* (New York: Sheep Meadow Press, 1979). Her many poems have appeared in journals, little magazines, and anthologies, and she won the nationally significant Avery Hopwood Prize for poetry. She has worked with Poets-in-the-Schools programs in Illinois and Alaska, and in northeast Florida she is the Project Director for JAXWRITE, a continuing national writing project undertaken in 1990. A few of Baron's titles suggest her thematic preoccupations: "Dreaming of the Doctor's Hands," "The baby dreams," "Winter child," "Reluctant love poem," "Christening," and "Laying on of Hands." Her current book of poems in progress is *Storyknife*.

William Slaughter, born in South Bend, Indiana, in 1943, grew up in La Porte, Indiana, later moving to West Lafayette near Purdue University where he completed his undergraduate degree, earning graduate degrees from the University of Washington and Purdue University. Coming to Jacksonville in 1972, to help open the new University of North Florida, he has offered American literature and culture as well as poetry-writing courses and workshops. On occasion, he and his wife leave their home, located across a street from the ocean, to go abroad. He has been Senior Fulbright Lecturer in Egypt and in China, and has taught in England. All three places enter into his poetry, which always centers in the self, no matter where the poem's "place" is. Slaughter has published more than 200 poems in international and well-known periodicals such as *Poetry, Chicago Review, Poetry Australia, North American Review, Canadian Forum, Poetry Wales, People's Daily* (in China), *Exquisite Corpse,* and *Critical Quarterly* (England). His first book is *Untold Stories* (Port Townsend, WA: Empty Bowl, 1990). His second book, by the same publisher, will soon appear as *The Politics of My Heart*.

In "Alibis" he writes,

> . . My subject
> has always been
> history
>
>
> vs. my own affairs.

As both a public man ("history") and a private man (his "own affairs"), his poems often center on contradictions, oppositions — love and death, the ambiguities of relationship, the profoundly divided self — and the importance of place to him. A few titles suggest these themes: "Love Song/Death Song," "Reporting from Cairo," "Laughing Man," "The Hostage," "Signing My Name," "Losing My Innocence," and "Burial Instructions."

In 1922, pilot Jimmy Doolittle used Pablo Beach to make aviation history when he took off from its smooth, hard-packed sand to become the first pilot to fly across our continent alone in less than a day. That heroic accomplishment earned him the U.S. Army's Distinguished Flying Cross, proved the practicality of transcontinental flight, and thrust him into literary legend. **Warren J. Brown**'s *Florida's Aviation History* (Largo, FL: Aero-Medical Consultants, Inc., 1980) describes similar aviation achievements in which Florida figures significantly. **Robert Hawk**'s *Florida's Air Force: Air National Guard, 1946-1990* (St. Augustine, FL: Florida National Guard Historical Foundation, 1990) focuses on Florida's 159th Fighter-Interceptor Squadron located at Jacksonville International Airport.

An incident off Jacksonville Beach 20 years after Doolittle alarmed Florida's coastal residents and prompted one of the state's most distinguished historians to write a major book. When a German U-boat torpedoed and sank the oil tanker *Gulfamerica* in April 1942, Floridians became aware of Nazi

rebuilt after the withdrawal of the Northern troops in 1863. On returning, refugees found their homes burned, trenches instead of streets, outlying farms devastated, and all ferry and dock facilities destroyed. Now the burgeoning metropolis, almost fifty percent black, boasted a population of about 7,500. Restoration was a painful process, but it was being accomplished. The St. James Hotel opened its opulent doors in 1869.

Whittington's account of nineteenth-century Jacksonville is historically accurate, while **Robert Wilder**'s *God Has a Long Face* offers a romantic view of the same growing city. Wilder's portrayal of Jacksonville's urban life is typical of novels about nineteenth-century cities: They view cities as exotic places of adventure, symbols of the positive excitement an able and eager traveler could expect to experience. Wilder's General Burgoyne ties up his ship at the Cowford dock and surveys the early-nineteenth-century scene:

> There was a brawling vigor about Jacksonville which delighted the General's rowdy soul and kept him in a state of perpetual excitement. Bay Street, running along the waterfront, was a boisterous thoroughfare of ship chandlers, warehouses, and seamen's dives. Freshly sawed yellow pine was piled high on the docks while cotton, indigo, and rosin crowded every foot of pier space awaiting shipment to the North.

By the 1880s, Jacksonville had earned the name the Winter City in Summerland for northern tourists coming to warm their skins in the Florida sun. The adventure of visiting downtown Jacksonville had changed.

By the time the railroad reached the city near the end of the century, Jacksonville had become a full-blown tourists' haven. One very literary visitor, the returning expatriate-American **Henry James** (1843-1916), spent a short time during 1905 in one of the Jacksonville hotels, observing at the time in his *American Scene* that

> I was...able, I found, to be quite Byronically foolish about the St. Johns River and the various structures, looming now through the darkness, that more or less adorned its banks.... That was the charm...the velvet air, the extravagant plants, the palms, the oranges, the cacti, the architectural fountain, the florid local monument, the cheap and easy exoticism, the sense of people feeding, off in the background, very much *al fresco*, that is on queer things and with flaring lights — one might almost have been in a corner of Naples or of Genoa.

This romantic view continues the nineteenth-century portrayal of cities, which even realist novelists such as James saw as places of exotic adventure. The transformation of American cities to symbols of corruption and industrial disasters was yet to come and would include Jacksonville.

H.L. Mencken (1880-1956), ever the ironic commentator on American life, drew "my first really juicy out-of-town assignment" from his newspaper, the *Baltimore Herald*, to cover the aftermath of the great Jacksonville fire of

May 1901. On this trip, he says, I "began to develop in a large way my theory that Service is mainly only blah." His comments, from his book *Newspaper Days: 1899-1906*, appear in the chapter called "The Gospel of Service." He solemnly informs readers that the Jacksonville blaze was the "largest blaze in American history between the burning of Chicago in 1871 and the burning of Baltimore in 1904." As he points out, the fire destroyed no fewer than "...2361 buildings, stretching over 196 city blocks and 450 acres.... All I can add to these statistics," he writes, "is that when I arrived by train, all set to load the wires with graphic prose, there seemed to be nothing left save a fringe of houses around the municipal periphery, like the hair on a friar's head." He then explains what many contemporary Americans have come to understand about service in the life of our cities.

After a survey of the gifts from various service organizations around the nation to help the Jacksonville citizens, Mencken reports on Boston's boxcar filled with oil stoves, woolen mittens from Montgomery, Alabama, heavy red underwear from Winston-Salem, North Carolina, 100 used horse blankets from Pimlico — but Jacksonville was sweltering in 80-degree heat at the time. Twenty coffins came from Baltimore, but no one had died in the fire. In addition, Baltimore had sent 100 cases of Maryland rye, but they had not arrived yet. He tried to obtain a statement of the mayor's gratitude, at his editor's demand, but the mayor "raised scruples about giving it to me," for "What if they were wrecked along the way, and the whole world learned the cars never arrived at all?" Such suspicions (the mayor's) and preoccupations (the editor's), together with the other lunacies, paint a picture of American urban intelligence on vacation, à la Mencken.

He closes his mirthful essay with a report of his return a year later "to find out how the town was making out." He writes,

> I found, as I expected, that the fire had been the luckiest act of God in all its history. The marsh that used to lie between it and the channel of the St. Johns River, generating mosquitoes and malaria, was now filled with the debris, and dozens of new warehouses were going up. A little while later Congress ordered the 19-foot channel dredged to 24 feet, and then to 30. During the next decade, the population of Jacksonville more than doubled, and today it is a metropolis comparable to Ninevah or Gomorrah in their prime, with the hottest night clubs between Norfolk and Miami, and so many indigenous salvage-crews of humanitarians that Florida can't contain them....

Certainly, contrasting views of this great city, such as those recorded by the awed Henry James and the ironic H. L. Mencken, still exist. The dualistic vision of cities, Jacksonville included, ranging from romantically charming to civilization in decline, continues to characterize literary portraits of cities.

Still another visitor to the city was a young man named **Will McLean** (1919-1990) from Chipley, later called "The Black-hatted Troubador," a folksinger and Florida original, in contrast to James or Mencken, for he dedicated his life to transforming the lore of Florida into the poetry of song throughout the state. In his *Florida Sand* (Earleton, FL: Lake & Emerald Publications, New Enlarged Edition, 1977) introduction, he tells at length of visiting Jacksonville with his grandfather, "one of the highlights in the man and boy's sojourn." At a traveling medicine show, the harmonica-and-banjo-playing one-man band held the boy spellbound; and the grandfather, on the train west, "talked so much" and "tears began to flood the man's eyes, running down his face to commingle with the boy's tears as they hugged each other."

This epiphany, this incandescent experience stayed with the young boy through his life, as though he grew up to give life to what his grandfather called "the boy's natural talent," to bring the pleasure to others his grandfather said "the boy brought him through his playing of church songs on his [mouth]-harp." At the trip's end, the grandfather turned the young Will McLean over to the boy's mother and new stepfather — and then departed forever from the boy.

The Jacksonville experience for this poet-singer was the inspiration for his life decision, the stimulus for the legend which Will McLean became. His song of Osceola crying from prison in Castillo de San Marcos in St. Augustine, called "Osceola's Last Words," or "The Ballad of Silver Springs," "Conch Island," "Blount's Fort," or "Land O'Gold" (on the St. Johns River) are among dozens of songs he left as a musical, folkloric legacy to Floridians.

Frederick Delius and his traveling companion Charles Douglas just before leaving England for Florida, February 1884. The composer worked for almost two years at his orange grove on the St. Johns River, before moving to Jacksonville.

A traveler driving west from Fort Caroline on Fort Caroline Road and then south on University Boulevard will come to Jacksonville University, a private university founded in 1934 in a wooded setting overlooking the St. Johns River. Of special note is the restored house of European composer Frederick Delius (1862-1934), located behind the gymnasium on the campus and moved there from its original location from just south of Jacksonville in Orangedale. Delius represents the refined heritage of early English settlers here. In 1884, Julius Delius sent his 22-year-old son Frederick from England to Florida to run an orange grove and thus begin a business career. Once he arrived and saw the run-down grove, Delius quickly lost whatever interest he might have had in oranges and began listening to the ballads of black laborers living nearby. On a visit to Jacksonville, he entered a music store and began plinking keys on a piano. A passing piano teacher, Thomas Ward, offered to give Delius piano lessons, and the rest is the Delius legend.

Eventually, Delius returned to Europe to study and compose the music which led to his fame and honor throughout the world. His works include the compelling *Florida Suite* and the opera *Koanga*, the first European opera set in America. His work entitled *Appalachia* became the sound track for the movie version of one of Florida's most famous novels, *The Yearling* by **Marjorie Kinnan Rawlings**. In Delius, Florida lost an orange grower but gained an important composer. Jacksonville promotes a Delius Festival of music each March to honor one of north Florida's most famous residents.

For further information about this important composer see *Frederick Delius* (New York: Vienna House, 1973) by **Thomas Beecham**; *Delius* (New York: Crowell, 1972) by **Eric Fenby**; *Delius* (Westport, CT: Greenwood Press, 1970) by **Arthur Hutchings**; *Delius* (New York: Octagon Books, 1972) by **Alan Jefferson**; *The Road to Samarkand: Frederick Delius and His Music* (New York: Scribner's Sons, 1969) by **Gloria Jahoda**; and *Delius: Portrait of a Cosmopolitan* (New York: Holmes & Meier, 1976) by **Christopher Palmer**.

Several Jacksonville schools and colleges have inspired historians to write about them: **Ralph D. Bald, Jr.** wrote *A History of Jacksonville University, The First Twenty-Five Years, 1934-1959* (Jacksonville: Jacksonville University, 1959). More recently, **George Hallam** wrote *Our Place in the Sun: A History of Jacksonville University* (Jacksonville: The University, 1988). **Samuel J. Tucker**'s *Phoenix From the Ashes* (Jacksonville: Convention Press, 1976) is a history of Edward Waters College. **Daniel L. Schafer**'s *From Scratch Pads and Dreams* (Jacksonville: University of North Florida, 1982) explains the first ten years of the University of North Florida history. **Robert Gentry** wrote *A College Tells Its Story: An Oral History of Florida Community College at Jacksonville, 1963-1991* (Jacksonville: Florida Community College at Jacksonville, 1991), which he asserts is "the first oral history of any educational institution in the United States in book form." Two high school histories also exist: **Lula F. Miller** edited *Perspectives, Fifty Years of Bartram School, 1934-1984* (Jacksonville: Paramount Press, 1983) and **George Hallam** wrote *Bolles: The Standard-Bearer* (Jacksonville: Bolles School, 1983) about The Bolles School in southside Jacksonville.

Several books feature particular parts or facets of the city's life. For example, **George Hallam**'s *Riverside Remembered* (Jacksonville: Drummond

Press, 1976) provides an account of one of Jacksonville's most historic residential suburbs. And **Dena Snodgrass**'s *The Island of Ortega* (Jacksonville: Ortega School, 1981) chronicles a history of an island in the St. Johns once owned by Don Juan McQueen.

Millions of travelers from northern states gather first impressions of a Florida city from Jacksonville, in much the same way as General Burgoyne, who arrived at Cowford by boat, and H.L. Mencken, who arrived by train, formed their impressions. In 1882, **George Barbour** described the city in his *Florida For Tourists, Invalids, and Settlers*:

> The streets are remarkably wide, and are nearly all shaded by long rows of mammoth live oaks, forming arcades of embowering green in winter as well as in summer. Good sidewalks of brick or planks contribute greatly to the comfort of pedestrians, but the streets themselves are too sandy for rapid or pleasant driving, and are 'heavy' for all vehicles.

At the corner of Bay and Liberty streets, a plaque commemorates the place where the Old Kings Road crossed the St. Johns River.

In the late 1890s, **Stephen Crane** (1871-1900), author of many stories and poems, as well as the two novels *The Red Badge of Courage* (1895) and *Maggie: A Girl of the Streets* (1896), stayed at the St. James Hotel, probably located on

Cora Taylor and Stephen Crane, August 23, 1899, about a year before Crane's death.

Duval Street between Laura and Hogan streets. His future wife, Cora Taylor, ran a brothel, the Hotel de Dream, on the southwest corner of Ashley and Hawk (now Jefferson) streets. Crane was sailing from Jacksonville for Cuba on the *Commodore* to report on the Cuban War when the ship sprang a leak and sank off Daytona Beach; drawing on that harrowing experience, he wrote "The Open Boat," which in 1934 Ernest Hemingway called one of the two perfect American stories in American literature. Cora Crane's legend inspired **Lillian Gilkes**, a Jacksonville resident when she began her research, to write the ambitious *Cora Crane: A Biography of Mrs. Stephen Crane* (Bloomington: Indiana University Press, 1968) and prompted **Peggy Friedmann** to research and publish "Jacksonville's Most Famous Madam," *Jacksonville* 17 (May/June 1980), pp.12-20. Cora Crane died in 1910, ten years after Stephen Crane, and was buried in Jacksonville's Evergreen Cemetery in Northside.

"The Court" was one of the hotels along "the row" which attracted many visitors, the most famous being the author Stephen Crane. This hotel, located at the corner of Ward and Davis Streets, suggests the sort of environment Cora's Hotel de Dream provided.

Jacksonville Authors

Merian C. Cooper, born in Jacksonville in 1893, was the scion of an old Georgia family and became one of the region's most accomplished sons as a Hollywood film producer/director in the 1930s and a traveler and popular novelist as well. Before he became an author and Hollywood mogul, he had led an exceptional military career, as Jan Sek, a Polish journalist working on Cooper's biography, reveals in notes he donated to the Florida Collection of the Jacksonville Public Library. Perhaps as background experience for his literary career, Cooper enlisted as a private in 1916 with the Second Georgia Infantry fighting Pancho Villa in the Mexican campaign. He left the military as a U.S. Air Force brigadier general, an adviser to General MacArthur in the Pacific war. Between those events, he rose from captain to colonel in the Polish Air Force, the creation of which he proposed to the Polish army commander in World War I. During the war, he was wounded more than once, imprisoned more than once over a ten-month period, and escaped from a Moscow prison to walk for 17 nights to the Latvian border, where he proceeded to rejoin his squadron. For this, he received the highest Polish military honor, the Crosses of Valour, in 1921.

Returning to civilian life, he moved to Hollywood to begin his second great career. Cooper produced and directed movies with Ernest B. Schoedsack: *Grass*, *Chang*, and *Four Feathers*. He produced several notable movies on his own: *Little Women*, *The Last Days of Pompeii*, *She*, and *King Kong* (1933), the classic science-fiction work, a fable for our time. For *this* work alone, his career is remarkable. He and Edgar Wallace conceived it in 1932 when he wrote it as a filmscript. A *King Kong* novelization by **Delos W. Lovelace** appeared in 1932 but has been reprinted (New York: Ace Books, 1974).

Cooper's globe-trotting adventures and his military experience helped him to develop a global outlook. His King Kong serves as a metaphor for the result — simultaneously wondrous and yet terrifying — of technological intrusions into Earth's natural environment, in the manner of Dr. Frankenstein's humane but destructive monster, Mary Shelley's creation more than a century earlier. His remarkable twentieth-century twist on this important fable endures in videos and late-night old movies and extends his reputation as one of our century's notable science-fiction creators.

Other impressive achievements include Cooper's becoming Pan Am's first director in 1930 and helping to launch Cinerama in the 1950s. His books include *Grass* (1925), *The Sea Gypsy* (co-authored with **Edward A. Salisbury**, 1924), and *Things Men Die For* (1927). His films starred John Wayne, Katherine Hepburn, and Fred Astaire, among other mythic stars. He died in San Diego in 1973 at 80 years of age.

George Dillon (1906-1968) was born in Jacksonville and lived in the family home on the northwest corner of Boulevard and Silver streets. He published three books of poetry: *Boy in the Wind* (1927), *The Flowering Stone* (1931), and *Flowers of Evil* (1936). In 1932 he won the Pulitzer Prize for poetry and in 1937 became editor of the important journal *Poetry: A Magazine of Verse*.

Teresa Holloway (1906-1989), was born in Apalachicola, Florida, which she once said "is hard to get to, and so the people become more colorful there." She moved to Jacksonville in 1939, owning and operating a ginger ale company for four years; from 1947 to 1967 she worked every biennium as an administrative assistant in the Florida Senate. She also taught writing workshops at Jacksonville University and Florida Community College. Holloway published 39 novels under her own name and the pseudonyms **Elizabeth Beatty** and **Margaret Vail McLeod**. Her popular nurse romance novels for young adults feature a young woman or girl as protagonist.

Some of her novels — for example *Government Girl* — feature Florida settings. As **Elizabeth Beatty,** Holloway wrote mysteries, such as *Jupiter Missile Mystery* and *Murder at Auction*. As **Margaret Vail McLeod** and **Teresa Holloway,** she wrote novels of young women in leadership jobs, such as *Captain Jane, River Rescue,* and *Lady Lawyer*. In addition, she scripted TV documentaries featuring Florida, such as *The Good Old Days,* an account of vanishing rural countryside Florida life. She also wrote numerous features for the Jacksonville newspapers and a political column on the Florida legislature in the 1950s. Her many stories have appeared in *The Saturday Evening Post, Ford Times,* and *Alfred Hitchcock Mystery Magazine,* among others.

Ann Hyman is a third-generation Floridian born in Bradenton, Florida, in 1936. After earning her undergraduate degree from Florida State University and spending a year as a journalist in Bradenton, she arrived in Jacksonville's Riverside in 1959 to become eventually features columnist and special projects writer for *The Florida Times-Union*. She has written numerous in-depth features on such Florida subjects as "the literary St. Johns," Mayport's history and present-day ambiance, and Dessie Smith Prescott, the woman who accompanied Marjorie Kinnan Rawlings on the Hyacinth Drift adventure described in Rawlings's *Cross Creek*. Hyman is the author of *The Lansing Legacy* (New York: David MacKay Company, Inc., 1974), a mystery novel, and the autobiography *Chaos Clear As Glass: A Memoir* (Atlanta, GA: Longstreet Press, 1991). Her mystery, while set in the fictional Port Charles, derives from Jacksonville locations: "In my mind, the novel's country club is Jacksonville's Timuquana Country Club, and the mansion is 'Los Cedros,' located in Ortega." In *Chaos,* her memoirs, she visits earlier places dear to her: her apartment in Riverside where she first lived in the early 1960s; Hopewell, "a little community of orange groves and strawberry fields in Hillsborough County"; and Anna Maria Island, near her Bradenton home. In her signature manner, she writes of her visit to Jacksonville as a high school junior:

> We were quartered in the George Washington Hotel [demolished, early 1970s], a classic, world-weary, Bogey-movie kind of a place with slow ceiling fans and dark polished wood, a hotel where high school kids went to their junior-senior proms and politicians stashed their whores and old couples celebrated their golden anniversaries and young naval aviators and their brides spent their wedding nights.

The middle section treats her remarkable trip in the late 1980s to Russia, "which changed my life." Hyman's writing has enlightened a generation about the arts, culture, entertainment, and even history of northeast Florida.

A plaque at Third and Lee streets, also visible from Interstate 95 North just beyond State Road 23, commemorates the birthplace of Jacksonville's **James Weldon Johnson** (1871-1938). From his autobiography *Along This Way* (1933; reprinted New York: Viking Press, 1968), one can learn a great deal about his early life in the city. His father, as headwaiter in one of the leading Jacksonville hotels, provided well for the Johnson family, and James led a secure and untroubled childhood, playing games and doing boyhood chores such as filling oil lamps, cleaning chimneys, helping with the dishes, and helping his grandmother with her bakery in her home. His father taught him Spanish and guitar playing; his mother taught him to play the piano. Baseball was his favorite sport, and from a professional player he learned special pitches that helped him win games for his team, the Domestics.

He attended Stanton, the only school for blacks, which took students through only the eighth grade. His parents sent him to Atlanta University to complete his high school education. Because Jacksonville was relatively free of Jim Crow restrictions on Negro citizens until into the twentieth century, he did not suffer from racial discrimination until he was an adolescent. In 1894, Johnson returned to his hometown where he became principal of Stanton at age 23; under his leadership, the school added one grade per year until it became Stanton High School, located now on West Thirteenth Street — and now called Stanton College Preparatory School.

James Weldon Johnson

Besides being principal of Stanton High School at Broad and Ashley streets, Johnson founded the nation's first daily newspaper for blacks, but lack of money ended the publication after eight months. After 18 months of study, and assisted by a young attorney, a member of a prominent white family, he became the first African-American admitted to the Florida Bar upon examination. He had little time for law practice, for he was still principal and had been elected president of the state teachers' association. After he received two royalty checks for musical works composed with his brother, J. Rosamond Johnson, just two years younger than he, the two men decided to move to New York in 1901 to try selling their music on Broadway. They spent the next four years there, writing more than 200 songs and collaborating with some of the most popular writers, singers, and actors of the day.

Johnson had written the words while his brother had composed the music of "Lift Ev'ry Voice and Sing," which became the official song of the National Association for the Advancement of Colored People (NAACP). Originally, they had created the song for a group of Jacksonville men planning a Lincoln's birthday celebration in 1900. Five hundred school children sang the song from

35

mimeographed copies on that occasion. When the two Johnson brothers moved to New York, they forgot about the song, but the youngsters of Jacksonville continued singing it, inspiring others to spread the stirring anthem throughout the South and eventually throughout the country. The song has reverberated through the years as an anthem of African-American pride, and more recently, while still inspiring African-American pride, the song evokes a common national experience when sung by racially mixed groups, typically along with "The Star-Spangled Banner."

The themes of this powerful anthem appear in these lines:

> Lift ev'ry voice and sing,
> Till earth and heaven ring,
> Ring with the harmonies of Liberty . . .

And later:

> We have come over a way that with tears has been watered;
> We have come, treading our path thro' the blood of the slaughtered,
>
> Out from the gloomy past.
> Till now we stand at last
> Where the white gleam of our bright star is cast. . .

And finally:

> Shadowed beneath Thy hand,
> May we forever stand
> True to our God, True to our native land.

The song is a living legacy from Johnson, one of Florida's most significant native authors.

Later, he became a U.S. Consul to Venezuela and to Nicaragua, married in 1910, and published the novel *The Autobiography of an Ex-Colored Man* (New York: Alfred A. Knopf, 1912). When he returned to New York from the consular service, he became editor of *The New York Age*, the nation's leading black journal founded by native Floridian (from Marianna) T. Thomas Fortune and financed by Booker T. Washington; helped to organize the American Society of Composers, Authors, and Publishers (ASCAP); and became the first African-American secretary of the NAACP, serving from 1920 to 1930 by organizing new branches, investigating riots, and helping to achieve equal voting rights. During this period, Johnson also became an important figure in the cultural revolution of the Harlem Renaissance, which flowered after the first World War through the Twenties.

In New York, the Johnson brothers again collaborated to create *God's Trombones: Seven Negro Sermons in Verse* in 1927, a dramatization of Biblical themes, delivered and often sung in the style of African-American worship and based on the idiom of the folk-preacher. For this stunning work, Johnson was given the Harmon Award. A sampling of his lyrics illustrates the power and majesty of his poetic rendering. The following are the first and fourth stanzas of the first sermon, called "The Creation":

> And God stepped out on space,
> And he looked around, and said:
> I'm lonely —
> I'll make me a world.

And the fourth stanza:

> Then God reached out and took the light in his hands,
> And God rolled the light around in his hands
> Until He made the sun;
> And he set that sun a-blazing in the heavens.
> And the light that was left from making the sun
> God gathered it up in a shining ball
> And flung it against the darkness,
> Spangling the night with the moon and the stars.
> Then down between
> The darkness and the light
> He hurled the world;
> And God said: That's good!

In his later years, he became Professor of Creative Literature at Fisk University and a lecturer at New York University and Columbia University on African-American history and art. In 1938, while on vacation in Maine, he was killed in an automobile accident. His funeral was held in Harlem.

On James Weldon Johnson Day, held during Jacksonville's sesquicentennial celebration in 1972, the City placed a plaque at his birthplace and sponsored several programs, one of which featured James Earl Jones reading from Johnson's poetry. A few words document the wisdom of his unusual and distinguished life. He wrote, "In large measure the race question involves the saving of black America's body and white America's soul."

For additional Johnson lore, consult the following books (all entitled *James Weldon Johnson*) by the following authors: **Ophelia Settle Egypt** (New York: Crowell, 1974); **Harold W. Felton** (New York: Dodd, Mead, 1971); **Robert E. Fleming** (Boston: Twayne, 1987); **Eugene D. Levy** (Chicago: University of Chicago Press, 1973); and **Jane Tolbert Rouchaleau** (New York: Chelsea House, 1988). **Ellen Tarry** wrote a novel about him entitled *Young Jim, The Early Years of James Weldon Johnson* (New York: Dodd, Mead, 1967).

Stetson Kennedy (1916-), internationally known as a folklorist, has authored several books, such as *Palmetto Country* (1942) and *Southern Exposure* (1946). He is also an advocate of social justice and human rights, whose investigative histories include *The Klan Unmasked* (1990) and *Jim Crow Guide to the U.S.A.* (1959). Kennedy was born in Jacksonville on Walnut Street, which was then downtown in a city of about 20,000 people. When he was five, his family moved to a place on Hedrick Street, in what was then Ingleside Heights — before Avondale or Riverside existed there. He grew up, as the eldest of five children, in this neighborhood, attending Lee High School, until he left for the University of Florida "in about 1930," he recalls. Subsequently, he lived in Key West, Miami, and other Florida locations while working on the Works Progress Administration (WPA) Writers Project in the Thirties. In the Forties he wrote landmark books about southern life and lore. During the 1950s he moved overseas, traveling throughout Europe and North Africa as a journalist and author.

In 1959 he returned to Fruit Cove, a community just south of Mandarin between Julington Creek and Switzerland, where he had maintained a residence since 1948, then moved for a time to the old Billard Home on Brady Road in Mandarin. In 1973, he and his wife Joyce Ann created 20-acre Lake Beluthahatchee (an Indian word meaning Nirvana on Water) in a 70-acre tract in Fruit Cove, off State Road 13, where they still live in their two-story cottage overlooking a cypress-sprigged lake, which, without the few houses dotting the shores, resembles a primeval Eden, complete with alligators, anhingas, hummingbirds, egrets, snakes, ospreys, lizards, bronze grackles, and the Kennedy cats. His home is as natural and comfortable as Kennedy himself. The house has a name — Lake Dwellers; one wonders if this man who has loved justice so passionately through his life and books is the spiritual descendant of the

Stetson Kennedy, folklorist and historian, social activist and internationally known journalist — also called "Beluthahatchee Bill" by his pal Woody Guthrie.

Indians who preceded him here.

Kennedy began to prepare for his first book *Palmetto Country* (1942; reprinted by Florida A & M University Press, 1989) when but a young man listening to stories and accents until he became an untutored expert on southern folklore. He put this talent and interest to use in the Thirties when he worked with **Carita Doggett Corse, Zora Neale Hurston,** and many other authors on the *Florida Guide*, a WPA Writers Project. As a journalist writer traveling about the state, he met and lived among ordinary people of all races and creeds, laying the basis for not only his folklorist expertise but his empathy for all those who experience the effects of social injustice through poverty, prejudice, and Jim Crow laws.

As a folklorist — or "pofolkist" as his pal **Woody Guthrie** dubbed him — Kennedy feels strongly that some of the very best literature about Florida or any place else exists in the oral tradition of the folk, its authorship usually collective and anonymous. Some of this lore, in the form of one-liners, occasionally called folksay, appears in a typical sample Kennedy collected as uttered by a black preacher in the Sea Island area during the "root-hog-or-die" days of the Great Depression: "Hear us, Oh Lord; we're down here gnawin' on dry bones!" Another sampling (an expurgated version appearing in *Palmetto Country*) is "Them Johnson Gals," a net-hauling sea chantey sung by the black crewmen of the menhaden fleet which, until the 1940s, operated out of Fernandina and Mayport (menhaden are small, inedible fish ground up in odiferous Jacksonville plants for use as fertilizer):

> Now, them Johnson gals is mighty fine gals.
> Walk around, Honey, walk around! (This refrain is sung after
>   each line, as crewmen walk in circle turning a winch to haul in nets)
> They's neat in the waist and has mighty fine legs.
> Great big legs, and teenincey feet.
> You feel her leg, and you wanna feel her thigh.
> You feel her thigh, and you wanna go on high!
> You go on high, and you fade away and die.
> They got sumpum under yonder called Jamaica jam.
> Hot as cayenne pepper, but good goddam!

The literary spice of the folk is a Kennedy specialty, and a significant part of his life and work gives voice to the real life of many cultural groups in Florida.

In 1991 the Archive of Southern Labor History at Georgia State University began work to produce a documentary for public television about the life of Stetson Kennedy. The title, *Southern Exposure: The Life and Times of Stetson Kennedy*, echoes its original model, Kennedy's *Southern Exposure* (1946; reprinted Gainesville: University Presses of Florida, 1991). The book is part of a tradition — maybe the start of a tradition: exposé journalism linking analysis to action, telling the truth and making clear the imperative for change. In it, Kennedy first identifies "The Problem of the South," explaining that the South became "the nation's economic problem No. 1," not because "... of any deficiency in human or natural resources," but rather because "...the bulk of its produce has been siphoned off by a few, leaving little or nothing for the many who produced it." He then projects "The Road Ahead," suggesting making racial discrimination and persecution illegal and bringing about equality through laws. He writes, however, that "White supremacy is going to die a hard death, almost as hard as slavery's." The present existence of school desegregation, voting rights laws, equal employment opportunity law, and other legal moves to bring about total equality suggest the prophetic nature of *Southern Exposure* — and thus the revival of interest in his books and the life of Citizen Kennedy.

Despite his grandfather's fighting for the Confederacy and an uncle prominent in the Ku Klux Klan, Kennedy took it upon himself during World

War II "...to infiltrate the hooded order with a view to doing all he could to cramp its style," as he put it. (Like all Klansmen, he used "Dr. Akai," for "a Klansman am I" as a secret way to signal his Klan membership when in a mixed crowd; his own pseudonym was John S. Perkins.) While the FBI reported his infiltration of the Klan *to* the Klan, Kennedy reported *his* experiences within the Klan to Drew Pearson, who broadcast them each week coast-to-coast by radio. Pearson called Kennedy "the Nation's number-one Klan-buster," and the Dragon sent an all-klaverns bulletin offering "$1,000 per pound of the traitor's [Kennedy's] ass, FOB Atlanta." His book *The Klan Unmasked*, originally published as *I Rode With the Ku Klux Klan* in a dozen languages around the world (London: Arco Publishers Ltd., 1954; republished for the first time in the U.S., Boca Raton: Florida Atlantic University, 1990), chronicles his early 1940s experiences inside the KKK and other racist/terrorist groups such as the American Gentile Army, Confederate Underground, and J.B. Stoner's Anti-Jewish Party. According to Klan historian Wyn Craig Wade in his *The Fiery Cross*, Kennedy's infiltration and exposure of the Klan was "the single most important factor in preventing a postwar revival of the Ku Klux Klan in the North."

Kennedy left the country in 1952 when he heard that a UN Committee on Forced Labor was canceling its hearings in New York because it could find no witnesses in the Western Hemisphere. Kennedy wired that he could produce witnesses; the committee chair replied that he would accept Kennedy as an expert witness IF he could get to Geneva, Switzerland in two weeks, at his own expense. He did not return home for eight years. During this time, his books appeared in foreign-language editions while he worked as a journalist in Europe, publishing his work in Jean-Paul Sartre's *Les Temps Moderne* ("Modern Times") and Alberto Moravia's *Nuovi Argomenti* ("New Argument"), among other places. Indeed, Sartre underwrote the publication of his book *Jim Crow Guide to the U.S.A.: The Laws, Customs, and Etiquette Governing the Conduct of Nonwhites and Other Minorities as Second-Class Citizens* (London: Lawrence & Wishart Ltd., 1959). The book teems with facts and examples, organized under such chapter titles as: "Who is Coloured Where," "Who May Marry Whom," "Who May Live Where," "Who May Study Where," or "Who May Travel How," and "Who May Work Where." One may hope this book will soon be considered solely a historical record of the past.

One tribute to Kennedy appears in three folk songs by **Woody Guthrie**, the fabled folksinger of the Thirties and Forties. Guthrie spent some time in Florida in the late 1940s and a year or two at Lake Dwellers with a woman named Aneeke in the early 1950s, when Kennedy was in Europe. One ballad, recorded in *The Klan Unmasked*, goes, in part,

> Beluthahatchee Bill, old Beluthahatchee Bill,
> Freedom-lovin', freedom-huntin', easy-ridin' Bill;
> You can swing me and hang me, and beat me to your fill,
> But you'll never slack my speed none, not Beluthahatchee Bill.

Guthrie could create legends with such lyrics, as well as the songs to express the suffering of the rural poor and the urban oppressed.

In 1992, even as he recently collected the $5,000 Cavallo Foundation Award for his life of "moral courage for the public benefit resulting in personal suffering and sacrifice," Kennedy, at 75, focuses on the future. He has at least a dozen book manuscripts, all in advanced stages, as projected publications. Among them are *After Appomattox: How the South Won the War* (scheduled for 1993); *Sand in Their Shoes* (an all-Florida folklore collection); *Grits & Grunts* (folkloric Key West); *Hate No More* (a universal prescription for ending ethnic and religious strife); *Naturalist Manifesto* (a "do or die" prognostication); *Land Be Bright* (selected works); and *Dissident-at-Large* (autobiography). Re-publication of his work has led to his presenting papers before several academic societies. He has appeared on national television talk shows, including CBS *Nightwatch* and in 1992 *Tony Brown's Journal*. Kennedy's work and ideas, once considered dangerous, are welcome and honored in this time of America's change.

Dell Lebo (1922-1979) lived in Florida from 1950, when he came to Florida State University as a graduate student, until his death in a scuba-diving accident. He published his first poetry in the university newspaper, the Florida *Flambeau*, in 1951, and moved to Jacksonville in 1954. Books by Lebo include *Poems and Verse, Book 1: The Metaphysical Poems, Book II: The Three Cornered Habit* (1966); *Intimations of Precariousness* (haiku) (1969); *Best Loved Poems of Dell Lebo* (1975); *Psychology in the Poetry of Dell Lebo* (1977); and *Festival of Life*, illustrated and co-edited (1978). Poems depicting Florida in a significant way include "First Impression," "Mrs. Johnson's Window," and "Head South." He served as Chief Psychologist at the Child Guidance Clinic in Jacksonville.

James Merrill (1926-), who spent his childhood in Jacksonville, says his memories of the city are "personal...how the river looked, tadpoles in Riverside Park, the war memorial,... how the air smelled... a boy's memories." He was born in New York, the son of financier Charles E. Merrill and his second wife, Hellen Ingram from Jacksonville's Riverside area; his parents' 1939 divorce reverberates throughout his work. A group of his poems first appeared in the national quarterly *Poetry*. *First Poems* appeared in 1951, after which he wrote two plays, *The Bait* (1953) and *The Immortal Husband* (1955). He then turned to the novel, with *The Seraglio* (1957).

His early work culminated with *Water Street* (1962), the title being Merrill's Stonington, Connecticut, address, where he has lived for many years, dividing his time between there and Greece. He wrote *Nights and Days* (1966), which won the National Book Award; *The Fire Screen* (1969); and *Braving the Elements* (1972), which won the Bollingen Prize for Poetry. He won the Pulitzer Prize for poetry with *Divine Comedies* (1976), which, with its three sections and a coda, was published in 1982 as *The Changing Light at Sandover* and won the National Book Critics Circle Prize. That same year, selections from his earlier books appeared in *From the First Nine: Poems 1946-1976*. *Late Settings* was published in 1985, and J.D. McCatchy edited a volume titled *Recitative: Prose by James Merrill* (San Francisco: North Point Press, 1986).

Several of his poems emanate from memories of Jacksonville. As he once said, "I wrote a poem called 'Water Hyacinths,' in which I used the lovely weeds as a metaphor for the disturbances in my grandmother's mind, thoughts that, like hyacinths, clogged the connective process. I also wrote a poem when she died, 'Annie Hill's Grave' — that was her maiden name — I tried to capture the experience of being suddenly at a graveside and seeing people I hadn't seen in years, and the unexpected spirit of sweetness encountered." The poems appeared in a book entitled *Country of 1,000 Years of Peace*. Merrill's poems reveal the pressure of fantasy, the abiding, unavoidable connections between fantasy and everyday life.

David Poyer (1950-), born in the coal country of northwest Pennsylvania, grew up in poverty and attended the U.S. Naval Academy in part because a full scholarship offered him a path to new opportunities. He was graduated in 1971 and served six years on destroyer and amphibious-type ships in the Atlantic, Mediterranean, Arctic, and Caribbean seas. He resigned in 1977 to pursue a writing career and spent six years struggling as a free-lancer before selling his first hardcover novel, *The Return of Philo T. McGiffen* (1983), the comic story of a plebe enduring hard knocks at the U.S. Naval Academy. By 1984, he had moved to Jacksonville when his wife, on active duty, was assigned to Mayport. Divorce followed the move, and he then lived in the Riverside-Avondale area from 1986 to 1991, writing five novels: *The Med* (1988), a navy novel set in the Mediterranean; *Hatteras Blue* (1989), a thriller about wreck diving in the Persian Gulf; *The Gulf* (1990), set in the Persian Gulf; *Bahamas Blue* (1991), a thriller-sequel to his 1989 book; and *The Circle* (1992). In 1991, after Poyer's great book successes, Universal Studios purchased film rights to *The Return of Philo T. McGiffen*.

Jacksonville figures occasionally in his story details. The best example occurs in *The Gulf*: helicopter pilot Claude "Chunky" Schweinberg, from Jacksonville, played football for Coach Bobby Bowden's FSU Seminoles, and, when hired by his uncle, an Ortega building contractor, to demolish a wall, did so by crashing an old Plymouth Fury into it at 45 mph while a fellow Navy pilot videotaped the event. The incident illustrates Poyer's humor and approach to character portrayal. His *Gulf*, *Med*, and *Circle* hero is Lieutenant Commander Dan Lenson, about whom Poyer intends to write a total of five novels. Having a million copies of his books in print for the first time in 1991, Poyer achieved financial success and critical acclaim. He then married Lenore Hart, an aspiring writer who was Community Relations Director for Jacksonville's downtown public library, and moved to Virginia's Eastern Shore. After living in relative poverty for more than a decade, Poyer said he is still adjusting to his affluent success: "I've towed this anchor for so long that, now that it's cut, I'm throwing up a big bow wave and feeling unsteady."

Mary Freels Rosborough, born in 1894, has resided in Jacksonville since her marriage in 1919 to George L. Rosborough. Born in Illinois, she nevertheless feels like a Florida native. She wrote, "I am almost a 'Florida Cracker,' having lived fifty years of my life here in Jacksonville." She has authored two Florida novels and nearly 50 short stories published in such magazines as *The Saturday Evening Post, McCalls, Collier's, Country Gentleman,* and *Everywoman,* from 1939 to 1974. Her first novel, *Don't You Cry For Me* (New York: Crowell,

1954), features tobacco farmers in north Florida along the Suwannee River and was originally published as a novelette in 1942 in *The Saturday Evening Post*. Another of her novels, *A Clear Place in the Sky* (New York: Crowell, 1955), features the Florida Everglades. Florida settings characterize nearly all of Rosborough's short stories. She wrote, in 1977, "I love living in Florida and it is an easy place to write but of course I'd write even if I were in Alaska or the South Pole."

Frank G. Slaughter has resided in Jacksonville since 1934, mostly in the Riverside area on Garibaldi and St. Johns Avenues, and now resides in the Ortega area. Born in 1908 in Washington, D.C., he grew up on a 225-acre tobacco farm near Oxford, North Carolina, earning his undergraduate degree at Duke University and his M.D. at Johns Hopkins in 1930 at age 22. Slaughter credits Dr. Wilburt C. Davison, his preceptor in medical school, for sharpening his "...interest in what may best be called the cultural side of medicine." As Slaughter put it in 1967, "Stored away deep in my mind even after forty years are still more seeds of medical lore, gained during those student days in Baltimore, and from these seeds will come other novels of medicine's heritage from history and the arts." By that year, Slaughter had already published 43 of his 62 books, six of them nonfiction and four swashbuckling adventure novels under his pseudonym, **C.V. Terry**. Through 1990, Slaughter's books have averaged more than a million sales per title, totaling over 100 million copies.

During Slaughter's eight years, from 1934 to 1942, as a surgeon at Jacksonvillle's Riverside Hospital, he purchased a $60 typewriter and wrote short stories at the rate of 100,000 words a year. In a five-year period, he sold only one story, for $12. He once met Marjorie Kinnan Rawlings while she was a hospital patient and asked her to review 15 pages of his work. Her comment: "Stick to operating." By 1938, he started his semi-autobiographical novel, *That None Should Die*, about a young doctor who, after graduation, begins his practice in a small southern community. Slaughter used this story to promote prepaid medical care without government interference, posing an alternative to socialized medicine. After revisions and six rejections of the novel, a

Frank G. Slaughter, Jacksonville resident for almost fifty years and author of 62 books.

local librarian showed it to a publisher's salesman, who persuaded an older writer/editor to work with Slaughter once more. Friends of the salesman at Doubleday Publishing Company passed the book to Thomas B. Costain, well-known novelist and editor-in-chief who had helped John Steinbeck with his writing. Doubleday published the book in 1941. The award-winning novel has remained in print somewhere in the world ever since. Doubleday continued to publish virtually all Slaughter's books (exceptions cited in these pages) which have been sold in 23 countries. (Slaughter's titles cited here without publishing information are by Doubleday; titles not published by Doubleday include complete publishing information.)

Drawing on experiences as a U.S. Army surgeon during World War II, he completed four novels, including his first of six Civil War novels and *In a Dark Garden* (1946), which became a best-seller. His growing success as an author prompted him in that year to quit medical practice permanently to write full time. The next year, Slaughter published *The Golden Isle* (1947), a historical novel set in early nineteenth-century Fernandina Beach about an English doctor kidnapped by a slave-trader and brought to Spanish Florida to treat his slaves. Slaughter researched his story by reading books mentioned earlier in this chapter: **T. Frederick Davis**'s book on Amelia Island and **Cabell** and **Hanna**'s *The St. Johns*, which provides an account of the legendary Zephaniah Kingsley and his Senegalese wife. Slaughter's other Florida novels include *Fort Everglades* (1951) about the Second Seminole War of 1835-42; *Storm Haven* (1953) about Florida during the Civil War; *The Warrior* (1956) about Osceola and the 1835 Seminole War; and *Countdown* (1970) about the NASA space program. These and his other books reflect Slaughter's practice of basing his books on real people and on "...historical events exactly as they happened according to the best information available."

Slaughter was unpleasantly surprised when his friends informed him that the Warner Brothers movie *Distant Drums* (1951), starring Gary Cooper, contained at least 20 scenes drawn from his novel *Fort Everglades* published earlier that year. Eventually, Slaughter's lawyers persuaded Warner Brothers to purchase, belatedly, the movie rights. Despite this negative episode, he worked on several Hollywood screenplays. Other Slaughter novels made into movies include *Sangaree* (1948); *The Song of Ruth* (1954), which became the film *The Story of Ruth*; *The Warrior* (1956), the story of Osceola which became the movie *Naked in the Sun*; *Doctors' Wives* (1967); and the more recent *Women in White* (1974), which became a popular four-part TV mini-series under the same title. The movies attest to and help extend the popularity of the typical Slaughter story: that of a young man (most often a doctor) on a personal mission (to free a captive or cure a sickness) with some love interest and a metaphorical victory over death.

His Biblical stories, based on a historical period or event, included *The Galileans: A Novel of Mary Magdelene* (1953); *The Crown and the Cross: The Life of Christ* (New York: World Publishing Company, 1959); *David, Warrior and King* (also World Publishing, 1962); *God's Warrior* (1967); and *The Sins of Herod*

(1968). One of his own favorites is *The Road to Bithynia* (1951), about St. Luke the physician and the early Christian church.

Among his nonfiction books is *Immortal Magyar: Semmelweis, Conqueror of Childbed Fever* (1950; re-published in New York: Collier, 1961), the biography of the tragic Hungarian obstetrician, Dr. Ignaz Phillip Semmelweis (1818-65), the discoverer of the benefits of antisepsis in surgery and a cure for childbed fever. This story sprang from one of those seeds of medical lore which caught Slaughter's attention when he was studying with his mentor Dr. Davison at Johns Hopkins. Other nonfiction books concern medical history, such as *The New Science of Surgery* (New York: Messner, 1946), which relates surgical progress until that time, and *Medicine for Moderns: The New Science of Psychosomatic Medicine* (New York: Messner, 1947). Slaughter's nonfiction writing attests to his lifelong interest in medical research, which he also transformed into fiction.

Assessing his chosen career, Slaughter says, "When I turned from medicine to free-lance writing, I promised my wife that, whenever my prospects in writing did not seem as rosy as I was certain they would be in active practice, I would seriously consider returning to surgery. As it happened, the question has never come up." In fact, Slaughter, at 84, was still signing contracts for foreign republication rights: six novels in France and two in Japan. And though he published his most recent novel in 1988, he was thinking of writing another in 1992.

O. (Orville) Z. (Zelotes) Tyler, born in Jacksonville in 1905, lived in the city except for his service periods in the army, in which he rose to the rank of colonel. While Tyler published poems and history, his one-of-a-kind book is *Osceola, Seminole Chief: An Unremembered Saga* (Winter Park, FL: Anna Publishers, 1976), a book in verse rendering this great Seminole chief's legend into a kind of heroic epic in the manner of Homer's *Iliad*. He explained his abiding interest in writing, in a 1977 letter from his summer home on Huckleberry Mountain near Asheville in North Carolina: "My grandmother and my mother, both natives of Jacksonville, wrote poetry" and "I taught history and poetry classes (off and on) at Florida Junior College and Jacksonville University for ten years." Tyler's most recent work of historical fiction is *Sweet Land of Liberty* (Pompano Beach, FL: Exposition Press of Florida, 1987), featuring both the colonial and the revolutionary war periods.

Jacksonville is the setting for a number of fictional works, including three novels by **Harry Crews**: *Car* (New York: Morrow, 1972) is about a man who eats a car for publicity in a used-car lot, probably just off Highway 17, which skirts the St. Johns River. Crews offers a comic vision of our national mania for the machine, and Jacksonville provides a metaphor for a nation in love with cars. This place of noise, metal-crunching, car-destroying, pulpmill-hazed urban mess constitutes a sort of alimentary canal for American technology. As such, Crews uses Jacksonville's west-side car lots as the place where cars and humans clash in a grotesque urban black comedy. *The Gypsy's Curse* (New York: Knopf, 1974) portrays a legless deaf mute, and *Scar Lover* (New York: Poseidon, 1992) features a young man suffering interior and exterior scars.

In *Scar Lover* Pete Butcher is one of the walking maimed of our society, who has landed in a boarding house in Jacksonville, with few skills, few illusions, and a job that keeps him sweltering in a boxcar all day. Running from a past that has scarred him and blamed him — a tragic accident has destroyed his family — he avoids all personal contact. Perhaps he is a male victim, estranged from life, when Sarah Loemer, an oddly beautiful girl next door, walks into his life. Slowly and sweetly, her feminine power pulls him back "...into the complications of love, family, death, and deliverance," as the book's dust jacket explains.

Baby Boy (New York: Putnam, 1973) by **Jess Gregg** takes a humorous, fictional look at a prisoner in the city; *Possum Trot* (New York: Carlton, 1968) by **Anne L. Harwick** takes place here; *Bridge to Nowhere* (New York: Norton, 1980) by **Larry R. Humes** offers a mystery about a thief who seems to jump off a Jacksonville bridge; *The Other Side of the Sun* (New York: Farrar, Straus & Giroux, 1971) by **Madeleine L'Engle** depicts a fictional Jacksonville called Jefferson; *Mainside* (New York: Random House, 1962) by **Paul Mandel** exposes the seamier side of life at a Jacksonville naval base.

For histories of the area see **James B. Crooks**'s *Jacksonville After the Fire, 1901-1919* (Jacksonville: University of North Florida Press, 1991); **T. Frederick Davis**'s *History of Jacksonville, Florida, and Vicinity, 1513 to 1924* (1925; reprinted by University of Florida Press, 1964); and the excellent **James Robertson Ward**'s *Old Hickory's Town: An Illustrated History of Jacksonville* (Jacksonville: Florida Publishing Co., 1982); Ward wrote this book in association with the distinguished Jacksonville historian, **Dena E. Snodgrass. Odell Griffith**'s *John Holliday Perry: Florida Press Lord* (Tampa: Trend House, 1974) describes the businessman who founded *The Jacksonville Journal* and became an important force in the Florida newspaper world, especially in the Panhandle. **Richard A. Martin**'s *The City Makers* (Jacksonville: Convention Press, 1972) chronicles the city in the last century; the same author wrote *A Century of Service* (Jacksonville: St. Luke's Hospital, 1973), tracing the history of the city's St. Luke's Hospital from 1873 to 1973, and he joined **Daniel L. Schafer** to write *Jacksonville's Ordeal by Fire: A Civil War History* (Jacksonville: Florida Publishing Co., 1984). **Jules L. Wagman**'s *Jacksonville and Florida's First Coast* (Northridge, CA: Windsor, 1988) emphasizes the twentieth century.

Other books provide historical accounts of parts of the Jacksonville community. **Seth H. Bramson**'s *Speedway to Sunshine* (Erin, Ontario: Boston Mills Press, 1984) records the story of the Florida East Coast Railway, the line that helped to render Jacksonville accessible to the rest of the country. **Lucy Ames Edwards**'s *Grave-Markers of Duval County, 1808-1916* (Jacksonville: Edwards, 1955) lists records from the Old City Cemetery. **Natalie H. Glickstein**'s *That Ye May Remember: Temple Ahavath Chesed, 1882-1982* (St. Petersburg: Byron Kennedy, 1982) offers information about Jacksonville's Jewish community. **Thomas Graham**'s *Charles H. Jones, Journalist and Politician of the Gilded Age* (Tallahassee: Florida A&M University Press, 1990) profiles one of the city's most important newspapermen. **Lawrence Mahoney**'s *Children and Hope* (Miami: Pickering, 1987) narrates the history of the Children's Home Society of Florida, founded in Jacksonville in 1902. **Arthur Neyle Sollee, Sr.**'s *The Engineer Speaks* (Jacksonville: Sollee, 1982) recounts the development of Jacksonville's roads. **Linda D. Vance**'s *May Mann Jennings: Florida's Genteel Activist* (Gainesville: University Presses of Florida, 1986) honors an important Jacksonville woman in the first decades of this century.

Architecture, an important feature of any city, has thus far inspired two presently available books about Jacksonville. **Robert C. Broward**'s *The Architecture of Henry John Klutho: The Prairie School in Jacksonville* (Jacksonville: University of North Florida Press, 1983) focuses on the Jacksonville career of Henry Klutho, who studied with Frank Lloyd Wright and who came to the city to help "rebuild a magnificent city on the ashes of the old one" after the 1901 fire. His Main Street home, completed in 1909 but severely altered after its move to 30 West Ninth Street, is the first Prairie-style house in Florida, perhaps even in the South, and has recently been restored. As Broward, a noted Jacksonville architect inspired by Frank Lloyd Wright, observed, "Even in its current degraded state Klutho's design stands proudly as a reminder of the excellence of his new directions in architectural design."

Wayne Wood's *Jacksonville's Architectural Heritage* (Jacksonville: University of North Florida Press, 1989) contains over 1,000 photographs and drawings, presenting an impressive record of Duval County's landmark sites. The book, useful for a walking/driving tour of the city's neighborhoods, serves as well for serious study. Among numerous architectural examples deserving mention is the downtown Jacksonville Terminal, now called the Prime F. Osborn III Convention Center, a popularly revered landmark located on West Bay Street. When completed in 1919, the terminal was the largest railroad station in the South, modeled indirectly after the ancient Roman Baths of Caracalla. The building is the greatest example in the city of the neo-Classical revival style. Wood's book provides photos of its construction phases and a typically useful descriptive history.

In the early part of this century Jacksonville claimed to be the World's Winter Film Capital. After *A Florida Feud* in 1908, over 30 film companies produced dozens of films in the city, partly to save money by using sunlight instead of studio lights. These companies eventually headed west to California when the people of Jacksonville objected to such practices as filming bank robberies on Sundays, calling in false alarms to shoot a film of speeding fire trucks, plunging cars into the St. Johns River for an action film, and the like. Henry Klutho, the noted architect, invested $40,000 in one of the film companies and lost that investment when other Jacksonville citizens did not likewise invest. He later lamented that he was first called "... a man of vision and ideas for the good of the town [but] later I was often told I was a fool." Film star Oliver Hardy, who with Stan Laurel formed the Laurel and Hardy comedy team, grew up in Georgia, but came to Jacksonville in 1913 to act for Lubin Motion Pictures as a comedian; he earned $5 a day and was guaranteed three days of work each week.

Kalem Studio, located near the present Blue Cross/Blue Shield building on Riverside Avenue, filmed dreams for the nation's silver screens in the early teens of this century.

Film star "Babe" Oliver Hardy (second from right) is pictured here in 1916 on location in Jacksonville with, from left, Pearl Bailey, Budd Ross, and Ethel Burton. Hardy later teamed with Stan Laurel for their legendary film careers.

Movies produced in Jacksonville include *From the Manger to the Cross* (1907), *Idol of the Stage* (1916), *A Corner in Cotton* (1916), and *Revenge of the Creature* (1955). *The Gulf Between*, shot in Jacksonville in 1917, became the first technicolor feature motion picture in the world and starred Grace Darmond and Niles Welch. **Richard Alan Nelson**'s *Lights! Camera! Florida!: Ninety Years of Moviemaking and Television Production in the Sunshine State* (Tampa: Florida Endowment for the Humanities, 1987) provides more historical background about Jacksonville's and all of Florida's film industry. Florida has regained some of its former status as a film center, for it now ranks behind only California and New York as the location for feature-length films.

MANDARIN TO POINTS SOUTH AND WEST: PICOLATA AND OLUSTEE

Mandarin

Several miles south of Jacksonville is historic Mandarin, named after a segmented orange, a variety brought to Florida from China in the 1840s. As a settlement, the community is older than Jacksonville and is known for homes more than 100 years old on the National Register of Historic Places. The river bluff was settled by the Timucuan Indians and visited by Spanish missionaries from the St. Augustine settlement. In the nineteenth century, steamships loaded citrus and vegetables at the three wharves along the Mandarin boardwalk, a half-mile-long wooden walkway connecting riverfront estates. The area still attracts travelers who drive through to admire its majestic live oaks forming a five-mile-long canopy arching over Mandarin Road, which meanders past orange groves along the river. Mandarin's orange trees, limbs bent low with fruit, inspired Harriet Beecher Stowe to call them the "trees of the Lord" and "the best worthy to represent the Tree of Life." Finally, Mandarin is well-known as the home of many artists, writers, craftsmen, and musicians, some with international reputations. South of Mandarin, Frederick Delius came to raise oranges — until he took up piano playing and the composing of music.

Those whose wit prompts them to enjoy tombstone lore may wish to visit Mandarin Cemetery. One much-visited marker offers the gravestone reader this inscription:

IN
MEMORY OF
GEORGE S. MOTT
Son of
Jacob C. and Mary C. Mott
of the state and
City of New-York
Shot by the Indians
May 18th in the year
of our Lord 1836
Aged 30 years

That the perpetrators of this
Cruel act may be forgiven
Is the prayer of his afflicted
And ever sorrowing Mother

According to legend, Mott, who had the dubious distinction of becoming Mandarin's first bigamist, had married Waha, the daughter of the local Timucuan chief, in tribal rites, neglecting to mention his wife and several children living in the North. Upon his return from a trip north, the Timucuans shot him before his boat landed.

Mandarin's best-known resident author was **Harriet Beecher Stowe** (1811-1896), author of 30 books, 11 of them novels, the most famous being *Uncle Tom's Cabin* (1851). She and her husband Calvin became winter residents here from 1867 to 1884. Her home at 12447 Mandarin Road no longer stands, and a Tiffany window dedicated to the Stowe family in the Episcopal Church of Our Saviour (located almost a half mile north of the Stowe homesite, which was across Mandarin Road from the present Community Club) was destroyed by Hurricane Dora in 1964. Even so, the church has replicated as its chapel wing the original interior (except for the crushed Stowe window) of the Church of Our Saviour that Stowe and her husband helped found. Harriet's father, Henry Ward Beecher, was probably the most famous preacher in the United States and certainly a strong influence on her activities and ideas.

The historical marker in front of the Community Club (originally built in 1869 as a branch of the Freedmen's Bureau at Stowe's urging to help educate black children) notes the purchase, by Harriet and Calvin Stowe, of a riverfront home on 30 acres of the Fairbanks Grant, one of the original land grants from the British Crown. Here she wrote the short stories and sketches she published as *Palmetto Leaves* (1873; reprinted by the University of Florida Press, 1968), a popular book about the beauties and benefits, as well as the stark realities, of Florida life. Her aim was to answer the many inquiries she received about her life in Florida. Among her subjects, she called the alligator "a delicate beast," wrote of a boat trip up Julington Creek, touted the school and church functions of the then-new Community Club (changed from the Freedmen's Bureau in 1870) as "a neat little pleasant place," and declared that "in this quiet bay... this [her home] is the place to read papers and books." Also in *Palmetto Leaves*, she wrote:

> For ourselves, we are getting reconciled to a sort of tumble-down,
> wild, picnicky kind of life, — this general happy-go-luckiness which
> Florida inculcates. If we painted her, we should not represent her
> as a neat, trim damsel, with starched linen cuffs and collar; she
> would be a brunette, dark but comely, with gorgeous tissues, a
> general disarray and dazzle, and with a sort of jolly untidiness, free,
> easy, and joyous.

The local steamboat that plied the waters between Jacksonville and Mandarin had an arrangement with Stowe that whenever it approached Mandarin she would go out to a writing table on her open porch — so the passengers could

Harriet Beecher Stowe and family on the front porch of the Stowe riverfront home in the winter of 1867, their wintering place until 1884. The "Stowe Cottage," as it was called, located across Mandarin Road from the present Mandarin Community Club, no longer exists. The traveler can find a historic marker on the community club grounds.

glimpse this famous American author "at work." This sort of public-relations gesture no doubt helped the sale of her books.

When the Stowes arrived in Mandarin, *Uncle Tom's Cabin* (1851) had long since become one of America's first runaway best-sellers, having sold 300,000 copies in its first year, making its author both rich and famous. Stowe, who had published her first article in 1834, at age 23, had vowed to write only for money, in order to have leisure and time for reflection — and be a mother to her children. Even during her Florida period, she toured, along with Mark Twain on occasion (who also visited her in Mandarin), New England in 1871 and the Midwest in 1872 to earn much money quickly and to promote her books. Her royalties alone were estimated at an average of $10,000-$20,000 per year from the 1850s through the 1870s.

As a pre-feminist, she championed many causes relating to the rights of women, including her controversial defense of Lady Byron, whom she came

51

to know during a trip to England and who confided in Stowe details about Lord Byron as a wife abuser. She also popularized writing as a career for women, proving that a woman could write a powerful novel, not just one of sentiment, as current stereotypes suggested. To write so much so profitably, she hired her unmarried sister Catherine to run her home. Despite Stowe's international reputation, she could not, as a nineteenth-century woman, sign her own publishing contracts — her husband had to sign for her. An intellectually quick and able man (a theologian, he was popularly known as "the professor"), though he had Bright's disease and was not physically strong, Calvin Stowe encouraged his wife in her work, living harmoniously with her as the husband of "the widow Stowe" (so named because she was often in the public eye, alone).

Moving to Florida, she felt some trepidation about what treatment she, as a northerner, might receive from the natives. Indeed, this was a widely held fear among Yankee tourists of the time, appearing as a complaint from a correspondent in the *New York Tribune* in 1877. Her pointed reply was printed in the *Tribune*, stating that she had "... received not even an incivility from any native Floridian." Unfortunately, nature was not so kind as the natives, for in 1880 the entire orange crop froze, a yearly hazard this far north, and Stowe openly wept upon seeing the resulting catastrophe when she arrived that year. Shortly after, she ceased coming to Mandarin. According to Mandarin historian Mary B. Graff, the Stowes' son Charles, "misguided by the feeling that his parents had not been treated well in Mandarin," had her house torn down in 1916 by offering "... lumber to all who would carry it away."

A modern novel featuring Mandarin is **William Du Bois**'s *A Season To Beware* (New York: Putnam's, 1956). For a history of the town see **Mary B. Graff**'s *Mandarin on the St. Johns* (1953; reprinted Gainesville: University of Florida Press, 1963), indispensable for understanding the history and lore of the area. At least four authors titled their biographies *Harriet Beecher Stowe*: **John R. Adams** (New York: Twayne, 1963); **Noel B. Gerson** (New York: Praeger, 1976); **Cathrene P. Gilbertson** (New York: Appleton Century, 1937); and **Robert E. Jakoubek** (New York: Chelsea House, 1989). **Edward Wagenknecht**'s account is called *Harriet Beecher Stowe: The Known and the Unknown* (New York: Oxford University Press, 1965). Some other excellent books deserve mention: For insider views see **Lyman Beecher Stowe**'s humorous and valuable *Saints, Sinners and Beechers* (Indianapolis: Bobbs-Merrill, 1934); **Catherine Beecher**'s *Woman Suffrage and Woman's Profession* (Hartford: Brown and Gross, 1871); and **Charles Stowe**'s *Life of Harriet Beecher Stowe* (Boston: Houghton, Mifflin & Co., 1889). *Runaway to Heaven, The Story of Harriet Beecher Stowe* (Garden City, NY: Doubleday, 1963) by **Johanna Johnston** provides more details about her life. *Harriet Beecher Stowe* (Hamden, CT: Archon Books, 1976) by **Margaret Holbrook Hildreth** is a bibliography of works about Stowe, and *Harriet Beecher Stowe* (Boston: G.K. Hall, 1977) by **Jean W. Ashton** is a reference guide.

Because of Stowe's feminism and because of new information about her life revealed through recently published letters, two forthcoming biographies should be of great interest. Their authors are **Joan Hedrick** of Trinity University in Hartford, Connecticut, and **Patricia Hill** of Wesleyan University in Middletown, Connecticut.

Picolata

South of Mandarin along the river and to the west of St. Augustine, Picolata may take its name from a Spanish phrase meaning *broad bluff*, referring to the ground on which early settlers built a Spanish fort. The Indians and Spanish used this narrow place to cross the river. **William Bartram** (1739-1828) came to Picolata to raise indigo in 1766. As the son of botanist John Bartram, who had founded in Philadelphia the first North American botanical garden in 1728, young William spent a number of years trying to find his calling: as an artist, surveyor, merchant, and farmer. He failed at all these pursuits. At Picolata he had neither wife nor friend nor neighbor within nine miles of his farm for help or companionship and so, discouraged over his unsuccessful crops, he returned to his father's home.

At that point a British doctor hired him to travel throughout the British colonies in the American South collecting rare plants and seeds that would withstand the bitter English winters and sketching birds and plants. During that trip William Bartram wrote *Travels Through North and South Carolina, Georgia, East and West Florida* (1791; New York: Viking Penguin Inc., 1988) and found his calling at last. He later became an eminent scientist and member of many learned societies. *Billy Bartram and His Green World* (New York: Farrar, Straus & Giroux, 1972) by **Marjory Bartlett Sanger** offers a biographical account of this great American traveler.

Bartram's *Travels* became important because it described clearly and evocatively the St. Johns River and the many curiosities of a rather unknown land, its flora, strange fauna, and Indians. *Travels*, published at a time when England's romantic movement was emphasizing a return to nature, prompted the great English romantics to borrow freely from his Florida descriptions, especially those of the St. Johns, for their poetry. Samuel Taylor Coleridge, for example, used Florida images in his remarkable works *The Rime of the Ancient Mariner, Kubla Khan*, and "Christabel." Other writers such as William Wordsworth, Robert Southey, and Thomas Campbell did likewise. *William Bartram* (Baltimore: The Johns Hopkins Press, 1933) by **N. Bryllion Fagin** traces the many uses of Bartram's *Travels* in English and European literature.

New England poet **William Cullen Bryant** visited Picolata in 1843 and wrote, "Here I find everything green, fresh, and fragrant, trees and shrubs in full foliage, and wild roses in flower. The dark waters of the St. John's [sic], one of the noblest streams in the country, in depth and width like the St. Lawrence, draining almost the whole extent of the peninsula, are flowing under my window. On the opposite shore are forests of tall trees, bright in the new verdure of the season." In another passage Bryant related how a group of

Indians ambushed a troupe of actors on their way to St. Augustine, killed them, dressed themselves in the actors' costumes, and pranced through the woods dressed as Othello and Richard III and Falstaff: a grotesque image of two cultures colliding.

Composer Frederick Delius came to Solano Grove in Picolata in 1884 to grow oranges, later abandoning life as a Florida farmer for international acclaim as a composer. A marker indicates the spot where Delius lived and where he first heard the singing of the black laborers, which influenced his music. A book describing music similar to that which Delius heard on the St. Johns is *Sinful Tunes and Spirituals: Black Folk Music to the Civil War* (Urbana: University of Illinois Press, 1977) by **Dena J. Epstein**, which includes a boat song used on the St. Johns at the time of the Second Seminole War.

Ruth Burnett's juvenile novel *The Picolata Treasure* (New York: Bouregy, 1974) takes place in this area, telling about the establishment of a wildlife preserve. In the novel, an armadillo saves the life of a human — quite unusual, but, like other Florida stories, buried Spanish treasure provokes intrigue and involved plots. [For more about Picolata see the next chapter.]

Orange Park

On the opposite side of the St. Johns and across the Buckman Bridge is the small city of Orange Park, originally the site of Laurel Grove when owned by Zephaniah Kingsley. No one knows why the name was changed, but perhaps the strong urge to commemorate the state's love affair with citrus and oranges is the answer.

Florida Pier Scott-Maxwell (1884-1962) was born in Orange Park and educated at home until age 10. Her Florida book is *The Measure of My Days* (1951; republished, New York: Knopf, 1968) about her childhood in Florida. By 1903 she had begun her writing career, and in 1910, she married John Scott-Maxwell and went to live in his native Scotland, becoming active there in the women's suffrage movement. In 1933 she began studying with Carl Jung and became an analytical psychologist, practicing in both Scottish and English clinics. In *Measure* she devotes a section to her Florida years, recalling that "When I was a child I went with my grandfather when he hunted wild turkey, or quail, driving through the roadless woods under great oaks shining as though newly washed by rain. Once on reaching a river I jumped from the wagon and running into the deep shade sat down on a large alligator, taking it for a half-buried log." Commenting on her later years, she observes in surprise that "Only a few years ago I enjoyed tranquility: now I am so disturbed by the outer world and by human quality in general that I want to put things right, as though I still owed a debt to life. I must calm down. I am far too frail to indulge in moral fervour." She lived 11 more years, to age 79, after publishing *Measure*.

Ann O'Connell Rust, who has resided in Orange Park since 1971, was born in 1929 in Canal Point, Florida, on Lake Okeechobee, where her parents were pioneers. After her graduation from Pahokee High School, she took a Miami modeling course and moved to New York in 1949, modeled for a while for the Huntington-Hartford Agency, and then married Allen Rust, who has become, since 1988, her editor and publisher. They traveled widely, finally settling in Orange Park, where Amaro, an acronym for "a Marjorie Ann Rust original," has designated their gown-design company, then a modeling and talent agency, and now a publishing company.

She began writing in 1984 during a lull in the filming of movies in this area. She and her associates, who tested actors for film companies, wanted to make movies in Florida with Florida actors and found they needed scripts. Her modeling business improved, however, so her first novel from Amaro — *Punta Passa*, named after the port across from Sanibel Island — was not published until 1988. Since then, however, Amaro has published *Palatka* (1989), *Kissimmee* (1990), *Monticello* (1991), and *Pahokee* (1992), which ends with the Florida hurricane of 1928, near her home town. These historical novels follow the lives of three Florida pioneer women from 1877 to 1928 in their different locations.

Madeleine L'Engle, the author of award-winning children's and young people's books, has deep roots in Florida. In a 1977 letter, she recalled her Florida ancestry: "... my mother's family arrived in Florida with that very first group of pioneers in the late 1500s." She treasures letters and memoirs written by these Florida forebears and handed down to her. Born in 1918 in New York, she spent several of her high school and college years in Florida and continued to visit her mother in Jacksonville after leaving home. "I wrote a great deal [in Florida] during vacations and from then on until my mother's death" in 1972. "I always wrote whenever I was visiting her." As she wrote in 1977, "My Florida roots are very strong in me and I am fortunate enough to visit almost every year and always write out on [a] dock in Orange Park."

She received the John Newbery Medal in 1963, the Hans Christian Andersen Runner-up Award in 1964, the Sequoyah Award in 1965, and the Lewis Carroll Shelf in 1965 for *A Wrinkle in Time*, which deals with the fifth dimension in the adventures of three young people in space and dramatizes the eternal struggle between good and evil. Florida figures prominently in *The Other Side of the Sun* (New York: Farrar, Straus & Giroux, 1971) and a non-fiction work about her mother entitled *The Summer of the Great-Grandmother* (New York: Farrar, Straus & Giroux, 1974). Other books by L'Engle include *Camilla* (1965), *The Arm of the Starfish* (1965), and *Circle of Quiet* (1972). She once wrote, "Each time I start a new book, I am risking failure.... Unless I'm willing to open myself up to risk [in relationships as well as books] and to being hurt, then I'm closing myself off to love and friendship." She lives in Goshen, Connecticut.

Hibernia

Across the river from Mandarin is the settlement of Hibernia, with the poetic name for Ireland. Hibernia, Mandarin, and Picolata all possess picturesque "carpenter Gothic" churches dating back to the days when river steamboats visited these towns. **Eugenia Price**'s *Margaret's Story* (New York: Lippincott & Crowell, 1980), a novel, relates the historical saga of Margaret Seton Fleming and her family from the 1830s to the 1880s. The church figures in

St. Margaret's Episcopal Church, Hibernia, ca. 1903, begun in 1875, built by Margaret Seton Fleming and her family. The first service in the church was her funeral in 1878.

the novel's action. See **Margaret Seton Fleming Biddle**'s *Hibernia: The Unreturning Tide* (New York: Vantage Press, 1974) for a history of the Hibernia area. She writes, at age 86, detailing life in Hibernia in the early 1800s, when the entire province of the Floridas had only a few thousand white persons and numerous, sometimes hostile Indians: "At this time there was one road — little more than a cart track — deep in sand and solitude, to the inland town of Middleburg.... The St. John's [sic] was the great highway of all that part of the country, the Main Street of Florida. Each plantation had its own eight-oar barge, manned by strong slaves, as a means of transportation on the river." For a description of this area from 1867 to 1874 see *Dear Jeffie* (Cambridge, MA: Peabody Museum Press, 1978) by **Jeffries Wyman**, edited by George E. Gifford, Jr.

Starke

Taking its name from either Madison Starke Perry, governor of Florida from 1857 to 1861, or Thomas Starke, a landowner in Volusia County, Starke is best known for Raiford, the nearby state prison.

James McLendon spent his first eighteen years in Union County where his father was a Raiford senior prison official. As he put it, "I was born in Gainesville on March 7, 1942, and was taken to the State Prison immediately." While in Florida, he worked at odd jobs such as shotgun guard at a road camp, brickyard laborer, and ice-cream truck driver, though when he left Florida for a few years he worked as a U.S. Marine infantryman, a sixth-grade and algebra teacher (he lost his job after an argument with the principal about his aversion to keeping his tie button buttoned), and a stockbroker, in Baltimore. In 1967, he decided to be a writer. After working on several southern daily newspapers, he worked at the *Key West Citizen* while he wrote *Papa: Hemingway in Key West* (Miami: E.A. Seemann Publishing Company, 1972). Over the next five years, McLendon wrote over 300 magazine articles and the biography of Del Layton, mayor of the town of Layton: *Pioneer in the Florida Keys* (Miami: E.A. Seemann Publishing Company, 1976). During that time, he also lived in Marathon, Islamorada, and Miami.

Once he became financially secure, he wrote *Deathwork* (Philadelphia: Lippincott, 1977), the first of a planned tetrology, which he called *The Sun Quartet*, dealing with a theme McLendon called "man's surge for freedom." The first book made him wealthy, enabling him and his nationally published photographer wife to divide their year between the Blue Ridge Mountain town of Blowing Rock, North Carolina, and the old city of Morelia, Mexico. *Deathwork*, which his editor called *faction*, recounted the minute-by-minute process in the electrocution of four criminals one morning at Raiford Prison. McLendon described his *Sun Quartet* as an explanation of the four stages of freedom: the absence of freedom, trapped with no hope (*Deathwork*); trying to get free but not getting free (*Eddie Macon's Run*, 1978); trying to get free and getting free (*Oro*, which he projected for writing in 1978-79); and finally being free, the essence of freedom (*Sun Man*, which he projected for writing in 1980-81).

Significantly, he wrote in a letter, July 13, 1977, "My novels are about me in one way or another. I was born a Cracker in North Florida and have since plugged into the big, wide world with all its up's and down's. I drew a lot of strength from my Cracker youth although I was always running from it. I've

Florida State Prison, Raiford, pictured September 1949. View of the watch tower and fence.

stopped running now and just write." McLendon did not live to tell his big Florida story. He died in 1982.

Connie May Fowler, a native Floridian, also features a small, unnamed town near her own St. Augustine which the locals in her novel *Sugar Cage* (New York: Putnam's, 1992) call The Prison Capital of the World as the town motto in order to lure "dumb Yankees" from "St. Augustine's oldest this and oldest that." The novel takes place partly in sugarcane fields and swamps to the south, but also in the unnamed prison, where the men, out of loneliness and prejudices, have created an annual Free Men and Prisoners Baseball Game. A poetically rendered book, the story features an unlikely community, perhaps a cross-section of Florida characters: a Haitian caneworker, an abandoned young boy, a philandering but loving husband, a dying intellectual, a grieving widow, a merry widow, a soldier facing death, and a little girl haunted by ghosts of her parents' past. **Sterling Watson**, a graduate of the creative writing program at the University of Florida and now professor on the Eckerd College faculty in St. Petersburg, also set his novel *Weep No More My Brother* (New York: Morrow, 1978) at Raiford.

Raiford was the prison in which Clarence Earl Gideon was serving a five-year sentence in the early 1960s for breaking into a Bay Harbor, Florida, pool hall in 1961; the U.S. Supreme Court eventually overturned his conviction because a lawyer had not represented him at his trial. The Gideon case was a landmark decision because it required that judges appoint a lawyer for a defendant who could not afford one. That case became the subject of *Gideon's Trumpet* by **Anthony Lewis** (New York: Random House, 1964). The novel became a film of the same name in 1979, starring Henry Fonda as Gideon. A work featuring Raiford Prison and other Florida prisons is *The Frank Murphy Story*, as told to **Thomas Helm** by **Frank Murphy** (New York: Dodd, Mead, 1968).

Marjorie Driggers's *History of Union County, Florida* (Lake Butler, FL: Union County Times, 1971) provides a record of the area, commemorating the county's fiftieth anniversary.

Olustee

Olustee, whose name comes from Seminole-Creek and means *blackfish*, is near the site where Confederate troops met Union troops in the largest Civil War battle on Florida soil. On February 20, 1864, in the Battle of Ocean Pond, reenacted each February at the battle site, the Confederate troops defeated the Union troops and, in the words on the monument there, "prevented a Sherman-like invasion of Georgia from the South." **William H. Nulty**'s *Confederate Florida: The Road to Olustee* (Tuscaloosa, AL: University of Alabama Press, 1990) points out that the diversion of 15,000 Confederate troops to north Florida from the defense of Savannah and Charleston delayed the reinforcement of the Army of Tennessee, which was desperately trying to keep Union troops out of northwestern Georgia.

A novel set in nearby Baker County is **Anne L. Harwick**'s *Possum Trot* (New York: Carlton Press, 1968), a story of sharecroppers there.

VIVA LA FLORIDA!

STETSON KENNEDY

Florida is assuredly one of the most written-about places on the planet — as this *Book Lover's Guide* to the state so abundantly attests. There were some very good reasons why the past five hundred years were productive of so much Florida literature, but what of the future? Will there be a natural and cultural Florida worth writing about?

When European palefaces first set foot on the Americas, they saw fit to dub the entire southeastern portion of the northerly continent "La Florida." That is to say, the hype and the Legend of Florida began right then and there. Seeing no sign of the hoped-for riches of Cathay, those first-comers (with apologies to the redskins who had come long before) sent rave reviews to the royalty and merchants back home about the flowers, forests, furs, and fisheries with which La Florida abounded and appended post scriptums of rumors of riches just over the horizon.

Thus the Legend of Florida was born and, thanks to all the scribes described in this guide and the General Development Corporation, has been spreading throughout the earth ever since. Back then as now, natural resources were regarded as anything which can be converted into cash, and in Florida's case this came to include the climate itself. "Salubrious" was the word which did the trick.

Florida was fortunate in having among its earliest chroniclers no lesser talents than Cabeza de Vaca, The Inca, and even conquistadors with a flair for the literary. Thereafter came such devoted sons of nature as botanist William Bartram; ornithologist John James Audubon, who set up his observatory on the Keys; John Muir, who while "traipsing from Fernandina to Cedar Key" resolved to thenceforth dedicate his life to "saving the wilderness from man, and man for the wilderness"; and poet Sidney Lanier singing praises to "the length and the breadth, and the breadth and the length, of the marvelous marshes of Glynn."

Later on, Florida was doubly blessed in having a Marjorie Kinnan Rawlings to immortalize the native Cracker culture and a Zora Neale Hurston to do the same for the black. To be sure, Marjorie's whites never lynched, and Zora's blacks never got lynched. But if the Florida those two depicted was on the Arcadian side, the fact is that in those days Florida was about as Arcadian as you could get, lynchings or no lynchings.

Another major conservator of our cultural heritage was the WPA [Work Projects Administration] Florida Writers Project, which during the latter half of the 1930s (when the mule was still the centerpiece of rural life) not only compiled the *Florida Guide* but in the process collected a vast treasure trove of Floridiana. Comprised of thousands of Florida folksongs, tales, oral histories, and ex-slave narratives, this material reposed for half a century in the Library of Congress before being brought back home to the folklife archive at White Springs.

As subject matter for writers, Florida has been undergoing profound changes ever since the advent of white folks and the blacks they brought in. Where blame is due, much of it must go to the former, since they were giving the orders; and, where credit is due, much of it must go to the latter, who did more than their share of the hard work of carrying out those orders.

My father gained an insight into the process when in the early 1920s he ventured into the terra incognita which was to become Miami. Nothing there but 'skeeters and 'gators, he came back to report. But then, after the real estate Boom of the mid-20s had done its work, he went back for another look. This time all he could say was, "My God, what money has done to this country!"

For better or worse, money has been doing things to Florida ever since. As I say in the Afterword of the 1989 reprint of my 1942 book *Palmetto Country*, "[After] looking back, around, and ahead...perhaps this much at least can be said with certainty: the palmetto has fared rather better than the country." Sometimes the Florida that man has made has embellished the Florida created by nature; but all too often it has been its despoliation and may yet prove its nemesis.

After wiping the peninsula slate clean of its indigenous peoples and cultures, the Europeans and their American-born descendants went about the business of converting Florida's natural resources into "filthy lucre." Timbering on a "cut out and get out" basis soon stripped the state of its forests of pine, cypress, and live oak (never again would the road to St. Augustine lie "stirrup deep in pine needles"). Strip mining for phosphate took its toll of the landscape and continues apace. Meanwhile, massive consumption and pollution have conspired to reduce the once-famous Florida seafood restaurant to featuring Alaskan king crab.

The very elements — air, sea, land, water — which made Florida what it was are at risk, all because there is money in pollution for someone. Unless we speedily call a halt and effect a turn-around, our Florida Welcome Stations may soon have to hand out, along with the free glass of orange juice, a warning: "DON'T breathe the air, drink the water, eat the fish, or bathe in the sun or sea!" Should it come to that, of course, it would no longer be Florida.

When Thor Heyerdahl of *Kon Tiki* fame went poking about in the caves of Easter Island far out in the Pacific off the South American shore, what he found were graven stone images of such creatures as ocelots and crocodiles, the living likes of which had never been seen in those parts.

Let us hope the day will never come when teachers of "Florida" will have to say, "Now, students, today we are going to watch a film made back in the 20th century, showing live and in motion such legendary species as the whooping crane, Key pigeon, Carolina parakeet, seaside sparrow, manatee, Florida panther, Florida black bear, Florida duck, Key deer, and other species which are no longer with us."

I have never been one to contend that only the "good ole days" were any good, or that the road back is the road ahead. What I do say is that where there is life there is bound to be culture, and this goes for modern, urban, industrialized man no less than for our rural, agricultural, pedestrian forebears. And yet at the same time I am painfully aware that we can consciously upgrade or downgrade our cultures and that commercialism is the worst possible arbiter of this vital aspect of our lives. We need to get our values straight, put our cultural well-being on the same footing as our environmental, economic, and physical — and adjust our public and private investments accordingly.

Perhaps the best prescription for a Florida worth living in and writing about is to see to it that the peoples who inhabit it know about it, love it, and care for it. To that end, the more of Florida we have on the bookshelves of our homes, schools, and libraries, the better the chances for keeping the Legend of Florida a living one.

Stetson Kennedy (1916-), who is mentioned in this chapter and the next one, is a native Floridian whose books about Florida and the South have recently been republished by the University Press of Florida.

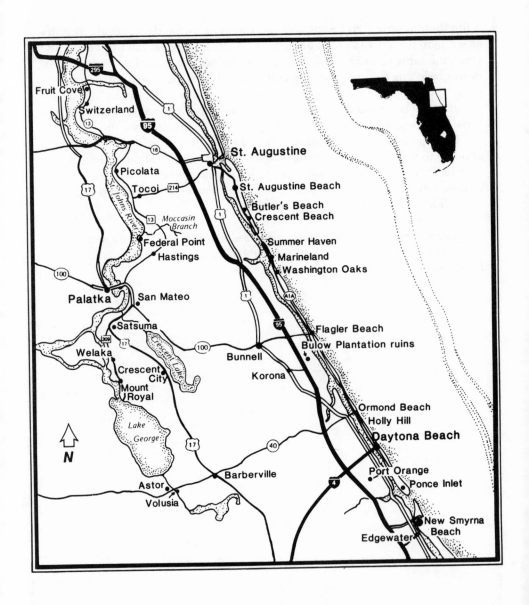

Fruit Cove
Switzerland
295
1
95
13
16
Picolata
Tocoi
St. Johns River
214
St. Augustine
St. Augustine Beach
Butler's Beach
Crescent Beach
1
Moccasin
Branch
13
Federal Point
Hastings
Summer Haven
Marineland
Washington Oaks
100
Palatka
San Mateo
1
A1A
Satsuma
309
95
Flagler Beach
Bulow Plantation ruins
17
Welaka
Crescent
Lake
100
Bunnell
Crescent
City
Korona
Mount
Royal
Lake
George
Ormond Beach
Holly Hill
Daytona Beach
17
N
40
Barberville
Port Orange
Ponce Inlet
4
Astor
Volusia
New Smyrna
Beach
Edgewater

2 ST. AUGUSTINE TO ASTOR

DAVID NOLAN

The Coastal Route: St. Augustine to Edgewater

Millions upon millions of visitors annually pass through this area, usually along interstate highways designed to funnel them, lemming-like, into the plastic worlds of Central Florida. What they miss in speeding by are many fascinating points of interest — quite a number of them even visible to the spectator without paying an admission fee. The triumphs and horrors of countless generations have left their remains — from prehistoric residents to the first European settlers to the latest round of developers of paradise.

A readable account of the region's history and some of its colorful characters can be found in *Florida's Golden Sands* by **A.J.** and **Kathryn Abbey Hanna** (Indianapolis: Bobbs-Merrill, 1950).

St. Augustine

St. Augustine, dating from 1565, is famed as the nation's oldest city — or, more exactly, as the oldest continuous European settlement on the continental United States. That is a distinction that the casual tourist will not be likely to miss. Everything is at least old, if not *olde* or *oldest*.

The city has been the subject and setting for shelves and shelves of books, from worthy literature to worthless trash. Most of St. Augustine fiction portrays some history — and quite a bit of St. Augustine's history has more than a small amount of fiction in it. One should expect no less in a tourist economy. When criticized for some of the exaggerations he peddled, one local entrepreneur replied simply: "You can't tell a man how to run his business."

Skepticism is warranted while walking these streets, but not in such a sour manner that appreciation of genuine folklore is lost. The spirit of the place was best captured by **Ring Lardner** (1885-1933) who had his fictional visitor in *Gullible's Travels* recount a day's itinerary:

"First, we went to St. George Street and visited the oldest house in the United States. Then we went to Hospital street and seen the oldest house in the United States. Then we turned the corner and went down St. Francis Street and inspected the oldest house in the United States. Then we dropped into a soda fountain and I had an egg phosphate made from the oldest egg in the Western Hemisphere." And so on.

The most complete listing of literature about the area is "Historical St. Augustine in Fiction" by Kevin McCarthy, which appeared in the 1978 edition of *El Escribano*, the annual journal of the St. Augustine Historical Society. The society also publishes an informative newsletter, *The East-Florida Gazette*, which draws its name from Florida's first newspaper, begun here in 1783 by Loyalist refugees from South Carolina during the American Revolution.

In 1782 Dr. William Charles Wells (1755-1817), whose family published the *South Carolina and American General Gazette*, arrived in St. Augustine with a printing press and, after assembling it, established the newspaper. His brother, John, later joined him and published books as well. The enterprise was abandoned when the British gave up control of Florida in 1784. The well-traveled printing press was taken to Nassau where it was used to launch yet another journal, *The Royal Bahama Gazette*.

The historical society library at 271 Charlotte Street contains the best collection of material about the city. The library has been claimed as a "second home" by the most popular author to write about St. Augustine in recent years, **Eugenia Price** (1916-). Her novel *Maria* (Philadelphia: Lippincott, 1977) is set at the Oldest House, 14 St. Francis Street, around the corner from the library. It is based on the life of a midwife who spent three decades in St. Augustine before her death in 1792. The book is so widely read by visitors that tour guides are used to people correcting their spiel based on "facts" from the novel. Many tourists who haven't yet read the book buy copies of it in the gift shop; and the historical society has also done a brisk traffic with its own pamphlet by **Patricia Griffin** researched by **Eugenia Arana**, *Mary Evans: A Woman of Substance*, subtitled *The Historical Basis for Eugenia Price's* Maria (St. Augustine Historical Society, 1977).

Another Price novel, *Margaret's Story* (New York: Lippincott & Crowell, 1980) is set partly at the nearby Fatio House, 20 Aviles Street, one of the city's outstanding restoration projects, sponsored by the Colonial Dames and open to visitors on a regular basis. Those curious as to Price's *modus operandi* will find of interest her companion nonfiction book, *Diary of a Novel* (New York: Lippincott & Crowell, 1980), which describes the writing of *Margaret's Story*. Though closely connected through her writing to the Ancient City, Eugenia Price always made her home elsewhere. Her favorite place to stay in St. Augustine was the upstairs front room at the Marion Motor Lodge, 120 Avenida Menendez, overlooking the bayfront.

So extensive has the writing been about St. Augustine that a visitor has the option of dividing it up according to taste. Different time periods, from Ponce de León to Martin Luther King, Jr., could be considered. Visitors can seek out buildings with literary associations, follow the footsteps of authors, and track down characters who appeared both in books and on these streets, either as residents or visitors.

One possible route might be the Heartbreak Tour of literary sites lost to the future. The old St. Johns County Courthouse, where three of Florida's finest novelists (Marjorie Kinnan Rawlings, Zora Neale Hurston, and Robert Wilder) were married, is now the site of a bank parking lot at the corner of Charlotte and Treasury streets.

The Buckingham Annex, where **James Branch Cabell** (1879-1958) spent most of his winters in St. Augustine (and where he pleaded with Marjorie Rawlings to explain to his wife that he was not unique in being unable to write with people traipsing through his room) is now gone, the site occupied by the Flagler College auditorium and gymnasium at the corner of Granada and Cedar streets.

The Valencia Hotel, 276 St. George Street, where both **Sinclair Lewis** (1885-1951) and **William Dean Howells** (1837-1920) stayed in 1916 is now a parking lot — only a low front wall and gate from the hotel remain. It was here that the meeting took place between the aged dean of American literature and the young man just embarking on his full-time writing career. The atmosphere was quite cordial, which made an occasion in 1930 all the more amazing. Lewis had just become the first American to win the Nobel Prize for literature, and he used his acceptance speech as an occasion to attack the by-then deceased Howells as a negative influence on American writing!

The old campus of Florida Memorial College, a black school where Zora Neale Hurston taught, Marjorie Kinnan Rawlings lectured, and Stetson Kennedy worked, seems destined to join these other vanished literary sites due to neglect, abandonment, vandalism, and arson. The current state of the remains can be seen on West King Street at Holmes Boulevard.

Quite an interesting tour could be made of the historic parking lots of St. Augustine, if only a sufficient number of tourists had the strength of vision to see things as they once were and not as they now appear.

A more conventional tour would focus on those buildings still standing, several of which have multiple literary associations.

Of the surviving grand hotel buildings of the Flagler era, which give the downtown such grace and majesty and the skyline its breathtaking quality, the Ponce de Leon (now Flagler College) had as guests over the years Mark Twain, Henry James, Sinclair Lewis, Edna Ferber, Thornton Wilder, Somerset Maugham, Sarah Orne Jewett, Maxwell Anderson, Mary Roberts Rinehart, and Stephen Vincent Benét, among others.

Henry James (1843-1916), the expatriate novelist, stayed at the Ponce in 1905 when, as the local society newspaper reported, he was "endeavoring to become familiar with the beauty and charm of his own country." The book that resulted from that sojourn, *The American Scene*, called it "an hotel of the first magnitude," noting that "it breaks out, on every pretext, into circular arches and embroidered screens, into courts and cloisters, arcades and fountains, fantastic projections and lordly towers...."

Ring Lardner gave a more down-to-earth description in his *Gullible's Travels* (Indianapolis: Bobbs-Merrill, 1917), the story of a social-climbing Chicago woman who drags her husband to Florida for the winter, hoping to meet some of the famous Four Hundred "society leaders." Mr. Gullible notes that his wife learned from her guidebook that the murals in the Ponce were worth seeing, "so we had to stand in front o' them for a couple hours and try to keep awake. Four or five o' them was thrillers, at that. Their names was Adventure, Discovery, Contest, and so on, but what they all should of been called was Lady Who Had Mislaid Her Clo'es."

Facing the Ponce de Leon is the slightly less elegant Alcazar, which Flagler made irresistible by adding a casino to the back. This hotel, the front of which is now St. Augustine's city hall, had a large literary clientele as well. The Indiana School writers, who so regularly populated the bestseller lists at the turn of the century, particularly favored it, including poet **James Whitcomb Riley** (1849-1916), novelist **Booth Tarkington** (1869-1946), and humorist **George Ade** (1866-1944), author of *Fables in Slang*. There was a scandal one year when Mr. and Mrs. George Ade registered at the hotel, since the humorist was a lifelong bachelor; it turned out to be a con man using Ade's name.

Finley Peter Dunne (1867-1936), who has been hailed as "our greatest humorist after Mark Twain" for his creation of Mr. Dooley, the genial Irish bartender with wise and witty comments on all variety of questions, spent his honeymoon at the Alcazar in 1903. Dunne was a good friend of Thomas Hastings, the architect from the firm of Carrère and Hastings, which designed the hotel and many other grand buildings of the Flagler era.

Another literary guest was **Albert Payson Terhune** (1872-1942), who achieved wide popularity with dog stories like *Lad* and also wrote two mysteries with Florida settings: *Black Caesar's Clan* (New York: A.L. Burt, 1922) and *The Secret of Sea-dream House* (New York: Harper, 1929).

A regular visitor for many years at the Alcazar was **William English Walling** (1877-1936), a prominent socialite and socialist journalist, whose article "Race War in the North" about a race riot in Springfield, Illinois, as that city prepared to celebrate the centennial birthday of Abraham Lincoln, touched the public conscience and helped lead to the founding in 1909 of the National Association for the Advancement of Colored People. Walling's wife, **Anna Strunsky** (1879-1964), had collaborated with **Jack London** on *The Kempton-Wace Letters* (1903) and appears as a character in **Irving Stone's** *Jack London: Sailor on Horseback* (1938).

In the courtyard of the Alcazar is the tomb of **Otto C. Lightner** (1887-1950), the founder of *Hobbies* magazine, who purchased the hotel in 1947 and opened the Lightner Museum whose gracious collection of antiques now occupies the rear section of the building. Lightner was the author of *The History of Business Depressions* (1922; reprinted New York: Burt Franklin, 1970).

The third surviving grand hotel, the Cordova, has served since 1968 as the St. Johns County Courthouse. Prior to that it hosted characters as diverse as five-and-ten magnate Frank Woolworth, Mrs. Tom Thumb, and the police dogs used during the 1964 civil rights demonstrations. The Cordova, rather than the neighboring Ponce or Alcazar, in 1891 drew the best-selling author of the Flagler era as a month-long guest. His name was **Archibald Clavering Gunter** (1847-1907) and, although almost universally forgotten today, his books like

Mr. Barnes of New York, Mr. Potter of Texas, and *Miss Nobody of Nowhere* were the rage of the time. If remembered at all nowadays, it is usually because he called the attention of his friend, actor DeWolfe Hopper, to a newspaper poem called "Casey At the Bat," which Hopper then immortalized in thousands of performances. Gunter spent his time here well, coming out afterwards with several Florida novels. *A Florida Enchantment* (New York: Home, 1892) was later made into a silent movie starring Sidney Drew.

Nearby at 83 King Street is Villa Zorayda, an often-overlooked building of great historic and architectural importance, with some literary associations as well. Built in 1883 as a winter home by **Franklin W. Smith** (1826-1911), Boston hardware merchant, reformer, and amateur architect, it began the process of re-introducing Hispanic architecture into the former Spanish colony of Florida. Smith also pioneered the use of poured concrete construction. Within a few years Standard Oil partner Henry Flagler adopted both the Spanish theme and the building material for his grand hotels and churches.

Smith, one of the great Victorian visionaries, died broke in 1911 and has been unjustly forgotten. The scope of his thinking is clearly given in his publications: *Design & Prospectus For The National Gallery of History & Art* (1891) and *Designs, Plans, and Suggestions for the Aggrandizement of Washington* (1900).

His daughter, **Nina Larré Smith** (later **Duryea**), published a collection of short stories called *Tales of St. Augustine* (Cambridge, MA: W.H. Wheeler, 1891), set in the various hotels of the Flagler era. Later, as Flagler continued his railroad south and established other resorts, she republished it as *Among the Palms* (New York: J.F. Taylor, 1903), with the settings changed to other cities, although, really, only the names are changed; the geography is always that of St. Augustine.

Randolph Caldecott grave, St. Augustine

The visitor may head in any direction from the heart of downtown and find places of literary association. Going west, at 8 Arenta Street is the Barbour House, the last in town to retain its original mansard roof. Its Charles Addams-like appearance increases with the reading of **June Moore Ferrell**'s *The House* (New York: Carlton, 1979), a spooky novel set there.

Evergreen Cemetery in West Augustine is the burial site of **Randolph Caldecott** (1846-1886), the celebrated British illustrator whom Maurice Sendak hailed as the father of the modern illustrated children's book. Indeed, the highest award in that field, given annually since 1938, is the Caldecott Medal, which Sendak won in 1964 for *Where the Wild Things Are* (1963). Caldecott was ill when he came to St. Augustine in 1885. Despite the city's reputation as a health resort, his condition worsened, and he died in February 1886 at the age of 39. Admirers paid for his headstone in the cemetery, which contains the wrong death date. For more about his final days, see John Cech, "Art Is Long; Life Isn't: Randolph Caldecott in America and in Florida," in the January 1981 issue of *The Florida Historical Quarterly*.

In 1991 the local public library had ceremonies to dedicate its Randolph Caldecott Children's Room, with two of his family members present. The Ancient City is headquarters for the Randolph Caldecott Society of America. Information is available from R.C.S.A., 112 Crooked Tree Trail, St Augustine, FL 32086.

Another literary landmark in West Augustine is the two-story house at 791 West King Street where Zora Neale Hurston lived while teaching at Florida Normal and Industrial Institute (later Florida Memorial College) in 1942.

Going south from downtown is a large, primarily residential area which contains many of the interesting old houses of the city. The childhood homes of three local boys who went on to make their mark in the literary world are here. **William McGuire** (1917-), who became editor of the Bollingen Series at Princeton University Press, executive editor of the collected works of Carl Jung, and a trustee of the Vladimir Nabokov Literary Trust, lived at 94 Cedar Street. McGuire's writings include *Bollingen: An Adventure in Collecting the Past* (1982) and *Poetry's Catbird Seat* (1988).

Zora Neale Hurston House, St. Augustine

The family home of **William DuBois** (1903-), who gained a reputation as a playwright, journalist, and novelist in New York, was at 11 Bridge Street. His play *Haiti* (1938) was one of the great hits of the Federal Theatre Project of the 1930s. An earlier play, *Pagan Lady* (1930), was set in a tourist town on the east coast of Florida. It was made into a movie by Columbia Pictures in 1931. His other writings include a mystery, *The Case of the Deadly Diary* (Boston: Little, Brown, 1940), set in New York and St. Augustine, and a novel, *A Season to Beware* (New York: Putnam, 1956), which has a Florida setting. His sister, **Virginia DuBois Edwards** (1910-1978), wrote an interesting historical pamphlet, *Stories of Old St. Augustine* (St. Augustine: C.F. Hamblen, 1973).

1 Palm Row was the home of **Michael Gannon** (1927-), author of two well-known Catholic histories: *Rebel Bishop* (Milwaukee: Bruce Publishing Co., 1964) and *The Cross in the Sand* (Gainesville: University of Florida Press, 1965), as well as the best-selling *Operation Drumbeat* (New York: Harper & Row, 1990) about German U-boat attacks on the American coast during World War II. Gannon has also served as chairman of the Historic St. Augustine Preservation Board.

William Dean Howells lived at 246 St. George Street during the early months of 1916, one of several winters that he came to the city. He was working on a novel with a local setting, but never completed it. He did, however, write a two-part series for *Harper's* magazine (April and May 1917) called "A Confession of St. Augustine," with illustrations by his son, the well-known architect John Mead Howells.

Next door at 250 St. George Street is what has been called for more than a century The Prince Murat House. Whether this is actually the "small house with a rather pretty garden" that Napoleon's nephew rented a few days after arriving in St. Augustine in 1824 has thus far eluded the documentary efforts of historians. It is, however, one of the Ancient City's oldest legends; of that there is no doubt. **Achille Murat** (1801-1847), a former crown prince of Naples (in the days before Waterloo), stayed in the city only a couple of months before buying a 1,200-acre plantation called Parthenope several miles to the south at the confluence of Moses Creek and the Matanzas River, an area still known as Murat's Point, where the ruins of a log cabin (there was no grand elegance on this plantation) survived into the twentieth century.

Murat later moved to Tallahassee, where he married a grandniece of George Washington. Firmly enshrined in the state's lore, he has inspired a novel, **Steve Glassman's** *Blood on the Moon* (Brooklyn, OH: Quality Publications, 1990), and a classic biography, **A.J. Hanna's** *A Prince in Their Midst: The Adventurous Life of Achille Murat on the American Frontier* (Norman, OK: University of Oklahoma Press, 1946).

Unfortunately forgotten have been the prince's own writings. One of his books was translated twice: in London as *A Moral and Political Sketch of the United States of North America* (London: E. Wilson, 1833) and in New York as *America and the Americans* (New York: W.H. Graham, 1849). An acute observation of life on the frontier where "every dispute is amicably terminated by the

St. Francis Inn courtyard and cottage, St. Augustine

fist," it surely deserves at least a fraction of the attention lavished over the years on the writings of his countryman and contemporary, Alexis de Tocqueville.

At 279 St. George Street is the St. Francis Inn, the city's oldest lodging place and one with long literary associations. It was once owned (as was the colonial Llambias House across the way at 31 St. Francis Street) by Dr. **William Hayne Simmons** (1784-1870). Physician, poet, politician, and promoter, Simmons was one of two commissioners who set out in 1824 from opposite ends of Florida, then met in the middle and decided on Tallahassee as the site for the new capital. Simmons had already written *Notices of East Florida* (1822; republished Gainesville: University of Florida Press, 1973), which was not only an early promotional work but also a pioneering ethnographic study of the Seminole Indians.

William J. Hardee (1815-1873), whose wife's family long operated 279 St. George Street as the Dummett House, was the author of *Rifle and Light Infantry Tactics* (1855), popularly known as Hardee's Tactics, which both sides used in the Civil War. Hardee, who served as a Confederate general, was the subject of a biography by **Nathaniel C. Hughes, Jr.**: *General William J. Hardee* (Baton Rouge: Louisiana State University Press, 1965).

The cottage in the picturesque courtyard of the St. Francis Inn was rented in 1933 by **Van Wyck Brooks** (1886-1963), who came to St. Augustine to begin work on his monumental literary history of the United States, the first volume of which, *The Flowering of New England* (1936), won the 1937 Pulitzer Prize for history. Brooks was lavish in his praise for the inn — then known as the Graham House — and even when he moved to larger quarters he returned there to eat two meals a day. Another literary guest at the Graham House was novelist **Gladys Hasty Carroll**, author of *As the Earth Turns* (1933).

The courtyard cottage was the first home shared by novelist **Edith Taylor Pope** (1905-1961) and her husband Verle, who later became president of the Florida Senate and was prominently mentioned as a possible candidate for governor. Her family home was nearby at 298 St. George Street, a house originally built about 1905 as winter residence for Simeon Baldwin (1840-1927), who served as governor of Connecticut and chief justice of that state's Supreme Court. Baldwin taught for 50 years at Yale Law School and wrote a number of books on legal subjects.

Edith Pope was one of the major local novelists of the twentieth century. Her first book was published while she was still in school, and her novel *Colcorton* (New York: Scribner's, 1944), which was set in Palm Valley and dealt with the theme of miscegenation, was a runner-up for the Pulitzer Prize. One of the characters was based on novelist Sinclair Lewis. It appeared in paperback in 1990 with an introduction by Rita Mae Brown as part of the Plume American Women Writers series, dedicated to bringing lost works back into print. Edith Pope's other works include *Not Magnolia* (New York: Dutton, 1928); *Old Lady Esteroy* (New York: Dutton, 1934); *Half Holiday* (New York: Dutton, 1938); *River in the Wind* (New York: Scribner's, 1954); and a children's book, *The Biggety Chameleon* (New York: Scribner's 1946). Her editor at Scribner's was the legendary Maxwell Perkins, who was persuaded to take on Pope by their mutual friend, Marjorie Kinnan Rawlings.

The old Flagler Hospital at 159 Marine Street is where Marjorie Kinnan Rawlings died on December 14, 1953, after suffering a cerebral hemorrhage at her Crescent Beach home.

Going north from the downtown area, there are also a number of literary sites. At 6 Valencia Street, right behind the Ponce de Leon Hotel, is a large winter cottage built in 1898 for the hotel physician, Dr. Frank Fremont-Smith, grandfather of book critic Eliot Fremont-Smith. Later, divided up, it became the Valencia Apartments and had at least two literary residents.

Bernadine Bailey (1901-), author of dozens of books for young readers, including *Juan Ponce de León* (Boston: Houghton Mifflin, 1958), lived there in the 1940s.

James Branch Cabell (1879-1958), lived at 6 Valencia in 1952, the last year before invalidism made it impossible for him to return to St. Augustine, which had been his regular winter home since 1935. The Ancient City figured prominently in most of his later books, both fiction and nonfiction. He collaborated with A.J. Hanna on *The St. Johns: A Parade of Diversities* (New York: Farrar & Rinehart, 1943) for the Rivers of America series. His novels *There Were Two Pirates* (New York: Farrar, Straus, 1946) and *The Devil's Own Dear Son* (New York: Farrar, Straus, 1949), with Ancient City settings, were dedicated to local residents Marjorie Kinnan Rawlings and Norton Baskin. His memoir *Quiet Please* was published by the University of Florida Press in 1952.

Going north along the bayfront, at 46 Avenida Menendez is the Chart House restaurant, formerly the Old Spanish Guest House, where novelist **John Dos Passos** (1896-1970) stayed while in St. Augustine in 1940. In a city where

71

many buildings have been reconstructed (particularly along St. George Street) to replace and replicate those carelessly demolished in the past, this building is of significance as the Ancient City's first reconstruction. In 1887 a huge fire swept the downtown area and destroyed a colonial coquina building on this site, the Carr House. It was reconstructed along the lines of the original, with one main exception: the building material used was not coquina, but rather the poured concrete that Henry Flagler was then using for his monumental hotels and churches.

A notable guest at the original Carr House back in the 1870s was **Constance Fenimore Woolson** (1840-1894), novelist and grandniece of James Fenimore Cooper. St. Augustine makes major and minor appearances in several of her books: *Rodman the Keeper* (New York: Appleton, 1880); *East Angels* (New York: Harper & Brothers, 1886); and *Horace Chase* (New York: Harper & Brothers, 1894). She also wrote a two-part series, "The Ancient City," for *Harper's* magazine (December 1874 and January 1875) that remains one of the best descriptions of the time between the Civil War and the arrival of Henry Flagler.

The apartment house at 24 Avenida Menendez is where **Gabriela Mistral,** (1889-1957), Chilean poet and diplomat, stayed when she spent a month in St. Augustine in 1939. She went on to receive the Nobel Prize for literature in 1945.

The most prominent site along the bayfront and the most popular tourist attraction in the area is the Castillo de San Marcos, operated by the National Park Service. This seventeenth-century masonry fort, which is the nation's oldest, has been through a variety of uses — military and non-military — over the centuries. The city's first golf course was on the fort green, and its walls were stormed in the 1951 movie *Distant Drums* with Gary Cooper. Rob Lowe ducked in and out of its various chambers in the 1987 film *Illegally Yours.*

The Castillo has been visited and commented upon by a number of authors. James Branch Cabell did some of his writing on the fort's terreplein. Sinclair Lewis visited with each of the three great loves of his life. Sidney Lanier and Henry James both left descriptions of it. Edith Pope used it on the dust jacket and in the text of her novel *River in the Wind* (New York: Scribner's, 1954). It makes cameo appearances in a variety of genres. French novelist **Jules Verne** (1828-1905) describes it in his Civil War novel set in Florida, *Texar's Revenge, or North Against South* (New York: Hurst & Co., 1887). Local romance novelist **Jackie Weger** mentions it in *Best Behavior* (Toronto, Canada: Harlequin Books, 1990). It also appears in the thriller *Florida is Closed Today* (New York: Leisure Books, 1982) by **Jack D. Hunter** (1921-), a St. Augustine resident best-known for his novel *The Blue Max* (1964).

The most famous prisoner held at the fort over the centuries was Osceola, after he was captured under a flag of truce south of town. He was then sent to South Carolina where he died. His exploits have been described in various ways, by novelists from Ned Buntline and Mayne Reid to Frank Slaughter and Robert Wilder. Walt Whitman wrote a poem entitled "Osceola" in *Leaves of*

Grass about the death of the Seminole leader. An interesting study that attempts to separate fact from fiction on this legendary figure is **Patricia R. Wickman**'s *Osceola's Legacy* (Tuscaloosa, AL: University of Alabama Press, 1991). The story of the fort itself is told in **Albert Manucy** and **Luis Arana**'s *The Building of Castillo de San Marcos* (St. Augustine: Eastern National Park & Monument Association for Castillo de San Marcos National Monument, 1977).

North of the fort, at 19 San Marco Avenue, is Warden Castle (now occupied by Ripley's Museum), which was built in 1887 as a winter cottage for William G. Warden of Philadelphia, a partner of John D. Rockefeller and Henry Flagler in the Standard Oil Company. A bit of local folklore says that, when Flagler tried to interest Warden in investing in St. Augustine, the latter declined, but said he would build a big house and watch Flagler go broke. Warden did, however, invest quite a bit — establishing the gas company and the St. Augustine Improvement Company, which dredged Maria Sanchez Lake and developed the surrounding real estate. One of his charities was a school for blacks called Warden Academy, whose principal, **J.B. Sevelli-Capponi**, wrote a book, *Ham and Dixie: A Just, Simple and Original Discussion of the Southern Problem* (St. Augustine: no publ., 1895), which deals with race relations in the Flagler era. Warden died in 1895, and the academy was later destroyed by fire.

In 1941 Warden's "cottage" was purchased by Norton Baskin, a career hotelman who was managing the Hotel Marion in Ocala. He remodeled it into the Castle Warden Hotel, which became a celebrated literary gathering place, not hindered by the fact that the same year he bought the hotel, Baskin married Pulitzer Prize-winning novelist **Marjorie Kinnan Rawlings** (1896-1953). They had a penthouse on the top floor, and horse-carriage drivers always pointed it out to tourists as the home of the author of *The Yearling*, making it difficult for her to get the peace and quiet she required to write.

Among the literary guests at the Castle Warden were novelist Zora Neale Hurston, mystery writer Mignon G. Eberhart, playwright Philip Barry, Pulitzer Prize-winning poet Margaret Widdemer, novelist Hamilton Basso, *One World* author (and presidential candidate) Wendell Willkie, and Sigrid Undset, Norwegian winner of the 1928 Nobel Prize for literature. **Barbara Speisman**'s play *Tea With Zora and Marjorie* is partly set at the Castle Warden.

Just west of the Castle Warden, at 12 Grove Avenue, is the house where **Ole E. Rolvaag** (1876-1931), Norwegian-American novelist and author of *Giants in the Earth* (1927), visited his cousin, L.J. Berdahl, who lived in St. Augustine.

The graceful Victorian home at 22 Water Street was built just before the Civil War and occupied by a school for freed slaves afterwards. In 1933 the writer and critic **Van Wyck Brooks** (1886-1963), recovering from a mental breakdown, rented the place and began writing after a lengthy bout of writer's block. He described it to his friend Lewis Mumford as "a huge old Southern house that was used as a hospital in the Civil War (there are still blood-stains on the parlor floor), with great airy bedrooms ten paces long, with up-stairs balconies at front and rear, over-looking a half-acre of forsaken garden," with palm and orange and a large magnolia "that covers us like an umbrella." He went on and on singing the praises and low prices of the place, causing Mumford to reply that another "dithyramb such as you wrote from St. Augustine" would not only cause the Mumford family to move there, but "after that other writers will come trooping down: there will be a colony and an Art Shoppe and gossip about it...and the prices will go up and in desperation we will all flee to Labrador!"

70 Water Street was the home from 1941-1943 of **Meredith Nicholson** (1866-1947), a leading figure in the Indiana School of writers, so many of whom sojourned in St. Augustine. His books include *The Hoosiers* (1900), *The House of a Thousand Candles* (1905), and *A Hoosier Chronicle* (1912). He came to the city after completing nearly a decade as an American diplomat in Paraguay, Venezuela, and Nicaragua.

27 Locust Street was for nearly half a century the home of author and artist **Langston Moffett** (1903-1989). His autobiographical novel, *Devil By the Tail* (1947), carried words of praise on the dust jacket from his friend Marjorie Kinnan Rawlings. When Moffett was in Italy in the early 1950s, the house was rented for a season to James Branch Cabell.

Prominent historian **Albert Manucy** (1910-) lived at 41 Abbott Street. He worked with the Federal Writers Project and the National Park Service and served as president of the Florida Historical Society. His books include *Florida's Menéndez* (1965) and the classic *The Houses of St. Augustine* (1962), both published by the St. Augustine Historical Society.

The grounds of the Mission of Nombre de Dios, San Marco Avenue between Ocean Avenue and Pine Street, are thought to represent the site of the first Catholic mass in St. Augustine. A statue by the sculptor Ivan Mestrovic (1883-1962) is on the grounds, along with a huge stainless-steel cross that is the city's tallest structure. Unfortunately lost in the process of creating the celebratory site was the home built by General Frederick T. Dent, brother-in-law of Ulysses S. Grant, and occupied for over two decades by Martin Johnson Heade (1819-1904), famous artist of the Luminist School whose career is recounted in Theodore Stebbins's *The Life and Works of Martin Johnson Heade* (New Haven, CT: Yale University Press, 1975).

At the rear of the mission grounds is a nineteenth-century cemetery that includes several graves of black Civil War soldiers. The small La Leche chapel in the cemetery area is a memorial to Martin D. Hardin (1837-1923), protégé of Abraham Lincoln and one of two Union generals (the other being John McAllister Schofield) who lived in St. Augustine's famous Union Generals House at 20 Valencia Street.

For many years the casket of Pedro Menéndez de Avilés, the city's founder, reposed in this chapel — one of the proudest local accomplishments of novelist **James Branch Cabell**. In the course of researching his novel *The First Gentleman of America* (New York: Farrar & Rinehart, 1942), Cabell learned that the Menéndez coffin had been presented, amidst great ceremony, to the Ancient City in 1924, then eventually consigned to a junk room in city hall. "I will unblushingly record," he wrote, "that it was I who re-discovered the forgotten casket of Menéndez, as well as I who stirred up a sufficiency of indignation, of remorse, and of thrift, among the people of St. Augustine, to bring about the removal of this coffin from out of a junk room into a chapel." After 16,000 tourists made "voluntary offerings" in the first three months after it was put on exhibition, Cabell admitted his "frank wonder that I should have thus become, though but temporarily, a public-spirited citizen, a benefactor of the Catholic Church, and a sound financier also, through enacting the public scold." In more recent times the Menéndez casket has been moved from the chapel to the gift shop, in close proximity to the soda machine — something that would no doubt re-ignite Cabell's wrath.

North of the mission grounds, on Magnolia Avenue between Myrtle and Dufferin, is the Fountain of Youth. Based on one of the oldest myths in our country it is in itself, apart from any historic claims or pretensions, of some literary interest. The discoverer of the site in 1909 was a colorful character named **Louella Day McConnell**, who came to St. Augustine after participating in the Yukon gold rush where, as legend has it, she was the original "Lady that's known as Lou" in **Robert W. Service**'s poem "The Shooting of Dan McGrew." She was the author, under the name **Luella Day**, of *The Tragedy of the Klondike* (1906). During World War I she was jailed as a German agent and only released after the Armistice was signed. **Theodore Dreiser**, who visited the Fountain of Youth in 1925, noted in his diary how she told him of surviving attempted poisonings by watermelon, by gas, and by Coca-Cola, and how the new messiah was to land at the Fountain of Youth. He thought her quite mad. Having survived the poisoning attempts, she died in an automobile accident in 1927 near Cross Creek.

Local lore and legends of Louella McConnell are considerable. According to one tale, when she was asked to stop fooling people with the claim of "rejuvenating waters," she shot back, "But there is iron in that spring! I know because I threw an old cookstove in it." It was only natural that such a character should find her way into literature, as McConnell did in the **Page Edwards** novel *American Girl* (New York: Marion Boyars, 1990).

The story of Ponce de León and the Fountain of Youth inspired Eugene O'Neill's play *The Fountain* (1926) as well as the 1895 opera by Frederick Delius, *The Magic Fountain*. An interesting historical examination of the origin of the myth can be found in **Leonardo Olschki**, "Ponce de León's Fountain of Youth," in *Hispanic American Historical Review* 21 (1941), pp. 361-85.

The "Lady that's known as Lou" was but one of many literary characters who have strode these streets. Mayor James Michael Curley (1874-1958) of Boston, the original for Frank Skeffington in **Edwin O'Connor**'s classic political novel, *The Last Hurrah* (1956), made a speech from the bandstand in the downtown plaza on the subject of city planning during the boom years of the 1920s.

William Jennings Bryan (1860-1925), three-time Democratic presidential candidate and a Florida resident during his final years, also spoke from the same pulpit on more than one occasion. For his role in the Scopes "Monkey"

Trial he became a leading character in the popular 1955 play *Inherit the Wind* by **Jerome Lawrence** and **Robert E. Lee**. Ironically, the other leading figure in that play, defense attorney Clarence Darrow (1857-1938), was spotted a few years later traversing this same plaza, though as a tourist rather than an advocate.

John L. Lewis (1880-1969), the head of the United Mine Workers union and leader of the Congress of Industrial Organizations (CIO) during its heyday in the 1930s, appeared thinly veiled as Benjamin Renwell Holt in the 1962 novel *Power* by **Howard Fast**. He also appeared, several times, as a guest at the Ponce de Leon Hotel and as a walker on the streets of St. Augustine, complete with bodyguards.

Memorial Presbyterian Church, ornate as a wedding cake and burial place of its builder, Henry M. Flagler, has been one of the great visual delights of St. Augustine for more than a century and ranks just next to the Ponce de Leon Hotel as a tribute to the artistry of its architects, Carrère and Hastings. Among those who preached there over the years was **Henry Martyn Field** (1822-1907), clergyman, author, and member of a prominent nineteenth-century family (one brother was a Supreme Court justice; another laid the first Atlantic cable). Field's books included one on Florida: *Bright Skies and Dark Shadows* (New York: Scribner's, 1890), which was dedicated to Henry Flagler. He also wrote biographies of two of his siblings and a host of popular travel books. Although he reached a wide public, he regretted in his later years that his brothers had accomplished great deeds, whereas he had merely recorded them. Perhaps he regretted too soon, for it was he, rather than his brothers, who later appeared as a main character in the best-selling novel by his grandniece, **Rachel Field**, *All This, and Heaven Too* (1938). In 1940 it became a movie starring Bette Davis and Charles Boyer.

Marjorie Kinnan Rawlings (1896-1953), though usually associated with Cross Creek, spent most of the last decade of her life in St. Augustine and served as president of the public-library association here during World War II. Some of the characters from her book *Cross Creek* also lived in St. Augustine. "My friend Zelma" Cason, who so objected to her portrayal in the book as "an ageless spinster, resembling an angry and efficient canary" that she sued Rawlings, was a social worker in the city for many years, living at different times at 28 St. Francis Street, 211 Arpieka Avenue (Apt. 7), and 6 Milton Street. She suffered a stroke in 1960 and spent her last years at the Gilmer Nursing Home, 189 San Marco Avenue. She died in 1963. **Patricia Nassif Acton** tells the dramatic story of the *Cross Creek* trial in *Invasion of Privacy* (Gainesville: University Presses of Florida, 1988).

Another character in *Cross Creek* is Ross Allen (1908-1981), the herpetologist who took Rawlings on a rattlesnake hunt in the Everglades. He had a famous reptile show at Silver Springs for many years. In the late 1970s he brought it to the Alligator Farm in St. Augustine and lived nearby at 13 Marilyn Avenue. In addition to his mention in *Cross Creek*, he was the subject of a biography for young adults: **Clarence J. Hylander**'s *Adventures With Reptiles:*

The Story of Ross Allen (New York: Messner, 1951), which was hailed by the *New York Times* as "a thrilling story and well worth reading."

Henry Fountain, who figures prominently in the *Cross Creek* chapter "Black Shadows," did not live in St. Augustine, but is buried at the U.S. National Cemetery (Section D, Plot 26) on Marine Street.

Finally, before leaving the downtown area, we should mention more recent historic events that have already made their way into several books, fiction and nonfiction. These were the dramatic 1964 civil rights demonstrations that focused international attention on the Ancient City and brought Martin Luther King, Jr. here for his last major campaign prior to the passage of the landmark Civil Rights Act of 1964. King went on later that year to receive the Nobel Peace Prize.

Sites connected with the civil rights movement include four black churches from which the marches began: Trinity United Methodist, 84 Bridge Street; St. Paul's A.M.E., 85 M.L. King Avenue; St. Mary's Baptist, 69 Washington Street; and First Baptist, 81 St. Francis Street. The focal point for marches was the Slave Market in the plaza. This was originally a public marketplace where a variety of things were sold, including slaves. A later generation of tourist promoters thought it quainter to label it a slave market, and this worked fine for the generation that made *Amos 'n' Andy* a top-rated radio program and saw only humor (and nothing offensive) in black-face minstrel shows. However, once it became a symbolic site for civil rights demonstrations, there began an effort to deny that any slaves had ever been sold there, contrary to much historic documentation.

McCrory's at 158 St. George Street was the site of the Ancient City's first lunch counter sit-in, a solo effort by Henry Thomas. He went on to become one of the original Freedom Riders, who in 1961 dramatically protested segregated bus stations in the South. Local legend, which has been repeated in some books, puts the original sit-in at Woolworth's (31 King Street), but this was corrected by Henry Thomas when he returned to receive the key to the city ("Will it open the jail?" he asked) at a Freedom Fighters Appreciation Banquet, March 28, 1992. The Monson Motel, 32 Avenida Menéndez, on the bayfront is where Martin Luther King, Jr. was arrested, and a widely reprinted photograph was taken of the manager pouring acid in the swimming pool to scare out an integrated group using the facility.

The Ponce de Leon Motor Lodge, 4000 U.S. 1 North, north of town, which opened in 1958 as an eventual replacement for the elegant Ponce de Leon Hotel downtown, is where Mrs. Malcolm Peabody, 72-year-old mother of the governor of Massachusetts, was arrested for asking to be served a meal while in an integrated group — one of the most publicized incidents of that eventful spring. The local sheriff put a sign behind his desk saying:

"St. Johns County famous jail.
Mrs. Peabody of the Boston Peabodys
Stayed here two nights
Reasonable fines...$35 and up."

St. Augustine, which had great experience in selling and promoting history, found it much less comfortable being the place where history was actually made. In more recent times it was not without some bitter opposition and much quoting of J. Edgar Hoover that Central Avenue was renamed to honor Martin Luther King, Jr. Many cities have streets named for him; this one is special because he actually walked on it in the course of making history.

St. Augustine has a long record of coming to terms with — and enshrining — earlier nemeses like Sir Francis Drake, James Oglethorpe, and Osceola. Some day this will extend to Martin Luther King, Jr., and a statue of him will be erected in the Slave Market. To fail to suitably note his presence, in a tourist economy, would, in the long run, be economic foolishness of the highest order.

The dramatic events of the civil rights movement in St. Augustine have been told in **David Colburn**'s *Racial Change and Community Crisis: St. Augustine, Florida, 1877-1980* (New York: Columbia University Press, 1985) and in the collection edited by **David J. Garrow**, *St. Augustine, Florida, 1963-1964: Mass Protest and Racial Violence* (Brooklyn, NY: Carlson, 1989). Episodes of it are also told in the memoirs of participants, such as **William Kunstler**'s *Deep in My Heart* (New York: Morrow, 1966); **William Sloane Coffin**'s *Once to Every Man* (New York: Atheneum, 1977); and **Paul Good**'s *The Trouble I've Seen* (Washington, DC: Howard University Press, 1975). Good also wrote a novel based on the events in St. Augustine: *Once to Every Man* (New York: Putnam, 1970). Those events figure loosely in **Jay Barbree**'s *The Hydra Pit*, a 1977 novel by a television newsman who covered St. Augustine.

Going east from downtown, the route crosses the scenic Bridge of Lions, from whose top the view back over the city skyline is picture-postcard perfect. Hailed when built in the 1920s as "the most beautiful bridge in Dixie" and listed on the National Register of Historic Places, it is periodically threatened with demolition by the Florida Department of Transportation.

The eastern end of the bridge lands in Davis Shores, a real estate development of the 1920s Florida boom by D.P. "Doc" Davis (1885-1926), who made a name for himself by creating saleable land where none existed before. In Tampa he had made a fortune by pumping Davis Islands up out of the bay and sought to repeat the feat (or at least the financial aspects of it) by pumping the bottom of the Matanzas River up onto the marshy north end of Anastasia Island to create building lots.

Davis published a special edition of the 1926 book *Florida* (New York: Harper & Brothers) by **Kenneth Lewis Roberts** (who would later win a Pulitzer Prize for his series of best-selling historical novels about the American Revolution). *Florida* said kind things about the Davis projects and was thus used as a selling tool by his employees. The author had visions of great riches, but the boom collapsed. D.P. Davis went out a porthole in the middle of the ocean, and the commercial edition of the book failed to sell more than 5,000 copies. It was not for another generation that Davis Shores was developed as a popular residential area, although not quite "America's foremost watering place" as D.P. Davis had promised.

What had previously been high ground on Anastasia Island is the area known as Lighthouse Park, which is one of Florida's pioneer beach areas, still containing Victorian cottages from the Flagler era. One of the most picturesque of these is the Octagon House, built in 1886, at 62 Lighthouse Avenue, which was owned for many years by artist Norman MacLeish (1890-1975), the brother of Pulitzer Prize-winning poet (and Librarian of Congress) **Archibald MacLeish** (1892-1982). The Octagon House had earlier been rented by **Mary Antin** (1881-1949), a Russian immigrant whose best-selling autobiography, *The Promised Land* (1912), was long used as a civics-class text in American public schools.

The lighthouse itself, completed in 1874, is the oldest surviving brick building in St. Augustine. It was designed by Paul J. Pelz (1841-1918), who was also the architect of the Library of Congress in Washington, D.C. The Junior Service League, in a decade-long effort, saved the 1876 Lightkeepers' House from destruction after fire had gutted it and has turned it into one of the Ancient City's outstanding museums.

South of Lighthouse Park is the St. Augustine Amphitheatre, built on the site of old coquina quarries in the 1960s as part of the celebration of the Ancient City's four-hundredth birthday. Since then it has been the home, each summer, of Florida's official state play, *Cross and Sword*, dealing with the founding of St. Augustine. The play was commissioned for the quadricentennial and is the work of **Paul Green** (1894-1981), who won the 1927 Pulitzer Prize for his play *In Abraham's Bosom*. He later collaborated with Richard Wright on the stage version of *Native Son*. In 1937 Green pioneered the outdoor historic drama with the production in North Carolina of *The Lost Colony*. Over the years he wrote similar plays for other states. The first performance of *Cross and Sword* was given on June 27, 1965, with two Florida governors in the audience. The amphitheatre grounds are a place of great beauty, natural and man-made, and a marker for the William Bartram Trail is located in the coquina gardens. Baseball fans will be interested to know that the seats in the amphitheatre came from New York's Polo Grounds when it was torn down and bear the logo of the New York Giants. Paul Green's last visit to St. Augustine came in 1980 when he met backstage with the cast, talked about the play, and signed autographs for the public.

St. Augustine Beach

South of the amphitheatre and Anastasia State Park is the city of St. Augustine Beach. Originally founded by Methodists just prior to World War I, it was one of the first beach areas in the state designed to be a summer, rather than winter, resort. It was known, variously, as Chautauqua Beach and Assembly Beach.

During the Florida boom of the 1920s, the internationally known pioneer of comprehensive city planning, **John Nolen** (1869-1937), was called in to redesign the area. Parts of his plan are still visible and others could, given the civic will, certainly be implemented. Nolen was the author of such seminal works as *Replanning Small Cities* (1912) and *New Ideals in the Planning of Cities, Towns, and Villages* (1919). From his office in Harvard Square he carried out many Florida projects during those boom years, including plans for Venice, Clewiston, and San Jose Estates in Jacksonville.

A number of writers were attracted to St. Augustine Beach in the 1930s and 1940s. **James Branch Cabell**, whose 1919 novel *Jurgen* (first a banned book, then a best-seller) was one of the literary events that ushered in the Roaring Twenties, rented the C.S. Smith cottage on the beach in 1936. He wrote to his friend Carl Van Vechten, "What I particularly like about St. Augustine Beach is the fact that every afternoon we find reserved for our bath the entire Atlantic Ocean. The circumstance appears dignified and ample."

Thornton Wilder (1897-1975), who had won Pulitzer prizes for his novel *The Bridge of San Luis Rey* (1927) and his play *Our Town* (1938), spent six weeks at St. Augustine Beach in the spring of 1940 working on his play *The Skin of Our Teeth*, which went on to win the Pulitzer Prize for drama in 1943. He told local newspaper reporter **Jane Quinn** (who went on to write several books herself) that he had been inspired to visit the area by memories of a family trip to St. Augustine when he was eight years old. He shared his routine with her: a walk on the beach, then a stint of writing. "One walk is good for a page," he said. He left this area to attend the premiere of the movie *Our Town*, but would return frequently over the years.

Another literary sojourner at the beach when Wilder was there was poet **William Rose Benét** (1886-1950), descendant of a St. Augustine family whose great-grandfather, Pedro Benet, was known as King of the Minorcans. Benét was courting the children's book illustrator, **Marjorie Flack** (1897-1958), who would soon become his fourth wife (they collaborated — he with verse, she with pictures — on a book about dolphins inspired by their time in the area: *Adolphus* [Boston: Houghton Mifflin, 1941]). He was also working on his 559-page autobiographical poem, *The Dust Which is God*, for which he received the Pulitzer Prize for poetry in 1942. Benét said, "St. Augustine Beach has been ideal — informal, with just the right amount of seclusion which is necessary for work."

The recently widowed playwright **Dorothy Heyward** (1890-1961) was also at St. Augustine Beach that year. She had collaborated with her husband, **DuBose**, on the stage version of his 1925 novel *Porgy* (in 1935, with the Gershwins, it became the folk opera *Porgy and Bess*). In 1948 she wrote a play, *Set My People Free*, about Denmark Vesey's slave uprising in Charleston in 1822.

In 1948 **Martha Gellhorn** (1908-), war correspondent and short-story writer who had first visited the area with her former husband, Ernest Hemingway, came to St. Augustine Beach and stayed in a cottage rented from Verle Pope.

In 1953 Dr. **Henry Seidel Canby** (1878-1961), a founder of the *Saturday Review of Literature*, biographer of Thoreau and Whitman, and longtime chairman of the board of judges of the Book of the Month Club, rented a cottage here with three generations of his family. A black woman who served as nursemaid for his grandchildren was arrested for going on the beach, which was reserved for "whites only." This prompted novelist **Marjorie Kinnan Rawlings** to write an angry letter to the editor of the *St. Augustine Record* protesting "the lack of simple courtesy and good manners on the part of a representative of the law." It was a harbinger of dramatic events in 1964 when several civil-rights "wade-ins" were held to protest segregation at the beach.

James McLendon (1942-1982), while a reporter for the *St. Augustine Record* in 1968-1969, lived at 1-14th Lane in St. Augustine Beach. He went on to write two popular novels: *Deathwork* (1977) and *Eddie Macon's Run* (1979), which were both made into movies. He also wrote a nonfiction book, *Papa: Hemingway in Key West* (Miami: Seemann Publishing Co., 1972). In his fiction he drew from the fact that the first decade of his life was spent within the walls of Raiford Prison, where his father was an official. McLendon once said, "The nicest people I ever met in my life, the kindest people, were the servants in our house, and they were all murderers. Dad wouldn't have a thief in the house."

Butler's Beach

South of St. Augustine Beach along State Road A1A is Butler's Beach, one of Florida's historic black beaches from the era of segregation. A park on both sides of the highway bears the name of its developer, Frank B. Butler (1885-1973), a black businessman who operated the Palace Market and College Park Realty in St. Augustine and was active in civic and political affairs. He is the subject of a biographical study by **Barbara Walch**, *Frank B. Butler: Lincolnville Businessman and Founder of St. Augustine, Florida's Historic Black Beach* (St. Augustine: Rudolph Hadley, 1992).

Crescent Beach

South of Butler's Beach is Crescent Beach, famous as the home of Florida's beloved novelist, **Marjorie Kinnan Rawlings** (1896-1953). With money she made from *The Yearling* she bought a small cottage atop a high dune at 6600 Broward Street. It was enlarged after World War II and was her main residence in the last decade of her life. One of her favorite short stories, "The Pelican's Shadow," is set here. Literary guests at the cottage included Robert Frost, Ernest Hemingway, Dylan Thomas, Zora Neale Hurston, and A. J. Cronin. This landmark of Florida's cultural heritage was threatened with demolition in the 1980s, as it was located on two valuable oceanfront lots and had been allowed to deteriorate. Fortunately, M. E. Streeter, an admirer of the author, purchased and saved it. Information about Rawlings's life at Crescent Beach can be found in *Selected Letters of Marjorie Kinnan Rawlings* edited by **Gordon Bigelow** and **Laura Monti** (Gainesville: University Presses of Florida, 1983) and *Marjorie Kinnan Rawlings: Sojourner at Cross Creek* (Woodstock, NY: Overlook Press, 1988) by **Elizabeth Silverthorne**. In the yard is the foundation of the cottage occupied by **Idella Parker**, author (with **Mary Keating**) of *Idella: Marjorie Rawlings' "Perfect Maid"* (Gainesville: University Press of Florida, 1992).

Marjorie Rawlings House, Crescent Beach

Crescent Beach makes a cameo appearance in **Carl Hiaasen's** serio-comic thriller, *Double Whammy* (New York: Putnam's, 1987). Crescent Beach is also the home of **Connie May Fowler,** author of the widely praised debut novel *Sugar Cage* (New York: Putnam's, 1992), which is set in this part of Florida.

Summer Haven

Going across Matanzas Inlet, one comes upon the century-old community of Summer Haven, long associated with the Mellon family of Pittsburgh. The large building in the compound on Mellon Court was formerly the Cove Tavern, where **John Dos Passos** (1896-1970) stayed in 1941. In his novel, *The Big Money* (New York: Harcourt, Brace, 1936), the final part of his *U.S.A.* trilogy, Dos Passos wrote about the Florida boom of the 1920s.

The picturesque cottage known as The Hut at 9177 Old A1A was owned by **Mary Mellon McClung,** author of the 1946 novel *Sheepshead Point* (Philadelphia: Dorrance), which is set in Summer Haven. The main cross street in the area has been named Gene Johnson Road in fitting tribute to a black man who for years put on legendary oyster roasts here that drew Gary Cooper and Marjorie Kinnan Rawlings, among other guests. Rawlings wrote of Johnson in her *Cross Creek Cookery* (New York: Scribner's, 1942). Unfortunately, the naming of the street did not prevent the demolition of his house along it in 1989. It is preserved only in watercolors by local artists C.B. Hinson and J.E. Fitzpatrick, and in the fond memories of those who attended Gene Johnson's oyster roasts.

Marineland

South of Summer Haven, going from St. Johns into Flagler County, is Marineland, the world's first oceanarium. Opened in 1938 and listed on the National Register of Historic Places in 1986, it was at one time Florida's leading tourist attraction and a famous literary gathering place. Columnists from Ernie Pyle and Eleanor Roosevelt to Russell Baker have written about Marineland. Robert Ripley and Grantland Rice made movie shorts there. Ilia Tolstoy, grandson of Russian novelist Leo Tolstoy, was one of its founders. Robert Benchley, whose grandson wrote *Jaws*, visited so often that he was named honorary mayor. Ernest Hemingway, Lowell Thomas, St.-John Perse, Alexander Woollcott, and Thornton Wilder were other literary guests. The Dolphin Restaurant at Marineland was run for many years by Norton Baskin, well-known raconteur and husband of novelist Marjorie Kinnan Rawlings.

Poet **William Rose Benét** and illustrator **Marjorie Flack** collaborated on a children's book inspired by Marineland called *Adolphus; or, The Adopted Dolphin & the Pirate's Daughter* (Boston: Houghton Mifflin, 1941). Poet **Don Blanding** wrote of Marineland in his collection of poems entitled *Floridays* (New York: Dodd, Mead, 1941).

The story of Marineland's first decades is told in **Ralph Nading Hill**'s *Window in the Sea* (New York: Rinehart, 1956). **John C. Lilly**'s *Man and Dolphin* (Garden City, NY: Doubleday, 1961) recounts some experiments carried out at the attraction. *High Peaks* (Lexington, KY: University Press of Kentucky, 1977) by **C(ornelius) V(anderbilt) Whitney** is the autobiography of the man who helped establish this tourist site and the adjacent Whitney Marine Laboratory.

Marineland is not merely a tourist attraction; in 1940 it became Florida's smallest incorporated municipality as well. One of the first aldermen was **Vernon Lamme**, archaeologist and author of *Florida Lore Not Found in the History Books!* (Boynton Beach, FL: Star Publishing Co., 1973).

Washington Oaks

South of Marineland is Washington Oaks Gardens, a state park that was formerly the winter home of Owen D. Young (1874-1962), chairman of the board of General Electric, founder of RCA, and *Time* magazine's Man of the Year for 1929. Young was also a noted book collector who gave a collection valued at hundreds of thousands of dollars to the New York Public Library. He was a close friend of Marjorie Kinnan Rawlings, and it was through him that she became interested in his hometown of Van Hornesville, New York, where she bought a home and worked on her final novel, *The Sojourner* (New York: Scribner's, 1953). Young was partly a model for the lead character in that book. He was also the subject of two biographies: **Ida M. Tarbell**'s *Owen D. Young: A New Type of Industrial Leader* (New York: Macmillan, 1932) and **Josephine Young Case** and **Everett Needham Case**'s *Owen D. Young and American Enterprise* (Boston: D.R. Godine, 1982).

Flagler Beach

One of the notable features of Flagler County is that so much of its beachfront is unbuildable, giving rare long ocean vistas from State Road A1A, unlike so many parts of coastal Florida where walls of condos block the view. Flagler County is one of Florida's newest (founded in 1917), smallest — and fastest growing.

Flagler Beach was incorporated in 1925, its famous pier built in 1927. The town was earlier called Ocean City Beach, but postal officials complained that name was too long. It is widely known for its outdoor farmers' market (open every Friday). It was in the ocean off Flagler Beach that Florida troubadour Gamble Rogers (1937-1991) died a hero's death while trying to save a Canadian tourist from drowning. In 1992 the state named in his honor the Gamble Rogers Memorial Recreation Area.

Flagler Beach was the home of **Marie E. Mann Boyd** (1865-1962), who as a girl set the type for the first newspaper in Daytona (published by her father, F.A. Mann). In 1920 she wrote *Florida Under Four Flags* (Daytona: Mills Publishing Co.), with a section on Indian legends that inspired artist Fred Dana Marsh's monumental statue at Tomoka State Park.

Bunnell

Inland from Flagler Beach is Bunnell, the county seat. The Flagler County Historical Society building at 204 East Moody Boulevard is an interesting bungalow once owned by the town druggist who filled the gabled ends of the house with different colored glass from medicine bottles. The 1926 county courthouse, across the street, is of architectural interest, as is the coquina Bunnell city hall nearby on State Street, a 1937 Works Progress Administration project. Cheap labor during the Depression made possible the last large-scale use of the distinctive native shellstone coquina as a building material in Florida.

Accounts of this area are given in **John A. Clegg**'s *The History of Flagler County* (Holly Hill, FL: Hall Publishing Co., 1976) and **Donna L. Helbing**'s *You Gotta Be Kiddin': A Composite of Folklore, Anecdotal Stories and Tall Tales From Flagler County Folks* (Bunnell, FL: Flagler County District School Board, n.d.). This compilation about ghosts, moonshine, courting, fishing, hunting, hurricanes, and tourist scams was sponsored by the school board and could be a model for other Florida counties to follow.

Korona

South of Bunnell, where Old Dixie Highway runs off U.S.1, is the Polish farming community of Korona. A Catholic church, built in 1914 by a group of immigrants and named for St. Mary, Queen of Poland, still features Sunday services in Polish. Next to the church is a coquina shrine to St. Christopher, patron saint of travelers, that was erected in 1935. This is one of several interesting ethnic settlements that give Florida its great diversity.

Bulow

Old Dixie Highway goes near the Bulow ruins, the remains of a vast sugar plantation destroyed during the Seminole War. John J. Audubon was a plantation guest in 1831, as he sought birds to paint for his landmark work. Information about his visit appears in **Kathryn Hall Proby's** *Audubon in Florida* (Coral Gables, FL: University of Miami Press, 1974). He praised his "most kind host" for "the most hospitable and welcome treatment that could possibly be expected." His, however, was not the universal opinion. John Bemrose, a young English druggist who served in the Seminole War (under a commander named Ichabod Crane, believe it or not), called Bulow a "demon," noting "he was quite young and handsome, yet I never heard of a good trait in his character. Dissipated and quarrelsome with his equals, tyrannical to his dependents, his hands dyed red with the blood of three of his slaves! Truly earth groaned under him and Hell must have groaned for him!"

The British novelist **J.B. Priestley** (1894-1984), who visited the ruins in 1967, thought, "It is surprising that no American writer has given us the Life and Times of John Joachim Bulow. Think what Voltaire or Anatole France could have done with this bitter tale!" Bulow did figure as a character in **Robert Wilder's** novel *Bright Feather* (New York: Putnam's, 1948).

The most recent writing has focused not on the person but the place; *Bulow Hammock: Mind in a Forest* (San Francisco: Sierra Club Books, 1989) is a nature book by **David Rains Wallace,** who had earlier won the 1984 John Burroughs Medal for natural history writing.

Bulow Creek State Park is the location of the Fairchild Oak, named in honor of plant explorer **David G. Fairchild** (1869-1954), a son-in-law of Alexander Graham Bell and author of the classics, *The World Was My Garden* (New York: Scribner's, 1938) and *The World Grows Round My Door* (New York: Scribner's, 1947), which have a place in every library of Floridiana. Fairchild Garden in Miami was named in his honor. An account of his career is given in *Plant Explorer: David Fairchild* (New York: Messner, 1961) by **Beryl Williams** and **Samuel Epstein.** Fairchild admired this tree when he came to Ormond Beach to work on his book *Garden Islands of the Great East* (New York: Scribner's, 1943), and he urged that it be saved. A marker at the site says, "This Live Oak tree is dedicated by the Lehigh Portland Cement Company to the memory of Dr. David Fairchild, the American botanist who introduced the soybean and many other valuable forms of plantlife to the U.S. As this tree has gladdened man's heart for 2000 years, so will Dr. Fairchild's legacy enrich the lives of future generations." The tree is of huge girth and spread, though 2,000 years is an exaggeration of Paul Bunyanesque proportions.

Two earlier figures in American botany (both natives of France) visited the area in 1788 as part of their explorations of Florida between St. Augustine and New Smyrna. **André Michaux** (1746-1802) and his teenaged son **François André Michaux** (1770-1855) used the material gathered to produce the pioneering study *Flora Boreali-Americana* (Paris, 1803; reprinted, New York: Hafner Press, 1974). A full-length biography of father and son is *André and François André Michaux* by **Henry** and **Elizabeth Savage** (Charlottesville, VA: University Press of Virginia, 1987).

Ormond Beach

Nearby is James Ormond Park, where, on a mound behind the restrooms, lies the tomb of James Ormond, for whose family the city is named. The inscription on the tombstone describes the pioneer who died in 1829 as "an honest man." *The Reminiscences of James Ormond* edited by **Elizabeth F. Smith** (Crawfordville, FL: Magnolia Monthly Press, 1966) tells the story of the family and its adventures in war and peace.

Beyond the Ormond tomb, Old Dixie Highway continues south to To-moka State Park. During the British period of Florida's history, this was Mt. Oswald Plantation, owned by Richard Oswald (1705-1784), a Scottish merchant and slave trader whose son was tutored by novelist Laurence Sterne (author of *Tristram Shandy*) and whose wife was execrated in verse by poet Robert Burns. Oswald is remembered today as one of the British peace commissioners who negotiated the settlement for the American Revolution. A monument to Oswald was erected in the park in 1976 as part of the bicentennial celebration. The story of Oswald's career is given in a master's thesis by **Thomas W. Taylor**, *"Settling a Colony Over A Bottle of Claret": Richard Oswald and the British Settlement of Florida* (Greensboro, NC: University of North Carolina, 1984).

An outstanding feature of the park is the statuary group, "The Legend of Tomokie," done by the famous sculptor and artist, Fred Dana Marsh (1872-1961). Marsh was inspired by the writings of **Marie E. Mann Boyd** on the Fountain of Youth legend and thought it could be expressed in monumental sculpture to help Florida capitalize on its history, as the people of the Hudson River area — where he had a studio — had done with the tales of Rip Van Winkle and Ichabod Crane. Marsh's statues were dedicated in 1957, and a decade later a museum of his work was opened in the park.

A native of Chicago who studied art in France and made his mark in New York doing industrial murals, Marsh came to Ormond Beach in the late 1920s and built one of the area's most distinctive beach houses, known as The Battleship, at 317 Ocean Shore Boulevard. In nautical moderne style, it included such idiosyncratic features as skeletons painted in a closet and a row of wooden horses along the seawall that had been rescued from merry-go-round junk heaps.

His son, Reginald Marsh (1898-1954), who visited The Battleship, was also a celebrated artist who, in addition to other works, illustrated books by Dreiser, Dos Passos, and James Fenimore Cooper. In 1971 the beach house was acquired by Embry-Riddle Aeronautical University as a home for its president.

South of it at 201 Ocean Shore Boulevard is The Doldrums, the Mediter-ranean-style beach house built in the 1920s for **George A. Zabriskie** (1868-1954), a wealthy flour manufacturer. He served as president of the New York Historical Society and wrote a number of books and pamphlets including

Landing of Ponce de León in Florida 1513 (New York: New York Historical Society, 1945); *Stephen Collins Foster* (Ormond Beach: The Doldrums, 1941); and, in a somewhat different vein, *Songs of the Azooks: Being a Collection of Verse and Worse Sung by that Ancient and Honorable Society of Golfers, by One of 'em* (Ormond Beach, FL: no publ., 1940). Zabriskie was active, both in New York and Florida, in saving historic landmarks from destruction.

The outstanding building in this city was the Ormond Hotel, built in 1887 and opened the next year. Connected with the hotel were a series of palmetto log cottages on Orchard Lane which were given Indian names by novelist **Kirk Munroe** (1850-1930), popular author of adventure stories for boys at the turn of the century and a lifelong friend of hotel manager John Anderson.

The original financial backer of the hotel was S.V. "Deacon" White (1831-1913), a congressman from New York and Wall Street speculator who was treasurer of Henry Ward Beecher's Plymouth Church in Brooklyn. White is said to have provided the legal expenses when Beecher was charged in a celebrated adultery case. In 1890 Henry M. Flagler bought the hotel, enlarged it (eventually to 186,000 square feet), and made it part of his chain of luxurious hostelries that spanned the east coast of Florida. A vast, rambling, wooden structure, it was sold by the Flagler interests in 1949, became a retirement home, and went through a series of owners who all began by announcing restoration plans; they mortgaged it heavily, then sold it or went broke. In 1986 the city condemned it and ordered it vacated. Its fate teetered for years this way and that, giving ulcers to those concerned with the great gap in Florida's heritage that would result from its loss. Demolition began in June 1992, and shopping center developer Milton Pepper earned a place in the history books as the man who destroyed the landmark. Gertrude Stein's comment about a city, that "There is no there there," seems applicable to Ormond minus its monumental hotel, and little credit is reflected on anyone who sought to profit from the situation.

Ed Sullivan (1902-1974), longtime king of Sunday night television, was, early in his career, a publicist for the Ormond Hotel. One of the events he promoted was a golf match between two of the nation's wealthiest octogenarians: banker George F. Baker (1840-1931) and oilman John D. Rockefeller (1839-1937).

Rockefeller had stayed at the Ormond Hotel — in what was referred to ever after as the Rockefeller Wing — prior to buying The Casements across the street at 25 Riverside Drive, where he wintered for the last two decades of his life, dying there at the age of 97. **Curt E. Engelbrecht's** *Neighbor John* (New York: Telegraph Press, 1936) tells the story of Rockefeller in Ormond Beach in both words and photographs. It has been reprinted in paperback by the Ormond Beach Historical Trust and is on sale at The Casements. The most recent extensive study of the oilman is *The Rockefeller Century* by **John Ensor Harr** and **Peter J. Johnson** (New York: Scribner's, 1988). The former Rockefeller home is now a cultural and civic center for Ormond Beach, having been rescued from a period of vacancy, vandalism, and neglect. Tours are given.

In his later years, Rockefeller was celebrated for handing out shiny dimes. At least one visitor turned the tables on him. After visiting with the millionaire in Ormond in 1928, humorist Will Rogers wrote: "The elder John D. made no effort to give me the customary dime, whereupon I took out one and gave it to him. He took it. I'll say he took it."

Rockefeller owned another house south of The Casements at 127 Riverside Drive which was used to accommodate staff and guests. This house had an interesting subsequent literary history. It was sold to **Albert F. Wilson** (1883-1940), an editor, author, and journalism professor at New York University, and his wife, **Ruth Danenhower Wilson**, a trustee of Bethune-Cookman College and author of *Jim Crow Joins Up: A Study of Negroes in the Armed Forces of the U.S.* (1944).

Their son, **Sloan Wilson** (1920-), wrote one of the landmark novels of the 1950s, *The Man in the Gray Flannel Suit* (1955), which was made into a 1956 movie with Gregory Peck. Among Wilson's other novels are two with Florida settings: *Janus Island* (Boston: Little, Brown, 1967) and *The Greatest Crime* (New York: Arbor House, 1980). His engaging memoir, *What Shall We Wear To This Party?* (New York: Arbor House, 1976), tells the story of his life in Florida and elsewhere. He later served as writer-in-residence at Rollins College in Winter Park, Florida, and as a director of the Council for Florida Libraries.

Another resident of Riverside Drive was former congressman **George Shiras III** (1859-1942), a trustee of the National Geographic Society and frequent contributor to its magazine. Shiras, in the legislative field, took special pride in bills putting migratory birds and fish under federal protection. As a photographer, he invented a technique for taking flash pictures of wild animals in their natural habitat. His photos won gold medals at the Paris and St. Louis expositions and helped to revolutionize the look of *National Geographic*, which began publishing them in 1906 — despite the protests of two geographers who resigned in a huff, complaining that "wandering off into nature is not geography."

In 1935 the society published Shiras's two-volume *Hunting Wildlife With Camera and Flashlight*. He also wrote *Justice George Shiras, Jr., of Pittsburgh: Associate Justice of the United States Supreme Court, 1892-1903* (1953), a posthumously published biography of his father, who also was a winter resident of Ormond Beach.

As Shiras was an expert on fauna, so also could Ormond boast the presence of one of the great experts on flora: **Oakes Ames** (1874-1950), professor of botany at Harvard and author of the classic *Economic Annuals and Human Cultures* (1939) that helped to shape modern thinking in the field. Son of a governor of Massachusetts, and grandson and namesake of the main figure in the Crédit Mobilier scandal of the 1870s, Ames had the kind of extended family that cries out for the writing of a multi-generational saga. His wife, Blanche, was the daughter of Adelbert Ames (1835-1933), a Union general in the Civil War who afterwards served as governor and senator from Mississippi and, in his nineties, was the favorite golfing partner of his Ormond neighbor, John D. Rockefeller. Blanche Ames's grandfather was Benjamin F. Butler (1818-1893), congressman, governor, presidential candidate, and Union general who earned from his enemies such flattering sobriquets as "Beast" and "the butcher of New Orleans."

Blanche Ames was a talented botanical artist and collaborated with her husband on *Drawings of Florida Orchids* (1947; reprinted Stanfordville, NY: E.M. Coleman, 1979). She also wrote *Adelbert Ames: General-Senator-Governor* (New York: Argosy-Antiquarian Ltd., 1964). The extended Ames family owned a number of houses in Ormond, with names like The Whim, The Porches, and The Last Straw. Literary members of the family include **Evelyn Ames** (1908-1990), an award-winning writer of children's books, as well as the memoir *Daughter of the House* (1962) about growing up in Hartford's Nook Farm, an area made famous by Mark Twain and Harriet Beecher Stowe. **George Plimpton** (1927-), a grandson of Oakes Ames, has been editor of the *Paris Review* and author of several popular books on his adventures as an amateur in professional sports. Ames Point Park on South Beach Street between Central and Mound avenues preserves the family name and some of its handiwork in the area of horticulture.

The Ormond Woman's Club at 42 North Beach Street, which formerly housed the public library, was built in 1916 according to designs by Ogden Codman, a well-known Boston architect and longtime friend of novelist **Edith Wharton** (1862-1937). He collaborated with her on her first commercial book, *The Decoration of Houses* (1897). The publisher had small hopes for it, but it struck a responsive chord and is still used today by old-house restorers. Wharton's most famous work was done solo in the area of fiction, and she recorded with amusement in her memoirs how, years later, an enthusiastic woman sailed up to her to say, "I'm so glad to meet you at last, because Ogden Codman is such an old friend of mine that I've read every one of the wonderful novels he and you have written together." It was at Codman's chateau south of Paris that Wharton suffered the stroke from which she died in 1937. The Ormond Woman's Club building was listed on the National Register of Historic Places in 1984.

For many years 345 Grove Street was the home of **Joe Haldeman** (1943-), who began his writing career after being wounded in the Vietnam War. His first novel was the semi-autobiographical *War Year* (1972). He won both Hugo and Nebula awards for the best science-fiction novel of the year with *The Forever War* (1974). Later work included the script for the Space Pavilion at Disney World (1979) and the novel *The Hemingway Hoax* (1990). A critical study of his work is **Joan Gordon**'s *Joe Haldeman* (Mercer Island, WA: Starmont House, 1980).

Ormond is also the home of **Jeanne Hines**, prolific author (**Valerie Sherwood**) of historical romances that have sold millions of copies. Among her books are *Rich Radiant Love*, *Wild Willful Love*, *Rash Reckless Love*, and *Bold Breathless Love*. Romance novelist **Elaine Raco Chase** lived in Ormond for several years and taught a writing class at The Casements.

Other writing teachers in Ormond over the years have been **Barbara Cameron**, author of several Harlequin and Silhouette romance novels, and **Joyce Sweeney**, whose first book *Center Line* (New York: Delacorte, 1984) —

partly set in Florida — won the Delacorte Press Prize for outstanding first young-adult novel. Sweeney's later young-adult novels include *Right Behind the Rain* (1987), *The Dream Collector* (1989), and *Face the Dragon* (1990). Authors active in the Ormond Writers League include **Audrey Parente** and **Evelyn Kelley Combs.**

The city has two noteworthy place names with literary backgrounds. One is Seton Lane, a street named for **Ernest Thompson Seton** (1860-1946), well-known naturalist, one of the founders of the Boy Scouts and Campfire Girls, and author of *Wild Animals I Have Known* (1898) and *The Trail of an Artist-Naturalist*, an autobiography published in 1940. The other place name is Number Nine Plantation, one of the area's interesting old buildings, dating from 1895 and located at 2887 John Anderson Drive. The name was taken from the popular novel *Sevenoaks* (1875) by **J.G. Holland** (1819-1881), in which a group of wanderers gives numbers to their temporary camps. Number Nine was the last of them. The founder of the plantation at Ormond considered eight other sites before settling on the ninth. Number Nine Plantation gained fame in the twentieth century for its jellies and preserved fruits which were shipped to a distinguished clientele around the nation and the world.

Books about the history of the city include *The Colonization of Ormond, Florida* (DeLand, FL: E.O. Painter, 1931) by **Ada Green Hinkley** and two by **Alice Strickland**: *The Valiant Pioneers* (Miami: University of Miami Press, 1963) and *Ormond-on-the-Halifax* (Holly Hill, FL: Southeast Printing and Publishing Co., 1980).

Holly Hill

South of Ormond, on the mainland side is Holly Hill, originally called Palmetto when settled in 1867 by W.W. Ross, the brother of Senator Edmund Ross of Kansas, who cast the deciding vote against conviction in the impeachment trial of President Andrew Johnson — what one historian called "the most heroic act in American history." John F. Kennedy included a chapter about Senator Ross in his Pulitzer Prize-winning *Profiles in Courage* (1956). W.W. Ross abandoned his homestead by 1870 and a later settler renamed the place Holly Hill after his old home in Delaware. Ross Point Park on Riverside Drive honors the pioneer at the original town site.

The residence at 121 15th Street in Holly Hill was the final home of **James Calvert Smith** (1879-1962), whose work earned him the accolade "historian with a paintbrush." After a long career in New York, where he did covers for the *Saturday Evening Post* and worked with Charles Dana Gibson and Norman Rockwell, Smith retired to his native Florida in the 1940s. Some of his paintings depicting important events in American history are hung in the Library of Congress. Paintings he did of Florida history can be found at the Castillo de San Marcos, the St. Augustine Historical Society, and the Halifax Historical Society. A number of them have been made into postcards.

Of architectural interest is the Holly Hill city hall, 1065 Ridgewood Avenue, a WPA project constructed of coquina during the Great Depression.

Daytona Beach

The whole area from Ormond Beach south has become melded into one metropolitan statistical area, the component parts delineated by legal boundaries rather than green spaces or rural areas. Daytona Beach comprises several earlier settlements linked together over the years into a single city.

The Seabreeze section on the oceanside peninsula was originally a separate town with an interesting history. **Helen Wilmans** (1831-1907) and her husband, **C.C. Post** (1846-1907), settled this area in 1892. They both had been journalists in Chicago, where they met. She had lived in California during the gold rush, and he had worked in Georgia with the Populist leader Tom Watson. In Seabreeze they started a printing and publishing business, built hotels (including the Colonnades and the legendary Princess Issena), an opera house, an amusement pavilion, and an ocean pier. They also planned a University of Psychical Research, for the crusade of their final years was to turn the area into "The Home Temple of Mental Science." Toward this end, they published a newspaper called *Freedom*, and Wilmans wrote several books: *The Blossom of the Century* (1893); *Conquest of Poverty* (1899); and her autobiography, *A Search for Freedom* (1898).

Post became the first mayor of Seabreeze in 1901, the same year the post office began prosecuting them for mail fraud. According to the *New York Times*, Wilmans "claims power to heal any disease or affliction, including poverty, by a method of concentrating her thought on the patient taking the treatment, and for such service she solicited remittances of $3 a week or $10 a month." Wilmans Boulevard and University Boulevard in the Seabreeze area recall this early period of development. The Princess Issena continued as one of the state's most interesting hotels until the 1970s, when it was torn down to create a vacant lot.

A later mayor of Seabreeze was **Pleasant Daniel Gold**. After a career in life insurance, Gold went into the motion-picture business with **Thomas Dixon** (1864-1946), author of *The Clansman* (1905), on which D.W. Griffith's controversial 1914 movie, *The Birth of a Nation*, was based. In 1920 Gold moved to Seabreeze and over the next decade wrote several books, including the historical novel *In Florida's Dawn* (Jacksonville, FL: H. & W.B. Drew Co., 1926), which later appeared in a 1931 printing as *The Rack*, and two nonfiction works: *History of Volusia County, Florida* (DeLand, FL: Painter Printing Co., 1927) and *History of Duval County, Florida* (St Augustine: Record Co., 1928).

At the time Seabreeze was settled, there was already a lighthouse at the southern end of the oceanside peninsula at an area long (and honestly) called Mosquito Inlet. That name fell prey in the 1920s to the booster spirit and was changed to the more marketable Ponce de Leon Inlet. The lighthouse already had literary associations, and they would soon grow dramatically. The designer in the early 1880s of the Mosquito Inlet Lighthouse was **Francis Hopkinson Smith** (1838-1915). The great-grandson and namesake of a signer of the Declaration of Independence, Smith was a man of many talents. As an engineer he designed not only lighthouses, but also the foundation for the Statue of

Liberty. As an artist he provided illustrations for poems by Lowell, Holmes, and Whittier. And in 1891 his first novel, *Colonel Carter of Cartersville*, proved so successful that he abandoned engineering to devote himself to writing.

The man in charge of building the lighthouse was General Orville H. Babcock (1835-1884), who had been a top aide to Ulysses Grant in the Civil War — even acting as advance man for Lee's surrender at Appomattox. When Grant was elected President, Babcock served as his private secretary, until he got caught up in the Whiskey Ring scandal in 1875. He avoided conviction, but lost the President's confidence and his White House job. Babcock purchased land surrounding the lighthouse with the intention of developing it, but did not live long enough. He died in a drowning accident at the inlet on June 2, 1884.

The lighthouse was finally completed in 1887. A decade later it served as a beacon for storm-tossed passengers in a ten-foot dinghy from the sunken steamship *Commodore*, which had set out from Jacksonville with the intention of running guns to Cuba for the insurgency against Spanish rule. "The lighthouse of Mosquito Inlet stuck up above the horizon like the point of a pin," wrote **Stephen Crane** (1871-1900), who survived 30 hours in the dinghy and turned what he called "the best experience of his life," not only

Lilian Place, where Stephen Crane stayed in Daytona Beach

into a front-page story for a New York newspaper ("Stephen Crane's Own Story") but, more enduringly, into his most famous short story, "The Open Boat," as well as the lesser-known "Flanagan and His Short Filibustering Career."

After the publication in 1895 of his classic Civil War novel, *The Red Badge of Courage*, Crane had become much in demand as a war correspondent, and it was this that had brought him to Florida to see if he could sneak into Cuba to provide a first-hand report on the hostilities there. His trip almost ended in the ocean off Daytona Beach. When Crane finally made it to shore, he was taken to spend the night at 111 Silver Beach Avenue, a Victorian house now known as Lilian Place that is one of the oldest surviving buildings in the area.

In 1986 a group of underwater archaeologists conducted salvage operations on what it believed to be the remains of the sunken *Commodore* in 80 feet of water about 12 miles off Daytona Beach.

The lighthouse that was designed by one novelist and served as a beacon for another is now open to the public, to the delight of many who enjoy climbing to the top of lighthouses. And it continues to inspire writers. It appears in one of the stories in *Out of the Blue* (New York: Putnam's Sons, 1943), a collection by **Robert Wilder** (1901-1974), who is the perfect literary companion to the Daytona Beach area.

Wilder's works include a trilogy of novels all published by G.P. Putnam's Sons of New York: *God Has a Long Face* (1940), *Bright Feather* (1948), and *The Sea and the Stars* (1967), tracing the history of the area from Spanish colonial times to the condomania of the twentieth century. His 1942 novel *Flamingo Road* (New York: Putnam's) was made into a 1949 movie with Joan Crawford and later a TV series with Morgan Fairchild.

The son of a dentist with offices at 102 1/2 South Beach Street, Wilder was propelled into a writing career after winning a dollar prize in a school story contest. Though his career took him to Broadway, Hollywood, and Mexico, he returned periodically to Daytona, sometimes for extended stints, as in 1948-1949 when he wrote his novel *Wait For Tomorrow* (New York: Putnam, 1950) while staying at the Surf and Sand Apartments. After finishing his daily quota of pages, he hastened to the Daytona Beach Tennis Club.

One of Wilder's Daytona contemporaries, black rather than white, who made his mark in the world was **Howard Thurman** (1900-1981), who was raised by his grandmother, a former slave, at 614 Whitehall Street. He was the co-founder of the interracial non-denominational Church for Fellowship of All Peoples in San Francisco. Influenced by the teachings of Mahatma Gandhi, Thurman provided a bridge to a later generation of civil rights leaders, including Martin Luther King, Jr., who was a graduate student at Boston University while Thurman was serving as the first black dean of that school's Marsh Chapel. Thurman wrote more than 20 books on race and religion. His memoirs, *With Head and Heart: The Autobiography of Howard Thurman* (New York: Harcourt Brace Jovanovich, 1979), and *Howard Thurman: Portrait of a Practical Dreamer* (New York: John Day Co., 1964) by **Elizabeth Yates** provide details of his life. One of the many honors Thurman received was the Mary McLeod Bethune Medallion from Bethune-Cookman College in 1958, named for the single most outstanding resident in Daytona's history.

Mary McLeod Bethune (1875-1955) never wrote a book (although she tried at the end of her life to do her memoirs, and asked her friend Marjorie Kinnan Rawlings to help get them under way), but she has been the subject of a large number of them: biographies entitled *Mary McLeod Bethune* by **Cather-**

ine Owens Peare (New York: Vanguard, 1951); **Emma Gelders Sterne** (New York: Knopf, 1957); **Rackham Holt** (Garden City, NY: Doubleday, 1964); **Eloise Greenfield** (New York: Crowell, 1977); **Patricia McKissack** (Chicago: Children's Press, 1985); **Milton Meltzer** (New York: Puffin Books, 1988); and **Malu Halasa** (New York: Chelsea House, 1989); as well as *The College Built on Prayer* by **Jesse Walter Dees** (Daytona Beach: Bethune-Cookman College, 1953) and *She Wanted To Read* by **Ella Kaiser Carruth** (New York: Abingdon Press, 1966). Even with all these volumes, many aimed at younger readers, there is still an opening for a good adult biography, warts and all, to help future generations understand how Bethune rose from the South Carolina cotton fields to become a White House adviser, college founder and president, and organizer of the National Council of Negro Women. She became the first black to receive an honorary degree from a white college in the South — at Rollins College in Winter Park, Florida, in 1949.

Her house at Bethune-Cookman College, 640 2nd Avenue, is open to the public. Among the literary exhibits is a signed copy of *The Yearling* from Marjorie Kinnan Rawlings, as well as autographed pictures of Langston Hughes and James Weldon Johnson.

Bethune was able to get support for her school, founded in 1904, from many wealthy winter residents of the Daytona area. A building on campus is named for one of them, **Harrison Rhodes** (1871-1929). A popular novelist and playwright, Rhodes was best known for the Broadway version of *Ruggles of Red Gap* (1915). He wrote a novel, *Flight to Eden: A Florida Romance* (New York: Holt, 1907), and collaborated with **Mary Wolfe Dumont** on *A Guide to Florida for Tourists, Sportsmen and Settlers* (New York: Dodd, Mead, 1912), an invaluable description of the state at the end of the Flagler era.

Among her other accomplishments, Bethune was credited with creating a more positive atmosphere in race relations than that found in neighboring cities, so in 1946 Daytona was chosen by Branch Rickey as a spring-training site when Jackie Robinson (1919-1972) began the modern integration of baseball. Racial conditions were not so good, however, that he could stay at a hotel with the rest of his team. Instead, he and his wife of three weeks, Rachel, occupied an upstairs apartment in the home of Joseph and Dufferin Harris at 337 Spruce Street.

Rachel Robinson returned to Daytona in 1990 to unveil a statue of her late husband at the former City Island Ball Park, which had been renamed in his honor the year before. The statue by Canadian sculptor Jules LaSalle is based on one that stands outside Montreal's Olympic Stadium, but is modified to show the ballplayer's pigeon-toed stance and the uniform he wore in Daytona. A bronze plaque notes "this is the site of the first racially integrated spring training game which was played on March 17, 1946 between the Brooklyn Dodgers and Montreal Royals. Hall of Fame legend Jackie Robinson played for Montreal, the Brooklyn farm team, thus marking an historic event in the struggle to achieve equality of opportunity in modern major league baseball." The story of that eventful spring training and the career that followed is told by several writers: **Jules Tygiel**, in *Baseball's Great Experiment: Jackie Robinson* *and His Legacy* (New York: Oxford University Press, 1983); **Carl Rowan** with **Jackie Robinson,** in *Wait Till Next Year* (New York: Random House, 1960); and **Jackie Robinson** as told to **Alfred Duckett,** in *I Never Had It Made* (New York: Putnam, 1972).

Daytona Beach has a long and interesting baseball history. Stan Musial played in town at the beginning of his career — as a pitcher — and worked in the off-season at the local Montgomery Ward store. Hall of Fame pitcher Red Ruffing was a minor-league manager here. A long-time Daytona resident was Fred Merkle (1888-1956), a valued member of John J. McGraw's New York Giants. He had the misfortune to make one mistake which overshadowed all else he did in his career. In what was for many years the greatest dispute in baseball history, Merkle was charged with failing to touch base in a crucial game that cost his team the 1908 pennant. According to one reference book, "Fans invented the terms 'boner' and 'bonehead' to apply to Merkle's play." The incident is described in detail in **Lawrence S. Ritter**'s baseball classic, *The Glory of Their Times* (New York: Macmillan, 1966). Merkle, who was a pioneer among ballplayers in playing bridge and golf, was a partner in a small Daytona business that manufactured fishing floats. His house still stands, although without historic marker, at 616 South Palmetto Avenue.

One of the legendary pranks of spring training took place in Daytona in 1915 when the pioneer aviator Ruth Law was to drop a ball from her plane to see if Brooklyn manager Wilbert Robinson could catch it. At the last minute a grapefruit was substituted (Casey Stengel took credit for it), and as it smashed and oozed over Robinson he screamed, "Jesus, I'm killed! I'm dead! My chest's split open! I'm covered with blood!" An account of the incident is given in **Robert Creamer,** *Stengel: His Life and Times* (New York: Simon and Schuster, 1984) as well as in the pictorial history of Daytona aviation by **Dick** and **Yvonne Punnett,** *Thrills, Chills & Spills* (New Smyrna Beach, FL: Luthers, 1990).

Aviation is only one aspect of speed with which Daytona is associated. Its greatest fame has come from automobile racing. The nearby Birthplace of Speed Museum, located in an architecturally significant building at 160 East Granada Boulevard in Ormond Beach, gives historic perspective on the sport, as do some of the exhibits in the excellent Halifax Historical Museum at 252 South Beach Street (across from Jackie Robinson Ballpark). The first movie made in the area was *Automobile Races at Ormond, Florida* in 1905 by the pioneering camera artist **G.W. "Billy" Bitzer,** author of the film memoir *Billy Bitzer: His Story* (New York: Farrar, Straus and Giroux, 1973). More recently the area came to the screen with Tom Cruise in *Days of Thunder* (1990). Racing has also figured in a number of books aimed at younger readers: for instance, **William Butterworth**'s *Return to Daytona* (New York: Grosset & Dunlap, 1974) and *Wheel of a Fast Car* (New York: Grosset & Dunlap, 1969). For a history of racing see **William Neely**'s *Daytona U.S.A.* (Tuscon, AZ: Aztex, 1979) and **Alice Strickland**'s "Florida's Golden Age of Racing," *Florida Historical Quarterly* 45 (January 1966), pp. 253-68.

Olds Hall at 340 South Ridgewood Avenue has an interesting story that recalls the early days of automobiles in Daytona Beach. Originally the Arroyo Gardens Hotel built during the 1920s boom, and later renamed the Daytona Terrace, it was purchased in 1942 by Ransom E. Olds (1864-1950), of Oldsmobile fame, as a retirement home for ministers and missionaries. For further information see **Arthur C. Archibald's** *Olds Hall* (1963).

The racing events for cars and motorcycles, the spring break for college students, and the pseudo-Las Vegas flavor of its beach area have combined to give Daytona a certain aura of raunchiness. So it is perhaps doubly amazing that the area once benefited from the promotional efforts of that pillar of American wholesomeness, Norman Rockwell (1894-1978). The city's advertising agency, looking for a new approach, came up with the idea of contacting Rockwell and was fortunate enough to do it when he was weatherbound at his northern home with temperatures below zero. The chance to work in the sunshine was more appealing to him than the $5,000 offered. He did half-a-dozen scenes, mostly with local models, of family groups at the beach — to be used on billboards and in newspaper and magazine advertising. He also obliged with kind words, saying "I don't know why they have to sell this place. I think it's just wonderful." He spoke to the local Rotary Club and was the honored guest at a reception of the Chamber of Commerce held April 4, 1961, at the historic Halifax River Yacht Club, 331 South Beach Street. When Rockwell died in 1978, the Daytona daily paper reprinted the most famous of his sketches, depicting two tourists sunbathing while their hometown newspaper prominently shows the headline, Blizzard.

There have been other efforts in the cultural field to tone up Daytona's image. The city has been proclaimed the Official American Summer Home of the London Symphony Orchestra, which has been performing in town since the mid-1960s. It has resulted in the appearance of many distinguished musicians and a couple of authors as well.

In the summer of 1967, the British novelist and playwright **J.B. Priestley** (1894-1984) and his wife, archaeologist and writer **Jacquetta Hawkes**, rented a furnished house on Crescent Ridge Road and observed the orchestra and its surroundings. The result was Priestley's book *Trumpets Over the Sea* (London: Heinemann, 1968), which gives interesting but acid comments on everything he came in contact with, not all of it accurate. He claimed he was unable to find a bookstore in Daytona, although the city directory listed a number of them, albeit some of the religious or greeting-card variety. He complained of the rented house. "We turned on a shower upstairs and water gushed through a hole in the dining-room ceiling." And he soon concluded, "I had made a fool of myself, and on a large and expensive scale too." He shares his foolishness with the readers of the book in a readable, if not always good-humored, way.

Notable in another area was **Rupert J. Longstreet**, founder and editor of the *Florida Naturalist* (1927-1949) and president of the Florida Audubon Society (1930-1936), whose standard work, *Birds in Florida* (Tampa: Trend House), went through a number of editions between 1931 and 1969. An educator by profession (Robert Wilder was one of his students), he lived at 610 Braddock Avenue and has been honored with the naming of the R.J. Long-street Elementary School at 2745 South Peninsula Drive. His other books include (with **R.L. Goulding**) *Stories of Florida* (Auburn, AL: Prather, 1931) and *The Story of Mount Dora, Florida* (Mount Dora, FL: Mount Dora Historical Society, 1960).

Daytona's pioneer newspaper, the *Halifax Journal*, made its first appearance on February 15, 1883. It was printed on cloth when the necessary paper supplies failed to arrive. The editor and publisher, **Florian Alexander Mann** (1837-1924), later put out the first newspaper in Ormond in 1890 and wrote two historical novels: *Story of the Huguenots* (St. Augustine: Mann & Mann, 1898) and *The Story of Ponce de Leon* (DeLand, FL: Mann, 1903).

A more recent literary resident is **Walter M. Miller, Jr.** (1923-), author of the science-fiction classic *A Canticle for Leibowitz* (1960), who lived for many years at 513 Hillside Avenue and 403 Lenox Avenue. Also a Daytona Beach resident is **Edward S. Fox** (1911-), whose works include *Massacre Inlet* (Garden City: Doubleday, 1965), a novel for younger readers about the slaughter of the French Huguenots by the Spaniards under Pedro Menéndez in 1565. Fox is a nephew of the celebrated Virginia author John Fox, Jr. (1863?-1919), who wrote *The Little Shepherd of Kingdom Come* (1903).

In a city catering to tourists, there would naturally be short-term residents of note. **James Calvert Smith** (1879-1962), the historian with a paintbrush, lived in 1947 at 108 South Coates Street. Some of his paintings are in the Halifax Historical Museum, 252 South Beach Street. **Robert Lewis Taylor** (1912-), who won the 1959 Pulitzer Prize for fiction for *The Travels of Jamie McPheeters*, which he followed with the Florida-based novel *A Journey to Matecumbe* (New York: McGraw-Hill, 1961), lived in Daytona in 1971-1972 at the Bellair Apartments, 2727 North Atlantic Avenue, and in 1975-1976 at Peck Plaza, 2625 South Atlantic Avenue.

A winter visitor earlier in the century was **Elizabeth Bacon Custer** (1842-1933), author of several books, the best-known being *Boots and Saddles* (1885), about her husband, General George Armstrong Custer (1839-76). Her biography, *General Custer's Libbie*, has been written by **Lawrence A. Frost** (Seattle: Superior, 1976).

One area in which speed has not served Daytona well is the speed with which local landmarks have been demolished. Perhaps nowhere is this more heartbreaking than in the case of **Zora Neale Hurston** (1891?-1960), the famous black novelist who died in a welfare home and was buried in an unmarked grave in Fort Pierce, Florida, three decades before her books all came back into print, with her 1937 novel, *Their Eyes Were Watching God*, selling at the rate of 20,000 copies a month.

The first home Hurston ever owned was the houseboat Wanago. The second, and last, was its successor, Sun Tan. She lived on them in the 1940s at the Howard Boat Works, 633 Ballough Road, where, she wrote, "all the other boat owners are very nice to me. Not a word about race." Unfortunately, the boat works, long a Daytona landmark, has recently been demolished — yet another bit of precious heritage carelessly dispensed with.

Novels with Daytona Beach settings include **Edgar A. Anderson's** *Day Number 142* (New York: Dorrance, 1974); **Howard Bloomfield's** *Last Cruise of the Nightwatch* (Englewood Cliffs, NJ: Prentice-Hall, 1956); and **Stewart Sterling's** *Kick of the Wheel* (New York: Prentice-Hall, 1957).

Information about the area's past can be found in **Ianthe Bond Hebel's** *Centennial History of Volusia County, Florida* (Daytona Beach: College Publishing Co., 1955); **Michael G. Schene's** *Hopes, Dreams, and Promises: A History of Volusia County, Florida* (Daytona Beach: News Journal Corporation, 1976); and **Henry B. Watson's** *Bicentennial Pictorial History of Volusia County* (Daytona Beach: News-Journal Corporation, 1976).

Port Orange

South of Daytona is Port Orange — actually the third location of a town of that name — which began after the Civil War as a settlement for freed slaves organized by former Union officers. Literary residents of the city include **Sam Harrison**, winner of the 1987 Nelson Algren Short Story Award and author of the 1990 first novel *Walls of Blue Coquina* (San Diego: Harcourt Brace Jovanovich), which was set on Florida's gulf coast as was his second, *Birdsong Ascending* (San Diego: Harcourt Brace Jovanovich, 1992).

Thomas Block (1945-), an airline captain who piloted everything from gliders to the Goodyear blimp and contributed a long-running column to *Flying* magazine, combined his interests in aviation and writing to produce a popular series of airplane adventure and suspense tales. The first, *Mayday* (1980), was a Literary Guild Book Club selection. Others include *Orbit* (1982), *Forced Landing* (1983), *Airship Nine* (1984), and *Skyfall* (1987).

Robert W. Walker (1948 -), a prolific author in several genres, including mystery and horror, is a Port Orange resident and English instructor at Bethune-Cookman College. The first book he wrote was a young adult novel about the Underground Railroad that took slaves to freedom before the Civil War: *Daniel Webster Jackson and the Wrongway Railway* (1982). His horror novel *Razor's Edge* (New York: Pinnacle Books, 1989) has a Florida setting.

Gamble Place on Spruce Creek in Port Orange was formerly owned by James Gamble (1836-1932) of Procter & Gamble. One of its features is the Snow White Cottage, designed by a member of the family and based on the dwarfs' house in Walt Disney's famous movie. Tours may be arranged through the Daytona Museum of Arts and Sciences (904 255-0285), which manages the property.

New Smyrna Beach

New Smyrna Beach is one of the early, though not continuous, settlements of Florida, with Indian mounds testifying to the occupancy of many centuries, and with the story of the Minorcans providing an important contribution to its folklore.

When the British took control of Florida in the 1760s, there were many efforts to develop a plantation economy in what had previously been an isolated military outpost of the Spanish empire. The largest development scheme was that of Dr. Andrew Turnbull (1720-1792), who planned to grow indigo (richly prized for dye making), using indentured laborers from the Mediterranean, particularly the island of Minorca. Turnbull named the colony after his Greek wife's home town of Smyrna (which is now the Turkish port city of Izmir).

The naturalist **William Bartram** (1739-1823), who accompanied the surveyor laying out the lines of the settlement, noted later in his *Travels* that "All this ridge was then one entire orange grove, with live oaks, magnolias, palms, red bays, and others."

Turnbull's colony, so blithely projected to bring prosperity and fortune, soon degenerated into a horror story, and in 1777 the Minorcan colonists made their way to St. Augustine, where the governor, earning Turnbull's undying enmity, gave them their freedom. The Minorcans stayed on through many changes of flags and became a people as distinctive to Florida as the Cajuns are to Louisiana, though less heavily promoted by the tourism agencies (even in St. Augustine, in the historic Minorcan Quarter, where most of the restoration effort has taken place, the area is promoted to tourists as the Spanish Quarter).

The New Smyrna colony and the Minorcan story have given birth to a literature in both fact and fiction. **Archibald Clavering Gunter** (1847-1907), the best-selling novelist of the Flagler era, wrote a two-part novel under the rubric *The Power of Woman* (New York: Hurst, 1897) with the component parts *Susan Turnbull* and *Ballyho Bey* that helped to tarnish Turnbull's reputation.

Dr. **Carita Doggett Corse** (1892-1978), a Turnbull descendant, entered the fray in 1919 with a nonfiction study, *Dr. Andrew Turnbull and the New Smyrna Colony of Florida* (revised, St. Petersburg: Great Outdoors Publishing Co., 1967), which is understandably favorable to her ancestor. Corse later headed the Federal Writers Project in Florida.

In 1926 the story again appeared in fiction with *Spanish Bayonet* by **Stephen Vincent Benét** (1898-1943), whose great-grandfather, Pedro Benet, was known as King of the Minorcans and who had heard the tales passed on through generations of his family. Benét had never visited Florida before he wrote the novel, but did come to speak to the St. Augustine Historical Society in 1941 on "The Human Side of History" to an audience that included Carita Doggett Corse!

Later studies include **E.P. Panagopoulos's** *New Smyrna: An Eighteenth Century Greek Odyssey* (Gainesville: University of Florida Press, 1966), which concentrates on the Greek members of the colony; **Philip D. Rasico's** *The Minorcans of Florida: Their History, Language, and Culture* (New Smyrna Beach, FL: Luthers, 1990); and **Patricia C. Griffin's** *Mullet on the Beach: The Minorcans of Florida, 1768-1788* (Jacksonville: University of North Florida Press, 1991).

The 1975 study, *Minorcans in Florida: Their History and Heritage* (St. Augustine: Mission Press) by **Jane Quinn**, was sponsored by the twentieth-century King of the Minorcans, X.L. Pellicer (1900-1990), whose ancestor, Francisco Pellicer, led the Minorcan hegira from New Smyrna to St. Augustine in 1777.

In front of New Smyrna's city hall, 210 Sams Avenue, is a plaque honoring Turnbull. Across the street, in interesting juxtaposition, is one in memory of the Greek members of the Minorcan colony. Both were placed there by different sponsors in 1968 as part of the celebration of the city's two-hundredth birthday.

Robert Turnbull (1775-1833), son of the colony-building doctor, became New Smyrna's first native-born author. His 1796 *Visit to the Philadelphia Prison* was published in both London and Paris to considerable comment. A prominent figure in the political life of South Carolina, he played a role in the suppression of Denmark Vesey's 1822 slave uprising. Turnbull's best-known work was *The Crisis: or, Essays on the Usurpations of the Federal Government* (1827), originally a series of newspaper articles, which became a kind of textbook for the nullification movement and one of the theoretical underpinnings for the eventual Civil War. His admirers erected a monument to his memory in Charleston.

New Smyrna was periodically abandoned and resettled. Jacob Rhett Motte, an army surgeon who visited during the Seminole War, found it "almost reduced to a state of primitive wildness from its long desertion" and noted: "This was the spot where Turnbull first established his Minorcan colony, and the ruins of the original occupants' dwellings are still visible in the distance, adding a melancholy feature to the landscape, from a retrospective association of the sufferings there endured." **Charles W. Bockelman**'s *Six Columns and Fort New Smyrna* (Daytona Beach: Halifax Historical Society, 1985) is about the fort that was used as a supply depot from 1837 to 1855 during the Seminole Indian wars.

In 1853 **John McAllister Schofield** (1831-1906), later a Union general in the Civil War, passed through on his way to a military posting. He wrote in his memoirs: "At New Smyrna Mrs. Sheldon provided excellent entertainment during the ten days' waiting for the mailboat down Mosquito Lagoon and Indian River, while Mr. Sheldon's pack of hounds furnished sport." The long delay was occasioned by the fact that the mailboat captain "divided his time fairly between carrying the United States mail and drinking whisky, but he never attempted to do both at the same time."

The foundations of the Sheldon house, where Schofield stayed, are still visible in the park at North Riverside Drive and Julia Street. *Visible* is an understatement: they are the most obvious historic remains in town, and one need only walk around the park and read the markers to see what is also New Smyrna's greatest historic problem: exaggeration. If the city had more tourists, it could probably vie with St. Augustine in the number of tall tales told about its past. These foundations have been attributed to a fort, to Turnbull's "palace" (though not on Turnbull's land), or — more recently — to a church that served the Minorcan colony. It is hard to see that a serious history of New Smyrna can be written until the origin of these foundations, which the WPA excavated in the 1930s, is firmly established — even if they turn out to be not so ancient or colorful as generations of residents have been led to believe. To learn the truth should be a point of civic pride.

Another historic feature of New Smyrna is the grave in the middle of the street. Canova Drive, south of the Riverview Hotel, has an island in it with the tomb of Charles Dummett (1844-1860), black son of the white orange grower Douglas Dummett, who is considered the father of Indian River citrus. According to **John McPhee** in *Oranges* (New York: Farrar, Straus and Giroux, 1967): "The son, Charles, shot himself when he was sixteen. His death was called an accident, but some people on Merritt Island thought he had done it because of the shame he was made to feel for having Negro blood." It is ironic that the son's final resting place has kept even the notoriously unsentimental road builders at bay, while his celebrated father, who died 13 years later, lies buried in an unmarked grave.

Poet **Sidney Lanier** (1842-1881), who visited in 1875 while preparing a guidebook to Florida for a railroad company, wrote enthusiastically of this area: "The waters are full of fish in great variety; the woods abound in deer and other game; and the whole land amounts to a perpetual invitation to the overworked, the invalid, the air-poisoned, the nervously prostrate people, to come down with yacht and tent, with rod and gun, and rebuild brain, muscle, and nerve."

Within a decade, that perpetual invitation was taken up by a wealthy New York stockbroker, Washington Everett Connor (1849-1935), who bought large acreage in the area and became to New Smyrna what Flagler had been to St. Augustine, Henry Plant to Tampa, and John B. Stetson to DeLand. His Ronnoc Groves (*Connor* spelled backwards) grew not only the obligatory oranges, but had extensive vineyards from which he produced his own wine.

Connor could afford it. As the primary stockbroker for robber baron Jay Gould, he had made a million dollars on a single deal back when that was real money. He built a bridge connecting downtown with the beach, planted palm and oak trees to beautify the area, and donated a library (the building, which later served as a garden center, has recently been moved to the park opposite city hall, awaiting renovation and a new lease on life).

He also interested himself in the antiquities of the area, particularly the ruins of what he thought to be an old Spanish mission (later research has shown it to be a sugar mill from the 1830s). The story grew better and better, and the place came to be known as Columbus Chapel. A state historic site, it can still be visited today at 600 Old Mission Road.

Washington Connor was probably not the first, and certainly not the last, to tell tall tales about the past; but it is ironic because his second wife became one of Florida's leading historians. In 1913 he married Jeannette Thurber (1872-1927), whose mother founded the National Conservatory of Music in New York, brought Antonin Dvorak to this country, and figures as a character in Joseph Skvorecky's novel *Dvorak in Love* (1987). Spurred on by the gift of the sugar mill — or Columbus Chapel — ruins from her husband, **Jeanette Thurber Connor** proceeded to ransack the Spanish archives for early records of Florida. In the course of this she met another researcher, John B. Stetson, Jr. (1884-1952), and together they founded the Florida State Historical Society (not to be confused with the Florida Historical Society) in 1921. Their organization embarked on an ambitious publication program of high-quality historical studies. Many of them have since been reprinted, and original editions are highly valued by collectors. Among the volumes Jeanette Thurber Connor translated and edited for the series were *Pedro Menéndez de Avilés: Memorial* by *Gonzalo Solis de Meras* (1923); *Colonial Records of Spanish Florida* (two volumes, 1925 and 1930); and *The Whole & True Discouerye of Terra Florida* by **Jean Ribaut** (1927). Unfortunately, the death of Mrs. Connor in 1927 and financial reverses suffered by John B. Stetson, Jr., in the stock market crash of 1929 brought an end to the historical society and its program. Perhaps the finest tribute to their work was given in her *New York Times* obituary: "It is said that Mrs. Connor and Mr. Stetson together had copies of every Spanish historical paper relating to the early Florida settlements, so that if all the libraries in Spain were to be destroyed the historical facts would still be available." Modern researchers like Dr. Eugene Lyon have demonstrated that there are, indeed, more documents to be uncovered in Spain and so are advancing the work that Connor and Stetson sponsored in their own time.

Washington Connor was not without his critics. One was **John Y. Detwiler**, editor of the *New Smyrna Breeze*, who published two pamphlets: *First Settlement in America* and *Early History of New Smyrna*. While attacking Connor's exaggerations, however, Detwiler mainly sought to prove that New Smyrna was the original St. Augustine of Pedro Menéndez. Detwiler's house at 307 South Indian River Road is one of the oldest in the area — and notable also as the home of New Smyrna's first woman mayor, his daughter Hannah Detwiler Bonnet (1891-1977).

Detwiler was a pioneer journalist in New Smyrna, but not the first. The city's earliest newspaper was the *Florida Star*, launched in 1877 by the Coes, a family of printers originally from Waterbury, Connecticut, who had settled a homestead four miles west of New Smyrna in 1875 in an area that came to be named Glencoe. According to an 1878 note by Dr. J.M. Hawks, "They live in a frame house built by themselves, a few rods south of Mr. Sellecks and perhaps 80 rods from Lewis H. Bryan's."

Although the newspaper was sold (and later moved to Titusville and Cocoa) after the father of the family died in 1879, one of the sons, **Charles H. Coe** (1856-1954), left his mark on Florida literature with a book, *Red Patriots: The Story of the Seminoles*, first published in 1898 and reprinted as part of the Bicentennial Floridiana Facsimile series in 1974 by the University Presses of Florida. Among Coe's later works of local interest was the pamphlet *Debunking the So-Called Spanish Mission Near New Smyrna Beach, Volusia County, Florida* (Daytona Beach: Fitzgerald Publications, 1941).

Friendlier to Connor was another area historian, **Zelia Wilson Sweett** (1897-1980), co-author (with **J.C. Marsden**) of *New Smyrna, Florida: Its History and Antiquities* (DeLand, FL: Painter, 1925). She worked with the Federal Writers Project in the 1930s and lived at 128 North Riverside Drive.

Walter Miller's childhood home, New Smyrna Beach

One unmarked literary landmark of the city is at 705 South Magnolia Street. This one-story stuccoed bungalow has been modified with a modern front enclosure and curving entrance ramp, reflecting its recent use as a chiropractor's office. Its significance derives from the fact that it was the childhood home of **Walter M. Miller, Jr.**, born in New Smyrna in 1923, who wrote the classic *A Canticle for Leibowitz* (1960) and won a Hugo Award for best novelette in 1955 for *The Darfsteller*. His masterpiece, which has sold over a million copies, was placed in context by one early reviewer who wrote: "*A Canticle for Leibowitz* belongs in the same category as Aldous Huxley's *Brave New World*, George Orwell's *1984*, and contemporary works such as Nevil Shute's *On the Beach*...." Orville Prescott hailed it as "A remarkable science-fiction novel that soars above the level of science-fiction in the realm of satire, parable, allegory and philosophy." Some say it is the best science-fiction novel ever written.

Because the railroad runs through New Smyrna, a famous author died there. **Albert Bigelow Paine** (1861-1937), the biographer and literary executor of Mark Twain, had spent the winter in south Florida and was en route to New York when he became ill and was hospitalized at New Smyrna. He died there, four weeks later, on April 9. An obituary noted: "A member of the Pulitzer Prize committee for many years, he had just finished reading a novel which may bring its author the award next month." The Pulitzer prize that year was won by *Gone With the Wind*. Paine had written dozens of books, one of which contributed a memorable phrase to the language; the title of his 1901 novel,

The Great White Way, came to be the standard designation for Broadway and New York's theater district.

At 611 Oliver Drive in New Smyrna lived **Nixon Smiley** (1911-1990), retired veteran of many years with the *Miami Herald*. His books like *Florida: Land of Images* (Miami: Seemann Publishing Co., 1972) and *On the Beat and Offbeat with Nixon Smiley* (Miami: Banyan, 1983) have done much to foster public interest in Florida's heritage.

New Smyrna is also the location of the Atlantic Center for the Arts, 1414 Art Center Avenue, which opened in 1982. It brings in well-known artists several times a year to work for three weeks with specially selected students. Among the writers who have participated are Allen Ginsburg, Lawrence Ferlinghetti, Edward Albee, Bobbie Ann Mason, Mary Lee Settle, and James Dickey. The facility is used year-round by cultural groups and has a gallery open to the public.

Edgewater

Edgewater is another of those Florida places whose name has been changed in the quest for riches at the expense of its history. It was founded in 1871 and named Hawks Park. During the real-estate boom of the 1920s, people complained that, when spoken fast, it sounded like Hog's Park so they had the state legislature change it to the easier-to-sell Edgewater. The boom collapsed before the little village could be turned into a great metropolis.

The shame of it is that the original name reflected the founding role in the community of one — or two — of the truly outstanding characters in Florida history: Dr. **John Milton Hawks** (1826-1910) and his wife, Dr. **Esther Hill Hawks** (1833-1906). Both of the Doctors Hawks were authors — although

Hawks House in Edgewater

in one case it took more than a century for the book to appear — but that was just one of many talents they evinced in long and interesting careers.

Both were physicians and schoolteachers. John was superintendent of schools in Volusia County after the Civil War, and during the war Esther taught what may have been the state's first integrated public school. Both were advocates of women's rights and activists in the antislavery cause. Both served during the Civil War with black troops in the South Carolina Sea Islands, an episode of history described in **Thomas Wentworth Higginson's** *Army Life in a Black Regiment* (1870) and **Willie Lee Rose's** *Rehearsal for Reconstruction* (1964).

John Hawks worked with other Union officers at the end of the war to establish the Florida Land and Lumber Company, which tried to settle black soldiers at Port Orange. That attempt failed, but he continued his activities in Florida. In 1870 he met an Ohio businessman named Matthias Day, who was looking for a site to develop. Hawks traveled with him to the Halifax River, and Daytona Beach was the result. He wrote two notable books: *The Florida Gazeteer* (New Orleans: Bronze Pen Steam Book and Job Office, 1871) and *The East Coast of Florida* (Lynn, Mass.: Lewis & Winship, 1887), which would both merit reprinting for the light they shed on an interesting period in the state's history.

The writing of Esther Hawks took longer to appear, but acquired the excitement of a whodunit in the process. In 1975 an apartment building in Essex County, Massachusetts, was being renovated. Someone going through the mounds of trash found several diaries, which proved to be those in which Esther Hawks noted her day-to-day Civil War experiences in Florida and South Carolina. Internal evidence indicated there was another diary. Had it already been found by someone who did not realize its importance? The discovered volumes, edited by Gerald Schwartz, were published in 1984 by the University of South Carolina Press as *A Woman Doctor's Civil War: Esther Hill Hawks' Diary*.

When Esther died in 1906, she left $1,000 to establish a library, and it is fitting that her picture, along with one of her husband, hangs today in the Edgewater Public Library at 103 West Indian River Boulevard. In front of the building is a memorial bronze plaque to the doctors, dedicated in 1969 by the local American Legion. Best of all, a fine and meticulously preserved collection of the Hawks papers is available in the library.

John Hawks is buried in the Edgewater Cemetery on U.S. 1, and the Hawks house is still standing at 114 North Riverside Drive, a landmark awaiting historic recognition and tender loving care.

THE RIVER ROUTE: FRUIT COVE TO ASTOR

The St. Johns River, beloved by placid fishermen and befouled by smelly paper manufacturers, ranks with the Nile for its rare north-flowing waters and with the Mississippi as a once (and future?) center of the steamboat trade. Winslow Homer painted along its banks, Frederick Delius played music, John

J. Audubon hunted birds, and the Bartrams sought out new varieties of plants to share with the world.

After the Civil War, when the tourism industry started in earnest, this was the route visitors took: up (because of the flow, rather than down, as the geography would seem to indicate) the St. Johns and its lakes and tributaries to places like Enterprise, Sanford, Silver Springs, Palatka, Green Cove Springs, and Mandarin. The river route reigned supreme until the railroad replaced the steamboat as the way of getting around the peninsula.

Edward Mueller's *Steamboating on the St. Johns* (Melbourne, FL: Kellersberger Fund of the South Brevard Historical Society, 1980) tells in words and pictures the story of that vanished era. Two books, *The St. Johns: A Parade of Diversities* (New York: Farrar & Rinehart, 1943) by **Branch Cabell** and **A.J. Hanna** — part of the famous Rivers of America series — and Congressman **Charles Bennett'**s *Twelve on the River St. Johns* (Jacksonville: University of North Florida Press, 1989), deal with interesting characters whose lives and reputations intertwined with the area. Many of the settlements, communities, towns, and cities along the river have had their brushes with literature and writing people.

Fruit Cove

Fruit Cove, founded in 1871, was an outgrowth of the Orange Fever that brought settlers to Florida after the Civil War to seek their fortunes in citrus. The name of the settlement reflects the times and was bestowed by its founder, Reverend **Theophilus Wilson Moore** (1832-1908), a native of North Carolina with a lifelong passion for horticulture. Moore was a minister of the gospel and author of *The Analysis and Exposition of Our Lord's Sermon on the Mount* (1886) and *The Book of Revelation* (1897), but for many settlers of that era the true bible was another of his books: the widely known work popularly christened *Moore's Orange-Culture*. First published in 1877, it sold out and was succeeded by a revised and enlarged second edition in 1881. A third edition came in 1884, with an expanded title that reflected the changing times and hopes of a larger geographical market; it was called *Treatise and Hand-book of Orange Culture in Florida, Louisiana and California* (New York: E.R. Pelton, 1884) rather than the simple *Florida* which had graced the first two editions. His son, T.V. Moore (1857-1927), represented St. Johns County in the state legislature from 1889-1890, then moved south to the Indian River and finally Miami, where he became known as the Pineapple King.

Switzerland

The community south of Fruit Cove, settled a century earlier, takes its name from the former home of its founder, Francis P. Fatio (1724-1811), who established New Switzerland Plantation after the British took control of Florida from Spain in the 1760s. **Eugenia Price'**s novel *Margaret's Story* (New York: Bantam, 1980) deals with the Fatio family.

A modern-day descendant of Francis Fatio is **Madeleine L'Engle** (1918-), author of the classic *A Wrinkle In Time* which received the 1963 Newbery Medal for "the most distinguished contribution to American literature for children," and many other books. She tells the story of her family, its lore and legends, in *The Summer of the Great-Grandmother* (New York: Farrar, Straus & Giroux, 1974). The Fatio plantation is long gone, but a marker in front of the Switzerland Community Church recalls its historic importance to the area.

One of the colorful figures of Florida history was born a slave at New Switzerland Plantation. Louis Pacheco (1800-1895) learned to read and write, eventually mastering four languages. Employed as an interpreter during the Seminole wars, he survived the Dade Massacre and lived among the Indians as a free man. The celebrated attempt to return him to slavery is dealt with in the **Joshua R. Giddings** work, *The Exiles of Florida* (1858, reprinted Gainesville: University of Florida Press, 1964). In 1892 the elderly Pacheco returned to New Switzerland and was reunited with the Fatio daughter who had taught him to read so long before. He died there at the age of 94 and was buried at his birthplace. The next year he appeared as a character in **Kirk Munroe**'s novel *Through Swamp and Glade: A Tale of the Seminole War* (New York: Scribner's, 1896). A biographical sketch is given in Kenneth W. Porter's "The Early Life of Luis Pacheco Né Fatio," *Negro History Bulletin* (December 1943).

Stetson Kennedy (1916-), author of *Palmetto Country* (1942) — a volume in the American Folkways series edited by Erskine Caldwell — is a longtime resident of Switzerland. Kennedy's fascinating career has included service with the Federal Writers Project in the 1930s; infiltrating the Ku Klux Klan in the 1940s and exposing them in *Southern Exposure* (Garden City, NY: Doubleday, 1946) and *I Rode With the Ku Klux Klan* (NY: Arco Publications, 1954); an independent "color-blind" candidacy for the U.S. Senate in 1950 (after Claude Pepper had been defeated in a searing primary campaign by George Smathers); and presidency of the Florida Folklore Society in the 1980s — all of which make his autobiography an eagerly awaited book. An account of his activities is given in **Wyn C. Wade**'s *The Fiery Cross* (NY: Simon & Schuster, 1987).

Kennedy inherited property in Switzerland from his father at a time when there were only 87 residents in the area. He later wrote: "My piece of land, which embraces a small lake, lies on the outskirts, with no neighbors within shouting distance. My wife and I came in like pioneers and began to clear the land and make a home. We decided to call the place Beluthahatchee — a Seminole Indian name meaning Nirvana on Water." Folksinger **Woody Guthrie** (1912-1967) visited there and wrote a song about "Beluthahatchee Bill." Three of Kennedy's books were brought out in paperback editions by the state's university presses in 1990: *Palmetto Country, The Klan Unmasked*, and *Jim Crow Guide: The Way It Was*. A fourth, *Southern Exposure*, came out in 1991.

Switzerland has grown beyond the hamlet he first knew. It now bristles with new subdivisions, some of whose streets bear Swiss appellations while others are named after the local road-kill. Bombing Range Road, named for its historic use during World War II, was deemed not sufficiently saleable and was prettified to Greenbriar Road. The main artery through the area is State Road 13, designated by the Florida legislature in 1981 as the William Bartram Scenic Highway, due to efforts of local garden clubs and others. By 1988 the

State Department of Transportation planned to cut down many of the ancient overarching live oaks that made it scenic. Massive protests prompted the governor to intervene and stop the slaughter.

Picolata

The naming of the route was appropriate because **William Bartram** (1739-1823), with his father John, had explored the St. Johns River in the 1760s. Among other events, they witnessed the meeting that resulted in the 1765 Treaty of Picolata, delineating which parts of Florida were open for British settlement and which were reserved for the Indians.

When John Bartram (1699-1777) returned to Pennsylvania, William decided to stay in Florida and seek his fortune as a planter of rice and indigo at Picolata. Henry Laurens, a family friend who would later succeed John Hancock as president of the Continental Congress, visited there in the summer of 1766 and wrote a dismal description of "Poor Billy Bartram, a gentle mild young man, no wife, no friend, no companion, no neighbor, no human inhabitant within nine miles of him, the nearest by water, no boat to come to them and these only common soldiers seated on a beggarly spot of land, scant of bare necessities, and totally devoid of the comforts of life, except an inimitable degree of patience, for which he deserves a thousand times better fate." By 1767 Bartram was gone from Picolata, though he returned to Florida in the 1770s and wrote, as a result, his memorable *Travels Through North & South Carolina, Georgia, East & West Florida* (1791), which remains in print two centuries later.

Bartram's *Travels* has come to have significance in a wide number of areas, including botany, history, ethnology, architecture, and — certainly not least — literature. Not only is it highly regarded as a piece of writing but it also inspired poets like Samuel Taylor Coleridge and William Wordsworth, and was plagiarized by the French novelist Chateaubriand and the American Washington Irving. For more details, see **E.P. Panagopoulos**, "Chateaubriand's Florida and His Journey to America," *Florida Historical Quarterly* 49 (1970-71), pp. 140-52.

It is one of the scandals of Florida history that no effort has been made to locate and mark the site of Bartram's plantation. With the winds of development roaring in the area, some land will have to be put aside, and what would be more appropriate than a William Bartram Nature Preserve and Botanical Garden on the site of his old plantation? It may have been located in the vicinity of Palmo Fish Camp Road on Six Mile Creek, and there may be the possibility of finding archaeological remains of Bartram's occupancy.

In a state which has so often celebrated Bartram's tenure here, such an undertaking does not seem to be beyond the realm of possibility. But then again, a fragile wildflower named Bartram's Ixia, found only in northeast Florida, was denied admission to the Federal Endangered Species list in 1990 after lobbying by the state's forest industry and developers. Even after two centuries there is a certain wariness about honoring Bartram fully. It can still endanger profits to be an advocate of nature with the fervor of Bartram.

A number of books have been written about the Bartrams. The prominent novelist **Josephine Herbst** (1897-1969) traced the careers of father and son in *New Green World* (New York: Hastings House, 1954), the first volume in the American Procession series. **N. Bryllion Fagin**'s *William Bartram, Interpreter of the American Landscape* (Baltimore: The Johns Hopkins Press, 1933) examines his influence on authors around the world. Also worth a place in any Florida library are **Ernest Earnest**'s *John and William Bartram, Botanists and Explorers*, (Philadelphia: University of Pennsylvania Press, 1940); **Helen Cruickshank**'s *John and William Bartram's America* (New York: Devin-Adair, 1957); and **Edmund Berkeley** and **Dorothy Smith Berkeley**'s *The Life and Travels of John Bartram* (Tallahassee: University Presses of Florida, 1982) as well as the collection edited by the same authors, *The Correspondence of John Bartram 1734-1777* (Gainesville: University Press of Florida, 1992). Two highly regarded juvenile biographies are **Marjory Bartlett Sanger**'s *Billy Bartram and His Green World* (New York: Farrar, Straus & Giroux, 1972) and **Ann** and **Myron Sutton**'s *Exploring with the Bartrams* (Chicago: Rand McNally, 1963). The father's writings on Florida are included in **William Stork**'s *A Description of East Florida, with a Journal kept by John Bartram* (1769; reprinted, Ann Arbor, MI: University Microfilms International, 1981). The contributions of the Bartrams are put into context in two other studies: **Alfred Kazin**'s *A Writer's America: Landscape in Literature* (New York: Knopf, 1988) and **Stephen Spongberg**'s *A Reunion of Trees: The Discovery of Exotic Plants and Their Introduction Into North American and European Landscapes* (Cambridge, MA: Harvard University Press, 1990).

During the steamboat era of the 1800s, Picolata came to prominence as the gateway to the Ancient City. Visitors, some of them literary, would go up the St. Johns to Picolata and then take the stage, run by James Riz (1799-1859) and his Colee in-laws, to St. Augustine. A century and a half later, the Colee family still operates horse carriages that take tourists through the nation's oldest city: a fascinating multi-generational saga that awaits only a pen to write it down.

A mile north of Riz's landing lived the legendary **John Lee Williams** (1775-1856), who in 1824 with Dr. William Hayne Simmons selected Tallahassee as the site of Florida's capital. He was the author of two classics: *A View of West Florida* (1827; reprinted, Gainesville: University Presses of Florida, 1976) and *The Territory of Florida* (1837; reprinted, Gainesville: University of Florida Press, 1962). Though he suffered from years of poverty and marital desertion, a contemporary account reported: "His mind retained its vigor to the last, and within a week of his death he was actively employed in various literary avocations, among which was the preparation of an improved edition of his History, which he had very nearly completed. At the very moment the paralytic stroke, from which he died, seized him, he had the pen in his hand writing a novel, the scene of which was laid in China!"

In 1842, during the Second Seminole War, a young lieutenant fresh from West Point boarded with Williams while stationed at Picolata. His name was William Tecumseh Sherman (1820-1891), and at least this theater of war he did not find hell. His descriptions were glowing: "It is a very beautiful spot indeed. Magnificent live oak trees shade the yard, enclosing my splendid quarters, and the St. Johns, a noble sheet of water, about one and a half miles broad, adds beauty to the whole. In fact I would much prefer being here to St. Augustine, for 'tis like being in the country with all the advantages of both town and country, for with a good horse I can ride over at any time in a couple of hours, get books, see the ladies, etc."

A year later the man often called the Father of American Poetry landed at Picolata and took the stage for St. Augustine. **William Cullen Bryant** (1794-1878) found that the driver was also a tour guide, pointing out where various events in the Seminole War had taken place: "he showed us the spot where a party of players, on their way to St. Augustine, were surprised and killed. The Indians took possession of the stage dresses, one of them arraying himself in the garb of Othello, another in that of Richard the Third, and another taking the costume of Falstaff." Today there is a historic marker on County Road 208 about a mile and a half west of Interstate 95 at the site of the 1840 attack on the theatrical troupe led by Coacoochee (Wildcat). The incident formed the basis for a short story, "Seminole Attack" by **Theodore Pratt** (1901-1969) in *Florida Roundabout* (New York: Duell, Sloan and Pearce, 1959). A free-verse account of the life of the colorful Indian leader is **Arthur Francke**'s *Coacoochee: Made of the Sands of Florida* (DeLeon Springs, FL: Painter Printing Co., 1986). **Edith Pope** used Coacoochee as a character in her novel *River in the Wind* (New York: Scribner's, 1954), as did **Frank Slaughter** in *The Warrior* (Garden City, NY: Doubleday, 1956).

Picolata received its share of knocks from those who passed through. Henry Benjamin Whipple (1822-1901) noted in his diary for January 27, 1844, that he "very demurely walked up to the (what shall I call it?) Hotel! no! tavern! no but to the frame or skeleton of the building where weary wayfarers wait impatiently for a boat to remove them from this dreary hole." He added, "of one thing I am certain, the inn keeper wisely concluded no man ever stopped at his house twice & so he made the most of his charge."

Whipple, who was a brother-in-law of Florida historian George Fairbanks, returned a decade later, when warm climate was prescribed for his wife's ill health. By that time he had become an Episcopal priest, and he preached while his wife recuperated, holding missionary services on a plantation at Picolata, among other places. In 1859 he became the first bishop of Minnesota and earned renown as a friend and advocate of the Indians, who called him Straight Tongue — no small honor in the age of the forked one. In 1880 he wrote the preface to **Helen Hunt Jackson**'s *A Century of Dishonor*, an indignant chronicle of the government's treatment of the Indian, that was followed by her land-mark novel on the subject, *Ramona* (1884).

General Sherman's enthusiasm for Picolata did not extend to his Civil War aide-de-camp, **George Ward Nichols** (1831-1885), who in 1870 wrote: "A more disgraceful, disheartening abomination than Picolata and its stage line I never met with in all my travels." His travels, of course, included Sherman's blazing trail through Georgia, which Nichols chronicled in a best-seller: *The Story of the*

Great March (1865), based on his wartime diary. When he tried, a year later, to recast the same material as fiction in *The Sanctuary*, it fell flat.

Nichols was in Cincinnati with his general after the war when he met and married Maria Longworth. She founded the famous Rookwood Pottery Company, and he authored two more books: *Art Education Applied to Industry* (1877) and *Pottery: How it is Made, its Shape, and Decoration* (1878).

But for Picolata, Nichols could not find a single good thing to say. He recalled for his readers in *Harper's* magazine a tale of Buckingham Smith (1810-1871), the scholar and diplomat from St. Augustine who sent his wife home from Madrid with the parting words: "Good-by, and God bless you. You are comfortably provided for your voyage. You are all safe until you reach Picolata, and then Heaven alone can help you."

The significance of Picolata soon declined, not because of bad press, but because technological innovation rendered the stage line obsolete. In 1875 the poet **Sidney Lanier** (1842-1881), writing a guidebook to the state, described Picolata as "a place formerly of some importance as the landing for passengers bound to St. Augustine, but now of only historic interest."

In the next decade, however, despite diminishing traffic, a new chapter in the significance of the area began with the arrival of Frederick Delius (1862-1934). Fleeing his family textile business in England, Delius arrived in 1884 in a "state of complete mental demoralization" supposedly to grow oranges at Solano Grove. He found golden apples of little interest compared to the excitement he felt hearing the singing of his black grove hands; "it was then and there that I first felt the urge to express myself in music," he recalled years after. Among the productions of his distinguished career as a composer were the *Florida Suite* (1888); the 1895 opera *The Magic Fountain*, drawing on the legend of the Fountain of Youth; and *Appalachia*, which was used in the musical sound track for the movie adaptation of Marjorie Kinnan Rawlings's *The Yearling*.

Though his time at Picolata was brief (1884-1885 and a return stay in 1897) it was of key significance to his life for, as his sister wrote, "it was there he found his soul." The composer has been the subject of a number of books, including **Clare Delius**'s *Frederick Delius: Memories of My Brother* (London: Ivor Nicholson & Watson, 1935); **Sir Thomas Beecham**'s *Frederick Delius* (New York: Knopf, 1960); and **Gloria Jahoda**'s *The Road to Samarkand: Frederick Delius and His Music* (New York: Scribner's 1969). For more about the music that African-Americans produced along the St. Johns River see **Dena J. Epstein**'s *Sinful Tunes and Spirituals, Black Folk Music to the Civil War* (Urbana, IL: University of Illinois Press, 1977).

The afterlife of the Delius property is equally fascinating. In 1915 the British author **D.H. Lawrence** (1885-1930) turned his thoughts to fleeing his native land. His novel *The Rainbow* had been banned as obscene, his pacifist sympathies were at odds with a nation mobilizing for World War I, and his loyalty was suspect because his wife, Frieda, was a cousin of the enemy's leading air ace, "Red Baron" Manfred von Richthofen. He projected a Utopian colony called Rananim and recruited other writers like Aldous Huxley to join him. They invited philosopher Bertrand Russell to be their president. For a location, they approached Frederick Delius about the possibility of settling at Solano Grove. Delius replied that the climate would be a death sentence for Lawrence's tuberculosis, but that, even so, Solano Grove was no longer his. He had given it, in gratitude, to the German conductor Hans Haym, who introduced Delius's music to a public audience. Thus was Picolata's chance to be a stellar location of twentieth-century literature reduced to one of the great what-ifs of Florida's cultural history.

There is a marker at Solano Grove on State Road 13, noting it was the home of composer Delius, but the intrepid explorer will be unable to find the house because in 1961 it was moved to the campus of Jacksonville University. There, according to Gloria Jahoda, it was restored "to an unknown splendor of two antique pianos and oriental rugs and gleaming white paint, and put. . . between the Swisher Athletic Gymnasium and a music practice hall. It is flanked also on one side by a basketball court and on the other by an archery range where suntanned coeds in tight short shorts send what look like Cupid's arrows into a row of large multicolored bullseyes."

Thus do styles in preservation change. The Jacksonville music lover, Mrs. Henry Richmond, who found the Delius house in near collapse at Picolata, kept it from vanishing forever. But, by moving it, she removed it from its essential context and, not for the first or last time, took one of St. Johns County's cultural treasures north to Duval County at a period when local people had not the wit or wisdom to save it. She also promoted the Delius Association, which since the early 1960s has put on an excellent annual festival in Jacksonville that is one of the state's musical highlights. Part of the 1992 festival was the dedication at Solano Grove of a bronze bas-relief portrait of Delius by sculptor Derby Ulloa, set on a column of native coquina rock. Now, however, is a time of correction. Plans should be made to return the Delius house to Solano Grove and to see that Solano Grove is preserved in perpetuity as a place sacred to the cultural heritage of Florida. To fail to do so would be to compound the lack of wisdom that nearly lost it in the first place.

Solano Grove, even without the house, has become a place of pilgrimage for music lovers in general and members of the London Symphony Orchestra (which has long made Daytona Beach its summer home) in particular. It was in connection with the LSO's 1967 appearance that British novelist and music lover **J.B. Priestley** (1894-1984) visited Solano Grove and did a painting of the St. Johns River as he imagined it must have appeared to Delius. An account of the trip is given in his book *Trumpets Over the Sea* (London: Heinemann, 1968).

Another modern pilgrim was the popular Florida writer **Gloria Jahoda** (1926-1980), a Delius biographer, who has a fascinating chapter in *The Other Florida* (New York: Scribner's, 1967) following in the footsteps of the composer and finding in West Augustine a nonagenarian black woman, Julia Sanks, who had worked and sung for him and helped inspire his music.

The area, though not this particular site, also appears between hard covers in **Ruth Burnett's** mystery-romance *The Picolata Treasure* (New York: Thomas Bouregy and Co., 1974).

What citrus was to Picolata in the nineteenth century, turpentine was in the twentieth. A study of the naval-stores industry (as it was called) in the area is found in **James M. Smith** and **Stanley C. Bond**'s *Stomping the Flatwoods* (St. Augustine: Historic St. Augustine Preservation Board, 1984).

Tocoi

Tocoi is the community that replaced Picolata as the main transfer point from water to land on the route to St. Augustine. This was due to Dr. John Westcott (1807-1888), a former surveyor-general of Florida, who ascertained the route was shorter and made it technologically more advanced with his St. Johns Railroad. This was a powerful name for what was, at least in the beginning, a rather feeble operation. It was renowned primarily for its slowness. When an outraged customer protested that its rates were extortionate, Westcott calmly replied: "Quite true, sir, tho' I want to tell you this; you will travel longer over this line than over any other line in the U.S. for the same sum." **Greville Bathe**'s *The St. Johns Railroad 1858 to 1895* (St. Augustine, 1958) is an illustrated history written to celebrate its hundredth anniversary. Bathe (1883-1964) was an engineer and inventor who retired to St. Augustine and authored several books.

Tocoi has a point of literary significance, if only in a genealogical sense. A German-born cabinetmaker-turned-farmer whose career, while still in his thirties, had taken him halfway around the world and through blood-curdling adventures in the Holy Land, settled in Tocoi in the 1850s, hoping to find peace in a bucolic setting. But the Civil War broke out, and he was soon impressed, unwillingly, into Confederate service. He was taken prisoner, paroled, and in later years continued his journey on to California. A modern Voltaire, in a new *Candide*, might have done justice to his odyssey. A grandson did want to write of him at length, but never did — although he wrote notably of many other things, winning both Pulitzer and Nobel prizes. The name of the grandson, as of the grandfather, was John Steinbeck (1902-1968). Son of one and father of the other was yet another John Steinbeck, born in Florida in 1862, who was, according to one biographer, "the prototype for the many strong, silent Westerners in his son's fiction, men who repress their feelings and who are made stern by the effort to carve out a life under difficult circumstances."

Moccasin Branch

The Potato Belt lies south and east of Tocoi: Elkton; Molasses Junction; Spuds; and Hastings, the Potato Capital. One of the most interesting of these communities is Moccasin Branch, settled over a century ago and home to many Minorcan farming families.

St. Ambrose Catholic Church is the heart of the community (take St. Ambrose Church Road west from Elkton, pass Elvis Presley Boulevard, and look for the sign). The parish grounds consist of several Victorian and early twentieth-century buildings set in a scenic live-oak grove. The annual St.

Ambrose Fair, which has been going on for more than a hundred years, is a north Florida event not to be missed. The St. Ambrose Centennial Committee prepared a history of the community: *The Branches: Springs of Living Water* (Green Cove Springs, FL: Emerald Printing Co., 1975).

A literary resident of the area was **Ernest Matthew Mickler** (1940-1988). His book *White Trash Cooking* (Berkeley, CA: Ten Speed Press, 1986) was one of the surprise best-sellers of 1986, drawing praise from people as diverse as Helen Hayes, Harper Lee, and J. William Fulbright. With sales of over 300,000 copies, Mickler treated himself to a modern home on three acres at Moccasin Branch in December 1986. He worked on a second collection of recipes, stories, and photos which was published as *Sinkin Spells, Hot Flashes, Fits and Cravins* (Berkeley, CA: Ten Speed Press, 1988) just two weeks before his death from AIDS.

Federal Point

Just across the county line from St. Johns into Putnam, and right on the river is the picturesque Victorian community of Federal Point. Slave-trader **Zephaniah Kingsley** once owned it and later left it to his wife, Anna, the daughter of an African chief. Kingsley, a legendary figure in Florida history, was the author of a pamphlet with the backbreaking title *A Treatise on the Patriarchal, or Co-operative, System of Society As it Exists in Some Governments, and Colonies in America, and in the United States, Under the Name of Slavery, With its Necessity and Advantages*, which went through four editions between 1828 and 1834 and was reprinted in 1970 by Books for Libraries Press of Freeport, New York. Kingsley also wrote *The Rural Code of Haiti* (1837).

His career is described in **Philip S. May's**, "Zephaniah Kingsley, Nonconformist (1765-1843)," *Florida Historical Quarterly* 23 (January 1945), pp.145-59. May, a lawyer and president of the Florida Historical Society, was a friend of Marjorie Kinnan Rawlings and her attorney in the *Cross Creek* trial. He interested Rawlings in writing a novel about Kingsley, but she ultimately gave it up unable to find a sympathetic character. May continued to encourage other writers to take it on, and Edith Pope used some of the Kingsley story in her novel *Colcorton* (New York: Scribner's, 1944).

John Francis Tenney is often called the Father of Federal Point. A native of New Hampshire, he first came here in 1859, but left with the outbreak of the Civil War as his sympathies were with the Union. Returning after the war, "Squire" Tenney served as mayor, postmaster, and justice of the peace in addition to his careers as farmer and hotelier. The Groveland House, which he built, still stands at 181 Commercial Avenue. He was the author of the posthumously published *Slavery, Secession, and Success: The Memoirs of a Florida Pioneer* (San Antonio, TX: Southern Literary Institute, 1934).

Palatka

Palatka is the largest city and governmental seat of Putnam County, which was named for Benjamin A. Putnam (1801-1869), who served as speaker of the

Florida House of Representatives, surveyor-general of the state, and first president of the Florida Historical Society. Located on the west side of the St. Johns River, the area was visited in the 1760s and 1770s by naturalist **William Bartram**, who wrote of it in his *Travels* (1791). A modern retracing of his journey through the vicinity is included in **Mark Derr's** *Some Kind of Paradise: A Chronicle of Man and the Land in Florida* (New York: William Morrow, 1989).

During the Seminole War of 1835-1842, Palatka came to prominence as a military outpost, attracting some soldiers whose names are writ large in history. Three of them figured in the presidential politics of the nineteenth century: Zachary Taylor, who won in 1848; Winfield Scott, who lost in 1852; and William Tecumseh Sherman, whose 1884 vow that "I will not accept if nominated and will not serve if elected" is almost as famous as his earlier remark that "War is hell."

Palatka is the location of one of north Florida's outstanding antebellum homes, Sunny Point, 110 Madison Street, built for Judge Isaac Bronson in the

Bronson House in Palatka

1850s. Now known as the Bronson-Mulholland House, it is open to the public on Sunday, Tuesday, and Thursday afternoons, along with the adjacent Putnam Historic Museum. It was once threatened with demolition, but saved by the efforts of the local historical society. It was added to the National Register of Historic Places in 1972 and restored as a bicentennial project later in that decade. Among those involved in the effort was **Lora Britt**, longtime editor of the *Palatka Daily News* and author of *A Century for Christ* (Palatka, FL: Brittany House, 1975) and *My Gold Coast* (Palatka, FL: Brittany House, 1984).

Isaac Bronson (1802-1855) was a Democratic congressman from upstate New York from 1837 to 1839. Defeated for re-election, he was appointed by

President Martin Van Buren as U.S. judge for the Eastern District of Florida. He lived in St. Augustine for several years, then moved to Palatka, where his family played a leading role in social and political life. George Bancroft (1800-1891), the once-popular historian now mainly remembered as the father of the U.S. Naval Academy at Annapolis, visited Palatka in 1855 and noted in a letter to his wife that the hotel was "full of persons come on to honor Miss Bronson's wedding."

One of Bronson's latter-day relatives who made his reputation with a pen was **George Bronson Rea** (1869-1936), a war correspondent with Stephen Crane and Richard Harding Davis during the Spanish-American War. He was the first newspaperman to reach the battleship *Maine* after it was blown up in Havana harbor and wrote the book entitled *Facts and Fakes About Cuba* (1897). He later moved to China, where he published *Far Eastern Review* and served as an adviser to Dr. Sun Yat-sen during that country's revolution. In his final years he wrote another book, *The Case for Manchukuo* (1935), reflecting his work as international spokesman for the Japanese puppet government in Manchuria. An account of Rea's far-flung career is given in **Joyce Milton's** *The Yellow Kids: Foreign Correspondents in the Heyday of Yellow Journalism* (New York: Harper & Row, 1989).

Isaac Bronson deserves at least a footnote in history for bringing to Florida as his clerk a New Yorker named **George R. Fairbanks** (1820-1906), who became a prominent politician, editor, author, orange grower, and — despite his northern antecedents — Confederate. He is best remembered as an early president of the Florida Historical Society and, as Michael Gannon has written, "Florida's first serious historian in the English language."

Fairbanks's pioneering *History and Antiquities of the City of St. Augustine, Florida* appeared in 1858, with later editions in 1868 and 1881. In 1975, the University Presses of Florida reprinted it as part of the Bicentennial Floridiana Facsimile series. A.J. Hanna wrote: "One of the advantages of this book is that it was written before the manufacture of romantic legends for the entertainment of tourists." Fairbanks's later *History of Florida* (Philadelphia: Lippincott, 1871) was dedicated "To the memory of my honored friend Isaac H. Bronson, the first judge of the United States District Court, Northern District of Florida, a citizen whose life and public virtues shed lustre upon the state of his adoption." Fairbanks's *History* had subsequent editions in 1898 and 1904, and for many years was used as the standard textbook on the subject.

Fairbanks's brother-in-law, Henry Benjamin Whipple (1822-1901), who later became Episcopal bishop of Minnesota and was noted for his efforts on behalf of the Indians, came to Florida in 1853 for his wife's health and preached at Palatka "in an old tumble-down warehouse." He befriended Isaac Bronson, then in ill health, and wrote in his memoirs: "It was a pleasure that I was able to raise the means to build the church that now stands in Palatka, in which many invalids have found comfort in the winter months."

That church, St. Mark's Episcopal, exists to this day as one of Palatka's significant landmarks, surviving a 1919 plan to demolish it and construct a new one in the Mediterranean Revival style. A wooden building with Gothic features, St. Mark's may be considered the forerunner for a whole series of churches in that style built along the St. Johns River three decades later by the contractors McGuire and McDonald. St. Mark's was designed in the offices of Richard Upjohn (1802-1878), who did New York's Trinity Church and was founder and first president of the American Institute of Architects. He was the subject of the biography by **Everard M. Upjohn**, *Richard Upjohn, Architect and Churchman* (New York: Columbia University Press, 1939).

One distinguished Episcopalian who began his career at St. Mark's was Albion W. Knight (1859-1936), who later became bishop of Cuba, the Canal Zone, and New Jersey. He served as chancellor of the University of the South from 1913 to 1922. St. Mark's Church was added to the National Register of Historic Places in 1973.

During the Civil War, Palatka swung back and forth between Union and Confederate control. Local legend has it that the walls of the Bronson House were covered with insults left by the soldiers of one side to the enemy who were about to succeed them in holding the area.

Early in the war the yacht *America*, which had a decade before won the international yachting trophy that became the America's Cup, was taken south of Palatka after a period as a Confederate blockade runner, and scuttled to prevent capture. The Union forces found it anyway, salvaged it, and put it into service as part of their blockading fleet. The incident is told in **Charles Boswell's** *The* America: *The Story of the World's Most Famous Yacht* (New York: David McKay, 1967).

Palatka was often visited by The Swamp Fox of the Confederacy, **J.J. Dickison** (1816?-1902), whose exploits as a guerrilla warrior earned him that and other nicknames: the "Gray Fox," the "War Eagle," and, simply "Dixie." His *Military History of Florida* (Atlanta: Confederate Publishing Co., 1899) was part of a series covering the events of the war, state by state, by southern participants. His wife, **Mary Elizabeth Dickison** (1832?-1913), recounted his career in *Dickison and His Men* (1890; facsimile reprints in 1962 by University Presses of Florida, Gainesville, and in 1984 by San Marco Bookstore, Jacksonville).

One visible symbol of the end of Reconstruction in Florida came in 1877 when Governor George B. Drew appointed Dickison as the state's adjutant general. Part of the Dickison legend was his capture in 1864 at Horse Landing, near Palatka, of the Union gunboat *Columbine*. **Branch Cabell** and **A.J. Hanna** wrote that it "was perhaps, in all naval record, the sole ship of war to be taken by cavalry." Dickison saved and hid away a lifeboat from the *Columbine* and used it a year later, at the end of the war, to help John C. Breckenridge, former Confederate secretary of war (and, before that, vice president of the United States), escape to Cuba. That adventure is recounted in **A.J. Hanna's** *Flight Into Oblivion* (Richmond: Johnson Publishing Co., 1938).

From the Union perspective, Palatka is referred to many times in *A Woman Doctor's Civil War: Esther Hill Hawks' Diary* (Columbia, SC: University of South Carolina Press, 1984) edited by **Gerald Schwartz**.

After the war, Charlotte Henry operated a school for freed slaves in the Bronson House. She later married Nathaniel White, the brother of S.V.

"Deacon" White, the New York congressman, astonomer, and Wall Street speculator who built the Ormond Hotel and was a close friend of Henry Ward Beecher. Beecher's wife visited the area, and his sister Harriet Beecher Stowe, who had a winter home at Mandarin, wrote that Palatka was "an unusually pretty, attractive-looking place for a Florida settlement."

The years following the Civil War were a kind of golden age in Palatka's history, due to a confluence of factors. It was the era of Golden Apples, when people not only around the nation, but even across the oceans thought to get rich by growing oranges — and Palatka was just below the frost line and thus suitable for citriculture. It was the age of the steamboat, and the broad St. Johns River reached Palatka before becoming narrow and twisty, so the city became a significant port. The steamboats brought in the first flood of tourists, and the popular trip of the time was up the Ocklawaha River to Silver Springs. The boats for that journey left from Palatka.

Several hotels were built, and Palatka, christened the Gem City of the St. Johns, became a major resort. **Wanton S. Webb**, a contemporary observer, wrote: "To see Palatka at its best one should arrive there of a pleasant afternoon, and be impressed with its well-kept streets, with orange trees on either side, under which are seen the promenaders from the North, or lounging on the spacious piazzas of the hotels. As twilight steals on, electric lights illuminate the surroundings, and, with music in the air floating from the parlors of the hotels, the scene is suggestive of life in Italy, and directly in contrast with the frozen North."

Among the wealthy winter resorters were Isaac Ellwood, the Barbed-Wire King, who had a home near St. Mark's Church, and his one-time ace salesman, John W. Gates, who docked his yacht nearby at the foot of Madison Street. Gates (1855-1911) was a prominent figure among the robber barons of the Gilded Age, playing a role in the founding of U.S. Steel and Texaco, among others. But he is best remembered by his nickname, "Bet-a-Million," as the most legendary gambler in American history. He has been the subject of two biographies: **Robert Warshow**'s *Bet a Million Gates* (1932) and **Lloyd Wendt** and **Herman Kogan**'s *Bet a Million! The Story of John W. Gates* (1948).

Other well-known historical figures who came through town were Thomas Edison, William Jennings Bryan, and Buffalo Bill Cody. **William Cullen Bryant** (1794-1878), the aged Father of American Poetry, came in 1873 after visiting his friend, Harriet Beecher Stowe, downriver at Mandarin. His descriptions of Palatka and the Ocklawaha River trip to Silver Springs are included in "Letters of William Cullen Bryant from Florida," *Florida Historical Quarterly* 14 (April 1936), pp. 255-274.

Southern poet **Sidney Lanier** (1842-1881) in his guidebook, *Florida* (1875; facsimile reprint Gainesville: University of Florida Press, 1973), noted, "the Florida world is hopelessly divided as to whether it is spelled Pi- or Pa-latka." It was a long-standing dispute that ended that very year when the post office finally settled on *Palatka*. It was, wrote Lanier, "a considerable resort for consumptives" — a matter of great personal concern as his own life would be cut short by that disease. He also remarked that the Palatka newspaper was "noted for alligator-stories to such an extent that its editor is universally known as Alligator Pratt."

Another literary visitor in the steamboat age was **Henry Wheeler Shaw** (1818-1885). Along with Mark Twain, he was one of the kings of the lecture circuit, calling himself Josh Billings, Saturnine Philosopher, and earning a place in Bartlett's *Familiar Quotations* for his saying: "The wheel that squeaks the loudest is the one that gets the grease."

John Muir (1838-1914), writer, naturalist, and founder of the Sierra Club, visited in 1898 and penned a description of the large trees along the river that appeared in the work edited by **Linnie Marsh Wolfe**, *John of the Mountains: The Unpublished Journals of John Muir* (Boston: Houghton Mifflin, 1938).

Palatka also made cameo appearances in several novels of the time, including **William T. Adams's (Oliver Optic)** *Down South: or, Yacht Adventures in Florida* (Boston: Lothrop, Lee & Shepard, 1880); **Frank Stockton's** *A Jolly Fellowship* (New York: Scribner's, 1880); **Robert Boit's** *Eustis* (Boston: James R. Osgood & Co., 1884); and **Mary Jane Holmes's** *The Cromptons* (New York: G.W. Dillingham Co., 1902).

Other visitors in those times included some of America's early archaeologists. **Jeffries Wyman** (1814-1874), the first director of the Peabody Museum at Harvard and a man whose career was memorialized in prose by **Oliver Wendell Holmes** (*Atlantic Monthly*, November 1874) and in verse by **James Russell Lowell**, was a frequent sojourner after the Civil War while preparing the posthumously published *Fresh Water Shell Mounds of the St. John's River, Florida* (Salem, MA: Peabody Academy of Science, 1875). A collection of sketches and letters to his young son, many from this area, has more recently been brought out as **Jeffries Wyman's** *Dear Jeffie* (Cambridge, MA: Peabody Museum Press, 1978), edited by **George E. Gifford, Jr.**

A few years later, **Clarence Bloomfield Moore** (1852-1936), the pioneer archaeologist from Philadelphia, conducted research in the area and prepared *Certain Sand Mounds of the St. Johns River, Florida* (Philadelphia: The Levytype Co., 1894).

The arrival of Standard Oil partner Henry Morrison Flagler in Florida in the 1880s had a great effect on the Gem City, but not what people there had hoped. "When he heard that a delegation from neighboring Palatka wanted to visit to sell him on the virtues of their city, he said he would arrange to be out of town. He did everything he could to discourage those with dollar signs in their eyes."

Some of the oilman's associates did dip into the real estate market with an attempt to turn East Palatka into President City where the streets running in one direction would bear the names of presidents of the United States, while those running in the other would be named after the vice presidents. The entire town was to radiate out from a central park called the Capitol, and the developers predicted that "A person's political preferences may influence him as to what street he may see fit to reside upon." Nothing came of it.

Something did come, however, of Flagler's railroad development in Florida. It started to sound the death knell for the steamboats that had been so important to Palatka's development. Water hyacinths, which clogged the river and hindered navigation, were another factor. Freezes in the 1890s destroyed the citrus groves and convinced winter resorters to head farther south. Palatka came into the twentieth century not as a tourist mecca but as a workaday city.

Henry Flagler, a founding father to so many places in Florida, was more of a harbinger of doom for Palatka, but it was here that he found his first biographer. **Sidney Walter Martin** (1911-) was history teacher and athletic director at Palatka High School from 1932 to 1935. In the latter year he received his master's degree from the University of Georgia with a thesis about Flagler called *The Second Discovery of Florida*. This he later expanded to *Florida's Flagler* (Athens, GA: University of Georgia Press, 1949). Martin was also the author of *Florida During the Territorial Days* (Athens, GA: University of Georgia Press, 1944). He served as president of Emory University in Atlanta from 1957 to 1962 and as a trustee of the Ty Cobb Educational Fund.

The last, and longest-term, wealthy winter resident of Palatka was Judge James R. Mellon (1846-1934) of Pittsburgh, who first came in 1883. The next year he built a home at 424 Emmett Street that, though no longer maintained as it was in his day, remains one of the city's significant landmarks. The judge owned a bank and railroad in his native state and was a member of a family that has become legendary for its great wealth. His younger brother, Andrew Mellon (1855-1937), served as Secretary of the Treasury during the Roaring Twenties and founded the National Gallery of Art in Washington. **Matthew T. Mellon's** *The Watermellons* (n.p.: privately published by the author, 1974) is an account from within of the Mellon family in its resorting phase.

Larimer Memorial Library in Palatka

The judge engaged in charitable ventures in Palatka, as was expected from one of his standing, giving stained glass windows to the First Presbyterian Church, a war memorial to the courthouse, and land for a school (which was named in his honor). Most visible today is the Larimer Memorial Library building at 216 Reid Street, which was, as a plaque inside the door relates, "Erected to the memory of Rachel Hughey Larimer wife of James Ross Mellon 1930." The building, which is a gem of design, was used for over six decades and, when closed as a library, was planned to serve as an arts center. It was the work of the famous architect, H.J. Klutho (1873-1964), who had previously done the adjacent 1905 Palatka city hall (now, unfortunately, demolished) and the nearby James Hotel (St. Johns Avenue at 3rd Street) in 1916. **Robert C. Broward**'s award-winning *The Architecture of Henry John Klutho* (Jacksonville: University of North Florida Press, 1983) describes and illustrates these and other buildings.

Among the famous guests who stayed at James Mellon's home on Emmett Street was Billy Sunday (1863-1935), the former baseball player who became the most prominent evangelist of his time and inspired Carl Sandburg to write the poem "To a Contemporary Bunk-Shooter." Sunday appears as a character in **Charles Erskine Scott Wood**'s *Heavenly Discourse* (1927).

Even more closely connected with Palatka was Sunday's successor as celebrity evangelist, Billy Graham (1918-), who "gave his life to Christ," ironically, on the same day that Billy Sunday died. Graham was a 19-year-old student at Florida Bible Institute in Temple Terrace when he came to the Palatka area in 1938 to conduct eight days of revival meetings. He was invited back later that year to preach at Peniel Baptist Church, where the minister, Cecil Underwood, as Graham later recalled, "talked to me earnestly about becoming a Baptist and being baptized. I made a rather hasty decision to be both baptized and join the Peniel Baptist Church. I must hasten to say I never regretted that decision. About a year later I was ordained into the ministry by this church."

The old Peniel Church is maintained as a historic site. Its story is told in **Leola Smith Young**'s *The Peniel Lighthouse: History of the Peniel Baptist Church (Peniel), Palatka, Florida 1852-1982* (published by the author, 1982). More about the evangelist and his connection with the state is found in Lois Ferm's "Billy Graham in Florida," *Florida Historical Quarterly* 60 (October 1981), pp. 174-185.

During the difficult years of the Great Depression, government money was used to create both jobs and a thing of beauty in Ravine Gardens. Thomas B. Gillespie (1885-1985), the local paving contractor who headed the effort, later recalled: "The main industry we had then was a sawmill. I thought to myself, 'Who would want to come to Palatka to see a sawmill?'" Over 100,000 azaleas were planted around a natural ravine, creating a breathtaking sight during the blooming season. From its opening in 1935, it became Palatka's greatest tourist attraction. The city operated it until 1970, when it became a state park.

Palatka is one of the major cities bordering the Big Scrub area immortalized in the writings of **Marjorie Kinnan Rawlings** (1896-1953). Her first published novel, *South Moon Under* (New York: Scribner's, 1933), mentions Palatka and one of its major businesses, the Wilson Cypress Company. Wilson Cypress, founded in 1889, was said to be the second-largest such operation in the world during its heyday. Company attorney Arthur Corcoran and his wife, Marguerite, were particular friends of Rawlings.

Less happy for Rawlings were the Palatka connections with the long, drawn-out lawsuit around her 1942 book, *Cross Creek*. Zelma Cason (1890-1963), who charged Rawlings with invasion of privacy for her depiction in the story, was a social worker in Palatka, where she boarded with the family of J. Edward Preston; Mrs. Preston was a witness at the trial on Cason's behalf. Representing Zelma were Palatka attorneys J.V. and Kate Walton, father and daughter. The J.V. Walton house still stands at 605 North 3rd Street. Kate Walton lived her final years at 193 Walton Lane in East Palatka. **Patricia Nassif Acton** tells the story of the *Cross Creek* trial in her *Invasion of Privacy* (Gainesville: University of Florida Press, 1988).

World War II brought to international prominence Palatka native Joseph W. (Vinegar Joe) Stilwell (1883-1946), who served as American commander in the China-Burma-India theater as well as chief of staff of the Chinese Army and saw more frontline combat than any other four-star general. **Theodore H. White** (who would later gain fame for his series of books on the making of presidents) arranged and edited the works of Stilwell into *The Stilwell Papers* (New York: William Sloane Associates, Inc., 1948). Asia scholar John K. Fairbank called it "the most comprehensive and pungent indictment of a Chinese potentate ever set on paper." Novelist John P. Marquand wrote that "there has never been any memoir just like *The Stilwell Papers* and perhaps there will never be again."

The general, whose father had purchased an eight-acre tract on the St. Johns River near Devil's Elbow in 1882, was recognized posthumously by his native city on March 7, 1962, when the local U.S. Army Reserve Center and the street it was on were named in his honor (although the sign painters over the years have misspelled the name as *Stillwell*).

A quarter century after his death, Stilwell was again in the news when the doors that had been long closed between the United States and China began to open with President Nixon's well-publicized visit. The 1972 Pulitzer Prize for general nonfiction was awarded to **Barbara Tuchman** for her best-selling *Stilwell and the American Experience in China 1911-45* (New York: Macmillan, 1971), a book that provided background information for many people at a time of dramatic public-policy change.

Palatka appeared in a novel about the experience of a blinded veteran of World War II that was later made into a movie. The book was *Lights Out* (New York: William Morrow, 1945). On the screen in 1951 it became *Bright Victory*, starring Arthur Kennedy and Peggy Dow, with a minor part played by a struggling young actor named Rock Hudson. The author was **Baynard Kendrick** (1894-1977), who came by his knowledge of Palatka from having lived there in the 1920s, when he worked with the Selden Cypress Door Company, before launching his writing career. (The company has long since gone out of business, but its headquarters, taken over by Florida Furniture Industries, still stands at 722 River Street.)

His interest in the problems of the blind was of similarly long standing. During World War I (when he was the first American to volunteer for the Canadian Army) he met blinded soldiers who amazed him with their abilities. Between 1937 and 1961, Kendrick wrote 13 mysteries featuring a blind detective, Captain Duncan Maclain, and his seeing-eye dog. Three Maclain movies were made. During World War II Kendrick served as a consultant to the government on training blinded veterans, and, a few months after the war ended, his novel *Lights Out* appeared. When the Blinded Veterans Association was organized in 1945, Kendrick was elected sighted advisor and honorary chairman. The novel struck a responsive chord not only for the veterans but with an important sub-theme as well. The sightless white soldier from racially segregated Palatka gives a new meaning to the term *color-blind* when he unknowingly strikes up a friendship with a fellow veteran who is black.

Lights Out was Kendrick's first serious (as opposed to mystery) novel. He followed it three years later with *The Flames of Time* (New York: Scribner's, 1948), a Literary Guild selection set in north Florida during the late 1700s and early 1800s.

In 1951, groundbreaking ceremonies were held at Horse Landing south of Palatka (where Dickison's Raiders had captured the gunboat during the Civil War) for the Rodeheaver Boys Ranch, a home for troubled youth founded by **Homer A. Rodeheaver** (1880-1955), who gained fame as music director for evangelist Billy Sunday. He was the composer of many gospel songs, the best known being "Then Jesus Came." He was the author of several books, including *Song Stories of the Sawdust Trail* (1917) and *Twenty Years With Billy Sunday* (1936).

President Lyndon B. Johnson visited Horse Landing on February 27, 1964, when he came to press a button exploding a dynamite charge that marked the beginning of construction on the ill-fated Cross-Florida Barge Canal. One of the facilities at the boys ranch is Little Yankee Field, built in 1978 as a gift from New York Yankees owner George Steinbrenner.

Palatka's long and interesting baseball history resulted in at least one unflattering appearance in a book: **Pat Jordan**'s *A False Spring* (New York: Dodd, Mead, 1975). A Little League and high school pitching phenomenon, Jordan signed as a bonus baby with the Milwaukee Braves, then saw his career go ever downward until he spent two months with the Palatka Azaleas in 1962. He hated everything about it. "Palatka was a suffocating place, claustrophobic, and everything in it emitted an overwhelming sense of decay." He recounted the vines that crept into the ballpark and tripped up players, and an instance when a snake slithered on the field and time out was called while a player beat it to death with a baseball bat. Jordan's negativism toward the city was probably not unrelated to the fact that it was the place where his professional career ended. He did go on, however, to meet greater success as a writer, frequently contributing to *Sports Illustrated* and publishing several books, including *Black Coach* (1971) and *The Suitors of Spring* (1973).

The most famous name in baseball also figured in Palatka's history. Babe Ruth (1894-1948) taught at Ray Doan's All-American Baseball School in the Azalea Bowl in 1941, living at the H.O. Hamm House, 422 River Street. Palatka was also the birthplace of the man Ruth once said was the greatest player he had ever seen: John Henry "Pop" Lloyd (1884-1965), who was elected to the Baseball Hall of Fame in 1977. During a career that stretched from 1905 to 1932, Lloyd compiled a batting average of .365 to .370 in the Negro Leagues. He was often called "the Black Wagner" after the white star, Honus Wagner, who once commented, "After I saw him I felt honored that they would name such a great player after me." Atlantic City, New Jersey, named its baseball field after Lloyd in 1949, but Palatka has yet to honor its famous native son. More about his life and times appears in **Robert W. Peterson**'s *Only the Ball Was White* (Englewood Cliffs, NJ: Prentice-Hall, 1970) and **John Holway**'s *Voices From the Great Black Baseball Leagues* (New York: Dodd, Mead, 1975).

In 1930, Lloyd's Lincoln Giants became the first black team to play in New York's Yankee Stadium. They drew a crowd of nearly 20,000 fans for a game to benefit the fledgling Brotherhood of Sleeping Car Porters, the pioneer black labor union then being organized by another Putnam County native, **A. Philip Randolph** (1889-1979). The son of a minister in the African Methodist Episcopal Church, Randolph retained vivid lifelong memories of accompanying his father on the steamboat to Palatka, where they would be met by oxcart and taken to the rural site where open-air services were held. The congregation, being small and poor, sometimes paid the preacher in produce rather than cash. The most complete account of the labor leader's growing up in Florida is given in **Jervis Anderson**'s *A. Philip Randolph: A Biographical Portrait* (New York: Harcourt Brace Jovanovich, 1973).

Lloyd and Randolph are just part of Palatka's rich black heritage. Novelist **Zora Neale Hurston** (1891?-1960) also came through town on her folklore-collecting expeditions. **Mary McLeod Bethune** (1875-1955) taught at a Presbyterian Mission School in Palatka from 1899 to 1903, augmenting her income as an agent for the Afro-American Life Insurance Company. She was involved in defending a black man accused of murder in a celebrated case described in "Who Was the Phantom Killer of Train #10?" in *Master Detective* (June 1934). It was a dream she had in Palatka which inspired her to move to Daytona and start what became Bethune-Cookman College. The story of her Palatka years is given in **Rackham Holt**'s *Mary McLeod Bethune* (New York: Doubleday, 1964).

A contemporary of Bethune's in Palatka was the multi-talented Dr. **Daniel Wallace Culp**. Born a slave in South Carolina, D.W. Culp graduated in 1879 from Princeton Theological Seminary and became a minister, principal of Stanton School in Jacksonville, and a physician. While practicing in Palatka, Culp edited the important book *Twentieth Century Negro Literature* (1902; reprinted, NY: Arno Press, 1969), which included chapters by such prominent figures as Booker T. Washington, James Weldon Johnson, Mary Church Terrell, and George Washington Carver.

In the mid-twentieth century, when Palatka was more renowned for bass fishing than for tourism, one of its landmarks was a floating one: a charter fishing boat named *Noah's Ark*, operated by Noah Tilghman. Some of the anglers who used it were Babe Ruth, Gary Cooper, and Jimmy Stewart. A best-selling poet (*Jimmy Stewart and His Poems*, 1989) as well as an actor, Stewart wrote an article about his Palatka experiences, "Paddling After the Largemouth Bass," *Ford Times*, June 1968, pp. 2-6. *Noah's Ark* was purchased in the 1980s by the Mission Inn resort at Howey-in-the-Hills, Florida, and re-christened *La Reina*.

Palatka is the home of the Florida School of the Arts, 5001 St. Johns Avenue, which opened in 1976 as the first state-supported professional arts school for high school and college students seeking careers in art, dance, and theater. The school's gallery offers changing exhibits, and plays are presented in the theater on a regular basis. FloArts (as it is called) is involved in the production of the official state play, *Cross and Sword*, in St. Augustine.

Books dealing with Palatka that have appeared in recent years include **Brian Michaels's** *The River Flows North: A History of Putnam County* (Palatka, FL: Putnam County Archives and History Commission, 1986) and **Ann O'Connell Rust's** *Palatka* (Orange Park, FL: Amaro Books, 1989), one of a series of historical romances by the author set in different Florida cities.

Another mention came in 1989 when a Palatka woman, Carrie White, was recognized by the *Guiness Book of World Records* as the oldest living person on earth. She died at Putnam Memorial Nursing Home in 1991 at the age of 116.

Given its varied and interesting history, it is ironic that Palatka is perhaps best known today for the jokes told about it. "Palatka bashing" is a popular north Florida sport. The city does suffer an unfortunate paper mill aroma at times, and the main route through town is largely devoid of trees, but a block or two to either side are large neighborhoods of old buildings listed on the National Register of Historic Places. So, the joke is largely on those who zoom through rather than wander around.

Rollestown

South of Palatka on Highway 17, just beyond a tattoo parlor and right outside a barbed-wire and chain-linked enclosure, is a wayside park, complete with picnic tables and trash dumpster, that boasts two historic markers. One is for William Bartram; the other, for Rollestown, the settlement he visited here more than two centuries ago.

It was second only to Andrew Turnbull's Minorcan colony at New Smyrna as a grandiose development scheme of the British period (1763-1783) in Florida's history. The moving spirit behind the project was **Denys Rolle** (1725-1797), a British member of parliament. What has given it a particular cachet in Florida lore and legend was his scheme to populate it with reformed prostitutes and pickpockets, redeeming their souls (and filling his coffers) through honest (and exceptionally hard) labor.

"But it seems," wrote William Bartram, "from an ill-concerted plan in its infant establishment, negligence, or extreme parsimony in sending proper recruits and other necessaries, together with a bad choice of citizens, the settlement by degrees grew weaker, and at length totally fell to the ground. Those of them who escaped the constant contagious fevers, fled the dreaded place, betaking themselves for subsistence to the more fruitful and populous regions of Georgia and Carolina."

Rolle later developed his extensive holdings with the more traditional slave labor, but his hopes of great riches were dashed when, as part of the settlement of the American Revolution, control of Florida was returned from Britain to Spain. He moved his establishment to Exuma, in the Bahamas, and, like other dispossessed British developers, filed claims for his losses. A book he wrote in 1765, *The Humble Petition of Denys Rolle*, has been reprinted as part of the Bicentennial Floridiana Facsimile series (Gainesville: University Presses of Florida, 1977).

A century later, **Mrs. Henry Ward Beecher** (1812-1897) spent some time writing at the site of the old settlement. She was the author of *Motherly Talks with Young Housekeepers* (1873) and *All Around the House; or, How to Make Homes Happy* (1879), but was best-known as the wife of the era's most celebrated preacher, who was also the defendant in its most notorious adultery trial. The book she was working on was *Letters From Florida* (New York: Appleton, 1879), and in it she wrote: "At Rollestown, part of the old foundations of Rolle's mansion were used only a few weeks since as the foundation of the present cottage where I now write, and I have picked up the glazed bricks that were used in building the houses for his tenantry. The old earthworks and rifle-pits built to protect them from the Indians are still to be seen here."

In 1951, Florida Power and Light built a huge electrical facility on the site of Rollestown.

Going south along the river route are many communities whose names are telltale signs of their origin in the age of Orange Fever that followed the Civil War: Pomona, Satsuma, Fruitland, and Seville.

San Mateo

Among those who sought their fortune growing fruit was a northern Baptist clergyman named **Putnam Peter Bishop** (1823-1896), who settled at San Mateo. Active in political, religious, and agricultural affairs, P.P. Bishop wielded a busy pen. Among his writings was a novel *The Psychologist* (New York: Putnam's, 1886), said to have been based on characters he knew in Florida.

Satsuma

Satsuma was the home in the 1950s and 1960s of Tyler Gatewood Kent (1911-1988), who called his 80-acre estate on the St. Johns River "Hermit's Cove." Kent had been charged during World War II, while serving in the American embassy in London, with betraying secret allied codes to Germany. He was a stormy figure as publisher from 1959-62 of the *Putnam County Weekly Sun*, a newspaper known for its extremist political views. Kent's career is discussed, in brief, in **Richard J. Whalen's** *The Founding Father* (New York: Signet Books, 1966) and at length in **Ray Bearse** and **Anthony Read's** *Conspirator: The Untold Story of Tyler Kent* (New York: Doubleday, 1991).

Welaka

One of the settlements that pre-dates the war and has an Indian rather than a horticultural name is Welaka. It is the subject of **Mati Belle Reeder's** *History of Welaka, 1853-1935* (Welaka: s.n., 1976). Beecher Point in the Welaka area draws its name from the famous nineteenth-century family, one of whose members was Harriet Beecher Stowe, author of *Uncle Tom's Cabin* and a winter resident of Mandarin, Florida.

Mount Royal

Mount Royal is famous for its Timucuan Indian mound, which William Bartram described in his *Travels*, and which pioneer archaeologist Clarence B. Moore partially excavated in the 1890s. The Northeast Florida Anthropological Society made it the focus of restoration efforts in the 1980s. A state historic marker was dedicated in 1983 at the corner of County Road 309 and Fort Gates Ferry Road.

Crescent City

Scenically located between two lakes and boasting many outstanding examples of Victorian architecture, Crescent City is a candidate for anyone's short list of Florida's best-kept secrets. One of its landmarks, listed on the National Register of Historic Places, is the Hubbard House at 600 North Park Street, poised on a hill overlooking Crescent Lake. It was the home of the famous American entomologist **Henry Guernsey Hubbard** (1850-1899). He was a member of a prominent Detroit family which had major holdings in this

Hubbard House in Crescent City

area and is credited with the first large-scale growing of camphor in Florida. Hubbard moved to Crescent City to oversee the family interests after his brother's accidental death by drowning in 1879. Surrounding his house he created Hubbard Park, a well-known semitropical garden. A Harvard-trained scientist, he worked with the U.S. Department of Agriculture, doing valuable work on economic entomology. Of particular importance was his *Report on the Insects Affecting the Orange* (Washington: 1885), which was long considered the standard work on the subject. He developed the Riley-Hubbard Emulsion, a kerosene-soap treatment that was widely used to protect oranges from insect pests. A memoir of his life and work is given in *Proceedings of Entomological Society of Washington* 4 (1901) pp. 350-360. His premature death came after a long battle with tuberculosis.

Crescent City is best-known as the birthplace of **A. Philip Randolph** (1889-1979), black labor leader and recipient of the Presidential Medal of Freedom. His father, James William Randolph, was a minister of the African Methodist Episcopal Church in Crescent City. The family later moved to Jacksonville, where the future union organizer received his education before settling in New York in 1911. He became a socialist, and with **Chandler Owen** (1889-1967) put out a radical magazine called *The Messenger*. The two also wrote *Terms of Peace and the Darker Races* (1917) and *The Truth About Lynching* (1917).

In 1925, Randolph organized the Brotherhood of Sleeping Car Porters, which became the first major black labor union. He also served as vice president of the AFL-CIO. Equally important were his civil rights activities. In 1941, he threatened to lead a march on Washington to protest job discrimination in the defense industries, convincing President Franklin Roosevelt to establish a Fair Employment Practices Committee. In 1948, a similar campaign resulted in President Harry Truman's issuing an executive order calling for an end to racial segregation in the armed forces. In 1963, Randolph was the chairman of the March on Washington for Jobs and Freedom, introducing Dr. Martin Luther King, Jr., to make his "I Have a Dream" speech.

Randolph has been the subject of a number of books. **Jervis Anderson's** *A. Philip Randolph: A Biographical Portrait* (New York: Harcourt Brace Jovanovich, 1973) is the most detailed. His professional career is dealt with in **Paula F. Pfeffer's** *A. Philip Randolph, Pioneer of the Civil Rights Movement* (Baton Rouge: Louisiana State University Press, 1990) and **William H. Harris's** *Keeping the Faith: A. Philip Randolph, Milton P. Webster, and the Brotherhood of Sleeping Car Porters, 1925-37* (Urbana, IL: University of Illinois Press, 1977). A longtime co-worker, **Anna Arnold Hedgeman**, has written about him in *The Trumpet Sounds: A Memoir of Negro Leadership* (New York: Holt, 1964) and *The Gift of Chaos: Decades of American Discontent* (New York: Oxford University Press, 1977). There have been a number of biographies for younger readers, including **Daniel S. Davis's** *Mr. Black Labor* (New York: Dutton, 1972) and volumes entitled *A. Philip Randolph* by **Sally A. Hanley** (New York: Chelsea House, 1989); **Bob Waymer** (Atlanta: Elloree Co., 1990); and **Sarah E. Wright** (Englewood Cliffs, NJ: Silver Burdett Press, 1990). A. Philip Randolph was honored on a U.S. postage stamp in 1989 and was named to the Railroad Hall of Fame in 1991. A suitable memorial, however, has not yet been established in his birthplace.

Barberville

Going south from Crescent City, Highway 17 crosses into Volusia County and goes through agricultural areas like Pierson, the Fern Capital. The story of the settlements in this part of the county is given in **Arthur E. Francke, Jr.'s** *Volusia: The West Side* (DeLand, FL: West Volusia Historical Society, 1986) and **William Dreggors** and **John Hess's** *A Pictorial History of West Volusia County, 1870-1940* (DeLand, FL: West Volusia Historical Society, 1986).

Barberville, settled in 1882 by J.D. Barber, who gave it his name and served as postmaster, has been since 1978 the home of a living history museum called the **Pioneer Settlement for the Creative Arts**. It began with two old school buildings and over the years, a bridge tender's house, train depot, blacksmith shop, turpentine still, and other vanishing species have been added. Exhibits, craft demonstrations, and an annual heritage festival are among the ways they seek to preserve the pioneer spirit. (Monday through Saturday; 904 749-2959)

Volusia

West of Barberville, where Highway 40 meets the St. Johns River, is the old town of Volusia, whose successive waves of settlement have left it littered with archaeological artifacts. Some of these are available for viewing at the Volusia Museum, 1958 Alice Drive, (904 749-2280) established in 1982 and open Wednesday through Saturday. Literary travelers will be particularly interested in the exhibits dealing with Marjorie Kinnan Rawlings and *The Yearling*. The museum founder, Lillian Dillard Gibson, is the daughter of Barney Dillard (1864-1962), who told Rawlings some of the stories used in the novel. His memoirs have been published in **Lillian Dillard Gibson's** *Early Days in Volusia* (Volusia, FL: R. Alex Gibson, 1975). She has produced several other volumes, including *Annals of Volusia* (Volusia, FL: R. Alex Gibson, 1978); *To Hell'N Blazes* (Volusia, FL: R. Alex Gibson, 1981); and *Florida Yarns* (St. Johns Press, 1985). Barney Dillard's house, where Rawlings stayed and cooked and talked and took notes in the 1930s, stands nearby at 1968 Alice Drive.

A landmark of the area is what was long, and justly, called the Dillard Oak. This huge tree was threatened with destruction in 1926 by the state road department, but Barney Dillard stood under it, shotgun in hand, reciting the famous poem:

> Woodman, spare that tree,
> Touch not a single bough!
> In youth it sheltered me
> And I'll protect it now.

He kept watch until a delegation from the Daughters of the American Revolution and the United Daughters of the Confederacy made its way to Tallahassee to convince the governor to save it. The live oak, on Route 40 just east of the river, was designated a historic site in 1978 and has a marker which — alas — just calls

Dillard Oak in Volusia

it the Volusia Oak and doesn't mention Dillard's heroic role in preserving it. In the shade of the old oak tree on October 8, 1980, the first Bartram Trail marker in the Deep South region was placed by the Pierson Garden Club.

Astor

Across the river from Volusia is the town of Astor, named for Colonel William Astor (1829-1892), a member of the family that was once America's wealthiest. He had citrus, real-estate, and railroad interests in Florida. Astor has been the home of **Alice Strickland**, former curator of the Fred Dana Marsh Museum at Tomoka State Park and leading historian of Ormond Beach. Her works include *The Valiant Pioneers* (Miami: University of Miami Press, 1963);

Ormond-on-the-Halifax (Holly Hill, FL: Southeast Printing and Publishing Co., 1980); and *Ashes on the Wind: The Story of the Lost Plantations* (Daytona Beach, FL: Volusia County Historical Commission, 1985).

Another local resident is **Albert Wass** (1908-), a prolific author in both English and Hungarian. His works include the mystery *Deadly Fog at Deadman's Landing* (Astor, FL: Danubian Press, 1979), which is set in this area, and *The History of Astor on the St. Johns, Astor Park and the Surrounding Area* (Astor, FL: Danubian Press, 1982).

Beyond Astor lies the Big Scrub country, immortalized in the writings of Marjorie Kinnan Rawlings.

HISTORIES OF FLORIDA: AN UPDATE

WILLIAM S. COKER

For those interested in a brief review and discussion of the published histories of Florida, two studies stand out. The first one, by James A. Servies, is called *A Bibliography of West Florida. (4 vols.) 3rd Edition (Pensacola: University of West Florida, 1982)*. It begins with Gonzalo Fernández de Oviedo y Valdes, *La Historia General de las Indias* (1535), and progresses chronologically through 1971. Vol. 3 is the index. Vol. 4, the supplement, includes works omitted in the first two volumes and continues through 1981. There are references to many of the early histories of Florida: Brinton (1859), Fairbanks (1871), Winsor (1884), Chipley (1885), Webb (1885), Campbell (1892), Rerick (1902), *Makers of America* [Florida edition] (1909), Serrano y Sanz (1912), Chapin (1914), Cutler (1923), Brevard (1924), Dau (1934), Kenny (1934), Cash (1938), Barcia Carballido (1951), and Dovell (1952). Unfortunately, Servies did not include all of the histories of Florida in this work.

The second bibliography of Florida histories, edited by Paul S. George, is entitled *A Guide to the History of Florida* (New York: Greenwood Press, 1989). It is a compilation of essays by historians, librarians, archivists, archaeologists, curators, etc., relating to the history of Florida. Part One ("The Historical Literature") covers each era chronologically from aboriginal Florida to the present. There are references to many Florida historians and their works, but not all of them were included. Part Two ("Archives and Sources") is a comprehensive survey of where the documents pertaining to Florida history can be found.

As for the histories of Florida in print today, there is no traditional, up-to-date history textbook available at the college and university level. Charlton W. Tebeau's *History of Florida* (Miami: University of Miami Press, 1980) has not been revised or updated since 1980. It is fairly comprehensive for the post-1821 period, but its coverage of the colonial era, from the earliest period to 1821, is relatively brief. This volume seems to have been the outgrowth of an earlier study of Tebeau and Ruby Leach Carson, *Florida from Indian Trail to Space Age: A History*, 3 vols. (Delray Beach, FL: The Southern Publishing Company, 1965).

There are many excellent new, or relatively new, books about various aspects of Florida's history. However, unless the book attempts to cover Florida history in its larger context, it is not included here. Some years ago, historians began a new approach to Florida history by compiling pictorial histories of the state. That trend continues.

In 1955, Rembert W. Patrick prepared a volume, *Florida Under Five Flags* (Gainesville: University of Florida Press), 140 pp., which was intended for

Floridians and visitors and could "be read in a short evening." It contains many illustrations and maps.

Ten years later, Richard J. Bowe's *Pictorial History of Florida* (Tallahassee: Historical Publications, Inc., 1965), 160 pp., appeared. Bowe hoped that his book would "stimulate a greater interest on the part of all Floridians, and their visitors, in the monumental importance of compiling and promulgating the heritage of Florida which is truly the birthplace of our nation" (p. 6).

In 1975, to celebrate the American bicentennial, Joan E. Gill and Beth R. Read edited another pictorial history, *Born of the Sun* (Hollywood, FL: Florida Bicentennial Commemorative Journal, Inc.), 192 pp. Many Florida historians contributed to this work.

Two years ago, Jerrell H. Shofner assisted by Milly St. Julien compiled a volume for the Florida Historical Society entitled *Florida Portrait: A Pictorial History of Florida* (Sarasota, FL: Pineapple Press, 1990), 255 pp, 270 photographs.

The latest pictorial history of Florida came off the press in March 1992: William S. Coker and Jerrell H. Shofner assisted by Joan Morris, *Florida: From the Beginning to 1992* (Houston, TX: Pioneer Publications), 204 pp., 445 maps and illustrations. This volume was prepared for the Florida Columbus Hemispheric Commission. There are ten chapters on the colonial era and ten chapters on the post-1821 period. Given its size, it is comprehensive in its coverage of Florida history.

Continuing the tradition of pictorial histories, Michael V. Gannon has just completed *Florida: A Short History* (150 pp., 83 illustrations) for the University Press of Florida. It should be available early in 1993. Gannon is also working on a multi-authored volume, "The History of Florida," for the State of Florida's sesquicentennial celebration in 1995.

Taking a somewhat different approach, Allen C. Morris has for years compiled *The Florida Handbook*, which includes a significant amount of information about Florida government and many Florida-related topics. The latest edition is 1991-1992, published by the Peninsular Publishing Company of Tallahassee. This volume, which is updated every two years, has been used as a textbook in the public schools.

There are, of course, several books designed as textbooks about Florida history for the public schools, but no effort will be made to detail those histories here.

As this is being written, there is no comprehensive, high-quality, up-to-date textbook on Florida history for the college or university level. However, recently Coker and Shofner agreed to prepare a 900-page fully documented manuscript on the subject. That should be in print in a couple of years.

Dr. Coker is Professor Emeritus at the University of West Florida.

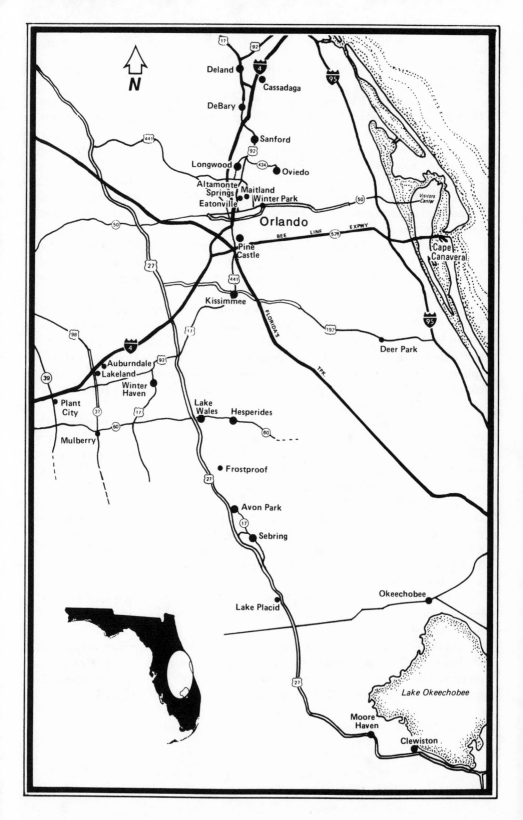

3 DELAND TO LAKE OKEECHOBEE

RICHARD ADICKS

DeLand

The city of DeLand takes its name from a New York manufacturer of baking powder who purchased property there in the 1870s and in 1883 founded a Baptist-affiliated academy which would become the oldest chartered university in Florida. Henry DeLand gave his own name to the school but subsequently suggested that it be known by the name of a generous contributor, John B. Stetson, the hat manufacturer.

Stetson University's main campus in DeLand (its college of law is today located in St. Petersburg) consists of over 30 buildings on 100 beautifully landscaped acres. Among its special features is the DuPont Ball Library, which has more than 200,000 books and periodicals, as well as the Florida and southern Baptist archives.

Stetson University attracted two of DeLand's most recognized writers. **Guy Owen** (1925-1981) who was born in Clarkton, North Carolina, earned B.A., M.A., and Ph.D. degrees at the University of North Carolina at Chapel Hill and taught at Davidson College and Elon College before arriving at Stetson in 1955. Owen, who taught at Stetson until 1962 and then moved to North Carolina State University, is best known for his novel *The Ballad of the Flim-Flam Man* (New York: Macmillan, 1965), which was made into a movie by Twentieth Century-Fox in 1966. Other books include *Cape Fear Country and Other Poems* (1958); *Season of Fear* (1960); and *Journey for Joedel* (1970).

William E. Taylor, born in Newark, New Jersey, in 1920, taught at Stetson University from 1957 to 1985, when he retired to live in New Smyrna Beach. Before coming to Stetson, he taught at Lincoln Memorial University and directed the Lincoln Museum there. He has published *Man in the Wind* (Crescent City, FL: New Athenaeum Press, 1960); *Devoirs to Florida* (Homestead, IL: Olivant Press, 1968); *Twenty Against the Apocalypse* (Orange City, FL: St. Johns River Press, 1979); and other verse.

When Bill Taylor came to Stetson, Guy Owen introduced him to the circle of poets who met at Lake Como, a tourist village between Palatka and Crescent City, where Evelyn Thorne and Will Tullos published a poetry magazine called *Epos*. Owen and Taylor would go there to talk about modern poetry with a coterie that included **Warren French**, the Steinbeck scholar, then teaching at Stetson; Jo and Jim Palmer, graduate students from Gainesville; **Fanny Ven-**

Elizabeth Hall, Stetson University

tadour, an American whose poems were printed during the many years she lived in France; and **Miller Williams,** who was destined to win the Prix de Rome.

At Stetson, Owen and Taylor edited and published *Impetus,* a journal in which the work of many a Stetson poet first appeared in print. Many poets and novelists were nurtured at Stetson, including **Malcolm Glass** from Winter Park, now at Austin Peay State University in Tennessee; **Charles Nelson,** who still lives in DeLand and who wrote an epistolary novel about Vietnam, *The Boy Who Picked the Bullets Up* (1981); **Louis Phillips,** now writing plays and poems in New York; and **Gail White**, poetry editor for the *Piedmont Literary Review* in Blacksburg, Virginia. Songwriter and poet **Rod Taylor** also graduated from Stetson and now lives in southern California. Novelist **Robert Wilder**, who attended public schools in Daytona Beach, spent his army days in World War I at Stetson, enjoying the congenial rigors of military training.

Though DeLand has not been the subject of as many novels as has been coastal Volusia County, **Edith Everett Pope's** *River in the Wind* (New York: Scribner's, 1954) is set in a grove near DeLand, and **Robert Wilder's** popular *Flamingo Road* (New York: Putnam, 1942) is locally regarded as having been based on political corruption and scandals in DeLand and Volusia County. It was made into a movie in 1949 with Joan Crawford and more recently into a TV series.

The history of DeLand was first recorded in **Helen Parce DeLand's** *The Story of DeLand and Lake Helen, Florida* (DeLand, FL: Louis H. Walden, 1928; reprinted by the West Volusia Historical Society, 1990). Since then, the city's history has been dealt with in *Reflections: 100 Years of Progress* (DeLand, FL: City of DeLand Centennial, 1976) and in *Volusia: The West Side* (DeLand, FL: West Volusia Historical Society, 1986) by **Arthur E. Francke, Jr., Alyce Hockaday Gillingham**, and **Maxine Carey Turner**. For more about the university see **Harry C. Garwood's** *Stetson University and Florida Baptists* (DeLand, FL: Florida Baptist Historical Society, 1962) edited by **Edward A. Holmes, Jr.**; **E. Earl Joiner's** *A History of Florida Baptists* (Jacksonville: Convention Press, 1972); and **Gilbert L. Lycan's** *Stetson University: The First 100 Years* (DeLand: Stetson University Press, 1983).

Cassadaga

Several miles east of Interstate 4 south of DeLand is Cassadaga, named after a place in New York State. The Florida site is a 35-acre camp for Spiritualists, who believe that they can communicate with the spirit world. They work in and around the huge 80-year-old Cassadaga Hotel and the Andrew Jackson Davis Education Building, the latter named after one of the founders of American Spiritualism. For the history and description of this Spiritualists' camp see **Robert Harrold's** *Cassadaga* (Miami: Banyan, 1979).

DeBary

This town, named after Baron Frederick de Bary, the German who once held a franchise for Mumm's champagne in North America, is home to a museum-mansion that de Bary built in 1871. The mansion featured indoor plumbing, an elevator, a wooden swimming pool, and a collection of rare birds. Presidents Grant and Cleveland, writer Harriet Beecher Stowe, and many European notables were guests on this large hunting and fishing preserve. For more about the baron see **Edith G. Brooks's** *Saga of Baron Frederick de Bary & de Bary Hall, Florida* (DeBary, FL: Convention Press, 1968) and **Ruth Ericksen's** *Frederick de Bary, The Man and His Mansion* (Sanford, FL: Emickson, 1964).

Sanford

In the years after the War Between the States, a settlement grew on the south shore of Lake Monroe at Mellonville, the site of Fort Mellon during the Second Seminole War (1835-1842). Henry Sanford bought 12,000 acres west of Mellonville in 1871 and established a town that he named for himself. Eventually the town of Sanford absorbed Mellonville. Sanford became the county seat when Seminole County was carved out of Orange County in 1913.

The poet **Stephen Caldwell Wright** (1946-) was born and still lives in Sanford and teaches multi-cultural studies at Seminole Community College. Wright went to Florida Atlantic University for his B.A., Atlanta University for his M.A., and Indiana University of Pennsylvania for his Ph.D. Winner of the 1984 Gwendolyn Brooks Poetry Prize and the 1988 International Poets Academy Award, he has published his work in several chapbooks and recently collected many of his poems in *Making Symphony: New and Selected Poems* (1987). He has also written several plays, and his short story "Pearl" appears in the 1989 edition of *New Visions: Fiction by Florida Writers* (Orlando: Arbiter Press, 1989). Wright, whose poetry is rich in homage to his family and their influence, says, "Everybody should have the same level of respect for language that my family instilled in me."

Elvira Garner's novels for children, *Ezekiel* (New York: Holt, 1937) and *Ezekiel Travels* (New York: Holt, 1938), are set in Sanford. *Orange Winter: A Story of Florida in 1880* (New York: Longmans, Green, 1931) by **Marjorie P. Medary** is a tale of pioneers traveling down the Ocklawaha River and up the St. Johns to Sanford. Somewhere in this vicinity north of Orlando is the site of the fictional Fort Repose, the scene of **Pat Frank**'s novel about World War III, *Alas, Babylon* (Philadelphia: Lippincott, 1959); in the story the survivors of a nuclear attack which destroys much of the United States must abandon their modern, electricity-driven gadgets and return to the old ways of living. **Sam Harrison**'s *Birdsong Ascending* (Orlando: Harcourt Brace Jovanovich, 1992) is a novel set in contemporary times in Calhoun, a fictional town near Sanford.

Arthur Francke, Jr. documents the early history of Sanford in *Fort Mellon, 1837-1842* (Miami: Banyan, 1977) and *Early Days of Seminole County, Florida* (Sanford, FL: Seminole County Historical Commission, 1984). For more about the town's namesake see **Joseph A. Fry**'s *Henry S. Sanford* (Reno, NV: University of Nevada Press, 1982). Fry calls him "the most important single contributor to the development of Florida's late-nineteenth-century citrus industry." Journalist **Peter Schaal**, who came to Sanford in 1912 to become news and sports editor of the local newspaper and later Seminole County correspondent for the *Orlando Sentinel*, the Jacksonville *Florida Times-Union*, and the Associated Press, has recorded many reminiscences in *Sanford As I Knew It, 1912-1935* (Sanford, FL: Schaal, 1970). **Katherine Bishop** has written about local happenings in her *Sanford Now and Then* (Sanford, FL: Bishop, 1976), as did **J.N. Whitner** in her 1910 *A Tale of a Mosquito* (Sanford, FL: Woman's Club of Sanford, 1970). Another local author, **Altermese Smith Bentley**, has written

DELAND TO LAKE OKEECHOBEE

Georgetown, The History of a Black Neighborhood (Sanford, FL: Bentley, 1989). Also see **Margaret Sprout Green**'s *Lake Mary's Beginnings and the Roaring Twenties in Lake Mary and Sanford, Florida* (Chuluota, FL: Mickler House, 1986).

A Sanford boy who went on to write a number of books about baseball is **Red Barber**. Born Walter Lanier Barber in Columbus, Mississippi, on February 17, 1908, he received the name *Lanier* because of a distant relative, the great southern poet Sidney Lanier. When he was ten, his family moved to Sanford, where Red attended high school and worked at jobs like picking celery and driving a truck. As he later wrote,

> I was working as a day laborer in 1928 at any odd job I could get, down in Sanford, Florida. Things were bona fide tough. In 1927 Florida had gotten hit by a depression — two years, as it turned out, before the rest of the country —and by summer of '28 it was hard to get a job of any kind, and when you got one, it was from daylight to dark for two dollars a day...and back-breaking. I figured that that way I wasn't going anywhere, I might as well head up to the University at Gainesville and work my way through school. I didn't know what I'd study — but I had nothing to lose. Nothing.

At the University of Florida in Gainesville he found work at the radio station and went on to become the announcer for the Brooklyn Dodgers and later the New York Yankees. He now lives in Tallahassee and once a week comments on sports during *Morning Edition* on National Public Radio. Among his books are *The Rhubarb Patch* (1954), *Rhubarb in the Catbird Seat* (with Robert Creamer, Garden City, 1968), and *Walk in the Spirit* (1969).

Oviedo

Oviedo, settled in the late 1860s, was named in 1879 by a Swedish postmaster after the city in northern Spain. For over a century it was an agricultural community, producing citrus and celery, but in the 1980s agriculture declined, and Oviedo has been growing as a residential community since then. Mickler's Floridiana, the preeminent dealer in new Florida books, can be found at 151 West Broadway in Oviedo. It is owned and operated by Sam Mickler, who bought the enterprise from Thomas and Georgine Mickler in 1985 and moved it to Oviedo from Chuluota. Mickler's annual catalog is available from P.O. Box 1450, Oviedo, Florida 32765, or by calling 407 365-6425. *Oviedo: Biography of a Town* (Orlando: Adicks and Neely, 1979) by **Richard Adicks** and **Donna M. Neely** recounts the history of Oviedo's first century. **Wesley Ford Davis**'s novel, *The Time of the Panther* (New York: Harper, 1958), is set in a sawmill town nearby. Some incidents in **Zora Neale Hurston**'s *Jonah's Gourd Vine* (Philadelphia: Lippincott, 1934) take place in Oviedo. It appears as the town of Valdez in **Beverly Coyle**'s *The Kneeling Bus* (New York: Ticknor and Fields, 1990).

Wyatt Wyatt, author of *Catching Fire* (New York: Random House, 1977), *Deep in the Heart* (1980), and several short stories, lives in the Whitney-Wolcott House on Lake Charm. Wyatt was born in Oklahoma and lived in various parts of the United States before coming to Florida in 1970 to teach in the department of English at Florida Technological University (now the University of Central Florida).

Richard Adicks, who also lives on Lake Charm, is the editor of *Le Conte's Report on East Florida* (Gainesville: University Presses of Florida, 1978) and author of *A Court for Owls* (Sarasota: Pineapple Press, 1989), a novel about Lewis Powell, one of the conspirators in the assassination of Abraham Lincoln.

Southeast of Oviedo on State Road 419, halfway to Chuluota, is the community known as Taintsville, so named in the early 1970s by Mary Preston Gross. Soon after settling in the home she calls Beau Lac, Gross heard a workman say that the place "tain't in Oviedo and tain't in Chuluota." She obtained permission from the Department of Transportation to put up a pair of Taintsville signs, but the signs are often missing, spirited away by souvenir hunters. The nearby Flying Seminole Ranch, an airfield for gliders and small aircraft, was dubbed the Taintsville Airport until it passed out of use. Under the imprint of Beau Lac Publishers of Taintsville, **Mary Preston Gross** has written and published *Florida's Fantastic Fauna and Flora* (1970) and a number of books on protocol for army wives.

The poet Robert Frost (1874-1963) and the conductor Leopold Stokowski (1882-1977) visited Beau Lac several times before it received its present name and when it was the home of Mr. and Mrs. Robert P. Lamont. Lamont was the son of Robert Patterson Lamont, President Herbert Hoover's secretary of commerce from 1929 to 1932. In March 1957, during one of Frost's visits, Professor Alfred Hanna of Rollins College came to call with books for him to autograph, but Hanna was unable to induce the poet to speak at Rollins.

Chuluota

Five miles southeast of Oviedo on State Road 419 is Chuluota, which takes its name from Creek Indian words meaning "pine island" and may have been so called as early as the 1860s. Book-lovers have known Chuluota since 1963 as the home of the best-known dealers in books about Florida. After operating Book Tracers in Orlando from 1960 to 1963, Thomas and Georgine Mickler moved to a spacious two-story house on Lake Drive in Chuluota and launched Mickler's Floridiana, Mickler's Antiquarian Books, and Mickler House Publishers. For three decades they have stimulated research and writing about Florida. In 1985 they sold Mickler's Floridiana while retaining Mickler House Publishers and Mickler's Antiquarian Books, with its noteworthy library of out-of-print Florida books, maps, and memorabilia. Their address is P.O. Box 38, Chuluota, Florida 32766, and their telephone number is 407 365-3636.

Boyhood in the piney woods of Chuluota started **Herbert Stoddard** (1889-1970) on his way to becoming a world-renowned ornithologist. Stoddard, who lived in Chuluota from 1893 to 1900, later studied quail throughout the Southeast and in 1931 published the work called "the Bob White Bible":

The Bob White Quail: Its Habits, Preservation, and Increase (Quincy, FL: David Avant, 1992). In his *Memoirs of a Naturalist* (Norman, OK: University of Oklahoma Press, 1969), Stoddard wrote nostalgically about pioneer life in Chuluota.

Longwood

When E.W. Henck, a Bostonian, came to Florida in the early 1880s to found Longwood, he named it for a district in his native city. Like many towns in Florida, Longwood has been restoring its older homes, many of which are open to tourists. The Bradley-McIntyre House was used as the model for the mansion in **Patricia Muse**'s *Eight Candles Glowing* (New York: Ballantine Books, 1976), a novel set in the Florida Keys. The so-called Grant House was supposed to have been built by General Ulysses S. Grant and used while he wrote his memoirs. This apocryphal story may have been started by the owner who wanted to sell the 12-room, three-story building, a beautiful house that the Central Florida Society of Historic Preservation moved from nearby Altamonte Springs in 1973.

Longwood has been the home of **Robert Newton Peck** since 1977. Peck, who was born in Vermont in 1928 and went to Rollins College for his B.A. degree, has been a soldier, a lumberjack, a paper mill worker, and an advertising executive. Peck describes himself as "Author of 55 books, 100 poems, 35 songs (words and music), creator of 3 TV specials on ABC, winner of the Mark Twain Award, ragtime piano player, stand-up comic, lousy dancer, enthusiastic yet untalented athlete, habitual show-off." His best-known novel, *A Day No Pigs Would Die* (1972), sprang from his experience as a hog-killer. Peck has written other books for readers of all ages, including *Millie's Boy* (1973); *Soup* (1974); *The Seminole Seed* (Sarasota: Pineapple Press, 1983); *Hallapoosa* (1988); and *The Horse Hunters* (1988).

Philip Deaver, winner of the 1986 Flannery O'Connor Award for Short Fiction and author of *Silent Retreats* (1988), a short-story collection, has lived in Longwood since 1984. Deaver, who has lived in the Midwest and in Virginia and has been a teacher and a college administrator, now works for a consulting firm and writes "between the hours of 9 P.M. and 2 A.M."

Altamonte Springs

Robert Adams (1934-1990) was born in Danville, Virginia, and moved to Altamonte Springs in 1945. He did not start writing until 1969, but soon became a prolific novelist. His forte was fantasy, and he became an expert on ancient armor. Adams wrote 18 novels in his Horseclans fantasy series, six in his Castaways in Time series, and two in his Stairway to Forever series before he died of cancer in Apopka in 1990.

Maitland

This city, named after Seminole War soldier Captain William Seton Maitland, was the home of **Allen Drury** during the late 1960s and early 1970s while he was writing his novel about the space program, *The Throne of Saturn* (Garden City, NY: Doubleday, 1971). Drury worked with Rollins College English professor Marion Folsom and **Marjory Bartlett Sanger** in organizing and supporting the Rollins College Annual Writers' Conference starting in 1968. Among Drury's other novels are three published by Doubleday in Garden City, New York: *Advise and Consent* (1959), which won him the Pulitzer Prize in 1960 and a Doctor of Letters degree from Rollins College in 1961; *Pentagon* (1986); and *Preserve and Protect* (1968).

For more about the town, see *Fort Maitland* (Maitland, FL: Fort Maitland Committee, 1936) by **Alfred Jackson Hanna**.

Eatonville

"I was born in a Negro town," wrote **Zora Neale Hurston** (1891?-1960). "I do not mean by that the black back-side of an average town. Eatonville, Florida, is, and was at the time of my birth, a pure Negro town — charter, Mayor, council, town marshal and all. It was not the first Negro community in America, but it was the first to be incorporated, the first attempt at organized self-government on the part of Negroes in America."

Zora Neale Hurston (center) and friends

Eatonville was named in 1888 for a white Union veteran, Joshua (or Josiah) C. Eaton. Zora Neale Hurston was born when the town was new, probably in 1891, though she claimed a 1901 birth date. Her father, the Reverend John Hurston, was at one time mayor of Eatonville. He and her mother, Lucy, were the models for John and Lucy Pearson in *Jonah's Gourd Vine* (Philadelphia: Lippincott, 1934). They lived on the site bounded now by West, Lime, People, and Lemon streets; the house has long been gone.

Zora Neale Hurston's memories of Eatonville are woven into her writing: her lively autobiography, *Dust Tracks on a Road* (New York: Arno Press, 1942); her novel *Their Eyes Were Watching God* (Philadelphia: Lippincott, 1937); the aforementioned *Jonah's Gourd Vine*; a collection of sketches that she called "The Eatonville Anthology" (1926); and such short stories as "The Gilded Six-Bits" (1933) and "Sweat" (1926). A central scene in her fiction is Joe Clarke's store, now the R & R grocery store at Kennedy Boulevard and West Street, and of course her father's church, the Macedonia Baptist Church, which in her day was on the south side of Eaton Street between West and East streets.

Zora Neale Hurston's childhood in the small town where she "used to take a seat on top of the gate-post and watch the world go by" ended soon after she was nine. Her mother died, her father remarried, and Zora was sent to Jacksonville to live with a brother and attend school there. Her adolescent years were marked by a struggle against poverty. Working as a wardrobe girl for a traveling theatrical company, she made her way to Baltimore, where she left the company and attended Morgan Academy. Later she attended Howard University sporadically, earning an associate degree. She went to New York, where she became part of the Harlem Renaissance and attended Barnard College.

In 1927 and 1928, supported by grants, Hurston returned to Eatonville and to other parts of Florida to gather folklore. In 1932 she spent the summer again in Eatonville, gardening happily and writing *Mules and Men* (Philadelphia: Lippincott, 1935), her collection of folk tales.

When publisher Bertram Lippincott asked Hurston if she were working on a novel, she told him she was and immediately rented a room in Sanford in order to start work on the story that became *Jonah's Gourd Vine*. Hurston's subsequent years were spent in New York, the Carolinas, Jamaica, Haiti, and Honduras writing and collecting folklore. After a humiliating experience in which she was unjustly charged with seducing a young boy, she left New York and worked as a maid in Miami. From 1952 to 1956 she lived in Eau Gallie while she continued to write, and for a time lived in Cocoa and on Merritt Island. In 1958, sick and needy, she moved to Fort Pierce. In January 1960 Zora Neale Hurston died in the St. Lucie County welfare home in Fort Pierce and was buried in a pauper's grave. There is talk of reburying her remains in Eatonville.

For the standard biography of Hurston, see **Robert E. Hemenway**'s *Zora Neale Hurston* (Urbana, IL: University of Illinois, 1977). A biography for young readers is **Janelle Yates**'s *Zora Neale Hurston: A Storyteller's Life* (Staten Island:

Ward Hill Press, 1991). Selections from Hurston's folklore, essays, and her fiction are in **Zora Neale Hurston's** *I Love Myself When I Am Laughing* (Old Westbury, NY: Feminist Press, 1979) edited by **Alice Walker**. *Zora in Florida* (Orlando: University of Central Florida Press, 1991) edited by **Steve Glassman** and **Kathryn Lee Seidel** treats in more detail different aspects of her life and writing in the state. Among the many recent publications about Hurston's work are **Karla F.C. Holloway's** *The Character of the Word: The Texts of Zora Neale Hurston* (Westport, CT: Greenwood Press, 1987) and **Mary E. Lyons's** *Sorrow's Kitchen: The Life and Folklore of Zora Neale Hurston* (New York: Scribner's Sons, 1990). The history of Eatonville is chronicled in **Frank M. Otey's** *Eatonville, Florida: A Brief History* (Winter Park, FL: Four-G Publishers, 1989). *Zora! Zora Neale Hurston: A Woman and Her Community* (Orlando: Sentinel Communications Company, 1991) edited by **N.Y. Nathiri** brings alive the relationship between Hurston and Eatonville.

Since 1990 the Preserve Eatonville Community organization has sponsored an annual festival in January commemorating Zora Neale Hurston and her achievements. The Zora Neale Hurston National Museum of Fine Arts at 227 East Kennedy Boulevard (Monday through Friday, 10 A.M. to 4 P.M.; available on weekends for special tours; 407 647-3307) exhibits works of African-American visual artists in six shows a year.

Winter Park

Winter Park, platted and named in 1881 by Loring Chase and Oliver E. Chapman, has long prided itself on being a literary and artistic colony and has attracted a galaxy of writers and artists. It is the site of Rollins College, established in 1885, and its Cornell Fine Arts Center (Tuesday through Friday, 10 A.M. to 5 P.M; Saturday and Sunday, 1 to 5 P.M.; closed Monday; 407 646-2526). At 133 East Welbourne Avenue is the Charles Hosmer Morse Museum of American Art (Tuesday through Saturday, 9:30 A.M. to 4 P.M.; Sunday, 1 P.M. to 4 P.M.; closed Monday; 407 644-3686), which exhibits an outstanding collection of Louis Comfort Tiffany stained glass; for more about that collection see *The "Lost" Treasures of Louis Comfort Tiffany* (New York: Doubleday, 1980) by **Hugh F. McKean**, a former president of Rollins College. Every spring the Winter Park Art Festival attracts artists from all over the nation. For more about the college and surrounding town see *Winter Park Portrait, The Story of Winter Park and Rollins College* (Beachwood, OH: West Summit Press, 1987) by **Richard N. Campen**. Also see **Jack Lane's** *Rollins College* (Tallahassee: Rose Printing Co., 1980).

Olin Library at Rollins College is particularly rich in several ways. Its Floridiana Collection is one of the most comprehensive collections of printed materials about the state, covering material written in many languages; its Union Catalog of Floridiana lists materials about Florida that are located around the country. Other collections in the library and archives are the Benjamin Franklin Collection, containing books by and about Franklin; the Hispanic Collection, encompassing Spain, Portugal, and Hispanic America;

Rollins College

the Rittenhouse Collection of poetry with its 1,200 volumes of poetry, especially American poets, and some 1,500 letters from poets; the Nehrling Collection of botany and horticulture; the Walt Whitman Collection of books by and about the great American poet. The horseshoe-shaped walkway in front of the Mills Memorial Building (the former library) is lined with stones from the home towns and regions of over 800 famous writers, artists, and philosophers. Part or all of each plaque comes from a site associated with the notable person. Called The Walk of Fame, the ground-level collection includes stones from Martin Luther King, Jr.'s Atlanta, Winston Churchill's Kent, England, and Emily Dickinson's Amherst, Massachusetts.

Near the library is a house dedicated to **Constance Fenimore Woolson** (1840-1894), the grandniece of American novelist James Fenimore Cooper. The house contains her books, manuscripts, furniture, and other memorabilia. She was born in New Hampshire and lived in Cleveland, Ohio, Cooperstown, New York, and St. Augustine, Florida. In several novels, all published by Harper in New York, she used Florida as a setting: *East Angels* (1886), *Horace Chase* (1894), and *Rodman the Keeper* (1886). Her niece, Clare Benedict, built the house on the Rollins campus to honor the writer. For more about Woolson's life and work see **Rayburn S. Moore**'s *Constance Fenimore Woolson* (New York: Twayne, 1963) and **Cheryl B. Torsney**'s *Constance Fenimore Woolson* (Athens, GA: University of Georgia, 1989).

The Literary Colony of Winter Park, Florida (Winter Park, FL: The College Press, 1943) listed 171 authors and their 781 works. Many of the authors were attracted by temperate climate, the area's cultural and literary activities, and Rollins College. Among the authors who came to Winter Park over the years was **Winston Churchill** (1871-1947), who was not related to the British prime minister. Author of *The Crisis* (1901), *Richard Carvel* (1899), and other novels, Churchill died in Winter Park shortly after arriving in March 1947. **Ray Stannard Baker** (1870-1946), journalist, biographer of Woodrow Wilson, and author of several novels under the name of **David Grayson**, spent several winters in the area. New York author **Irving A. Bacheller** (1859-1950) moved to Winter Park in 1918 and became a trustee of Rollins College. Bacheller built a home, Gate o' the Isles, on the Isle of Sicily in Lake Maitland, where he continued to write. His best-known books include *Eben Holden* (1900), *The Light in the Clearing* (1917), and *Dawn* (1927).

In his honor, Rollins College established the Irving Bacheller Professorship of Creative Writing. The first to hold the professorship was **Edwin Granberry** (1897-1988), who was born in Meridian, Mississippi, and lived in Lake City, Florida, as a youth. Granberry attended the University of Florida and earned his B.A. at Columbia University. From 1922 to 1924 he studied with **Thomas Wolfe** and others in George Pierce Baker's 47 Workshop at Harvard University. Granberry, who came to Rollins in 1933 and was named Bacheller Professor in 1940, is best known for his short story, "A Trip to Czardis" (1932), which he expanded into a novel with the same name in 1966. Other books, all published by Macaulay in New York, were *The Ancient Hunger* (1927), *Strangers and Lovers* (1928), and *The Erl King* (1930). In later years, Granberry collaborated with cartoonist **Roy Crane** on the Buz Sawyer comic strip. The current Irving Bacheller Professor is **Jean West**, who has published *Holding the Chariot* (Winter Park, FL: Open House, 1976) and other poetry.

Associated with the literary life of Winter Park was the Alabama Hotel on Lake Maitland. Among the writers who stayed at the Alabama was **Harlow Shaply** (1886-1972), the astronomer who wrote *Of Stars and Men* (1958). Now renovated as condominiums, The Alabama was opened in 1922 or 1923, and the proprietors from about 1932 on were Noella LaChance Schenck and her husband, Henry Schenck. Noella Schenck recalled the day Edwin Granberry drove to the hotel followed by a touring car carrying **Sinclair Lewis** (1885-1951) and his secretary, who stayed overnight. **Dorothy Thompson**, who once was married to Lewis, stayed at the Alabama at the same time as Lewis, but, wrote Noella Schenck, "whether it was planned or accidental I never knew."

Her most vivid recollection involves **Margaret Mitchell** (1900-1949). Mitchell and her husband had been staying with Ed Granberry and his family in December 1938 until a passerby recognized her, thus jeopardizing her anonymity. Granberry took the couple to the Alabama Hotel, where the Schencks, sworn to silence, registered them as Mr. and Mrs. Munnerlin. They stayed for several days, while one inquisitive guest told the hoteliers repeatedly that he thought he recognized "that young woman" from somewhere. During her sojourn at the Alabama Hotel, Margaret Mitchell received a telegram informing her that 600,000 copies of *Gone with the Wind* had been sold. Later Ed Granberry and his family spent ten days with Margaret Mitchell at her mountain home in North Carolina. Granberry called her "the brightest, the most scintillating, the most compassionate spirit we have ever known."

In front of the Alumni House at Rollins are buried the ashes of one of Rollins's most noted alumni, **Rex Beach** (1877-1949), and those of his wife. Beach, a native of Michigan who grew up in Tampa, attended Rollins from 1891 to 1896. "I went there," he wrote, "for the same reason I ate bananas — it was cheap and I was told it would give me all I needed." Beach was restive under the college's restrictions, objecting that "faculty and students alike prayed without provocation." (The school was established by the Congregational Church.) He was suspended from the college once — for rowing a boat on Sunday, he said, but local tradition has it that he slipped a girl into the dorm. In later years, Beach became reconciled with his alma mater. He served as president of the Rollins Alumni Association, gave generously to Rollins, and held the world premiere of the movie of his novel *The Barrier* at the Baby Grand Theatre (later the Colony Theatre) on Park Avenue in Winter Park.

Rollins College played a large role in the nurturing of **Zora Neale Hurston**. In 1932, after she had returned from New York, she became acquainted with Hamilton Holt, the president of Rollins; Edwin Osgood Grover, the librarian and "professor of books"; and professors Robert Wunsch and John Rice. They all urged her to perform three folk concerts at the college. One of them, *From Sun to Sun*, was based on *The Great Day*, a show that she had produced in New York. Hurston took the show to Eatonville and other Florida communities. Wunsch read her story "The Gilded Six-Bits" to his creative-writing class and sent it to the editors of *Story* magazine, who bought it.

A poet who taught at Rollins for many years — rather, a teacher who wrote poetry — was **Wilbur Dorsett** (1913-1980). Dorsett's *Lightning in the Mirror* (Winter Park: Dorsett, 1980) and *Shards* (Winter Park: Dorsett, 1977) are volumes of Shakespearean sonnets reflecting the joys, amusements, and frustrations of teaching. Dorsett's drama *A Song for Rollins* (1966) celebrated the Rollins community in a delightful compendium of folklore and legend, including the popular jingle about the Dinky Line, the railroad that connected Winter Park and Orlando:

Some folks say that the Dinky won't run.
But folks, let me tell you what the Dinky done!
She left Orlando at half past one
And reached Rollins College at the setting of the sun!

For many years, a distinctive Rollins tradition was the Animated Magazine, founded by President Hamilton Holt. Each spring the Animag brought to campus distinguished speakers, among them Presidents Franklin Delano Roosevelt and Harry Truman, Cordell Hull, Edward R. Murrow, Greer Garson, Lillian Gish, J. Edgar Hoover, Mary McLeod Bethune, Jane Addams, and the novelists Rex Beach, Marjorie Kinnan Rawlings, Faith Baldwin, and Zona Gale. Many were invited, but not all chose to answer the call. In 1936 President Holt besought Robert Frost to speak at the Animated Magazine, but Holt's six-minute limitation drew a negative response from the poet. Frost wrote back: "I can never be drawn into a show like your living magazine. My talents, such as they are, don't lend themselves to crowded programs. It is the rarest thing for anyone to ask me to speak or read in chorus. People have learned that my modest kind of entertainment is better when it has the occasion all to itself."

Winter Park and Rollins College boast two important figures in the writing of Florida history: **Alfred Jackson Hanna** (1893-1978) and **Kathryn Abbey Hanna** (1895-1967). A.J. Hanna, who was born in Tampa and graduated from Rollins in 1914, spent more than 60 years associated with the college: as registrar, assistant to the president, assistant treasurer, first vice president, trustee, chair of the history department, director of inter-American studies, and finally as professor emeritus of history. In 1941 he married Kathryn Abbey, who for 15 years had been head of the department of history, geography, and political science at Florida State College for Women (now Florida State University). A.J. Hanna is the author of *A Prince in Their Midst* (Norman, OK: University of Oklahoma Press, 1946) and *Flight Into Oblivion* (Bloomington, IN: Indiana University Press, 1959). With **James Branch Cabell**, he wrote *The St. Johns* (New York: Farrer & Rinehart, 1943) in the Rivers of America series. Together, A.J. Hanna and Kathryn Abbey Hanna wrote *Lake Okeechobee* (Indianapolis: Bobbs-Merrill, 1948), *Florida's Golden Sands* (Indianapolis: Bobbs-Merrill, 1950), *Confederate Exiles in Venezuela* (1960), and *Napoleon III in Mexico* (1971).

Sloan Wilson (1920-), a former resident of Ormond Beach, Florida, was already an established writer when he came to Winter Park in 1980. The author of *Man in the Gray Flannel Suit* (1955), *A Summer Place* (1958), and other novels, Wilson taught creative writing for a year at Rollins College and lived in Winter Park until 1989, when he moved to Richmond, Virginia.

Few writers have made more of an impact on the writing of science fiction and fantasy than has **Andre Norton** (1912-). Writing under her own name as well as those of **Andrew North** and **Allen Weston**, Norton has more than a hundred titles to her credit and has won a dazzling array of national and international awards. She was born in Cleveland, Ohio, and worked for a number of years as a librarian and editor before devoting her full time to writing. Norton moved to Casselberry in Seminole County with her mother in

Marjory Bartlett Sanger

1966 and to Winter Park in 1980. Her works include science fiction such as *Sea Siege* (1957, 1987) and *Flight in Yiktor* (1986); fantasy such as the Witch World series; as well as historical, Gothic, and mystery novels.

The name of **Marjory Bartlett Sanger** (1920-) is known well to readers of books on nature. She was born in Baltimore, came to Winter Park in 1959, and has long maintained a close relationship with Rollins College and with the Winter Park community. She helped found the Rollins College Annual Writers' Conference in 1968 and served on the conference board until 1977. Sanger's books on Florida include *Mangrove Island* (Cleveland, OH: World Publishing Co., 1963); *Cypress Country* (Cleveland, OH: World Publishing Co., 1965); *World of the Great White Heron* (New York: Devin-Adair, 1967); *Checkerback's Journey: The Migration of the Ruddy Turnstone* (Cleveland, OH: World Publishing Co., 1969), which she claims as her favorite; *Billy Bartram and His Green World* (New York: Farrar, Straus & Giroux, 1972); and *Forest in the Sand* (New York: Atheneum, 1983).

Many other writers call Winter Park home and have drawn inspiration from its ambiance. **Jess Gregg**, a student of Edwin Granberry at Rollins College, has remained in Winter Park to write *The Glory Circuit* (New York: St. Martin's Press, 1962); *Baby Boy* (New York: Putnam, 1973), and *The Other Elizabeth* (New York: Rinehart, 1955). **Malcolm Glass,** who was born in Winter Park in 1936, earned his B.A. degree at Stetson University in 1958 and M.A. at Vanderbilt in 1961. Glass, who has taught at Austin Peay State College in Clarkesville, Tennessee, since 1962, has published *Bone Love* (1978) and other poems. **Omar S. Castañeda** wrote *Cunuman* (Sarasota: Pineapple Press 1987) in Winter Park. **Edgar L'Heureux** has published two volumes of short stories: *The Clay of Vases* (1988) and *The Dollar Collar* (1986). L'Heureux is also editor of a semi-annual literary journal, the *Sabal Palm Review*. **David Posner**, author of more than 12 volumes of poems, including *The Sandpipers* (1976), lived in Winter Park for several years until his death in 1985. The city also counts authors of children's books among its writers: **Loreen Leedy**, who has a degree in art, writes and illustrates books in her Winter Park studio. Starting with *A Number of Dragons* (1985), she has published more than ten books. **W.B. Park** has written and illustrated six children's books, including *The Costume Party* (1983) and its sequel, *Bakery Business* (1983). Sisters **Jeni** and **Lisa Bassett** have written *Beany and Scamp* (1987) and Jeni Bassett has illustrated other books.

An early novel set in Winter Park is **William Drysdale's** *The Fast Mail: The Story of a Train Boy* (Boston: Wilde, 1896). **Wyatt Wyatt's** comic novel, *Catching Fire* (New York: Random House, 1977), takes place in Winter Park, much of it at the fictitious Hotel Paradise, based on the Langford Hotel on New England Avenue.

Orlando

For many people the name of Orlando evokes thoughts of a tourist destination, where "world" upon "world" beckon travelers from all over the planet. But the self-proclaimed City Beautiful has its literary side as well. In the spring Shakespeare is brought to life in the open air at Lake Eola Park by the Orlando Shakespeare Festival. Another event, the Orlando Sentinel Book Fair, a celebration of books, of reading, and of literacy, takes place annually at Lake Eola Park as part of Orlando's Arts in April festival. The city's name may be of Shakespearean origin — from the character Orlando in *As You Like It*. Lending support to this theory is the existence of a Rosalind Street in Orlando, where, at the corner with Central Boulevard, stands the public library. However, the generally accepted theory of the origin of the city's name is that it comes from Orlando Reeves (or Rees), a pioneer said to have been killed by Seminoles in the vicinity of Lake Eola about 1835.

George Garrett (1929-) was born in Orlando and started his formal education at St. Luke's Cathedral School. An "indifferent student" (so he says), he went on to Delaney Street Grammar School (the same school attended earlier by **Mary Lee Settle**) and to Cherokee Junior High School before bearing that indifference to Sewanee Military Academy. Garrett tells of learning to swim in a lake in Winter Park when the Rollins College swimming coach, Fleetwood Peeples, threw him off a dock to let him sink or swim.

"For reading," Garrett says, "we had all the riches of my father's one great extravagance — an overflowing library of some thousands of books. Books of all kinds in bookcases and piles and on tables everywhere in the house. Everybody read and read. And so did I. I remember reading Kipling and Stevenson and Dickens and Scott sooner than I was able to. And you could earn a quarter anytime for reading any one of the hard books that my father thought anybody and everybody ought to read."

George Garrett

Garrett's father, George Garrett, Sr., was a lawyer who "ran the Ku Klux Klan, then a real political power, completely out of Kissimmee, Florida. And lived to enjoy the victory. Took on the big railroads — the Atlantic Coast Line, the Florida East Coast, the Seaboard, and the Southern — and beat them again and again." Garrett graduated from Princeton in 1952, then served in the army in Trieste and Austria. His fiction, poetry, and plays draw upon his experience, but also range much beyond, showing his versatility and agility. His short stories *In the Briar Patch* (Austin, TX: University of Texas Press, 1961) include a story set at Wekiva Springs, and his early novel *The Finished Man* (New York: Scribner, 1959) is about an idealistic politician in the central Florida town of Oakland. Other novels include three set in Elizabethan England, all published by Doubleday of Garden City, New York: *Death of the Fox* (1971), *The Succession: A Novel of Elizabeth and James* (1983), and *Entered from the Sun* (1990). Garrett's six volumes of poems have been gathered into *The Collected Poems of George Garrett* (1984).

George Garrett has been a scriptwriter in Hollywood and has taught at Wesleyan University, Rice University, Hollins College, the University of South Carolina, Columbia University, the University of Michigan, Florida International University, Bennington College, and the Atlantic Center for the Arts. He is now professor of creative writing at the University of Virginia.

Other writers have immigrated to Orlando and found it a congenial place to write. **Iris Tracy Comfort** was born in Racine, Wisconsin, and has pursued her career in central Florida. She manages a wildlife sanctuary near Lake Helen and lives much of the time in Orlando. Comfort worked as a newspaper reporter in St. Paul, Minnesota, and as a public-relations executive in Milwaukee and Chicago before coming to Florida. Her novels include *Echoes of Evil* (1977), *Joey Tigertail* (1973), and *Shadow Masque* (1980).

Mildred Elwood Lawrence grew up in Illinois and Michigan, then moved to Boynton Beach, Florida, in the 1940s with her husband. He edited newspapers in Boynton Beach and in Eustis, while she wrote feature articles. After they settled in Orlando in 1951, Lawrence wrote children's books based on her experiences in Florida. All were published by Harcourt Brace in New York. *Once at the Weary Why* (1969) is set in central Florida, while *A Starry Answer* (1962) and *One Hundred White Horses* (1953) are set in the Cape Canaveral-Indian River area. *Inside the Gate* (1968) and *Sand in Her Shoes* (1949) take place in south Florida. St. Augustine in 1767 is the setting of *Indigo Magic* (1956).

Another author of books for young readers is **Kathryn Vinson (Kay Williams)**, who was born and reared in Cordele, Georgia, but has made Orlando her home for many years. Two of her novels are *The Luck of the Golden Cross* (Philadelphia: Lippincott, 1960) about youthful sponge fishermen at Tarpon Springs and *Run With the Ring* (1965) about a blind runner.

Jill Pelaez, who was born in Puerto Rico and has lived in ten states, has published a volume of short stories, *Donkey Tales* (1971), and other works. She earned B.A. and M.A.T. degrees from Rollins College and taught at Lake Highland Preparatory School.

Edward "Ed" Hayes, now retired from his duties as book editor of the *Orlando Sentinel*, writes a weekly column in the *Sentinel*, Heydays, and is the author of a novel, *The Day of the Game* (1981). With his wife, **Betty Ann Weber**, Hayes authored *The Florida One-Day Trip Book* (McLean, VA: EPM, 1990).

Sam Hodges, a feature writer for the *Orlando Sentinel*, has published *B-Four* (1992), a comic novel blending newspaper reporting with Civil War reenactment.

About eight miles east of Orlando, on Alafaya Trail, is the University of Central Florida, which originated as Florida Technological University in 1968

University of Central Florida Library

and underwent a name change in 1978. In its English department are a number of writers. **Roland Browne**, professor emeritus, has published *The Holy Jerusalem Voyage of Ogier VIII, Seigneur d'Anglure* (1975), *The Rose Lover's Guide* (1974), and scores of articles. **Stephen Becker**, now retired as visiting lecturer, is the author of *When the War Is Over* (1969), *The Chinese Bandit* (1975), *The Blue-Eyed Shan* (1982), and other novels, essays, and translations. **Judith Hemschemeyer** has published several volumes of poetry, including *The Ride Home* (1987) and a translation, *The Complete Poems of Anna Akhmatova* (1990). **Don Stap**'s books include poetry — *Letter at the End of Winter* (1987) — and a nonfiction work about ornithologists in South America entitled *A Parrot Without a Name* (1990). **Pat Rushin**'s *Puzzling Through the News* (1991) is a volume of short stories. **Gail Regier** has published short stories, essays, and poems in a variety of journals. Two UCF writers, Wyatt Wyatt and Richard Adicks, have been mentioned earlier. The *Florida Review*, published semiannually at the University of Central Florida and edited by Russell Kesler, features the fiction and poetry of writers from Florida and all regions of the United States.

Jerrell Shofner

Another University of Central Florida professor who writes about Florida is **Jerrell Shofner**, former chair of the history department and one of the state's most distinguished historians. Among his many publications are *Nor Is It Over Yet: Florida in the Era of Reconstruction, 1863-1877* (Gainesville: University Press of Florida, 1974); *History of Jefferson County* (Tallahassee: Sentry Press, 1976); *Daniel Ladd, Merchant Prince of Frontier Florida* (Gainesville: University Press of Florida, 1978); *History of Apopka and Northwest Orange County, Florida* (Apopka: Apopka Historical Society, 1982); *Orlando: The City Beautiful* (Tulsa, OK: Continental Heritage Press, 1984); and *Jackson County, Florida: A History* (Marianna, FL: Jackson County Heritage Association, 1985).

Orlando and central Florida have been the locale of several novels. They include **Hugh B. Cave**'s *The Nebulon Horror* (New York: Dell, 1980); **Luanna Churchill**'s *Bride of the Unliving* (New York: Lennox Hill Press, 1974) and *Shadow on the Moon* (New York: Lennox Hill Press, 1974); **Paul Erickson**'s *One Step Forward* (New York: Pageant Press, 1957); **Peggy Gaddis**'s *At Granada Court* (New York: Arcadia House, 1959); **Richard Glendinning**'s *Too Fast We Live* (New York: Popular Library, 1954); **Jannette Hodges**'s *Back Country* (New York: Pageant Press, 1958); **Clayton A. Lerch**'s *The Last Hope* (Orlando: Sunrise Publications, 1956); **John D. MacDonald**'s *The Drowner* (Greenwich, CT: Fawcett, 1963); **Eugenie Reid**'s *Mystery of the Carrowell Necklace* (New York:

Lothrop, Lee & Shepard, 1965); **James Q. Roop**'s *Billy Brahman* (New York: Greenwich Book Publishers, 1960); **Nancy Spofford**'s *The Day of the Bear* (Chicago: Follett Publishing Co., 1964); **Donald Tracy**'s *The Hated One* (New York: Simon & Schuster, 1963); **Laurence Vershel**'s *Between Grief and Nothing* (New York: Exposition Press, 1973); **Harry Whittington**'s *A Woman on the Place* (New York: Ace Books, 1956); and **William Yarish**'s *The Rancher* (New York: Carlton Press, 1978). The mystery writer **John Lutz** has written about Orlando in his tales of the detective Fred Carver: *Tropical Heat* (1986), *Scorcher* (1987), and *Kiss* (1988), all published by Henry Holt in New York.

There have been several histories of Orlando and of Orange County in addition to Jerrell Shofner's work noted earlier. **Eve Bacon** wrote *Orlando: A Centennial History* (Chuluota, FL: Mickler House), of which Volume I (1875-1925) appeared in 1975, and Volume II (1926-1975) in 1977. Others are *More Than a Memory*, the bicentennial history of Orlando by **Becky Karst**, **David Stark**, and **Jacob Stuart** (Orlando: Robinsons, 1975) and **Baynard Kendrick**'s *Orlando, A Century Plus* (Orlando: Sentinel Star, 1976). For more about the city see the autobiography of one of its mayors, **Carl T. Langford**'s *Hizzoner the Mayor* (Orlando: Chateau Publishing Co., 1976) and the memoirs of a civic leader, **J. Thomas Gurney**, in *Summing Up or A Walk Through a Century* (Orlando: Burney, 1992). For the story of a dishonest Orlando policeman known as the "Florida Fox" see *The Most Wanted Man in America* (New York: Stein and Day, 1975) by **John William Clouser** with **Dave Fisher.**

Disney World, southwest of Orlando, claims to be one of the most popular tourist attractions in the world. With the addition of thousands of hotel/motel rooms and shops catering to the tourist, the theme park has had a major impact on central Florida. For more about the attraction see **Richard R. Beard**'s *Walt Disney's Epcot Center: Creating the New World of Tomorrow* (New York: H.N. Abrams, 1982) and **Leonard E. Zehnder**'s *Florida's Disney World: Promises and Problems* (Tallahassee: Peninsular Publishing Co., 1975). A novel that alludes to the ultra-successful amusement park in central Florida is **William Hegner**'s *Rainbowland* (Chicago: Playboy Press, 1977), a book that illustrates the strong influence such a park has on the state's economy, ecology, and living conditions. **Clark Blaise**'s novel *Lunar Attractions* (Garden City, NY: Doubleday, 1979) is about a boy growing up in this area before the coming of Disney World.

Pine Castle

Once a distinct town, Pine Castle has been virtually absorbed by Orlando, although it still maintains its identity with a Pine Castle Folk Arts Center at 6015 Randolph Street (Monday through Friday, 10 A.M. to 12 P.M. and 1 P.M. to 4 P.M.; telephone 407 855-7461) and a pioneer festival every October. The town was named by **Will Wallace Harney** (1832-1912), who came to Orange County in 1869, homesteaded 160 acres of land, and called the home that he built the Pine Castle. Harney was born in Indiana and graduated from

Transylvania University in Kentucky. He studied law and taught in Louisville and practiced law for a short time before becoming editor of the *Louisville Democrat*. After marrying Mary Randolph of New Orleans in 1868 and settling in Orange County, Harney wrote many articles for northern journals, which are credited with inducing readers to move to Florida in the 1870s and 1880s. Mrs. Harney died in 1870, leaving one son, William Randolph Harney. Will Wallace Harney published a volume of sketches and poems in 1909, *The Spirit of the South*, dedicating them to his son.

Kissimmee

The name of this town is pronounced with the accent on the second syllable. It may come from an Indian name that means *mulberries yonder*.

Kissimmee has been the headquarters of the Florida Cattlemen's Association, the heart of the cattle country of southern Florida, and the home of the annual Silver Spurs Rodeo. Much of the surrounding Osceola County is used for cattle raising, especially Brahman cattle. Visitors may be unaware that Florida ranks among the top ten states in beef-cattle production. *Florida Cowman, A History of Florida Cattle Raising* (Kissimmee, FL: Florida Cattlemen's Association, 1976) and *American Brahman: A History of the American Brahman* (Houston: American Brahman Breeders Association, 1982) both by **Joe A. Akerman, Jr.**, point out how vital this industry is to the state. A novel about cattle raising in this area is **Rex Beach's** *Wild Pastures* (New York: Farrar & Rinehart, 1935), which ranges as far south as Fort Myers in its setting. A novel based on local ranch life is **Leila O. Keen's** *The Cowpoke's Wife* (New York: Carlton Press, 1969). For a vivid description of the nineteenth-century Florida cowboys and their difficult, dreary life see "Cracker Cowboys of Florida" in **Frederic Remington's** *Crooked Trails* (New York: Harper, 1899; reprinted as a facsimile by Bonanza Books, 1974).

Other novels that take place in the area include *Buzzard Barbara* (New York: Manor Books, 1978) by **Bernice Barber (Barbara Berne)** and *The Kissimmee Kid* (New York: Lothrop, Lee, & Shepard, 1981) by **Vera** and **Bill Cleaver**. A story of The Shadow (Lamont Cranston) was set not far away at Intercession City in **Walter Gibson's** *City of Ghosts* (New York: Street & Smith, 1939). **Betty Metzger** has edited *The History of Kissimmee* (St. Petersburg: Byron Kennedy & Co., 1983?). Two county histories are *Osceola County: The First 100 Years* (Kissimmee, FL: R.G. Cody, 1987) by **Aldus M.** and **Robert S. Cody**; and *History of Osceola County* (Orlando: Inland Press, 1935) by **Minnie Moore-Willson**.

Deer Park

Farther east on U.S. 192 near Deer Park is the largest cattle ranch in America, the 300,000-acre Deseret Ranch run by the Mormon Church. Half the size of Orange County, this working ranch has more than 50,000 head of cattle; the 80 hard-working ranchhands live up to the name Deseret, a Mormon word meaning *industry*. This entire region, the St. Cloud-Kissimmee-Deer Park area, is described in **Alma Hetherington**'s book, *The River of the Long Water* (Chuluota, FL: Mickler House, 1980).

Lakeland

Southwest of Kissimmee along busy Interstate 4 is Lakeland, named to commemorate the many lakes in its city limits. Lake Morton, home to many swans and ducks, received its original pair of swans from the Queen of England. Lake Hollingsworth is the site of Florida Southern College, founded in 1885, and originally called the South Florida Seminary when it was in Orlando. The school had several different names and sites (Sutherland, Clearwater, and then Lakeland in 1922). Frank Lloyd Wright, who developed his idea of organic architecture to combine the best of the environment with the purpose of the buildings, designed several buildings on the Lakeland campus. For more about the college see **Harris G. Sims**'s *The Story of Southern College* (Lakeland, FL: Florida Southern College, 1935); **Charles T. Thrift**'s *Through Three Decades at Florida Southern College, Lakeland, Florida* (Lakeland, FL: Florida Southern College, 1955); and **Theodore M. Haggard**'s *Florida Southern College, Lakeland, Florida: The First 100 Years* (Lakeland, FL: Florida Southern College, 1985). As for literature, **Lois Lenski**'s *Strawberry Girl* (Philadelphia: Lippincott, 1945) is set in this area, as is **Nazon H. Arnold**'s *Rusty's Travels* (Boston: Lothrop, Lee & Shepard, 1931). The 1961 movie entitled *The Marriage-Go-Round* with Susan Hayward and James Mason included scenes filmed on the Florida Southern campus.

Novelist **Wyatt Blassingame** (1909-1985) taught at Florida Southern College from 1948 to 1951 and then lived in Anna Maria north of Sarasota for many years. Born in Demopolis, Alabama, he was the author of over 600 stories and articles. In *The Golden Geyser* (New York: Doubleday, 1961) he profiled many of the Floridians who figured prominently in the Florida boom of the 1920s. Some of his other Florida works are *Live From the Devil* (Garden City, NY: Doubleday, 1959) about cattle raising in Florida; *Osceola: Seminole War Chief* (Champaign, IL: Garrard, 1967); *Jake Gaither: Winning Coach* (Champaign, IL: Garrard, 1969) about the very successful football coach at Florida A & M University); *Wonders of Alligators and Crocodiles* (New York: Dodd, Mead, 1973); *The Everglades* (New York: Putnam, 1974); and *Ponce De León* (New York: Chelsea House, 1991).

For more about Lakeland and Polk County see **Hampton Dunn**'s *Yesterday's Lakeland* (Tampa: Bay Center Corp., 1976) and **Louise Frisbie**'s *Yesterday's Polk County* (Miami: Seemann Publishing Co., 1976). Inter-racial conflicts in Lakeland are recorded in **Willard B. Gatewood, Jr.**'s *"Smoked Yankees" and the Struggle for Empire: Letters from Negro Soldiers, 1898-1902* (Urbana, IL: University of Illinois, 1971).

Ernest Hemingway's first wife, Elizabeth Hadley Mowrer, died in Lakeland in 1979 at the age of 89. In *A Moveable Feast* Hemingway described the love triangle in Paris that led to his divorce from Mowrer and his eventual marriage to Pauline Pfeiffer, who later lived with him in Key West.

In east Lakeland off U.S. 92 is Acton, settled in 1884 by a group of Englishmen and named for the English author Lord Acton (1834-1902), a learned historian and planner of *The Cambridge Modern History*. The town lasted ten years, until the great freeze of 1894-95. During that decade the residents lived a British life, engaging in polo, fox hunting, and cricket.

Plant City

Located farther west near Interstate 4, Plant City was named after Henry B. Plant, who built a railroad from Sanford to Tampa and helped develop this area of Florida. For more about the city see **Quintilla Geer Bruton** and **David E. Bailey, Jr.**'s *Plant City: Its Origin and History* (St. Petersburg, FL: Valkyrie Press, 1977).

Author **John Keasler** (1921-) was born in Plant City. Among his writings that deal with Florida are the novels *Surrounded on Three Sides* (Philadelphia: Lippincott, 1958); *Keyhole* co-authored with **C. DeWitt Coffman** (Englewood Cliffs, NJ: Prentice-Hall, 1972); and the children's book, *The Christmas It Snowed in Florida* (Coconut Grove, FL: Hurricane House, 1962). He published numerous short stories and articles for leading magazines and worked for the *Miami News*. *Keyhole* is a factual account of the humorous side of the American hotel industry and features many Florida hotels; in *Surrounded on Three Sides*, Keasler foresaw the overcrowding of Florida.

Mulberry

South of Lakeland is the small town of Mulberry, named after a mulberry tree that used to be in the vicinity; railroad workers used it as a depot site for four large phosphate plants in the area. Phosphate mining dominates the region with both good economic results and bad environmental effects. The Mulberry Phosphate Museum one block south of State Road 60 off State Road 37 has 3,000 specimens, some from 15 million years ago, and all found in the surrounding area. An estimated 25,000 people a year visit the museum, including 10,000 schoolchildren who marvel at the life-size diorama with its Pleistocene creatures. (Tuesday through Saturday, 813 425-2823.)

Several novels take place in and around Polk County: **Harry Crews's** *Naked in Garden Hills* (New York: Morrow, 1969); **Sara Lucille Jenkins's** *Year in Paradise* (New York: Crowell, 1952); **Lillian B. McCall's** *The Unconquerable, A Florida Historical Novel* (New York: Exposition, 1958); and **Bess Rooks's** *The Bottom Rail* (New York: Vantage, 1960). Nonfiction works about Florida phosphate and the fossils found in it include **Arch Fredric Blakey's** *The Florida Phosphate Industry* (Cambridge, MA: Harvard University Press, 1973); the Florida Defenders of the Environment's *Phosphate Mining in Florida: A Source Book* (Tallahassee: Environmental Service Center, 1984); **S. David Webb's** *Pleistocene Mammals of Florida* (Gainesville: University

Presses of Florida, 1974); and **Marian Murray**'s *Florida Fossils* (Tampa: Trend House, 1975). **John Frasca**'s *The Mulberry Tree* (Englewood Cliffs, NJ: Prentice-Hall, 1968) is a nonfiction account of how local authorities jailed an innocent man after a series of minor robberies in the town.

Auburndale

East of Lakeland on U.S. Highway 92 is the town of Auburndale, named after a town in Massachusetts and thus honoring British writer Oliver Goldsmith (1728-1774), who wrote in *The Deserted Village* (1770): "Sweet Auburn! loveliest village of the plain,/Where health and plenty cheer'd the laboring swain."

Winter Haven

A developer named P.D. Eyclesheimer platted this city in 1884 and gave it the attractive name because he wanted to promote it as immune to the ravages of cold weather. Winter Haven has been a popular city for writers. **Vera** and **Bill Cleaver** made it their home for years. Bill (1920-1981) was born in Seattle and served in the U.S. Air Force for many years; Vera (1919-) was born in North Dakota but grew up in Florida. Together they wrote more than 20 books, including the following that Lippincott of Philadelphia published: *Ellen Grae* (1967), *Where the Lilies Bloom* (1969), *The Mimosa Tree* (1970), and *Dust of the Earth* (1975). The Cleavers have said of their writing life: "We would rather observe than be observed. We don't play golf or bridge. We go to bed at ten o'clock and are up by six, which is to say we work a lot. If one can be in love with work, that is the way it is with us."

Winter Haven is also the home of **Velma Seawell Daniels**, the author of several inspirational novels: *Patches of Joy* (1976), *Kat: The True Story of My Calico Cat* (1978), *Celebrate Joy!* (1981), and *Fountain of Love* (1983).

John and **Jane Perry**, who live on a lake in Winter Haven, have written over 20 books, chiefly on natural history and ecology, including a number of Sierra Club guides. In 1992 Pineapple Press (Sarasota, FL) will publish their book *The Nature of Florida*.

Richard Bach, an aviator and author who was born in Oak Park, Illinois, and lived in California, has made his home near Winter Haven for several years. Bach, winner of the 1974 Nene Award for *Jonathan Livingston Seagull* (1970), has also published *A Gift of Wings* (1974), *The Bridge Across Forever* (1984), *One: A Novel* (1988), and other books. **Larry Smith**'s *Taildraggers High* (New York: Farrar, Straus & Giroux, 1985) is set in the citrus-grove country near Winter Haven. Several chapters of **Russell Banks**'s *Continental Drift* (New York: Harper and Row, 1985) take place in Oleander Park, a fictional Polk County town. The history of Winter Haven can be found in **Josephine G. Burr**'s *History of Winter Haven, Florida* (Winter Haven, FL: L. Burr, 1974) and **M.F. Hetherington**'s *History of Polk County, Florida* (St. Augustine: Record Co., 1928; reprinted by Mickler House, Chuluota, FL, 1971).

Lake Wales

In 1879 Sidney Wailes surveyed the land around the present city and renamed one of the larger lakes, Lake Wailes. The spelling of the name altered as time went by, and in 1915 the new post office was named Lake Wales.

Edward Bok (1863-1930) built a home at Mountain Lake near Lake Wales and chose nearby Iron Mountain as the site of his famous Singing Tower, where he installed some of the finest carillons in the world and which he called the Taj Mahal of America. Bok, born in the Netherlands, came to the United States when he was six and worked his way to wealth and fame in classic Horatio Alger fashion. He began as an office boy, rose to advertising manager and editor of various newspapers and magazines, and earned fame from 1889 to 1919 as editor of the *Ladies' Home Journal*. To make the Horatio Alger analogy complete, Bok married Mary Louise Curtis, his publisher's daughter. His best-known book is *The Americanization of Edward Bok* (New York: Scribner's, 1920), which won him the 1921 Pulitzer Prize for biography. Although Bok, who died at his Mountain Lake home in 1930, had said that he did not want the carillon structure to be a monument to him, he was buried at the foot of the Singing Tower. Poet **Don Blanding** wrote of this tower in his collection of poems entitled *Floridays* (New York: Dodd, Mead, 1945): "The Singing Tower holds aloft its carillon of bells/While from its carven marble shaft the sweetest music swells." For more about Bok and his magazine see **Salme Harju Steinberg's** *Reformer in the Marketplace: Edward W. Bok and the Ladies' Home Journal* (Baton Rouge: Louisiana State University Press, 1979).

Histories of Lake Wales include **Janyce Barnwell Ahl's** *Crown Jewel of the Highlands: Lake Wales, Florida* (Lake Wales, FL: Lake Wales Library Association, 1983) and **Dorothy Kaucher's** *They Built a City* (Orlando: Kirstein, 1970). **Ken Morrison,** a past president of the National Audubon Society, has recorded his 25 years as director of the Mountain Lake Sanctuary in *Mountain Lake Almanac* (Sarasota: Pineapple Press, 1984). A novel that takes place near Lake Wales is **Cecil M. Miller's** *The Echo* (New York: Vantage Press, 1966).

Hesperides

Nine miles east of Lake Wales on Highway 60, nestled amid orange groves, lies this classically named town. The Hesperides, three daughters of Atlas, lived in a remote western land, tending the golden apples of Hera. To guard the apples from the Hesperides themselves as well as from others Hera had sent a dragon named Ladon who coiled around the tree. Hercules's eleventh labor was to steal the golden fruit (oranges? grapefruit?). Having been warned not to seize the fruit himself, Hercules killed Ladon by shooting an arrow over the wall; he shouldered the earth in Atlas's place while he sent Atlas to carry out the theft. Then, pretending to need to get a pad to protect his aching neck, Hercules tricked Atlas into giving him the apples and taking the earth again onto his back.

Frostproof

The self-explanatory name was supposedly bestowed by cowboys who herded their cattle to town during the winter months. Part of **Lawrence Dorr's** collection of short stories, *A Slow, Soft River* (Grand Rapids, MI: Eerdmans, 1973), takes place near Frostproof, where the author was a cowboy and a missionary at one time. The cowboys who worked in the area are some of those that **Jim Bob Tinsley** commemorates in *He Was Singin' This Song* (Orlando: University Presses of Florida, 1981); the book, especially the chapter entitled "Bad Brahma Bull," is about the musical heritage of Florida's cowboys.

Avon Park

O.M. Crosby of Danbury, Connecticut, president of the Florida Development Company, chose this site about 1885. He went to England to recruit settlers for the town and persuaded Mr. and Mrs. William King from Stratford-upon-Avon to relocate across the Atlantic. They named the town for Shakespeare's birthplace. For more about the Florida town see **Leoma Bradshaw Maxwell's** *The First Hundred Years of Avon Park, Florida* (Avon Park: Historical Society, 1980?).

Sebring

Founded in 1912, the town was named for George Eugene Sebring, a pottery manufacturer from Sebring, Ohio. For many years the town hosted the famous Sebring 12-hour Race of Endurance. A novel about those races is **Tom Pace's** *Afternoon of a Loser* (New York: Harper & Row, 1969); two 1961 racing movies take place in Sebring: *The Green Helmet* and *The Checkered Flag*.

Rex Beach (1877-1949), the author who was once called the Victor Hugo of the North, made his home at 2107 Northeast Lakeview Drive in Sebring for the last years of his life. Born in Atwood, Michigan, Beach came to Tampa in 1886 when his father chose a warmer climate in which to raise fruit trees. Rex attended Rollins Preparatory School and subsequently Rollins College, running a laundry to pay his tuition. He dabbled at the study of law and at professional football, then set out for the Klondike in 1900. He never made it as far as he intended, but tried mining at Nome. When he came home, he decided to write about the life he had seen in Alaska. *Pardners* (1905) was his first book; his second was *The Spoilers* (1906), which has been made and re-made into movies.

Prospering from more than 30 novels of rugged he-men and the movies made from his books, Beach returned to Florida in 1926 to buy land and farm. On 7,000 acres near Sebring and 5,000 acres near Indiantown, he used scientific methods of cattle raising and produced two crops of celery a year on 70 acres between Avon Park and Sebring. The raising of gladiolus bulbs made him a second fortune. He even tried to start a flower-bulb enterprise in Orizaba, Mexico, but this venture failed. In 1926 he gave a reporter this tough-minded assessment of Florida: "Florida is the only pioneer state left in

Rex Beach

the Union. I hope the reformers don't get here and spoil it all. We need some sort of sanity and tolerance. Today Florida is that center.... I wish a Catholic could be elected president.... The Protestants have failed miserably." Among his many novels, he set *Wild Pastures* (New York: Farrar & Rinehart, 1935) in the cattle land of south Florida. His autobiography is *Personal Exposures* (New York: Harper, 1940). In 1949 at the age of 72, in despair over his wife's death, growing blind and unable to write, and suffering from cancer of the throat, Beach shot himself. The Girl Scout loghouse at 442 South Eucalyptus Street has in its cornerstone a few of Beach's novels; a nearby tree bears a commemorative bronze marker.

Other local authors include **Park** and **George DeVane, Courtney Ryley Cooper,** and poets **Carrow DeVries** and **Louise C. Moshier.** The city police department at 307 North Ridgewood Drive features a wall mural done by artist Charles Knight in 1942 as part of the federal government's program to use artists during the Depression; entitled "Prehistoric Life in Florida," the mural depicts the saber-toothed tiger as it roamed through Florida eons ago.

One can find the history of Sebring in several books, including *The Fifty Years of Sebring, 1912-1962* (Sebring, FL: Sebring Semi-Centennial Committee, 1962); *History of Sebring, Highlands County, Florida* (Sebring, FL: Chamber of Commerce History Committee, 1965); and **Alec Ulmann**'s *The Sebring Story* (Philadelphia: Chilton, 1969).

East of Sebring is the Kissimmee River, a waterway that the Army Corps of Engineers tampered with and eventually straightened. That river is the site of "The Haunted Kissimmee River" in *Florida Folktales* (Gainesville: University Presses of Florida, 1987) edited by **J. Russell Reaver. Kyle S. Van Landingham**'s *Pioneer Families of the Kissimmee River Valley* (no publisher, 1976) is a history of the nineteenth-century settlers in the area. A book about 18 of the major rivers of Florida is *The Rivers of Florida* (Sarasota: Pineapple Press, 1990) by **Del** and **Marty Marth**; the chapter on the Kissimmee River by **Lee Hinnant** explains how environmentalists are succeeding in forcing engineers to restore the river to its original, meandering bed. The Marths, two of Florida's most distinguished and prolific journalists, also edit the annual *Florida Almanac*. Two other books about Florida's rivers are *The Rivers of Florida* (New York: Springer-Verlag, 1991) edited by **Robert J. Livingston** and *Rivers of Florida* (Atlanta: Southern Press, 1974) by **Henry Marks** and **Gene Britt Riggs**.

Lake Placid

In 1927 Melvil Dewey (1851-1931), the inventor of the Dewey Decimal System, advocate of spelling reform, and founder of the Lake Placid Club in New York, bought 3,000 acres in Florida and convinced the legislature to change the name from Lake Stearns to Lake Placid. Dewey set about developing a subtropical extension of the Lake Placid Club and oversaw the building of a clubhouse, guest buildings, and a golf course.

Okeechobee

A fierce battle was waged near Okeechobee on December 24, 1837. Colonel Zachary Taylor and a band of 1,000 soldiers fought hand to hand with about 500 Seminole Indians, led by Billy Bowlegs. Federal forces won the Battle of Okeechobee, called the only major conventional battle of the Second Seminole Indian War. Lasting only three hours, the battle resulted in the death of 14 Indians and 26 U.S. soldiers, but it made Taylor the hero of the Seminole War and led to his nomination as the Whig candidate for President of the United States; he was elected to office in 1848 but died two years later. For more about the battle see **Willard Steele**'s *The Battle of Okeechobee* (Miami: Archaeological and Historical Conservancy, 1987) and **Dorothy May Dunsing**'s novel *The Seminole Trail* (New York: Longmans, Green, 1956).

This area is the site of **Edison Marshall**'s novel *The Lost Colony* (Garden City, NY: Doubleday, 1964), which speculated that members of Sir Walter Raleigh's sixteenth-century lost colony on Roanoke Island might have wandered to Florida and intermarried with the Indians. For a history of the city and vicinity see *Lawrence Will's Cracker History of Okeechobee* (St. Petersburg: Great Outdoors Publishing Co., 1964) by **Lawrence Will** and *The History of Okeechobee County* (Fort Pierce, FL: Van Landingham, 1978) by **Kyle S. Van Landingham** and **Alma Hetherington. Alto Adams, Jr.**'s *A Cattleman's Backcountry Florida* (Gainesville: University Presses of Florida, 1985) covers ranches in Okeechobee, St. Lucie, and Osceola counties.

Lake Okeechobee

From an Indian word meaning *big water*, Okeechobee with its 700 square miles is the second-largest freshwater lake totally within one state in the United States. (Lake Michigan is the largest.) Lake Okeechobee, which does not have a natural outlet, is very shallow, averaging only about 13 feet. Originating about 6,000 years ago, the lake used to form a large river, 50 miles wide and 6 inches deep, that flowed south through the Everglades to the Gulf of Mexico. After Florida became a state in 1845, private developers were encouraged to drain this land to make more arable acreage. Between 1881 and 1885 Hamilton Disston built 40 miles of canals to lower the water level of this area. He bought 4 million acres of land around the lake for $1 million and built a sugar factory, but irrigation problems and the panic of 1893 worked against him.

Worse was to come. In 1926 a hurricane raised a wall of water that killed 300 Moore Haven residents on the southwestern edge of the lake. In 1928 another hurricane killed approximately 2,000 people. President-elect Herbert Hoover inspected the area and directed the U.S. Army Corps of Engineers to build a huge dike around the lake. Canals and dikes around the lake regulate the depth of the water and aid the irrigation of southern Florida.

Lake Okeechobee was the setting for **Vinnie Williams**'s *The Fruit Tramp* (New York: Harper, 1957) and **May Nickerson Wallace**'s *The Plume Hunters Mystery* (New York: McKay, 1956). For a history of the lake see **Alfred Jackson Hanna** and **Kathryn Abbey Hanna**'s *Lake Okeechobee: Wellspring of the Everglades* (Indianapolis: Bobbs-Merrill, 1948), part of the American Lakes series.

Moore Haven

Moore Haven was called Emmet Harbor in **Richard Powell**'s *I Take This Land* (New York: Scribner's, 1962), a novel that describes this area between 1895 and 1946.

Clewiston

South of Okeechobee on Highway 27 is Clewiston, a company town of cracker box twenties-style houses built around the U.S. Sugar Corporation, the largest sugar manufacturer in the country. There's even a company whistle that goes off every afternoon at 4:30 to announce the end of a workday. The Clewiston Inn is Deep South in decor with a white-columned front entrance and a restaurant that features some of the best Southern cooking in the state. Off to one side of the wood-paneled lobby is the Bird Room Bar, a cozy, intimate lounge with a mural of the local bird-life covering all four walls. A section of **Zora Neale Hurston**'s *Their Eyes Were Watching God* (Philadelphia: Lippincott, 1937) dealing with migrant workers takes place near Lake Okeechobee, as does a **MacKinlay Kantor** short story about love and revenge among the local fishermen entitled "No Storm on Galilee" in *Florida Short Stories* (Gainesville: University of Florida Press, 1989) edited by **Kevin McCarthy**.

THE POETRY OF FLORIDA

JANE ANDERSON JONES & MAURICE J. O'SULLIVAN

In 1565 Nicholas Le Challeux, returning to France from the ill-fated French Huguenot expedition to Florida, wrote a brief lament which he titled "An Octet...Upon Arriving in His Home, in the Town of Dieppe, Hungry." ["Huitain par ledit Auteur arrivé en sa maison, en la ville de Dieppe, ayant faim."] That lyric, written the year after Shakespeare was born and four decades before the settlement of Jamestown, represents the first-known American poem or, more precisely, the first poem about America by a European known to have visited there. Le Challeux's "Octet" has also proven emblematic for Florida's poetry: not only has much of the writing that followed been the product of visitors, it often reflects needs yet unfulfilled.

During the years of European occupation that followed, poetry about *La Florida* reflected colonial desires for wealth and inhabitable land. Spanish poets offered idiosyncratic accounts of the terrain, its natives, and the conquistadores, ranging from Juan de Castellanos's *Elegias de varones illustres de Indias* (1589), with its idealized portrait of an Edenic land filled with noble savages and explored by a chivalrous Ponce de León, to Fray Alonso Gregorio de Escobedo's account of a hostile world thick with treacherous infidels (c. 1598). British poems revealed a similar ambivalence, especially in works by authors who had never visited the territory. A Renaissance lyric, "Have You Not Hard of Floryda" (1564?), describes a "savage pepell" who "in the mold find glysteryng gold/And yt for tryfels sell," while Oliver Goldsmith warned British settlers to avoid Florida's "torrid tracts" and "ravaged landscape" in *The Deserted Village* (1770).

After the United States acquired Florida, American writers began exploring the possibilities of their new southern frontier. On a visit to St. Augustine for his health during the winter of 1827-28, the young clergyman Ralph Waldo Emerson wrote a number of poems about North America's oldest city in his *Journals*. Although he notes the residents' "unsocial eye" and misses his native New England ("The exile's bread is salt"), he also senses a mythic quality in the land:

> The faint traces of romantic things
> The old land of America
> I find in this nook of sand
> The first footprint of that giant grown.

In addition to this romantic past, poets like Walt Whitman found inspiration in the new possession's tropical nature ("Orange Buds by Mail from Florida") and doomed Seminoles ("Osceola"). The Seminole Wars, in fact, inspired the most ambitious nineteenth-century poem about Florida, Albery Allson Whitman's epic *The Rape of Florida* (1884), reissued the following year as *Twasinta's Seminoles*. In Spenserian stanzas, Albery Whitman uses the Seminole removal as a metaphor for the American rape of paradise.

The trials and challenges of the nineteenth and early twentieth centuries, which encompassed the Seminole War, slavery, the Civil War, Reconstruction, road and railroad building, cattle herding, turpentine camps, and citrus groves, generated a folk poetry of diverse accents, from "Gator Can't Run" and "I Want to Go Back to Georgia" to "Conch Talk" and "Miami Hairikin." While Alton Morris's *Folk Songs of Florida* (1950) offers the most extensive anthology of the Anglo-American folk poetry, generous samples of work by other cultures can be found in Zora Neale Hurston's *Mules and Men* (1935), the Work Projects Administration's *Florida: A Guide to the Southernmost State* (1939), Stetson Kennedy's *Palmetto Country* (1942), Frances Densmore's *Seminole Music* (1956), Gloria Jahoda's *The Other Florida* (1967), and Wiley Housewright's *Music and Dance in Florida 1565-1865* (1991).

During the first half of the twentieth century, Florida became a source of inspiration for a number of important figures. James Weldon Johnson, a Jacksonville native, practiced law and school administration before moving north to help shape the Harlem Renaissance with *God's Trombones* (1927), seven verse sermons that recreated the language and imagery Johnson had experienced in the black churches of his youth. Heading in the opposite direction, Hart Crane spent time in Key West and began writing a series of lyrics very different from his epic *The Bridge* (1930). He completed this final collection, *Key West: An Island Sheaf*, just before his suicide in 1932.

As Florida became a tourist mecca, visiting poets were alternately enchanted and disillusioned by their visits. Wallace Stevens, the Connecticut insurance executive who refashioned American poetry, found in the Keys a pattern of sensuous images around which he organized many of the poems in his first two books, *Harmonium* (1923, reissued 1931) and *Ideas of Order* (1935). A decade later Elizabeth Bishop offered a slightly less idealized vision of Florida's mythic landscape in her *North and South* (1946). Three other figures who drew attention to the state's poetry during these years were Don Blanding, whose witty *Floridays* (1941) helped launch a successful speaking career; Vivian Yeiser Laramore, Florida's first poet laureate whose annual volume of *Florida Poets* during the thirties published the work of both natives and visitors; and Edward Osgood Grove, who founded the Angel Alley Press in Winter Park to publish a series of poetry chapbooks.

When the state's population exploded after World War II, the number of poets grew in proportion. An eclectic mix, they include natives like Pulitzer Prize–winner Donald Justice, transplants like the state's current poet laureate Edmund Skellings, and visitors like May Swenson. In Florida's Panhandle, the protean Van Brock helped found the Anhinga Press and introduced a talented group of new poets. Many established figures, like Peter Meinke, Donald Caswell, E. MacArthur ("Mac") Miller, and Jean West, have encouraged new generations of writers in Florida's colleges and universities. Those new generations with their rich variety of voices range from Enid Shomer's *Stalking the Florida Panther* (1987) and David Bottoms' *Scavengers at the Bibb County Dump*

(1980) to Yvonne Sapia's *The Fertile Crescent* (1983) and Ricardo Pau-Llosa's *Cuba* (1992). Together with poets like Carolina Hospital, Justin Spring, Silvia Curbelo, Alison Kolodinsky, Dionisio D. Martinez, and Lola Haskins, they have continued to extend America's oldest poetic tradition.

Jane Anderson Jones, an associate professor at Manatee Community College in Venice, Florida, and Maurice J. O'Sullivan, a professor at Rollins College in Winter Park, Florida, and the co-editor of The Florida Reader, *have edited a forthcoming anthology of Florida poetry.*

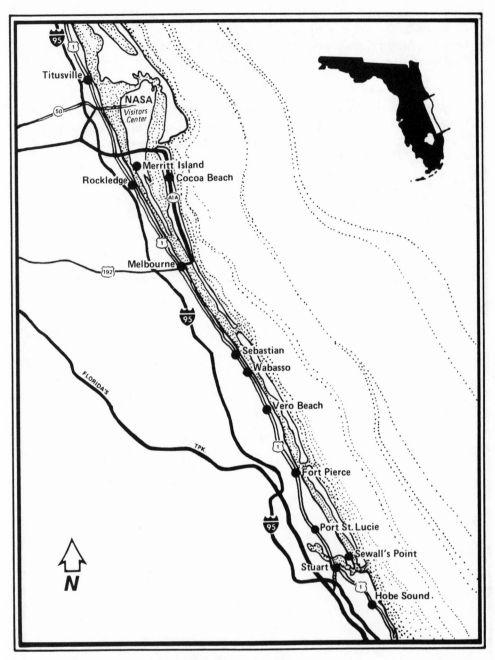

(Map for southern part of this section on p. 183)

168

4 TITUSVILLE TO FORT LAUDERDALE

STUART B. MCIVER

Titusville

Lying on the northern edge of America's gateway to the Space Age is Titusville, a city with roots tracing back to the day of the steamboat. In the nineteenth century, Titusville, the Brevard County seat, was the northernmost port on the Indian River, a coastal, saltwater lagoon, stretching nearly 150 miles down to Jupiter in Palm Beach County, lengthened in part by man-made canals. In his 1891 *On the Indian River* (Chicago: Charles H. Sergel), **C. Vickerstaff Hine** wrote: "It is this 'streak of silver sea,' this glittering chain of linked bays and coves and sunny sounds, this sun-kissed line of sapphire waters, that makes the Indian River Country the Riviera of America...a poem of pleasure." **Walter R. Hellier,** in his *Indian River — Florida's Treasure Coast* (Coconut Grove, FL: Hurricane House, 1965) was less effusive when he wrote that the Indian River "is not really a river. It has no source nor mouth, nor flowing current. It is neither all fresh nor all salt...we would call it brackish. It is still one of the most beautiful and picturesque bodies of water on the North American continent." Novels that take place on the Indian River include *One Hundred White Horses* by **Mildred Lawrence** (New York: Harcourt, Brace, 1953) and *No Place For a Woman* by **Laura Saunders** (New York: Avalon, 1955).

Titusville, at the river's head, acquired its name in 1873 when an early settler, the autocratic free-booter, hotelier and saloon-keeper, Colonel Henry T. Titus, named a little pioneer settlement after himself. The city today is home to many from the world of high technology as well as to novelist **Betty Sue Cummings**. A native of Stone Gap, Virginia, she has written an historical novel about the Second Seminole War (1835-1842) from the point of view of Indian families caught up in the war. *Say These Names — Remember Them* (Sarasota: Pineapple Press, 1984) ranges from central Florida down to the Everglades west of Fort Lauderdale. She has also written an environmental novel for young adults about the Indian River, *Let a River Be* (New York: Atheneum, 1978).

Merritt Island/Cocoa Beach

Just east of Titusville lies Merritt Island, an unincorporated area named for a Seminole War captain. It owed its nineteenth-century fame to an orange

Patrick D. Smith

grove started on the island by Captain Douglas Dummitt of Barbados. Skillful grafting developed the Dummitt Grove from which Florida's Indian River oranges evolved.

Merritt Island's fame today thrusts upward and outward from its location as home for the National Aeronautics and Space Administration's (NASA) Kennedy Space Center. It is also home to one of Florida's most eminent writers, **Patrick D. Smith** (1927-). A native Mississippian, Smith has written six novels, four of them set in Florida: *Forever Island* (New York: Norton, 1972) in the Big Cypress/Everglades area; *Angel City* (St. Petersburg: Valkyrie Press, 1974) in the migrant camps near Homestead; *Allapattah* (New York: Manor Books, 1979) in the Big Cypress; and *A Land Remembered* (Sarasota: Pineapple Press, 1984), a saga of three generations of the MacIvey family, ranging from central Florida cattle country down to Lake Okeechobee, to Henry Flagler's Palm Beach and to Miami in the wild years of the 1920s land boom. Smith's work captures a side of Florida far removed from the glitz, glamour, or criminality that many see. He writes instead of displaced Seminoles, struggling migrants, and the cowmen and women who kept families together under pioneer hardships.

That his writings touch the heart is shown by the universal appeal of such works as *Forever Island*, which has now carried this story of the American Indian into 46 languages. His books are popular in Russia, which he has visited as the guest of the Union of Writers of the USSR. *Angel City* was made into a 1980 Movie of the Week by CBS, starring Ralph Waite, and Smith himself has been the subject of a Public Broadcasting System special: *Visions of Nature: Patrick Smith*. His books have won many awards and have brought him nominations for both the Pulitzer and Nobel prizes. Two Patrick Smith readers published by Sarasota's Pineapple Press have combined four of his novels; the first reader (1987) has *Forever Island* and *Allapattah*, while the second one (1989) has *The River Is Home* (his first novel) and *Angel City*.

The northern end of Merritt Island is shared by NASA's Kennedy Space Center and the Merritt Island National Wildlife Refuge. Egrets, herons, ibis, and ducks coexist with much larger birds that soar far above the island's saltwater marshes. From Merritt Island humans first ventured forth to the moon. Sensing the magnitude of the achievement, visitors began flocking to the area on launch days, eager to see history at its most spectacular unfold before their eyes. Motels are filled and highways are packed with the earth-bound seeking a vantage point from which to watch the great rockets break free from gravity's hold.

Even without the thrill of a blast-off, the Kennedy Space Center is well worth visiting. Bus tours sanctioned by NASA conduct visitors to the Vehicle Assembly Building, one of the world's largest structures, bigger by far than the Empire State Building; to Complex 39, the launch site for the Apollo moon missions, Skylabs, and the space shuttles *Columbia*, and the tragic *Challenger*; and to the Astronaut Training Building. As far back as 1947 test missiles were launched from nearby Cape Canaveral, which juts out into the Atlantic just across the Banana River from Merritt Island. Canaveral, first sighted by Ponce de León in 1513, means *canebrake* in Spanish. From the cape the first successful U.S. satellite, *Explorer I*, was launched on January 31, 1958.

In May 1961 President John F. Kennedy gave the young space program a goal: to land a man on the moon and return him safely to Earth before the decade ended. By 1964 an accelerating NASA expanded onto 140,000 acres on Merritt Island, less than ten percent of which has been utilized to date; the rest has been left to wildlife. As employment in the aerospace industry soared, small, old South towns near the cape turned into high-tech mining camps. The space community, staffed with intelligent, highly educated people at work in intense, exciting jobs, boasted at one time the highest average income in the country. With the money and the pressure came a high divorce rate as well as serious drug and alcohol problems.

These human rather than technological problems of the space society are depicted in novels by two of Florida's most prolific authors. **Frank Slaughter** (1908-), the surgeon/novelist from Jacksonville, has made life at Spaceport City the subject of his fifty-second novel, *Countdown* (Garden City, NY: Doubleday, 1970). Slaughter exposes the basic insecurity that dwells within the so-called "aerospace beast."

Martin Caidin (1927-), a former Cocoa Beach resident now living in Gainesville, has written more than 120 fiction and nonfiction books, 59 of them set in Florida, mostly in space country. In *The Cape* (Garden City, NY: Doubleday, 1971), he paints a searing picture of life in Cocoa Beach for those caught in the stresses of the space program. He also wrote *Spaceport, U.S.A.* (New York: Dutton, 1959) about the cape. Most of Caidin's fiction, however, falls into the science fiction or action/adventure category. His novel, *Marooned* (1964), is about astronauts unable to bring their spaceship back to Earth; it became a popular 1969 motion picture starring Gregory Peck. *Four Came Back* (1968) is a novel about a rescue that the space center devises for a space laboratory. A later book, *Cyborg* (1972), spun off two well-known TV series: *The Six Million Dollar Man* and *The Bionic Woman*.

Like Caidin, many other science-fiction writers have been inspired by the futuristic world of the cape. **Ben Bova** (1932-), a six-time winner of the Hugo Award who now lives in Naples, has written some 75 books. Among these is *The Kinsman Saga* (New York: St. Martin's Press, 1987), a novel of global collapse and space colonization; the book contains a major section set at Cape

Canaveral. The Kennedy Space Center and Cape Canaveral are featured prominently in *The Trikon Deception* (New York: Tor, 1992) by Bova and former astronaut, **William Pogue**.

Long before Caidin and Bova began writing about a Florida spaceport, the rich imagination of French novelist **Jules Verne** (1828-1905) brought forth the preposterous notion of space travel. As far back as 1865, when the horse was the

The Space Shuttle *Columbia* lifts off from Kennedy Space Center, June 5, 1991.

fastest form of surface transportation, he wrote *From the Earth to the Moon* (Mattituck, NY: Aeonian Press, 1976). With a rare stroke of foresight he placed his launch site in Florida but not on Merritt Island, instead picking Tampa Town. A more recent trip to the moon is recounted in *Stowaway to the Moon: The Camelot Odyssey* by **William R. Shelton** (Garden City, NY: Doubleday, 1973).

Although most of the books on the spaceport have been written by either science-fiction or nonfiction science writers, several mainstream American authors of major stature have been drawn to the coupling of man's highest technology and the mystery of an unknown world. These authors include James Michener, Norman Mailer, both Pulitzer Prize winners, and Tom Wolfe.

In 1976 **James Michener** (1907-) became deeply interested in the space program. Six years later his novel, *Space* (New York: Random House, 1982), told the story of NASA's complex operations. Scientists, engineers, astronauts, and politicians parade across its 622 pages, providing an informative account of a vast, wide-ranging venture. **Norman Mailer** (1923-) covered the 1969 moon shot for *Life* Magazine, then developed the three lengthy installments into *Of a Fire on the Moon* (Boston: Little, Brown, 1970). Mailer's book was concerned with the cultural origins and effects of technology. **Tom Wolfe** (1931-), a leading figure in the New Journalism school of writing and author of *The Bonfire of the Vanities* (1987), approached the world of space through the eyes of the military pilots picked to be America's first space travelers, men who would be known as astronauts, men who would have to have the "right stuff." He titled his penetrating story of the heroes of the Space Age and their families *The Right Stuff* (New York: Farrar, Straus, Giroux, 1979); it became a 1983 major motion picture.

Among the novels set in the area are *Operation Moon Rocket* (New York: Universal, 1968) by **Nick Carter**; *The Throne of Saturn* (Garden City, NY: Doubleday, 1971) by **Allen S. Drury**; *Girl on Witches Hill* (New York: Harcourt, Brace, 1963) by **Mildred Lawrence**; *Julie Jones, Cape Canaveral Nurse* (New York: Ace, 1963) by **Suzanne Roberts**; *The Happy Hollisters and the Mystery at Missile Town* (Garden City, NY: Doubleday, 1961) by **Jerry West**; and *Mike Mars at Cape Canaveral* (Garden City, NY: Doubleday, 1961) by **Donald A. Wollheim**.

A number of nonfiction accounts of various aspects of the space program have been written, among them *Cape Canaveral* (St. Petersburg: Valkyrie Press, 1974) by **Harriett Carr**; *Gateway to Space* (New York: Morrow, 1960) by **Charles Combs**; *History of NASA, America's Voyage to the Stars* (New York: Exeter Books 1984) by **John** and **Nancy DeWaard**; *The Missilemen* (Garden City, NY: Doubleday, 1960) by **Mel Hunter**; *The Illustrated History of NASA* (New York: Gallery Books, 1986) by **Robin Kerrod**; *Challenger, a Major Malfunction* (Garden City, NY: Doubleday, 1987) by **Malcolm McConnell**; *Mission, an American Congressman's Voyage to Space* (San Diego: Harcourt Brace Jovanovich, 1988) by U.S. Congressman **Bill Nelson** of Melbourne with **Jamie Buckingham**; *Cape Kennedy: America's Spaceport* (Little Rock, AR: Pioneer, 1966) by **C.W. Scarboro** and **Stephen B. Milner**; *Liftoff: The Story of America's Spaceport* (New York: Dutton, 1968) by **L.B. Taylor, Jr.**; and *Space Travel, a History* (New York: Harper & Row, 1985) by **Wernher von Braun** and **Frederick I. Ordway III** with **David Dooling**.

Rocketry has not been the only futuristic pursuit at Cocoa Beach, which is named, like its sister city, Cocoa, for its plentiful growth of coconut palms. In a secluded conference room at his oceanfront estate, Pumpkin Center, **Allen H. Neuharth** assembled a team of Gannett Company employees on February 29, 1980. Their mission was to create a national newspaper. The result, *USA Today*, has not generally been regarded as a boon to the literary scene, but its impact on the publishing world has been a moonshot in its own right. Neuharth has written of this venture in his autobiography, *Confessions of an S.O.B.* (New York: Doubleday, 1989). Another book on the launching of *USA Today* is *The Making of McPaper: the Inside Story of USA Today* (1987) by **Peter Prichard**, the paper's managing editor.

Cocoa was also the final home of novelist **Frances Gaither** (1889-1955), author of *Follow the Drinking Gourd* (1940) and *Double Muscadine* (1949). A novel set in Cocoa Beach is **Babs Deal's** *It's Always Three O'Clock* (New York: McKay, 1961).

Rockledge

Just south of Cocoa on the mainland lies Rockledge, named for the rock that crops out in ledges along the western shore of the Indian River. Established in 1875, Rockledge proved a popular nineteenth-century winter resort for Northerners, many of whom enjoyed the rich birdlife in Indian River country. Rockledge in the twentieth century was the home of **Allan** and **Helen Cruickshank**, the husband-wife team of photographer/ornithologists, who wrote 14 books on birds. Helen Cruickshank has also written *Flight into Sunshine* (New York: Macmillan, 1948) and edited *William Bartram in Florida*

1774 (Cocoa, FL: Florida Federation of Garden Clubs, 1986). The area near Rockledge is the site of **Jess Gregg**'s novel, *The Glory Circuit* (New York: St. Martin's Press, 1962) about tent preachers.

Melbourne

South of Rockledge lies Melbourne, the largest city in the cape area. An 1870s town, Melbourne owes its name to the Australian city. Melbourne author **Elaine Stone** has written a history of the county, *Brevard County: From Cape of the Canes to Space Coast* (Northridge, CA: Windsor Publications, 1988). **Floyd** and **Marion Rinhart**, authorities on pioneer photography who winter on Melbourne Beach, have written *Victorian Florida: America's Last Frontier* (Atlanta: Peachtree, 1986); the book contains a section on early photographs of Indian River country.

Among the local histories one might examine are *Melbourne Village: The First Twenty-five Years (1946-1971)* by **Richard C. Crepeau** (Orlando: University of Central Florida Press, 1988), which tells the story of the small town west of Melbourne that became the site of an experiment by three women from Dayton, Ohio, who wanted to find economic solutions to the Depression; *Melbourne Sketches* by **Louis J. Hole** (Melbourne, FL: Kellersberger Fund of the South Brevard Historical Society, 1975); *Melbourne, Florida Postal History, 1880-1980* by **Fred A. Hopwood** (Melbourne, FL: Kellersberger Fund of the South Brevard Historical Society, 1981); two works by **Georgiana Greene Kjerulff** and published by the Kellersberger Fund: *Tales of Old Brevard* (1972) and *Troubled Paradise: Melbourne Village, Florida* (1987); two works by **Frank J. Thomas**: *Early Days in Melbourne Beach, 1888-1928* (Cocoa Beach, FL: Jet Press, 1968) and *Satires and Unsatires on Melbourne Beach* (Melbourne Beach, FL: Frank J. Thomas, 1976); and *Melbourne: A Century of Memories* (Melbourne, FL: Melbourne Area Chamber of Commerce Centennial Committee, 1980). For a description by its former principal of the innovative teaching at Melbourne High School see *The Nongraded High School* by **B. Frank Brown** (Englewood Cliffs, NJ: Prentice-Hall, 1963).

A number of authors live or have lived in the Melbourne and Melbourne Beach area, among them Colonel **Larry Guarino**, *A P.O.W.'s Story: 2801 Days in Hanoi* (1990); **Fred Hopwood**, *Steamboating on the Indian River* (Author, 1983); **Sybil Leek**, *The Complete Art of Witchcraft* (1971); **Richard Newhafer**, *On the Wings of the Storm* (New York: Morrow, 1969), a novel about Palm Beach; **M.M. Parker**, *Big Phil's Kid* (New York: Meredith Press, 1969), another novel about Palm Beach; **Cecil Stoughton**, *The Memories: JFK, 1961-1963* (1973); **Marian Van Atta**, *Growing & Using Exotic Foods: Living off the Land* (Sarasota: Pineapple Press, 1991); and **Bernard Wiseman**, *Morris and Boris, Three Stories for Children* (1974). Melbourne was at one time the home of **Michael Shaara**, who won the 1975 Pulitzer Prize for *The Killer Angels*, his historical novel about the Battle of Gettysburg.

Robert F. Marx lives in a Space Age town, Satellite Beach, but writes about sunken treasure ships from an earlier age. Among his many books on diving and underwater exploration are his autobiography, *Always Another Adventure* (1967); *The Lure of Sunken Treasure* (1973); *Buried Treasure of the United States: How and Where to Locate Hidden Wealth* (1978); *Into the Deep: The History of Man's Underwater Exploration* (1978); and *Shipwrecks in Florida Waters* (Chuluota, FL: Mickler House, 1985).

Brevard County is not without small towns whose names reflect classical literary figures. On Merritt Island lies the town of Orsino, named after the Duke of Illyria in William Shakespeare's *Twelfth Night*. Valkaria, south of Melbourne, was named by its early Swedish settlers after the Valkyries of Scandinavian mythology, warrior maidens who attended the chief god Odin and brought back to his hall, Valhalla, the souls of brave heroes slain in battle. Valkaria was the scene of a climactic automobile race in *Race the Tide* (New York: Silhouette Books, 1982) by **Mia Maxam (Ethel Crews).**

Sebastian

Those traveling south on Federal Highway leave Brevard County and enter Indian River County at the bridge over the Sebastian River, named by Spanish explorers for the martyred St. Sebastian. In November 1924 a group of outlaws traveling north failed to make it across the bridge, cut down instead by a hail of bullets from the law. The outlaws, the Ashley Gang, now a Florida legend, were the subject of a popular book, *The Notorious Ashley Gang; A Saga of the King and Queen of the Everglades* by **Hix C. Stuart** (Stuart, FL: St. Lucie Printing Co., 1928). The king was John Ashley, and his queen, or moll, was Laura Upthegrove. In its decade of crime the gang ranged up and down Indian River country and the Everglades.

From Bankers Bluff on the southern edge of the town of Sebastian, a bird lover can look across at Pelican Island, the site of a famous pelican and plume-bird rookery at the turn of the century. Endangered by marauding plume hunters, the birds found a measure of protection when President Theodore Roosevelt made Pelican Island the nation's first national wildlife refuge in 1903. Among the many nineteenth-century ornithologists who visited the Indian River was **Frank Chapman** of the American Museum of Natural History. Chapman, who was editor of *Bird Lore*, the forerunner of today's *Audubon* magazine, wintered at a nearby lodge and later wrote *Camps and Cruises of an Ornithologist* (New York: Appleton, 1908), partly about Pelican Island. **Elizabeth S. Austin's** *Frank M. Chapman in Florida: His Journals & Letters* (Gainesville: University of Florida Press, 1967) includes additional interesting material on the island. Other books about the island include **Robert M. McClung's** novel *Scoop: Last of the Brown Pelicans* (New York: Morrow, 1972) and **Joseph E. Brown's** nonfiction work, *The Return of the Brown Pelican* (Baton Rouge: Louisiana State University Press, 1983).

Wabasso

On July 24, 1715, a hurricane struck a Spanish treasure fleet south of Cape Canaveral, killing 700 seamen and sinking ten ships. Two-and-a-half centuries later Kip Wagner, a construction worker living in Wabasso who had caught treasure fever, formed a group of salvors into the Real Eight Corporation and, in the winter of 1961, found the riches from that Spanish plate fleet of 1715. One can read the story of their six-million-dollar discovery in *Pieces of Eight* (New York: Dutton, 1966) by **Kip Wagner** as told to **L.B. Taylor, Jr.** Also **Robert F. Burgess** and **Carl Clausen** (the state marine archaeologist assigned to monitor the salvage effort) retell the story of the discovery from a different point of view in their *Florida's Golden Galleons: The Search for the 1715 Spanish Treasure Fleet* (Port Salerno, FL: Florida Classics Library, 1982).

Much has been written about that treasure hunt and discovery. **Alan K. Craig** gives a numismatic study of the coins in his *Gold Coins of the 1715 Spanish Plate Fleet* (Tallahassee: Florida Bureau of Archaeological Research, 1988). *Artifacts of the Spanish Colonies of Florida and the Caribbean, 1500-1800, Volume I: Ceramics, Glassware, and Beads* (Washington, DC: Smithsonian, 1987) by **Kathleen Deagan** and *Sunken Treasure on Florida Reefs* (Lake Worth, FL: Cross Anchors Salvage, 1987) by **Robert "Frogfoot" Weller** also discuss the discovery. Just south of the inlet on State Road A1A visitors can learn more about the quest for treasure at the McLarty State Museum, which is on the site of an old salvage camp Spanish divers used when they tried to recover the fleet's gold and silver. This stretch of southeast Florida is appropriately known as the Treasure Coast.

Across from the barrier island on the mainland, south of Sebastian, lies a strangely named town, Wabasso, where people since the 1890s have made their living from Indian River citrus. Its first settlers, who hailed from Ossabaw, Georgia, came up with *Wabasso* simply by spelling their hometown backward.

In 1943 an unlikely couple came to Wabasso to grow fruit and ship it elsewhere. They were the distinguished poet, **Laura Riding** (1901-1991), who had spent most of her adult life in Europe, and her husband, **Schuyler B.**

Laura Riding Cottage

Jackson (? - 1968), a poet, critic, and former contributing editor for *Time* magazine. Riding published four novels, three collections of short stories, seven works of nonfiction, and 15 volumes of poetry, including *Collected Poems* (1938), *Selected Poems: In Five Sets* (1973), and *The Poems of Laura Riding* (1980). A major influence on modern poetry (although she wrote no poems after the late 1930s), the literary collaborator and mistress of poet and novelist Robert Graves, and a member of the Fugitives group of Southern poets based in Nashville, Tennessee, she was also the recipient of the Mark Rothko Award in 1972, a Guggenheim Fellowship in 1973, and the Bollingen Prize in poetry in 1991, the year she died. For more about her see *Robert Graves: The Years With Laura, 1926-1940* by **Richard Perceval Graves** (New York: Viking, 1990); *The Enemy Self: Poetry and Criticism of Laura Riding* by **Barbara Adams** (Ann Arbor, MI: UMI Research Press, 1990); and two books by **Joyce Piell Wexler**: *Laura Riding's Pursuit of Truth* (Athens, OH: Ohio University Press, 1979) and *Laura Riding, A Bibliography* (New York: Garland, 1981).

Vero Beach

The Indian River County seat is Vero Beach, named after Vero Gifford, the wife of the town's founder. An affluent winter resort and retirement area, Vero Beach has one of big-league baseball's most complete spring-training facilities. **Roger Kahn**'s *The Boys of Summer* (New York: Harper & Row, 1972) contains passages about Dodgertown and Vero Beach. Among the other baseball books about the state is **Peter Golenbock**'s *The Forever Boys* (New York: Carol Publishing Group, 1991), a look at Florida's Senior Professional Baseball League.

Vero Beach is home to a number of authors, among them **Cecily Crowe**, whose gothic novels include *Bloodrose Abbey* (1985). **Edwin Lanham** (1904-1975) wrote a number of novels and mysteries, including *Slug It Slay* (1946); *Murder on My Street*, set in Bath, England (1958); *Passage To Danger* (New York: Harcourt, Brace & World, 1961), a novel set in Fort Lauderdale and the Florida Keys; *Speak Not Evil* (1964); and *The Clock at 8:16*, a story set in the Far East (1976). Research by Florida historian and former Vero Beach city manager **Eugene Lyon** in the Archives of the Indies in Seville, Spain, helped pinpoint the location of a treasure-laden Spanish galleon off the Florida Keys. His *The Search for the Atocha* (Port Salerno, FL: Florida Classics Library, 1985; revised and updated as *Search for the Motherlode of the Atocha*, 1989) remains one of the most fascinating of all the state's treasure books.

Vero Beach is the home of **Kathryn Ryan**, author of *A Private Battle* (New York: Simon and Schuster, 1979), the story of the last days of her husband, Cornelius Ryan, who was dying of cancer. Kathryn Ryan had collaborated with her husband on his noted books on World War II, *The Longest Day* (1959), *The Last Battle* (1966), and *A Bridge Too Far* (1974). Co-author with comedian Alan King of *Anybody Who Owns His Own Home Deserves It* (1962), she has also written in her own right the novel *The Betty Tree* (1972).

One of Vero's principal manufacturers is Piper Aircraft. **Fred E. Weick** of Piper, in collaboration with **James R. Hansen**, NASA historian, has written of his experiences in *From the Ground Up: The Autobiography of an Aeronautical Engineer* (Washington, DC: Smithsonian Institution Press, 1988).

Several authors of books for children and young adults call Vero Beach home. These include **Betty Cavanna**, who has written 11 books, her most recent being *Banner Year* (1987). **Debra Frasier** wrote the environmental children's book *On the Day You Were Born* (1991). Among **Patricia Stone Martin**'s eight books are *Christa McAuliffe: Reaching for the Stars* (1987); *Jesse Jackson, a Rainbow Leader* (1987); and *Samantha Smith: Little Ambassador* (1987), all from Rourke Publishers of Fort Pierce. A novel that takes place in Vero Beach is *Troubled Journey* (Philadelphia: Lippincott, 1969) by **Richard Lockridge**. For a history of the city see *Florida's Hibiscus City: Vero Beach* (Melbourne, FL: Brevard Graphics, 1968) by **J. Noble Richards**. A volume presenting an overall picture of the Vero Beach area is *Florida's Historic Indian River County* (Vero Beach, FL: Mediatronics, Inc., 1975) by **Charlotte Lockwood**.

For a description of what life was like in this area in the last century see *Stories of Early Life Along Beautiful Indian River* (Stuart, FL: Stuart Daily News, 1953) by **Anna Pearl Leonard Newman**. South of Vero Beach on Route A1A are two sites with intriguing names: Starvation Point and Little Starvation Cove.

Fort Pierce

South of Vero Beach lies St. Lucie County. In 1565 the Spanish bestowed the name of the martyred Santa Lucia of Syracuse upon a fort near Cape Canaveral. A variation of the name has since been used to designate the county, the small town of St. Lucie, the larger city of Port St. Lucie, a river, an inlet, and a canal extending from the river to Lake Okeechobee. The county seat of this citrus and cattle world is Fort Pierce, which dates back to the Second Seminole War. The fort, built in 1838, traces its name to its first commanding officer, Lieutenant Colonel Benjamin Kendrick Pierce, a brother of President Franklin Pierce. *Our Worthy Commander: The Life and Times of Benjamin K. Pierce, in Whose Honor Fort Pierce Is Named* (Fort Pierce, FL: Indian River Community College Historical Data Center, 1976) by **Louis H. Burbey** gives a history of the man.

At the end of the 1950s **Zora Neale Hurston**, one of America's first black female novelists, was struggling against poverty and failing health. She worked as a librarian in the space program at Patrick Air Force Base, lived for a time on Merritt Island, and then in 1957 moved to Fort Pierce. She tried teaching and freelancing for a local paper, but after a stroke she was forced to enter the county welfare home. When she died in January 1960, she was buried in an unmarked grave in the Garden of the Heavenly Rest, a pauper despite a lifetime of achievement. Her books include the memorable novel, *Their Eyes Were Watching God* (1937), and a compendium of folklore, *Mules and Men* (1935), both published by Lippincott of Philadelphia. After she died, a local minister summed up her life when he said: "'The Miami paper said she died poor. But she died rich. She did something.'"

In the late summer of 1973 **Alice Walker** (1944-), whose *The Color Purple* would win the Pulitzer Prize a decade later, came to Fort Pierce, "Looking for

Zora," as she entitled a chapter in *In Search of Our Mother's Garden* (San Diego: Harcourt Brace Jovanovich, 1983). She wrote: "We are a people. A people do not throw their geniuses away. And if they are thrown away, it is our duty as artists and as witnesses for the future to collect them again for the sake of our children, and, if necessary, bone by bone." Walker found Hurston's grave and placed on it a stone which reads:

Zora Neale Hurston
"A Genius of the South"
1901 - - - 1960
NOVELIST, FOLKLORIST
ANTHROPOLOGIST

One can find the cemetery and Hurston's gravestone at the dead-end of North Seventeenth Street and Avenue S. For more about her see **Robert E. Hemenway**'s *Zora Neale Hurston — A Literary Biography* (Urbana: University of Illinois Press, 1977); **Adele S. Newson**'s *Zora Neale Hurston: A Reference Guide* (Boston: G.K. Hall, 1987); **Paul Witcover**'s *Zora Neale Hurston* (New York: Chelsea House, 1991); and editors **Steve Glassman** and **Kathryn Lee Seidel**'s *Zora in Florida* (Orlando: University of Central Florida Press, 1991)

Jim Bishop (1907-1987), author and syndicated columnist, came to Fort Pierce in 1960 from his Florida home in Hallandale to cover an extraordinary murder trial for the Hearst newspapers. His publisher was alerted to the trial via a note from Palm Beach from the widow of a famous writer, **Joseph Hergesheimer,** who had lived in and written about the exclusive winter resort in the 1920s. Hit men hired by one judge had kidnapped and then murdered a prominent Palm Beach judge, C.E. Chillingworth, and Mrs. Chillingworth. Authorities had the trial moved to the St. Lucie County Courthouse to escape the intense feeling aroused in the Palm Beaches. "Fort Pierce," Bishop wrote in his autobiography, *A Bishop's Confession* (Boston: Little, Brown and Co., 1981), "was a little cracker town which clung to Route 1 for its life. You could buy gasoline if you waited until the man put his toothpick on top of the cash register." Bishop's reports formed the basis for his book, *The Murder Trial of Judge Peel* (New York: Simon & Schuster, 1962). **Ernie Hutter**, a reporter for the *Palm Beach Post* who had covered the double murder of Judge and Mrs. Chillingworth wrote a more complete account of the case: *The Chillingworth Murder Case* (Derby, CT: Monarch Books, 1963).

Local authors have written about other topics, including land and sea adventures. For example, **Jan McGowan**'s *Heart of the Storm* (New York: Pocket Books, 1989) tells a suspenseful story set during the nineteenth-century Seminole War. From the Port of Fort Pierce, Edwin A. Link, inventor of the Link trainer, used to train Allied pilots in World War II, launched treasure and oceanographic ventures through his Harbor Branch Oceanographic Research Center. In her *Sea Diver* (New York: Rinehart, 1959), his widow, **Marion Link**, wrote about his many projects in Florida and the Caribbean. Perhaps Fort Pierce's most famous resident was Beanie Backus (1906-1990), one of Florida's best-known landscape painters and the subject of *A.E. Backus: Florida Artist* by local historian **Olive Peterson** (Fort Pierce, FL: Fort Pierce Art Gallery, 1984).

Those interested in learning more about the area should see **Walter R. Hellier**'s *Indian River — Florida's Treasure Coast* (Coconut Grove, FL: Hurricane House, 1965) and his *Palmetto Rambler* (New York: Vantage Press, 1973) about the history of the area. **Kyle S. Van Landingham** has compiled *Pictorial History of Saint Lucie County, 1565-1910* (Fort Pierce, FL: St. Lucie Historical Society, 1976). A richly illustrated book with full-color photographs of wildlife on a St. Lucie County ranch is *A Cattleman's Backcountry Florida* (Gainesville: University Presses of Florida, 1985) by the prominent Fort Pierce attorney, **Alto Adams**. **Charles S. Miley**, editor of the *Fort Pierce News Tribune* for many years, has written *Miley's Memos* (Fort Pierce, FL: Indian River Community College, 1979), recounting the area's history since 1914, and **Lucille Rights** has written *A Historical View of Fort Pierce and the Indian River Environmental Community* (Fort Pierce, FL: St. Lucie County Schools, 1979). Among the novels set in the area is *The Captain's Lady* (New York: Farrar & Rinehart, 1950) by **Basil Heatter**.

Port St. Lucie

Port St. Lucie is built along the shores of the north fork of the St. Lucie River. A Port St. Lucie resident, **Mark Jackson**, writes under the exotic pseudonym of **Kano Shinichi**. His *Ninja Men of Iga* was published in 1989 by Dragon Books, an imprint of Unique Publishing at Burbank, California.

Stuart

Stuart, named after the settlement's first telegraph operator and Florida East Coast Railway station agent, is the Martin County seat. Its earlier name, Potsdam, was changed to Stuart after railroad conductors "called out loudly as the train approached the station: 'Pots-dam, Pots dam-pots-' much to the consternation and disapproval of the 1895 ladies." The county is blessed with beautiful waterways: the Indian River, the north and south forks of the St. Lucie, and — farther to the south — the Loxahatchee River. No one writes more perceptively of these jungle rivers than **Ernest Lyons** in *My Florida* (New York: A.S. Barnes & Co., 1969):

> Their jungle scenery of cabbage palms, live-oaks and water maples, bordered by lush giant ferns, spider-lilies and custard apples, enveloped by wild asters, moon vines and fox grapes, is so dense that it takes the stiffest breeze to ripple the water.... They are precious places wrapped in a magic spell which can not endure the encroachment of housing or development. The moment a house appears on one of these banks, the illusion of being far away and deep in a jungle will be broken.

In addition to *My Florida*, Lyons has published a second volume of his columns from the *Stuart News* entitled *The Last Cracker Barrel* (New York: Newspaper Enterprise Association, 1975). In the spring of 1992 Lyons' home at 315 Seminole Street in Historic Downtown Stuart was designated a Literary Landmark by the Literary Landmarks Association.

Love of nature and concern for the environment emerge often as themes for Martin County's authors. **Edwin A. Meninger**, editor of the *Stuart News* and the brother of the founders of the famed Meninger Clinic in Topeka, Kansas, wrote *Flowering Trees of the World: For Tropics and Warm Climates* (1962), *Seaside Plants of the World* (1964), *Fantastic Trees* (1967), *Flowering Vines of the World: An Encyclopedia of Climbing Plants* (1970), *Color in the Sky: Flowering Trees in our Landscape* (1975), and *Edible Nuts of the World* (1977). **Frederic B. Stresau** wrote *Florida, My Eden* (Port Salerno, FL: Florida Classics Library, 1986) about exotic and native plants for tropical and subtropical landscaping. A powerful environmental work is *The River Killers* by **Martin Heuvelmans** (Harrisburg, PA: Stackpole Books, 1974) about the problems of the Kissimmee River Valley, Lake Okeechobee, and the St. Lucie Inlet.

Among the novelists who have lived in Stuart is **James Gould Cozzens**, winner of the 1949 Pulitzer Prize for *Guard of Honor* (New York: Harcourt, Brace, 1948), which takes place at Orlando's air force base; Cozzens died in Stuart in 1978 at the age of 74. **Sharon Sanders**'s 1987 mystery, *Night Shadows* (New York: Avalon Books), is set in Palm Lake, a fictional Martin County town. *The Jupiter Lighthouse Mystery* (Tequesta, FL: Rendezvous Publications, 1986) was written by Stuart author **Fred St. Laurent**. **Cena Christopher Draper** is the author of the popular children's book, *The Worst Hound Around* (1979). A "literary" work in nearby Jensen in the 1890s was a newspaper called *The Match-Maker*, in which one enterprising young man successfully rectified the scarcity of marriageable young women in the area; his widely circulated newspaper helped to populate the area through numerous marriages between local young men and those young women willing to leave the comforts of their childhood homes to begin a new life in the wilds of south Florida.

Sewall's Point

Sewall's Point, a high tip of land overlooking the St. Lucie and Indian rivers, was named for an early settler. **Hugh de Laussat Willoughby** served as the first president of the Sewall's Point Land Company in the 1890s. Willoughby was a remarkable man, an early automobile racer, a designer and builder of seaplanes, and a noted canoeist. In 1897 he and his navigator crossed the Everglades by canoe in just 15 days, an adventure that he described in his book, *Across the Everglades* (Philadelphia: Lippincott, 1898). A half-century later publisher **William M. Kiplinger** and his son, **Austin H. Kiplinger**, who publish *The Kiplinger Letter* and the magazine, *Changing Times*, picked Sewall's Point as their vacation home.

The Martin County Historical Society operates two museums worth visiting: the Elliott Museum, which contains the society's permanent art and historical collection, and the Gilbert's Bar House of Refuge, the only surviving refuge for shipwrecked sailors of the six built in 1876. The director of both museums, **Janet Hutchinson**, is the author of *History of Martin County* (Hutchinson Island, FL: The Martin County Historical Society, 1975).

Hobe Sound

South of Stuart an area emerges filled with confusing place names from classical Greek and Roman mythology. The Indians called the area near the Loxahatchee River Jobe or Jove, originally pronounced *Hoe-Bay*. From this the Spanish evolved the name Hobe Sound for the lower part of the Indian River. Carrying it a bit further, they named the barrier island on the east side of the waterway, Jupiter (a variation of Jove), a name which was then adopted for a Seminole War fort built farther south. That area would become Jupiter in Palm Beach County, and another town farther south would be given the name Juno. To continue the naming spree the operators of the Lake Worth Railway named two station stops on their eight-mile railroad Mars and Venus. No wonder a writer for *Harper's* magazine christened it the Celestial Railway. In the 1890s the area was jokingly called the Galaxy.

Confusion spills over to this day. The ultra-exclusive oceanside resort community on Jupiter Island is often called Hobe Sound, but the town of Hobe Sound is actually a small, working-class town on the west side of the lagoon, previously named Olympia. Little has been written about Hobe Sound; its wealthy, powerful, old-money residents, who look down on Palm Beach, prefer as low a profile as possible. **Cleveland Amory** in *The Last Resorts* (New York: Harper, 1952) has written a fascinating account of life on the island, and **Stephen Birmingham** examines the resort as one of several in Florida in his portrait of the American social establishment, *The Right People* (Boston: Little, Brown, 1968). Two notable writers have made the resort their home: the socialite playwright, **Philip Barry** (1896-1949), and the novelist, **John Marquand**, whose *The Late George Apley* won the 1938 Pulitzer Prize; Marquand (1893-1960) bought a small winter home which he called Nervana at Hobe Sound in 1946 and stayed there until he sold the house in 1952.

The first white visitors to Jupiter Island arrived on September 23, 1696, when the British barkentine, *Reformation*, foundered just off the island. Among the 24 survivors were a party of Quakers bound from Jamaica to Philadelphia. Their leader, **Jonathan Dickinson**, became the first white man to write about the life of Indian tribes along the southeast coast of Florida. His *Jonathan Dickinson's Journal or God's Protecting Providence, Being the Narrative of a Journey from Port Royal in Jamaica to Philadelphia between August 23, 1696 and April 1, 1697* was published in Philadelphia in 1699. A best-seller, it was reprinted 16 times before fading in popularity during the Civil War; Florida Classics Library of Port Salerno in southern Martin County republished it in 1988. An historical marker has been erected on U.S. 1 at the entrance to Jonathan Dickinson State Park, three miles west of the beach where the survivors made landfall.

Jupiter

Jupiter proclaims itself to the southbound traveler through its bright red lighthouse, set on a point of land where the Indian and Loxahatchee rivers meet and then flow out to sea at the treacherous Jupiter Inlet. The north-

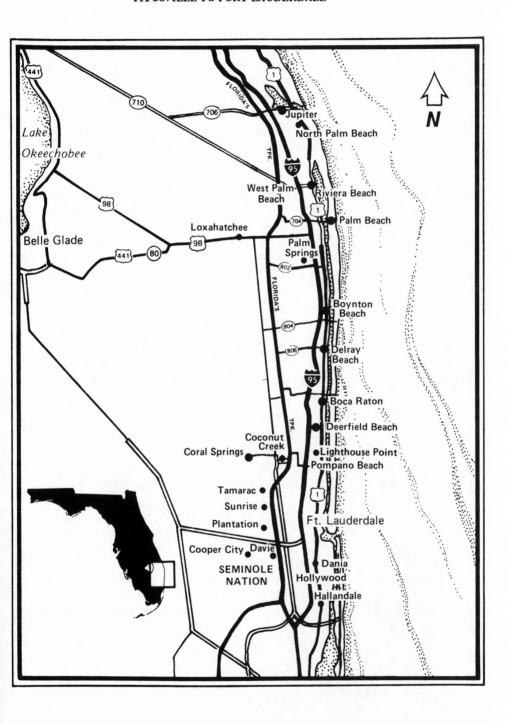

ernmost town in Palm Beach County as well as the county's oldest settlement, Jupiter dates back to 1838, when it was first called Fort Jupiter during the Second Seminole War. The lighthouse, 105 feet tall, was first lighted in 1860, then darkened for most of the Civil War.

Bessie Wilson DuBois lived much of her long life on the southside of the inlet, where Indian River steamboats completed their voyage south. She has written four short books about Jupiter and its surrounding country: *Shipwrecks in the Vicinity of Jupiter Inlet* (1975); *A History of Juno Beach and Juno, Florida* (1978); *The History of Jupiter Lighthouse* (1981); and *The History of the Loxahatchee River* (1981). More of the rich lore of the area is available in **Elsie Dolby Jackson**'s *Loxahatchee Lament: Reminiscences of Jupiter, Florida, Where Pioneers Lived into the Space Age*, Volumes 1 and 2 (Jupiter, FL: Cary Publications, 1978).

Jupiter and its sister city, Tequesta, boast two popular authors of romance novels: **Sydney A. Clary** of Jupiter and **Edith Delatush** formerly of Tequesta. Clary, who also writes as **Sara Chance** and **Sherry Carr**, is the author of 28 novels. Four, written under the Chance name, are set in Palm Beach County: *Her Golden Eyes* (New York: Silhouette, 1983), *A Touch of Passion* (New York: Silhouette, 1986), *Shadow Watch* (Toronto: Harlequin, 1988), and *Fire in the Night* (Toronto: Harlequin, 1989). Edith Delatush under her own name has written *Hand in Hand* (1985); as **Edith St. George**, she has written *Midnight Wine* (1981) and *Velvet is for Lovers* (1984); as **Alyssa Morgan**, she has written *No Other Love* (1983). Finally, *Sailor Jim's Cave* (New York: Dodd, Mead, 1951) by **W.J. Pat Enright**, the pseudonym of **Walter Joseph Enright**, is a novel that takes place near Jupiter, and *Bud Baker, Racing Swimmer* (New York: Hastings, 1962) by **C. Paul Jackson** takes place near Juno Beach to the south.

Elmore Leonard

North Palm Beach

Heading south from Jupiter, U.S.1 leads into the residential city of North Palm Beach, the home of one of America's leading tough-school crime writers, **Elmore Leonard** (1925-), who divides his time between Detroit and his winter residence in the Old Port Cove section of North Palm Beach; he formerly wintered in Pompano Beach. A master of dialogue, Leonard captures the feel, the sound, and the action of the Gold Coast crime scene. Eight of his 32 novels have been set at least in part in south Florida: *Gold Coast* (New York: Bantam, 1980); *Split Images*

(New York: Arbor House, 1981); *Cat Chaser* (New York: Arbor House, 1982); *Stick* (New York: Arbor House, 1983); *La Brava* (New York: Arbor House, 1983); *Glitz* (New York: Arbor House, 1985); *Maximum Bob* (New York: Delacorte, 1991); and *Rum Punch* (New York: Delacorte, 1992). *Split Images* deals with a Palm Beacher who murders a Haitian gardener just for the fun of it. In *La Brava* Leonard has created film noir in book form in telling the story of a former movie queen whose career had blossomed in the film-noir era. The book contains scenes in the South County Mental Health Center in Delray Beach, where his stepdaughter had once worked. *Maximum Bob*, the story of a Cracker judge in Palm Beach County, ranges from the Gold Coast towns of West Palm Beach, Boynton Beach, and Ocean Ridge all the way to the world of Belle Glade alligator poachers. Much of the action in *Rum Punch* occurs in nearby Palm Beach Gardens, including a murder in the city's big shopping mall, The Gardens. For more about this significant Florida author see **David Geherin's** *Elmore Leonard* (New York: Continuum, 1989).

Riviera Beach

South of Jupiter and North Palm Beach lies the town of Riviera Beach, which owes its name change from Oak Lawn to a chance remark of a visitor who described it as the Riviera of America. Most of the city lies west of Lake Worth, like Indian River, a coastal lagoon. Part of the city, however, occupies Singer Island, which fronts on the ocean. A winter resident who lives on the northern part of the island is the noted novelist, **Marilyn French**, one of America's most eloquent voices for the feminist cause. Her novels include the acclaimed *The Women's Room* (1977), *The Bleeding Heart* (1980), and *Her Mother's Daughter* (1987).

Riviera Beach authors have written several mysteries and suspense thrillers. A recent Mafia story is *A Present for Santa* (New York: St. Martin's Press, 1986) by **Jim Burke**, a former CIA intelligence officer and FBI agent; his book ranges from Europe to Hong Kong to Tahiti, but from time to time it touches down in Palm Beach, West Palm Beach, and even Lake Okeechobee for a little fishing action. **Tom Pace** has written three mysteries set to some extent in the Riviera Beach area: *Afternoon of a Loser* (New York: Harper, 1969); *The Treasure Hunt* (New York: Harper, 1970); and *Fisherman's Luck* (New York: Harper, 1971). *Sideswipe* (New York: St. Martin's Press, 1987), a crime novel by Miami author **Charles Willeford**, also contains scenes set in Riviera Beach in a non-oceanic subdivision called Ocean Pine Terraces. Novelist **Frederick Exley**, author of *A Fan's Notes* (1968) and *Pages from a Cold Island* (1975), stayed briefly in Riviera Beach.

A History of Riviera Beach, Florida, edited by **Lynn Brink**, was published in 1976 by the Bicentennial Commission of Riviera Beach. **Charles C. Foster** has assembled a photo-history of *Conchtown USA: Bahamanian Fisherfolk in Riviera Beach, Florida* (Boca Raton: Florida Atlantic University Press, 1991). An interesting account of the Bahamian community in the town is contained in **Stetson Kennedy's** *Palmetto Country* (1942; reprinted Tallahassee: Florida A & M University Press, 1989).

Palm Beach

In 1878 the Spanish brig, *Providencia*, washed ashore south of the Jupiter Lighthouse, laden with coconuts which soon took root on the island. In less than a decade the resulting palms would give the island its name, Palm Beach, a place that would become one of the world's ritziest winter resorts, one which would draw the attention of many writers in the years ahead.

In the late nineteenth century Henry M. Flagler, one of the founders of Standard Oil of Ohio, began building railroads and hotels along Florida's east coast. At Palm Beach he built the world's largest resort hotel, the Royal Poinciana. On the west shore of Lake Worth he constructed a service town which he named Westpalmbeach, later opened up to three words. His railroad reached West Palm Beach in 1894 at roughly the same time the hotel was finished. That winter the era of Palm Beach began.

Flagler's goal was to bring the cream of United States society to his exclusive winter resort via his railroad. Three biographies of Flagler give details of his long life: *Florida's Flagler* (Athens, GA: University of Georgia Press, 1949) by **Sidney Walter Martin**; *Henry Flagler: The Astonishing Life and Times of the Visionary Robber Baron Who Founded Florida* (New York: Macmillan, 1986) by **David Leon Chandler**; and *Flagler, Rockefeller Partner and Florida Baron* (Kent, OH: The Kent State University Press, 1988) by **Edward N. Akin**.

To give his third wife, the former Mary Lily Kenan, the mansion she craved, Flagler built Whitehall on the eastern shore of Lake Worth in 1902. The marble palace today houses both the Henry M. Flagler Museum and the tragic memories of Mary Lily. After Flagler's death in 1913 at age 83, his widow, America's wealthiest woman, married Robert Bingham, a beau from her pre-Flagler days. A strong suspicion persists to this day that he later murdered her for her money. Books that deal with the alleged murder of the mistress of Whitehall include *The Binghams of Louisville: The Dark History Behind One of America's Great Fortunes* (New York: Crown, 1987) by **David Leon Chandler**; *House of Dreams: The Bingham Family of Louisville* (New York: Random House, 1988) by **Marie Brenner**; *Passion and Prejudice: A Family Memoir* (New York: Knopf, 1989) by **Sallie Bingham**; and *The Patriarch: The Rise and Fall of the Bingham Dynasty* by **Susan E. Tifft** and **Alex S. Jones** (New York: Summit, 1991).

"The Royal Poinciana Hotel which once stood in Palm Beach was the grandest of all grand hotels of all time," wrote **Theodore Pratt** in *That Was Palm Beach* (St. Petersburg: Great Outdoors Publishing Co., 1968). The Ponce, as it was called, could accommodate as many as 2,000 guests. Its remarkable impact on American society was not lost on America's authors. The Royal Poinciana appears in many historical novels, among them Pratt's *The Flame Tree* (St. Petersburg: Great Outdoors Publishing Co., 1950), the second volume in his Palm Beach trilogy; **Thea Coy Douglass's** *Royal Poinciana* (New York: Donald I. Fine, 1987), which tells the story of people who worked at the hotel; and **Patrick Smith's** *A Land Remembered* (Sarasota: Pineapple Press, 1984), in which Smith's cowman proves a bit too rough-hewn for the hotel's snobbish pretensions. **Ring Lardner's** *Gullible's Travels*, a long short story, is a contem-

Royal Poinciana Hotel plays host to the cream of American society in the winter of 1896.

porary account; Lardner, commenting on the size of the Ponce's dining room wrote, "From one end of it to the other is a toll call."

Flagler's luxury resort did not escape the scathing assessment of the expatriate novelist, **Henry James**, who wrote in *The American Scene* (1907) of Flagler's Palm Beach world: "There as nowhere else, in America, one would find Vanity Fair in full blast...."

Even after Flagler's death the momentum of Palm Beach continued. The fashionable, illegal gambling casino of Colonel E.R. Bradley and **Addison Mizner's** Mediterranean architecture combined to enhance the glory of the resort.

The flamboyant Mizner, whose architecture was once described as "Bastard-Spanish-Moorish-Romanesque-Gothic-Renaissance-Bull-Market-Damn-the-Expense Style," has inspired a number of books, among them Pratt's novel, *The Big Bubble* (New York: Duell, Sloan & Pearce, 1951). In addition to Mizner's autobiography, *The Many Mizners* (New York: Sears, 1932), nonfiction works about him include *Florida Architecture of Addison Mizner* (New York: William Hellburn, 1928) by **Ida Tarbell**; *The Legendary Mizners* (New York: Farrar, Straus & Young, 1953) by **Alva Johnston**; *Addison Mizner* (Palm Beach: Norton Gallery and School of Art, 1977) by **Christina Orr**; *Architect to the Affluent* (Fort Lauderdale: Gale Graphics, 1983) with sketches by William Olendorf and text by **Robert Tolf**; and *Mizner's Florida* (Cambridge, MA: MIT Press, 1984) by **Donald W. Curl**. In addition, Addison Mizner's rascal of a brother has inspired two biographies: *The Fabulous Wilson Mizner* (New York: Henkle, 1935) by **Edward Dean Sullivan** and *Rogue's Progress* (New York: Putnam's, 1975) by

John Burke. Barbara D. Hoffstot's *Landmark Architecture of Palm Beach* (Pittsburgh, PA: Ober Park Associates, 1974) is also about the town's beautiful homes.

Other books and stories about Palm Beach include *The Reluctant Cinderella* (New York: Bouregy & Curl, 1952) by **Jennifer Ames (Maysie Greig)**; *White Pants Willie* (Indianapolis: Bobbs-Merrill, 1932) by **Elmer Davis;** *Dead Right* (Philadelphia: Lippincott, 1956) by **Spencer Dean (Prentice Winchell)**; one of **F. Scott Fitzgerald**'s most famous stories: "The Rich Boy" from *All the Sad Young Men* (1926); *Eileen Duggan* (1952), *Make-Believe Mother* (1958), *The Girl Outside* (1960), *Palm Beach Girl* (1962), and *Everglades Nurse* (1964) all by **Peggy Gaddis** and published by New York's Arcadia House; *Tropical Winter* (New York: Knopf, 1933) by **Joseph Hergesheimer;** *Double Down* (New York: Dutton, 1991) by **Tom Kakonis;** the Palm Beach novels of **Arthur Somers Roche**, such as *The Pleasure Buyers* (New York: Macmillan, 1925) and *Devil-May-Care* (New York: Grosset & Dunlap, 1926); and "Palm Beach Santa Claus" from *Runyon à la Carte* by **Damon Runyon** (Philadelphia: Lippincott, 1949).

A light-hearted and entertaining account of Palm Beach up until the early post-World War II era is provided by **Cleveland Amory** in *The Last Resorts* (New York: Harper, 1952). Nonfiction books on Palm Beach include *Palm Beach County: An Illustrated History* by **Donald W. Curl** (Northridge, CA: Windsor Publications, 1986); *Palm Beach* by **Hans W. Hannau** (Garden City, NY: Doubleday, 1968); *Palm Beach Houses* (New York: Rizzoli, 1991) by **Shirley Johnston;** Judge **James R. Knott**'s three short historical volumes: *Palm Beach Revisited* (1987), *Palm Beach Revisited II* (1988), and *The Mansion Builders* (1990), all self-published; *Yesterday's Palm Beach* by **Stuart McIver** (Miami: Seemann Publishing Co., 1976); *Palm Beach: The Place, the People, Its Pleasures and Palaces* by **John Ney** (Boston: Little, Brown, 1966); and *Palm Beach, A Century of Heritage* by **Wilma Bell Spencer** (Washington, DC: Mount Vernon Publishing Co., 1975).

Theodore Pratt

For many years **Theodore Pratt** (1901-1970) was the principal author mining the Palm Beach lode. Of his 35 books 17 had Florida settings. Five of them were made into movies, including his most famous novel, *The Barefoot Mailman* (New York: Duell, Sloan and Pearce, 1943), the first volume in his Palm Beach trilogy, for which he earned the title literary laureate of Florida. The story of the pioneer mailman depicted the southeast Florida of the 1880s. *The Flame Tree* (New York: Dodd,

Mead, 1950), a novel whose title is another name for the royal poinciana tree, moved forward into the 1890s with action at Flagler's huge hotel and the famous Bradley casino. The final book in the trilogy, *The Big Bubble* (New York: Duell, Sloan & Pearce, 1951), deals with the great Florida land boom of the mid-1920s. Addison Mizner appears thinly disguised as architect Adam Paine.

From 1934 till his death in 1970 Pratt lived in Lake Worth, in a Mizner house in Boca Raton, and in Delray Beach. Two other Pratt books worth noting are *Seminole* (New York: Fawcett Gold Medal Books, 1954), a novel about Osceola, and *Florida Roundabout* (New York: Duell, Sloan & Pearce, 1959), a collection of his short stories, including "Five to Seven, Palm Beach." Under the pseudonym of **Timothy Brace** he wrote four mystery novels, two of them set in Palm Beach County: *Murder Goes Fishing* (New York: Dutton, 1936), which takes place in Palm Beach, and *Murder Goes in a Trailer* (New York: Dutton, 1937), which takes place in a mobile-home park in Briny Breezes. In 1941 Pratt wrote a *Saturday Evening Post* article about the squalid living conditions in the migrant labor camps near Belle Glade; based on this material, he followed up with a screenplay for a 1942 Warner Brothers movie called *Juke Girl*, whose male lead was played by Ronald Reagan.

In the 1960s a Palm Beach resident, **Edward Albee**, whose father had been a force in vaudeville, made a major impact on America's theater. His *A Delicate Balance* (1966) and his *Seascape* (1975) each won Pulitzer prizes. His best-known work, however, was *Who's Afraid of Virginia Woolf?*, the 1963 winner of the Drama Critics Circle Award and later (1966) a successful motion picture starring Elizabeth Taylor and Richard Burton.

In the early 1960s the frequent visits to Palm Beach by President **John F. Kennedy** began to build further interest in the town. Kennedy had spent his long convalescence from a back operation during the 1950s at the Kennedy compound and there wrote his Pulitzer Prize-winning *Profiles in Courage* (1956). By the end of the decade **Richard Newhafer's** *On Wings of the Storm* (New York: Morrow, 1969) had appeared, followed shortly by the first of **John Ney's** young-adult novels about Ox Olmstead, a rich Palm Beach lad. The books in this series are *Ox, The Story of a Kid at the Top* (Boston: Little, Brown, 1970); *Ox Goes North* (New York: Harper & Row, 1973); *Ox Under Pressure* (Philadelphia: Lippincott, 1976); and *Ox and the Prime Time Kid* (Sarasota: Pineapple Press, 1985). In 1971 **Charles Willeford's** *The Burnt Orange Heresy* (New York: Crown), a suspense novel about the art business, was published.

Robert P. Davis has had four novels published: *The Pilot* (New York: Morrow, 1976); *Cat Five* (New York: Morrow, 1977), the story of a major hurricane striking Palm Beach; *Control Tower* (New York: Putnam, 1980); and *The Divorce* (1980). The popular novelist, **Phyllis A. Whitney**, turned her attention to Palm Beach in 1980 with her *Poinciana* (Garden City, NY: Doubleday). Three years later **John McIlvain** wrote *Worth Avenue* (New York: Seaview/Putnam, 1983), in which the high life of the town is symbolized by its famous street of fashionable shops and restaurants. Novelist **Arthur Maling** wrote the following about the famous Worth Avenue:

Architecturally, it was nothing to brag about. Only three blocks long, narrow and congested, it was lined on both sides with low buildings that had a vaguely Mediterranean air. But the junior-size palm trees that stood at attention along the sidewalk, the casual display of absurdly expensive merchandise in the shopwindows, the Pucci-clad women walking French poodles, the Jaguars, Porsches and Cadillac convertibles parked at the curb gave the street an atmosphere of price-be-damned prosperity that I'd never seen anywhere else.

Judith Green presents another contemporary picture of the place in *Sometimes Paradise* (New York: Knopf, 1987).

Pat Booth

The first novel to bear the name of the town was **Cornelius Vanderbilt, Jr.**'s *Palm Beach* (New York: Macaulay, 1931), a love story about a poor boy and a rich girl. More than a half-century later **Pat Booth** picked the same name for her blockbuster novel, the most popular book ever written about the ritzy watering hole. The novel has been described accurately as "steamy," a story from the "land of sun-drenched sex and champagne-drenched parties." A Londoner, Booth now lives in Palm Beach a short distance from the Kennedy compound. In 1985 *Palm Beach* was published in hardback by Crown and in its many paperback editions by Ballantine. The action moves through many familiar Palm Beach settings: Worth Avenue, the Flagler Museum, Cafe L'Europe, the Kennedy compound, even Green's Drug Store. Following the success of *Palm Beach*, Booth wrote *The Sisters* (1987); *Beverly Hills* (New York: Crown, 1989), containing scenes in the Everglades area near Lake Okeechobee; and *Malibu*, (1990). In *Miami* (New York: Crown, 1992) she returned to south Florida for her story locale.

Booth's *Palm Beach*, which she dedicated to **Roxanne Pulitzer** after meeting her at an aerobics class, presents as its heroine Lisa Starr, a West Palm Beach aerobics instructor. Lisa, however, is not based on Pulitzer, whose stormy life is a compelling story in its own right. Following a celebrated divorce trial in which she lost the custody of her twin sons, **Roxanne Pulitzer** with **Kathleen Maxa** wrote a best-selling nonfiction account of her experiences: *The Prize Pulitzer* (New York: Villard, 1987). Her second book, *Twins* (New York: Villard, 1990), deals with the long-term effect of divorce on children in a

Roxanne Pulitzer

decadent Palm Beach society. Her third book, *Facades* (New York: Villard, 1992), is set in the Palm Beaches, New York, and Aspen.

Palm Beach is the setting for **Bob Shacochis**'s short story, "Hot Day on the Gold Coast," published in *Easy in the Islands* (New York: Crown, 1985). **Terry Cline** has written a crime novel, *Reaper* (New York: Donald I. Fine, 1989), about a psycho who seeks revenge after a Palm Beach psychic ruins his life with her astrological forecasts. **Dan Norman** and **Kristy Montee**, a husband-wife team writing under the penname, **Kristy Daniels**, set scenes in their 1987 novel, *Hot Type* (New York: Fawcett), at Whitehall and at the Palm Beach Polo Club west of downtown in Wellington.

Other novels about Palm Beach are **George Abbot's** *Tryout* (New York: Playboy, 1979); **Rory Harrity's** *Customer's Man* (Englewood Cliffs, NJ: Prentice-Hall, 1969); **Richard** and **Frances Lockridge's** *With One Stone, A Captain Heimrich Mystery* (Philadelphia: Lippincott, 1961); **Arthur Maling's** *Loophole* (New York: Harper and Row, 1971); **M.M. Parker's** *Big Phil's Kid* (New York: Meredith Press, 1969); and **Eleanor Ratigan's** *Deep Water* (New York: Lothrop, Lee & Shepard, 1961).

Palm Beach was for a time the home of **Morris West** (1916-), author of novels of intrigue and adventure. His most famous work was *The Shoes of the Fisherman* (1963). The city was also the residence of writer **Terry Garrity,** who was first known to the reading public as "**J**"; her 1970 best-seller was called *The Sensuous Woman*. Later with her author/brother **John Garrity**, she wrote *Story of "J": The Author of The Sensuous Woman Tells the Bitter Price of Her Crazy Success* (1984). John Garrity is the author of several books on sports, including *The George Brett Story* (1981) and *The Traveler's Guide to Baseball Spring Training* (Kansas City: Andrews and McMeel, 1990).

West Palm Beach

Many of the books about Palm Beach contain numerous scenes in West Palm Beach, a city so close that action flows back and forth between the two locales. A notable book set in West Palm Beach is **Warren Adler's** *The Sunset Gang* (New York: Viking, 1977), a collection of short stories about life at Century Village, a predominantly Jewish retirement community on the west side of town that his parents had lived in. **Lucia St. Clair Robson**, who had first read about Osceola in her fourth-grade class in West Palm Beach, years later wrote *Light a Distant Fire*, a novel about the great Seminole leader (New York: Ballantine, 1988). Her latest novel, her fourth, *The Tokaido Road* (1991), is set in feudal Japan. **Louis Capron** wrote many books and articles about the Seminoles and the Seminole wars, among them *The Gold Arrowhead* (New York: Howell, Soskin, 1943); *The Blue Witch* (New York: Henry Holt, 1957); *White Moccasins* (New York: Howell, Soskin, 1963); and *The Red War Pole* (Indianapolis: Bobbs-Merrill, 1963). For murals from one of the area's most famous books, **Theodore Pratt**'s *The Barefoot Mailman* (New York: Duell, Sloan and Pearce, 1943), see the main post office in West Palm Beach; in 1940 artist Stevan Dohanos placed there six large paintings depicting scenes of the way barefoot mailmen carried mail along the beaches from the Jupiter Lighthouse to Miami in the 1880s.

Shortly before World War II, **Edwin O'Connor** worked as a radio announcer for the West Palm Beach station WJNO, which would later also employ Roxanne Pulitzer. O'Connor, who based his novel *The Oracle* (Boston: Little, Brown, 1951) on that experience, also wrote the memorable *The Last Hurrah* (1956) about an Irish-American politician's final run for office and *The Edge of Sadness* (1961), which won the 1962 Pulitzer Prize for fiction. **Paul Patti** drew heavily on his experience as a Lake Worth police officer to write *Silhouettes* (New York: St. Martin's Press, 1990), a mystery about a husband and wife detective team based in West Palm Beach. **Scott Eyman**, film critic for the *Palm Beach Post*, has written three books on the movies: *Flashback: A Brief History of Film* (1986), co-authored with **Louis Giannetti**; *Five American Cinematographers* (1987); and *Mary Pickford: America's Sweetheart* (1990).

In her *Public Faces, Private Lives: Women in South Florida, 1870s-1910s* (Miami: Pickering Press, 1990) **Karen Davis** focuses on early south Florida as seen through the eyes of the women who cooked the meals, washed the clothes, taught the children, and, all too often, lived out their days in loneliness and isolation.

Growth and water are at the heart of south Florida's environmental problems. **Lamar Johnson**, chief engineer of the Central and Southern Florida Flood Control District, traced the state's water-control problems from the nineteenth century into the 1950s in his *Beyond the Fourth Generation* (Gainesville: University Presses of Florida, 1974). **John Strawn**'s *Driving the Green: The Making of a Golf Course* (New York: HarperCollins, 1991) observes Palm Beach County's environmental problems from a different point of view; in telling his story of how a real-estate developer's golf course is built, Strawn presents a contemporary picture of the strains between growth and environmental concerns. The golf course, Ironhorse, is built on land once owned by Henry Flagler and later by billionaire John D. MacArthur, Florida's wealthiest resident and largest landowner in the latter half of the twentieth century. Developer MacArthur, the brother of Charles MacArthur, co-author of the famous play, *The Front Page* (1928), is the subject of *The Stockholder* (New York: Lyle Stuart, 1969) by **William Hoffman**.

Just to the west of West Palm Beach lies the developer community of Wellington, named after the Duke of Wellington. The town has the Palm Beach Polo Club, which appears in Booth's *Palm Beach* and *The Prize Pulitzer* as well as in *Hot Type.* The community is also the home of **Robert Lacey,** author of *Little Man,* (Boston: Little, Brown, 1991), a biography of the famed south Florida mobster, Meyer Lansky. Lacey's other works include *Ford: The Men and the Machine* (1986) and a number of books about royal families in Great Britain and Saudi Arabia.

Loxahatchee

Just beyond Wellington, Palm Beach County assumes a decidedly agricultural vista. Loxahatchee is best known for its citrus groves and for an attraction named Lion Country Safari. **Frederick Buechner**'s *Lion Country* (New York: Atheneum, 1971), a book about a shady clergyman who operates in the West Palm Beach area, contains scenes set at the animal park. The name *Loxahatchee,* which is Armadillo in the book, is Seminole for *turtle creek.* It traces its name, however, not to the river, which lies to the north, but to the nearby Loxahatchee Slough.

Belle Glade

To the west, Palm Beach County fronts on Lake Okeechobee, the second-largest freshwater lake totally within one state in the United States. (Lake Michigan is the largest.) Appropriately, its name is an Indian word meaning *big water.* Water flowing south from the lake feeds into the Everglades. Drainage of the Glades in the early twentieth century produced rich farmland where winter vegetables and sugarcane are grown, usually by large agribusinesses. Of particular interest to the many authors who have written about the lake country have been the migrant laborers and two deadly hurricanes which struck the area in the 1920s.

The climax of **Zora Neale Hurston**'s masterwork, *Their Eyes Were Watching God* (Philadelphia: Lippincott, 1937, reprinted in paperback, University of Illinois Press, 1978), occurs near Belle Glade (the belle of the Glades) where Janie and Tea Cake have gone to work in the fields. "To Janie's strange eyes, everything in the Everglades was big and new. Big Lake Okechobee [sic], big beans, big cane, big weeds, big everything.... Ground so rich that everything went wild.... People wild too." Tragically the winds were wild when they came in September 1928 and drove the water into the fields, killing nearly 2,000 people. "It [the wind] woke up old Okechobee [sic] and the monster began to roll in his bed. Began to roll and complain like a peevish world on a grumble."

The wind that "woke up" the lake formed the heart of **Lawrence E. Will**'s *Okeechobee Hurricane and the Hoover Dike* (St. Petersburg: Great Outdoors Publishing Co., 1978), the best nonfiction account of the devastating hurricane, one of the worst storms in American history. Will wrote five local-color books on the lake country, all published by Great Outdoors Publishing Company of St. Petersburg. The others were *Cracker History of Okeechobee* (1964), *Okeechobee Boats and Skippers* (1965), *Okeechobee Catfishing* (1965), and *Swamp to Sugar Bowl: Pioneer Days in Belle Glade* (1968). The Lawrence E. Will Museum at the Belle Glade Library preserves much of the lore of the lake.

"You either hate this swamp and you leave it, or you hate it and **remain,**" **John Dufresne** writes of Belle Glade in his short story, "What Follows in the Wake of Love," published in *The Way Water Enters Stone*, a collection of short stories (New York: Norton, 1991). **Elmore Leonard** used Belle Glade as a setting in *Maximum Bob* (New York: Delacorte, 1991), as did **Nell H. Scullen** in *Cam* (New York: Pageant, 1951). **Judith Richards**, like her husband, author **Terry Cline**, has been drawn to Palm Beach County settings; her *Summer Lightning* (New York: St. Martin's, 1978) and *After the Storm* (Atlanta: Peachtree, 1987) tell of the area through a young boy's eyes.

Nearly all of this country's sugarcane is grown in the rich black soil near the shores of the lake. **Alec Wilkinson**'s *Big Sugar: Seasons in the Cane Fields of Florida* (New York: Knopf, 1989) is a damning exposé of the industry and its exploitation of migrant labor.

Palm Springs

A return to the east leads into Palm Springs on the south side of West Palm Beach. The town is the home of **Angelica Carpenter** and her mother, **Jean Shirley**, co-authors of two biographies for young people: *Frances Hodgson Burnett: Beyond the Secret Garden* (1990) and *L. Frank Baum: Royal Historian of Oz* (1992). Carpenter, a Palm Springs librarian, is also executive director of the Book Fest of the Palm Beaches, an annual celebration of books and reading. A novel that takes place in the area is *The Samson Touch* by **Charles Whited** (New York: Signet, 1975).

Lake Country

Early settlers referred to the group of communities at the lower end of Lake Worth as lake country. From these would emerge Lake Worth, Hypoluxo, Lantana, Boynton Beach, Briny Breezes, and Ocean Ridge. In 1872 the Pierce family of Chicago came to a Lake Worth island called Hypoluxo, a Seminole word for *big water all around — no get out*. Young **Charles W. Pierce** wrote a lengthy manuscript about growing into manhood on Lake Worth in the days before Flagler. Edited by Professor **Donald Walter Curl** of Florida Atlantic University, his story, *Pioneer Life in Southeast Florida* (Coral Gables, FL: University of Miami Press, 1970), contains a first-hand account of the duties of the barefoot mailman. Pierce was one of that hardy breed.

A later history of the area is *Early Lantana, Her Neighbors and More* by **Mary Collar Linehan** (St. Petersburg: Byron Kennedy & Co., 1980). Lantana, named for a tropical plant that grows in the area, would in time win a measure of publishing fame as the home of the *National Enquirer*.

Martha Moffett of Lake Worth uses Briney [sic] Breezes as the setting for her 1989 novel, *Keepaway* (New York: Bantam), the story of a woman's battle to retain custody of her son. The novel also makes excellent use of another famous piece of south Florida landscape: Interstate 95. Ocean Ridge, just to the north, appears as a locale in Elmore Leonard's *Maximum Bob* (1991).

Boynton Beach

Boynton Beach, named for its founder, Major Nathan Boynton, is the scene of many of the interlocking events that make up the narrative in *The Kneeling Bus* (New York: Ticknor & Fields, 1990) by **Beverly Coyle**. The author, now an English professor at Vassar College, weaves a gentle, humorous tale about Carrie Willis, a young girl growing up in the 1950s, the daughter of a liberal Methodist minister. Ann Peyton of Florida Atlantic University's English department has called Coyle "the southern Protestant's answer to Flannery O'Connor."

An unusual husband-wife team of authors resides in Boynton Beach: **Rob** and **Trish MacGregor**. They have written one book together: *The Making of Miami Vice* (New York: Ballantine, 1986), the story of the television series. Rob has written six others under two different names, and Trish has written 12 mysteries under three different names. Most of her books under the name of **Alison Drake** take place in the Florida Keys. As **Trish Janeshutz** and **T.J. MacGregor** she has positioned most of her mysteries in the Miami area. In her two most recent T.J. MacGregor books she makes use of Palm Beach County locales: the Everglades in *Kin Dread* (New York: Ballantine, 1990) and Lake Okeechobee and West Palm Beach in *Death Flats* (New York: Ballantine, 1991). Four of Rob MacGregor's books are about Indiana Jones, an archaeologist who operates in the movies far from Florida.

Rob and Trish Janeshutz MacGregor

Boynton Beach was also the home of **Pat Frank** (1908-1964), who wrote the best-selling *Alas, Babylon*, first published in 1959 and reprinted by Bantam Books in 1976. Nearby Everglades settings appear, too, in short-story anthologies and collections. For example, *Stalkers* (New York: New American Library, 1990) contains "Lizardman" by **Robert R. McCammon**, and *Starwind* (Columbus, OH: Ohio State University Press, 1978) has "Skunk Ape Retreat" by **Ginger Curry** of Boynton Beach. For more about the role of the Catholic Church in the area see *Catholicism in South Florida, 1868-1968* (Gainesville: University Presses of Florida, 1984) by **Father**

Michael J. McNally, a professor of history at the local St. Vincent de Paul Regional Seminary.

Delray Beach

Directly south of Boynton Beach is the resort city of Delray Beach, whose name is possibly a corruption of the Spanish *del rey*, meaning *of the king*, or as some believe simply a name adopted from a neighborhood in Detroit. Whatever its origin the city acquired a reputation in the 1930s and 1940s as an artists' colony, attracting poets, authors, and cartoonists. The artist **Woody Cowan** created Our Boarding House, starring Major Hoople, while **Fontaine Fox** produced the popular comic strip, Toonerville Trolley. In 1936-1937 the distinguished poet, **Edna St. Vincent Millay,** lived in Delray Beach. Many members of this informal group met for breakfast at the Arcade Tap Room on Atlantic Avenue. For more information about these writers see **Lora Sinks Britt's** *My Gold Coast: South Florida in Earlier Years* (Palatka, FL: Brittany House Publishers, 1984).

In 1958 **Theodore Pratt** moved from his home in the Old Floresta section of Boca Raton to a more secluded spot on Delray's Brady Boulevard. During this period he wrote *Handsome's Seven Women* (Greenwich, CT: Fawcett, 1959); *Tropical Disturbance* (New York: Fawcett Gold Medal Books, 1961); *The Lovers of Pompeii* (Derby, CT: Monarch Books, 1961); *The White God* (1963); and *The Money* (New York: Duell, Sloan and Pearce, 1965).

The early days of Delray Beach are described in *The Lonesome Road* (Miami: Center Printing, 1965) by **Olive Chapman Lauther.** Highland Beach, just south of oceanside Delray is the home of two travel writers and restaurant critics: **Robert Tolf,** who has also written a book on Mizner: *Addison Mizner, Architect to the Affluent* (Fort Lauderdale: Gale Graphics, 1983); and **Molly Arost Staub,** author of *Pirate's Passion* (1990). A novel set in the area is **Robert Wilder's** *Walk With Evil* (New York: Fawcett, 1957).

Boca Raton

The southernmost city in Palm Beach County is Boca Raton, a name that is a variation of the Spanish for *rat's mouth*, thought by some to be a reference to dangerous rocks in the Boca Raton Inlet. The city, which has developed into a prestigious address for business and affluent winter residents, is also the location for Florida Atlantic University (FAU). For more about this school see **Roger H. Miller's** *Florida Atlantic University: Its Beginnings and Early Years, The Inside Story* (Boca Raton: Florida Atlantic University, 1989).

Shortly before his death in 1970, **Theodore Pratt** donated his collection of notes, manuscripts, correspondence with his publishers, and records of manuscript submissions and rejections to FAU. The Theodore Pratt Room at the S.E. Wimberly Library houses the collection, along with his easy chair, books, photographs, a painting, and other Pratt memorabilia. FAU also houses the **Thomas Burnett Swann** Collection. Swann (1928-1976), a member of the FAU faculty, wrote a number of fantasy books and short stories as well as poems and one book of literary criticism, *The Classical World of H.D.*, a study of the poetry of Hilda Doolittle (1963). Among his books are *Wolfwinter* (1971), winner of the Phoenix Award for fantasy, and *The Tournament of Thorns* (1976). Seven of his novels have been published in Germany. The Thomas Burnett Swann Fund has been used to underwrite science-fiction and fantasy conferences at FAU and to encourage writing, teaching, and research into these genres. For a closer look at the author, see *Thomas Burnett Swann: A Brief Critical Biography and Annotated Bibliography* (Boca Raton: Florida Atlantic University Foundation, 1979) by **Robert A. Collins**, professor of English at FAU. Dr. Collins, with Robert Latham, a Stanford University graduate student, formerly of Boca Raton, edits *Science Fiction & Fantasy Book Review Annual*, containing short reviews and scholarly essays.

Several FAU faculty members have written noteworthy books, among them the historical works of **Donald Curl** and several books on the Seminoles by **Harry A. Kersey, Jr.** Professor Kersey's *Pelts, Plumes, and Hides: White Traders among the Seminole Indians, 1870-1930* (Gainesville: University Presses of Florida, 1975) examines the Indian trading posts established in South Florida after the Seminole Wars. Other books by Kersey include *The Seminole World of Tommy Tiger* (Tallahassee: Florida State Division of Archives, 1982), a young-adult novel co-authored with **Voncile Mallory**, and *The Florida Seminoles and The New Deal, 1933-42* (Boca Raton: Florida Atlantic University Press, 1989). **Robert J. Huckshorn**, Florida Atlantic University's Associate Vice President for Academic Affairs, Boca Raton and Northern Palm Beach Center, author of 10 books on American politics, has edited *The Government and Politics of Florida* (Gainesville: University of Florida Press, 1991). **Julian Rice**, professor of English, also writes about the American Indian; he has written three books about the Sioux: *Lakota Story Telling: Black Elk, Ella DeLoria and Frank Fools Crow* (1989), *Black Elk's Story, Distinguishing Its Lakota Purpose* (1991), and *Deer Women and Elk Men, The Lakota Narrative of Ella DeLoria* (1992). **Carol McGuirk** is the author of a book on Scotland's favorite poet: *Robert Burns and the Sentimental Era* (1985). Poet **Susan Mitchell**, Mary Blossom Lee Professor in Creative Writing at FAU, has written two books of poetry: *The Water Inside the Water* (1983) and *Rapture* (1992). **Faith Berry**, associate professor, English, is the author of a biography of a noted black writer, *Langston Hughes: Before and Beyond Harlem* (1983). In addition she edited and wrote the introduction to *Good Morning, Revolution: Uncollected Social Protest Writings by Langston Hughes* (1992).

Boca Raton is also the home of **Otto Bettmann** (1903-), founder of the famed Bettmann Archive, one of the world's great picture libraries, and director of FAU's Department of Pictorial Research. Among his many books are *The Good Old Days — They Never Were* (1974), *The Bettmann Archive Picture History of the World* (1978), *The Delights of Reading: Quotes, Notes & Anecdotes* (1987), and the autobiographical *The Picture Man* (Gainesville: University of Florida Press, 1992).

A winter resident of Boca Raton is **Arthur Ashe, Jr.**, the first African-American to win the Wimbledon men's tennis championship. Ashe is the author of the three-volume *A Hard Road to Glory: A History of the African-Ameri-*

can Athlete (1988). **Drollene Brown** has written two juvenile nonfiction books: *Sybil Rides for Independence* (1985) and *Belva Lockwood Wins Her Case* (1987). For a history of Boca Raton see **Jacqueline Ashton's** *Boca Raton: From Pioneer Days to the Fabulous Twenties* (Boca Raton: Dedication Press, 1979). For more about one of the most grandiose buildings in the city, the Boca Raton Hotel and Club, see **Stanley Johnson's** *Once Upon a Time, The Story of Boca Raton* (Miami, Seemann Publishing, 1979). For a selection of oral interviews of residents and a history of the black settlement in Boca Raton see **Arthur S. Evans, Jr.** and **David Lee's** *Pearl City, Florida: A Black Community Remembers* (Boca Raton: Florida Atlantic University Press, 1990).

Deerfield Beach

Set in the northeast corner of Broward County, Deerfield Beach owes its name to its early deer population. In his *Hunting and Fishing in Florida, Including a Key to the Water Birds Known to Occur in the State* (1896; New York: Arno, 1970), **Charles B. Cory** (1857-1921) described the hunting grounds near the Hillsboro River, where he stalked not only deer but also panther. The first naturalist to study the Florida panther, Cory has been memorialized in the zoological name of the big cat: *Felis concolor coryi*. An article he wrote about the animal has been reprinted in **Jim Bob Tinsley's** *The Florida Panther* (St. Petersburg: Great Outdoors Publishing Co., 1970).

Among the authors who made Deerfield Beach their home was **Susan B. Anthony** (1917-1991), grandniece and namesake of the famous suffragist. Dr. Anthony, a feminist herself, has written eight books, including her autobiography, *The Ghost in My Life* (1979). **Mary Unterbrink** has written *Jazz Women at the Keyboard* (1983), *Funny Women* (1987), and *Manatees: Gentle Giants in Peril* (St. Petersburg: Great Outdoors Publishing Co., 1984), a book which has gone into more than a dozen printings.

Dr. **Nelson M. Blake** (1908-), Syracuse University professor of history and author of such books as *The Road to Reno: A History of Divorce in the United States* (1962), *Novelists' America: Fiction as History, 1910-1940* (1969), and *A History of American Life and Thought* (1972), retired to Deerfield Beach, then found himself fascinated by Florida's battles with its water problems; he had earlier written *Water For the Cities: A History of the Urban Water Supply Problem in the United States* (1956). The result of his research was *Land Into Water — Water Into Land: A History of Water Management in Florida* (Tallahassee: University Presses of Florida, 1980), a highly acclaimed study of the state's water policies.

Coral Springs

One of the newest towns in Broward County, Coral Springs, named after Coral Ridge Properties, the company that developed it, is the locale of a novel reaching considerably further back in time than the town's founding in 1963. As **Lynn Armistead McKee** dug with the Broward County Archaeological Society on sites in the Coral Springs/Parkland area, she looked back 2,500 years into a prehistoric world. From these glimpses came *A Woman of the Mists* (New York: Berkley, 1991), a coming-of-age story in an America long before the arrival of white settlers, and *Touches the Stars* (New York: Diamond Books, 1992).

Coral Springs is the home of **Joyce Sweeney** and the setting for her fourth young-adult novel, *Face the Dragon* (New York: Delacorte, 1990). Much of the action occurs at a mythical high school, based roughly on Coral Springs High, while other scenes occur at the adjacent city of Coconut Creek and at the Anglin Pier in Lauderdale-by-the-Sea. An earlier book, *Center Line* (New York: Delacorte, 1984), winner of the 1984 Delacorte Award for a first novel, makes extensive use of Daytona Beach and Ormond Beach locales. Sweeney's other books are *Right Behind the Rain* (1987), *The Dream Collector* (1989), and *Piano Man* (1992).

Coral Springs author of historical romances is **Robyn Carr**, whose *Chelynne* (1980), *The Blue Falcon* (1981), and *The Braeswood Tapestry* (1984), were all published by Little, Brown. For the history of a very young city see *Coral Springs: The First Twenty-five Years* by **Stuart McIver** (Norfolk, VA: Donning Co., 1988).

Coconut Creek

Coconut Creek, named for its palm trees and waterways, is the location of the north campus of Broward Community College. It is also the home of **Sidney Pink**, the author of *So You Want to Make Movies: My Life as an Independent Film Producer* (1990). Pink used to produce "spaghetti Westerns" in Europe; in Hollywood he gave Dustin Hoffman his first movie role. Pink also produced the first commercial 3-D color feature film, *Bwana Devil* (1952), starring Robert Stack and Barbara Britton.

Pompano Beach

Named for the delicious fish caught off its shores, Pompano Beach, the second-oldest city in Broward County, was for many years a major producer of winter vegetables, but is now better known as an oceanside resort and the winter home of the Goodyear blimp. A number of famous authors have lived here: **Henry Klinger** (1908-), **Lawrence Sanders** (1920-), **Jerome Weidman** (1913-), and **Elmore Leonard** (1925-). Klinger, who was born in New York City and moved to Florida in 1969, was executive story-editor for Twentieth Century-Fox for 40 years and was involved in the making of such films as *The Grapes of Wrath*, *The Boston Strangler*, and *The Poseidon Adventure*; his novels include *Lust for Murder* (1966) and *Three Cases of Shomri Shomar*.

Most of the crime novels by Sanders, who lives in an oceanfront condominium, are set in New York, for example *The Anderson Tapes* (1970), *The First Deadly Sin* (1973) and the series of "sin" books that followed, and *The Sixth Commandment* (1979) and a series of "commandment" books. His 1982 *The Case of Lucy Bending* (New York: Putnam, 1982) and his 1991 *McNally's Secret* (New York: Putnam), however, take place on Florida's Gold Coast. Like Sanders, Weidman also used New York locales extensively in most of his novels, such as his 1937 *I Can Get It For You Wholesale*. His successful adaptation of this work for the stage introduced Barbra Streisand to Broadway. Weidman also wrote *Fourth Street East* (1971), *Tiffany Street* (1975), *Before You Go* (1976), *The Price Is Right* (1976), *The Sound of Bow Bells* (1962), *The Temple* (1977), and *Family Fortune* (New York: Simon & Schuster, 1978), a story that takes place in the Pompano Beach area.

Of the four authors cited here only Elmore Leonard, who knows the scene well, has made extensive use of area locales in his books. In 1968 he bought his mother a small motel a block away from the ocean, and that may have given him data for the *Cat Chaser* (New York: Arbor House, 1982), in which his protagonist, George Moran, runs the Coconut Palms Resort Apartments on Pompano Beach. A guest observes that the motel sports no palm trees. "Some bugs ate 'em," said Moran.

Pompano's Farmers' Market west of the resort area served as a significant locale in Miami author **Jim Shaffer**'s *Peterbilt to Laredo* (New York: St. Martin's, 1989), the story of a truck driver's eventful trip from Pompano to Texas; Peterbilt is the top-of-the-line in American trucks. Pompano Beach is also the setting for part of **Beverly Coyle**'s fictional work, *The Kneeling Bus* (New York: Ticknor & Fields, 1990). **Opal Menius**, a Pompano resident, is the author of three books for juveniles: *The Empty Cup* (1951), which has been translated into German; *Patsy's Best Summer* (1959); and *No Escape* (New York: Elsevier/Nelson Books, 1979), which utilizes the beaches of south Florida in its story line. Menius has conducted numerous writing workshops in the South and participated in the first Liberian Writers Workshop in Monrovia, West Africa. The Gold Coast is also the setting for two novels worth mentioning: **Sholem Asch**'s *Passage in the Night* (New York: Putnam's Sons, 1953), which takes place between Palm Beach and Hollywood, Florida; and **Philip Wylie**'s *They Both Were Naked* (Garden City, NY: Doubleday, 1965), a fishing story which takes place between Palm Beach and Fort Lauderdale.

Two other area authors deserve mention. The child of deaf parents, **Ruth Sidransky** wrote *In Silence: Growing Up Hearing in a Deaf World* (1989), a book that showed deep insight into the world of the hearing-impaired and one that made her a sought-after lecturer around the country. **Tucker Halleran**, a winter resident of Lighthouse Point, wrote a pair of crime novels that featured a private eye named Cam McCardle in a town called Cypress Beach: *A Cool Clear Death* (New York: St. Martin's, 1984), which is set in the Broward area and Daytona Beach, and *Sudden Death Finish* (New York: St. Martin's, 1985), which deals with organized crime in settings ranging from Gold Coast trailer parks to a Key West artists' colony.

Lighthouse Point is also the home of **Stuart McIver**, whose seven books on south Florida are *Yesterday's Palm Beach* (Miami: Seemann Publishing Co., 1976); *The Greatest Sale on Earth* (Miami: Seemann Publishing Co., 1980); *Fort Lauderdale and Broward County: An Illustrated History* (Woodland Hills, CA: Windsor Publications, 1983); *100 Years on Biscayne Bay* (Coconut Grove, FL: Biscayne Bay Yacht Club, 1987); *Coral Springs: The First Twenty-five Years* (Norfolk, VA: Donning Co., 1988); *Glimpses of South Florida History* (Miami:

Florida Flair Books, 1988); and *True Tales of the Everglades* (Miami: Florida Flair Books, 1989).

Among the other novels set in the area are *Mary Jane Tonight at Angels Twelve* (Garden City, NY: Doubleday, 1972) by **Martin Caidin**; *The Venture* (Nashville, TN: Charter House, 1978) by **Jack Cummings**; *Blood Coast* (Smithtown, NY: Exposition, 1980) by **Michael Gora**; and *Spaniard's Gift* (New York: Pocket Books, 1977) by **Elizabeth Welles**.

Fort Lauderdale

Broward's county seat and largest city, Fort Lauderdale was incorporated in 1913 and has developed into a world-famous resort and cruise port as well as the financial and cultural center of Florida's second most populous county. Founded as a fort in 1838, during the Second Seminole War, Fort Lauderdale traces its name back to Major William Lauderdale, who built a stockade on the banks of the New River. He was really a minor character in the history of Florida, as evidenced in **Cooper Kirk**'s biography, *William Lauderdale: General Andrew Jackson's Warrior* (Fort Lauderdale: Manatee Press, 1982). A second temporary fort was built on the river, and a third, more substantial fortification was added to Fort Lauderdale in an area now called Bahia Mar. For more about early Fort Lauderdale see *Historical, Mysterious, Picturesque New River* compiled by **Austin Smith** (Fort Lauderdale: Friends of the Library of Fort Lauderdale, Florida, 1979).

The Bahia Mar area was the site of Broward County's first and last legal hanging. On August 17, 1929, convicted murderer, rumrunner, and alien smuggler James Horace Alderman was hanged for killing a Secret Service agent and two Coast Guardsmen when they tried to stop his smuggling of illicit whiskey. A federal judge in Jacksonville ordered that Alderman be hanged in Dade County, but officials there claimed they did not know how to hang anyone, and so the site was moved to the Coast Guard station in Fort Lauderdale. One of the Coast Guardsmen present, 17-year-old **Hal M. Caudle**, later wrote a book about the execution: *The Hanging at Bahia Mar* (Fort Lauderdale: Wake-Brook House, 1976). Also see "Rumrunner's Career Ends in Hanging" by **Darrell Eiland** in *Mostly Sunny Days: A* Miami Herald *Salute to South Florida's Heritage* edited by **Bob Kearney** (Miami: Miami Herald, 1986), pp. 152-155. **Marjory Stoneman Douglas** wrote about such rumrunning in "Twenty Minutes Late for Dinner," which is collected in *Nine Florida Stories by Marjory Stoneman Douglas* edited by **Kevin M. McCarthy** (Jacksonville: University of North Florida Press, 1990), pp. 74-96.

Bahia Mar was also the home of one of America's most famous fictional detectives, **John D. MacDonald**'s Travis McGee. MacDonald (1916-1986), who called McGee "a knight in slightly tarnished armor — a thinking man's Robin Hood," wrote 21 McGee novels, each of them bearing a color in its title, from the first, *The Deep Blue Good-By* (Greenwich, CT: Fawcett, 1964), to the last, *The Lonely Silver Rain* (New York: Knopf, 1985). The action of the McGee stories ranged across a large landscape, but all of them started at Slip F18. There was, in fact, no Slip F18, but the Bahia Mar Resort and Yachting Center, which lies

Aerial, Bahia Mar Marine, home of Travis McGee.

between Fort Lauderdale Beach on Route A1A and the Intracoastal Waterway, renamed Slip 610 and marked it with a plaque. On February 21, 1987, the Literary Landmarks Association designated Slip F18 a literary landmark and gave countless MacDonald fans a site to commemorate one of Florida's most popular writers, a man who could write such passages as the following about his detective-hero's boat:

> Somebody came burbling into their slip, and the *Busted Flush* heaved a little, sighed a little, as the slow bow wave came by.... Another surge moved the *Flush*. In the sense of movement a boat is a living thing. It is a companion in the night. Each boat has its own manner and character. The *Flush* is an amiable, stubborn old brute. Like a fat dog, she can be made to run, but not for very long, and then will pretend more exhaustion than she feels.

For more about this significant writer and his detective/protagonist see *John D. MacDonald and the Colorful World of Travis McGee* by **Frank D. Campbell, Jr.** (San Bernardino, CA: Borgo Press, 1977).

One of MacDonald's last pieces of writing was commissioned by the Library of Congress through its Center for the Book and its affiliate, the Florida Center for the Book. Entitled *Reading for Survival* (Washington, DC: Library of Congress, 1987), the small book, which starts at Slip F 18, presents MacDonald's views on the importance of reading. This work, which takes the form of a dialogue between Travis and his friend Meyer, was completed just a few months before MacDonald's death on December 28, 1986.

A close-up of Slip F 18.

Long before MacDonald made Bahia Mar the subject of fiction, a writer of vast popularity appeared at the site. His name was **Edward Zane Carroll Judson** (1823-1886), but the reading public knew him as **Ned Buntline**, the originator of the dime novel. Ned served in the Fort Lauderdale area during the Second Seminole War and later wrote his "Sketches of the Florida War," which were published in *Western Library and Journal and Monthly Magazine* in 1844-1845. After his dishonorable discharge from the army during the Civil War, he headed west, met William F. Cody, gave him the name Buffalo Bill, and wrote sensationalized dime novels about a new American hero.

Since Buntline, many famous authors have made their way to Fort Lauderdale. Among those who have lived in the city are **John Knowles** (1926-), author of *A Separate Peace* (1959) and winner of the William Faulkner Award, and **Dick Francis** (1920-), whose crime novels of the horse-racing world have captured a worldwide readership. Their books are set in distant locations. Not so the 1960 novel that **Glendon Swarthout** wrote. His *Where the Boys Are* (New York: Random House), a tale of the rites of spring break, brought more attention to Fort Lauderdale than any other book ever written about it, an effect intensified further when it was made into a popular 1960 motion picture. The beach became so overrun with vacationing college students in later years that the city took measures to discourage their annual spring madness.

Just after World War II ended, a strange event occurred at the Fort Lauderdale Naval Air Station, which is now the Fort Lauderdale/Hollywood International Airport. Five Navy TBM Avengers with 15 aboard took off on a training mission. No trace of these planes was ever found, and a Martin PBM on a rescue mission for them out of Melbourne also disappeared with 13 aboard. These events provided the foundation for the grisly legend which has spawned a number of books, some of them by Fort Lauderdale authors. In 1974 **Dick Winer** wrote *The Devil's Triangle* (New York: Bantam), and that same year **Charles Berlitz**, a member of the famed linguistic clan, published *The Bermuda Triangle* (Garden City, NY: Doubleday). **Martin Caidin**'s novel, *Three Corners to Nowhere* (New York: Bantam, 1975), is also about the disappearance of a jet in the Bermuda Triangle.

Fort Lauderdale hotels have provided at least temporary residence for writers. The Riverside Hotel, the oldest in downtown Fort Lauderdale, was long the winter home of the famous newspaper poet, **Edgar A. Guest** (1881-1959), whose most famous collections of poems were *A Heap of Living* (1916) and *Life's Highway* (1933). In 1949 he even wrote a poem called "Riverside

Dick Francis

Shufflers," a paean to the vigorous retirement sport of shuffleboard at the hotel. The poem includes such lines as "Oh! here is a most exciting game,/Designed for the blind, the deaf and the lame."

In 1961 **Robert Ruark** (1915-1965), syndicated columnist and author of the best-selling novel, *Something of Value* (1955), needed a quiet place to complete a second novel about Africa. His former secretary, now a Fort Lauderdale real-estate salesman, lined him up a quiet suite at the Escape Hotel (now the Tiffany House retirement home) on Fort Lauderdale Beach, where he finished *Uhuru* (1962).

Novelist **Rita Mae Brown**, who lived in Fort Lauderdale as a young girl, later wrote *Southern Discomfort* (New York: Harper & Row, 1982) and *Rubyfruit Jungle* (New York: Bantam, 1988). An engineer who switched to writing mysteries, **Robert Fish**, a resident of the Coral Ridge section of Fort Lauderdale, won the 1963 Edgar Allan Poe Award for the best first mystery of the year, *The Fugitive*. Many of his mysteries are set in Brazil, where he lived for many years. His *Mute Witness* became the 1968 Steve McQueen movie, *Bullitt*.

In recent years Fort Lauderdale has continued to attract mystery and crime writers. **Cherokee Paul McDonald** served for a decade as a Fort Lauderdale police officer before resigning in 1980 from fatigue. His first novel, *The Patch* (New York: Popular Books, 1986), blended his Vietnam and Fort Lauderdale police experiences into a tense crime story. He followed it in 1988 by *Gulf Stream* (New York: Popular Books), a story of drug smuggling set in south Florida. His book with the greatest impact, however, has been *Blue Truth* (New York: Donald I. Fine, 1991), a nonfiction account of what a police officer's life is really like. It opens with the force of a billy club: "It was a hard-metal trinity: the badge, the gun and the handcuffs. Each was cold and heavy with inherent power and responsibility; each was forged with precise purpose."

Another Fort Lauderdale author who writes both fiction and nonfiction about the south Florida crime scene is **Richard Smitten**. His novel, *Twice Killed* (New York: Avon, 1987), is set in Colombia, the Caribbean, and Key West. He followed with two true-crime books: *The Godmother: The True Story of the Hunt for the Most Bloodthirsty Female Criminal of Our Time* (New York: Pocket Books,

1990) and *The Man Who Made it Snow* (New York: Simon & Schuster, 1990) by **Max Mermelstine**, as told to **Robin Moore** and Richard Smitten.

Another well-known author of true-crime books is **Hank Messick**, who lived for a number of years in Fort Lauderdale's Rio Vista section. Messick, author of many books on organized crime, wrote several books about crime in south Florida and the nearby islands, among them *The Silent Syndicate* (New York: Macmillan, 1967); *Syndicate in the Sun* (New York: Macmillan, 1968); *Syndicate Abroad* (New York: Macmillan, 1969); and *Lansky* (New York: Putnam, 1971).

Fort Lauderdale is home, too, for **Donn Pearce**, who wrote *Cool Hand Luke* (New York: Scribner's, 1965), a novel about life in a central Florida prison camp. It became a popular 1967 movie starring Paul Newman. Pearce also

wrote *Dying in the Sun* (New York: Charterhouse, 1974), nonfiction about people living out their days in such Broward County locales as Fort Lauderdale, Pompano Beach, Tamarac, and Dania.

The husband-and-wife newspaper team of **Dan Norman** (Deputy Managing Editor, *Fort Lauderdale Sun-Sentinel*) and **Kristy Montee** write under the name **Kristy Daniels**. Two of their books use newspaper backgrounds: *Hot Type* (New York: Fawcett, 1987), set principally in Miami, and *Jewels of Our Father* (1991), set in San Francisco. A third book is *The Dancer* (1984). **John de Groot**, also a member of the *Sun-Sentinel* staff, has written a one-man

Donn Pearce

play about Ernest Hemingway: *Papa* (Boise, ID: Hemingway Western Studies Center, 1989). **Thomas Swick**, the newspaper's travel editor, is the author of *Unquiet Days: At Home in Poland* (1991).

Rules of Prey (1989), a gripping tale about a serial killer in Minnesota's Twin-Cities, was written by **John Sandford**, the pseudonym of a Pulitzer Prize-winning journalist. When he worked in Fort Lauderdale he was known by his real name, **John Camp**, city editor of the *Miami Herald*'s Broward bureau.

Crying in the Wilderness (New York: Avon, 1983) by **Floydene Partain** takes the reader back into the fifteenth century as the Spaniards began their conquest of the New World. The story involves a Jewish family coping with the Spanish Inquisition and a Haitian family struggling with Spanish domination of their island. A famous Fort Lauderdale author of books on self-actualization, a kind of personal philosophy, is **Wayne Dyer**; his books include *Your Erroneous Zones* (1977) and *The Sky's the Limit* (1981).

Jan Rogozinski is the author of three books, the latest being *A Brief History of the Caribbean: From the Arawak and the Carib to the Present* (1992).

Several of the smaller towns in the Greater Fort Lauderdale area have served either as settings for fiction or as home for nonfiction authors. The smallest town in Broward County, Lazy Lakes, population 36, is the setting for **T.J. MacGregor's** mystery, *Hidden Lake* (New York: Ballantine, 1987). Lauderdale-by-the-Sea is the site of important action in **Joyce Sweeney's** *Face the Dragon* (New York: Delacorte, 1990), as well as the home of **Martha Munzer** (1900-), author of seven books on city planning and the environment published by Alfred Knopf and most recently *A History of Lauderdale-by-the-Sea* (Lauderdale-by-the Sea: JMG Publishing, 1990).

Greater Fort Lauderdale in recent years has begun to emerge as a literary center of some consequence. The Broward County Main Library in downtown Fort Lauderdale houses the Florida Center for the Book, the first such state affiliate of the Center for the Book in the Library of Congress in Washington, D.C. The Florida Center for the Book sponsors and promotes programs throughout the state which highlight the relevance and importance of books, reading, and libraries in everyday life. The area is also headquarters for the Council for Florida Libraries, the Book Group of South Florida, an organization of Gold Coast book professionals, The Fontaneda Society, a group of book collectors, and the Florida Freelance Writers Association founded by **Dana Cassell**.

Among the other novels set in and around Fort Lauderdale are **Clark Blaise's** *A North American Education* (Garden City, NY: Doubleday, 1973); **Frank Conroy's** *Stop-Time* (New York: Viking, 1967); **C. Paul Jackson's** *Big Play in the Small League* (New York: Hastings House, 1968); **Edwin Lanham's** *Passage to Danger* (New York: Harcourt, Brace, 1961); **Will McGill's** *The Folly of Foley in Ft. Lauderdale* (New York: Carlton, 1974); and **Philip Wylie's** *The End of the Dream* (Garden City, NY: Doubleday, 1972).

Several books have been published on the history of Fort Lauderdale and Broward County. *Checkered Sunshine: The Story of Fort Lauderdale, 1793-1955* (Gainesville: University of Florida Press, 1966) was written by **Philip J. Weidling** and **August Burghard**. Weidling is also the author of *Secret of the Old Bridge* (New York: David McKay, 1963), a young-adult novel set in old Fort Lauderdale. A later history, and the only one including the entire county, is *Fort Lauderdale and Broward County: An Illustrated History* by **Stuart McIver** (Woodland Hills, CA: Windsor, 1982). *Glimpses of South Florida History* by **Stuart McIver** (Miami: Florida Flair Books, 1988) has historical articles about the people and events that shaped the area's history, as does the author's *True Tales of the Everglades* (Miami: Florida Flair Books, 1989). One can find a good description of the 1920s era in Fort Lauderdale in *My Early Days in Florida From 1905* by **Albert W. Erkins** in collaboration with August Burghard (Fort Lauderdale: Wade-Brook House, 1975). **Bruno Carl Schmidt** collected his poems and songs about Fort Lauderdale in his *Song of Broward* (Fort Lauderdale: Schmidt, 1968). **Paul A. Gore's** *Past the Edge of Poverty: A Biography of Robert Hayes Gore, Sr.* (Fort Lauderdale: R. H. Gore Co., 1990) tells the story of his grandfather, the millionaire businessman and publisher of the Fort Lauderdale *Sun-Sentinel*. **Donald L. Maggin's** *Bankers, Builders, Knaves and Thieves:*

The $300 Million Scam at ESM (Chicago: Contemporary Books, 1989) is an exposé of how ESM Government Securities, Inc., of Fort Lauderdale joined forces with an Ohio savings and loan institution to speculate in futures — with disastrous results. *Stranahan's People* (Fort Lauderdale: Stranahan High School, 1975) contains oral-history interviews done by students, and *A Biographic History of Broward County* by **Bill McGoun** (Miami: The Miami Herald, 1972) contains descriptions of the important people in the area's history. Joe Davis's paintings and Jim Scully's photographs present a waterfront view of the city in *Visions and Views: Fort Lauderdale, Venice of America* (Boca Raton: Social Issues Resources Series [SIRS], 1992).

West Broward

The largest West Broward city south of Coral Springs is Plantation, built on land formerly used as a plantation. A resident of the city is novelist **Carl Hiaasen**, who was born in nearby Fort Lauderdale. Hiaasen, a columnist for *The Miami Herald*, has written four novels and co-authored two more set primarily in the Miami area and the Keys. His books can be characterized as black comedy, suspense-thrillers laced with telling insights into Florida's environmental dilemma. (More about him in the next chapter.) The city for several years was home to author **Paul Erdman**, whose novels about shenanigans in the world of international high finance included *The Billion Dollar Sure Thing* (1973), *The Silver Bears* (1974), *The Crash of '79* (1976), and *The Last Days of America* (1981). **James Randi** is the author of *The Mask of Nostradamus* (1990). **Miriam Ownby**, an environmental writer, has written a guidebook, *Explore the Everglades* (Kissimmee, FL: TeakWood Press, 1992).

Just to the north of Plantation lies Sunrise, where famed mystery writer **Brett Halliday** lived in his later years; Halliday was creator of fictional detective Mike Shayne. Sunrise, which was originally called Sunset, was planned as a retirement community, but the local retirees changed the name to the more optimistic Sunrise.

Tamarac is the home of **Will Eisner** (1917-), artist, cartoonist, and author of such works as *A Pictorial Arsenal of America's Combat Weapons* (1960), *America's Space Vehicles* (1962), and *Comics & Sequential Art* (1985). Farther to the south is the town of Pembroke Pines, the home of **Tom McHale**, a Philadelphian who wrote *Principato* (1970) and *Farragan's Retreat* (1971) and was one of the five original founders of the Book Group of South Florida; he committed suicide in Pembroke Pines in 1982.

The oldest city in West Broward is Davie, named after the man who developed it after early twentieth-century drainage canals in the Everglades produced rich farmland. It houses an educational complex, consisting of a branch of Florida Atlantic University, Nova University, and Broward Community College (BCC). A member of the BCC faculty in the 1960s was **Harry Crews**, who used Broward locales and events in *Karate is a Thing of the Spirit* (New York: William Morrow, 1971), most memorably a Fourth of July fireworks and beauty contest at the Dania pier. Davie is the home of novelist **Barbara Parker**, whose *Running Mates* (New

York: NAL/Onyx, 1991) deals not with jogging but with politics. For a history of the town see **Victoria Wagner**'s *The History of Davie and Its Dilemma* (Fort Lauderdale: Nova/NYIT University Press, 1982).

Cooper City, named for its developer, Morris Cooper, is the home of **Marilyn Campbell**. Her first novel, *Daydreams*, a romantic comedy set in Hollywood, Florida, was published under her pseudonym, **Marina Palmieri** (Bensalem, PA: Meteor Books, 1991). Her second book, a futuristic romance, *Pyramid of Dreams* (Champaign, IL: Leisure Books, 1992), opens in Fort Lauderdale and heads into an alien world via the Bermuda Triangle.

Dania

The county's first (1904) incorporated city, Dania, on the ocean south of Fort Lauderdale, was named for the Danish settlers who founded it. Among Dania's writers have been **Edmund Skellings**, named Florida's poet laureate in 1980 by Governor Bob Graham to replace **Vivian Laramore Rader** of Miami, who had held the post from 1931 until her death in 1973. Skellings's books include three published by the University Presses of Florida: *Heart Attacks* (1976), *Nearing the Millenium* (1977), and *Showing My Age* (1978), which includes a poem about fishing from the Dania pier:

> Someone has caught a hideous fish,
> Spiny and speckled,
> Dull brown and battleship grey,
> Nothing anyone would stuff on a wall.

Skellings, who makes extensive use of contemporary electronic and computer techniques in his work, has had some of his poetry "published" in video cassettes. In 1979 he was nominated for the Nobel Prize in literature.

John Dufresne (1948-), a Dania resident, teaches creative writing at Florida International University in nearby North Miami. A poet and a short-story writer who has won numerous literary awards, Dufresne has received critical acclaim for his short-story collection, *The Way Water Enters Stone* (New York: Norton, 1991). These stories, peopled with blue-collar characters on the fringe of society, are set both in the Northeast and the South, with one story, "What Follows in the Wake of Love," in Belle Glade.

Dania Beach is one of the places featured in *Workdays* by **Bob Graham** (Miami: Banyan, 1978), written while he was successfully campaigning for governor. The book, while clearly a political gimmick at the time, does give a good picture of workers around the state, especially monolingual Spanish speakers, handicapped people, and civil servants. Graham spent days working at various jobs around Florida, a practice he continued from time to time after he became governor and later U.S. senator.

Hollywood

Christened Hollywood-by-the-Sea by its founder, Broward's second-largest city was named for California's movie capital. Florida's early attempts to establish a movie industry are recounted in **Richard Alan Nelson**'s *Florida and* *the American Motion Picture Industry, 1898-1980* (New York: Garland, 1982). To the west of Hollywood lies the Everglades, the subject of a 1969 children's book by **Lucy Salamanca**, a Hollywood resident. Her adventure book, *Lost in the Everglades* (New York: Golden Press, 1971), won the Lucille Ogle Literary Award for the best original children's story for ages eight to 12. The author's background is unusual for a delver into the Glades. In addition to being Lucy Salamanca, she also answered to the name of **Countess del Barco-Lodron** and the **Marquesa de Colonetta**. She had previously written *Tommy Tiger of the Seminoles* (New York: Franklin Watts, 1961). A more recent Hollywood author is **James Swain**, whose 1989 tale of magic, *The Man Who Walked Through Walls*, was published by St. Martin's in New York.

A present-day Hollywood author is novelist **Theresa Di Benedetto**, whose *Wildflower* (1989) won the *Romantic Times Magazine* Reviewers' Choice Award as best historical western of the year. Her second book, *Silver Mist* (New York: Berkley/Diamond, 1990), takes place in Dunnellon, Florida, when the nineteenth-century discovery of phosphate turned the little town into a booming mining camp. She has also written *Western Winds* (1991); a Cival War romance, *A Corner of Heaven*, as **Theresa Michaels** (1991) and *Desert Sunrise*, under the name **Raine Cantrell** (1992).

Two books have been written about the city: *History of Hollywood* by **Virginia Elliot Ten Eick** (Hollywood, FL: City of Hollywood, 1966) and *Tales of Old Hollywood* by **Don Cuddy** (Decatur, IL: Spectator Books, 1977). For more on Hollywood's founder, Joseph W. Young, see "Joe Young's Mighty Plan" by **Joan McIver** in *Mostly Sunny Days: A* Miami Herald *Salute to South Florida's Heritage* edited by **Bob Kearney** (Miami: Miami Herald, 1986).

Seminole Nation

Many of the stories and folk tales of the Seminole Indians are handed down by word of mouth. **James Billie**, chairman of the tribe and collector of these tales throughout Florida's Seminole Nation, is preserving them by converting them into songs, a group of which have been recorded on his album, *Native Sun*, and on a 24-minute video cassette of the same name (distributed by Pineapple Press, Sarasota, FL). Of particular note is his popular song, "BigAlligator, much played on Lake Okeechobee area music stations in 1986.

In 1990 the tribe published *Echoes in the Wind, the Seminole Indian Poetry* of **Moses Jumper, Jr.** (distributed by Pineapple Press, Sarasota, FL), the first instance of a Seminole's work appearing in book form. In a sense, however, an hereditary influence was at work here. Moses Jumper's mother, **Betty Mae Jumper,** the only woman ever elected chief of the tribe, had previously published a pamphlet, *God's Word Came in Wagons* (Hollywood: Seminole Communications, 1988), a religious account of her family's move from Indiantown to the Seminole reservation in Hollywood. Esteemed as the tribal storyteller, Betty Mae Jumper has also narrated six popular Seminole folk tales for a 28-minute videotape, *The Corn Lady: Seminole Indian Legends as told by Betty Mae Jumper,* (Margate, FL: AIMM Productions, 1992).

My Work among the Florida Seminoles by **James Lafayette Glenn** and edited by **Harry A. Kersey, Jr.** (Gainesville: University Presses of Florida, 1982) is an account of the man who was in charge of the Seminole Agency at Dania in the 1930s. In 1990 the Fort Lauderdale Historical Society published **David M. Blackard's** *Patchwork & Palmettos: Seminole-Miccosukee Folk Art since 1820*, an examination of the Seminole artistic tradition. For more about the languages spoken by the Seminoles and Miccosukees see *Languages of the Aboriginal Southeast* edited by **Karen M. Booker** (Metuchen, NJ: Scarecrow, 1991).

Hallandale

Established in 1898, Hallandale bears the name of its founder, Swedish minister Luther Halland. In later years it would veer far away from its religious roots as it became a haven for illegal gambling casinos. Books on Meyer Lansky — *Little Man* by **Robert Lacey** (Boston: Little, Brown, 1991) and *Lansky* by **Hank Messick** (New York: Putnam, 1971) — treat this phase of Hallandale history, which extended into the early 1950s. **William McGoun** has written the only history of the city, *Hallandale* (Hallandale, FL: Hallandale Historical Society, 1976).

Hallandale would later become the home of **Jim Bishop**, author of *The Day Lincoln Was Shot* (1955), *The Day Christ Died* (1957), *A Day in the Life of President Kennedy* (1964), and *FDR's Last Year* (1974). Bishop's autobiography, *A Bishop's Confession* (Boston: Little, Brown, 1981), contains material on Florida locales, particularly South Broward, Miami, and Fort Pierce.

THE COMMUNITY OF THE BOOK IN FLORIDA

JEAN TREBBI

Is there a community of the book in Florida? Is the reader of *The Book Lover's Guide* a part of it? My answer is a definite yes.

The community of the book in Florida, as this guide testifies, is alive and well, connecting and enriching the literary life of people who share a common interest — books. Authors are linked to editors, publishers, booksellers, librarians, wholesalers, literary agents, critics, book reviewers, translators, collectors, and ultimately readers to writers.

Bringing readers and writers together is a special role of the Florida Center for the Book. "In 1977, the Center for the Book in the Library of Congress was established on the assumption that a community of the book exists and that it can be mobilized to keep books and reading central in our lives and in the life of our democracy," writes John Cole, Director of the Center for the Book. The Florida Center for the Book, founded in 1984 as the first state affiliate of the National Center for the Book, is headquartered at Broward County Main Library in Fort Lauderdale and has literary partners across the state promoting books, reading, and libraries.

An early Florida Center for the Book project is also one of the country's longest-running author interview programs. *Library Edition* can be seen on cable TV in South Florida. Produced with support from Selkirk Communications, the program features informed interviews with best-selling authors, highly prized writers, and those with first books.

Writers continue to come to Florida in Hemingway's footsteps. In a 1936 letter to Soviet critic Ivan Kashkin, Hemingway wrote, "I wish you could come down here, the weather is wonderful now, like the finest sort of spring day and it is wonderful out in the Gulf stream.... I am going to fish tomorrow, and write the next day."

Fort Lauderdale is home to two active writers' organizations. The Book Group of South Florida has more than 50 writers who are current members. The Florida Freelance Writers Association has over a thousand members and publishes a *Directory of Florida Markets for Writers and PR Professionals* and presents numerous professional workshops throughout the state. Romance Writers of America has savvy and enthusiastic members in five Florida chapters, the newest in Tampa; and mystery writers are organizing chapters on both coasts. A helpful new directory, from White Tiger Publishing in Winter 1993, entitled *Writer's Southeast Handbook,* has more entries from Florida than the other Southeast states. It should be of tremendous value to writers identifying markets and readers looking for book-based organizations and events.

Florida's climate affects the literary life, particularly during the season. In northern Florida it parallels the academic year, and in subtropical south Florida the literary life heats up as fall temperatures drop and snowbirds and visitors meet resident book lovers at one or more of the frequently scheduled literary events. The mostly mild temperatures and blue skies are conducive to outdoor celebrations and account in part for Florida's many book fairs and festivals that celebrate the written word. Bernadine Clark describes them in detail in *Fanfare for Words: Bookfairs and Book Festivals in North America*, published by the Library of Congress.

Miami's International Book Fair is the largest in the country, attracting hundreds of thousands of people each November to hear internationally acclaimed authors lecture or read their works and to discover new writers and their books among the more than 300 publishers, booksellers, and exhibits of books for children and adults.

Sarasota's ABC Book Fair which focuses on authors, books, and cuisine, is held on the New College campus. In Fort Lauderdale, a Children's Reading Festival sponsored by Broward County Library presents authors signing books, artists, concerts, performances, storytelling, and creative writing workshops, which attract thousands of children and adults each spring.

The Florida Antiquarian Booksellers Association has sponsored a major antiquarian book fair since 1981 in St. Petersburg. About 90 dealers from New York, Florida, and in between create "a new Fourth Avenue" where rare and out-of-print books are easy to find. The Fort Lauderdale Antiquarian Book Fair stimulated publisher and bookman Fred Ruffner to organize a group of book collectors who meet regularly as the Fontaneda Society.

Fans and writers of science fiction and fantasy gather annually at Tropicon in South Florida, and in 1992 Orlando hosted Worldcon, the science-fiction and fantasy biggie, as it celebrated its 50th anniversary.

The Key West Literary Seminar, described in more detail in the Florida Keys chapter, has established an international reputation for excellence and ambiance in its ten-year history. Its literary walking tours are conducted year round, and Hemingway's house is one of Florida's most frequently visited literary landmarks.

The Council for Florida Libraries, based in Fort Lauderdale, has provided statewide leadership for Friends of Libraries and many of Florida's literary events and organizations, including the Key West Literary Seminar.

In many cities and towns, Friends of the Library groups support and organize book-based projects and literary programs for book lovers. Annual or continuous book sales at libraries, book and author luncheons and dinners, author readings and receptions supplement local tax revenue for libraries and draw readers together, enriching their social and literary lives and the book culture of the state.

Byblos is the special events committee of the Broward Public Library Foundation, which originated the Night of Literary Feasts and Day of Literary Lectures. It raises funds, linking the literati to a Florida lifestyle, featuring a dozen distinguished authors in a weekend of public events including lectures and book signings and ticketed dinner parties, waterway cruises, and receptions.

Parents who want to share the joy of reading and raise readers are encouraged to bring children to story hours at local libraries year-round, and each summer public libraries offer reading programs for children to help get them hooked on books and develop into lifetime readers. In Orlando, the library has pioneered an early reading project to Catch 'Em in the Cradle, and the Florida Center for the Book has created Raise-A-Reader kits, which were distributed in Florida's hospitals to newborns and their mothers. The Martin County Memorial Hospital Foundation is one of the organizations continuing the Raise-A-Reader project, and Friends of Libraries U.S.A. is planning to expand the project nationwide.

The National Library Service for the Blind and Physically Handicapped, based in Daytona, provides books and magazines by mail on records or cassette for readers with special needs.

In Delray Beach, book lovers may browse at the showrooms of the Levenger Company among the modular wood and glass-front bookcases, library ladders, reading tables, high-tech lamps, and bookends, all Tools for Serious Readers, advertised in its catalog and sold by mail to book lovers worldwide.

Readers who want to develop their own book collections can find chain bookstores in malls and unique stores specializing in religious, new age, construction, and aviation books. Booklovers can find nautical books at Bluewater Books in Fort Lauderdale, and children's books fill Storylines in Boca Raton. Books & Books, with two locations in Coral Gables and Miami's South Beach, has become a must for serious booklovers. Mitchell Kaplan, owner and true bookman, also offers regular author readings and signings and is a major force in the Miami Book Fair. Liberties Fine Books and Music, which presents author readings and book signings, is bustling in Boca Raton. Ruby-fruit Books in Tallahassee specializes in publications from small presses and concentrates on alternate lifestyles. Students get hooked on books for life at Goerings in Gainesville, browsing leisurely among academic and general book titles and a wide range of magazines. Since 1965, Libreria and Distribuidora Universal has been providing new, old and rare books in Spanish for adults, students, and children in Miami and to other readers through its regular catalogs. St. Petersburg is home to Haslam's, one of Florida's largest book-stores, with a reputation of knowledgeable staff in both new and rare books. Nearby is the new Snoop Sisters Mystery Bookshoppe Boutique in Belle Air Bluffs. The Florida Antiquarian Booksellers Directory lists about three dozen dealers, a third of them located in the Tampa-St. Petersburg area.

Learning how to write or how to write better is taught in classes and programs for writers on many of Florida's college and university campuses. Noted novelists have long been connected with the University of Florida's creative writing program, and Florida International University's MFA program in Creative Writing has fine writer-teachers talented in a variety of literary genres. *The Guide to Writers Conferences*, published by Shaw Associates of Coral

Gables, is a national directory detailing hundreds of non-degree programs for writers. Its geographical index lists more than a dozen programs in Florida, and its conference calendar helps Florida writers plan their work and travel schedule. The Florida Center for the Book offers continuous five-session workshops on a variety of subjects for beginning and experienced writers, and in New Smyrna Beach the Atlantic Center for the Arts presents outstanding interdisciplinary residencies with major artists and gifted authors three times each year.

Florida bills itself as the State of the Arts and provides financial support of book culture. The Division of Cultural Affairs sponsors annual literary fellowships with typical awards of $5,000. Organizations may apply for grants to the Florida Arts Council to present literary programs and workshops, while the Florida Humanities Council, based in Tampa, funds scholarly interpretation and discussions of the written word which tell us about our lives and cultures. Some of the most informed discussions about books and ideas take place in communities throughout the state through funding by the Florida Humanities Council.

Books are not only read and written, but published in Florida. Pineapple Press, located in Sarasota, publishes general books of fiction and nonfiction which appeal to book lovers everywhere, and their Florida books have special interest for residents and those who want to read more about our physical, cultural, and political environment.

The University Press of Florida publishes scholarly books of research and reference as does SIRS (Social Issues Resource Series) in Boca Raton. CRC Press, also in Boca Raton, is an international publisher of hundreds of medical, scientific, and technical reference books each year.

Book lovers can stay in touch with the best of current literature listening to Dick Estelle, who reads the full text of current books on the Radio Reader program broadcast by National Public Radio affiliates. Even the morning newspapers are read aloud weekdays in Miami on WLRN's Radio Reading Service.

Book lovers are invited to visit literary landmarks for Zora Neale Hurston in Eatonville or Stephen Crane in Daytona Beach. John D. MacDonald's Slip F18 at Bahia Mar in Four Lauderdale marks the fictional home of Travis Magee and his boat, the *Busted Flush*. Key West, where Hemingway's house draws thousands of visitors each year, also boasts the newest literary landmark, Elizabeth Bishop's home.

Book lovers can explore the literary archives of Marjorie Kinnan Rawlings or John D. MacDonald at the University of Florida in Gainesville, or examine the Lois Lenski manuscripts and Kelmscott Press books at Florida State University's library in Tallahassee.

For book lovers at sea who pack books in their ditty bags, the Florida Center for the Book offers a Books Aboard Burgee, a marine flag that signals to boaters that books are aboard and that a book lover is interested in trading or talking about them.

The demise of the book has been forecast each decade with every new technological invention. Its portability continues to recommend it for independence and convenience. More than one survey reporting on favorite places to read has found that "in bed" is still the most frequent answer.

From the State Library in Tallahassee to the writers colony in Key West, the Community of the Book is thriving in Florida, largely due to the influx of readers, but also because so many authors continue to find, as Hemingway did, that Florida provides a creative climate in which to live and write, enriching the literary culture of our state.

Jean Trebbi is Executive Director of Florida Center for the Book, based in Broward County Library in Fort Lauderdale.

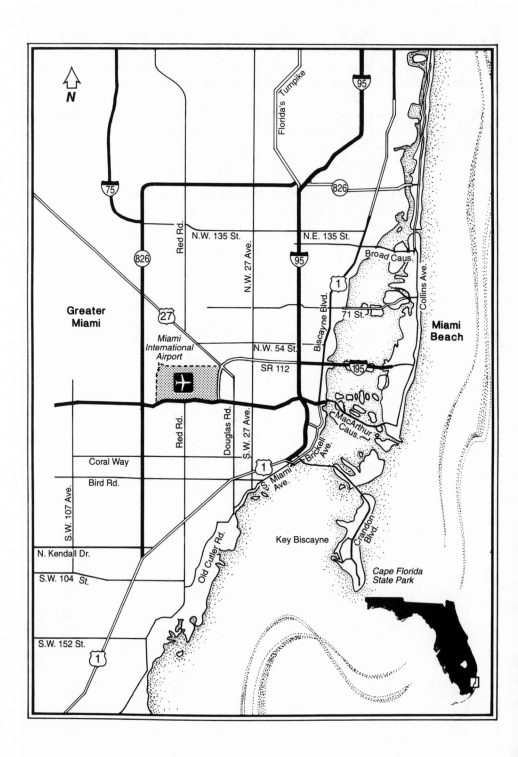

N

Florida's Turnpike

95

I-75

826

826

Red Rd.

N.W. 135 St.

N.E. 135 St.

N.W. 27 Ave.

95

Broad Caus.

Biscayne Blvd.

1

Collins Ave.

Greater Miami

US 27

71 St.

Miami Beach

Miami International Airport

N.W. 54 St.

SR 112

195

MacArthur Caus.

Red Rd.

Douglas Rd.

S.W. 27 Ave.

Brickell Ave.

Coral Way

1

S. Miami Ave.

Bird Rd.

S.W. 107 Ave.

Crandon Blvd.

Old Cutler Rd.

Key Biscayne

N. Kendall Dr.

S.W. 104 St.

Cape Florida State Park

S.W. 152 St.

1

216

5 GREATER MIAMI

GISELA CASINES

The city of Miami is one of the 27 municipalities of Dade County, but, because it is so well known, residents will usually say they are from Miami, regardless of which part of the county they hail from. Consequently, many of the local agencies, institutions, and businesses use a hyphenated combination of the city and the county name; for example, the largest community college in the United States is called Miami-Dade. In 1836, Dade, the nineteenth county of the state of Florida, was named after Major Francis L. Dade, who in the 1835 Seminole War was killed near Bushnell, Florida, in what came to be known as the Dade Massacre. Within its 2,109 square miles, Dade County encompasses a variety of locales and terrain: the eastern part is densely populated, the southwestern section has an important farming district, and the western border forms the eastern edge of the Everglades. Because of its proximity to that beautiful natural preserve, the county is often at war with the developers who want to continue inching west. Development into the untouched portions of Dade County has been so successful that sometimes during the dry season when brush fires start in the Everglades, some family homes are threatened.

Dade's other important natural resource, its people, offers striking variety: The Dade County Public School System serves students from more than 130 countries and from every state in the Union. Although the population increase had always been steady, it exploded in the 1960s with the arrival of thousands of Cuban refugees and in the 1980s with the Mariel boatlift and the influx of political refugees from Central America, especially Nicaragua and El Salvador. This meteoric growth has created numerous problems, which the media have frequently documented. In the last 30 years Miami has grown from a small town, which came alive during the winter tourist season, to one of the most important cities in the United States.

North Miami Beach

As one travels south from Broward County on Interstate 95, North Miami Beach lies southeast of the Miami Gardens Drive exchange (Northwest 183rd Street). Incorporated in 1926, the city has a misleading name because it is really on the mainland and not directly north of Miami Beach. However, like many Dade communities, it used the water association to attract residents.

217

Here lives **Dan Bentley-Baker** (1945-), a native of New Orleans, but a Miami resident since 1954. A former teacher, Bentley-Baker left the classroom to devote himself to writing, but he still finds time to teach courses in natural science at Miami-Dade's North Campus, 11380 Northwest 27th Avenue. In 1988, Pineapple Press published his book, *The Paper Boat*, a saga which looks at three souls as they migrate through seven incarnations. In addition, he has had stories published in the *Tampa Tribune Fiction Quarterly* and *Audubon* magazine.

Northern Dade County

One of the biggest attractions in northern Dade County is Joe Robbie Stadium, home of the Miami Dolphins football and the Florida Marlins baseball teams. Built entirely from private funds, it commemorates the late owner of the Dolphins. **C. Paul Jackson's** *Hall of Fame Flankerback* (New York: Hastings House, 1968) is a juvenile novel about a young man who plays for the Dolphins; another novel about professional football in Miami is **Milton J. Shapiro's** *The Hawk* (New York: Ace Books, 1975). Just north of the stadium is Calder Race Track, Miami's newest. One of **Damon Runyon's** short stories, "Pick the Winner" (1933) published in *Runyon on Broadway* (London: Constable, 1954), takes place at such a race track, although it was probably either Tropical Park or Hialeah Park.

Jeanette Stephens-El (1959-) organizes the annual Pan African Book Fair and the Black Arts Workshop. Originally from New Jersey but a resident of Miami since 1977, she is the author of a book of poems, *Rivers of My Mind* (1981).

Miami native **Elsie Fergueson** (1946-) also lives in the area. The poet, documentary scriptwriter, and children's book author has published her poetry in *Some of My Best* (New York: Macmillan, 1980) and *Young Distance Trainers* (Miami: Short Stop Publishers, 1987). In addition, she has also completed a documentary, *Haiti Sanctified*, an examination of Haitian culture, for the local educational television station.

Jamaican poet and playwright **Malachi Smith** (1956-) has been a Miami resident since 1987. His *Yankee Affair* was presented at the Phillip Michael Thomas Theatre, 12615 West Dixie Highway. Set in contemporary Miami, the play looks at a West Indian immigrant and his relationship with the new society in which he now lives. In 1985 Smith won the Jamaica Cultural Development Bronze Medal for *Until Death Do Us Part*.

In Palm Springs North, an unincorporated area named after Palm Springs, a section of Hialeah, is the home of **Beverly McGlamry** (1932-), whose specialty is writing historical sagas; for example, her *Family Bible* (1985) and *Goodly Heritage* (1986) use the colonial period as a backdrop. Under the name of **Kate Cameron**, she published *As If They Were Gods* (1987) and *Orenda* (1991). She is currently working on another historical novel based on the Calusa and Timucua Indians, early inhabitants of South Florida. **Charles Mink** of Hialeah has written *Princess of the Everglades* (Sarasota: Pineapple Press, 1991), a novel set in south Florida in the 1920s.

Nearby is the Country Club of Miami, both a development and a membership club. Now retired, but formerly in sales and marketing for Ashland Oil, is **Jim Shaffer** (1926-), who wrote *Peterbilt to Laredo* (New York: St. Martins, 1989), the story of a trip from South Florida to Laredo in a new Peterbilt. Shaffer himself undertook the journey; he finds Miami an "exciting" place for writers and believes that the city offers a "tremendous background for writing."

Opa-Locka

Heading south on Red Road to State Road 826, better known as the Palmetto Expressway, and then east to Northwest 27th Avenue, we exit south and find Opa-Locka. This municipality has perhaps the most exotic theme of all the early enterprises of the first twenty years of the century. Its founders, aviation pioneer Glenn H. Curtiss and James Bright, who also founded Miami Springs and Hialeah, decided on an Arabian-architecture theme, just as George Merrick had used Spanish-Italian architecture in Coral Gables. Many buildings in Opa-Locka exhibit an architectural style based on *Tales From the Arabian Nights*. One of the most striking examples is city hall, 777 Sharazad Boulevard. Opa-Locka's unusual name is a combination of two Seminole words, *opilwa* (swamp) and *lako* (big), a name chosen because of the hammocks nearby.

For a history of the city, see **Frank S. FitzGerald-Bush**'s *A Dream of Araby: Glenn H. Curtiss and the Founding of Opa-Locka* (Opa-Locka, FL: South Florida Archaeological Museum, 1976). For a biography of Curtiss see **Robert Scharff** and **Walter S. Taylor**'s *Over Land and Sea* (New York: David McKay, 1968).

Opa-Locka's two institutions of higher learning (Florida Memorial and St. Thomas) have very different histories. Originally established in Live Oak, Florida, in 1879, Florida Memorial College, 15800 Northwest 42nd Avenue, moved to this location in 1958. The county's only program in aviation administration is housed here.

St. Thomas University, located at 16400 Northwest 32nd Avenue, was established in the early 1960s by priests fleeing Cuba after Castro closed Villanueva University. The university is located on acres of pine trees, which one can easily see from the Palmetto Expressway, and used to be home to the Miami Dolphin training camp. Appropriately, the university offers a unique program in sports administration. **Mercedes García Tudurí**'s career closely parallels that of the institution. Born in 1904 in Cuba, she was dean of faculty at Villanueva and, soon after the opening of St. Thomas University, became professor of Spanish and philosophy. In addition to her numerous scholarly works, she has written four books of poetry. Her latest one, *Andariega de Dios: Tiempo de exilio* (New York: Senda Nueva de Ediciónes, 1983), looks at the exile experience and expresses longing for the country she left behind.

On Biscayne Boulevard (U.S. 1) and Northwest 151st Street is the North Miami campus of Florida International University (FIU) which occupies a large cypress preserve overlooking the Intracoastal Waterway. FIU's English department sponsors the Writers on the Bay series, which presents some of today's best writers reading from their works. Carolyn Forché, Louis Simpson, and Derek Walcott have participated in the program. In addition, the Creative Writing Program began in 1989 to publish *Gulf Stream*, a literary magazine which has attracted not only local writers but writers from all over the nation, including Ann Hood, Gerald Costanzo, and Dara Wier.

Since 1985 **Les Standiford** (1945-) has been director of the Creative Writing Program, which, even in its infancy, earned high praise. His short stories and poems have appeared in the *Kansas Quarterly, Descant,* and *Editors' Choice: The Best of the Small Presses.* This Ohio native recently published an eco-thriller, *Spill* (1991), in which a chemical spill threatens Yellowstone National Park. Acknowledging that "it takes about five or six years in a place to get to know it," Standiford will set his next novel in Miami. He believes that the city's "great cultural flux makes it very interesting."

In 1973 Florida International University hired **James "Jim" W. Hall** (1947-). A native Kentuckian, Hall for many years devoted himself to writing poetry. He published four books of poetry and saw his work appear in *Poetry, Antioch Review, North American Review,* and other prestigious literary magazines. In the 1980s he decided to try to write a mystery-thriller, a genre he much admires, and, in the tradition of Elmore Leonard and John D. MacDonald, published *Under Cover of Daylight* (1987). Thorn, a native of the Florida Keys who makes a living tying fishing flies, tries to solve the murder of his adoptive mother. In his quest, he learns how this murder ties in with a 20-year-old incident, in which he avenged the death of his parents by a drunk driver.

James W. Hall

Two years later, Hall published another novel, *Tropical Freeze* (1989), in which Thorn investigates the disappearance and eventual death of a good friend who was an FBI agent. The play with language evinced in the titles of the first two novels suggests Hall's poetic sensibility: the unexpected turn following *Under Cover* and the oxymoronic quality of *Tropical Freeze* prepare the reader for the poetic character of his prose; his training and work as a poet are evident in every page of his novels. His carefully crafted descriptions and his use of subtle understatement carry the reader not only through exciting plots, but through almost poetic prose. Both novels have been translated into Spanish, French, German, Japanese, Italian, Dutch, Swedish, and Danish and have been on the best-seller list in England.

In another mystery-thriller, *Bones of Coral* (1991), Hall took the death of the protagonist's father and the mystery of why the Florida Keys have so many cases of multiple sclerosis and tied the two into an exciting story. Norton also collected Hall's previously published short stories under the title of *Paper Products* (1990). In the almost 20 years Hall has lived in Miami, he has watched it undergo a tremendous transformation, but he likes what is happening to the city: "Rapid changes like these [the ones occurring now] are exciting for the writer," he says.

Another creative-writing professor at FIU is **John Dufresne** (1948-). He received the *Trans-Atlantic Review*/Henfield Foundation Award in 1984 for "After the Passing of Beautiful Devereaux" (Greensboro, NC: *Greensboro Review*, 1984) and the PEN Syndicated Fiction Award in 1984 for his "Surveyors," which first appeared in *Tropic* magazine and later in *Arizona* and *Republic*. In 1991 a collection of short stories, *The Way That Water Enters Stone*, was published by Norton to good reviews.

Born in Elizabeth, New Jersey, **Jeffrey Knapp** (1949-) has lived in Miami since 1975. Writing in the tradition of Dada-Surrealists, he has been published in *Ploughshares, Boston Review of the Arts, La Bête*, and *The Chapbook*. From 1975 to 1989, Knapp was director and artist-in-residence for the National Endowment for the Arts Poet-in-the-Schools program. He is also founder and editor of Dial-a-Poem (305-444-POEM).

Lynne Barrett (1950-), who joined the FIU creative writing faculty in 1987, recently won an award given by the Mystery Writers of America for "Elvis Lives," published in *Ellery Queen Magazine*; it has now been reprinted in *Best Mystery Stories, 1991* and *The Year's Best Mystery and Suspense* (1991). In 1988 Carnegie-Mellon published a collection of her short stories, *The Land of Go*. Barrett plans to have Miami as a setting for some of her future works.

A Miami resident since 1956, **Ronn Silverstein** (1950-) has been teaching in the English department since 1987. His first book-length publication, *Diary of a Glass Blower in Solitude* (Dunvegan, Ontario, Canada: Cormorant, 1990), was nominated for the Cambert Award for best first book of poetry. In addition, his work has appeared in *The Inner Ear, Poetry in Australia*, and *West Coast Review*.

South at 12615 Biscayne Boulevard is the Phillip Michael Thomas Miami Way Theatre, founded by *Miami Vice* star Phillip Michael Thomas. New Yorker **Robert Macbeth,** adjunct professor of theater at the University of Miami, has close ties with the theater. His play, *The Ritual*, was presented here to much acclaim. More recently, he has been concentrating on screenwriting.

Across the bay is Surfside, one of the municipalities on a group of islands east of the coast; the other important city on these islands is Miami Beach.

Paralleling the coastline, Collins Avenue (State Road A1A) joins many of the islands and is lined with hotels and condominiums. In **Edna Buchanan's** *Nobody Lives Forever* (New York: Random House, 1990), detective Rick Barrish's description of this famous avenue encapsulates Dade County's history of development: "You used to be able to drive down Collins Avenue, eyeball the big estates on the ocean — and actually see the water."

Surfside

A former subdivision of Miami Beach, Surfside became a separate municipality in 1935. Although the 1960s television series *Surfside Six* used this city's name, the houseboat in the show was actually moored on the Intracoastal Waterway in Miami Beach. Today Surfside is the home of **Eve Titus**, author of 21 children's books, mostly about mice, including *Anatole* (1956), *Anatole and the Cat* (1957), *Basil* (1958), and *Anatole and the Piano* (1966).

Isaac Bashevis Singer (1904-1991), one of Miami's most important literary figures, lived in Surfside. Winner of the 1978 Nobel Prize for literature and the world's foremost writer in Yiddish, Singer was born in Poland, the son of a rabbi. He arrived in the United States in 1935 with one published novel, *Satan in Goray* (1934), to his credit. Finding himself in this new land, he "was struck by a disease familiar to most exiled intellectuals, creative paralysis." Eventually

I.B. Singer

surmounting this block, Singer went on to a distinguished career and continued writing in Yiddish "despite his pessimistic views concerning the fate" of the language. Having lived most of his life in New York City, in 1973 he moved south to the Miami area. Because of his frail health, he spent his last three years at the Douglas Gardens Convalescent Home, while his wife resided in their Surfside home. During his life, local authorities renamed a Surfside street in his honor.

Singer's literary output is as prolific as it is varied, for he wrote even children's books. Although many of his works are set in

Jewish ghettos of Eastern Europe, they are universally admired because they address the problem of faith and relationships in modern times. Singer's extensive contributions to literature are legendary, but a few works deserve special mention. His first and probably best-known collection of short stories is *Gimpel the Fool and Other Stories* (1957), and his most-recognized novel is *The Spinoza of Market Street* (1961). His preoccupation with the fate of Judaism, the Jewish people, and Yiddish is also evident in his novel, *The Penitent* (1983), and his collection of short stories, *Love and Exile* (1984). His last book, *Scum*, appeared just a year before his death, and another just recently translated, *The Certificate*, was published in 1992. Hollywood turned its attention to his works by adapting his short story "Yentl, the Yeshiva Boy" into the movie *Yentl* (1983), starring Barbra Streisand; but Singer was dissatisfied with the movie's melodramatic rendition of his work. His *Enemies, A Love Story* (1969) became a film of the same name starring Ron Silver and Angelica Houston (1990). His short story about a storm in Miami Beach entitled "Alone" appears in *Florida Stories* edited by **Kevin McCarthy** (Gainesville: University of Florida Press, 1989).

Miami Beach

Directly south of Surfside is Miami Beach proper, a city known for its beautiful beaches, art deco, and huge hotels. Its three developers — Carl Fisher, Thomas Pancoast, and John S. Collins — decided to rename the area, which had been called Alton Beach, to capitalize on Miami's growing popularity. Having made a fortune on the patent he held for automobile headlights, Fisher provided most of the capital for the development. The city's most important thoroughfare honors Collins, who with Fisher dredged and cleared the land and built a bridge connecting the island with the mainland.

The southern tip of Miami Beach, which is called South Beach, is the oldest part and is best known for its many art-deco buildings. South Beach has become a hot spot on weekends, and its many outdoors cafés are crowded with both tourists and natives. Resident **Edna Buchanan** describes the city's charm in *The Corpse Had a Familiar Face: Covering Miami, America's Hottest Beat*: "It is a wild and wacky town where outlandish events occur."

For more about the city's unique buildings see **Barbara Baer Capitman's** *Deco Delights: Preserving the Beauty and Joy of Miami Beach Architecture* (New York: Dutton, 1988). For two accounts of Miami Beach's history, see **J.N. Lummus's** *Miracle of Miami Beach* (Miami: Miami Post Publishing Co., 1944) and **Polly Redford's** *Billion-Dollar Sandbar: A Biography of Miami Beach* (New York: Dutton, 1970). A more recent book is **David Scheinbaum's** *Miami Beach: Photographs of an American Dream* (Miami: Florida International University Press, 1990).

Among Miami Beach's many literary visitors were James Whitcomb Riley (1849-1916) and Tennessee Williams (1911-1983). Several writers also make their homes on the island, including **Judith Berke**, one of Dade County's most respected poets. A resident of the Beach since 1964, Berke published *White*

Morning (1989) and has had poems in *Gulf Stream, Atlantic,* and *American Poetry Review.* Her love of the Miami area can be seen specifically in two of her poems: "Vizcaya" (3152 South Miami Avenue) and "Coral Castle" (28655 South Federal Highway, Homestead). Miami inspires her because "when the sky is so huge and there are no mountains and there's nothing high, and everything is just sky, sky, sky, it's almost as if you have to fill the sky with your imagination."

A former winter visitor and a relatively new resident is **Thomas Harris** (1940-), author of *Red Dragon* (1981) and *The Silence of the Lambs* (1988), whose movie version starring Jodie Foster and Anthony Hopkins was one of 1991's most popular films and won an Oscar for Best Picture.

Virginia-born **John Rothchild** (1945-) has lived in Dade County since 1980. His irreverent look at Florida, *Up for Grabs* (New York: Viking, 1985), recounts his early days in the area and his sojourn in Everglades City. He is also the co-writer of Marjory Stoneman Douglas's autobiography: *Marjory Stoneman Douglas: Voice of the River* (Sarasota: Pineapple Press, 1987). Another work, *Going for Broke* (New York: Viking, 1988), examines Robert Campeau, whose purchase and subsequent sale of Allied and Federated department stores have greatly affected the South Florida economy.

Although no longer a Miami Beach resident, **John Katzenbach** (1950-) thrust Miami into the forefront of exciting settings for mystery-thrillers with *In the Heat of the Summer* (New York: Atheneum, 1982). In 1985 the novel was made into a movie, *The Mean Season,* starring Kurt Russell and Mariel Hemingway. Katzenbach's next novel was mostly set in Miami: *The Traveller* (New York: Putnam, 1986) is a mystery-thriller in which a serial killer kidnaps a photographer. A former reporter for both the *Miami News* and the *Miami Herald,* Katzenbach also set his recent novel, *Just Cause* (New York: Putnam, 1992), in Miami because the city is "crazier and wilder than anything you could think of."

Although works of fiction set in Dade County usually cover the county instead of focusing on a particular area, the following fictional works are set mostly in Miami Beach: **J.C. Conaway**'s *Miami Beach* (New York: Tower, 1976); **Peggy Dern**'s (**Peggy Gaddis**) *Nurse in Shadows* (New York: Arcadia House, 1965); **Davis Dresser**'s (**Brett Halliday**) *Marked for Murder* (New York: Dodd, Mead, 1945), *Pay-off in Blood* (New York: Dodd, Mead, 1953), *Weep for a Blonde* (New York: Dodd, Mead, 1957), *Murder in Haste* (New York: Dodd, Mead, 1961), *Murder Spins the Wheel* (New York: Dodd, Mead, 1966), *Million Dollar Handle* (New York: Dell, 1976), and many more detective novels featuring Mike Shayne; **Stanley Ellin**'s *The Bind* (New York: Random House, 1970) and *Star Light, Star Bright* (New York: Random House, 1975); **Merrill Joan Gerber**'s *Now Molly Knows* (New York: Arbor House, 1971); **Gerald Green**'s *The Lotus Eaters* (New York: Scribner's, 1959); **Albert Halper**'s *The Fourth Horseman of Miami Beach* (New York: Norton, 1966); **Syd Hoff**'s *Irving and Me* (New York: Harper and Row, 1967); **Evan Hunter**'s *Happy New Year, Herbie and Other Stories* (New York: Simon & Schuster, 1963); **Herbert Kastle**'s (**Herbert d'H. Lee**) *Miami Golden Boy* (New York: Bernard Geis, 1969); **David A. Kaufelt**'s *Late Bloomer*

(New York: Harcourt Brace Jovanovich, 1979); **Day Keene's** *Miami 59* (New York: Dell, 1965); **Rufus King's** *The Faces of Danger* (Garden City, NY: Doubleday, 1964); **Alfred D.** Laurence's *Hub-Dir-In-Budt: The Magic Maid of Miami Beach* (Miami Beach: Candid, 1962); **Elmore Leonard's** *La Brava* (New York: Arbor House, 1983), *Stick* (New York: Avon, 1983), *Glitz* (New York: Arbor, 1985), and *Get Shorty* (New York: Delacorte, 1990); **Milton Lesser's** (**C.H. Thames**) *Violence Is Golden* (New York: Bouregy & Curl, 1956); **Richard Pitts Powell's** *Tickets to the Devil* (New York: Scribner, 1968); **Frank Gill Slaughter's** *Women in White* (Garden City, NY: Doubleday, 1974); and **Philip Wylie's** *They Both Were Naked* (Garden City, NY: Doubleday, 1965), about a writer's difficulties in trying to live in expensive Miami Beach.

Miami Shores

The two parts of the name of this city suggest its geographic importance, with Miami just south of it and Biscayne Bay forming its eastern boundary. Settled in the 1870s by William Gleason and William Hurt, this charming village was incorporated in 1932. It has always been a residential community with enough commerce to satisfy its residents' needs. In 1940 Barry College, 11300 Northeast 2nd Avenue, was established on a 40-acre tract as a Catholic women's college. Today, it is co-ed and in 1981 changed its name from college to university to reflect more accurately its changing educational programs. For a history of Miami Shores, see **Bill Kofoed, Ray Smith,** and **Bernard Schwartz's** *Miami Shores Village, 1932-1982* (n.p., n.d.). Also see *Lemon City: Pioneering on Biscayne Bay, 1850-1925* (Miami: Banyan, 1976) by **Thelma Peters.**

One of the town's most important residents was **Vivian Laramore Rader** (1891-1973), Florida's second poet laureate — from 1931 to 1973. Very active in the literary life of Miami, Rader often sponsored poetry readings throughout the community and regularly published her poetry in the *Miami News.* Two of her books of poetry are *Hounds on the Mountain* (1937) and *Ode to Life and Selected Poems* (1967).

Jamaican **Geoffrey Philp** (1958-) currently resides in Miami Shores. A graduate of the University of Miami, Philp published *Exodus and Other Poems* (St. Croix, VI: University of Virgin Islands Press, 1990), in which he explores the immigrant experience. In addition, his poetry has appeared in *Appalachia Quarterly, Journal of Caribbean Studies,* and *Caribbean Review.*

Miami

South of Miami Shores lies the city of Miami. Incorporated in 1896, the city has become the gateway to Latin America, and its international airport is one of the nation's busiest. Those who wished to visit the area in the nineteenth century had no such entrée, however; they first had to go to Key West and then undertake a dangerous journey on a small boat up the coast. In 1838 on the north bank of the Miami River an army outpost, Fort Dallas, was established to keep the Seminole Indians in check. Among the novels chronicling the area are **Frank Gill Slaughter's** *Fort Everglades* (Garden City, NY: Doubleday, 1951) about the Second Seminole War and **Stephen Meader**'s *Everglades Adventure* (New York: Harcourt, Brace, 1957) about Fort Dallas after the Civil War.

In the 1870s on the south side of the river, the Brickell family established a store to serve both the newcomers and the Indians. The area continued to grow steadily until 1896 when Henry Flagler brought the railroad and ushered in Miami's first boom. He may have done so because of Julia Tuttle's persistence; some claim that she sent him orange blossoms after a particularly bad frost had killed many crops farther north and gave him choice real estate to lure him to the area. He accepted, and the railroad he built gave this fledgling city a chance to thrive. Julia Tuttle and other personages of south Florida are figures in **David Kaufelt**'s novel about early Florida: *American Tropic* (New York: Poseidon, 1986).

The second boom occurred in the 1920s when developers started "to turn Florida sand into gold, men cut up fruit groves to make subdivisions, filled in swampland and planted coconut palms and Australian pines." The area was becoming a tourist destination, but the devastation of the 1926 hurricane and the Depression ended the boom. The town did continue its steady growth, and, because thousands of tourists would take advantage of the balmy weather every winter, the aviation and tourist industries grew. Another boom began after World War II and thrust Miami into unprecedented growth in all economic sectors, but especially the banking industry.

Although the exact derivation of *Miami* remains a mystery, many scholars believe that it comes from the Seminole for *sweet water* because of the river that flows through it. Early spellings of the name include *Maama* and *Mayaimi*, and, finally, in 1877 the official spelling of the name was agreed upon. Miami originally encompassed all the territory south of the northern bank of Lake Okeechobee, a lake that was originally called Miami. In 1843 the village of Miami was platted on the south bank of the Miami River and in 1844 became the county seat of a very large county.

Just west of Biscayne Boulevard at Northeast 54th Street is an ill-defined section called Little Haiti because of the many Haitian immigrants who have settled there. One of its newest sites is the Market Place at Northeast 2nd Avenue and 59th Street, an open air shopping center with a distinctive Caribbean architecture. That this area will be of interest to writers in the future is suggested specifically by one of the best novels with a south Florida setting, **Russell Banks**'s *Continental Drift* (New York: Harper & Row, 1985).

The area's literary potential is also symbolized by one of its young writers, **Rudy Antoine** (1966-), who arrived in Little Haiti from his native Port-au-Prince in 1983. He is the winner four years in a row of the Inner City Poetry Award in the young-adult category presented by the Miami-Dade Public Library. Currently working on a book of poetry, he published in *Compages* (1988) "This is Krome" about the Krome Detention Center for illegal immigrants and "The Sun Will Rise" about Soweto.

West of Little Haiti is Liberty City, originally called Liberty Square. One of the first federally funded public housing projects, it was built in 1937. Nearby at 545 Northwest 48th Street is the former home of Pulitzer Prize-winner

Donald Justice

Donald Justice. Born in 1925, he resided at this house and at 1825 Northwest 47th Street and 1829 Northwest 46th Street; as an adult he lived in Coconut Grove and Coral Gables. In "A Winter Ode to the Old Men of Lummus Park, Miami, Florida," Justice describes the proud "old ghosts" who implicitly contrast with the more affluent winter tourists; the park at 404 Northwest 3rd Street is one of the area's oldest public parks and was named after the city's second mayor, J.E. Lummus. Justice also wrote the following poems about Miami: "Memory of a Porch, Miami, 1942"; "Variations on a Text by Vallejo"; "Memories of the Depression Years"; "Thinking about the Past"; and "Childhood." These poems are in **Donald Justice**, *Selected Poems* (New York: Atheneum, 1979). His short story, "The Artificial Moonlight" in *Florida Stories* (Gainesville: University of Florida Press, 1989), edited by **Kevin McCarthy**, is partly about the passing of the old in Miami in favor of the new.

Presenting many of her works at the theater at the Caleb Community Center, 5400 Northwest 22nd Avenue, is **Alice Johnson** (1927-), who tirelessly works to teach the children of different cultural groups in the area about each other. She has written ten docudramas for the local educational television station. Although her interests lately have led her to more theatrical endeavors, in 1976 she published a book of poems entitled *How to Feel Good about Yourself*.

Gigi Watson, journalist and poet, is a resident of Orchardville, a section of Liberty City. Her column in the *Miami Times*, "Chatter that Matters," is one of the most popular features of the newspaper. In 1991 the Dade County School Board published *Child, Please*, a collection of her poetry culled from her previous six books of poetry, as a text to be used in the classrooms. A lifelong teacher of French, Watson in the 1950s studied at the Sorbonne in Paris and for ten years served as an official translator for the Miss Universe pageant.

Spanish is the operative language at *Diario Las Américas*, 2900 Northwest 36th Street, the building that houses Miami's first Spanish-language newspaper, founded in 1953. Its current managing editor, **Luis Mario** (1935-), has been writing columns for the newspaper on poets and poetry since 1973; he published *Un poeta cubano*, his first book of poetry in the United States in 1971. His recent, seventh book of poetry, ... *la misma* (1989), is a continuation of his fifth, *Esta mujer...* (1983).

Nearby, Miami International Airport, one of the largest in the country, is the gateway for thousands of visitors from Latin America. The American Society of Landscape Architects gave the airport an honor award in 1979 because of the lush tropical plantings around the buildings. Several novels have been set at the airport including **David E. Fisher's** *The Last Flying Tiger* (New York: Scribner's, 1976) about several light planes. Two novels by **Robert P. Davis** are *The Pilot* (New York: Morrow, 1976) about an alcoholic pilot who retires to a career in cropdusting and *Control Tower* (New York: Putnam's, 1980) about job stress in a modern airport. **Robert J. Serling's** *From the Captain to the Colonel* (New York: Dial Press, 1980) is an informal history of Eastern Airlines, a company which had much to do with Florida's development in the twentieth century.

To the southeast of the airport on Biscayne Boulevard and 14th Street is the *Miami Herald* building, home to several journalists/authors. Established in 1910, it has won 11 Pulitzer prizes and is considered one of the nation's best newspapers and certainly one of the South's best. Its newsroom has been used as a set by director Sydney Pollack in *Absence of Malice* (1982), starring Sally Field and Paul Newman, and by director Philip Borsos in *The Mean Season* (1985) with Kurt Russell and Mariel Hemingway. **Nixon Smiley's** *Knights of the Fourth Estate: The Story of the Miami Herald* (Miami: Seemann Publishing Co., 1974) chronicles the growth of the paper until it became the largest in the world during the 1925-1926 land boom. In those days it minimized great disasters, e.g., destructive hurricanes, in the city, so as not to dissuade visitors and newcomers. For a history of the *Herald* in relation to one of its owners see *John Knight: A Publisher in a Tumultuous Century* (New York: Dutton, 1988) by **Charles Whited.**

Nixon Smiley (1911-), a longtime employee at the *Miami Herald*, wrote several books about Florida which Miami's Seemann Publishing Company produced: *Florida, Land of Images* (1972); *Crowder Tales* (1973), which has stories about a fictitious site in north Florida; *Yesterday's Miami* (1973); and *Yesterday's Florida* (1974). He collected many of his *Miami Herald* essays in *On the Beat and Offbeat* (Miami: Banyan, 1983).

Jim Bishop (1907-1987), whose syndicated column originated from this newspaper, was born in Jersey City, New Jersey. His accounts of historical events made history accessible to many who would not ordinarily read a history text. The first and most famous of his history books was *The Day Lincoln Was Shot* (1955), followed by others in the same vein, like *The Day Christ Died* (1957). His painstaking research is evident in the accuracy and enormous attention to detail in his writing.

Charles Willeford's (1919-1988) intimate knowledge of the area and its people is evident in all his Miami-based works. He was very successful with his Hoke Mosely series: *Miami Blues* (New York: Ballantine, 1984); *New Hope for the Dead* (New York: St. Martin's, 1985); and *The Way We Die Now* (New York: Random House, 1988). *Miami Blues* was made into a 1990 movie starring Alec Baldwin. Earlier he had written a novel about cockfighting in the Everglades entitled *Cockfighter* (New York: Crown, 1972).

Charles Whited, another *Herald* columnist/novelist, loved the Miami area and set part of his novel, *The Brandon Affair* (New York: New American Library, 1976), in the city; earlier he had written *The Decoy Man* (Chicago: Playboy, 1973).

On leave from the *Herald* is **Edna Buchanan** (1946-). Her *The Corpse Had a Familiar Face: Covering Miami, America's Hottest Beat* (New York: Random House, 1987) recounts her many years as a *Herald* crime reporter as does the sequel, *Never Let Them See You Cry: More Tales of Murder and Mayhem in Miami* (New York: Random House, 1992). Buchanan, who won the Pulitzer Prize for general reporting in 1986, has also turned to fiction and in 1990 published *Nobody Lives Forever* (New York: Random House), a mystery-thriller set in Miami. That Miami plays so prominent a role in her writing is not surprising because, as she says, "It's impossible to work or live here in Miami and not let it creep into your writing."

Two other *Herald* columnists take an off-beat look at living in this international city. Winner of the Pulitzer Prize for commentary (1988) is **Dave Barry** (1947-), whose column appears weekly in the newspaper's Sunday magazine, *Tropic*. Two of his works, *The Taming of the Screw* (1983) and *Homes and Other Black Holes* (1988), take a humorous look at the perils of owning a home. He reinterprets American history in *Dave Barry Slept Here* (1989). *Dave Barry's Greatest Hits* (1988), *Dave Barry Turns 40* (1990), and *Dave Barry Talks Back* (1991) further suggest the absurdity and humor he finds in life every day. Barry has become a major national humorist with a wide following.

Carl Hiaasen (1953-), a native of Fort Lauderdale, also revels in the sometimes-absurd reality of living in south Florida. In *Tourist Season* (New York: Putnam, 1986), his cast of characters includes terrorists, revolutionaries, a beauty queen, and a reporter-turned-private-investigator. In *Native Tongue* (New York: Knopf, 1991), the absurd reality plays out in a murder-mystery set in a fictitious theme park in north Key Largo. Hiaasen also wrote *Double Whammy* (New York: Putnam's, 1987) and *Skin Tight* (New York: Putnam's, 1989) and, with **William D. Montalbano,** *Powder Burn* (New York: Atheneum, 1981) and *Trap Line* (New York: Atheneum, 1982).

Just south of the *Herald* building is the MacArthur Causeway, named after General Douglas MacArthur. This beautiful road was often used in the filming of television's *Miami Vice*. On its south side is Government Cut, an artificially deepened channel often lined with cruise ships awaiting passengers. On the north side lie some of the most exclusive islands in Dade County. Celebrities Gloria Estefan and Don Johnson own homes on Star Island; Al Capone (1899-1947) lived at 93 Palm Island; and **Damon Runyon** (1880-1946), author of *Guys and Dolls*, lived in the 1930s at 271 Hibiscus Island, where he co-authored the farce, *A Slight Case of Murder* (1935), with Howard Lindsay. Runyon's three short stories with a Miami setting appear in *Runyon à-la-carte* (Philadelphia: Lippincott, 1949). Novelist **Sholem Asch** (1880-1957), who wrote *The Nazarene* (1939), *The Apostle* (1943), and *The Prophet* (1955), lived at 121 Hibiscus Avenue on the island in the 1950s.

Downtown Miami's Biscayne Boulevard takes its name from the adjacent Biscayne Bay. Most agree that the bay received its name from one of the area's first settlers, Don Pedro, el Biscaino, who was originally from Spain's Biscaya province. **Barry Jay Kaplan**'s *Biscayne* (New York: Simon and Schuster, 1988) is a novel that takes place in the area.

Writer **Andrew Glaze**, who worked for many years in journalism and public relations, has lived in this area since 1988. His *Damned Ugly Children* (1966) was named to the Notable Book List compiled by the American Library Association. In 1991 he published *Fury and Certainty*, and now that he has retired he plans to add to his six books of poetry.

At 6th Street is the former *Miami News* building, better known as Freedom Tower because in the 1960s it served as the processing center for thousands of Cuban refugees. Now renovated, it serves as an office building. Two blocks south is Bayside, which has become a favorite of tourists and residents. Built in the late 1980s by the Rouse Corporation, it has succeeded in bringing the citizens of Dade County back to downtown Miami to enjoy its beautiful architecture, many shops, boutiques, and restaurants. Different activities take place every weekend; the most important and largest is a great end-of-the-year party following the King Orange Jamboree Parade, where many Miamians congregate to welcome the new year.

Flagler Street, named after Henry Flagler, is the heart of downtown Miami. Before the advent of malls, this was the main shopping area for the residents of the county. Now it is also the most important business district in Dade, and during the day shoppers and office workers crowd the sidewalks. Two of the most striking office buildings are the Southeast Bank, 1 Southeast Financial Center, the tallest building in Miami, and the CenTrust Tower, 100 Southeast 2nd Street, designed by I.M. Pei and beautiful at night with its lit exterior. The Pei innovation has started a trend, and now many buildings throughout the county have lit their exteriors at night.

Miami-Dade Community College's Mitchell Wolfson New World Center campus, 300 Northwest 2nd Avenue, is in the midst of the downtown metropolis. Its students can submit their literary efforts to the award-winning literary magazine *Metromorphosis*. Started in 1987 and distributed campus-wide, the magazine provides internship experience for journalism students. **Michael Hettich** (1953-), who teaches English, received wide acclaim for his *A Small Boat* (1990). In addition, in 1987 he published *Lathe* and, in 1991, *Habitat*. Writing on Judaic themes is another English professor, **Victor Uszerowicz** (1955-), who has been published in *Response* and *Midstream*. The campus also houses the Prometeo Theater, one of Dade County's most important Spanish-language theaters. In Cuba, Prometeo presented avant-garde works and in

1972 was resurrected in the United States, offering quality theater to Miami's Spanish speakers and often touring the different Hispanic communities to bring theater to the people. The founder and director of the theater, **Teresa María Rojas,** has written four books of poetry: *Señal de agua* (1968), *La casa de agua* (1973), *Campo oscuro* (1977), and *Capilla ardiente* (Miami: Ediciones Isimir, 1980).

The Miami Book Fair International at Miami-Dade Community College is south Florida's major book event and the largest book celebration in the country. It takes place on the campus and features more than 100 writers and 300 or more exhibitors at a weekend streetfair. Begun in 1984, it attracts about 400,000 people, is covered by the Latin American and European media, and runs eight days every November. The three-day streetfair is the culmination of the event.

The beautiful Mediterranean-style Cultural Center which Philip Johnson designed and which rises one story above street level at 101 West Flagler combines the county's main public library, the Historical Museum of Southern Florida, and the Center for the Fine Arts, the county art museum.

Miami's oldest bar, established in 1912, is Tobacco Road, 626 South Miami Avenue, named after **Erskine Caldwell's** novel of the same name. Although Caldwell (1903-1987) lived in Dunedin, Florida, north of Tampa, he visited Miami quite frequently.

South of the Miami River is one of the county's most beautiful roads, Brickell Avenue. Named after William Brickell, the road is lined with banks and high-rise condominiums whose bold architectural attributes were featured on the opening sequence of *Miami Vice.* East of 8th Street on the Bay is the Four Ambassadors Hotel, so called because of its four towers. In 1973 **Celedonio González** (1923-) wrote an amusing novel in which the speaker is the hotel itself; titled *Los cuatro embajadores* (Miami: Ediciones Universal, 1973), the novel presents the happenings at the hotel, examining an assortment of employees and guests and their interactions. González also wrote two other novels which depict how the recently arrived Cuban exiles were coping with their new lives: *Los primos* (Miami: Ediciones Universal, 1971) and *El espesor del pellejo de un gato ya cadáver* (Miami: Ediciones Universal, 1978).

The area around Southwest 8th Street between 7th and 27th avenues is known as Little Havana because of the number of Cuban exiles who settled there. Along *Calle Ocho,* as 8th Street is better known, one can see old-timers hand rolling cigars and playing dominoes. Lately, this area has become a favorite of writers, many of whom use its uniqueness in their plots.

Douglas Fairbairn's *Street 8* (New York: Delacorte, 1977) is set almost entirely in this area; the following novels also include some scenes in Little Havana: **Christine Bell's** *The Pérez Family* (New York: W.W. Norton, 1990); **John Katzenbach's** *In the Heat of the Summer* (New York: Atheneum, 1982); **Paul Levine's** *To Speak for the Dead* (New York: Bantam, 1990); **John Sayles's** *Los Gusanos* (New York: HarperCollins, 1991); and **Virgil Suarez's** *The Cutter* (New York: Ballantine, 1991). **Peter Bart** and **Denne Bart Petitclerc's** *Destinies* (New York: Simon and Schuster, 1979) deals with the attempts of Cubans in Miami to overthrow Castro in Cuba. **Marcia del Mar's** *A Cuban Story* (Winston-Salem, NC: J.F. Blair, 1979) also takes place in the area.

Among the nonfiction books about the Cubans in Miami are *Pioneros Cubanos en U.S.A.* (Miami: no publisher, 1971) by **J. Isern** and *Cubans in the United States* (Westport, CT: Greenwood Press, 1984) by **Lyn MacCorkle**. Among the novels are *Cubanitos in a New Land* (Hialeah, FL: Mazan, 1975) by **Margaretta Curtin**; *The Nine Lives of Alphonse* (Philadelphia: Lippincott, 1968) by **James L. Johnson**; and *Flight From a Firing Wall* (New York: Simon & Schuster, 1966) by **Baynard Kendrick**.

In 1991 the Little Havana YMCA became the home of the Writer's Voice, which began at the New York West Side YMCA as a place where writers can find artistic support through workshops, awards, career-development programs, and other services. Under the original directorship of Carolina Hospital, the Writer's Voice, which has since moved to the Allapattah Y., aims to promote the literary arts among the community by sponsoring readings, awards, and general support for writers.

Also in Little Havana is La Casa del Preso, a boarding home for ex-political prisoners who have no family in the United States. While in Castro's prisons, many wrote poems, some of which were successfully smuggled out. Some of the most notable of these former political prisoner-poets are: **Angel Cuadra** (1931-), who wrote *Tiempo del hombre* (1977) and *Las señales y los sueños* (1988); **Angel Pardo** (1942-), whose works include *Neomambí* (1989) and *Entre rejas de Boniato/Behind Bars at Boniato* (1989); **Ernesto Díaz Rodriguez** (1939-), the author of *La campana del alba* (1984); **Salvador E. Subira Turro** (1938-), who wrote *Don Sinsonte de la palma* (1987); and **Jorge Valls** (1933-), who has published *A la paloma nocturna* (1984) and *Donde estoy no hay luz* (1984). Their poetry is testament to their strength of character and ability to survive harsh prison life.

On the western edge of Little Havana lies the Interamerican Center of Miami-Dade Community College, 699 Southwest 27th Avenue. One of its adjunct professors in Spanish, a man who has won six poetry prizes, including two of Spain's most prestigious, is **Amando Fernández** (1949-). After leaving Cuba and going to Spain in 1960, he moved to Miami in 1980. Since then, he has published eight books of poetry. His *Materia y forma* (1990) won the Luis de Góngora poetry prize, named after one of Spain's most important poets of the Renaissance, and his *Espacio mayor* (1991) won the Juan Ramón Jiménez Poetry Prize, named after the 1956 Nobel Prize winner.

Elsewhere in the southern section of the city lived **Enrique Labrador Ruiz** (1902-1991), who began writing in his native Cuba and published numerous books of short stories and fiction. One of his best known, *El pan de los muertos*, was originally published in Havana in 1958 and reprinted by Universal in 1988. Some of his other works include a short-story collection, *Carne de quimera* (1983); the novel *El laberinto de si mismo* (1933; reprinted 1983); and a collection of essays, *Cartas à la carte* (1991).

Colombian **Luis Zalamea** (1921-) has been living in the Miami area since 1967. This former translator for the United Nations has written in both English and Spanish. In 1965 Houghton-Mifflin published his *The Hour of Giving*, which describes the social situation in Colombia in the 1950s. Since then, Zalamea has written *Voces del destierro* (1984); *El círculo del alacrán* (Miami: Universal,1990), which satirically looks at Miami's Cuban exiles; and *Las guerras de la Champaña* (1992).

Christine Bell (1951-) was so inspired by the Mariel exodus that she wrote *The Pérez Family* (New York: W.W. Norton, 1990), a moving story of a political prisoner and his search for his family in Miami. The book suggests how in the twentieth century the family unit has been redefined. Her interest in the people of Latin America is also evident in her first novel, *Saint* (1985), set in South America.

Further south is the Vizcaya Museum and Gardens, 3251 South Miami Avenue. Built in 1916 by James Deering, owner of International Harvester, it offers south Floridians a European presence right on Biscayne Bay. **Judith Berke's** "Vizcaya" looks at the reality and unreality of this famous landmark, where past and present meet. Her poem recalls that Deering built the estate because "he can afford/a little culture now," yet he "liked to dress/as an explorer" while his "guests/in their splendid Greek and Arabian costumes" enjoyed this piece of Europe in early Miami. **Kathryn Chapman Harwood's** *The Lives of Vizcaya: Annals of a Great House* (Miami: Banyan, 1985) details the beginnings of this great mansion. *Florida Rediscovered*, compiled by **C. Douglas Elliott** and **Jeffrey D. Trammell** (Charlottesville, VA: Thomas Thomasson-Grant, 1988), includes photographs of this mansion and other Florida sites.

Several other writers deserve mention here. **Audrey Wurdemann** and her husband, **Joseph Auslander**, both died in Miami after long productive writing careers. Wurdemann (1911-1960), who was born in Seattle, had her first book of verse, *House of Silk* (1927), published when she was 16; her second book, *Bright Ambush*, won the Pulitzer Prize for poetry in 1935; she was the youngest poet ever to receive that award. She also wrote *Seven Sins, Splendour in the Grass*, and *Testament of Love: A Sonnet Sequence*. She is buried in Flagler Memorial Park in Miami. Her husband, **Joseph Auslander** (1897-1965), who was born in Philadelphia, collaborated with his wife in writing *The Unconquerables* (1943); *My Uncle Jan* (1948); and *The Islanders* (New York: Longmans, Green, 1951), about the conflicts between the old Greek culture in Florida and the American system. He joined with **Frank Ernest Hill** to write *The Winged Horse* (1927), a history of poetry for youngsters, and to edit *The Winged Horse Anthology* (1927), a widely used text in American schools. Joseph Auslander's other books of poetry were *Sunrise Trumpets* (1924), *Cyclops' Eye* (1926), *Hell in Harness* (1930), and *Letters to Women* (1930). He was poetry editor of *North American Review* and won the Robert Frost Prize for poetry.

Finally, poet **Larry Rubin** (1930-), who grew up in Miami and now teaches at the Georgia Institute of Technology, has written three books of poetry: *The World's Old Way* (Lincoln, NE: University of Nebraska Press, 1962), which includes some poems about Miami; *Lanced in Light* (1967); and *All My Mirrors Lie* (1975).

Coconut Grove

Just south of Vizcaya is Coconut Grove, whose history is almost as old as that of Miami. Originally called Jack's Bight, *bight* — meaning a bend or a small bay between two points of land, its name was changed in 1873 to Cocoanut Grove because of the abundance of coconut palms. When it was incorporated into the city of Miami in 1925, the *a* was dropped from the name. The history of this area is as colorful as some of its residents. In the 1870s the Edmund P.

Coconut Grove Playhouse

Beasley family moved into town; after the deaths of the Beasleys, Dr. Horace P. Porter, who had been living with them, made a claim on the land, which was eventually found to be invalid. During the time Porter had the land, he opened a post office with the name Cocoanut Grove. The area is also home to an early black settlement, comprised mainly of Bahamians who had come to work on Henry Flagler's railroad. Today the Grove is considered the Greenwich Village of Dade County, and its leisurely pace contrasts with the bustle of Miami. *Historic Coconut Grove: Self-Guided Tour* (Miami: Junior League of Miami, 1987) offers historical information about the area.

An important landmark is the Coconut Grove Playhouse, 3500 Main Highway, built in 1926 as a movie theater and converted in the 1950s. On January 3, 1956, it opened with the American premiere of **Samuel Beckett's** *Waiting for Godot* with Tom Ewell and Bert Lahr. The premiere was less than successful, perhaps because it baffled the audience and seemed too highbrow for the local scene. This theatrical event received national press, and among the celebrities in attendance were Joan Fontaine and Joseph Cotten. The second play presented boasted an international star, Tallulah Bankhead, in *A Streetcar Named Desire*. During the 1958-1959 season, **Tennessee Williams** tried to co-direct his *Period of Adjustment* with Owen Phillips, but eventually bowed out. Then in 1960 he supervised an early version of *Night of the Iguana*. More recently, during the 1985-86 season, **Edward Albee** (1928-) directed *Seascape*, starring Henderson Forsythe and Jacqueline Brooks. Now owned by the state of Florida, the playhouse is Miami's regional theater. **Carol Cohan**'s *Broadway by the Bay: Thirty Years at the Coconut Grove Playhouse* (Miami: Pickering, 1987) provides an extensive history of the playhouse, including a list of the more than 300 productions there. Because of its small-town charm, Coconut Grove continues to attract many with an artistic bent.

One of the early residents of the area was **Kirk Munroe** (1850-1930), who argued for the dropping of the *a* in the town's name. A writer of juvenile literature as well as adult fiction, Munroe recognized the literary potential of the area and often wrote about the Seminole Indians and the Everglades. Among his works with Miami settings are *Wakulla* (New York: Harper & Brothers, 1885) and *The Coral Ship* (New York: Chatterton, 1893). For more about him see **Irving Leonard**'s *The Florida Adventures of Kirk Munroe* (Chuluota, FL: Mickler House, 1975), a work that contains Munroe's autobiography, two articles about Florida, and a bibliography of his writings. Kirk Munroe's wife founded the Coconut Grove Library in 1895.

Kirk Munroe and Ralph Middleton Munroe (no relation) helped start the famous Biscayne Bay Yacht Club in 1887, as described in *One Hundred Years on Biscayne Bay, 1887-1987* by **Stuart McIver** (Miami: Seemann Publishing Co., 1980) and *The Commodore's Story* by **Ralph Middleton Munroe** and **Vincent Gilpin** (Miami: Historical Association of Southern Florida, 1985, a reprint of the 1930 edition). *Season of Innocence* by **Deborah A. Coulombe** and **Herbert L. Hiller** (Miami: Pickering, 1988) is about the Ralph Munroe family at their home, the Barnacle, in Coconut Grove; the Munroe family lived in the house

Marjory Stoneman Douglas

until 1973, when the state of Florida bought the property and restored the house and grounds.

The Coconut Grove House-keeper's Club at 2985 South Bayshore Drive was the scene of an incident that, according to the 1939 *WPA Guide to Florida*, was used by **Owen Wister** in *The Virginian* (1902). According to the *Guide*, visitors to the woman's club who had entrusted their children to the nursery for the day found that someone had switched the babies' identifying shawls — to the great confusion of the babies' parents.

Coconut Grove's most important figure, literary or otherwise, is **Marjory Stoneman Douglas** (1890-), not only a lifelong environmentalist, but also a journalist and writer. Born in Minneapolis, she arrived in Miami in 1915 and has lived in the same Coconut Grove house since 1926. She wrote a society column for the *Miami Herald*, which her father, Frank B. Stoneman, had founded. Invited by **Hervey Allen** to write for Rinehart's Rivers of America series, she chose to write about the Everglades rather than the small Miami River and describes the birth of the project thus: "There, on a writer's whim and an editor's decision, I was hooked with the idea that would consume me for the rest of my life." Because of the title of the series, she gave her work the title, *The Everglades: River of Grass* (New York: Rinehart, 1947; revised by Pineapple Press, 1988). Douglas describes the fragility and the beauty of this unique habitat. She continues to defend the environment and has lent her name to environmental causes. Among Douglas's many literary accolades is the O. Henry Award for her short story "He-Man," which is included in *Nine Florida Stories by Marjory Stoneman Douglas* edited by **Kevin M. McCarthy** (Jacksonville: University of North Florida Press, 1990).

Although preferring to write short stories, Douglas published a novel, *Road to the Sun* (New York: Rinehart, 1951), which she says "wasn't very good." In fact, she says that writing the novel "was a terrible struggle" because she was not used to writing such lengthy works. She set the novel in Miami before and after the boom of the 1920s, a time that she knew well. Her interest in the environment and Florida history can also be seen in her children's books, *Freedom River* (New York: Scribner, 1953) and *Alligator Crossing* (New York: John Day, 1959). Her *Florida: The Long Frontier* (New York: Harper & Row, 1967) is a history of the state. Her autobiography, which she wrote with **John Rothchild**, is *Marjory Stoneman Douglas: Voice of the River* (Sarasota: Pineapple Press, 1987).

Douglas was a founding member of south Florida's Fairchild Tropical Garden, 10901 Old Cutler Road, and the first editor of its *FTG Bulletin*. Thousands of visitors tour the gardens each year to see the variety of tropical plants, the largest such collection in the United States. As one of 19 botanical gardens in the country working to protect endangered species, it established The Center for Plant Conservation in 1984. For more about the garden see **Bertram Zuckerman's** *The Dream Lives on: A History of the Fairchild Tropical Garden, 1938-1988* (Miami: Banyan, 1988). **David Fairchild's** *Garden Islands of the Great East* (New York: Scribner's, 1944) is the story of Fairchild's collecting seeds in the Philippines, the Netherlands, and India for his garden. For a book on a wider area see *A Naturalist in Southern Florida* (Coral Gables, FL: University of Miami, 1971) by **Charlotte Orr Gantz**, a winter resident of Key Biscayne.

Sloan Wilson (1920-) during the 1970s lived on a boat in the Dinner Key Marina, 3400 Pan American Drive. A prolific writer, he is best known for *The Man in the Gray Flannel Suit* (1955) and *A Summer Place* (1958), both of which were made into movies.

Douglas Fairbairn (1926-) moved to the Miami area as a youngster. From his autobiography, *Down and Out in Cambridge* (New York: Coward, McCann, & Geoghegan, 1982), one gets a sense of early Coconut Grove where he lived. *Money, Marbles, and Chalk* (New York: Simon and Schuster, 1958) is set in Miami and deals with the adventures of a new boat captain and treasure seekers. Fairbairn, one of the first to write in English about the Cuban exiles, presents the volatile nature of some of the exiles, particularly when politics mixes with crime, in *Street 8* (New York: Delacorte Press, 1977). Although he originally wanted to call his novel *Calle Ocho*, the Spanish name for Eighth Street, his publishers felt that a Spanish title would not fare well in the market and forced him to change it.

E. Howard Hunt (1918-), who was born in Hamburg, New York, spent his childhood in Florida, attending elementary and junior high schools in Fort Lauderdale, where his father practiced law. In 1944, Hunt taught at the Air Force Intelligence School in Orlando, Florida, and during the Bay of Pigs invasion of Cuba (1961) stayed in Miami and Coconut Grove. His novels include *The Berlin Ending* (1973), *Undercover* (1974), and *The Hargrave Deception* (1980). *Bimini Run* (New York: Farrar, Straus, 1949) is set in Florida, as is the nonfiction *Give Us This Day* (New Rochelle, NY: Arlington House, 1973). Hunt returned to Miami in 1974 to stay.

Among the novels set in Coconut Grove is *Wilderness Teacher* (New York: Rand McNally, 1956) by **Zachary Ball**, the pseudonym of **Kelly Ray Masters**. For a history of how Pan American Airlines began operations at Dinner Key Marina under Juan Terry Trippe see **Lawrence Mahoney's** *The Early Birds, A History of Pan Am's Clipper Ships* (Miami: Pickering, 1987).

Key Biscayne

East of Coconut Grove is Key Biscayne, accessible from the Rickenbacker Causeway. Incorporated in 1991, it is one of the area's most exclusive communities; Richard Nixon had a vacation home there during his presidency. Some scholars believe that the first landfall made in the area was at Cape Florida, the southernmost tip of the island. In 1499 John Cabot rounded this point and named it Cape of the End of April. The only lighthouse in the county stands at the point. The islands have several beautiful and popular beaches, and the most famous tourist attraction is the Seaquarium, 4400 Rickenbacker Causeway.

Sherryl Woods (1944-), who has published more than 40 romance novels, moved to Miami in 1974 to work as television critic for the *Miami News*. In 1980 she began to write romances, and her first novel was *Restoring Love* (1982). Having set *A Kiss Away* (New York: Berkley, 1986) in Miami, she has now begun work on a Miami-based mystery series for Dell, which focuses, as she says, "not on glitzy Miami, but on real people." The first of the series is *Hot Property* (New York: Dell, 1992). Woods likes living near the sea because she is "creatively affected by being around water and the ocean."

Another Key Biscayne resident, **Susan Westfall** (1954-), began her career as writer-in-residence for the Coconut Grove Playhouse's touring company. A native Miamian, she "feels blessed because every day there's material created for [her] by the characters who are here." This love of the area is reflected in her plays, all of which are set in Miami. Her 1988 *Voices at the Mary Elizabeth Hotel* for New Theatre is a one-man show about an Overtown hotel that is being torn down to make way for Interstate 95. In *1962* (1989), she presents several persons at an elementary school in Miami during the October missile crisis. In her latest work, the musical *You Are Here* (1991), actors and characters comment on the city. She considers one of her most challenging commissions a 15-minute piece on the history of Miami that was performed during Queen Elizabeth's 1991 visit to the city.

Among the novels set in and around Key Biscayne is *Millionaires* (New York: Delacorte, 1972) by **Herbert d'H. Lee**, the pseudonym of **Herbert Kastle**. For a history of the island see *The Book of Key Biscayne* by **Jim Woodman** (Miami: Miami Post, 1961). A less savory part of the island was explored in *The Candy Murder Case* by **Paul Holmes** (New York: Bantam, 1966). The work covers the 1964 murder of financier Jacques Mossler in one of the apartments on Key Biscayne; his wife (Candace) and her nephew (Mel Powers) were indicted for the murder, but were acquitted in a trial.

Coral Gables

Like Orlando, Coral Gables calls itself the City Beautiful and is to the west of Coconut Grove. In 1919 entrepreneur George Merrick, seeing how fast Miami was growing, founded Coral Gables and paid William Jennings Bryan $50,000 to act as its spokesperson. The origin of its name, much like that of Miami, has never been fully ascertained; some say that it is a version of Gray Gables, the name of Grover Cleveland's Cape Cod home, while others say it described the first house built there, which had its gables decorated with coral rock. For more about the area see *George E. Merrick and Coral Gables, Florida* by **Kathryne Ashley** (Coral Gables, FL: Crystal Bay Publishers, 1985) and *Coral Gables in Postcards: Scenes from Florida's Yesterday* by **Samuel D. LaRoue, Jr.** and **Ellen J. Uguccioni** (Miami: Dade Heritage Trust, 1988).

An early Gables resident was **Effie Lawrence Marshall** (1873-1970), who wrote numerous novels based on the lives of famous women of the Bible. However, one of her novels, *The Flame Vine* (Portland, ME: House of Falmouth, 1964), is set in 1920s Miami. Juvenile-literature writer **Jean Lee Latham** (1902-) is still a Gables resident. The West Virginia native began writing in the 1950s and is best known for *Carry on, Mr. Bowditch* (1955), which was a 1956 selection for the Newbery Award for children's literature.

The 1956 Nobel Prize winner for literature, the Spanish writer **Juan Ramón Jiménez** (1881-1958), lived in Coral Gables for a while during the 1950s; he is best known for *Platero and I* (1957), Spain's best-known work after *Don Quixote*, and for being a father figure for such prominent poets as Lorca. A Republican during the Spanish civil war, Jiménez argued unceasingly all over the world defending the Republican cause. When the Republicans lost, he became disillusioned and stopped writing. While he was in the United States, the University of Miami invited him "to give a series of lectures." That Jiménez spent time in Coral Gables is not surprising due to "the fact that Coral Gables was so much like Andalusia," his birthplace. While convalescing at Doctors Hospital, 5000 University Drive, he was inspired by the beautiful view from his hospital room and wrote *Los romances de Coral Gables*, which can be found in *Tercera antología poética* (Madrid: Biblioteca Nueva, 1957). Several of the poems, like "Espacio," reflect the beauty of the city.

Hervey Allen (1889-1949), author of *Anthony Adverse* (1933), was a Gables resident and longtime supporter and trustee of the University of Miami. When **Robert Frost** moved to the area, their friendship, which had begun at Bread Loaf, a two-week summertime writers' conference in Middlebury, Vermont, blossomed. Allen was instrumental in convincing Frost to make the Miami area his winter home. As editor of the Rivers of America series, Allen also contacted **Marjory Stoneman Douglas** to see if she would write a book about the Miami River; instead of that project she suggested a book about the Everglades and proceeded to write the environmentally significant work *The Everglades: River* *of Grass* (New York: Rinehart, 1947). [See her essay in Chapter Seven of this *Book Lover's Guide* for background on her book.] For more about Allen see **Stuart E. Knee**'s *Hervey Allen, 1889-1949: A Literary Historian in America* (Lewiston, NY: Edwin Mellen, 1988).

Folklorist and short-story writer **Lydia Cabrera** (1900-1991) also made her home in Coral Gables. She was the foremost authority on Afro-Cuban folklore and religion, writing seminal works in this field, of which *El monte* (1957) is her best known. When she left her native Cuba in 1960, she continued writing both scholarly and creative works. In her first collection, *Cuentos negros de Cuba* (1940), and in her later *Ayapá, cuentos de Jicotea* (1971), she captured the essence of the Afro-Cuban experience in a series of folk tales. Following the tradition of mythology, she tried to explain, using Afro-Cuban folklore, the origins of things in the world in *¿Por qué?* (1948; reprinted 1972) and underscored the theme of the collection by beginning each tale with *why*. In a different vein, but still recalling her native land and trying to keep its memory alive even during exile, is her *Itinerarios del insomnio: Trinidad de Cuba* (1977).

Leslie Charteris (1907-), who also spent some time in Coral Gables, is best known for his *Saint* novels, which have been made into movies and a popular television series. *Meet the Tiger* (1929) and *Knight Templar* (1930) are two of the earliest novels in the series; *The Saint in Miami* (New York: Doubleday, Doran & Company, 1940) is set in Miami.

One of the new generation of Cuban-American writers is **Roberto G. Fernández** (1948-). Having written his first two novels in Spanish, *La vida es un especial* (Miami: Ediciones Universal, 1981) and *La montaña rusa* (Houston: Arte Público Press, 1985), in 1988 he published *Raining Backwards* (Houston: Arte Público Press), his first work in English. In all three novels, he takes a satirical and surrealistic look at the life of the Cuban exiles. Although he teaches Spanish at Florida State University in Tallahassee, whenever he comes to Miami, which is as often as he can, he stays in the Gables.

Prolific **Heather Graham Pozzessere** (1953-) publishes romance novels under three names: her own, **Heather Graham**, and **Shannon Drake**. Even though she has set her more than 60 novels in a variety of locales, she likes to use her hometown. Her first two novels had a Miami setting: *Tender Taming* (New York: Dell, 1983) and *When Next We Love* (New York: Dell, 1983). In addition, her *Tomorrow the Glory* (New York: Pinnacle Books, 1985) partly takes place at the mouth of the Miami River during the Civil War. For Harlequin/Silhouette of New York City, she has published the following Miami-set novels: *The Game of Love* (1986), *Angel of Mercy* (1988), *Borrowed Angel* (1989), and *Forever My Love* (1990).

Dade County's oldest institution of higher learning, the University of Miami, is an important part of the city. Established in 1926 "to attract students from Central and South America," the university has many literary associations. While in the area, **Robert Frost** and **Hervey Allen** were strong supporters of the English department. In the 1930s Frost participated in the school's Winter Institute of Literature. Among the visiting professors the department has had are Isaac Bashevis Singer and James Michener, who in the 1980s taught creative-writing courses. Distinguished alumnus and Pulitzer Prize-winner Donald Justice graduated from the university in 1945. The institution also promotes the literary arts through its two literary magazines. The older, *Carrel*, has been sponsored by the Friends of the Library for more than three decades. Although it began as a library journal, it now publishes poetry, fiction, and artwork of persons associated with the university. The younger magazine, *Epiphany*, presents the works of both graduate and undergraduate university students.

Among other writers associated with the university is a native of Vancouver, British Columbia, **Laurence Donovan** (1927-), who came to Miami at age 11 and grew up in the area now known as Little Havana. He has been with the university's English department since the early 1960s. The area's profound influence on him is evident in most of his poetry and art work, for he often illustrates his own verse. In "Sidewalks," he laments how Miamians no longer use them, and in "The Solar Heater Plant," he depicts old Miami. Both poems appear in *Spirit* (South Orange, NJ: Seton Hall University Press, 1989). Donovan frequently reviews poetry books and books about poets for the *Miami Herald*.

Also writing and teaching fiction at the university since the early 1960s is **Lester Goran** (1928-). Of his many novels, *The Paratrooper of Mechanic Avenue* (1960) is his most popular. However, *The Demon in the Sun Parlor* (New York: New American Library, 1968), set in Key Biscayne in the 1930s, received excellent reviews. Goran returns to a Miami setting in his next novel, *Under the Neon Moon*.

Evelyn Wilde Mayerson (1935-), author of many historical novels, set *No Enemy but Time* (Garden City, NY: Doubleday, 1983) in Miami Beach during World War II. The best-known of her seven novels is *Sanjo* (1979). Mayerson received the Sidney Taylor Award for children's literature for *Cat Who Escaped from Steerage* (1990). A former professor of psychiatry at Temple University and the University of South Florida, Mayerson now teaches fiction. She feels like a Miami native because she arrived in the city at age three. What she likes most about living in Miami is that the city has "an enormous amount of electricity created by our ethnic mix, our newness, and our vast natural resources"; because of this newness "one can forge his own place."

Three other writers are teaching in the English department of the University of Miami. Novelist **Kathleen Martell Gordon** combines fantastic elements and an Everglades setting in *Psychic and the Swamp Man* (New York: Viking Press, 1981). **Robert Gregory** (1947-), named the Best Poet in Miami in 1990 by the *New Times*, has written *Interferences* (Berkeley, CA: Poltroon Press, 1987); in addition, his poetry has appeared in *Caliban, Ariel*, and *Gulf Stream*. Miami Shores native **Peter Schmitt** (1958-) received high praise for *Country Airport* (Providence, RI: Cooper Beech Press, 1989); three poems in the book reflect life in Miami: "Frost in Miami," "Glance," and "A Day at the Beach."

Charlton Tebeau

One of Miami's most prolific writers, **Ana Rosa Nuñez** (1926-), has been a reference librarian at the university's Otto G. Richter Library since 1965. She has written or edited more than 19 books, including *Poesía en éxodo* (1970), a collection of the writings of exiled Cuban poets. Although she always writes in Spanish, she has published a bilingual collection of poetry, *Crisantemos* (1990). In *Uno y veinte golpes por América* (1991) she uses the Japanese haiku to address each nation of the New World.

David E. Fisher (1932-) has taught marine geology since the mid-1960s but also finds time to write fiction. Among his many works are *The Last Flying Tiger* (New York: Scribner, 1980), set in Miami; *Hostage One* (1989) about the kidnapping of the President; and *Fire and Ice* (1990), which examines the environment and particularly the greenhouse effect. Finally, **Gilbert L. Voss** (1918-1989), a distinguished oceanographer and marine biologist with the University of Miami's Rosenstiel School of Marine and Atmospheric Science, wrote such works as *Oceanography* (1972); *Seashore Life of Florida and the Caribbean* (Miami: Seemann Publishing Co., 1976); and *Coral Reefs of Florida* (Sarasota: Pineapple Press, 1988).

For more about the school see *The University of Miami: A Golden Anniversary History, 1926-1976* (Coral Gables, FL: University of Miami, 1976) by **Charlton W. Tebeau** (1904-). Tebeau, longtime chairman of the school's history department, wrote with **Ruby Leach Carson** *Florida: From Indian Trail To Space Age* (Delray Beach, FL: Southern Publishing Co., 1965). For 40 years he edited *Tequesta*, the journal of the Historical Association of Southern Florida, and wrote such Florida works as *Florida's Last Frontier: The History of Collier County* (Coral Gables, FL: University of Miami Press, 1957; updated 1966); *They Lived* *in the Park* (Coral Gables, FL: Everglades Natural History Association, 1963; revised in 1968 as *Man in the Everglades*); *Synagogue in the Central City: Temple Israel of Greater Miami, 1922-1972* (Coral Gables, FL: University of Miami Press, 1972); one of the best histories of the state: *The History of Florida* (Coral Gables, FL: University of Miami Press, 1971; updated 1980); and *The Story of the Chokoloskee Bay Country* (Miami: Banyan, 1976).

Directly across the street from the University of Miami is the National Hurricane Center, 1320 South Dixie Highway. The most important hurricane-tracking center in the hemisphere, it also is responsible for reporting on all tropical meteorology and tracks hurricanes both in the Atlantic region and in the eastern Pacific. During hurricane season (June 1 to November 30), the center is busy keeping the community and the nation informed of all tropical storms and hurricane activity. Among the hurricane novels that take place in South Florida are **Shelley Katz**'s *Alligator* (New York: Dell, 1977) and **Herman Wouk**'s *Slattery's Hurricane* (New York: PermaBooks, 1956). **José Carlos Millás**'s *Hurricanes of the Caribbean & Adjacent Regions, 1492-1800* (Miami: Academy of the Arts and Sciences of the Americas, 1968) is a chronological list of storms to hit the area. For a good book covering the entire state see

Morton D. Winsberg's *Florida Weather* (Orlando: University of Central Florida Press, 1990). **Marjory Stoneman Douglas**'s *Hurricane* (New York: Rinehart, 1958) gives a good description of hurricanes; the revised edition of that book (Atlanta: Mockingbird Books, 1976) left out the details of the Florida hurricanes. **Pauline B. Innis** and **Joseph Archibald**'s *Hurricane Fighters* (New York: McKay Co., 1962) is about the scientists who track down and study hurricanes.

South Miami

Around the Dixie Highway and Red Road (Southwest 57th Avenue) intersection is the city of South Miami. Its name is not quite accurate, for it really lies more directly south

Robert Frost

of Coral Gables than of Miami. However, that was not the city's first name; it was called Larkin, after one of its most important citizens, William A. Larkin, who established one of the first stores in the area. **Rhoda Ogden Protko's** *In and Around South Miami, 1776-1976* (South Miami, FL: South Miami Area Chamber of Commerce, 1976) provides information not only about the city but also about the county as a whole.

In the 1940s **Robert Frost** (1874-1963) moved to what is now 8101 Southwest 53rd Avenue and named it Pencil Pines; his estate, located "in a clearing of scrub pine," is on the National Register of Historic Places. Before settling here, he wintered for many years in different parts of the state, including Key West and Gainesville. Although his poetry does not reflect the influence of his Florida home, his biographers suggest that he changed the title of his 1961 book because of his living in South Miami. Having planned for many years to call it *The Great Misgiving*, Frost changed it to *In the Clearing* while he was recuperating in Pencil Pines from a bout of pneumonia. On March 17, 1962, **Charles Whited**, a reporter for the *Miami Herald*, published an interview with Frost in which he described Frost's house as a "New England cottage, ... simple, utilitarian, and screened from the world by heavy foliage." According to Whited, the yard was full of fruit trees, including avocadoes and mangoes, because Frost had come to be a farmer in his South Miami home. In a letter to Louis Mertins, Frost described his winters in the area as follows: "I am farming for a few weeks among the loquats and avocadoes of California's rival climate." In 1960, the University of Miami awarded Frost an honorary degree both for his work and for his many contributions to the university community.

Close to the area's Sunset Drive and Red Road intersection lived **Philip Wylie** (1902-1971), best known for his vitriolic *A Generation of Vipers* (1942). Wylie is also well known for his science-fiction novel, *When Worlds Collide* (1933), which he co-wrote with **Edwin Balmer**. Equally successful were the many stories about Miami fishing he published throughout his life in the *Saturday Evening Post*; some of these have been collected in *The Best of Crunch and Des* (New York: Rinehart, 1954); "Widow Voyage" in *Florida Stories* (1989) edited by **Kevin McCarthy** and *Crunch and Des* (New York: Lyons & Burford, 1990). He also used Miami as a backdrop for two novels: *Night unto Night* (New York: Grosset & Dunlap, 1944), which is set during World War II and has as one of the protagonists an aviation officer training in Miami Beach; and *The Disappearance* (New York: Holt, Rinehart & Winston, 1951).

Another science-fiction writer who calls South Miami home is **Gary Alan Ruse** (1946-). This Miami native first began publishing high-tech suspense novels, *Houndstooth* (1975) and *A Game of Titans* (1976), for instance. In the 1980s he turned to science fiction with *The Gods of Cerus Major* (1982) and *Deathhunt on a Dying Planet* (1988).

Judy Cuevas (1948-), writer of historical novels, has lived in Miami since 1970. Although her *Starlit Surrender* (1988) is set during the French Revolution and her *Black Silk* (1991) is set in Victorian England, she has plans to write in the near future a novel set in Miami.

Lawyer **Paul Levine's** (1948-) first novel spent 15 weeks on the *Miami Herald* best-seller list. He finds inspiration living in Miami because for a writer of crime fiction like himself "there's no better place to work in than Miami, especially if you like to lace your fiction with humor because it offers a wealth of raw material and a cornucopia of weirdness." As a former crime reporter for the *Herald*, Levine was able to draw from his experiences for both *To Speak for the Dead* (New York: Bantam Books, 1990) and *Night Vision* (New York: Bantam, 1991), a dark tale of serial murder.

Another former journalist, **Lois Wolfe** (1952-), has recently turned to writing historical romances. A native of West Virginia, she came to Miami in 1975. While at the *Miami Herald*, she wrote two columns: "Parenting" (1983-1985) and "Bookbeat" (1988-1991). Her novel *The Schemers* (1991), which is set at the end of the Civil War, presents a French-English-Egyptian conspiracy to save the South. Although she writes about nineteenth-century England and the United States, she believes that "the multicultural experience [of Miami] has made [her] more sensitive to the quiet cultural blend of the nineteenth century."

Eugenio Florit

Unincorporated Southern Dade

Unincorporated southern Dade County includes a number of residential communities; one of them is known as Westchester. **Eugenio Florit** (1903-), considered one of the best writers in Spanish, calls it home. Though he was born in Spain, his family moved to Cuba in 1918. A former professor of Spanish at Columbia University, Florit has lived in the United States since 1942. He moved to Miami in 1982 and continues to write, adding to his library of more than 30 published books. In 1955 he translated the works of contemporary American writers in *Antología de la poesía norteamericana contemporánea* (1955);

in addition, his own work has been translated into English. Despite the fact that he is fluent in the language, he has never written his own poems in English.

His first book of poetry, *32 poemas breves,* appeared in 1927, but one of his most respected is his second, *Trópico* (1930), where he describes the Cuban landscape, focusing on the countryside and the sea. His love and admiration of nature and especially of the Cuban and Spanish countryside is a theme evident throughout his work. However, some of his best writing turns inward, examining the self and the influences of the past; his *Conversaciones a mi padre* (1949) breaks ground by painting a realistic picture of his father, which suggests the poet's emotional and artistic maturity. Two of Florit's most recent collections of poems are *Castillo interior y otros versos* (1987) and *Las noches* (1988).

Hilda Perera (1926-) is another important figure in Cuban literature. She often writes for young people but is most recognized for her novels. She considers *Robledal* (1987) to be her best, although *Sitio de nadie* (1972) is her best known. In the latter she examines a Cuban family in the early 1960s as it prepares to leave the island seeking the freedom it had been denied. One of her works set in Miami is *Felices pascuas* (Barcelona: Editorial Planeta, 1977). Her *Free To Be Me* (Miami: Pickering Press, 1991), a translation of her Spanish-language novel entitled *Kiki,* is about Cuban children who came to Miami in the 1960s without their parents and then later had to help their parents adjust to life in America.

On 8th Street at 107th Avenue lies the University Park campus of Florida International University (FIU). The only state university in the area, FIU opened its doors in September 1972 with more than 5,000 students. *Visibility Unlimited* (Miami: Florida International University, 1976) by **Rafe Gibbs** describes the early years of the university.

Currently teaching on this campus is Hungarian-born **Peter Hargatai** (1947-), known both for his translations and his short stories. He has translated the work of **Atilla Jozsef,** the most important twentieth-century Hungarian poet. Hargatai's *Perched on Nothing's Branch* (1989) is a selection of Jozsef's best poetry. In addition, he has translated Hungarian folk tales which are compiled in *Magyai Tales* (1989). His *Budapestäl New Yorkig* (1989) is a collection of short stories in Hungarian and English. Most recently his stories have appeared in *Fodor's Budget Zion* (1991).

Adjunct professor **Virgil Suarez** (1962-) lived in California for many years but since 1986 has lived in Dade County, first in Hialeah and more recently in Coral Gables. His California upbringing is evident in his novel *Latin Jazz* (New York: William Morrow, 1989), which takes place alternately in Los Angeles and Havana during the Mariel boatlift. His interest in things Cuban can be seen in his latest work, *The Cutter* (1991), whose title refers to the protagonist's being forced to participate in the harvesting of sugarcane in order to be allowed to leave the island.

Several other writers at the university should be mentioned. Bilingual dramatist **Miguel González-Pando** (1941-) has held various administrative positions since he began working at FIU in 1973. One of his plays, *The Torch* (1988), creates in the audience the sense of political oppression that the characters are experiencing. In 1989 he wrote *Había una vez un sueño* and then did the English version of it — *Once Upon a Dream* (Houston: Arte Público, 1991). His *The Great American Justice Game* (1985) won a prize at Seattle's Multicultural Playwright's Festival. This Bay of Pigs veteran has completed a documentary presenting oral accounts of Cuba's history.

One of Miami's most respected writers has been at FIU since 1987. **Uva Clavijo** (1944-) has written three books of poetry and three collections of short stories, but has lately focused on the latter. She is most proud of *Ni verdad ni mentira y otros cuentos* (Miami: Ediciones Universal, 1977) and *No puedo más y otros cuentos* (Miami: Ediciones Universal, 1989). Influenced by Edgar Allan Poe, she likes to give her stories unexpected endings. In *No puedo más*, she experiments with point of view and explores the limit of one's endurance; the title, meaning *I can no more*, is indicative of man's struggle to survive and, frequently, his inability to do so. Another important literary figure is **Darden Asbury Pyron** (1942-), a founding member of the university's department of History. His *Southern Daughter: The Life of Margaret Mitchell* (1991) has received good critical response and was a Book of the Month Club selection.

Further south is Kendall Drive (Southwest 88th Street), which gives its name to another section of unincorporated Dade County. However, as late as the end of the nineteenth century, there was still a Seminole village at Kendall and 87th Avenue. The area's namesake was Henry John Boughton Kendall, vice president of British Land Company, which owned this tract. Henry Flagler boosted its development by choosing the land for one of the model groves which he would showcase as proof of the area's great value.

Nicole Rubel (1953-), who has written over 30 children's books, lives in Kendall. Her most popular stories are part of the Rotten Ralph series, published by Dial. One can see how living in Miami has influenced her writing by her frequent use of alligators. Her *It Came from the Swamp* (New York: Dial, 1988) was inspired by a story from the *Miami Herald* which touched upon how the westward movement of the population was affecting the eastern portion of the Everglades.

Here also is the Kendall Campus of Miami-Dade Community College, 11011 Southwest 104th Street. Its English department is home to three important area writers and sponsors a student literary magazine. *My Ambiance* started in 1987 and has won several awards; it presents the works of students on campus. Since 1965 **Ron DeMaris** has been teaching composition and creative writing at the Kendall campus. In the past few years, his poetry has appeared in *Nation* and *Ploughshares*. He frequently uses the Miami milieu in his poetry, as evidenced in "Net" (*American Poetry Review*) and "Pizarro" (*Sewanee Review*).

A former student of DeMaris and now associate professor of English, **Ricardo Pau-Llosa** (1954-) has written poetry both in Spanish and English; the versatile writer is also an expert in contemporary Latin American art and has written seven books of art criticism. His *Sorting Metaphors* (Tallahassee: Anhinga Press, 1983) won the Anhinga Poetry Prize. Moving away from an examination of language and particularly of metaphors, he addresses in *Bread of the Imagined* (Tucson: Bilingual, 1991) the problem of place, with the first part of the book dealing with poems about Miami and the tropics. In his most recent work, *Cuba* (1992), Mr. Pau-Llosa fondly mingles memories and stories of his native country, further moving his work toward the narrative. One of the reasons he likes living in Miami is that, as he says, "I live this close to Latin America and have access to a lot of Latin American culture, which allows me to live in close contact with that culture. In Miami, I can live in two cultural contexts in one place."

Carolina Hospital (1957-), editor of the ground-breaking *Cuban American Writers: Los Atrevidos* (Princeton, NJ: Ediciones Ellas/Linden Lane Press, 1988),

Felix Morisseau-Leroy

left Cuba in 1961 and has lived in Miami since 1966. Her poetry has appeared in *Linden Lane Magazine*, *Appalachia Quarterly*, *The Americas Review*, and *Confrontation*. With **Pablo Medina**, she has translated Cuban dissident poet Tania Díaz Castro's *Everyone Will Have to Listen* (1991) into English.

South of the Kendall area along Dixie Highway (U.S. 1) to 152nd Street lies yet another unincorporated area of Dade County. Perrine gets its name from Dr. Henry Perrine, who was killed by Indians in the 1840 Indian Key Massacre. Perrine had come to south Florida to try his luck in growing citrus trees when his medical practice proved unsuccessful. After Henry Flagler decided to continue his railroad south to Key West, this area grew tremendously because it was used as a supply depot.

Haiti's foremost poet has resided in Dade County since 1981. **Félix Morisseau-Leroy** (1912-) had to leave his country after he used Sophocles's *Antigone* to comment on Papa Doc Duvalier's dictatorship. He translated the play into Creole, juxtaposed Greek religion with voodoo, and pointed to the similarities between Kreon and Duvalier. Since his exile in 1959, he has lived in France, Nigeria, Ghana, Senegal, and Jamaica working in the theater as director and training actors. In Miami, where his son owns an import-export business, he has continued writing poetry and contributing to the local Haitian newspaper, *Haiti en march*, and has been actively involved in local productions of plays in Creole.

Morisseau-Leroy was the first Haitian poet to write in Creole instead of French. He saw his lifelong struggle to assert the superiority of Creole vindicated when the post-Duvalier Haitian constitution was written in both Creole and French. The Haitian government is now also increasingly using Creole as its official language. His first book of poems, *Plénitudes* (1939), was better received in France than in Haiti; but now his poem "Thank you, Dessalines" has become, as he calls it, "the poem of the people" because it was used as a rallying cry during the country's struggle against dictatorship. *Dyakout 1, 2, 3, 4* (1990) is a collection of his poetry; a *dyakout* is a bag used by peasants to carry items and by the voodoo priests to carry their wares. Morisseau-Leroy's works have been translated into French, German, Spanish, Russian, Chinese, Wolof (a language spoken in Senegal), Twe (one of the languages spoken in Ghana), and Fanti (another language of Ghana). There are two collections of his works in English: *Ten Selected Poems* (1978) and *Haitiad and Other Oddities* (1991).

Nova University administrator **Ralph Hogges** (1947-) has lived in Miami since 1972. His *The Next President of the United States* (1988) is the story of how a very poor boy attains the highest office. Hogges is also a poet, whose work appears in *The American Poetry Anthology* (1990), *Treasured Poems of America* (1990), and *Windows on the World* (1990).

To read more about Dade County and its history, see **E.V. Blackman's** *Miami and Dade County, Florida: Its Settlement, Progress and Achievement* (Chuluota, FL: Mickler House, 1977); **Laura Cerwinske's** *Miami: Hot and Cool* (New York: C.N. Potter, 1990); **David King Gleason's** *Over Miami* (Baton Rouge: Louisiana State University Press, 1990); **Tracy Hollingsworth's** *History of Dade County* (Miami: *Miami Post*, 1936); **William W. Jenna, Jr.'s** *Metropolitan Miami: A Demographic Overview* (Coral Gables, FL: University of Miami Press, 1972); **Bob Kearney's** *Mostly Sunny Days: A* Miami Herald *Salute to South Florida's Heritage* (Miami: Miami Herald Publishing Co., 1986); **Helen Muir's** *Miami, U.S.A.* (1953; republished Miami: Pickering Press, 1990) and *The Biltmore: Beacon for Miami* (Miami: Pickering Press, 1987); **Arva Moore Parks's** *Miami, Magic City* (Tulsa, OK: Continental Heritage Press, 1981); **Thelma Peters's** *Biscayne Country, 1870-1926* (Miami: Banyan, 1981); **Guillermo J. Grenier** and **Alex Stepick III's** *Miami Now!* (Gainesville: University Press of Florida, 1992); and **Jean Taylor's** *The Villages of South Dade* (St. Petersburg: Byron Kennedy, 1985?).

Three recent books have explored how Miami is coping with and surviving rapid changes: **T.D. Allman's** *Miami: City of the Future* (New York: Atlantic Monthly Press, 1987); **Joan Didion's** *Miami* (New York: Simon and Schuster, 1987); and **David Rieff's** *Going to Miami: Exiles, Tourists, and Refugees in the New America* (Boston: Little, Brown, 1987). Miami historian

Paul S. George has edited *A Guide to the History of Florida* (New York: Greenwood Press, 1989) with chapters written by experts on each of Florida's historical periods.

The Miami area has always been a source of inspiration to writers. The following is a list of novels and plays set in Miami by authors who have not lived in Dade County: **William Ard**'s *The Root of His Evil* (New York: Rinehart, 1957); **Russell Banks's** *Continental Drift* (New York: Harper & Row, 1985); **Mike Barry**'s *Miami Marauder* (New York: Berkley, 1974); **Wyatt Blassingame**'s *The Golden Geyser* (Garden City, NY: Doubleday, 1961); **Raúl de Cárdenas'** *Dile a la Fragancia que yo la quiero* (Los Angeles: no publisher, 1985) and *Luz divina, santera, espiritista de una a cinco* (Los Angeles: no publisher, 1986); **Harriet H. Carr**'s *Miami Tower* (New York: Macmillan, 1956); **Warren Pendleton Carrier**'s *Bay of the Damned* (New York: John Day Co., 1957); **Douglas Cook**'s *Chocker's Son* (New York: Comet, 1959); **Dorothy Cottrell**'s *Silent Reefs* (New York: William Morrow, 1953); **John Creasey**'s *Murder, London-Miami* (New York: Scribner, 1969); **Dorothy Erskine** and **Edward Everett Tanner**'s **(Patrick Dennis)** *The Pink Hotel* (New York: Putnam, 1957); **Maysie Greig**'s **(Mary Douglas Warren)** *The High Road* (New York: Arcadia House, 1954); **James Herlihy**'s *Midnight Cowboy* (New York: Simon and Schuster, 1965); **Rona Jaffe**'s *Family Secrets* (New York: Simon and Schuster, 1974); **David Allan Kaufelt**'s *Late Bloomer* (New York: Harcourt, Brace, Jovanovich, 1979); **Rufus King**'s *Murder Masks Miami* (New York: Doubleday, Doran & Co., Inc., 1939); **Lynn Kostoff**'s *A Choice of Nightmares* (New York: Crown, 1991); **Marston La France**'s *Miami Murder-Go-Round* (Cleveland, OH: World Publishing, 1951); **Susan Lennox**'s *Paradise Isle* (New York: Avalon Books, 1957); **John D. MacDonald**'s *The Last One Left* (Garden City, NY: Doubleday, 1967) and *The Scarlet Ruse* (Greenwich, CT: Fawcett, 1973); **Elaine Markson**'s *Home Again, Home Again* (New York: William Morrow, 1978); **Kelly Ray Masters'** **(Zachary Ball)** *Joe Panther* (New York: Holiday House, 1950) and *Swamp Chief* (New York: Holiday House, 1952); **Victoria McKernan**'s *Point Deception* (New York: Carroll & Graf Publishers, 1992); **Mildred Nelson**'s *The Island* (New York: Pocket Books, 1973); **Ellery Queen**'s *The Yellow Cat Mystery* (Boston: Little, Brown, 1952); **Judith Richards**'s *Summer Lightning* (New York: St. Martin's Press, 1978); **Harold Robbins**'s *79 Park Avenue* (New York: Knopf, 1955); **Jerome Sanford**'s *Miami Heat* (New York: St. Martin's Press, 1991); **Robert Kimmel Smith**'s *Sadie Shapiro in Miami* (New York: Fawcett Crest, 1977); **Charlotte Springer** and **Bob Springer**'s *Smuggler's Moon* (New York: Exposition, 1954); **Francis Wallace**'s *Kid Galahad* (Boston: Little, Brown, 1936); **Herman Weiss**'s *Passion in the Wind* (New York: Popular Library, 1977); **Lionel White**'s *Flight into Terror* (New York: Dutton, 1955); **Charles Williams**'s *Aground* (New York: Viking Press, 1960) and *The Sailcloth Shroud* (New York: Pocket Books, 1960); **Joy Williams**'s *The Changeling* (Garden City, NY: Doubleday, 1978); and **Prentice Winchell**'s **(Spencer Dean)** *Dishonor Among Thieves* (Garden City, NY: Doubleday, 1958).

Other fictional works set in Miami are **Electa Clark**'s *Spanish Gold and Casey McKee* (New York: David McKay, 1956); **Walter Farley**'s *The Black Stallion Challenged* (New York: Random House, 1964); **John Keasler**'s *The Christmas It Snowed in Florida* (Coconut Grove, FL: Hurricane House, 1962); **Ben Kerr**'s *Shakedown* (New York: Henry Holt, 1952); **Eleanor Frances Lattimore**'s *Lively Victoria* (New York: Morrow, 1952); **Theodore McCormick**'s *Dangerous Rescue* (New York: Funk & Wagnalls, 1964); **Mariana Prieto**'s *Tomato Boy* (New York: John Day, 1967); and **Suzy Wetlaufer**'s *Judgment Call* (New York: Morrow, 1992).

FLORIDA MYSTERIES

MAURICE J. O'SULLIVAN

Perhaps the earliest of Florida's fictional detectives, U.S. Revenue Detective Thomas Duff Mastic, appeared in Archibald Clavering Gunter's *Don Blasco of Key West* (1896). With its emphasis on action, its monochromatic conception of good and evil, its flat characters, and its stilted language — Mastic's first words are, "Hang me if I understand this!" — *Don Blasco* exemplifies the dime novel adventure popular in Victorian America. Florida's mysteries continued in this vein for the next four decades, with occasional forays into the traditions of romance and gothic novels. Under the influence of *The Black Mask* magazine and its hard-boiled heroes, however, the American mystery novel was undergoing a transformation, adding characterization and psychology to stories known primarily for intricate plots and exotic weapons.

The turning point for the detective novel in Florida was 1936. That year Dennis Wheatley produced the first of his four police dossiers, *Murder Off Miami*, a work which provided all the evidence necessary to solve a crime, including photos, letters, personal statements, and bits of physical evidence. While this work may be the purest police procedural ever published (if published is the right word), that same year the first two Florida series detectives appeared. Baynard Hardwick Kendrick introduced deputy sheriff Miles Standish Rice ("I'm Miles Standish Rice — the Hungry!") in *The Iron Spiders* and *The Eleven of Diamonds*; and Theodore Pratt, better known for his historical novels like *The Barefoot Mailman* (1943), assumed the pen name Timothy Brace to create the millionaire sportsman Anthony Adams for the first of three mysteries with characteristically Floridian settings: *Murder Goes Fishing*, soon followed by *Murder Goes in a Trailer* (1937) and *Murder Goes to the Dogs* (1938).

The last year of the thirties saw the emergence of Florida's first best-selling detective series when Davis Dresser, writing as Brett Halliday, opened the Miami office of Mike Shayne to investigate a *Dividend on Death*. In over 70 novels the tough redhead, with one hand reaching for a bottle of cognac and the other beckoning to his compliant secretary, Lucy Hamilton, helped make South Florida a pulp heaven. Maxwell Grant's The Shadow slipped into the state seven times to foil an ethnic mix of gangs from *The Yellow Band* (1937) to Nazis in the belated *Five Keys to Crime* (1945). Leslie Charteris's debonair Simon Templar materialized in *The Saint in Miami* (1940). Some years later Donald Hamilton's master spy, Matt Helm, ranged the coast from Pensacola (*The Shadowers* [1964]) to the Bermuda Triangle (*The Intimidators* [1974]). Like many seniors, the ageless Nick Carter, who first appeared as a tough urban detective in the series created by Ralph Hayes in 1886, finally found his way to the state in his reincarnation as a James Bondish spy in *Danger Key* (1966) and *Operation Moon Rocket* (1968). Even the Hardy Boys vacationed in the Keys long enough to solve the *Mystery of Smuggler's Cove* (1980). Many of these pulp series are the products of teams of writers working from a master outline. The Shadow series, for example, includes some 325 novels, all published originally in *The Shadow* magazine by Street & Smith under the pen name of Maxwell Grant. Although the series had a number of authors, the primary one was Walker Gibson, who wrote 282 of the stories.

In the years after Mike Shayne first arrived, three followers of the distinctively American tradition of Hammett and Chandler created a series of memorable works with tough heroes searching for truth in a corrupt and corrupting world. George Harmon Coxe's *Inland Passage* (1949) and *Never Bet Your Life* (1952) read like perfect vehicles for Bogart and Cagney. Stephen Ransome began his fine series of novels with the classic *noir* title, *So Deadly My Love* (1957); those which followed from *I'll Die for You* (1959) to *Trap #6* (1971) generally present respectable citizens forced to bend the law to discover justice. Donald Tracy's harder-edged novels do not always rely on respectable heroes, especially *The Hated One* (1963), a hard-boiled version of *To Kill a Mockingbird*. In a more classical vein, Mignon Eberhart used Florida for three elegantly plotted books which reflect her strong sense of place (*Unidentified Woman* [1943], *The White Dress* [1945], and *Another Man's Murder* [1957]); and John Creasey sent his relentlessly bourgeois Chief Superintendent Richard West on a transatlantic case in *Murder, London-Miami* (1969).

John D. MacDonald honed his craft through the fifties in a series of mysteries which combined brisk action and ironic social commentary. His early mysteries and thrillers, like *The Brass Cupcake* (1950), *Murder in the Wind* (1956), and *A Flash of Green* (1962), introduce themes of natural disaster and human corruption which would appear both in the McGee series and such bestsellers as *Condominium* (1977). In *The Deep Blue Goodbye* (1964) he unveiled Florida's most famous knight errant, Travis McGee. Living just off the edge of his fading paradise, on an elaborate houseboat, *The Busted Flush,* moored at Slip F-18, Bahia Mar Marina, Fort Lauderdale, McGee operates an extra-legal salvage business, collecting 50% of whatever he recovers to finance his frequently interrupted retirement. In twenty-one colorfully titled mysteries from *Bright Orange for the Shroud* (1965) and *Darker than Amber* (1966) to *The Dreadful Lemon Sky* (1974) and *The Lonely Silver Rain* (1985), the tough but vulnerable McGee mounts his electric blue Rolls Royce pickup, Miss Agnes, to battle evil.

MacDonald's influence has helped shape the work of four talented heirs-apparent to McGee's turf. Poet James Hall has his prickly hero Thorn roam the Keys in works like *Under Cover of Daylight* (1987) and *Squall Line* (1989), while W.R. Philbrick has had T.D. Stash interrupt his work as a fishing guide in *The Neon Flamingo* (1987) and *Tough Enough* (1989). An actual fishing guide, Sanibel Island's Randy Wayne White, draws on his background to link Florida with its Caribbean neighbors in his *Sanibel Flats* (1990). Trish Janeshutz, the author of *In Shadow* (1985) and *Hidden Lake* (1987), has used the name T.J. MacGregor to pair detectives Mike McCleary and Quin St. James in a series of mysteries that began with *Dark Fields* in 1986 and reached its seventh, *Spree*, in 1992.

A far more urban tradition traces its roots back to four stories about Florida's gamblers and jook joints that Damon Runyon included in *Runyon A La Carte* (1949). Runyon's mixture of memorable dialogue and idiosyncratic rogues has strong ties to Elmore Leonard's wise guys and hustlers attempting to survive a postmodern world. As he shifted his locale from Detroit to South Florida in works like *Cat Chaser* (1982), *LaBrava* (1983), *Stick* (1983), and *Maximum Bob* (1991), Leonard has found an ideal environment for his black comedies with their perfectly realized dialogue. Mixing a strong dose of Southern gothic into the same tradition, *Miami Herald* columnist Carl Hiaasen has written a series of novels which trace the dismantling of paradise. In *Tourist Season* (1986), a terrorist gang attempts to solve the tourist problem; in *Double Whammy* (1987), Skink, an ex-governor-turned-eco-terrorist, confronts professional bass fishermen; in *Skin Tight* (1989), plastic surgeons offer a cosmetic fountain of horrors; and in *Native Tongue* (1991), Skink returns to put his imprint on a new theme park. Three other works by Miami reporters which have explored similar territory are John Katzenbach's political *In the Heat of the Summer* (1982), Pulitzer Prize–winning crime reporter Edna Buchanan's wryly anecdotal *Nobody Lives Forever* (1990), and Suzy Wetlaufer's *Judgment Call* (1992).

Ed McBain (Evan Hunter) added to his urban 87th Precinct police procedurals a chillingly detailed series about lawyer Matthew Hope in fictional Calusa, a town strikingly similar to Sarasota. Hope works through his clients' labyrinthine cases in a series of novels with such ironically appropriate fairy-tale titles as *Goldilocks* (1978), *Cinderella* (1986), and *Three Blind Mice* (1990). In *Tropical Heat* (1986), *Scorcher* (1987), and *Kiss* (1988), John Lutz has P.I. Fred Carver, forced into retirement from the Orlando Police Department because of a disability, solve crimes in the heart of Disney and Daytona. Further south, Charles Willeford's Miami homicide detective Hoke Moseley, whose leisure suits and false teeth first appeared in *Miami Blues* (1984) and whose disabilities are primarily emotional, deals with a wide range of personal and professional crises, including retirement, in *New Hope for the Dead* (1985) and *Sideswipe* (1987).

As South Florida's public image has become more prominent and more sinister — cover stories in *Newsweek* and *Time* called Miami "America's Casablanca" and South Florida "Paradise Lost" — the state has become an increasingly attractive site for mystery novelists. Among the promising writers who have found inspiration in this rich ethnic and economic stew are Pulitzer Prize–winner Michael Shaara (*The Herald* [1981]), science-fiction novelist Martin Caidin (*Three Corners to Nowhere* [1975]), *The Man in the Gray Flannel Suit*'s Sloan Wilson (*The Greatest Crime* [1980]), perennial bestseller Lawrence Sanders (*McNally's Secret* [1992] and *McNally's Luck* [1992]), Joseph Koenig (*Floater* [1986]), C. Terry Cline (*Reaper* [1989]), and Lawrence Shames (*Florida Straits* [1992]). And three authors who have created notable series featuring women detectives have sent their sleuths south in recent years: Janice Law slipped Anna Peters into *The Shadow of the Palms* (1979); Sue Grafton had Kinsey Millhone visit Boca Raton in her second alphabetical adventure, *"B" is for Burglar (1985);* and Liza Cody's Anna Lee joined Florida's British expatriates in *Backhand* (1992).

Maurice O'Sullivan, a Professor of English at Rollins College, is the editor of Shakespeare's Other Lives *and co-editor of* The Florida Reader.

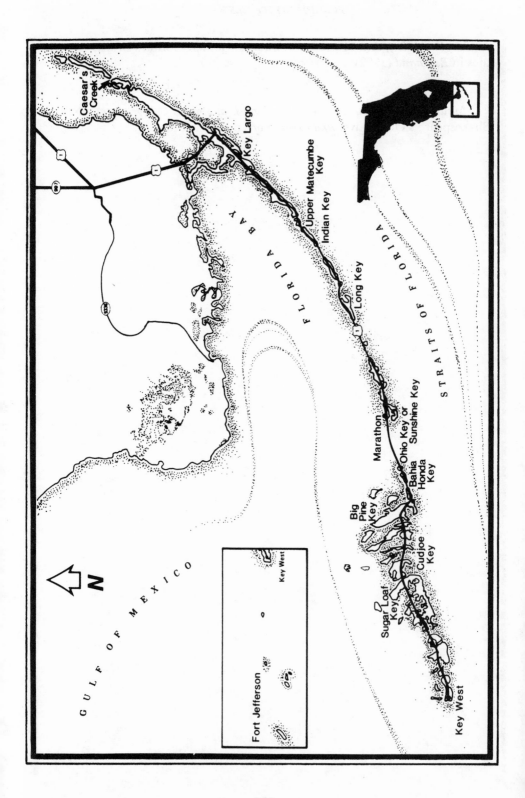

GULF OF MEXICO

FLORIDA BAY

STRAITS OF FLORIDA

Caesar's Creek

Key Largo

Upper Matecumbe Key

Indian Key

Long Key

Marathon

Sunshine Key

Ohio Key or

Bahia Honda Key

Big Pine Key

Cudjoe Key

Sugar Loaf Key

Key West

Fort Jefferson

Key West

N

6 THE FLORIDA KEYS

KEVIN M. MCCARTHY

The Florida Keys at the southeastern tip of the United States are well-known for their crystal-clear water, fishing, and relaxed lifestyles. They are less well-known for their contribution to Florida culture, especially her literature. That the Keys, especially Key West, have attracted so many writers over the years is probably due to their isolation from the mainland, closeness to nature, and tradition of nonconformity. The Keys have much to appeal to fiction writers: inaccessible nooks and crannies to bury murder victims, shallow harbors to hide pirates, and the constant threat of a summer hurricane barreling in from the open Caribbean. And while Key West is the gem of the Keys in terms of how many great writers it has attracted, the other keys have a place in a literary tour of the state. As Humphrey Bogart said in the movie *Key Largo*: "George was right. The Keys ARE different than anything I've ever seen."

Key Largo

Key Largo, meaning *large island* in Spanish, is one of the oldest place names on the North American coast. It was the site of the Humphrey Bogart-Lauren Bacall movie *Key Largo* (1948), which was based on a short story by **Maxwell Anderson**. Despite claims to the contrary by local restaurant and bar owners, the film was not shot in Key Largo other than a few scenes; as director John Huston wrote in his autobiography: "Since the major part of the action in *Key Largo* took place in a resort hotel, we were able to do most of the shooting in the Warner Brothers studio. A few mood shots were done in Florida." The popularity of the movie did, however, convince developers in the 1950s to change the name of the town from Rock Harbor to Key Largo and has spawned a profitable souvenir-selling business ever since. Another movie filmed there in 1978 was *Firepower* with Sophia Loren, James Coburn, and O.J. Simpson.

Several novels take place in the area, including **Edwin Lanham**'s novel of escape from Cuba, *Passage to Danger* (New York: Harcourt, Brace & World, 1961) and **Francoise Sagan**'s novel about the easy life, *The Wonderful Clouds* (New York: Dutton, 1962); **John D. MacDonald**'s *The Girl in the Plain Brown Wrapper* (Greenwich, CT: Fawcett, 1968) is a Travis McGee novel that takes place north of Key Largo. **Nikki Beare**'s *Pirates, Pineapples, and People* (Miami Beach: Atlantic, 1961) is about the history, tales, and legends of the Upper Florida Keys; **James A. Hathaway**'s *Key Largo: Island Home* (Coral Gables, FL: Key Largo Foundation, 1967) is a well-illustrated description of the island; and

Lois Simpson's *The Island of Key Largo, Florida, 1872-1983* (Mayfield, KY: Mayfield Printing Co., 1983) is a history of the island.

Among the litterateurs that Key Largo attracted, no one outdid **Ben Hecht** (1894-1964), author of novels, short stories, and plays. As he described in his autobiography, *A Child of the Century* (New York: Simon and Schuster, 1954, pp. 449-65), he arrived in Miami in 1925 at the height of the Florida real-estate boom and began to plot how he could make $2,500 a week for at least ten weeks. He conned some greedy businessmen into sponsoring a Key Largo treasure hunt, in which Hecht would lead society women and other celebrities on a search to find treasure conveniently hidden ahead of time on the island. When he could find no dowagers to join his hunt, Hecht paid an illiterate local man to "discover" some Spanish treasure. Dozens of reporters showed up to report the find, which led to swarms of would-be treasure-finders arriving, and Hecht's minions sold over $1 million in lots on Key Largo just before the real-estate boom went bust. Such schemes did much to tarnish the image of the state. For more about him see **Gene Burnett**'s, "Key Largo's Treasure Was Really Just Fiction," *Florida Trend* (January 1986), pp. 135-138, reprinted in *Florida's Past, Vol. 3*, (Sarasota, FL: Pineapple Press, 1991)..

Off Key Largo are shipwrecks that have attracted thousands of divers over the years. The deadly reef that runs along the Florida Keys, which is part of a living coral reef, is part of this country's first undersea park, the John Pennekamp Coral Reef State Park. Pennekamp was an editor at the *Miami Herald* who led the efforts to establish the park, which was opened to the public in 1963. For information about shipwrecks in the park that divers can visit see **Robert "Frogfoot" Weller**'s *Famous Shipwrecks of the Florida Keys* (Birmingham, AL: EBSCO Media, 1990), **Kevin M. McCarthy**'s *Thirty Florida Shipwrecks* (Sarasota: Pineapple Press, 1992), and **Steven D. Singer**'s *Shipwrecks of Florida* (Sarasota: Pineapple Press, 1992). **Oliver Griswold**'s *The Florida Keys and the Coral Reef* (Miami: Graywood Press, 1965) is a history of the area.

For more information about the lighthouses that warn ships about the deadly Florida reef just offshore see **Love Dean**'s *Reef Lights: Seaswept Lighthouses of the Florida Keys* (Key West: Historic Key West Preservation Board, 1982); **Elinor De Wire**'s *Guide to Florida Lighthouses* (Sarasota: Pineapple Press, 1987); and **Kevin M. McCarthy**'s *Florida Lighthouses* (Gainesville: University of Florida Press, 1990).

Caesar's Creek

North of Key Largo is Caesar's Creek, so named because of a pirate who lived there from about 1805 to 1815. One story says that he was an escaped slave who swam ashore from a sinking slave ship and set up operations in the northern keys, from which he preyed on passing ships. He may have joined Blackbeard or may have moved to Sanibel on Florida's west coast; other stories have him burying treasure in the creek that bears his name. For more about him see **Clifford Gardner**'s novel, *Black Caesar, Pirate* (Atlanta: Peachtree

Publishers, 1980), and **Love Dean**'s "Pirates and Legends" in *Florida Keys Magazine* (1st Quarter 1981), pp. 10-14.

The lighthouse on the offshore reef at Fowey Rocks had as one of its assistant keepers in the 1870s a young man who would later write one of the important histories of Key West. **Jefferson Browne** (1857-1937) had so much free time at the isolated lighthouse that he began reading law books to help him pass the time and became so absorbed in those books that, according to local lore, he never took a vacation. After 15 months at the lighthouse he traveled to Iowa and entered the University of Iowa Law School, from which he graduated with a law degree in only two years, partly because of his intense reading at the Fowey Rocks Lighthouse. He returned to the Florida Keys and became the attorney for Key West and Monroe County in 1880, later becoming an elected member of the Florida Supreme Court. He wrote *Key West: The Old and the New* (1912; reprinted Gainesville: University of Florida Press, 1973).

Plantation Key

South of Key Largo on Plantation Key is the town of Tavernier, named after the French pirate Tavernier or the Spanish "Cayo Tabona" ("Horsefly Key") or a misspelled sign ("tavern near"). For many years it has been the home of prolific science writer **Herbert S. Zim** (1909-). Along with many years of science teaching, Zim has written or edited over 100 books, many of them on scientific subjects and several on Florida, for example *Alligators and Crocodiles* (New York: Morrow, 1952) and *Guide to Everglades National Park and Nearby Florida Keys* (PLACE: Golden Press, 1960). His books on spiders, birds, sea shells, butterflies, trees, etc., have been very popular, reaching some two hundred million in print, with over a dozen titles passing the million mark. When asked why he and his wife chose to live in the Keys, he responded:

> I thought of finding a place where I could work more on books and sever my connections with the administrative aspects of academic life. At that time the Everglades National Park was being created; since I had worked with the Fish and Wildlife Service, I wanted to see the area with the hope of writing something about it. Eventually we did go down into the Everglades, and then drove down to the Keys. When the time came for us to make our choice, we debated strongly between the area around Patagonia in southwestern Arizona and the Florida Keys, choosing the latter because of the climate and because it was relatively closer to New York and publishing contacts. We've never regretted our choice, though we still like the Southwest immensely and go there as often as we can.

Upper Matecumbe Key

At the center of this island is a hurricane monument commemorating railroad workers killed in the 1935 Labor Day hurricane. The name *Matecumbe* may come from the Spanish *matar hombre* "to kill a man" because of the many shipwrecked sailors killed by Indians. **Robert L. Taylor**'s novel *A Journey to*

Wreckers at work

Matecumbe (New York: McGraw-Hill, 1961) and the movie *Treasure of Matecumbe* (1976) take place near here; Taylor lived in Islamorada on Upper Matecumbe Key in 1959 when he was writing the novel. A collection of stories about sunken treasure off the Upper Keys is **Jack Stark**'s *The Sponge Pirates and Other Florida Key Stories* (Miami: Hurricane House, 1962).

One of Florida's earliest written works began someplace in this vicinity when a young, 13-year-old Spanish boy on his way from South America to Spain was shipwrecked in 1545, just 53 years after Columbus came to the New World. When young Hernando d'Escalante Fontaneda swam ashore from the shipwreck that he survived off the Florida Keys, he fully expected to be killed by the Indians who were waiting for him. For some reason those Indians, who usually killed shipwreck survivors, decided to enslave him; for the next 17 years the young man worked for them, but all the time he was observing their customs, mastering their languages, traveling with them throughout Florida, and learning as much about the peninsula as he could. When he finally escaped and made his way back to Spain, he wrote a first-person narrative that is invaluable for what we can learn about sixteenth-century Florida. The *Memoir of Do. d'Escalante Fontaneda Respecting Florida* (Coral Gables, FL: Glade House, 1945), edited by **David O. True**, is one of the earliest works about Florida and one that subsequent historians would rely on for details about the land's geography, animals, plants, and Indians.

Indian Key

The Florida Keys are connected by the two-lane U.S. Highway 1, which begins in Key West and continues through Key Largo on up to Maine. Most businesses in the Keys refer to the nearest mile marker (MM) when indicating their position.

Off to the left from mile-marker 78 is historic Indian Key. One writer, who wrote that "perhaps no single piece of Florida real estate has absorbed more blood," described how Indians murdered 400 shipwrecked Frenchmen in the late 1600s and then how, in the 1830s, the famous wrecker, Jacob Houseman, lived there. Houseman was influential enough to have both Dade County established in 1836 and Indian Key named its county seat. During the Seminole Indian wars Houseman wrote to Congress, offering to kill the Indians in south Florida at $200 a head. The Calusa Indians under Chief Chekika heard about this and went to Indian Key, where they killed several of those living there at the time, including the famous botanist Dr. Perrine, but Houseman escaped.

For more about Houseman see **Basil Heatter's** novel entitled *"Wreck Ashore!"* (New York: Farrar, Straus & Giroux, 1969) and **Kaye Edwards Carter's** *The Rumskudgeon: Houseman, Wrecker of Indian Key* (Hialeah, FL: BPK Press, 1976). Among the articles about Dr. Henry Perrine are **Gene Burnett's** "Of Outraged Indians and Senseless Death," *Florida Trend* 18 (November 1975), pp. 80-82; **Webster Merritt's** "Dr. Henry Perrine, Versatile Florida Pioneer," *Journal of the Florida Medical Association* 39 (July 1952), pp. 45-50; and **Michael G. Schene's** "Indian Key," *Tequesta* 36 (1976), pp. 3-27. For more about the wreckers see **Birse Shepard's** *Lore of the Wreckers* (Boston: Beacon Press, 1961) and **Andre Norton's** fictional *The Opal-Eyed Fan* (New York: Dutton, 1977). **Michael G. Schene's** *History of Indian Key* (Tallahassee: Division of Archives, History and Records Management, 1973) is a good source.

One writer who found the Keys, especially their offshore waters, conducive for writing was **Charles Rawlings**, the first hus-

Charles and Marjorie Kinnan Rawlings

band of **Marjorie Kinnan Rawlings**, the Florida writer who made north-central Florida famous. After Charles and Marjorie bought an orange grove in Cross Creek in 1928, the rural setting inspired her to write *The Yearling* and *Cross Creek*, but alienated him, partly because it was so far from his beloved sea. When her *South Moon Under* was published in 1933 to good reviews, he decided to leave her, and they were divorced in November of that year. Although he never achieved the fame that Marjorie did, he wrote several good pieces about Florida, including a short story about a scuttled ship off the Florida Keys: "Johnny, Sail Your Luck!" in *Saturday Evening Post* Vol. 209 (May 22, 1937), pp. 5-7+.

Long Key

South of Key Largo is Long Key, whose name replaced the Spanish *Cayo Vivora* "Rattlesnake Key," so named because of the shape of the island rather than for any local reptiles, which are very rare on the Keys. The site was the scene of much carnage when a strong hurricane came ashore in October 1906 and killed many workers building Henry Flagler's railroad to Key West. In those days before weather satellites and instant radio communication those unfamiliar with the Keys sometimes found themselves at the mercy of the summer hurricanes that raced in from the Caribbean. Two novels about that hurricane and Flagler's railroad are **F.W. Belland**'s *The True Sea* (New York: Holt, Rinehart and Winston, 1984) and **Nora Smiley** and **Louise V. White**'s *Hurricane Road: A Novel of a Railroad That Went To Sea* (New York: Exposition Press, 1954). Despite warnings from native Keys people and from Miami editor Frank Stoneman, the father of author Marjory Stoneman Douglas, that the railroad line could not withstand another fierce hurricane, Flagler continued on with his project. He did not live to see the destruction caused by the 1935 Labor Day hurricane, which convinced his railroad heirs to sell out to the federal government and have a highway replace the rail line. For more about the railroad see **Pat Parks**'s *The Railroad That Died at Sea* (Brattleboro, VT: Stephen Greene Press, 1968) and **Rodman Bethel**'s *Flagler's Folly: The Railroad That Went to Sea and Was Blown Away* (Key West: Bethel, 1987?). Also see his *First Overseas Highway to Key West, Florida* (Key West: Bethel, 1989). **Benedict Thielen** based his novel, *The Lost Men* (New York: Appleton-Century, 1946), on the 1935 hurricane that did so much damage to the area.

Novelist **Ernest Hemingway** went by boat from Key West to the scene of the hurricane as soon as he could and helped with the rescue efforts of local officials. What he saw shocked him: "We were the first in to Camp Five of the veterans who were working on the Highway construction. Out of 187 only 8 survived. Saw more dead than I'd seen in one place since the lower Piave in June of 1918." He went on to write a vivid account of the tragedy five days after it happened and blamed faceless bureaucrats for not minding the hurricane warnings and taking responsibility for the veterans toiling under difficult conditions. Hemingway had his own recommendation for those bureaucrats: "...I would like to make whoever sent them there carry just one out through the mangroves, or turn one over that lay in the sun along the fill, or tie five together so they won't float out, or smell that smell you thought you'd never smell again, with luck when rich bastards make a war. The lack of luck goes on until all who take part in it are gone."

American author **Zane Grey** (1875-1939) fished in the local waters and had a nearby saltwater creek named for him. He and his brother, Romer, discovered the Florida Keys by chance in 1910, when, on their way to Mexico for tarpon fishing, they heard that yellow fever had broken out in Mexico. They then went by boat to Long Key, which at that time was a fishing village that Flagler had built. The fishing camp was on the ocean side and consisted of a three-story wooden hotel and several cottages; the docks were on the bay side, and a tunnel under the roadbed connected the two sides. Grey used Long Key, not only as a fishing escape, but also as a quiet place to write, and it was there that he wrote such works as *Wild Horse Mesa* (1928) and *Code of the West* (1934). He wrote about using light-tackle gear to catch sailfish and kingfish off Long Key in "Gulf Stream Fishing" in his *Tales of Fishes* (1919). In the Foreword to a book about saltwater fishing, he wrote the following about the place he had come to love, but which had been devastated by the hurricane: "It is sad to think that Long Key, doomed by a hurricane, is gone forever. But the memory of that long white winding lonely shore of coral sand, and the green reef, and the blue Gulf Stream will live in memory, and in such fine books as this."

Poet **Wallace Stevens** (1879-1955) went to Long Key in 1922 looking for a businessman who was fishing there. Stevens wrote a letter to his wife praising the place: "This is one of the choicest places I have ever been to. While it in no way resembles Byrdcliffe [the summer place where the Stevenses stayed in Woodstock, New York], it is about the same size and consists of a building like the Villetta in which you get your meals and a large number of cottages distributed around a cocoanut grove. The ground is white coral broken up, as white as this paper, dazzling in the sunshine. The whole place: it is an island, is no larger than the grounds on which the Hartford Fire has its building." **James McLendon**'s *Pioneer in the Florida Keys* (Miami: Seemann Publishing Co., 1977), tells the life of Del Layton, mayor of the town of Layton on Long Key.

Marathon

This town was named after the fifth-century B.C. battle between the Greeks and Persians. Just north of Marathon, between mile-markers 52 and 53, is a stream with the unusual name of Pull-and-be-damned Creek. For treasure-seeking off Marathon and the other Florida Keys see the first part of **Marion Clayton Link**'s *Sea Diver, A Quest for History Under the Sea* (New York: Rinehart, 1959).

In the 1930s, after Flagler's railroad had been washed away and before the U.S. government built U.S. 1 to Key West, travelers to the lower keys had to make the long trip in several stages. As novelist **John Dos Passos** described it:

> The railroad had folded and now you arrived by carferry from a point below Homestead on the mainland. There were three separate ferryrides and sandy roads through the scrubby keys between.

It took half a day and was a most delightful trip, with long cues of pelicans scrambling up off the water and manofwar birds in the sky and boobygulls on the buoys, and mullet jumping in the milky shallows.

Among the novels set in and around Marathon are **Adelaide Humphries's** *Doctor of the Keys* (New York: Thomas Bouregy, 1963); **Clifford Irving's** *On a Darkling Plain* (New York: Putnam's Sons, 1956) about the peaceful life there; **John D. MacDonald's** *Darker Than Amber* (Greenwich, CT: Fawcett, 1966), a Travis McGee mystery; and **Henry Hayes Stansbury's** *Hurricane in the Keys* (New York: Popular Library, 1968) about how a hurricane interferes with a fishing tournament. **Jerry** and **June Powell's** *Marathon: Heart of the Florida Keys* (Marathon, FL: Seagrape Publications, 1980) gives a good description of the area, including its fishing, wildlife, and local diversions. A work about the many birds of the Keys is **Earle R. Greene's** *A Lifetime with the Birds* (Ann Arbor, MI: Greene, 1966). A reprint of five articles from *Harper's New Monthly Magazine*, 1870-1895 is **Stuart D. Ludlum's** *Exploring Florida 100 Years Ago* (New York: Brodock & Ludlum, 1973).

Local author **Donald Hamilton**, who visited Florida in the early 1970s, wrote *The Intriguers* (Greenwich, CT: Fawcett, 1972), which ends in the neighborhood of a mythical Florida island called Robalo. Hamilton, whose 1973 stay resulted in *The Intimidators* (Greenwich, CT: Fawcett, 1974), is known for his creation of Matt Helm in such works as *The Ambushers* (1963), *The Shadowers* (1964), and *The Betrayers* (1966).

Ohio Key or Sunshine Key

Environmentalist **Rachel Carson** (1907-1964) worked on her 1955 book *The Edge of the Sea* (Boston: Houghton Mifflin, 1955) on Ohio Key. In that book she wrote about what that environment reminded her of: "I doubt that anyone can travel the length of the Florida Keys without having communicated to his mind a sense of the uniqueness of this land of sky and water and scattered mangrove-covered islands. The atmosphere of the Keys is strongly and peculiarly their own. It may be that here, more than in most places, remembrance of the past and intimations of the future are linked with present reality." **Marjory Bartlett Sanger's** *Mangrove Island* (Cleveland, OH: World Publishing Co., 1963) gives a good description of the formation and development of the many mangroves in the Keys. For a history of the Florida Keys from early times up until the Cuban Crisis of the 1960s see **Oliver Griswold's** *The Florida Keys and the Coral Reef* (Miami: Graywood Press, 1965).

Bahia Honda Key

This key, whose name means *deep bay* in Spanish and recalls a fact that the channel here is about 25 feet deep, has the 80-acre Bahia Honda State Recreation Area, a favorite haunt for botanists studying the numerous plants brought here by birds, winds, and water. **Shylah Boyd's** novel entitled *American*

Made (New York: Farrar, Straus & Giroux, 1975) is about a girl growing up on a key near Bahia Honda.

Big Pine Key

This key, the largest, highest, and most secure from hurricanes in the area, has Key Deer Refuge, a protected area for several hundred tiny key deer. For more about them see **Hope Ryden**'s *The Little Deer of the Florida Keys* (New York: Putnam's, 1978), **Joseph Lippincott**'s novel *The Phantom Deer* (Philadelphia: Lippincott, 1954), and **William J.** Weber's *Florida Nature Photography* (Gainesville: University Press of Florida, 1992). Here also is the Great White Heron National Wildlife Refuge; Winter Park author **Marjory Bartlett Sanger** wrote *World of the Great White Heron* (New York: Devin-Adair Company, 1967) about one of the beautiful birds that makes the Keys its home. **Lois Simpson**'s *History of Big Pine Key, Florida, 1873-1982* (Mayfield, KY: Simpson, 1982) is a long description of the island and its history. One of the isolated keys below Big Pine Key is the setting for a triple murder that sends **John D. MacDonald**'s Travis McGee on yet another risky case; MacDonald's last novel, *The Lonely Silver Rain* (New York: Knopf, 1985), was his seventy-sixth and the twenty-first Travis McGee book, making its author one of the most popular American writers in the twentieth century.

Cudjoe Key

This island, which is named after a forgotten "Cousin Joe" or the kudzu vine which grows throughout Florida's swamps, is the site of a diving expedition story in **Harrison** and **Mathilda Reed**'s *The Talbot Boys* (Maplewood, NJ: Hammond, 1961). **James D. Lazell, Jr.**'s *Wildlife of the Florida Keys: A Natural History* (Washington, DC: Island Press, 1989) gives a very thorough description of the mammals, birds, reptiles, amphibians, and insects of the Keys.

The gulf stream, which flows north along the Keys, is famous for its fishing, as **Ernest Hemingway** discovered when he fished out of Key West. He described this famous waterway in a letter to *Esquire* magazine in April 1936:

> In the first place, the Gulf Stream and the other great ocean currents are the last wild country there is left. Once you are out of sight of land and of the other boats you are more alone than you can ever be hunting and the sea is the same as it has been since before men ever went on it in boats. In a season fishing you will see it oily flat as the becalmed galleons saw it while they drifted to the westward; white-capped with a fresh breeze as they saw it running with the trades; and in high, rolling blue hills, the tops blowing off them like snow as they were punished by it, so that sometimes you will see three great hills of water with your fish jumping from the top of the farthest one and if you tried to make a turn to go with him without picking your chance, one of those breaking crests would roar down in on you with a thousand tons of water and you would hunt no more elephants, Richard, my lad.

Hemingway's famous work about fishing, *The Old Man and the Sea* (1952), won the 1954 Nobel Prize for literature.

Sugar Loaf Key

This island, so named either for the sugarloaf pineapples formerly grown here or for an Indian hill that resembled a loaf of sugar, still has standing one of the wooden towers used to house bats that would fly out each night to eat the hordes of mosquitoes that plague the area. Such a bat tower is featured in **Thomas McGuane's** novel, *The Bushwhacked Piano* (New York: Simon and Schuster, 1971), a humorous story that includes a description of an entrepreneur who paints the bats a day-glo orange so that people can watch them eating the bugs.

Among the more recent novels about the Florida Keys outside of Key West are the following: **Marilyn Cram Donahue's** *Sutter's Sands* (New York: Modern Promotions, 1971); **Dorothy Brenner Francis's** *Nurse of the Keys* (New York: Thomas Bouregy, 1974) and *Run of the Sea Witch* (Nashville, TN: Abingdon Press, 1978); **Jim Hall's** *Under Cover of Daylight* (New York: Norton, 1987) and *Tropical Freeze* (New York: Norton, 1989); **Adrienne D. McGillicuddy's** *In The Dark of the Moon* (New York: Vantage, 1980); **Patricia Muse's** *Eight Candles Glowing* (New York: Ballantine, 1976); **Ruth Hooker** and **Opal Smith's** *The Pelican Mystery* (Chicago: Albert Whitman, 1977); and **Ramona Stewart's** *Seasons of the Heart* (Putnam's, 1978).

The novels published in the 1960s include **Zachary Ball's** *Skin Diver* (New York: Random House, 1965); **Betty Brothers'** *Ra-Do and the Porpoises* (Big Pine Key, FL: Litoky Publishing Co., 1962) and *Triggerfish* (Fort Lauderdale: Wake-Brook, 1965); **Nick Carter's** *Danger Key* (New York: Universal-Award House, 1966); **Elinor Chamberlain's** *Mystery of the Moving Island* (Philadelphia: Lippincott, 1965); **Peggy Dern's** *The Persistent Suitor* (New York: Arcadia House, 1966); **Edward Fisher's** *Amazon Key* (New York: Abelard, Shuman, 1961); **Edith Hamill's** *The Craigshaw Curse* (New York: Meredith Press, 1968); **Wilma Pitchford Hays's** *Little Hurricane Happy* (Boston: Little, Brown, 1965); **Willard Manus's** *Sea Treasure* (Garden City, NY: Doubleday, 1961); **Ed McBain's** *The Sentries* (New York: Simon & Schuster, 1965); **Robert Merle's** *The Day of the Dolphin* (New York: Simon and Schuster, 1969); **Harry Whittington's** *Conolly's Woman* (Greenwich, CT: Fawcett, 1960); and **Sloan Wilson's** *Janus Island* (Boston: Little, Brown, 1967).

The novels published in the 1950s include **Cora Cheney's** *Key of Gold* (New York: Holt, 1955); **Dorothy Cottrell's** *Silent Reefs* (New York: William Morrow, 1953); **Kent Curtis's** *Cruise in the Sun* (Chicago: Ralph Fletcher Seymour, 1950); **Edith Hamill's** *A Nurse for Galleon Key* (New York: Avalon, 1957); **Margaret Bell Houston's** *Yonder* (New York: Crown, 1955); **Susan Lennox's** *Paradise Isle* (New York: Avalon, 1957); **Laura Cooper Rendina's** *Lolly Touchberry* (Boston: Little, Brown, 1957); and **Richard Watkins's** *Hurricane's Secret* (New York: Harcourt, Brace, 1950).

Among the movies set in the Keys are *It's Hot on Sin Island* (1964) and *Combat* (1927). For an illustrated history of the area see **Stan Windhorn** and **Wright Langley**'s *Yesterday's Florida Keys* (Miami: Seemann Publishing Co., 1974). **Joy Williams**'s *The Florida Keys* (New York: Random House, 1987) is a good history and guide to all of the Keys. Other works include **Charles Mann Brookfield**'s *They All Called It Tropical: True Tales of the Romantic Everglades National Park, Cape Sable, and the Florida Keys* (Miami: Data Press, 1964) and **Frank Papy**'s *Cruising Guide to the Florida Keys* (Ridgeland, SC: F. Papy, 1990).

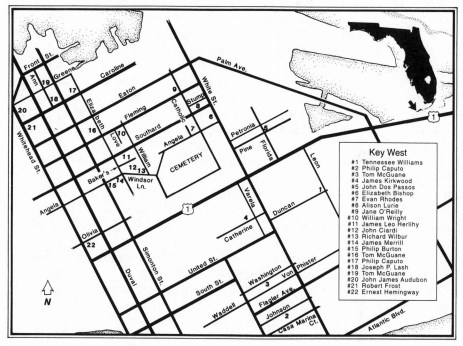

Key West
#1 Tennessee Williams
#2 Philip Caputo
#3 Tom McGuane
#4 James Kirkwood
#5 John Dos Passos
#6 Elizabeth Bishop
#7 Evan Rhodes
#8 Alison Lurie
#9 Jane O'Reilly
#10 William Wright
#11 James Leo Herlihy
#12 John Ciardi
#13 Richard Wilbur
#14 James Merrill
#15 Philip Burton
#16 Tom McGuane
#17 Philip Caputo
#18 Joseph P. Lash
#19 Tom McGuane
#20 John James Audubon
#21 Robert Frost
#22 Ernest Hemingway

Key West

Of the many writers who have lived and worked in Key West, we have chosen to mention a handful because of their unique contributions to American literature. The primary source for the following information is **Lynn Mitsuko Kaufelt**'s *Key West Writers and Their Houses* (Sarasota: Pineapple Press, 1986, updated 1991) and sources mentioned with the different writers; **George Murphy**'s *The Key West Reader: The Best of Key West's Writers, 1830-1990* (Key West: Tortugas Ltd., 1989) has fiction, nonfiction, and poetry about the city, and the museum at the East Martello Tower on South Roosevelt Boulevard near the airport has an authors' section with books and displays about the city's prominent writers. Presuming that most visitors will be coming in on U.S. 1 (North Roosevelt Boulevard), we begin there.

A book lover would take a left at Leon Street and go three blocks to 1431 Duncan Street, where **Tennessee Williams** (1911-1983) lived from 1949, when he bought the house, until he died. When he first came to Key West in the early 1940s to rewrite *Battle of Angels* (on which his play, *Orpheus Descending* [1958], was based), he stayed at a boarding house, the Tradewinds, on the southeast corner of Caroline and Duval; other writers, like Christopher Isherwood, Carson McCullers, Francoise Sagan, and Gore Vidal, sometimes joined Williams at the piano bar in the Tradewinds. Williams later moved to a hotel on the corner of Duval and Fleming streets, La Concha, and finished another play, *Summer and Smoke* (1948). In 1949 he moved to the old Bahamian house on Duncan Street and there wrote another play, *Night of the Iguana*, and set *The Gnadiges Fraulein* (1966) in a Key West-type place called Cockalooney Key. The Academy Award-winning film version of his play, *The Rose Tattoo*, was filmed in Key West in 1956. When he was in town, many people tried to see him: "He was the biggest tourist attraction on Key West, even bigger than the Hemingway house. The powers that were on the island decided to call a new wing of the library the Tennessee Williams Wing, perhaps hoping for a large cash donation. Tennessee gave them a tape of himself, reading his poetry, and told them they could use it to raise money for the library"; an example of his poetry is "The Diving Bell" in **George Murphy's** *The Key West Reader* (Key West: Tortugas Ltd., 1989), pp. 229-230. The Tennessee Williams Fine Arts Center at Florida Keys Community College opened in 1980 with a new Williams play: *Will Mr. Merriweather Return From Memphis?* At a memorial service following his death in 1983, a reader read **Wallace Stevens's** "The Idea of Order at Key West," a poem that Williams especially liked. For more about Williams see **Marsha Bellavance-Johnson's** *Tennessee Williams in Key West and Miami* (Ketchum, ID: Computer Lab, 1989).

Continuing west four blocks to White Street, then south eight blocks, we come to Casa Marina Court. **Philip Caputo** (1941-) lived for a while at 1101 Casa Marina Court in one of the island's larger houses. The pink house facing the Atlantic Ocean has a screened-in pool and a large amount of space, a rarity in Key West. In that house he wrote *Indian Country* (1987), a novel about a troubled Vietnam veteran. (More about Caputo later.)

Three blocks north, at 1011 Von Phister, lived novelist **Thomas McGuane** (1939-). Born in Michigan and educated at Michigan State University, the Yale School of Drama, and Stanford University, he finished his first novel, *The Sporting Club* (1968), and then moved to Key West, which he had visited with his father on a fishing trip in the early 1950s. He and his family first lived in a two-house-converted-to-one at 123-125 Ann Street before moving to Von Phister. There he finished *The Bushwhacked Piano* (New York: Simon and Schuster, 1971) and *Ninety-Two in the Shade* (New York: Farrar, Straus and Giroux, 1973), both of which are set in Key West. He later moved back to Old Town to 416 Elizabeth Street. When Key West lost its charm, he moved to Montana, although he occasionally returns to Key West for sailing and fishing.

Five blocks north, at 1023 Catherine Street, was the home of **James Kirkwood** (1930-1989). Kirkwood, who spent most of his life as a stage and screen actor, won — with four others — the 1976 Pulitzer Prize for drama for *A Chorus Line*. His novels include *Good Times/Bad Times* (1968), *American Grotesque* (1970), *P.S. Your Cat Is Dead!* (1972), *Some Kind of Hero* (1975), and

Hit Me With a Rainbow (1980). He also wrote *Diary of a Mad Playwright* (1989). Other residents of the Conch Grove Compound were writers Albin Krebs and Lynn and David Kaufelt, publisher Ross Claiborne, and literary agent Jay Garon.

On the other side of U.S. 1 and two blocks north to 1401 Pine Street is the former home of **John Dos Passos** (1896-1970), author of such works as *Manhattan Transfer* (1925), *The 42nd Parallel* (1930), *The Big Money* (1936), and *Mid-Century* (1961). Having originally arrived in Key West simply because he boarded the first train in central Florida and found out it was going to Key West, he came to like the town and encouraged his friend, Ernest Hemingway, to visit there. Dos Passos became a member of Hemingway's "Mob," acquired the nickname "Dos," and joined the other members (J.B. Sullivan, Henry Strater, Hamilton Adams, Waldo Pierce, Joe Russell, and Captain Eddie Saunders) in May 1928 at the Overseas Hotel, a three-story, 100-room structure at 917 Fleming Street — at the cost of $1 a day. Dos Passos met his wife, Kathy, at the Hemingways' house in 1934 and, after marrying her, rented the Conch house on Pine Street. Dos Passos spent much time in Key West, as described in **James McLendon's** *Papa: Hemingway in Key West* (Miami: Seemann Publishing Co., 1972), and it was there that he worked on *In All Countries* (1934) and *Three Plays* (1934). He described a fishing trip with Hemingway in "Under the Tropic," which is in **George Murphy's** *The Key West Reader* (Key West: Tortugas Ltd., 1989), pp. 85-93.

Proceeding west on Pine Street to White Street and then north, we come to 624 White Street, the former home of poet **Elizabeth Bishop** (1911-1979), author of *Brazil* (1962), *Collected Poems* (1969), *Geography III* (1976), and *Collected Prose* (1984). Having originally come to Key West in the late 1930s for its famous fishing, she learned to appreciate the town's special light and colors that influenced her painting; some of her watercolors of Key West scenes are on her book jackets. In 1946 she sold her house with the stipulation that subsequent owners make no structural changes to it. Two of her Key West poems, "A Norther — Key West" and "The Bight," are in **George Murphy's** *The Key West Reader* (Key West: Tortugas Ltd., 1989), pp. 32-34.

Three blocks west on Angela Street is Catholic Lane near the city cemetery. Author **Evan Rhodes** bought a Conch cottage at 621 Catholic Lane in 1977 and there wrote *An Army of Children* (1978), *On Wings of Fire* (1981), *Bless This House* (1982), *Forged in Fury* (1982), *Valiant Hearts* (1983), and *A Distant Dream* (1984), as well as the libretto for his musical that is based on his novel, *The Prince of Central Park* (1975). After selling his house there, he moved 15 miles north to the Saddlebunch Keys.

Two blocks north between Frances and White streets, at 1116 Stump Lane, is a house owned by **Alison Lurie** (1926-), a professor of English at Cornell who lives in another house in Key West's Casa Marina section. She is the author of fiction: *Love and Friendship* (1962), *The Nowhere City* (1965), *Imaginary Friends* (1967), *Real People* (1969), *The War Between the Tates* (1974), *Only Children* (1979), *Foreign Affairs* (1984 — which won the 1985 Pulitzer Prize for fiction); and nonfiction such as *The Language of Clothes* (1981) and *Don't Tell the*

Grown-ups (1990). Her juvenile books include *The Heavenly Zoo* (1979), *Clever Gretchen and Other Forgotten Folktales* (1980), and *Fabulous Beasts* (1981). A selection about Key West from *The Truth About Lorin Jones* (Boston: Little, Brown, 1988) is in **George Murphy**'s *The Key West Reader* (Key West: Tortugas Ltd., 1989), pp. 143-170.

Two blocks north, on the corner of Frances and Fleming streets, was the home of **Jane O'Reilly** (1936-), the author of two nonfiction books: *The Girl I Left Behind* (1980) and *No Turning Back* (1990), which she wrote with **Barbara Ferraro** and **Patricia Hussey**. The first book is a collection of her magazine essays; the second is about two nuns battling with the Vatican over women's right to choose about abortion. O'Reilly, a founding editor of *Ms.* magazine and a writer for such magazines as *Time* and *Vogue*, has lived in Key West since the early-1980s.

Approximately four blocks west on Fleming Street between William and Elizabeth streets is Love Lane. **William Wright** (1930-), who lived at 712 Love Lane near the town's pink library, began coming to Key West in 1972 and has written such books as *Ball: A Year in the Life of the April in Paris Extravaganza* (1972), *Heiress: The Rich Life of Marjorie Merriweather Post* (1978), *Pavarotti, My Own Story* (1981 — with **Luciano Pavarotti**), *The Von Bulow Affair* (1983), *Lillian Hellman: The Image, The Woman* (1986), and *All the Pain That Money Can Buy: The Life of Christina Onassis* (1991).

Two blocks south and off Elizabeth Street is tiny Baker's Lane. Author **James Leo Herlihy** (1927-) lived at 709 Baker's Lane, a place he owned from 1969 until he left Key West for southern California in 1972; one can still see the peace signs he had carved into the posts on the front-porch railing. His plays include *Blue Denim* (1958) and *Stop You're Killing Me* (1970); his fiction includes *The Sleep of Baby Filbertson and Other Stories* (1959), *All Fall Down* (1960), *Midnight Cowboy* (1965), *A Story That Ends With a Scream, and Eight Others* (1967), and *The Season of the Witch* (1971). Tennessee Williams was his mentor while the two of them lived in Key West, and they would often go swimming in the summer at dusk off the Monroe County pier.

One block south off Elizabeth Street is the Windsor Lane Compound, where **John Ciardi** (1916-1986) stayed and **Richard Wilbur** (1921-) lives. Ciardi is best known as a poet (*How Does a Poem Mean?* [1959], *In the Stoneworks* [1961], *Person to Person* [1964], *The Strangest Everything* [1966], *For Instance* [1979], *Selected Poems* [1984]), as a translator (*The Purgatorio* [1961] and *The Divine Comedy* [1977]), and as a nonfiction writer (*A Browser's Dictionary and Native's Guide to the Unknown American Language* [1980] and *A Second Browser's Dictionary and Native's Guide to the Unknown American Language* [1983]). Ciardi, who spent the last ten winters (mid-1970s to mid-1980s) in Key West with his wife, Judith, wrote "Audit at Key West" about the town he had come to love; it is in **George Murphy**'s *The Key West Reader* (Key West: Tortugas Ltd., 1989), pp. 51-52.

Richard Wilbur (1921-), who lives in the Windsor Compound with his wife, Charlee, has won such major awards as the 1957 Pulitzer Prize for poetry and the National Book Award for poetry for *Things of This World* (1956) and the 1989 Pulitzer Prize for *New and Collected Poems* (1988); he was the co-recipient of the Bollingen Prize for translation in 1963 for *Tartuffe* and for poetry in 1971 for *Walking to Sleep* (1969) and was the 1987-1988 poet laureate of the United States.

Back on Elizabeth Street, at 702 Elizabeth Street, is where poet **James Merrill** (1926-) has spent the winters since 1979 with writer **David Jackson**. The house, which had been built in the Bahamas, dismantled, and barged to Key West, was reconstructed around 1840 on the island's highest point: Solares Hill, all of 18 feet above sea level. Merrill won the 1977 Pulitzer Prize for poetry (for *Divine Comedies*), the National Book Award twice (for *Nights and Days* [1967] and *Mirabell: Books of Number* [1979]), and the Bollingen Prize for poetry. His "Clearing the Title" and "Monday Morning," which are found in **George Murphy**'s *The Key West Reader* (Key West: Tortugas Ltd., 1989), pp. 184-188, are about Key West.

Nearby, at 608 Angela Street, was the home of **Philip Burton** (1904-), who came to Key West in 1974 for health reasons. He wrote *Early Doors: My Life and the Theatre* (1969), *The Sole Voice: Character Portraits from Shakespeare* (1970), and *You, My Brother: A Novel Based on the Lives of Edmund & William Shakespeare* (1973). Burton was actor Richard Burton's step-father.

Two blocks north on Elizabeth Street is one of three homes that novelist **Thomas McGuane**, mentioned earlier, lived and worked in. When he moved from his house on Von Phister to a two-story Conch house in Old Town at 416 Elizabeth Street, he proceeded to write *Panama* (New York: Farrar, Straus and Giroux, 1978), a story set in Key West about the difficulties of coping with sudden fame. He may have used the excellent resources of the nearby library, which has a fine collection of Key West newspapers and memorabilia.

Two blocks north of that site is another place where **Philip Caputo** lived: 621 Caroline Street. Having been born near Oak Park, Ernest Hemingway's birthplace, Caputo has often been compared to the great writer in career (both were foreign correspondents) and in winning the Pulitzer Prize (Caputo shared his 1972 award for a voting-fraud investigation in Chicago). Caputo claims that he went to Key West, not to be near Hemingway's house, but to be able to write and fish. For an example of Caputo's writing on the fishing off Key West and Cuba see "The Ahab Complex" in **George Murphy**'s *The Key West Reader* (Key West: Tortugas Ltd., 1989), pp. 37-50. Caputo's first book, the nonfiction *A Rumor of War* (1977), did so well that he became a full-time writer. When he and his wife and two young boys were living in this Caroline Street house in the late 1970s, he rented a small cigarmaker's cottage off the nearby Lopez Lane off Eaton Street in order to write. His second book, the novel *Horn of Africa* (1980), is about a CIA operator in Ethiopia. He also wrote another novel, *Del Corso's Gallery* (1983), in his Lopez Lane cottage. His latest work is *Means of Escape* (1991).

Two blocks west of the cottage at 217 Ann Street is where **Joseph P. Lash** (1909-1987) spent his winters beginning in the late 1970s. He wrote *Dag Hammarskjold, Custodian of the Brushfire Peace* (1961) when he was the United Nations' correspondent for the *New York Post*; *Eleanor Roosevelt: A Friend's*

Memoir (1964); *Eleanor and Franklin: The Story of Their Relationship, Based on Eleanor Roosevelt's Private Papers* (1971), which won the 1972 Pulitzer Prize and National Book Award for biography; *Eleanor: The Years Alone* (1972); *From the Diaries of Felix Frankfurter* (1975); *Roosevelt and Churchill: A Study of Their Relationship* (1976), which won the 1978 Samuel E. Morison Award for history; *Helen and Teacher: The Story of Helen Keller and Anne Sullivan Macy* (1980); *Love, Eleanor: Eleanor Roosevelt and Her Friends* (1982) collected letters; *Life Was Meant to Be Lived: A Centenary Portrait of Eleanor Roosevelt* (1984); *A World of Love: Eleanor Roosevelt and Her Friends, 1943-1962* (1984) more letters; and *Dealers and Dreamers: A New Look at the New Deal* (1988) published posthumously.

One block north of where Lash wintered is yet another place where novelist **Thomas McGuane** lived when he first came to Key West in the late 1960s: a house made from two houses joined together at 123-125 Ann Street. In the former cigarmaker cottages from the 1880s McGuane wrote much of *The Bushwhacked Piano* (New York: Simon & Schuster, 1971), which captures the mood of downtown Key West.

Three blocks away, at 205 Whitehead Street on one of the main streets of the town, is the **John James Audubon** House-Museum, where the famous ornithologist stayed when he arrived in 1832, although it was then called the John Geiger House. While in the Keys, Audubon found the nearly extinct white-crowned pigeon, which he named the Key West pigeon, and the great white heron. Among his works are *The Birds of America* (1937) and *Ornithological Biography* (1831-1839). **Kathryn Hall Proby**'s *Audubon in Florida* (Coral Gables, FL: University of Miami Press, 1974) gives a description of his 1831-1832 travels in Florida.

South of Audubon's house is where poet **Robert Frost** lived at 410 Caroline Street, in the little green cottage at the back. He and his wife also stayed at 707 Seminole Street when he first visited Key West in 1934-1935. He was not very enchanted with Key West, however, as evidenced in this passage from a 1935 letter: "There is no sanitation. The water is all off the roofs and after it goes through people I don't know where it goes. Everything is shabby and even dilapidated." Part of his disillusionment may have been due to the fact that the federal government was running the city and questioning newcomers like the Frosts as to their suitability for staying in the place.

Six blocks south of there on Whitehead Street is the most famous literary site in Key West, the home of **Ernest Hemingway** (1899-1961) at 907 White-head Street. After the 1926 publication of *The Sun Also Rises*, Hemingway and his second wife, Pauline, came to Key West in 1928 at the suggestion of his friend, John Dos Passos. Hemingway owned the home from 1931 until 1961 and lived there with wife Pauline and their two sons, Patrick and Gregory, until he went off with Martha Gellhorn. Although he wrote such books as *A Farewell to Arms* (1929), *Death in the Afternoon* (1932), *Green Hills of Africa* (1935), *To Have and Have Not* (1937), and *For Whom the Bell Tolls* (1940) in the studio on top of the poolhouse, he set only *To Have and Have Not* (New York: Scribner, 1937) in the town; in fact, that is the only novel he set in America. In a 1935

Ernest Hemingway

David

Sloppy Joe urinal. Key West holds an annual Hemingw
a look-alike contest and other events meant to recall th
For more about how the town affected Hemingway s
Papa: Hemingway in Key West (Miami: Seemann Publi
Brasher's "Hemingway's Florida" in *Lost Generation Jou
1973), pp. 4-8, **Arnold Samuelson**'s *With Hemingway: .
Cuba* (New York: Random House, 1984), and **Marsha
Ernest Hemingway in Key West (Ketchum, ID: Computer

Some of the other writers who have made Key West
literary capital over the years include **John Malcolm B
Ellison** (1914-), **Nancy Friday** (1937-), **Jim Harrison
(1914-), **William Henry Manville** (1930-), **Norman Rc
Sackler** (1929-1982), **Shel(by) "Uncle Shelby" Silverst
Stewart** (1922-), **Robert Stone** (1937-), **Peter Taylor** (
Thompson (1939-).

Finally we should note here **David A. Kaufelt** (193
essay in this chapter on Key West: "Writers in Paradise
and educated at the University of Pennsylvania and Ne

Trop
Span
of a l
1993
the a
1986

York:
Athe
ner's
Simo
(Stam
(New
Knop
**Richa
Richa
cott,

273

worked in New York City as an advertising copywriter and at the Henry Street Settlement. After he moved to Key West in 1979, he became the coordinator of the Key West Literary Festival and president of the Founders Society of the Tennessee Williams Fine Arts Center. His early novels included *Six Months with an Older Woman* (1973), *The Bradley Beach Rumba* (1974), *Jade* (1978), *Spare Parts* (1978), *Late Bloomer* (New York: Harcourt Brace Jovanovich, 1979) — set in Miami Beach, *Midnight Movies* (1980), *The Best Table* (1981), *The Wine and the Music* (1981), *Silver Rose* (1982), *Souvenir* (1983), *American*

felt

New York: Poseidon Press, 1986), a generational novel about three
ds who sailed with Ponce de León to the New World and the beginning
g line of Floridians, and *The Fat Boy Murders* (New York: Pocket Books,
irst in a series of mysteries. Kaufelt's wife, **Lynn Mitsuko Kaufelt**, is
nor of *Key West Writers and Their Houses* (Sarasota: Pineapple Press,

ong the fiction set in Key West are **Louis Capron's** *The Blue Witch* (New
enry Holt, 1957); **Barbara Corcoran's** *A Dance to Still Music* (New York:
um, 1974); **Patricia D. Cornwall's** *Body of Evidence* (New York: Scrib-
ons, 1991); **Franklin W. Dixon's** *Mystery of Smuggler's Cove* (New York:
& Schuster, 1980, reprint); **William K. Eakins's** *Key West, 2720 A.D.*
rd, CT: Knights Press, 1989); **Dorothy Brenner Francis's** *Keys of Love*
ork: Thomas Bouregy, 1975); **James W. Hall's** *Bones of Coral* (New York:
1991); **Burt Hirschfield's** *Key West* (New York: William Morrow, 1978);
l Lockridge's *Encounter in Key West* (Philadelphia: Lippincott, 1966);
l and **Frances Lockridge's** *Death by Association* (Philadelphia: Lippin-
52); **David Loovis's** *The Last of the Southern Winds* (New York: Scribner,

1961); **Thomas McGuane**'s *Ninety-Two in the Shade* (New York: Farrar, Straus and Giroux 1973) and *Panama* (New York: Farrar, Straus and Giroux, 1978); **Frances McGuire**'s *Keys to Fortune* (New York: Dutton, 1954); **Thomas Sanchez**'s *Mile Zero* (New York: Knopf, 1989); **Nora K. Smiley**'s *Our Southernmost Children* (St. Petersburg: Great Outdoors Publishing Co., 1954); **Jack Stark**'s *Loggerhead* (Miami: Seemann Publishing Co., 1972); **Ramona Stewart**'s *Age of Consent* (New York: Dutton, 1975); **Daoma Winston**'s *The Traficante Treasure* (New York: Lancer Books, 1968); and **Bernard Wolfe**'s *In Deep* (New York: Knopf, 1957). Poet **Hart Crane** (1899-1932), who may never have visited Key West but who committed suicide by jumping from a boat off the Keys, wrote poems like "O Carib Isle!" and "Key West" about the town; they are reprinted in **George Murphy**'s *The Key West Reader* (Key West: Tortugas Ltd., 1989), pp. 59-61. That book has also reprinted **Wallace Stevens**'s poems entitled "The Idea of Order at Key West" and "O Florida, Venereal Soil."

Among the nonfiction works about Key West or its people are **Chris Sherrill** and **Roger Aiello**'s *Key West: The Last Resort* (Key West: Key West Book & Card Co., 1978), **L.P. Artman, Jr.**'s *Key West History* (Key West?: Artman, 1969), **Betty Miller Brothers**' *Wreckers & Workers of Old Key West* (Big Pine Key, FL: Litoky, 1972), **Alex Caemmerer**'s *The Houses of Key West* (Sarasota: Pineapple Press, 1992), **Christopher Cox**'s *A Key West Companion* (New York: St. Martin's Press, 1983), **Joseph T. Durkin**'s *Confederate Navy Chief: Stephen R. Mallory* (Columbia, SC: University of South Carolina Press, 1987), **Howard S. England**'s *Fort Zachary Taylor* (Key West: England, 1977), **George Hall**'s *Key West* (London: Osprey, 1991), **Joan & Wright Langley**'s *Key West: Images of the Past* (Key West: C.C. Belland & E.O. Swift, 1982) and their *Old Key West in 3-D* (Key West: Langley Press, 1986), **Stan Windhorn** and **Wright Langley**'s *Yesterday's Key West* (Miami: Seemann Publishing Company, 1973), **Walter H. Norman**'s *Nicknames and Conch Tales* (Tavernier, FL: Norman, 1979), **Kathryn Hall Proby**'s *Mario Sanchez: Painter of Key West Memories* (Key West: Southernmost Press, 1981), **Louise V. White** and **Nora K. Smiley**'s *History of Key West* (St. Petersburg: Great Outdoors Publishing Company, 1959), **Sharon Wells**'s *Portraits: Wooden Houses of Key West* (Key West: Historic Key West Preservation Board, 1979) and her *Forgotten Legacy: Blacks in Nineteenth Century Key West* (Key West: Historic Key West Preservation Board, 1982), **L. Glenn Westfall**'s *Key West: Cigar City, U.S.A.* (Key West: Historic Key West Preservation Board, 1984), **Louise White**'s *Key West* (St. Petersburg, FL: Great Outdoors Publishing Company, 1965), and **Henry Alan Green** and **Marcia Kerstein Zerivitz**'s *Mosaic: Jewish Life in Florida* (Gainesville: University Press of Florida, 1992).

Fort Jefferson

Sixty-eight miles west of Key West is Fort Jefferson, one of the most impressive sights in all of Florida, especially for those who fly out in one of the little planes from Key West. The fort, which can be reached only by boat or plane, is a huge nineteenth-century prison-fort which had as its most famous prisoner Dr. Samuel Mudd, the doctor who set the broken leg of John Wilkes

Fort Jefferson

Dr. Samuel Mudd

Booth, the assassin of President Lincoln. Several movies, for example, *His Name Was Mudd* (1979) and *The Prisoner of Shark Island* (1936), were filmed in the area. Dr. Mudd, who was imprisoned here for four years before President Andrew Johnson pardoned him in 1869, distinguished himself in 1867 during a yellow-fever epidemic that felled 270 of the 300 men at the fort. For more about him see **Samuel Carter III**'s *The Riddle of Dr. Mudd* (New York: Putnam 1974) and **Hal Higdon**'s *The Union vs. Dr. Mudd* (Chicago: Follett, 1964). **Alexander Key**'s novel, *Island Light* (Indianapolis: Bobbs-Merrill, 1950), portrays a Confederate soldier who escapes from Fort Jefferson. The fort, which was to have been the largest of a series of seacoast defenses in the nineteenth century from Texas to Maine, was begun in 1846 and, although under construction for 30 years, was never finished. See **Rodman Bethel's** *A Slumbering Giant of the Past: Fort Jefferson, U.S.A. in the Dry Tortugas* (Miami: Florida Flair, 1979).

John Dos Passos wrote the following passage about a visit to the fort:

Waldo [Pierce] set up his easel at one of the embrasures of the vast stone fort and painted. I had my cot and notebook in another shady nook. The sun was hot and the tradewind cool. The place was enormous and entirely empty. We kept expecting to meet poor old Dr. Mudd coming out of one of the tunnels. No sound but the querulous shrieking of the terns. The water was incredibly clear, delicious for swimming. We saw no shark or barracuda, only a variety of reef fish: yellowtails, angelfish, searobbins, all sorts of tiny jewellike creatures we didn't know the names of swarming under the coralheads. A couple of days went by; it was one of the times I understood the meaning of the word halcyon.

Three novels that take place on these isolated keys are **Theodore McCormick's** *Dangerous Rescue* (New York: Funk & Wagnalls, 1964); **Darwin Porter's** *Butterflies in Heat* (New York: Manor, 1976); and **Bryce Walton's** *Hurricane Reef* (New York: Crowell, 1970).

Enroute to Fort Jefferson from Key West the pilot of a locally arranged guided tour may point out the site of Florida's most famous shipwreck: the *Atocha*, which Mel Fisher found in 1985 after it had lain relatively undisturbed since 1622. For more about the search and eventual discovery of the ship see **Eugene Lyon's** *The Search for the Atocha* (Port Salerno, FL: Florida Classics Library, 1985; it was revised as *Search for the Motherlode of the Atocha* in 1989) and **R. Duncan Mathewson III's** *Treasure of the Atocha* (New York: Dutton, 1986). Also see **Eugene Lyon's** "The Trouble With Treasure," in *National Geographic* (June 1976), pp. 787-809 and **Robert F. Burgess's** *They Found Treasure* (New York: Dodd, Mead & Co., 1977), pp. 51-75. Mel Fisher is one of the Floridians interviewed and profiled in **William L. Pohl** and **John Ames's** *Speaking of Florida* (Jacksonville: University of North Florida Press, 1991).

WRITERS IN PARADISE

DAVID A. KAUFELT

For the past 60 or so years, Key West — this coral rock at the end of the rainbow, this southernmost end of the line — has been home and work place to a surprising number of American literary giants. Hemingway called it the "St. Tropez of the poor." Tennessee Williams called it home. John Hersey, who winters here, isn't talking. That's all right; everyone else is.

The Key West Literary Festival, which has taken place the second weekend of each January for the past ten years, attracts local and imported world-class writers who come and talk (talk, talk) about their writing. Sincere public television camera crews from Miami, Dusseldorf, and London have documented the phenomenon. Magazine articles (*People, Time, Vanity Fair*) have all focused on the fact that Key West is that extraordinary entity, a place where writers gather to live and work.

One mile long, four miles wide, 150 miles from Miami, 90 from Havana, Key West has more writers per capita than any other city in the country. As of now, 50 or so published writers, five of them Pulitzer Prize winners, are knocking themselves out over state-of-the-art word processors, battered typewriters, and chewed pencils (Hemingway said a good day's work was seven pencils) producing works of lasting merit and/or saleability.

The question being asked with increasing frequency by both media and academia is why. Herewith are some potential answers. But first a little background.

Ponce de León, searching for an island to call his own in 1513, discovered the Florida Keys, named them The Martyrs for their tortured, twisted shapes, and then ignored them. He was after bigger game (not the Fountain of Youth, but gold for his sovereign). In 1821 Key West became a United States territory (along with the rest of Florida, unwillingly ceded by the Spanish); the pirates were asked to leave, and the island city was established as a United States naval base, which it still is. Key West became the richest city per capita in the country in 1850, thanks to its salvage industry. (Ships would go down off the coast, foundering on Key West's coral reef; salvagers could keep what they salvaged.) Cuban cigarmakers, fleeing Spain's conscription laws, came in 1868. Henry Morrison Flagler arrived with his Overseas Railroad, spanning the 29 Florida Keys at enormous fiscal and human cost.

Artists had already succumbed to Key West's subtropical climate. Audubon came in 1832; Winslow Homer and Frederic Remington followed. Despite Flagler's railroad, Key West remained remote, a stopover for those headed for Havana. But all that changed in 1928 with the Overseas Highway. Though one still had to take a ferry or two, the trip from the mainland could now be made by car and Key West became just accessible enough. Writers began to arrive, attracted by Key West's near-tropical climate, its turquoise waters, piratical past, and deserved reputation as a wide-open town.

Hemingway, America's first great literary media celebrity, an early master of publicity spin, came via Cuba from Europe in 1928 on the recommendation of his friend, John Dos Passos, who had visited during a walking tour. Hemingway arrived at the beginning of his fame and the onset of his personal myth. His life in Key West was well chronicled in Pathé newsreels and *Life* magazine, helping to create an image of Key West as a writers' haven.

Other writers followed to bask in Papa's and Key West's sunshine, though poets Robert Frost and Wallace Stevens arrived on their own. Frost wintered in the still-existent little green cottage at the back of Jessie Porter Newton's mansion and said Key West "...is a very, very dead place because it has died several times. It died as a resort of pirates, then as a house of smugglers and wreckers...then as a winter resort boomtown." Wallace Stevens described Key West as being "too poor for gardens." But during the 1930s, which were poor indeed (10,000 of the 12,000 residents were on the dole and Mr. Roosevelt was considering closing down the island city), Stevens spent his winters at the Casa Marina Hotel, Flagler's grand luxe Mediterranean establishment on the Atlantic side of the island.

Poet and prose writer Elizabeth Bishop came on a fishing trip in the late thirties and stayed; Tennessee Williams arrived in 1941, staying in the slave quarters behind the no-longer-existent Tradewinds guest house, rewriting his play, "gathering," as he said, "experiences." "I was so happy then," he told Lynn Kaufelt (my wife), a few years before his death when she interviewed him for her book, *Key West Writers and Their Houses* (Sarasota: Pineapple Press, 1986). "I adored Key West which was a small time place.... I'm very sorry to say, my dear, that Key West is becoming a big time place, in a small way."

In the fifties and sixties another generation of writers arrived, searching for the freedom that the end of the rainbow, the last dropping-off place, promised. For the most part they found it. James Leo Herlihy lived and worked in Old Town. He now lives in Los Angeles but he remembers Old Town "as a low budget *film noir* mood piece; the Key West of today [is] a multimillion-dollar tropical fantasy in blazing color."

Thomas McGuane chose Key West as his home because "I didn't want to lose touch with American culture. I wanted to get out on the most scrambled edge of this one." He now spends a lot of time on his ranch in Montana though he often comes back for the bone fishing and the atmosphere, feeling his years here were most important to his writing. "It is nice to arise from the latest effort," he says, "go out the door, and find that life reinforces one's worst suspicions. There's nowhere like Key West for guaranteeing this satisfaction."

In the last decade or so, as Key West has become even more accessible via jet plane, fax, and computer modem, the island city would seem to have come into its full flowering as a literary community. Writers come and often come back again. Here's a partial list: Novelists Phil Caputo, Robert Stone, Thomas Sanchez, Marie Claire Blaise, Irving Weinman, James Hall, John Leslie, Bill Manville, Evan Rhodes, Peter Taylor, and Joy Williams. Playwright Jerry

Herman. Biographer William Wright. Novelist Ramona Stewart. Audubon chronicler Katherine Proby. Children's writer Shel Silverstein. Social commentator Nancy Friday. Poet Judith Kazanthkis. *Esquire* Fiction Editor Rust Hills. Publishers Bill Grose, Sam Lawrence, and Frank Taylor. One of the world's more important literary photographers, Rollie McKenna. And the list goes on.

What's more, James Merrill, who many consider one of America's best living poets, winters in Key West. So do Richard Wilbur (another contender for Best American Poet) and John Malcolm Brinnin.

There is something to be said for the comfort of living and working among one's own kind. However, when young and/or would-be writers ask if they should come to Key West to create, wondering if the reflected glory of those mentioned here might not rub off, wondering if "the curious mix of people" might not provide them with "material," I usually recommend Perth Amboy. More unpublished, unwritten writers get lost in the saloons and salons of Key West than you would care to know about. I think that one had better know who he/she is before flying down to the end of nowhere, schlepping personal computer, anxious to meet and mix.

And if a writer is intent on going to hell with himself in a truly epic way, there are any number of elaborate hells waiting for him in the back streets of Key West. That razor-thin edge of danger that makes up the outer perimeter of this island is attractive to certain writers in both the Hemingway and Tennessee Williams persuasions.

Certainly the houses and places writers live can have a strong effect on their work. Key West's tin-roofed, Dade County–pine cottages, decorated with New England gingerbread and furnished with South Sea Isles bamboo settees are mighty alluring. In her aforementioned book, Lynn Kaufelt writes that "the reason so many writers thrive in Key West is that the houses they write in and the houses around them are filled with the traditions and the histories and the life that help spark that elusive creative fire." The late Jimmy Kirkwood agreed, saying that Key West "is a nice place for lost people who are a little tilted." As are many of the houses they live in.

Freud believed that we are at our most creative during our first five years of life, before society puts constraints on our imagination. Key West is a child's universe, a Technicolor beach and ocean world where the denizens, no matter what their age, wear shorts and cut-off jeans, polo shirts, and sneakers; it's a treasure island where we ride bicycles, hobnob with pirates and ghosts, fish and swim and stay up late at parties reminiscent of early birthday fetes (except the pools are sometimes filled with gin). It's a Peter Pan sort of place where writers are free to relive their earliest and most creative years, where storytellers may work out — and sometimes live out — their fantasies.

When I first met Tennessee Williams a couple of decades ago in the bar of the hotel in New York where he would later die, he asked me what I wanted to be. Blushing and guffawing, stumbling over the simple but to me incredibly presumptuous words, I shamefacedly admitted I wanted to be (cough, gasp) a writer. Tennessee could be a very kind man and he was kind that evening. He looked me in the eye and said, "I have a small bit of advice for you, David." And that is, I prompted. "Travel light, my boy. Travel light."

I know of no place in the world where a writer can travel lighter than in Key West.

David A. Kaufelt is the author of eleven novels, including American Tropic, *a generational novel about Florida. His* The Fat Boy Murders *(New York: Pocket Books Hardcover, 1993) is the first in a series of mysteries.*

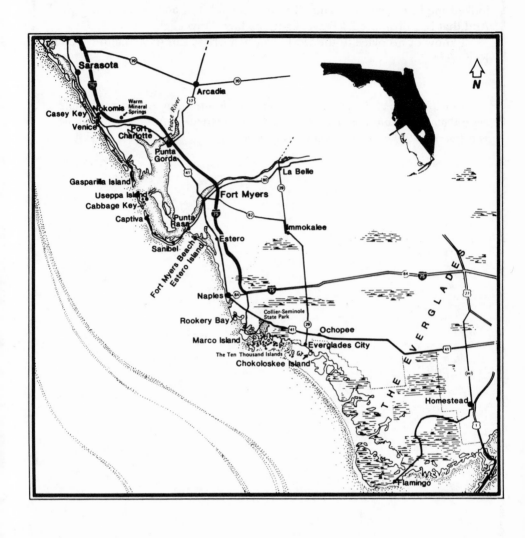

7 HOMESTEAD TO SARASOTA

DAVID WARNER

Homestead

Southwest of bustling Miami and northwest of fishing/diving adventures in the Florida Keys lie Homestead and the Everglades. Homestead was named at the turn of the century when railroad employees came to farm or homestead the rich land; the name *Homestead* was written across the freight car that was used as a depot. Today the city seems caught between two worlds: busy Miami to the northeast and the vast, brooding Glades to the west. Homestead calls itself the City of Bicycles for having originated the idea of bikeways. In August 1992 Hurricane Andrew swept through and did much damage to Homestead and the surrounding area.

Local author **Donald Vincent Smith** (1933-)has lived in Florida since 1957. Born in Fitzgerald, Georgia, Smith was a student at the University of Miami (1958-1959) and later worked first as an insurance underwriter, a traffic agent, and in publishing through his own firm, Olivant Press, in Atlanta. He is also the editor-in-chief of *Weid: The Sensibility Revue*, a Florida-based international literary review. Works by Smith include *Five Sonnets* (1967), *Tired-love Poems* (1968), *New Poems* (1968), *Odyssey* (1969), *New Review Poems* (1976), and *Fatherland* (1976).

Coral Castle on U.S. 1 three miles north of Homestead is Edward Leedskalnin's monument to love: he built the carved, coral-rock house to win back his former girlfriend. Leedskalnin, who weighed only 120 pounds, carved over 1,000 tons of coral rock, some of it weighing up to 30 tons, with handmade tools. It was a feat which engineers still cannot explain and is impressive fodder for the literary imagination.

The trip from Florida City to Flamingo along Route 27 is long and desolate but offers numerous spots from which to see the primitive beauty of the Glades. What one doesn't see is the squalor and inhuman conditions of labor camps back from the main roads, but this is the picture that **Patrick D. Smith** presents in *Angel City* (1978; reprinted by Pineapple Press, 1988), a novel about the cruel realities in the migrant labor camps located between Homestead and Florida City. Similar to **Edward R. Murrow**'s 1960 TV documentary, *Harvest of Shame*, which described the plight of Florida migrant workers, Smith's novel, which became the 1980 movie *Angel City*, antagonized local camp managers but helped draw national attention to the terrible working conditions endured

283

by immigrant workers. *Summer Lightning* (New York: St. Martin's Press, 1978) by **Judith Richards** is another novel set in a south Florida labor camp.

The impetus behind the founding of Everglades National Park at Flamingo goes back to Theodore Roosevelt, the first environmentalist President. In May 1904, William Dutcher, president of the National Audubon Society, secured state legislation to protect non-game fowl. The Audubon Society then employed at its own expense four game wardens to watch over endangered bird rookeries in the state. The cause of conservation suffered a temporary setback when plume poachers killed one of the agents, Guy Bradley, in the Glades in 1905; today at East Cape west of Flamingo, a stone plaque commemorates Bradley. In 1908, another agent, C.G. Mcleod, was murdered near Charlotte Harbor. For more about the slaughter of the birds see "Plumes" by **Marjory Stoneman Douglas** in *Nine Florida Stories by Marjory Stoneman Douglas* (Jacksonville: University of North Florida Press, 1990), edited by **Kevin M. McCarthy** and *They Saved Our Birds* (New York: Hippocrene Books, 1973) by **Helen Ossa**.

In 1910, the New York legislature enacted a bill outlawing the commercial use of American wild-bird feathers. Since New York was the center for the millinery industry, the law acted as a great deterrent to the poachers, but they were still able to sell their wares to foreign buyers who then shipped them back into the United States. Finally, an aroused public conscience, along with a change in fashion, made wearing bird feathers highly unpopular and brought an end to poaching.

Botanists ranging from David M. Fairchild, who founded the Fairchild Tropical Garden at Coconut Grove, to **John Kunkel Small**, who came to Florida in 1907 to collect plant specimens for the New York Botanical Garden, envisioned a federally owned park in the Glades as early as 1916. In his book, *From Eden to Sahara* (Lancaster, PA: Science Press, 1929), Small wrote:

> Here is a unique El Dorado, mainly a tongue of land, extending hundreds of miles into tepid waters, reaching, almost to the Tropic of Cancer, where the floristics of temperate, subtropic, and tropic regions not only meet, but mingle; where the animals of temperate regions associate with those of the tropics. As much as possible of this natural history museum should be preserved, not only for its beauty, but also for its educational value, for it is within easy reach of the majority of the population of the United States.

Despite increased calls for establishing a national park in the Everglades, it wasn't until December 6, 1947, that President Harry Truman dedicated the 1.4 million-acre park.

Myriad forms of plants and wildlife, many of them endangered, call the Glades home. The following quote on a stone plaque in the park reflects the idea of our relationship with the natural order and the interconnectedness of life on Earth:

To produce 1/10 pound of human flesh requires one pound of bass meat, which requires ten pounds of small fish, which requires a hundred pounds of tiny crustaceans, mollusks, worms, insect larvae, and copepods, which requires 1000 pounds of microscopic plant and animal plankton and mangrove detritus, which requires the sun, unpolluted water, an unobstructed flow of freshwater and protected estuaries.

Western writer **Zane Grey** (1875-1939) fished the nearby waters of Florida Bay and described them in *Tales of Southern Rivers*:

Mystery hovered over this forbidden place, neither land nor water nor forest, yet a combination of all three. Though the sun shone brightly and the sky was azure and the breeze breathed off a summer sea, this wilderness of waterways and endless ramifications of mangrove forest did not invite with the bright face of nature, did not beckon to the adventuring soul. It repelled. It boded ill. It was of the salt, hard, caustic, bitter. Never before had I seen a forest that did not lure. But this was not a forest; it was a sinister growth out of the coral.

Grey made the fishing camp at Long Key in the Florida Keys more popular and gulf-stream fishing better known to his readers; some of his descriptions of fishing in Florida Bay no doubt also attracted a good number of anglers.

Flamingo

Flamingo, the name of this frontier village, evokes an image of flocks of translucent pink flamingos circling grassy swamps during the last magic moments of a vermillion-tinged Glades sunset, but nothing could be further from the truth. Flamingos were never native to south Florida but once flew over seasonally in large numbers from Cuba and the Bahamas. At one time the most distinctive feature of Everglades wildlife, the population was reduced to several hundred by plume hunters during the late-nineteenth and early-twentieth centuries when bird feathers were in vogue as decoration on women's hats; the birds were rarely sighted after that. A work about the Flamingo area is *A Dredgeman of Cape Sable* (St. Petersburg: Great Outdoors Publishing Co., 1967) by **Lawrence E. Will**, the Cracker historian of the Everglades.

Ochopee

Back on the Tamiami Trail and near the turn-off to Everglades City is Ochopee, a settlement whose name means *field* or *farm* in Seminole. The town claims to have the country's smallest post office: a seven-by-eight-foot tool shed. This type of setting is part of **Padgett Powell**'s novel, *A Woman Named Drown* (New York: Farrar Straus Giroux, 1987).

Chokoloskee Island

147-acre Chokoloskee Island, three miles south of Everglades City on Highway 29, has a name that means *old house* and is a monument to Calusa know-how. Built on discarded oyster shells piled up by generations of Indians, the island is an engineering marvel but has become better known for its bloodshed, crime, and mystery.

The area was little known and hardly charted by white men until the turn of the nineteenth century. At that time, fewer than 300 people resided between Punta Rasa at the northernmost edge of the Ten Thousand Islands and Cape Sable to the south. The islands' isolation attracted many refugees from the law. They hunted and fished and killed birds and animals for their hides and generally kept to themselves. One writer lists seven unwritten laws of the area:

1. Suspect every man.
2. Ask no questions.
3. Settle your own quarrels.
4. Never steal from an Islander.
5. Stick by him, even if you do not know him.
6. Shoot quick, when your secret is in danger.
7. Cover your kill.

Peter Matthiessen

One such fugitive from the law is described in **Peter Matthiessen's** novel, *Killing Mister Watson* (New York: Random House, 1990). After reputedly killing a man in Columbia County, Florida, Ed Watson escaped to the Oklahoma Indian territory where he was rumored to have run with the James Gang and murdered the notorious woman outlaw, Belle Starr. When Watson moved to south Florida, he bought a sugar plantation at Cape Sable, to which he lured itinerant workers with the promise of good wages; he then killed them in lieu of payment. On October 24, 1910, when Watson boated to Chokoloskee Island for supplies, a mob surrounded and killed him. Watson's story is related by a series of Florida Cracker characters who knew him in the Ten Thousand Islands.

Smallwood's General Store at the southern end of Chokoloskee Island, the place where Watson was executed, houses a Cracker museum. For more about the island see **Charlton W. Tebeau's** *The Story of the Chokoloskee Bay Country* (Coral Gables, FL: University of Miami Press, 1955; Miami: Banyan, 1976).

Everglades City and The Ten Thousand Islands

A half-hour east of Naples, south on Highway 29 off U.S. 41, Everglades City and the Ten Thousand Islands are a world apart in pace and surroundings. No beaches. No bright lights. And the only nightlife is the occasional call of a night heron or a mullet jumping in the moonlit river. All around, one can find peace and quiet and the haunting beauty of the Glades. Everglades City's Rod & Gun Club has served as a meeting place for four presidents and celebrities ranging from actor John Barrymore to author Zane Grey. Today the inn retains the charm of a late nineteenth-century resort with its white-washed, clapboard siding, canary-yellow shutters, and knobby cypress-paneled lobby featuring an upside down, open-mouthed gator overlooking a green-baized pool table.

Among the novels set in the area are several that feature such gators in the wild. **Shelley Katz**'s *Alligator* (New York: Dell, 1977), an exciting novel about a huge gator's battle of wits with several skilled hunters, takes place near Everglades City, as does **George Laycock**'s *King Gator* (New York: Norton, 1968) about a gator's fight for survival and **George X. Sand**'s *Iron-Tail* (New

Everglades City Rod and Gun Club

York: Scribner, 1971).

The state park system runs a cruise of the Ten Thousand Islands, countless, tiny mangrove islets off the southwest tip of Florida. The 2.5-hour tour leaves at different times according to the season (800 233-1821).

The first people to arrive in the area were the Calusa Indians in 1500 B.C. They lived there until around A.D. 1800, when diseases like smallpox and syphilis wiped out their last vestiges. For more about them see *The Evolution of the Calusa* (Tuscaloosa, AL: University of Alabama Press, 1988) by **Randolph**

J. Widmer and *Missions to the Calusa* (Gainesville: University of Florida **Press**, 1991) edited by **John H. Hann**. Until recent times, the islands' non-Indian inhabitants have retained a degree of self-sufficiency rare in this computerized age. Through the years the islands have provided food and shelter for numerous hermits, the most famous of whom was Roy Ozmer, who lived alone on Pelican Key for over 30 years before hurricane Donna forced him to retreat to the mainland.

Modern-day Everglades City was founded by Memphis ad magnate, Barron Collier (1873-1939), who made his fortune buying up the placard rights for buses, subways, and trolley cars in major cities. Collier first came to the area on vacation in 1911. By the 1920s, he was dredging the area and establishing Everglades City, which he made the nerve center for his extensive holdings in southwest Florida — 1.3 million acres of swampland including most of present-day Collier County. By 1923, he owned more of the state than anyone else.

Writer **John Rothchild**, co-author of *Marjory Stoneman Douglas: Voice of the River* (Sarasota: Pineapple Press, 1987), an autobiography of the great environmentalist pioneer, gives a description of Collier's domain in his book, *Up for Grabs* (New York: Viking Press, 1985), much of which is set in Everglades City:

> The Barron River had Collier's first name, the county had his last; Everglades City had been his company town, dug up and platted by his engineers, populated by his employees, financed by his bank. The old stucco buildings were all Collier buildings, erected in the 1920s, the city sewer plant and the water plant were originally the Collier utilities, the older men whom we saw cleaning their traps along Collier's river were ex-Collier fishing guides....

The Tamiami Trail was Collier's road, his dynamite crews blasted and loosened the oolitic rock, and his giant shovel machines followed behind, scooping and piling the rubble into the two-lane passage, raised a few inches above the surrounding wetlands. It cost Collier several million dollars to complete this highway, a feat that was equated with the digging of the Panama Canal.

Later additions to the town included a bank, a railroad station, and a theater. Unfortunately for his heirs, Collier lost most of his fortune during the Depression, at which point his Florida development was terminated.

Today one still sees the remnants of Collier's dream. A four-spoked hub is the focus of incoming traffic, and the central boulevard has a grassy median with Victorian-style street lamps running down its center. Then, too, there are the Cracker box houses constructed for Collier's employees and the abandoned courthouse with its pseudo-Grecian facade resembling, in Rothchild's words, "a dowager lost in high grass." Collier's stern Germanic portrait hangs alongside the upside-down alligator in the lobby of the Rod & Gun Club.

During the 1880s and 1890s, steamboat loads of wealthy tourists used to patrol the present-day Barron River taking potshots at local wildlife. The pink flamingo population was greatly depleted by 1900, when the federal government finally passed laws protecting wildlife. In the years since, the surrounding glades have gained a reputation as prime smuggling territory, starting with the illegal exportation of flamingo feathers for ladies' hats and continuing up to the present with alligator hides, Prohibition booze, moonshine, and, more recently, marijuana or *square grouper*, as the floating bales are dubbed locally.

Wind Across the Everglades, a 1958 movie dealing with the real-life murder of a federal wildlife officer by plume pirates (see Everglades National Park), written by **Budd Schulberg** and starring Burl Ives and Gypsy Rose Lee, was filmed around Everglades City. Other movies filmed in the area were *Flipper* (1963), *Thunder and Lightning* (1977), and *Pirates Key* (1980).

For information about the hundred-mile inside water route from Everglades City to Flamingo on Florida Bay, see **William G. Truesdell**'s *A Guide to the Wilderness Waterway of the Everglades National Park* (Coral Gables, FL: University of Miami Press, 1969). Also see *The Everglades: From Yesterday to Tomorrow* (New York: Putnam, 1974) by **Wyatt Blassingame**; *On Preserving Tropical Florida* (Coral Gables, FL: University of Miami Press, 1972) by **John C. Gifford**; and *Everglades Country* (New York: Viking, 1973) by **Patricia Lauber**. *Forty Years in the Everglades* by **Calvin R. Stone** (Tabor City, NC: Atlantic, 1979) is about the area from the 1930s to the 1970s.

Collier-Seminole State Park

Fifteen miles southeast of Naples off U.S. 41, the 6,423-acre Collier-Seminole State Park is home to such endangered species as the Florida black bear, the mangrove fox squirrel, the red-cockaded woodpecker, and the manatee. The park also contains exhibits about the area, featuring the construction of the Tamiami Trail across the Glades. For more about the people and events associated with this part of Florida see **Will Horne**'s *Tales of the Tamiami Trail* (St. Petersburg: Great Outdoors Publishing Co., 1966). The Tamiami Trail (U.S. 41) out of Miami's Southwest Eighth Street is a 70-mile road that heads west through the Everglades and the Big Cypress Swamp. For a description of the many gloomy, Poe-like mansions in the small towns near the Everglades see **Edith Hamill**'s (**Jean F. Webb**) *The Craigshaw Curse* (New York: Meredith Press, 1968), a mystery about ghosts and murder. English critic and writer **Alistair Cooke** described the land in a series of essays about America; his description of the area outside Miami is poetic:

> Within a half-hour Miami is a memory of a Hollywood musical to a man stranded on the Amazon. An eagle circles against a purple sky. A buzzard flaps away from some dark carrion on the road ahead. You stop your motor and see no living thing. But the loneliness, and the awe of living close to a jungle before it was ever tamed into lumber or tailored into farms or gardens, is intensified by the insane symphony of sound that strikes your ear. Over a bubbling, rumbling percussion of bullfrogs, you will hear the chuck-chuck of tropical woodpeckers, the wheezy sigh of bull-rats, a low slush of alligator.

The park and the surrounding county, which is larger than the state of Delaware, were named for the aforementioned Barron Collier. **James McMullen**'s *Cry of the Panther* (Sarasota: Pineapple Press, 1984) is about a Vietnam War vet's mystic identification with an endangered Florida panther; **Roger Caras**'s *Panther!* (Boston: Little Brown, 1969) also describes a panther in the swamp.

Marco Island and Rookery Bay

South of Naples, on Route 951, off Highway 41, is Marco Island, home to some of the poshest resorts in the state. **Marion Spjut Gilliland** recounts the early history of the island in two books: *Key Marco's Buried Treasure* (Gainesville: University of Florida Press, 1989) and *The Material Culture of Key Marco, Florida* (Gainesville: University Presses of Florida, 1975). Halfway between Marco Island and Naples and several miles to the west of Route 951 is Rookery Bay, an isolated part of the Gulf coast particularly rich in wildlife and foliage. **Raymond S. Dasmann**'s *No Further Retreat: The Fight to Save Florida* (New York: Macmillan, 1971) describes the delicacy of the environment here and elsewhere in south Florida.

Seminoles

The Seminole Indians are a southeastern Indian tribe who speak the Muskogee language. In the 1700s, some Creek Indians came to Florida from Georgia and intermarried with runaway slaves; the name *Seminole* means *runaways* or *those who separate*. After the Second Seminole War (1835-1842) about 3,800 of the Seminoles were relocated in the Oklahoma Indian territory, but some 300 refused to go and simply withdrew into the Everglades. Today the 1,500 Seminoles who live in central and southern Florida are related to those 300 Indians who stayed behind.

For historical information about these Indians see *Big Cypress, A Changing Seminole Community* (New York: Holt, Rinehart and Winston, 1972) and *The Seminole* (New York: Chelsea House, 1989) by **Merwyn S. Garbarino**; *The Seminole and Miccosukee Tribes: A Critical Bibliography* (Bloomington, IN: Indiana University Press, 1987) and *The Florida Seminoles and the New Deal, 1933-1942* (Boca Raton, FL: Florida Atlantic University Press, 1989) by **Harry A. Kersey, Jr.**; *Africans and Seminoles* (Westport, CT: Greenwood Press, 1977) by **Daniel F. Littlefield, Jr.**; *The Seminoles* (Norman, OK: University of Oklahoma Press, 1957) by **Edwin C. McReynolds**; *A Seminole Sourcebook* (New York: Garland, 1987) edited by **William C. Sturtevant**; and *Creeks and Seminoles: Destruction and Regeneration of the Muscogulge People* (Lincoln, NE: University of Nebraska Press, 1986) by **J. Leitch Wright, Jr.**

Among the novels dealing with the Seminoles are **Zachary Ball**'s *Joe Panther* (New York: Holiday House, 1950) and *Swamp Chief* (New York: Holiday House, 1952); **Iris T. Comfort**'s *Joey Tigertail* (Lexington, MA: Ginn, 1973); **Dee Dunsing**'s *The Seminole Trail* (New York: Longmans, Green, 1956); and **Patrick D. Smith**'s *Forever Island* (New York: Norton, 1973) and *Allapattah* (1979;

reprinted by Pineapple Press with *Forever Island*, 1987). *A Woman Set Apart* (New York: Dodd, Mead, 1963) by **William** and **Ellen Hartley** is the story of Deaconess Hariett Bedell, a remarkable woman who ministered to the local Indians.

The Everglades

The Glades panorama doesn't appeal to everyone. At first glance, the place appears flat, desolate, and foreboding, a mangrove swamp filled with gators and water moccasins. One can drive for miles down U.S. 41, the old Tamiami Trail, without any apparent change of scenery. The eye of a careful observer, however, can find a sort of brooding beauty in the Everglades and a variety of wildlife almost unparalleled in the world. Occasionally a weathered sign advertises alligator wrestling or airboat rides or a Seminole Indian reservation. These attractions are usually behind a sagging wooden fence — their ticket booths empty, the owners having moved elsewhere. Seminole women at work at such roadside attractions are featured in *Floridians At Work, Yesterday and Today* (Macon, GA: Mercer University Press, 1989) by **Margaret Gibbons Wilson.**

In her ground-breaking book, *The Everglades* (New York: Rinehart, 1947; reproduced by Banyan, 1979), author and naturalist **Marjory Stoneman Douglas** (1890-) christened the Glades a *River of Grass*. Its heart is a shallow, freshwater river, 50, 60, even 70 miles wide at places, no more than a few inches deep, that flows south from Lake Okeechobee into Florida Bay, an 850-square mile body of water, with borders on the Gulf and the Atlantic, whose depth ranges from three to six feet. Warmed by a hot subtropical sun, the Glades' shallow water provides a natural breeding place and refuge for plant and animal life including over 300 species of birds, 1,000 varieties of seed-bearing plants, 120 species of trees, 25 kinds of orchids, and a variety of bromeliads. The Everglades is also home to 11 endangered species including the American crocodile, the southern bald eagle, the West Indian manatee, and the Florida panther. Indeed, there exists a wealth of wildlife to be examined in detail by anyone with the least trace of adventure in his soul.

For more about this area of Florida, read **Louise Lee Floethe**'s *Sea of Grass* (New York: Scribner, 1963); **George X. Sand**'s *The Everglades Today: Endangered Wilderness* (New York: Four Winds Press, 1971); and two books by **Charlton W. Tebeau**: *They Lived in the Park: The Story of Man in the Everglades National Park* (Coral Gables, FL: Everglades Natural History Association, 1963) and *Florida's Last Frontier: The History of Collier County* (Coral Gables, FL: University of Miami Press, 1966).

The more than 70 novels that take place in the Glades deal with the area's vastness and inaccessibility, its flora and fauna, its vulnerability to hurricanes, and the Seminoles. Among the novels published since 1950 are **Paul Allen**'s *Apeland* (New York: Viking, 1976); **Virginia Anderson**'s *Storm Front* (New York: Bantam-Doubleday, 1992); **Helen Barney**'s *The White Dove* (New York: Crown, 1956); **Henry Chapin**'s *Tigertail, The Game Chicken* (New York: W.R. Scott,

1965); **Marjory Stoneman Douglas**'s *Freedom River* (New York: Scribner, 1953) and *Alligator Crossing* (New York: J. Day, 1959); **Mel Ellis**'s *Ironhead* (New York: Holt, Rinehart, and Winston, 1968); **William C. Emerson**'s *Belle of the Everglades* (New York: Pageant, 1958); **William Harrington**'s *Scorpio 5* (New York: Coward, McCann & Geoghegan, 1975); **Ann K. Hartman**'s *Adventure in the Everglades* (New York: Exposition, 1955); **Ida Haskins**' *Adventures on the Airboat Trail* (Miami: Seemann Publishing Co., 1973); **Frederick W. Keith**'s *Danger in the Everglades* (New York: Abelard-Schuman, 1957); **R.R. Knudson**'s *You Are the Rain* (New York: Delacorte, 1974); **George W. Meader**'s *Everglades Adventure* (New York: Harcourt, Brace, 1957); **Charles Mink**'s *Princess of the Everglades* (Sarasota: Pineapple Press, 1991), a recent novel about a 10-year-old girl rescued from the glades by Thomas Edison, Henry Ford, and Charles Lindbergh; **Fran Podulka**'s *The Wonder Jungle* (New York: Putnam, 1974); **Theodore Pratt**'s *Escape to Eden* (Greenwich, CT: Fawcett, 1953); **Ann Rush**'s *Florida Nurse* (New York: Avalon, 1956); **Budd Schulberg**'s *Wind Across the Everglades* (New York: Random House, 1958); **Frank Slaughter**'s *Fort Everglades* (Garden City, NY: Doubleday, 1951) and *The Warrior* (Garden City, NY: Doubleday, 1956); **Herman Weiss**'s *Passion in the Wind* (New York: Popular Library, 1977); and **Ester Wier**'s *The Winners* (New York: McKay, 1966).

Naples

The wealthiest city in Florida, Naples, which was named after the southern Italian city of the same name, has a neon-free beauty that its residents cherish. An Australian pine-lined beach and a long fishing pier add to the city's allure, as do its huge beach-front mansions. The area is the setting for **Theodore Pratt's** novel, *Big Blow* (Boston: Little Brown, 1936), about the local farmers' difficulties with insects and weather. **John D. MacDonald's** *Bright Orange For the Shroud* (Greenwich, CT: Fawcett, 1965), a Travis McGee thriller involving crooked land deals and high-speed boat chases, is also set in Naples. **Louise Bergstrom's** *The House of the Evening Star* (New York: Avalon, 1976) takes place on a fictional key off the southwest coast of Florida, as does **Edwin Granberry's** *A Trip to Czardis* (New York: Trident Press, 1966).

The 1985 murder of two members of a prominent local family is the subject of three books: *Blood Relations, The Exclusive Inside Story of the Benson Family Murders* (San Diego: Harcourt Brace Jovanovich, 1987) by **John Greenya**, *The Serpent's Tooth, A Family Story of Greed, Betrayal, Vengeance and Multiple Murder* (New York: Harper & Row, 1987) by **Christopher P. Andersen**, and *Money to Burn, The True Story of the Benson Family Murders* by **Michael Mewshaw** (New York: Aytheneum, 1987). For a personal account of the city, read *Early Naples and Collier County* (Naples, FL: Collier County Historical Society, 1973) by **Earl L. Baum.**

Several significant writers have made their home in Naples over the years. One of them is **Ben Bova** (1932-). Bova, whose interest in space and high technology was first stimulated by a childhood visit to Philadelphia's Fess Planetarium, is the former editor of *Omni* and *Analog* magazines and has won the coveted Hugo award (the Oscar of science fiction) six times. His more than 75 novels and nonfiction works include *As on a Darkling Plain* (1972) about a machine that permits personal disputes to be settled on a simulated background; *The Kinsman Saga* (1987) about astronaut Chester A. Kinsman, a character based on Bova himself; and *Voyagers* (1981) about an extraterrestrial intelligence that serves as a metaphor for our present technology. Bova believes: "A science fiction story is one in which some aspect of future science and technology is so important that if you took that aspect out of the story it would collapse.... The archetype of all this is Mary Shelley's novel *Frankenstein*. She was one of the first to take this kind of story out of the realm of magic and the supernatural and say, 'This new thing we call science might be able to do something like this....'" Having worked with the likes of Woody Allen (*Sleeper*), George Lucas (*THX-1138*), and Gene Roddenberry (*Star Trek*), Bova states further: "While it can be good entertainment, most of the science fiction out of Hollywood bears...the same relationship to published science fiction that Popeye does to naval history."

Novelist **Robin Cook** (1940-) is known as the Master of the Medical Thriller. His ten novels all deal with medicine except *Sphinx*, which was made into a 1981 movie starring Frank Langella and Lesley-Anne Down. Cook, himself once a doctor, explains: "Part of my motivation to go to medical school was having been inundated by the media's glowing portrayal of medicine.... I grew up watching Ben Casey. He was this intelligent, angry, young guy who was going to conquer the world and stamp out disease.... So when I went to medical school, I felt cheated, that maybe I'd gone to the wrong school.... [But] I found out it was that way everywhere.... One thing that really shocked me was this great heterogeneity in the medical profession. There are great doctors and there are lousy doctors. I mean, some are so abominable; it's a joke."

Cook was later drafted and sent out as a doctor on a nuclear sub. It was during this time that he wrote his first novel, *The Year of the Intern* (1972). "Now, when doctors ask me how I find time to write, I tell them to think about joining the navy," jokes Cook. Because *The Year of the Intern* was not a best-seller, the young writer went back to read it again. To his dismay, he found it was boring. To become better known, Cook decided that his next book would have to be a best-seller. "I went to the best-seller list and began a study," he explains. "I found one genre that kept popping out: the mystery-thriller. So I read a lot of them and came up with what made a mystery and what made a thriller.... [A] mystery is when the writer gives the reader different information than he gives the main character, who is always one step ahead.... In a thriller, you know what the main character doesn't know. You see a scary house and say, 'Don't go in there.' And, of course, he does."

In *Coma* (1977) Cook's first best-seller, he used the methods he had found in other best-sellers. *Coma* was later made into a successful 1978 movie starring Genevieve Bujold and Michael Douglas. Cook's other works include *Brain* (1981), *Fever* (1982), *Godplayer* (1983), and *Mutation* (1989).

According to Random House's biography of **Robert Ludlum** (1927-), their best-selling author, he "is not now nor has he ever been: a CIA agent, a retired general, an international lawyer, a Nazi spy, a member of the Mafia, or any of the other identities of the numerous heroes and villains from his 16 novels of international intrigue. He is instead a former actor and theatrical producer who, when he was 40 years old, decided to change careers and try his hand at writing."

Ludlum's first book, *The Scarlatti Inheritance* (1971), was a *New York Times* best-seller, a Book of the Month Club selection, and a major paperback. From then on, he produced one best-seller a year until 1981, when he switched publishers and began producing one every two years. Ludlum begins writing at 4:30 every morning. He edits his work in longhand as he writes, then sends a copy to his secretary in Connecticut. She transcribes it on a word processor and sends a copy back to him. Ludlum then turns it over to his wife for a critique. According to Ludlum: "I write every day, and it's not a question of having to. It's a matter of *wanting* to. I think you always need to be honing these skills. And there always has to be an idea. There is no time off from thinking; it's a constant job. I'm going to keep on writing, because I see no reason to ever stop."

Ludlum's dedication has produced 18 best-sellers including *The Rhineman Exchange* (1974), *The Gemini Contenders* (1976), *The Matarese Circle* (1979), *The Aquitaine Progression* (1984), and *The Icarus Agenda* (1988). His best-seller, *The Bourne Identity* (1980), was made into a 1988 TV mini-series, as was its sequel, *The Bourne Supremacy* (1986).

Phyllis Luxem (1907-), who was born in Waupaca, Wisconsin, and moved to Naples in 1962, wrote *The Secret of Cypress Manor* (New York: Avalon, 1974), a gothic romance set in Naples that contains a detailed description of southwest Florida flora and fauna. In addition, she is the author of 29 light romances or career novels, the heroines of which are nurses, school teachers, and librarians.

Estero

Fifteen miles south of Fort Myers on U.S. 41 is Estero, a town whose Spanish name means *estuary*. The historic site of Koreshan is five miles south of Highway 865 on U.S. 41 (813 992-0311). A Chicago doctor, Cyrus Tweed, bought a thousand acres of land in Estero, and in 1893 he and 175 followers set out to create a New Jerusalem. Christening himself Koresh, Hebrew for *Cyrus*, Tweed established a communal society that farmed the land, believed that humans live on the inside of the globe, and practiced total birth control. Problems arose when Tweed, who was supposed to be immortal, died in 1908 and a hurricane washed his tomb out to sea. In 1962, the settlement's last four survivors deeded the land to the state for a park. For a description of the architecture and history of the place, read *Koreshan Unity Settlement, 1894-1977* (Winter Park, FL: Architects Design Group of Florida, 1977) by **G.M. Herbert** and **I.S.K. Reeves V.**

During the Second World War, Nazis experimented with Tweed's idea concerning the globe. They sent a group of scientists to an island in the Baltic Sea where they trained their infrared equipment upward to photograph the

British fleet in the Atlantic. If Tweed's theory that humans live on the concave surface of the earth had been correct, the photograph should have come out. Needless to say, the experiment failed; for more information about it, see the June 1946 issue of *Popular Astronomy*, pp. 277-278.

The Koreshans established *The American Eagle*, a political weekly, in 1906 and later developed it into a highly respected horticultural magazine. After a brief suspension of the paper, Hedwig Michel revived it in 1965 as a monthly devoted to the conservation of the state's natural resources. The early issues are valuable for historians, genealogists, and scholars of early farming methods.

Immokalee

Immokalee, 21 miles east of Fort Myers on Route 846, is a town whose name comes from the Seminole meaning *tumbling water* or *his home*. Corkscrew Swamp Sanctuary is an 11,000-acre wilderness area featuring the 700-year-old bald cypress, the oldest tree in eastern North America. A 1.75-mile nature walk provides a view of subtropical flora and fauna including wood storks, alligators, wading birds, and air plants (813 657-3771). Much of the surrounding area, called the Caloosahatchee River region, is described in **Florence I. Fritz's** *Unknown Florida* (Coral Gables, FL: University of Miami Press, 1963).

La Belle

This small town at the intersection of Routes 29 and 80 was named by a local man in honor of his two daughters, Laura and Belle. A part of *The Night of Camp David* (New York: Harper & Row, 1965), **Fletcher Knebel's** novel depicting a Southern politician who becomes President, takes place in La Belle. Knebel is also the author of *Seven Days in May* (1962) and *Trespass* (1969).

Cabbage Key

Located off Captiva Island and approachable only by boat, this beautiful, subtropical island was once home to the world-renowned mystery writer, **Mary Roberts Rinehart** (1876-1958). Rinehart, the author of novels and plays including *The Circular Staircase* (1908), *The Truce of God* (1922), *The Door* (1930), *The Wall* (1938), *Episode of the Wandering Knife* (1950), *The Swimming Pool* (1952), and *The Bat* (1920, with **Avery Hapwood**), began writing in 1903 to provide her family an income after its fortunes plummeted due to unsuccessful stock-market investments. In subsequent years, she became one of America's most highly paid writers. Her home on Cabbage Key was built atop a Calusa Indian shell mound in 1938. Today the Rinehart house is operated as a rustic, six-room resort with six working fireplaces, five porches, and a restaurant-bar papered with thousands of one-dollar bills, signed and posted by customers over the years. A water tower offers a beautiful view of the surrounding area.

Sanibel – Captiva

The nearby islands of Sanibel and Captiva, famous for their shelling and their wildlife preserves, are reached by a toll bridge on Route 867. Legend has it that the infamous pirate, José Gaspar, held Mexican girls captive on Captiva, hence the name. Sanibel was named after Santa Isabella, queen of Aragon and Castille

The Darling National Wildlife Refuge on Sanibel was named after conservationist **"Ding" Darling** (1876-1962), a political cartoonist for the *New York Herald Tribune* who won the Pulitzer Prize in 1924 and 1943. Darling was the head of the U.S. Biological Survey (which later became the U.S. Fish and Wildlife Service) and helped establish the National Wildlife Federation. He was also on the board of directors of the National Audubon Society. The refuge, encompassing more than 5,000 acres, consists of saltwater mangroves and freshwater marsh and attracts over 300 species of birds (813 472-1100).

For more about the island see **George R. Campbell**'s *The Nature of Things on Sanibel* (1978; revised & published by Pineapple Press, 1988); **Lynn Stone**'s *Sanibel Island* (Stillwater, MN: Voyageur Press, 1991); **Charles J. Wilson**'s *The Indian Presence* (Sanibel, FL: Sanibel-Captiva Conservation Foundation, 1982); **Elinore M. Dormer**'s *The Sea Shell Islands* (Tallahassee: Rose, 1979); **Linda Firestone** and **Whit Morse**'s *Sanibel & Captiva* (Richmond, VA: Good Life Publishers, 1978); and **Florence Fritz**'s *The Unknown Story of World Famous Sanibel and Captiva (Ybel y Cautivo)* (Parsons, WV: McClain, 1974) — Fritz was the first woman mayor of Fort Myers. A story about a young egret on the islands is **Griffing Bancroft**'s *Snowy* (New York: McCall, 1970). Literary footnote: Clarence Hemingway, Ernest Hemingway's father, lost his retirement money in land speculation on Sanibel during the 1920s and shortly thereafter committed suicide.

Several well-known authors have lived on Sanibel and Captiva. **Anne Morrow Lindbergh** (1906-), who was born in Englewood, New Jersey and married the American hero, Charles Lindbergh, wrote novels and poetry. When poet John Ciardi criticized her book, *The Unicorn and Other Poems, 1935-1955* (New York: Pantheon, 1956), hundreds of irate women readers came to her defense. As the *Woman's Home Companion* described the rally, "Her books are a gift to all women who hope for individual expression while they make peanut-butter sandwiches, iron clothes, and dream."

Anne Morrow Lindbergh

Punta Rasa

Located on Route 867 near the mainland end of the Sanibel-Captiva toll bridge is Punta Rasa, a name that means *flat point* in Spanish and aptly describes the coastline. During the late 1800s, it was a prosperous cattle town with overflowing hotels and raucous saloons, where Florida cattlemen drove their herds for shipment to Cuba and the Caribbean. Located at the end of the cable line between Florida and Cuba, it was the first town in the United States to receive word of the sinking of the U.S.S. *Maine* on February 15, 1898, the event that precipitated the Spanish-American War.

Fort Myers

One of the nation's fastest-growing cities, Fort Myers was named after U.S. Army General Abraham Myers, who established a fort in 1850 during the Third Seminole War.

In 1915, British novelist **D.H. Lawrence** (1885-1930) planned to start Rananim, a Utopian community in Florida. In a letter to his friend, William Hopkins, Lawrence wrote that he wanted to "sail away from the world of war and squalor and found a little colony where there shall be no money, but a sort of communism as far as the necessaries of life go..." It would be "a community... established upon the assumption of goodness in the members instead of the assumption of badness." In a later letter to his friend and patron, Lady Ottoline, he wrote that it would be "a small world for those who wanted to escape the temporal and 'consider the big things.'" Other residents of the community were to have included Lady Ottoline, composer Phillip Heseltine (alias Peter Warlock), artist Dorothy Brett, and writers Aldous Huxley, Michael Arlen (author of *The Green Hat*), and Katherine Mansfield. Lawrence would lecture on immortality, and mathematician/philosopher Bertrand Russell would lecture on ethics. Lawrence offered the presidency to Russell, but he declined. At first Lawrence went to composer Frederick Delius, who owned property in Picolata near St. Augustine, but Delius argued that the damp climate would be fatal for the tubercular Lawrence. Lawrence then heard of cheap property available at Fort Myers and began making inquiries. At the last moment Lawrence discovered that he could not leave England without an official exemption from military conscription during World War I. When he went to take the exam, he waited two hours before deciding that he did not want to risk hearing bad news about his health. As a result, Lawrence's plans for the Utopian community fell by the wayside, never to be retrieved.

Thomas Edison's (1847-1931) Winter Home, a 14-acre riverfront estate at 2350 McGregor Boulevard, is today a museum (813 332-7799). Among the displays are the patents for Edison's 1,097 inventions, light bulbs that have been burning 12 hours a day since 1910, an Indian banyan tree that dominates the front yard, and mementos of his two friends and neighbors, Henry Ford and Harvey Firestone. The house, built in Maine and shipped south in sections, was the first prefabricated house in America. Edison's swimming pool, reinforced with bamboo instead of steel, has never leaked or cracked since its construction in 1900; it is filled by a 1,100-foot artesian well which also supplies the underground irrigation system for the gardens. A tour of the gardens reveals many of the fascinating trees and plants that the great man cultivated.

In 1887, Edison offered to set up an electric lighting system for Fort Myers free of charge if the city would provide the poles. The city, however, turned him down, reasoning that the poles were too expensive and electricity would be dangerous and might scare the cows. Despite this and other arguments with the city, Edison claimed that Fort Myers was "as near heaven as (he) ever hope(d) to be." Every February, The Edison Pageant of Light commemorates his many achievements.

For more about Edison, see **Florence Fritz's** *Bamboo and Sailing Ships: The Story of Thomas Alva Edison and Fort Myers, Florida* (Fort Myers: no publisher, 1949). For more about Edison, Ford, Firestone, and Charles Lindbergh and the time they spent in Fort Myers, see *Uncommon Friends* (San Diego: Harcourt Brace Jovanovich, 1987) by **James D. Newton.** Among the novels set in the area are *Rogue's Coat* (Garden City, NY: Doubleday, 1949) by **Theodora McCormick Dubois** and *Fifty Fathom Klondike* (New York: Funk & Wagnalls, 1959) by **Prentice Winchell (Stewart Sterling).** For a history of the city, see *Yesterday's Fort Myers* (Miami: Seemann Publishing Co., 1975) by **Marian Godown & Alberta Rawchuck** and *The Story of Fort Myers* (Fort Myers: Island Press, 1982) by **Karl H. Grismer. Richard Powell's** *I Take This Land* (New York: Scribner's, 1962) is a novel

Richard Powell

which concentrates on the period between 1895 and 1946, especially the coming of the railroad. Two books by **E.A. "Frog" Smith** containing local folklore are *Frog Smith's Scrapbook* (Fort Myers?: Author, 1978) and *Crackers and Swamp Cabbage* (1975). *Medical Nostalgia* (New York: Pageant Press, 1970) by **Edwin L. Rasmussen** is about medical practices in Fort Myers at the beginning of the twentieth century.

One of the most popular local authors, **Richard Powell** (1908-), was born in Philadelphia and moved to Fort Myers in 1946. From 1946 to 1956, he wrote several mysteries with Florida settings that Simon & Schuster published: *And Hope To Die* (1947), *Shark River* (1950), *Shell Game* (1950), and *A Shot in the Dark*

(1952). Three other Powell novels that Scribner's published also take place in Florida: *Pioneer, Go Home* (1959), *I Take This Land* (1962), and *Tickets to the Devil* (1968). *Pioneer, Go Home* was made into the 1962 movie, *Follow That Dream*, shot in Levy County, Florida, and starring Elvis Presley. Powell, whose novel *The Philadelphian* (1956), is his most famous work, describes himself as a "Philadelphian by birth, education and culture and a southwest Floridian by emotion."

Gasparilla Island

Southeast of Port Charlotte is Gasparilla Island, named after the infamous though probably mythical Spanish pirate, José Gaspar (1783-1824). Legend has it that Gaspar used the island as his base of operations, capturing 40 ships and murdering their crews and passengers. About to be captured by the British, he tied an anchor about his neck and leaped to his death rather than face execution.

For more about Gaspar and the surrounding area see several books by **Jack Beater**: *The "Gasparilla" Story* (Fort Myers, FL: Wordshop House, 1952); *Islands of the Florida Coast* (Fort Myers, FL: Beater, 1956); *True Tales of the Florida West Coast* (Fort Myers, FL: Beater, 1959); and *The Life and Times of Gasparilla* (Fort Myers, FL: Beater, 1968); also see *The Sea Adventurer* (New York: Dell, 1957) by **Jack Beater** and **Robert MacLennon**.

The beautifully restored, turn-of-the-century fishing village of Boca Grande is on Gasparilla. Before roads extended this far south, America's First Families boarded trains to get to the Gasparilla Inn built in 1912. The world-renowned tarpon fishing off Boca Grande's shores has attracted such notables as Presidents Theodore Roosevelt and Herbert Hoover, writers Zane Grey and Mary Roberts Rinehart, boxer Gene Tunney, and countless other wealthy visitors from around the world. For more about this exclusive resort see **Charles Dana Gibson**'s *Boca Grande, A Series of Historical Essays* (Boca Grande, FL: C.D. Gibson, 1982). The lighthouse at the southern tip of the island is featured on the cover of **Elinor De Wire**'s *Guide to Florida Lighthouses* (Sarasota: Pineapple Press, 1987); **Kevin M. McCarthy**'s *Florida Lighthouses* (Gainesville: University of Florida Press, 1990) also describes this lighthouse and others in Florida.

Punta Gorda

The wide point leading into Charlotte Harbor was first sighted in 1513 by Spanish explorer Ponce de León. He christened it Punta Gorda or *Fat Point* and spent several weeks in the area until he was attacked by Calusa Indians. When he returned in 1521 with two boatloads of colonists to start a short-lived colony, he was wounded by the same Indians and died shortly thereafter in Cuba. A park and shrine commemorate Ponce de León's stay in the area.

During the 1880s, the state offered land grants to railroads to expand their systems. As a result, railroad mogul Henry Plant built a line from Jacksonville to Tampa in 1883, and Florida Southern Railway brought the first train south to Punta Gorda in 1886. It was extended to Fort Myers in 1904.

Punta Gorda is the destination of a family in **William C. Anderson's** novel, *The Headstrong Houseboat* (New York: Crown, 1972). *Punta Gorda and the Charlotte Harbor Area: A Pictorial History* (Norfolk, VA: Donning, 1986) by **Vernon Peeples** contains rare photographs of the area as well as a readable history of the towns and islands there. For an analysis of a part of the community see *Indian Springs Cemetery in Punta Gorda, Florida* (Port Charlotte, FL: Charlotte County Genealogical Society, 1988) edited by **Betsey Lambert**.

Warm Mineral Springs

Twenty miles south of Venice to the east of U.S. 41 is Warm Mineral Springs, a natural freshwater spring with a year-round temperature of 87 degrees. The springs serve as a natural depository for prehistoric human and animal bones over 10,000 years old including those of sloths and mammoths. In 1958, archaeologists began underwater exploration of the springs. In 1977, a diver discovered the bones of a saber-toothed tiger near those of a young man who had been intentionally buried in the once-dry sinkhole. These bones are the earliest human remains discovered in North America.

Walter Farley and Teena

Venice

Venice was named after the renowned Italian City of Canals and is the winter home of the Ringling Brothers and Barnum and Bailey Circus, which features public shows during the winter season.

Noted Venice writer, **Walter Farley** (1915-1989), was born in Syracuse, New York. He began writing his world-renowned novel, *The Black Stallion*, while still a boy, creating in fiction the horse he couldn't have in real life: "The splendid wild black horse fulfills a universal fantasy of childhood — finding identity in nature; taming the untamed forces." Mable R. Robinson, Farley's teacher at Columbia University, worked with him and encouraged him to submit the manuscript to Random House, which published it in 1941.

Farley wrote 34 children's novels which have been published in 22 countries. According to the critics: "The enduring appeal of (his) work is best explained by looking at the underlying values. Examples of courage, independence, and a 'can-do' attitude leap off every page of these fast-moving, gripping adventure stories."

Farley married Rosemary Lutz, a Manhattan Powers model, in 1945. They came to Venice in 1946, though they spent summers at their Pennsylvania farm. According to Farley: "You ought to pursue your hobby..., not become a lawyer so you can spend your spare time pursuing your hobby.... Imagination can help you reach into the heavens to grasp an idea, bring it down to earth, and make it work.... You have to become one with the horse to be a fine rider. I have that feeling at the typewriter."

Farley's books include *The Black Stallion Returns* (1945), *Son of the Black Stallion* (1947), *The Island Stallion* (1948), and *The Black Stallion Legend* (1983). A critically acclaimed series of films based on *The Black Stallion* was produced by Francis Ford Coppola. The children's wing of the Venice-Nokomis library is dedicated to Farley, and an exhibit there features his Smith-Corona typewriter and the manuscript pages of *The Black Stallion*, along with his riding boots, bridle, trophies, silver cups, and photographs from his life.

Other Venice writers include **Roy Chandler** (*Alaskan Hunter, Arrowmaker*); **Matt Christopher** (*Power Play, Longshot for Paul*, and over 25 juvenile books); **Elizabeth Foster** (*Friend of the Singing One, Lyrico, Long Hungry Night*); **Peg M. Gaertner** (*Bending the Twig*); **Joseph Harrington** (*Blind Spot, The Last Doorbell*); **Wilma Pitchford Hays** (*Siege, Little Hawaiian Horse*); **Jeannette Letton** (*Cragsmore, Don't Cry Little Sister, The Haunting of Cliffside*); **Fay Le Meadows** (*Little Silver Cloud, One Flying Bird*); and **Franklin E. Meyer** (*Me and Caleb, Me and Caleb Again*).

A useful guide to the area is *Venice and the Venice Area* (Venice, FL: Sunshine Press, 1969) by **George E. Youngberg** and **W. Earl Aumann**. Youngberg was the engineer in charge of laying out Venice in 1925 when the city was formed as a retirement community by the Brotherhood of Locomotive Engineers. Also see *Venice: Journey from Horse and Chaise* (Sarasota: Pine Level Press, 1989) by **Janet Snyder Matthews**. *Once Upon a Time in Southwest Florida* (Venice: Gondolier Publishing, 1982) by **Fred Harris** has profiles of early settlers along Florida's lower gulf coast, including **Edward Zane Carroll Judson**, known as the father of the dime novel when he wrote under the name **Ned Buntline**. **Wyatt Blassingame's** novel, *Live From The Devil* (Garden City, NY: Doubleday, 1959), describes the nineteenth-century cattle wars that used to plague the area.

Casey Key

Casey Key is a tiny subtropical key 15 miles south of Sarasota on Albee Road off U.S. 41. At Casey Key's northern exit, via Blackburn Point Road, an old-fashioned swing bridge spans the Intracoastal Waterway; the bridge operator walks out to the middle of this one-lane bridge and throws long-handled switches to activate the bridge which swings open instead of rising to accommodate boat traffic.

Two authors who made Casey Key their home deserve mention. **Richard Jessup** (1925-1982) spent eleven years in the merchant marine and then took up writing, eventually publishing over 60 crime and thriller novels. His most famous novel, *The Cincinnati Kid* (1963), was later made into a popular 1965 movie starring Steve McQueen and Edward G. Robinson. His other novels include *A Rage to Die* (1955), *Commander Vengeance* (1957), *The Deadly Duo* (1959), *The Hot Blue Sea* (1974), and *Threat* (1981), about the inner rage of a returning Vietnam War vet. The other author on Casey Key was publisher and naturalist **Joseph E. Lippincott** (1887-1976), who wrote two children's books set in Florida: *The Wahoo Bobcat* (Philadelphia: Lippincott, 1950) and *The Phantom Deer* (Philadelphia: Lippincott, 1954).

Nokomis

Nokomis, a town 15 miles south of Sarasota on U.S. 41, was named after the grandmother in Longfellow's classic poem, *Hiawatha*:

> Thus was born my Hiawatha,
> Thus was born the child of wonder;
> But the daughter of Nokomis,
> Hiawatha's gentle mother,
> In her anguish died deserted
> By the West-Wind, false and faithless,
> By the heartless Mudjekeewis.

Peace River

The Peace River was called *Peas* by the Seminoles after the cowpeas or black-eyed peas which grew on its banks. This name was converted to *Peace* by the early settlers due to the peace and serenity of the slow-moving river. The Peace River begins at Lake Hamilton in Polk County and runs through Arcadia southwesterly to Charlotte Harbor. For a description of the river, read *Rivers of Florida* (Atlanta: Southern Press, 1974) by **Henry Marks** and **Gene Britt Riggs** and *Florida by Paddle and Pack* (Miami: Banyan Books, 1979) by **Mike** and **Pat Toner**. Peace River's early inhabitants are described in *Florida's Peace River Frontier* (Orlando: University of Central Florida Press, 1991) by **Canter Brown Jr.** *and Peace River Pioneers* (Miami: Seemann Publishing Co., 1974) by **Louise Frisbie.**

Arcadia

Arcadia, 70 miles east of Sarasota on Route 72, has a name that goes back to Arcadia, Greece, an area often used by poets to symbolize peace and serenity. Ironically, in the late-eighteenth and early-nineteenth centuries, this was a rough cattle town with frequent cattle wars and gunplay in the streets. Famed painter **Frederic Remington** (1861-1909) traveled to the area on a writing assignment from *Harper's Weekly* in 1895; he was to write about cowboys in a part of the country that was still frontier. Even though the United States Census declared in 1890 that the frontier no longer existed in this country, Florida still had frontier conditions, especially south of Orlando in the decades before the influx of settlers. When Remington visited the Florida towns of Punta Gorda and Arcadia and saw his first Cracker cowboys, he described them as "wild-looking individuals, whose hanging hair and drooping hats and generally bedraggled appearance would remind you at once of the Spanish-moss which hangs so quietly and helplessly to the limbs of the oaks out in the swamps." His essay had a scathing description of cattle-stealing in the area and depicted the town in very negative terms.

The local cowboys who work on ranches today are joined each year in mid-March and early July by professional wranglers for the Arcadia Rodeo. One of Florida's best-known cowboys, Bone Mizell, lived in the Arcadia area. For more about him and about the DeSoto County cattle wars of the 1890s see *Florida Cow Hunter: The Life and Times of Bone Mizell* (Orlando: University of Central Florida Press, 1990) by **Jim Bob Tinsley**. *A Pictorial History of Arcadia and DeSoto County* (St. Petersburg: Byron Kennedy, 1984?) by **George Lane, Jr.** has photographs of early life in the area. **Mark Lane's** nonfictional *Arcadia* (New York: Holt, 1970) is based on a series of local murders.

Eight miles west of Arcadia lie the remains of one of Florida's ghost towns: Pine Level. Once the largest city in DeSoto County, Pine Level had a court-house, jail, stores, two churches, warehouses, and many homes. "The saloons outnumbered the other businesses by 14 to 1 and as the town was the only watering hole for many thirsty miles, Saturday night was a riotous evening of gambling, drinking, shootings and just plain 'raisin' hell.'" Today the town is gone, but ghosts are said to remain. For more about the Sarasota Gang that once operated out of the town see *Gangs and Gangsters* (New York: Ballantine, 1974) by **Hank Messick** and **Burt Goldblatt**.

On a ranch near Myakka River State Park live a husband-wife team who have been very successful in writing and illustrating books, especially science fiction. Illustrator **Don Maitz** has had 175 commissioned works by major publishers like Doubleday and Simon & Schuster. Writer/illustrator **Janny Wurts** has had nine novels published, including *Daughter of the Empire* (1987) and *Servant of the Empire* (1990), both with **Raymond E. Feist**.

Sarasota

South of Bradenton on Highway 41 is Sarasota, which most likely took its name from a forgotten Calusa Indian name. According to popular myth, it was named for Sara Sota, Hernando De Soto's beautiful and entirely fictional daughter. An Indian prince allowed himself to be taken prisoner by the Spaniards so that he could be near his true love, Sara Sota. In captivity, he fell sick, and Sara nursed him back to health. As a result, she, too, became sick and died. The prince and a hundred braves buried her at sea, then chopped their canoes with tomahawks and sank themselves.

The Sarasota area over the last 60 or so years has played host to a number of writers and artists. It was home to the Ringling Brothers and Barnum and Bailey Circus from 1928 to 1960, and it has a fine concert hall, the Van Wezel, that can accommodate 1,778 people. The causeway off to the right at the city marina leads to St. Armands Key, with its elegant stores and boutiques, and beyond to Lido Beach and Longboat Key.

Bowsprit Lane on Longboat Key was home to the notorious Carl Coppolino, who in 1965 was accused of killing his wife, Carmela. Coppolino was acquitted of the charge of first-degree murder of an army officer in New Jersey but was found guilty in 1967 of second-degree murder in the poisoning of Carmela. For more about the trial see *The Trials of Dr. Coppolino* (New York: The New American Library, 1968) by **Paul Holmes** and *No Deadly Drug* (Garden City, NY: Doubleday, 1968) by **John D. MacDonald**.

Back in Sarasota at the corner of U.S. 41 and Gulfstream Avenue is a plaque commemorating the founding of the city in 1885 by a group of Scottish families. Coincidentally, Sarasota is the home of America's first golf course, a two-holer built by Colonel J. Hamilton Gillespie, a Scotsman, in 1886. By 1905, Gillespie's obsession with golf produced a nine-hole course and a clubhouse on a 110-acre tract. In 1923, he died while playing his course.

The Ringling Museum of Art on U.S. 41 near the airport houses the largest extant collection of works by Reubens, the great seventeenth-century Flemish painter, as well as a fine collection of baroque art from the seventeenth, eighteenth, and nineteenth centuries (813 355-1660). Each March, a Medieval Fair features a human chess match, madrigal singers, jugglers, and other performers out of the Middle Ages.

Close by is the Ca'd'Zan, or House of John (Ringling). Ringling founded the Ringling Brothers Circus, which winters in nearby Venice, and traveled extensively in Europe where he became an art connoisseur and collector. His 1925 mansion, which was modeled after the Doge's Palace in Venice, Italy, has 32 beautiful rooms furnished with *objects d'art* from around the world. His 500 art works include paintings by El Greco, Gainesborough, Hais, Rembrandt, Reynolds, Tintoretto, Valasquez, and Veronese, as well as Reubens.

Ringling was full of contradictions. Though an art connoisseur, he was shocked by the representation of his wife and himself as a nude couple at the front of the building. Hardly a gourmet, he was addicted to hash and ice cream. In 1929, when his beloved wife died, he was heartbroken. He later married a widow, Emily Haag Buck, but made her sign a waiver-of-rights in regard to his estate. After the wedding, Emily tore up the waiver. On their divorce, Ringling was forced to settle the matter in court.

Ringling lost control of the circus to trusted friends and sank deep in debt. Still he refused to sell his valuable art collection. At his death in 1936 he had $311 in the bank though his estate was valued at $23.5 million. He left Emily one dollar and willed Ca'd'Zan and his art collection to the state of Florida, which took possession in 1946 after much litigation. The nearby Ringling Museum of the Circus features exhibits about the history of the circus (813 355-5101).

For more about Ringling and the circus, read *The Circus Kings, Our Ringling Family Story* (Garden City, NY: Doubleday, 1960) by **Henry Ringling North** and **Alden Hatch**; *Those Amazing Ringlings and Their Circus* (Caldwell, ID: Caxton Printers, 1967) by **Gene Plowden**; and *The Unlikely Legacy* (Sarasota: Aaron Publishing, 1979) by **Kenneth Mathews** and **Robert McDevitt**. A book about a key figure in the Ringling circus is **Gene Plowden**'s *Merle Evans: Maestro of the Circus* (Miami: Seemann Publishing Co., 1971). A 1978 made-for-TV movie entitled *The Great Wallendas*, about the famed family of trapeze artists, was filmed in the Sarasota area. A book about Ringlings' nephew and heir, John Ringling North, is *A Ringling by Any Other Name: The Story of John Ringling North and His Circus* (Metuchen, NJ: Scarecrow Press, 1989) by **Ernest Albrecht**.

The Asolo Center for the Performing Arts, adjacent to the Ringling Museum on U.S. 41, houses the state's official theater troupe and holds performances from September to July (813 351-9010). Its mainstage was constructed using plaster casts and moldings from an old opera house in Dunfermline, Scotland. The original Asolo Theater, housed on the grounds of the Ringling Museum and used for performances from 1960 until the new Asolo Center was constructed in 1989, was built in Asolo, Italy, in 1798 and shipped to Florida in 1949. It is the only original eighteenth-century Italian theater in America.

Mote Marine Laboratory on City Island, founded by shipping magnate Bill Mote, specializes in shark studies. Other fields of study include fish enhancement, red tide, biomedical issues, chemical fate and effects, turtles and marine mammals, and other problems affecting west central Florida. It employs close to 80 people, including 20 doctoral-level scientists, and includes a large aquarium and educational center.

Marine biologist **Eugenie Clark**, once employed by Mote, has written several books dealing with the sea including *Lady With a Spear* (New York: Harper, 1953) and *The Lady and the Sharks* (New York: Harper & Row, 1969). *The Desert Beneath the Sea* (New York: Scholastic, Inc., 1991), her latest book, written with **Ann McGovern**, is meant to awaken children's interest in the undersea world.

Finally, Siesta Key, off U.S. 41 on Route 72, is the setting for **John D. MacDonald**'s *Condominium* (Philadelphia: Lippincott, 1977), a novel about shoddy developers and an oncoming hurricane. *Condominium* was later made into a 1979 made-for-TV movie starring Dan Haggerty and Ralph Bellamy. Another novel, **Thomas Helm**'s *Hurricane Coming!* (New York: Dodd, Mead, 1964), also describes the destructive power of a storm.

For more about Sarasota see **Karl H. Grismer**'s *The Story of Sarasota* (Sarasota: M.E. Russell, 1946), **Jeff Lahurd**'s *The Quincentennial*, and **Del Marth**'s *Yesterday's Sarasota* (Miami: Seemann Publishing Co., 1977). *Edge of Wilderness: A Settlement History of Manatee River and Sarasota Bay* (Tulsa, OK: Caprine Press, 1983) by **Janet Snyder Matthews** gives a history of the area from prehistoric times to the twentieth century. A more recent book by Matthews is *Sarasota: Journey to Centennial* (Tulsa, OK; Continental Heritage Press, 1985). **Dennis R. Cooper**'s *The Florida West Coast Symphony Orchestra* (Sarasota: Florida West Coast Symphony Orchestra, 1974) tells the history of the orchestra, which is based in Sarasota. A different look at the surrounding county is found in **Elmer G. Sulzer**'s *Ghost Railroads of Sarasota County* (Sarasota: Sarasota County Historical Commission, 1971). A number of novels are set in and around Sarasota, including **Janice Law**'s *The Shadow of the Palms* (Boston:

Houghton, Mifflin, 1979). The Historical Society of Sarasota County publishes *Sarasota Origins* with articles about the area's history.

Liars' Lunch

The Liars' Lunch is a loose rendezvous of Sarasota writers and artists who meet to exchange ideas and gossip. It is reminiscent of similar gatherings in eighteenth-century England and that famous Manhattan literary huddle, the Algonquin Round Table. The Liars' Lunch used to meet every Friday afternoon from 1 to 3 at the old Plaza Hotel (later Merlin's Bar and Restaurant). Today it meets downtown at Coley's, a restaurant and bar.

The idea behind the lunch originated in November 1952, when Pulitzer Prize-winning novelist, **MacKinlay Kantor**, hosted a luncheon at the Orange Blossom Hotel for writers **Norton Weber, Joe Millard**, and **Dick Glendinning**. According to Glendinning, the writers "dreaded the thought of anything that smacked of being an 'Authors' Club' made up of hopeful writers in search of panaceas, magic formulae and the name of a good agent.... Yet the lunch at the Orange Blossom went so smoothly that those present...decided that what made this lunch different was the fact that they met primarily as friends who happened to be in the same profession."

The locale for the lunch was later switched to the Plaza Hotel, which suited the group perfectly since it was "more like a club than a restaurant...with its pseudo-Spanish theme and ill-assorted frills...and its food chosen from a menu that may not have seen a change since opening day in 1928." The group met in the Plaza Hotel over a span of 36 years, except for an interval when the hotel closed and Merlin's opened.

An undated letter sent out around that time contains several paragraphs that come as close to a definition of the group as anything ever attempted:

> All talk of bylaws, constitutions and baskets to needy writers will be discouraged. Anyone proposing a Story Laboratory for mention in *Writers' Digest*, or chatty papers on Helpful Hints to Writers, or little talks and book reviews or anything else which has no proper place in a gathering of this sort will be hooted into the men's room where he will please flush himself down the drain....Attendance would indicate that you are probably there. Absence tends to suggest the opposite. In any case, no one will be altogether sure.

Kantor was the unofficial leader of the group. "He was grand guru, and pretty much set the tone in the old days," says novelist-playwright, Joe Hayes. A tall, trim man with a military bearing, Kantor was an unabashed patriot who cherished the old-fashioned values like integrity and valor. A quick man with a story or joke, he could apparently recite the lyrics of most popular songs written since 1900 and could tell five or six versions of the same joke.

From the beginning, the gathering was an all-male enclave, a practice that led to the barring of playwright **Lillian Hellman**, who was in town with *New Yorker* humorist, **S.J. Perelman**. Perelman had been invited to the lunch, but, when he learned about the no-women-allowed rule, he refused to attend without Hellman. Naturally, Hellman, too, was miffed.

Out-of-town writers attending over the years have included political satirist **Art Buchwald, Erskine Caldwell** (*God's Little Acre, Tobacco Road*), **James T. Farrell** (*Studs Lonigan*), **Buckminster Fuller** (theoritician and scientific writer who invented the geodesic dome), Watergate conspirator and author **E. Howard Hunt, William Inge** (*Come Back, Little Sheba Picnic*), **Budd Schulberg** (*On the Waterfront, What Makes Sammy Run?*), and **Thornton Wilder** (*Our Town, The Skin of Our Teeth*). At one lunch, when the subject of productivity came up, it was discovered that the eight people present had published over 300 books.

Sometime in the late 1950s, liars' poker, a game played with the serial numbers of currency instead of cards, was introduced to Sarasota via Manhattan and promised to be a solution to the problem of guests who felt politeness demanded that they buy a round of drinks. Since that time, three rounds of liars' poker have been played for drinks, and a record of wins and losses was kept. At first, the records, illegible chicken scratchings scribbled on the backs of cocktail napkins, canceled checks, or whatever else was at hand, were stored behind the bar, but deciphering them became a real problem. Next, the records were moved to the molding of a frame containing group member Jim McCague's photo. One morning, a cleaning woman was straightening the frame when the paper slips came tumbling down. Figuring them to be dinner orders that never made it to the kitchen, she cleaned up the evidence and dumped it in the trash with the intention of saving some poor waiter his job. After that, Dick Glendinning kept the records until his death in 1987. Since then, MacKinlay Kantor's son, Tim, keeps them.

An inscribed plaque is presented at the end of each year to the worst liar. Winners over the years have included novelists MacKinlay Kantor, Borden Deal, and Richard Jessup, historians Phillip Van Doren Stern and Carl Carmer, songwriter Nick Kenny, and cartoonist Dik Browne.

Though most of the lunches have passed without incident, there have been exceptions. For example, novelist **John D. MacDonald** was bitten on the ear by a Pulitzer Prize-winning writer, and then there was the excluded war novelist who used to occupy the next table and make his presence felt by glaring ominously in the group's direction. **Clifford Irving** showed up fresh from being sentenced to a jail term for his fake autobiography of Howard Hughes, only to find that the forewarned members had gathered elsewhere. As Glendinning put it: "There had been crises and stormy scenes, bruised egos and punctured balloons..., emotional walk-outs and irritated boycotts. But all of these were inevitable in a group of unreconstructed individuals who refused to be anything but themselves."

Sarasota has had a number of authors as residents over the years. **Roy Basler** (1906-1989), who was born in St. Louis, Missouri, headed the English departments of several southern colleges before joining the staff of the Library of Congress in 1952. An authority on the Civil War, he specialized in the study of Lincoln and wrote *The Lincoln Legend* (1935), *Lincoln* (1962), and *A Short History of the Civil War* (1967).

Dik Browne (1917-1989), who was born in New York, moved to Sarasota in the early 1970s. He was the creator of the popular comic strip, Hagar the Horrible, which is circulated to over 1,800 newspapers nationwide. He was also co-creator with Mort Walker (of Beetle Bailey fame) of the strip Hi and Lois, with a circulation of over 1,100 papers. Brown was the recipient of an unprecedented two Reubens awarded by the Cartoonists' Association of America. He is survived by two sons, Chris and Chance, who carry on the strips.

Carl Carmer (1893-1976) and his wife, Elizabeth, an illustrator, spent nearly 30 winters in Sarasota. Carmer was a folklorist and historian who edited the Rivers of America and Regions of America series and wrote *The Hudson* (1939). He was also the interpreter of four albums of regional folklore and adapted folk stories for Walt Disney's *Melody Time*. Carmer wrote *Hurricane Luck* (New York: Aladdin, 1949), a children's novel with a Florida setting and published a book of poetry, *Deep South* (1930), while wintering in Florida. His most famous book was *Stars Fell on Alabama* (1930). While a visiting professor at the University of Alabama, Carmer compared the state to the Belgian Congo: "The Congo is not more different from Massachusetts or Kansas or California. So I have chosen to write of Alabama not as a state which is part of a nation, but as a strange country in which I once lived and from which I have now returned." Later a popular song was recorded with the same name derived from a night in the late 1800s when a meteor shower fell on Alabama.

Tom Chamales (1924-1960) wrote two blockbuster war novels: *Never So Few* (1957) about the Burma campaign in World War II and *Go Naked in the World* (1959) about veterans returning from that war. (Remember the excluded war novelist who used to glare ominously in the direction of the table occupied by the Liars' Lunch?) He died in 1960, two weeks before the publication of *Forget that I Ever Lived* (1960). *Never So Few* was made into a 1959 film starring Frank Sinatra and Steve McQueen. Chamales was part of a famous writing colony in Marshall, Illinois, established by Lowell Handy, the wife of a wealthy industrialist, and novelist **James Jones**. A vicious young writer on the make based on Chamales plays a key role in one of Jones's lesser-known novels, *Go to the Widowmaker* (1967). Chamales received only lukewarm critical praise; one reviewer stated: "Perhaps the final verdict on *Never So Few* should be that Chamales is neither a sound novelist nor a clear thinker, but that he certainly is one whale of a story teller about war." However, *Never So Few* was a best-seller. Chamales died tragically in a fire after falling asleep with a lighted cigarette in a New York hotel room.

Lary Crews (1946-) is the author of a series of paperback mystery novels that take place in southwest Florida and feature a girl reporter named Veronica Slate. These include *Kill Cue* (1988), *Extreme Closeup* (1989), and *Deadly Sacrifice* (1991), all published by New York's Lynx Books.

Babs Deal (1929-) lived at Sarasota and Casey Key for many years with her writer-husband, **Borden Deal** (1922-1985). She has contributed short stories to major magazines like *McCall's*, *Redbook*, and *Cosmopolitan*, and her stories have been anthologized in *Love and Marriage*, *Best Detective Stories of 1961*, and *Love, Love, Love*. Her novels include *Night Story* (1962), about life in a southern town after dark; *The Grail* (1963), which applies the Arthurian legend to the workings of a Southern college football team; *High Lonesome Road* (1968), about a country singer based on the legendary Hank Williams, Sr.; *The Walls Came Tumbling Down* (1968), about an aborted baby hidden for years within the walls of a Southern sorority; and *Goodnight, Ladies* (Garden City, NY: Doubleday, 1978), about the breakup of her marriage and a consequent identity crisis. *Summer Games* (Garden City, NY: Doubleday, 1972) about an artist and his wife who amuse themselves with drink, games, and gossip until a hurricane brings tragedy into their and their friends' lives and *The Crystal Mouse* (Garden City, NY: Doubleday, 1973) about a recently widowed woman who begins to hear strange noises in a deserted condo on the beach both take place in Cape Haze, a fictionalized Sarasota.

Babs Deal, who was born in Scottsboro, Alabama, met her husband, novelist Borden Deal, while attending Hudson Strode's famous creative-writing class at the University of Alabama. Following their marriage, they moved to Mobile, Alabama, where Borden wrote copy for a local radio station while attempting to sell his novel. His wife, who took up writing on a dare from her husband, specializes in the tight, psychological novel, as opposed to her husband's broad, sprawling, sociological novels. The couple divorced in 1976. Babs Deal presently lives in Opelika, Alabama.

Borden Deal (pseudonym **Lee Borden**) was born in New Albany, Mississippi, and moved to Sarasota in 1964. He grew up on a rural Mississippi tenant farm, as he put it, "about fifteen miles [southwest] of William Faulkner." In high school he took a job maintaining the school typewriters so he could learn to type. During the Depression, he joined the Civilian Conservation Corps and was sent to Oregon to fight forest fires. Later while riding the rails, he watched a friend cut in half by the train's wheels. His life and work were devoted to defending the underdog, and his novels concern what has come to be known as the New South (as opposed to the Old South of moonlight, magnolias, and mint juleps).

His works include *Walk Through the Valley* (1956), *Dunbar's Cove* (1957), *The Insolent Breed* (1959), *Dragon's Wine* (1960), and *The Tobacco Men* (1965 — based on notes by Theodore Dreiser). His political trilogy about an aspiring southern governor consists of *The Loser* (1964), *The Advocate* (1968), and *The Winner* (1973). *The Least One* (1967) and *The Other Room* (1974) are autobiographical novels about growing up poor in Mississippi. Florida locations figure prominently in *A Long Way To Go* (Garden City, NY: Doubleday, 1965) and *Interstate* (Garden City, NY: Doubleday, 1970). In addition, Deal published over 100 short stories, his most famous being "Antaeus," which is included in numerous anthologies including *The Best Short Stories of 1962*.

Dunbar's Cove, a novel about the Tennessee Valley Authority (TVA) dam project in the Tennessee mountains, was made into a classic 1960 movie, *Wild River*, directed by Elia Kazan and starring Montgomery Clift and Lee Remick. *The Insolent Breed* was the basis for a Broadway musical about country music entitled *A Joyful Noise*. *Bluegrass* (1976), a novel about Kentucky horse-breeding farms, was a 1988 made-for-TV movie starring Cheryl Ladd and Mickey

Rooney. Two days after Borden's death on January 23, 1985, word was leaked to the press at his earlier request that he had been the author of a series of sexy paperback originals: *Her* (1970), *Him* (1972), *Us* (1973), which sold many copies and were written under the pseudonym of Anonymous.

Louise Lee Floethe (1913-) moved to Sarasota from New York in 1950. All of her books (most of them for children) have been written in Florida, and two of them — *The Fisherman and His Boat* (New York: Scribner, 1961) and *Sea of Grass* (New York: Scribner, 1963) — have Florida settings. Her other works include *Fountain of the Friendly Lion* (1966), *A Thousand and One Buddhas* (1967), *Floating Market* (1969), and *Jungle People* (1971).

Richard "Dick" (1917-1987) and **Sally Glendinning** (1913-), who came to Sarasota in 1950, collaborated on three juvenile novels published by Garrard of Champaign, Illinois, which focus on Sarasota's circus: *Circus Days Under the Big Top* (1969), *Gargantua: The Mighty Gorilla* (1974), and *The Ringling Brothers: A Circus Family* (1972). Dick Glendinning's novels include *Carnival Girl* (1956) and *Terror in the Sun* (1952). His Florida-set novels include *Who Evil Thinks* (New York: Fawcett, 1952), a thriller, and *Too Fast We Live* (New York: Popular Library, 1954), about small citrus groves being taken over by large combines. Sally created the Jimmy and Joe series of juvenile books; her other works include *Thomas Gainesborough: Artist of England* (1969) and *Queen Victoria: English Empress* (1970).

Alden Hatch (1902-1977) was born in New York and died in Sarasota. He wrote fiction, journalism, and history, but is best remembered for his biographies, including *General Ike: A Biography of Dwight D. Eisenhower* (1946), *Franklin D. Roosevelt: An Informal Portrait* (1947), *George Patton: General in Spurs* (1950), and *Buckminster Fuller: At Home in the Universe* (1974).

Lillian Hellman (1905-1984) spent two winters at a Sarasota beach house in the company of *New Yorker* humorist, **Sidney Perelman**, and **Francis and Albert Hackett**, the famous husband-wife screenwriting team who wrote the *Thin Man* series of movies starring William Powell and Myrna Loy. Her lover and companion, writer **Peter Feibelman**, writes about their sharing a house on Siesta Key in the late 1960s in his book, *Lilly: Reminiscences of Lillian Hellman* (New York: Morrow, 1988).

Rust Hills (1924-), who was born in Brooklyn, is the fiction editor of *Esquire* magazine and the author of humorous works entitled *How To Retire at Forty* (1973), *How To Do Things Right* (1974), and *How To Be Good* (1976). His wife is Sarasota novelist, Joy Williams.

Evan Hunter (1926-) grew up in Manhattan's Italian Harlem, and later taught in a New York City vocational school. These experiences served as the basis of his first novel, *The Blackboard Jungle* (1954), which was later made into a popular 1955 film starring Glenn Ford and Sidney Poitier. He has written under the pseudonyms **Richard Marstan**, **Hunt Collins**, and **Ed McBain**. Having published over 60 novels, he is best known as the author of the 87th Precinct series of police novels published by Simon & Schuster. His other works include *Buddwing* (1964), *Me and Mr. Stennes* (1976), and *The Chisholms* (1976). *Buddwing* was also made into a film starring James Garner. Only one of his novels, *Goldilocks* (New York: Arbor House, 1976), has a Florida setting. He first came to Sarasota in 1975.

Ted Irwin (1907-), who was born in New York City, was once managing editor of *Look* and *Cue* magazines and is the author of two novels: *Collusion* (1933) and *Strange Passage* (1935).

MacKinlay Kantor (1904-1977) was born in Webster City, Iowa, and lived on Siesta Key near Sarasota from 1931 until his death. Although his first novel, *Diversey*, was written in 1927, it was only with the publication of *Long Remember* (1934) that he gained critical and financial success. His other works include *The Voice of Bugle Ann* (1935), *Angleworms on Toast* (1942), *Happy Land* (1943), *Missouri Bittersweet* (1965), *Beauty Beast* (1968), and *Valley Forge* (1975). His verse-novel, *The Best Years of Our Lives* (1946), was made into the Academy Award-winning movie of the same name directed by William Wyler and starring Frederick March and Myrna Loy. *The Day I met A Lion* (1968) is a collection of his nonfiction articles. His *Andersonville* (1955), a novel about the infamous Confederate prisoner-of-war camp, won the Pulitzer Prize in 1956. Only one of Kantor's novels, *The Noise of their Wings* (New York: Coward-McCann, 1938), takes place in Florida. Several of his short stories, however, are set in the state and deal with Florida Crackers (see Lake Okeechobee). In 1950, Kantor received the Medal of Freedom for his work as a war correspondent in Korea.

MacKinlay Kantor

In his later years, Kantor's ultra-conservative views often clashed with those of his liberal writer friends, but they admired him nonetheless. According to Joe Hayes, "In his presence one felt amused, warmed, sometimes irritated, often exhilarated, but always alive." For an engaging memoir of Kantor, see his son **Tim Kantor**'s book *My Father's Voice: MacKinlay Kantor Long Remembered* (New York: McGraw Hill, 1988).

Nick Kenny (1895-1975) was a *New York Daily Mirror* entertainment columnist, a poet in the Edgar

Guest vein, and a songwriter who composed such sentimental standards as "Love Letters in the Sand," "Little Old Cathedral in the Pines," and "There's a Gold Mine in the Sky."

Larry L. King (1928-) was born in Putnam, Texas, and lived in Sarasota during the late 1960s and early 1970s. He worked for President Johnson as an administrative assistant and edited *Capitol Hill* magazine. He quit to write a novel about a southern governor entitled *The One-Eyed Man* (1966), which was accepted by the Book of the Month Club but was a critical failure. This prompted King to begin working in nonfiction. King's other books include *Wheeling & Dealing* (1978), with Lyndon Johnson protégé, **Bobby Baker**; and three collections of articles: *And Other Dirty Stories* (1968); *The Old Man & Lesser Mortals* (1974); and *Of Outlaws, Con Men, Whores, Politicians, and Other Artists* (1980). King's best-known work is the play, *The Best Little Whorehouse in Texas*, based on an article in *Playboy* and written in collaboration with **Peter Masterson**. For an amusing rendition of the making of the play and the later 1982 movie version of *Whorehouse*, starring Burt Reynolds and Dolly Parton, read King's *The Whorehouse Papers* (1982). King's *None But a Blockhead: On Being a Writer* (New York: Viking, 1988) contains a description of the Liars' Lunch and brief descriptions of novelists MacKinlay Kantor and Borden Deal and songwriter Nick Kenny.

William Manchester (1922-), who was born in Attleboro, Pennsylvania, has wintered in Sarasota since 1985. A sickly and often homebound child, Manchester remembers reading such classic historians as Ruskin, Macaulay, and Carlyle before the age of ten. He is that rare bird — a bonafide historian with a popular following, whose massive tomes have sold millions of copies. Specializing in world leaders, Manchester has written about General Douglas A. MacArthur, Prime Minister Winston Churchill, and President John F. Kennedy. His most controversial book, *Death of a President* (1967), was a detailed account of the Kennedy assassination. Though his books have sold countless copies, Manchester doesn't think of himself as a commercial writer. "When you're writing, you can't be thinking of the marketplace," he says.

The uncluttered, spacious study in his Longboat Key home is symbolic of his straight, no-nonsense approach. The study has a wooden work table with a cup of freshly sharpened pencils, book shelves filled with reference works and first and foreign editions of his many books, some family pictures, and a coffee maker. Covering the walls are his books' dust jackets, mementos of his foreign-correspondent days, and a Purple Heart citation which he won while serving in the marine corps during World War II. Manchester's output — the number and length of his books — would stagger most writers. In the mornings he edits what he wrote the day before, then writes for five hours in the afternoons, and does research in the evenings. When speaking of writing, Manchester borrows a quote from one of his favorite writers, a friend and former associate from his *Baltimore Sun* days, H.L. Mencken: "Writing does for me what milking does for the cow."

Manchester's works include *Disturber of the Peace* (1951), a biography of Mencken; *Arms of Krupp* (1968), a study of the famed German munitions family; *The Glory and the Dream: A Narrative History of America, 1932-1972* (1975), a

1,397-page account of those years by a self-confessed member of the Swing Generation; *American Caesar* (1978), a study of General Douglas A. MacArthur; and *The Last Lion* (1983, 1987, 1990), a trilogy about British Prime Minister Winston Churchill.

Joe Millard (1908-) was born in Canby, Minnesota, and came to Florida in 1947. He is the author of *Edgar Cayce* (1958), *The Cheyenne Wars* (1964), and *The Incredible William Bowles* (Philadelphia: Chilton, 1966). He wrote novelizations of the following films: *For a Few Dollars More* (1967); *The Good, the Bad, and the Ugly* (1967); *The Last Rebel* (1970); *Chato's Land* (1972); *Cahill, U.S. Marshall* (1973); *Thunderbolt and Lightfoot* (1974); and as **David Wilson**, *The Corpse Maker* (1974). In addition, he has contributed articles to such well-known magazines as *Argosy, True, Holiday,* and *Good Housekeeping.* Millard began in advertising and was the editor of *How To Sell* magazine and *National Mortician.*

Robert Plunket (1945-) was born in Greenville, Texas, and moved to Sarasota in 1985. He wrote the highly acclaimed humorous novel, *My Search for Warren Harding* (1983), which *Time* magazine called "hilarious"; it is the story of a Harding scholar's search for the long-lost mistress of President Harding. Plunket has contributed articles to many major publications including the *New York Times* and wrote a monthly column, Mr. Chatterbox, for *Sarasota* magazine. He has also acted in several films including Martin Scorsese's *After Hours* (1985). He often uses the ripe manure of such supermarket tabloids as *The Star* and *The National Enquirer* to fertilize his imagination.

According to Plunket: "I'm not really a writer. I'm just a person with a lot of axes to grind. My idol is Paul Harvey, the radio commentator. How I wish I could get my own radio show! Then I could attract much more attention with less effort. It would be a call-in format. I would give people advice and then force them to listen to records I like."

Plunket's latest novel, *Love Junkie* (1992), is the story of a social-climbing housewife who becomes obsessed with a hunky porn star and falls headlong into the pre-AIDS nightlife of New York. In a front-page review in the *New York Times Book Review,* novelist Jay McInerney called the novel a "comedy of manners with a time bomb ticking behind the curtains." *The Los Angeles Times* said the book was "full of enchanting sentences that you could find in no other book.... Robert Plunket is some kind — some bizarre but lovable kind — of genius." According to Plunket's mother, Dolores, however: "It's an excellent book. But I'm going to tell my friends they are too young to read it." Plunket is currently working on a novel set in Sarasota.

Sam Raphaelson (1896-1983) was born in New York City. He is the author of numerous stage plays, screenplays, and short stories. His plays include *The Jazz Singer* (1925), *The Wooden Slipper* (1933), *Skylark* (1939), *The Perfect Marriage* (1944), *Hilda Crane* (1950), and *Two Acts in October* (1974). Among his screenplays are *The Smiling Lieutenant* (1930), *One Hour With You* (1932), *Trouble in Paradise* (1932), *The Merry Widow* (1934), *Angel* (1937), *The Shop Around The Corner* (1939), *Heaven Can Wait* (1943), *Hilda Crane* (1956), and *But Not For Me* (1958).

Raphaelson had this to say about the movie version of his play, *The Jazz Singer,* a landmark 1927 film that initiated the era of the talkies: "Jolson didn't have any comedy dialogue. The man's a terrific comedian — and a lousy actor. They gave him 'dramatic' scenes — that is, 'straight' scenes — terribly written synopsis dialogue — and he didn't try to play them; he just read them. It was embarrassing. A dreadful picture. I've seen very few worse." However, he did see the future of the sound film: "I could see tremendous possibilities, once I heard sound on film. You heard background noises; as you went through the East Side, you heard the street sounds, and so on. I could see a whole new era had come into the theater. But from this particular picture, you wouldn't have much hope for the possibilities of that era." Raphaelson, who had turned down earlier Hollywood offers as "degrading," was more than willing to sign up with RKO at $750 per week after he lost all his savings in the 1929 stock-market crash.

Laura Cooper Rendina (1902-) was born in Northampton, Massachusetts, and moved to Siesta Key in 1946. She is the author of eight children's books and numerous short stories published in magazines like *The Ladies' Home Journal* and *Seventeen*. All of Rendina's novels have been written in Florida, and all were published by Little Brown. *Holly Touchberry* (1957) is the story of a young girl's experiences at Sarasota Junior High. *World of Their Own* (1963) deals with a group of Florida children on a summer work project in the tobacco fields of Connecticut. Her other books include *Roommates* (1948), *Debbie Jones* (1950), *Summer For Two* (1952), *My Love For One* (1955), *Trudi* (1959), and *Destination Capri* (1968).

William Shirer (1904-), who was born in Chicago was a reporter for the Paris branch of the *Chicago Tribune* from 1925 to 1927. He originally wanted to be a fiction writer, but, as he explained, "After a year in Paris, I was beginning to know myself well enough to see that, as [my colleague] Jim [Thurber] said of himself, I was not going to be a Fitzgerald or a Hemingway or a Dos Passos or even a lesser creator of fiction and poetry. I had another disposition. Whereas they...had turned inward to find the sources of their creativity..., I was beginning to turn outward...to what was going on in the world."

Shirer became a foreign correspondent in Paris, London, Geneva, Rome, Dublin, Vienna, and Prague, and in 1937 went to work for CBS radio as a correspondent in Vienna and Berlin. He served as a war correspondent from 1939 to 1945 and was a radio commentator from 1941 to 1947. He was blackballed during the McCarthy era for his support of the Hollywood Ten, and it was then that he began researching his most famous work, *The Rise and Fall of the Third Reich* (1960), which won the National Book Award in 1961. His other works include *Berlin Diary 1934-1941* (1941), *Twentieth-Century Journey: A Memoir of a Life and the Times: Volume I: The Start 1904-1930* (1976), and *Ghandi: A Memoir* (1980). *Berlin Diary* became a TV mini-series.

Ralph Smith is the creator of the Captain Vincible comic strip and works with Chris and Chance Browne on Hagar, the Horrible.

Ben Stahl (1910-1987) is primarily known as an artist, illustrator of over 800 *Saturday Evening Post* stories (including the Horatio Hornblower series by E.S. Forrester), and co-founder of the Famous Artists School, a noted Chicago correspondence course. He also wrote and illustrated *Blackbeard's Ghost* (1965), which won the Sequoia Award for best children's book and was made into a 1967 Disney movie starring Peter Ustinov. *The Secret of Red Skull* (1971), another children's book, was written by Stahl and illustrated by his son.

Philip Van Doren Stern was born in Philadelphia in 1900. He wrote 40 books and was a noted editor at Knopf and Simon & Schuster. He specialized in the Civil War and is the author of *The Man Who Killed Lincoln* (1939), *The Drums of Morning* (1942), *An End to Valor* (1958), and *Robert E. Lee: The Man and the Soldier* (1963). He is best known for what was originally a Christmas greeting entitled *The Greatest Gift* that he sent out to friends concerning a man about to commit suicide. *The Greatest Gift* was the basis for Frank Capra's 1946 Christmas classic movie, *It's A Wonderful Life,* starring James Stewart and Donna Reed.

Phil Troyer is the author of *Father Bede's Misfit* (1986), a poignant novel about a dyslexic boy's coming of age at a northern New Mexico monastery.

Irving Vendig (1903-) is the creator of the long-running soap opera, *The Edge of Night,* and wrote for radio for over 50 years.

Joy Williams (1944-) was born in Chelmsford, Massachusetts, and came to Sarasota in 1965 to work as a researcher and data analyst for Mote Marine Laboratory on Siesta Key. She is married to *Esquire* fiction editor Rust Hill. Her first novel, *State of Grace* (1973), was nominated for the National Book Award. Two of her novels, *Breaking and Entering* (New York: Vintage, 1988) and *The Changeling* (Garden City, NY: Doubleday, 1978) take place in Florida. She is also the author of numerous short stories, many with Florida settings, which have been published in *Esquire, Paris Review,* the *New Yorker, Grand Street,* and *Ms,* and are included in the *Best American Short Stories of 1964, 1985, 1986, and 1987.* Her stories may also be seen in such noted anthologies as the *O'Henry Prize Story Collection* (1966), *Best of the Little Magazines* (1969), and *Esquire Fiction Anthology* (1973); *Taking Care* (1987), a collection of her short stories, received much critical acclaim. Williams has also written *The Florida Keys: A History and Guide* (New York: Random House, 1986).

Her characters inhabit an absurd, nihilistic world. In her Sarasota novel, *Breaking and Entering,* a young man and his wife spend their lives breaking into expensive beach homes, and living there until the absentee owners are due to return: "Willie loved living in other people's houses and sleeping in their beds. He wore their clothes and drank their liquor, jumped in their pools and watched himself in their mirrors. Breaking into houses and living the ordered life of someone else appealed to Willie."

HOW I WROTE MY EVERGLADES BOOK

MARJORY STONEMAN DOUGLAS

[Marjory Stoneman Douglas, now 102 years old, is considered one of the first authorities on the Everglades because of her 1947 book entitled *The Everglades: River of Grass*. She recently made the following comments about two of her books.]

My Everglades book was for the Rivers of America series that Rinehart and Company published. The editor wanted me to write about the Miami River, but I said that the Miami River is part of the Everglades system, and he then agreed that I could write about the Everglades. When I began to study the Everglades, I found it was a river and not a swamp. That was my contribution to our knowledge of Florida. Before then everybody thought it was just swamps, but it's not; it's running water, and that makes it a river; a river is a body of fresh water moving more in one direction than another. I worked with the state hydrologist who was studying the ground water of southeastern Florida, Garald Parker, who was then over at the courthouse and who did a wonderful book on the water of southeastern Florida [*Water Resources of Southeastern Florida* by Garald Parker and others].

My book took me about four years to write and came out in 1947. Writing that book did not require a lot of trips in the Everglades because I had already been working on the committee to make the Everglades a national park and knew a good deal about them. Anyway, you can't take a trip into the Everglades; you can only go on the Tamiami Trail or U.S. 1 down to the park. You don't go walking in the sawgrass glades. I don't, at any rate.

That book has had a lot of influence on environmentalists. It finally sold in paperback to Mockingbird Books; then in 1988 I wrote an update chapter for Pineapple Press, who published a revised edition of it in hardcover. Last year it sold over 11,000 copies, and I'm still getting royalties, thank goodness. It is the only book of its kind and was the first to talk about the Everglades in any complete way. For research I used to go to Tallahassee and worked with the state hydrologists and engineers and people like that. I had some help, but unless they were professional, they didn't know much about the Everglades because everybody thought they were swamps.

One other note about the Everglades. There is an area we call east Everglades where Dade County has allowed people to build one house to 40 acres. I don't know when that was begun, but it was after we had defined the Everglades and talked about it, and it should never have been allowed. The east Everglades was right there at the high water mark, and the people had no business being in there at all; in fact I don't want to see any agriculture in south

Florida around the Everglades at all. It doesn't belong here because of what it will do to the water system. We haven't got enough soil in south Dade. We have only a foot-and-a-half of arable soil, and the tomatoes from south Dade are not particularly good.

We're fighting to have the Everglades preserved, and I think we have a very good chance; what we are trying to do is to restore the Kissimmee River. One of the greatest needs is to get Lake Okeechobee cleaned up; it's highly polluted. Officials have allowed the dairy farmers on the northeast coast to dump their untreated cow manure into the lake and have allowed the sugar people to back-pump irrigation water full of pesticides and fertilizer into the lake, which is completely polluted but which has to be cleaned up. Water is a big issue, has been a big issue, and will continue to be. We now know that much of our rain comes from the evaporation of the wet Everglades. The minute officials let the Everglades dry up we won't have any more rain. It's of the greatest possible importance that the Everglades should be kept wet.

I was fortunate to find something that hadn't been written about. That's one of the things that people don't know about writing; finding a new field that is not crowded with writers is very fortunate. A book on the Miami River would not have been as successful because the river is too short. It is only valuable as part of a system.

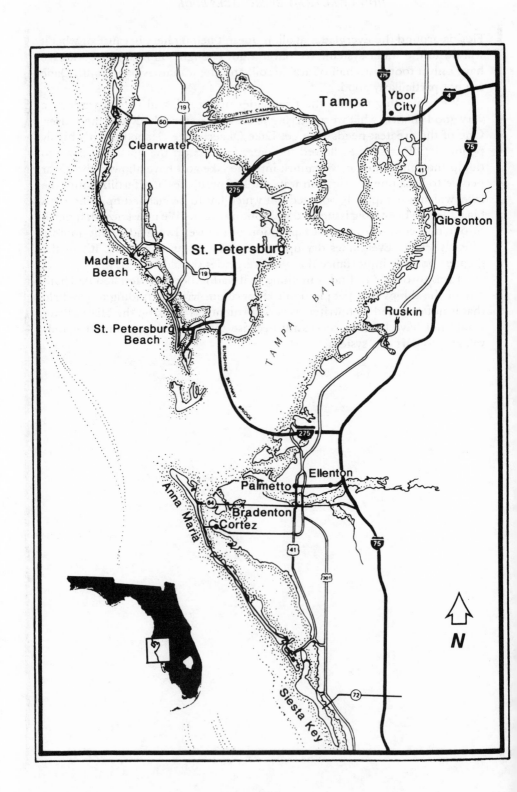

8 SIESTA KEY TO TAMPA

EDGAR W. HIRSHBERG

Siesta Key

Siesta Key, one of the barrier islands that juts out into Sarasota Bay to form the Inland Waterway off Sarasota, is connected to the mainland by three bridges but still has an insular atmosphere. Despite the implications of its name — a good place for long afternoon naps — it has been the home of one of the most prolific and successful modern American writers of fiction, **John D. MacDonald**. During the 35 years he resided in the Sarasota area, most of them on Siesta Key, he wrote over 70 novels and more than 500 short stories. The circulation of his works has gone into the millions of copies in nearly two dozen foreign languages as well as English, and most of his novels are still in print.

His beginnings were unspectacular. He was born on July 24, 1916, in Sharon, Pennsylvania, the son of a respectable local businessman. The family moved to Utica, New York, where he was educated through high school, graduating from Utica Free Academy in 1932. He attended the Wharton School of Finance at the University of Pennsylvania, then transferred to Syracuse University, where he graduated with a degree in Business Administration in 1938. In 1939 he earned an M.B.A. from the Harvard Graduate School of Business. Meanwhile he married Dorothy Prentiss, and their first and only son, Maynard John Prentiss MacDonald, was born. In 1940, John D. received a commission as a lieutenant in the U.S. Army, went overseas in 1943 to the China-Burma-India Theater of Operations, and ended up in the Office of Strategic Services — now the CIA — involved in extremely top-secret activities in Ceylon. While there he wrote his first short story, "Interlude in India," which he sent home to his wife, who submitted it to *Story* magazine, which published it in the July-August 1946 issue.

MacDonald never really stopped writing after receiving his first check — for $25 — from *Story*. He deluged the pulp magazines, such as *Doc Savage, Dime Detective, Black Mask,* and *Startling Stories,* and gradually started selling his work. He and his small family moved to Florida in 1952, where they settled in the Sarasota area, first renting a small house on Casey Key, then buying a permanent dwelling on Point Crisp Road on Siesta Key. Later they built a handsome tin-roofed Florida-style house with a porch on all four sides, facing Midnight Pass on Sarasota Bay. In those two homes MacDonald wrote most of his formidable body of fiction and several works of nonfiction.

MacDonald's chief claim to fame was his creation of Travis McGee, self-styled beach bum, salvage expert, detective, and therapist who was based on his houseboat *The Busted Flush*, docked in Berth F18 at the Bahia Mar marina in Fort Lauderdale, where a plaque memorializes the spot forever. However, MacDonald never considered himself a writer of mystery and detective stories only. In fact, more than half of his production has been in other genres. Yet much of the recognition he received honored his mystery and detective fiction: the Grand Prix de Littérature Policière for the French version of *A Key To The Suite* in 1964, the Grand Master Award from the Mystery Writers of America in 1972, and the American Booksellers Association award for the best mystery in 1980 (*The Green Ripper*). On the other hand he won the Ben Franklin Award for the best short story to appear in a mass-circulation magazine for "The Bear Trap" (*Cosmopolitan*, v. 138, no. 5 [May 1955] p. 70+), which had nothing to do with mystery or detection. It was a family story about a married man's memory of a youthful tragedy involving his high school sweetheart. And in 1971 he received the George Arents Pioneer Medal from Syracuse University for his contributions to American literature in general. The citation accompanying his honorary Ph.D. from Hobart and William Smith Colleges presented in 1978 praised him for setting an example "to those who seek to paint a contemporary picture of mankind with the medium of the printed word." With his 1980 honorary Ph.D. from the University of South Florida was a citation stating that the university "takes pride in honoring you as one of our nation's greatest living writers of fiction in an indigenously American mode."

MacDonald dealt with many themes and ideas in the novels and stories that he wrote between the late 1950s and his death on December 28, 1986, from complications that developed after open-heart surgery. Though he considered that his primary obligation to his readers was to tell a good story, he had much to say about contemporary social and moral issues. He once remarked that he felt he had the right to "try to move my suspense novels as close as I can to the 'legitimate' novels of manners and morals, despair and failure, love and joy.... I shall continue with my sociologist asides, with McGee and Meyer's dissertations on the condition of medicine, retirement, education, face lifting, ear mites, road construction, white-collar theft...billy rock, low fidelity and public service in America today." As commentaries on the state of the nation and the world, the Travis McGee novels and many of his others are effective and discerning social documents as well as good stories. MacDonald insists on taking a moral stance, on distinguishing good from evil, and there is never any doubt about which side he is on.

For more about MacDonald see *John D. MacDonald and the Colorful World of Travis McGee* by **Frank D. Campbell, Jr.** (San Bernardino, CA: Borgo Press, 1977); *A Bibliography of the Published Works of John D. MacDonald with Selected Biographical Materials and Critical Essays* by **Walter** and **Jean Shine** (Gainesville: Patrons of the Libraries, University of Florida, 1980); *John D. MacDonald* by **David Geherin** (New York: Ungar, 1982); *John D. MacDonald* by **Edgar W. Hirshberg** (Boston: Twayne, 1985). Hirshberg also edits and publishes the *JDM*

Bibliophile, a magazine about MacDonald, his life, works, and related matters, which has come out twice a year since 1965. The *Bibliophile*, with help from the English department at the University of South Florida in Tampa, has sponsored four major conferences concentrating on MacDonald; two have taken place at Bahia Mar in Fort Lauderdale, home port of *The Busted Flush*.

Anna Maria Island

North of Bradenton Beach is Anna Maria Island, named by Spanish explorer Ponce de León in 1513 for the Spanish king's wife. In 1539, Spanish explorer Hernando de Soto landed at the northern tip of the island and began his trek to the Mississippi River by land. De Soto National Park is located along the shores of the Manatee River Park where employees, dressed in costumes of the period, demonstrate sixteenth-century weapons. Films, demonstrations, and a short nature trail are also on the grounds (Daily 8 A.M. to 5:30 P.M.).

Among the local authors are two that deserve mention. **Wyatt Blassingame** (1909-1985) was born in Demopolis, Alabama, and moved to Anna Maria Island in the late 1940s. He wrote several novels including two with Florida settings: *Live from the Devil* (New York: Doubleday, 1959) about Florida cattlemen from 1900 to the 1940s and *Halo of Spears* (New York: Doubleday, 1962) about late nineteenth-century chain gangs. He specialized, however, in juvenile nonfiction; his books in this field include *Great Trains of the World* (1953), *First Book of the Seashore* (1964), *Men Who Opened the West* (1966), *Story of the Boy Scouts* (1968), *Jake Gaither, Winning Coach* (1969), *Medical Corps Heroes of World War II* (1969), and many others.

In the summer of 1952, writer **Joseph Arnold Hayes** (1918-) spent six weeks on Anna Maria Island writing *The Desperate Hours* (1954; New York: Carroll & Graf, 1985), a novel that was later made into a popular Tony Award-winning play starring Paul Newman and Fredric March. A 1955 movie version starred March and Humphrey Bogart. Hayes wrote all three versions (novel, play, screenplay). An Indianapolis native, he has spent part of each year in Florida since 1952, and has written two Florida-set novels: *Missing and Presumed Dead* (New York: New American Library, 1976) and *The Ways of Darkness* (New York: Morrow, 1986). His other novels include *Don't Go Away Mad* (1962), *The Third Day* (1964), *The Deep End* (1967), *Like Any Other Fugitive* (1972), *The Long Dark Night* (1974), and *No Escape* (1982). His stage plays include *The Desperate Hours* (1955) and *Calculated Risk* (1962); his screenplays include *The Young Doctors* and *The Third Day*. According to Hayes, "The trend, in uncertain times, toward nihilism, in society and literature, seems destructive, the one feeding on the other. When have times ever been certain? How did all this whining start and where will it end? If one does not like the world as it is (and who could?), then his job is to change it — by criticism, protest, politics — and not to sit and wallow in his own sour juices."

Cortez

Cortez, with a name that reminds us of the great Spanish explorers who may have passed through the area, is a quaint fishing village seven miles west of Bradenton off Cortez Road. In *Finest Kind: A Celebration of a Florida Fishing Village*, (Macon, GA: Mercer University Press, 1985) his book about the area, **Ben Green** (1951-), a native, describes Cortez in environmental terms:

> Cortez is a community of about 500 people located on Sarasota Bay, seven miles west of the city of Bradenton in Manatee County. It was settled in the 1880s by North Carolina fishermen who came south seeking one thing: mullet. The tens of thousands of Northern retirees who have settled in the state in the last two decades have come seeking one thing as well: to spend their retirement years in the sun. At one point in time, these two motivations might have been compatible, but they aren't any longer.
>
> This little village is on the brink of being destroyed in the next ten years unless the onslaught of condominiums, housing developments, and shopping malls is stopped or controlled.

Green studied writing at Florida State University before transferring to Brandeis University, where he majored in sociology. He became the writer-editor of Florida's AFL-CIO newsletter out of Tallahassee and later became a nonfiction fellow at the well-known Bread Loaf Writers' Conference. His most recent work is *The Soldier of Fortune Murders: A True Story of Obsessive Love and Murder-for-Hire* (New York: Delacorte, 1992) about three brutal 1985 murders, two of them in north-central Florida.

Bradenton

Bradenton takes its name from Dr. Joseph Braden, a pioneer sugar planter who built his house there in 1854. Today Bradenton is less well-known than neighboring Sarasota, but has its share of sugar-sand beaches, golf courses, and historic sites dating back to the 1800s. The South Florida Museum in downtown Bradenton has ancient Florida artifacts, including displays of Indian culture and Civil War memorabilia (Tuesday through Saturday 10 A.M. to 5 P.M.; Sunday 1 to 5 P.M.). **William Zinsser's** *Spring Training* (New York: Harper & Row, 1989) gives a description of the Pittsburgh Pirates' 1988 spring-training camp there.

A native Bradentonian who worked at the local newspaper is **Ann Hyman** (1936-). After earning her B.A. degree from Florida State University in 1958, she became a reporter for the *Bradenton Herald* (1958-1959) and then Jacksonville's *Florida Times-Union* (1959-1960). She is the author of *The Lansing Legacy* (1974) and *Chaos Clear As Glass: A Memoir* (1991) and presently resides in Jacksonville. (For more about her see Chapter One of this *Guide*.)

For more about the town see **Arthur C. Schofield's** *Yesterday's Bradenton* (Miami: Seemann Publishing Co., 1975). For a history of the region along the Manatee River see *The Singing River* by **Joe Warner** in collaboration with **Libby**

Warner (no publ., 1986). A specialized book about the county is **Robert E. King's** *A History of the Practice of Medicine in Manatee County, Florida* (Bradenton, FL: Manatee Memorial Hospital, 1985). A book about one of the area families is **Norman J. Pinardi's** *The Plant Pioneers* (Torrington, CT: Rainbow Press, 1980), which is about the Reasoner Family and their Royal Palm Nursery, the oldest continuously operating nursery in the state.

Palmetto

This town north of Bradenton got its name from the area's palmetto palms. Palmetto is the setting of **Jamie Lee Cooper's** novel, *The Great Dandelion* (Indianapolis: Bobbs-Merrill, 1972), about the reunion of the children in a family, and of **Donald J. Plantz's** novel *Sweeney Squadron* (Garden City, NY: Doubleday, 1961), about the training of an army air corps squadron at a nearby base. For a history see **Ruth E. Abel's** *One Hundred Years in Palmetto* (Palmetto: Palmetto Centennial Association, 1967).

Ellenton

East of Palmetto on U.S. 301, Ellenton is the site of the Gamble Plantation, the only Confederate shrine in Florida and the oldest building on the state's west coast. On the 3,000-acre sugar plantation is the 1850 mansion fronted by 18 beautiful pillars and furnished with varied Civil War mementos. This house was the hiding place of Judah Benjamin, the secretary of state of the Confederacy, who fled to England at the end of the Civil War (Daily 9 A.M. to 5 P.M.; tours begin on the hour; 813 722-1017) For more about Benjamin see **Eli N. Evans's** *Judah P. Benjamin: The Jewish Confederate* (New York: Free Press, 1988); **Robert Douthat Meade's** *Judah Benjamin, Confederate Statesman* (1943; New York: Arno Press, 1975); and **Simon I. Neiman's** *Judah Benjamin* (Indianapolis: Bobbs-Merrill, 1963). Another fine account of the flight of Benjamin and the other members of the Confederate cabinet is **A.J. Hanna's** *Flight Into Oblivion* (Bloomington, IN: Indiana University Press, 1959). Benjamin eventually reached England, where he had a distinguished career as a lawyer for 17 years.

Farther north on U.S. 301 and east at Parrish on State Road 62 is Duette, the site of Florida's smallest and last one-teacher school; the school, which served kindergarten to fourth grade, had 14 pupils in 1978. For more information about the surrounding county see **Joe G. Warner's** *Biscuits and 'Taters: A History of Cattle Ranching in Manatee County* (St. Petersburg: Great Outdoors Publishing Co., 1980).

Ruskin

Ruskin, farther north on U.S. 41, is the only Florida town named after a literary figure, John Ruskin (1819-1900), the British Victorian writer and socialist. Established as a socialist colony around 1908, Ruskin remained a center of socialism until about 1920, when repeated crop failures, due to the ineptness of early idealistic would-be farmers who did not take advantage of the rich soil, caused the demise of the colony. When more knowledgeable farmers in the 1930s began to take advantage of the frost-free location and loamy soil, rich crop yields began to bring prosperity to the little town. Its year-round crops of garden vegetables continue to feed much of the eastern half of the United States. The Ruskin Woman's Club building is on a historical site, an area that was part of Ruskin College in the early part of this century. A novel set in the vicinity is **John R.** Feegel's *Death Sails the Bay* (New York: Avon, 1978).

Gibsonton

The little town of Gibsonton, named for its founder, James B. Gibson, played an unusual role in science fiction. In an uncanny prediction of what would happen in the 20th century, 19th-century French science-fiction writer **Jules Verne** (1814-1905) described a rocket's take-off for the moon from Florida from a spot about 50 miles from Orlando. But instead of **Cape Canaveral,** Verne chose a site near Tampa, where he had a cannon shoot off the rocket on its trip to the moon. That fictional launch in *From the Earth to the Moon* (1865; New York: Dodd, Mead, 1962) took place more than a century before NASA would send the first Americans to the moon. Verne was amazingly accurate: the fictional trip begins in Florida, lasts four days, and involves three men in a rocket. In the book, a gun club from Baltimore was in charge of the actual launching of the rocket, but its members could not decide whether the launch site should be in Florida or Texas.

A fierce rivalry developed between the two states, with Texas marveling that "a wretched little strip of country like Florida" would compare itself to the great state of Texas. Texans declared that the force of the cannon shot would tear up the Florida peninsula. The gun club finally chose Bell Shoals just east of present-day Gibsonton for the launch. The 1939 *WPA Guide to Florida* pointed out that for 50 years many people thought that machinery found along the Alafia River near Gibsonton was originally part of the monstrous cannon that sent the rocket to the moon in Verne's novel. Jules Verne Park in **Tampa** at Interbay and Ballast Point boulevards near the pier honors the great writer.

St. Petersburg Beach

The spectacular 15-mile-long, 175-foot-high Sunshine Skyway Bridge leads into St. Petersburg. The original two-lane bridge, built in 1954 as Florida's largest public-works project at a cost of $22 million, was expanded by another two-lane bridge in 1971. It is so high that ocean-going ships can pass beneath it. Part of the bridge was destroyed in 1980 when a ship plowed into it during a heavy storm; 35 people died when a bus, three cars, and a pickup truck plunged 150 feet into the waters below.

Just across the bridge to the left is Eckerd College. Founded as Florida Presbyterian College, it changed its name to honor a local businessman who has done much to support the school. Located on a picturesque 280-acre campus, the school is well known for its liberal arts and sciences, as well as its

Peter Meinke

artists' series, its college theater, and the showing of classic films. The student literary magazine at Eckerd College, *The Siren*, comes out once a year and is limited to writing by students at the college.

Peter Meinke (1932-) has been director of the writing workshop at Eckerd College since the mid-1960s. With a Ph.D. from the University of Minnesota in 1965 and experience teaching in high school and at different universities both here and abroad, he brings to Eckerd College a diverse background and a publishing record of poetry and fiction. His poetry has appeared in such journals as *New Republic, Cosmopolitan, Antioch Review,* and *Southern Poetry Review.* He won the O. Henry Award for short fiction in 1983 for "The Ponoes" and in 1986 for "Uncle George and Uncle Stefan," as well as the Flannery O'Connor Award for short fiction in 1986 for *The Piano Tuner.* His other books include *Howard Nemerov* (1968), *The Night Train and the Golden Bird* (1977), *The Rat Poems* (1978), *Trying to Surprise God* (1981), *Nightwatch on the Chesapeake* (1987), and *Liquid Paper* (1991). For more about him see *Dictionary of Literary Biography* Vol. 5: *American Poets since World War II* (Detroit: Gale, 1980), part 2, pp. 41-45.

Meinke's colleague in the writing-workshop program is novelist **Sterling Watson** (1947-), who has published three critically acclaimed novels: *Weep No More My Brother* (New York: Morrow, 1978), *The Calling* (Atlanta, GA: Peachtree Publishers, 1986), and *Blind Tongues* (New York: Delta Books, 1989).

Also in residence during the winter months is **James Michener** (1907-), internationally famous novelist, who, Meinke reports, often helps individual students in the writing workshop. He is a member of ASPEC, the Association of Senior Professionals at Eckerd College, which maintains permanent on-campus residential headquarters for its membership.

A former writer-in-residence at Eckerd in 1975-1976 was **James Nolan** (1947-), who lived and wrote in Florida from 1965 to 1969 and in 1975 and 1976. Born in New Orleans, he worked on the Upward Bound project in St.

Sterling Watson

Petersburg and taught creative writing. His book of poetry entitled *Why I Live in the Forest* (1974) was written while he was in St. Petersburg. He spent much of the 1970s living and working in Central and South America, Europe, India, and the Orient; as a result, his poetry shows the influence of other cultures. He has also written *What Moves Is Not the Wind* (1980) and translated **Pablo Neruda's** *Stones of the Sky* (1980).

Back on the Pinellas Bayway, a condominium-packed causeway and a drawbridge lead to St. Petersburg Beach, site of The Don Ce-Sar Resort Hotel, which is situated on the beach facing the Gulf of Mexico; the second word in the name has three different spellings: Cesar, Ce-Sar, Ce-sar. Built in the 1920s at the height of the Florida real-estate boom, this towering pink edifice dominates the surrounding scene. Recently designated a National Historic Landmark, it is an outstanding example of the Spanish-Moorish-cum-Florida architecture that was so popular in the early decades of this century. During World War II fortunate U.S. Army Air Corps trainees used it as a barracks, and it later served as a regional headquarters for the Veterans Administration. It reverted back to its original function in the 1960s and is now a prosperous high-class beach resort.

The picturesque hotel has formed a background for several literary and dramatic productions. "The Don" was one of the stories in **Sandra Thompson**'s collection, *Close-Ups* (Athens, GA: University of Georgia Press, 1984), which won the Flannery O'Connor Award for short fiction. The film *Health,* with Carol Burnett and James Garner, was shot at the hotel in 1979. **Lary Crews,** a Sarasota writer, used it for the scene of much of the action in *Extreme Close-Up* (New York: Lynx Books, 1989), his second novel about Veronica Slate, a statuesque, auburn-haired St. Petersburg-based disc jockey. Crews drew on his experiences working on the 1985 film *Cocoon,* which was also shot at the Don and in the vicinity, for his background material.

At one time or another the plush hotel has housed such notables as baseball star Lou Gehrig, lawyer Clarence Darrow, and actor Cary Grant. For more about it see **June Hurley**'s *The Don Ce-Sar Story* (St. Petersburg: Partnership Press, 1974). Among items of interest it mentions other famous people who stayed there; for example, the Yankees baseball team spent three seasons at the hotel on the condition that the players would be able to have a steak every morning and as much milk as they could drink. **F. Scott Fitzgerald** and his wife, Zelda, stayed at the hotel in the early 1930s while he was revising *Tender Is the Night* (1934). Fitzgerald wrote the following about the place:

> The Don Ce-sar Hotel in Pass-A-Grille [which borders St. Petersburg Beach] stretched lazily over the stubbed wilderness, surrendering its shape to the blinding brightness of the gulf. Opalescent shells cupped the twilight on the beach and a stray dog's footprints in the wet sand staked out his claim to a free path round the ocean. We walked at night and discussed the Pythagorean theory of numbers, and we fished by day. We were sorry for the deep-sea bass and the amberjacks — they seemed such easy game and no sport at all. Reading the *Seven Against Thebes*, we browned on a lovely beach. The hotel was almost empty and there were so many waiters waiting to be off that we could hardly eat our meals.

For more about this area see **Frank T. Hurley, Jr.**'s *Surf, Sand, and Post Card Sunsets: A History of Pass-a-Grille and the Gulf Beaches* (St. Petersburg: Hurley, 1977). **Gil Brewer**'s *And the Girl Screamed* (New York: Fawcett, 1944) is a novel that takes place nearby in a pre-1950 setting.

St. Petersburg

The city of St. Petersburg was named for the original St. Petersburg, Russia, by the president of the Orange Belt Railroad, Peter Demens, a Russian immigrant to America. For more about him see *Full Steam Ahead! The Story of Peter Demens, Founder of St. Petersburg, Florida* (St. Petersburg: Great Outdoors Publishing Co., 1987) by **Albert Parry**. In south central St. Petersburg, off Park Street, stands a plaque memorializing the landing site of the Spanish explorer Pánfilo de Narváez, who landed near here in 1528 with the first large group of Europeans in the present United States; he had several hundred soldiers, 40 horses, and a number of fierce dogs to chase away Indians. This was 37 years before the 1565 founding of St. Augustine, 79 years before the 1607 founding of Jamestown, and 92 years before the 1620 landing of the Pilgrims at Plymouth Rock. One of the city's claims to fame took place on January 1, 1914, when St. Petersburg pilot Tony Jannus inaugurated scheduled airline transportation by carrying the first paying passenger in history across Tampa Bay, taking off from the St. Petersburg waterfront in his Benoist flying boat and landing on the Hillsborough River in Tampa 23 minutes later. That first passenger was former St. Petersburg mayor A.C. Pheil, who paid $400 for the privilege. The flight is commemorated by a plaque at the entrance to the city's municipal pier. Airfare was $5 for a one-way ticket, but it cut quite a bit of time from the 2.5-hour boat trip or the 12-hour train trip between the two cities. For more about this flight see **Gay Blair White's** *The World's First Airline, The St. Petersburg-Tampa Airboat Line* (Largo, FL: Aero-Medical Consultants, 1984) and **Hampton Dunn's** *Yesterday's St. Petersburg* (Miami: Seemann Publishing Co., 1973).

Also located in St. Petersburg on Central Avenue is the largest and probably the best-stocked bookstore in the Southeast — Haslam's. Its rambling premises, which dominate a city block, house some 300,000 books, some new, some old, both hardback and paperback. It was founded in 1933 and has been run by the Haslam family since its beginnings as a small magazine-and-book exchange. Charles Haslam, who served a term as president of the American Booksellers Association, took over from his parents and ran it until his death in 1983. His wife Elizabeth is now in charge, and the store is still prospering, with the help of the rest of the family. One member of that family, Ray Hinz, has a letter from a satisfied customer taped to his desk so he can see it from time to time; the letter says that, if you have lived right, when you die you get to go to Haslam's.

Harrison Arnston, who lives in Palm Harbor, is a successful writer of mystery and suspense stories. His latest works are *Act of Passion* (1991) and *Trade Off* (1992).

William T. Brannon (1906-1981) first came to Florida in 1925 at the age of 18. He worked as a writer then editor for the city's *Tourist News* (1925-1930) and also joined the staff of the *St. Petersburg Times* as a reporter (1925-1928) and later as a columnist (1929-1930). In 1930 he moved to Chicago and began his career as a crime writer producing over 5,000 true-crime stories for such publications as *Master Detective* and *True Detective* and over 1,000 stories of general interest. In 1950 and 1951, he won the Edgar Allan Poe Award of Mystery Writers of America for outstanding crime writing. He returned to settle permanently in Florida in 1963, where he lived in St. Petersburg in an apartment on Snell Isle. Brannon, who employed seven pseudonyms, wrote a short story, "The Perfect Secretary," which is set in the fictional Florida town of Palmview. He died in St. Petersburg.

Gil Brewer (1922-1983) came to Florida in 1947, and kept St. Petersburg as his home base, although he traveled extensively and had other residences throughout the country. With the publication of his first novel, *13 French Street* (New York: Fawcett, 1951), he began a long career of writing paperback originals. Many of his 30 crime novels have a Florida background, including *Satan Is a Woman* (New York: Fawcett, 1951); *So Rich, So Dead* (New York: Fawcett, 1951); *And the Girl Screamed* (New York: Fawcett, 1956); *Little Tramp* (New York: Fawcett, 1957); *The Red Scarf* (New York: Bouregy, 1958); *Sugar* (New York: Avon, 1959); and *Play It Hard* (Derby, CT: Monarch Books, 1960); his series character was Al Mundy. He also published over 350 short stories and novelettes, some of them under the pseudonym **Eric Fitzgerald** or **Bailey Morgan**. For a more complete list of his many publications see editor **John M. Reilly's** *Twentieth-Century Crime and Mystery Writers* (New York: St. Martin's, 1985).

Johnnie Clark's first book, *Guns Up* (1984), an autobiographical novel about his experiences fighting in the Vietnam War, achieved considerable critical and popular success. It was followed by *Semper Fidelis* (1988), the first of a series of war novels, this one also set in Vietnam. Second in the series was *The Old Corps* (1990), about World War II. Clark is planning two more.

Linda Crockett Gray (1943-), also known as **Linda Crockett** and **Christina Crockett**, lives and works in St. Petersburg, interspersed with stays in Bermuda. She has published several successful works in genres ranging from romance novels to horror and the supernatural. Among the latter are *Scryer* (New York: TOR, 1987) and *Tangerine* (New York: TOR Books, 1988). *Song of the Seabird*, a Harlequin Superromance published in 1985, takes place on the mythical barrier island of Palm Shores off Florida's west coast and is dedicated to the "workers of miracles at the Suncoast Seabird Sanctuary, Indian Shores, Florida." Scheduled for 1992 publication are *Carousel* from TOR Books and *Safelight* from New American Library.

Richard Fontaine Hill (1941-), a St. Petersburg native who attended St. Petersburg Junior College, Florida State University, and the University of South Florida, from which he earned a B.A. and an M.A., still lives in St. Petersburg. He published his first novel, *Ghost Story* (New York: Liveright, 1971), and wrote a screenplay for it for Warner Brothers in 1972; the novel's setting is St. Petersburg. He is a prolific short story writer and has published in such magazines as *Harper's, Esquire, Rolling Stone, Playboy, Penthouse, Cosmopolitan, Village Voice, American Review,* and many others. The death of his friend Jack Kerouac in 1969 at the young age of 47 had a great effect on Hill, who has taken care to stay healthy.

Alice M. Putnam (1916-) is a successful writer of children's books. Her latest is *Westering* (1990), a historical novel about an 11-year-old boy's adventures traveling in a wagon train from Missouri to Oregon in 1850. Other children's books by Putnam include *The Spy Doll* (1979), *The Whistling Swan* (1981), and *That New Guy* (1987). In 1991 two of her adult novels were published by Avalon in New York: *Murder in the Morning*, a mystery, and *Love's Sweet Refuge*, a romance set against a St. Petersburg background and also inspired by the Suncoast Seabird Sanctuary in Indian Shores.

Robert Turner came to Florida in 1954 and lived in St. Petersburg until 1959; he was public-relations director of Weeki Wachee Springs in 1958. Born in 1915 in New York City, he is the author of suspense and western novels, as well as several hundred short stories. His novel *Mafia: Operation Cocaine* (San Diego, CA: Pyramid Publications, 1974), under the pseudonym **Robert Morgan**, has a Florida setting. Many of his stories have been reprinted abroad, including a short story, "Christmas Gift" (1957), a police procedural set in St. Petersburg.

Harry Whittington (1915-1989) was born in Ocala and spent most of his life in St. Petersburg, his last years in nearby Indian Rocks Beach. He was the author of some 200 novels, hundreds of short stories and novelettes, and numerous film and television scripts. He used more than a dozen pseudonyms in his career, including **Harriet Kathryn Myers**, **Clay Stuart**, **Hondo Wells**,

Harry White, and **Ashley Carter.** Among his most popular works are his southern-Gothic Ashley Carter books: *Master of Blackoaks* (1976), *Sword of the Golden Stud* (1977), and *Taproots of Falconhurst* (1978). Books in which Florida figures prominently include *Cracker Girl* (New York: Beacon Books, 1953), *Saturday Night Town* (Greenwich, CT: Fawcett, 1956), *A Woman on the Place* (New York: Ace Books, 1956), *Heat of the Night* (1958), *Connolly's Woman* (Greenwich, CT: Fawcett, 1960), *Journey Into Violence* (Pyramid Books, 1960), *Rampage* (New York: Fawcett, 1978) — as Harry Whittington, and *The Outlanders* (New York: Jove, 1979) — as **Blaine Stevens.** For a list of his many books and an interview with him see *Contemporary Authors* Vol. 5, New Revision Series (Detroit: Gale Research Company, 1982), pp. 561-564. Acknowledged in France as a master of *noir* fiction, he was honored by having an entire issue of the magazine *Les Amis du Crime No. 5* (March 1980) dedicated to him and his work. In 1979 the *West Coast Review of Books* gave him its Silver Award for *Panama*, by Ashley Carter, as "best paperback original based on facts," and its Bronze Award for *Rampage*, written under his own name, as "best contemporary novel in paperback original."

Among the short-term residents of the city have been several that we should mention. **George Washington Cable** (1844-1925), author of such works as *Old Creole Days* (1879), *The Grandissimes* (1880), and *Madame Delphine* (1881), spent the 1924-1925 winter in the city with his third wife, Hannah Cowing; he died in St. Petersburg on January 31, 1925.

Edward Field (1924-) lived in St. Petersburg in the fall of 1972, when he was a visiting poet at Eckerd College; his parents live in Miami Beach, and he visits them there throughout the year. His major books of poetry include *Stand Up, Friend, With Me* (1963); *Variety Photoplays* (1967); a book of Eskimo translations entitled *Eskimo Songs and Stories* (1974); *A Full Heart* (1977); and *Stars in My Eyes* (1979). He was born in Brooklyn, New York, and resides there now.

Jack Kerouac (1922-1969), author of *On the Road* (1957) and *The Dharma Bums* (1958) and closely associated with the Beat Generation, lived at 5155 Tenth Avenue North in the mid-1960s and then at 5169 Tenth Avenue North; the term "Beat Generation" refers to those men and women in the 1950s who rejected conventional values and adopted new ways of living away from ordinary society. On October 20, 1969, after suffering a massive internal hemorrhage, he was rushed to St. Anthony's Hospital, where he died on October 21. For more about him, including his final days in St. Petersburg, see **Tom Clark**'s *Jack Kerouac* (San Diego: Harcourt Brace Jovanovich, 1984), especially p. 216; and **Gerald Nicosia**'s *Memory Babe: A Critical Biography of Jack Kerouac* (New York: Grove Press, 1983), especially pp. 656-664. Kerouac is buried in Lowell, Massachusetts. For more about his widow, Stella, see "St. Petersburg: A Visit with Stella Kerouac" in **Barry Gifford**'s *Kerouac's Town* (Berkeley, CA: Creative Arts Book Company, 1977), pp. 37-54. For picturesque details on Kerouac's activities at the Wild Boar, a tavern in Tampa he frequented along with a coterie of University of South Florida professors and students, see *Kerouac at the "Wild Boar" & Other Skirmishes*, compiled by John

Montgomery (San Anselmo, CA: Fels & Firn Press, 1986), especially "Requiem for a Madman, Bum & Angel," by Lawrence R. Broer, pp. 11-14, and "Jack Kerouac — End of the Road," by Larry Vickers, pp. 22-25.

J(ack) R(ichard) Salamanca was born in St. Petersburg in 1922 and grew up in Florida, Virginia, New York City, and Washington, D.C. His published novels include *The Lost Country* (1958), which was later filmed as *Wild in the Country* (1961) with Elvis Presley; *Lilith* (1961); *A Sea Change* (1969); and *Embarkation* (1973). He now teaches in the English department at the University of Maryland.

Among the fictional works set in St. Petersburg are the following: **Beatrice Brandon's** *The Court of the Silver Shadows* (Garden City, NY: Doubleday, 1980); **Marguerite Speer Cross's** *Whitie* (New York: Vantage, 1977); **Tove Jansson's** *Sun City* (New York: Pantheon, 1976); **Ring Lardner's** short story, "The Golden Honeymoon" (reprinted in *Florida Stories* [Gainesville: University of Florida Press, 1989] edited by Kevin McCarthy); **Milton Paul Magly's** *The Bell(e)s of Saint Petersburg* (New York: Exposition, 1963); **Eugenie C. Reid's** *Mystery of the Second Treasure* (New York: Lothrop, 1967); and **Don Tracy's** *The Big Brass Ring* (New York: Trident Press, 1963).

Histories of the area include **Raymond Arsenault's** *St. Petersburg and the Florida Dream, 1888-1950* (Norfolk, VA: Donning, 1988); **John A. Bethell's** *Bethell's History of Point Pinellas* (St. Petersburg: Great Outdoors Publishing Co., 1962); **Frederick Eberson's** *Early Medical History of Pinellas Peninsula* (St. Petersburg: Valkyrie Press, 1978); **Karl H. Grismer's** *History of St. Petersburg* (St. Petersburg: Tourist News Publishing Co., 1924); **Page S. Jackson's** *An Informal History of St. Petersburg* (St. Petersburg: Great Outdoors Publishing Co., 1962); and **June Hurley Young's** *Florida's Pinellas Peninsula* (St. Petersburg: Byron Kennedy, 1984). For some fine photographs of the city see **Hampton Dunn's** *Yesterday's St. Petersburg* (Miami: Seemann Publishing Co., 1973). Also see **Walter P. Fuller's** *St. Petersburg and Its People* (St. Petersburg: Great Outdoors Publishing Co., 1972) and **Del Marth's** *St. Petersburg: Once Upon a Time* (St. Petersburg: The City of St. Petersburg Bicentennial Committee, 1976). An interesting example of local history is *Our Story of Gulfport, Florida*, compiled by the Gulfport Historical Society (St. Petersburg, 1985), a compendium of historical and descriptive sketches about the small community located on the city's southwestern fringes.

One of the most important influences in the literary life of St. Petersburg during the past quarter century or so has been **Marjorie Schuck**, poet, publisher, editor, and one of the community's outstanding leaders. She established the Valkyrie Press in 1972, and since then the company has published nearly 300 titles in both hardback and paperback in such classifications as art, classical studies, biography, fiction, folklore, history, the occult, philosophy, religion, and many others. Valkyrie books have appeared in foreign languages, and the company has maintained a cooperative publishing arrangement with the German publishers, Lorber Verlag. **Patrick D. Smith's** *Angel City* (1978; reprinted by Pineapple Press, 1989) was produced as a major

Marjorie M. Schuck

TV movie in 1980 by CBS-TV and has been shown intermittently ever since. In addition, Schuck edited and produced *Poetry Venture*, an internationally circulated magazine of poetry, to which some of the outstanding poets of our generation contributed works, from 1968 through 1979, along with *Poetry Venture Quarterly Essays*, 1968-71. Representative of the company's recent publications having to do with Florida is **Richard Marvel**'s *The New Oz: The Wizard Revisited* (Valkyrie Publishing House, 1992). Schuck was instrumental in the founding of the Pinellas Arts Council and conceptualized the Florida Suncoast Writers' Conference and has been actively involved in its 20-year history. Administered by the English department of the University of South Florida (USF) in Tampa, the conference is held on USF's St. Petersburg campus and has attracted about 400 writers and aspiring writers who study under the guidance of some 25 novelists, poets, editors and other established literary figures.

Other literary activities in the St. Petersburg area include the St. Petersburg Writers' Club, which meets on the first and third Thursday at 1900 Thirty-fourth Street North; and *Pinawar*, the Pinellas Authors and Writers Association, which meets Saturday mornings at the Highland Recreational Complex in Largo. There is also a fledgling chapter of the Mystery Writers of America in the area. Finally, the Florida Bibliophile Society, which was founded in 1983 and is headquartered in Largo (P.O. Box 3887, St. Petersburg, FL 33731), has a newsletter and meetings for interested book lovers; Ormond Beach also has a chapter of the Society.

Madeira Beach

Madeira Beach, west of St. Petersburg and named after the Portuguese island off the Atlantic coast of Africa, was home for author **Damon Knight** for many years before he moved to Oregon. Born in 1922 in Baker, Oregon, Knight has written numerous science-fiction novels and in 1956 won the Hugo Award for best science-fiction criticism, much of which was collected in *In Search of Wonder* (1956). Works by Knight include *Beyond the Barrier* (1964), *Mind Switch* (1965), *Three Novels* (1967), and *The Futurians: The Story of the Science Fiction "Family" of the 30's That Produced Today's Top SF Writers and Editors* (1977). For a discussion of Knight and a list of his 45 books and his periodical publications, see *Twentieth-Century American Science-Fiction Writers* Part 1 (Detroit: Gale Research Company, 1981), pp. 239-242.

Also a resident of Madeira Beach is **Carol J. Perry**. In recent years School Book Fairs has published five of her books for young adults: *Sand Castle Summer* (1988), which was also published in Germany and republished as *Going Overboard* in 1991; *13 and Loving It* (1989); *My Perfect Winter* (1989); *Make Believe Love* (1989); and *Sister vs. Sister* (1991). She has also written a play, *Two On, Two Out*, scheduled for production at a local dinner theater, and has sold more than 100 nonfiction articles to various national and regional periodicals. In addition, she is currently president of the Bay Area Professional Writers' Guild and presents seminars on travel writing and fiction.

Frank C. Strunk

Another Madeira Beach resident, **Frank C. Strunk**, has embarked on a successful literary career with the publication in 1991 of his first novel, *Jordon's Wager*, a murder mystery set in the mountains of eastern Kentucky. Berkley Jordon is the hero, and Strunk has already sold his second novel about him to Walker.

In nearby Seminole, another St. Petersburg suburb, lives **Skip Harris**, a young poet who has had two books of his poems published by The Write Press of St. Petersburg: *Banjo Picker* (1989) and *Florida Fishin'* (1990).

A fictional work that takes place in this area is *The*

Court of Silver Shadows (Garden City, NY: Doubleday, 1980) by **Robert Krepps (Beatrice Brandon)**.

Tampa

Across Tampa Bay on Interstate 275 is Florida's third-largest city, which takes its name from an Indian word meaning *a nearby place* or *split wood for quick fire*; it was the site of Fort Brooke, established in 1824 as an important fortification in the First Seminole War. Settlers moving in around the fort established the city of Tampa, which now has a population of nearly 300,000.

Ybor City

One of Tampa's most interesting sections historically is Ybor City, now partially restored. Bordered roughly on the north by Interstate 4, on the south by Sixth Avenue, and running east to west from about Twentieth Street to Fourteenth, the district became the birthplace of the American cigar industry when Vicente Martinez Ybor, a Spanish entrepreneur, erected a big cigar factory late in the nineteenth century and brought his workers with him, mostly from Havana and Key West, to supply the labor. Other manufacturers followed his lead, and cigarmaking and Cuban politics combined to make the ethnic enclave that grew around the factories where the workers lived into a hotbed of activity. Many structures remain in their original form, or have been restored, and the two dozen or so historical plaques distributed throughout the area tell a fascinating story of revolution and intrigue, of José Marti's organizing of Cuban freedom fighters with speeches on the steps of the

Circulo Espagnol, Ybor City

tobacco factories, of Teddy Roosevelt's Rough Riders, and of the activities of the immigrants who worked here. Just south of what is now Ybor Square is a shrine dedicated to Marti (1835-1895) that was erected near the place where two Spanish agents tried to poison him in 1893. Later Marti, known as the George Washington of Cuba, forgave them and freed them, and the two spies joined him in the successful fight for Cuba's independence.

One part of those cigar factories that we should mention here were the *lectores*. Their function was to read to the tobacco workers to keep them entertained while they rolled cigars by hand, each at his own desk in a huge room. The lectores were almost always well-educated men with good voices who read in faultless Spanish, keeping it up for hours as they sat in their elevated chairs in the middle of the room so that everyone could hear. They often read from the classics; the Russians like Tolstoy and Dostoyevsky were favorites. They also kept their listeners abreast of current events. In the 1930s their point of view seems to have become increasingly liberal, and at least one strike was inspired by the owners' banning lectores, substituting music, because of the inflammatory nature of their readings. As the factories became more mechanized, the use of lectores decreased and finally stopped. During their heyday they were always paid by the workers, at 25 cents per day from each one, never by the owners.

For more about Marti see **Lorraine Williams Garrett's** *José Marti* (Washington, DC: Pan American Union, 1944); **Juan Marinello's** *José Marti* (Madrid, Spain: Jucar, 1972); **Peter Turton's** *José Marti* (London, England: Zed, 1986);

Cigarmakers

337

and **C. Neale Ronning**'s *José Marti and the Emigré Colony in Key West* (New York: Praeger, 1990).

At 1823 Ninth Avenue is a museum and archive of great historical interest, which forms a sort of cultural nucleus, along with the neighboring Ybor City branch of Hillsborough Community College. The commercial center for tourists is Ybor Square, housed in the old Ybor Cigar complex, the biggest of the Ybor City cigar factories originally built in the 1890s. The square contains restaurants and shops offering a wide variety of food and merchandise, including one shop where hand-rolled cigars are still made. Just north of the square is El Pasaje, an old red-brick, Spanish-style hotel and restaurant of considerable architectural interest. Such notables as Teddy Roosevelt and General John Pershing patronized it in its prime, and it now functions as a fairly upscale restaurant. Adjacent to it is the Cuban Club, once, together with the Italian Club, the Spanish Club, and the Circulo Marti-Maseo, the focal point in the lives of most of the people of Ybor City. These clubs provided social gathering places for the various ethnic groups comprising the population, which consisted largely of tobacco workers and their families. The clubs also took care of the workers' health needs by means of a unique system of health care which was really a form of early socialized medicine, one of the first and most successful of such systems to operate anywhere, with its own staff of doctors and nurses, its own hospitals and pharmacists, all available to its

Cuban Club, Ybor City

membership at a modest cost. Remnants of the system still exist, but are not much in evidence because of the flight of ethnic elements of Ybor City's population to other parts of Tampa.

The area has retained some of its unique characteristics, with the original wrought-iron balconies still in place fronting some of the old buildings whose nineteenth-century architecture has survived. There are several art galleries and book stores; the famous Columbia Restaurant, nearly a century old with its elaborate rococo Spanish decor, still reigns supreme as the area's chief tourist attraction for lovers of good Spanish food. "Back to Ybor City Day" is celebrated each October, recalling the old days with an art show and various Latin festivities and events.

Consummate historian of Ybor City and presently the official historian of Hillsborough County is **Anthony P. "Tony" Pizzo** (1912-), who was brought up in Ybor City and knows more about how things were during its heyday in the 1920s and 1930s than anyone else. His *Tampa Town*, subtitled *The Cracker Village with a Latin Accent* (Coconut Grove, FL: Hurricane Press, 1968), is a full-length treatment of Ybor City and its varied antecedents. His *The Italian Heritage in Tampa* is a major essay in *Little Italies in North America* (Ontario, Canada: Multicultural History Society, 1981) and a fine example of Pizzo's scholarship. He collaborated with USF history professor **Gary Mormino** in a third historical work, *Tampa, The Treasure City* (Tulsa, OK: Continental Heritage Press, 1983). Pizzo has written numerous articles in academic as well as popular periodicals and is regarded as the primary authority on Tampa's Latin heritage.

The Wonderful Life of Angelo Massari: An Autobiography (New York: Exposition Press, 1965), translated by **Arthur D. Massolo,** details the life of an unschooled Sicilian immigrant who went on to become a successful business-man in Ybor City. *The Immigrant World of Ybor City: Italians and Their Latin Neighbors in Tampa, 1885-1985* (Champaign, IL: University of Illinois Press, 1987) by **Gary R. Mormino** and **George E. Pozzetta** and *Afro-Cubans in Ybor City* (Tampa: no publ, 1986) by **Susan D. Greenbaum** provide good ethnic histories of the place. The best illustrated account is *A Pictorial History of Ybor City* (Tampa: Trend Publishers, 1975) by **Charles E. Harner.**

Another writer closely associated with Ybor City is **Jose Yglesias**, who was born in Tampa in 1919. His hometown provided inspiration for many of his works, often centering on the progress made by Cuban refugee families as they adjusted to American life. His novels include *A Wake in Ybor City* (New York: Holt, Rinehart and Winston, 1963); *The Goodbye Land* (New York: Pantheon, 1967); *In the Fist of the Revolution: Life in a Cuban Country Town* (New York: Pantheon, 1968); *An Orderly Life* (New York: Pantheon, 1968); *Down There* (New York: World, 1970); *The Truth About Them* (New York: World, 1971) about his youth in Ybor City in the 1920s and 1930s; and *The Kill Price* (Indianapolis: Bobbs-Merrill, 1976). He now lives in North Brooklyn, Maine.

Three novels that deal with the Spanish-American War and its effect on the Latins of Tampa are *The Year of the Spaniard, a Novel of 1898* (Garden City, NY: Doubleday, 1950) by **Henry Castor**; *The Little War of Private Post* (Boston:

Little, Brown, 1960) by **Charles Johnson Post**; and *Abraham's Wife* (New York: Vanguard Press, 1953) by **Francis J. Thompson**.

Situated downtown on the Hillsborough River, the building that houses the University of Tampa was originally constructed by railroad tycoon Henry B. Plant (1819-1899) between 1888 and 1891, as a luxury hotel named after him. Designed to rival Henry Flagler's Ponce de Leon Hotel in St. Augustine, it is an imposing combination of Moorish and Florida-Spanish architecture, featuring red-brick archways, a rambling piazza about a quarter-of-a-mile long which wealthy hotel patrons traversed by rickshaws, and 13 silver-tinted minarets which puncture the Tampa skyline with an exotic panache. Plant and his wife spent over a million dollars to furnish the hotel with antiques from around the world, and the hostelry was patronized by the rich and famous until after World War I. A feature of the plush landscaping was the DeSoto Oak, which still stands on the supposed site of the explorer Hernando de Soto's meeting with the Indians in 1539.

University of Tampa

When the Spanish-American War started in 1898, Tampa was used as an assembly point for the U.S. forces. Colonel Theodore Roosevelt and his officers moved into the Plant Hotel while their troops of Rough Riders camped on the banks of the river. Novelist **Stephen Crane** (*The Red Badge of Courage* and "The Open Boat") also stayed at the hotel on his way to the war, which he covered as a correspondent. For further details see **James W. Covington** and **C. Herbert Laub**'s *The Story of the University of Tampa* (Tampa: University of Tampa Press, 1955) and **Harris W. Mullen**'s *A History of the Tampa Bay Hotel* (Tampa: University of Tampa Foundation, 1966).

The hotel fell on bad times with the advent of the Great Depression and the city of Tampa took it over. In 1933 it was leased to the University of Tampa, which was then in its second year of operation, and the school has grown and prospered ever since. Recent books by its graduates include **Connie May Fowler's** *Sugar Cage* (New York: Putnam's, 1992), a novel set in a town that resembles Starke, Florida. The *Tampa Review* is the prestigious literary journal of the University of Tampa which comes out once a year and publishes work by some of the nation's outstanding writers. Fiction editor is **Andy Solomon,** a critic of national prominence and a finalist in the 1991 National Book Critics Circle Citation for Excellence. **Richard Mathews,** the editor, teaches at the university. His collection of Florida poems, *A Mummery,* was published in 1970 by the Konglomerati Press in St. Petersburg. He was co-editor, with **Richard Wilber,** of *Subtropical Speculations* (Sarasota: Pineapple Press, 1991), an anthology of stories by Florida science-fiction writers. Poetry editors **Donald Morrill** and **Kathryn Van Spanckeren** are both poets of considerable prominence. The student literary magazine at Tampa University is called *Quilt* and publishes student writing. The University of Tampa has an active creative-writing program and sponsors a series of lectures and readings by outstanding authors.

One of Florida's nine public universities, the University of South Florida (USF) was founded in 1956 and opened to students in the fall of 1960. It was the first major state university in America purposely planned and built entirely in this century; it is also Florida's first state university located in a major metropolitan center. The USF campuses, forming a string of anchor points for a metropolitan area rapidly becoming a megalopolis along the west coast of Florida, are within reach of more than two million people — roughly one sixth of the state's population — in the 15-county area they serve. The Tampa campus has about 23,000 students; other campuses are located in St. Petersburg, Lakeland, Fort Myers, and Sarasota; New College in Sarasota, formerly a private liberal-arts college, became a part of USF in 1975 but retains its distinctive academic program and the status of an honors college.

The library of the main campus houses the collection of the Florida Historical Society, probably the most complete and varied selection of works concerning the state and its history that is available. The library possesses the Hampton Dunn Collection of Florida books, as well as a number of photographs that **Hampton Dunn** used in his *Florida, A Pictorial History* (Norfolk, VA: Donning Co., 1988). The University of South Florida sponsors the annual Florida Suncoast Writers' Conference, held each February on its St. Petersburg campus. The English department offers several courses in writing and an M.A. in creative writing. Annual fiction, poetry, and science-fiction contests are open to USF students. There is also a writers' guild which meets periodically on campus.

Several present and former members of the USF faculty have produced literary and scholarly works of considerable consequence. **Wesley Ford Davis,** who was born near Orlando in 1921, left Florida and did not return until 1964, when he joined the University of South Florida English department. His short stories have rural southern settings, and some are science-fiction and fantasy. His most important work was *The Time of the Panther* (New York: Harper, 1958), a novel about a young man coming of age in the woods of central Florida. Retired from the faculty, Davis now lives in Temple Terrace.

341

Kenneth Kay (1915-1990), born in Atlanta, came to Florida in 1966 after an eventful career in the U.S. Air Force. He joined the English faculty in 1969 and taught advanced expository writing until shortly before his death. He was a prolific writer of short stories, which were published in such periodicals as *The Saturday Evening Post, Country Gentleman, Argosy*, and others. His novels include *Trouble in the Air* (1959), *The Chengtu Strain* (1976), *Disposable People* (1986), *The Man Who Must Not Die* (1987), and, with **Marshall Goldberg**, *The Anatomy Lesson* (1974).

Among those members of the present English faculty who have written about Florida are the following:

Virginia Anderson, affiliated with the English department as a teaching assistant, has written two novels about horses and horseracing: *King of the Roses* (1983) and *Blood Lies* (1989). Her latest novel is a murder mystery set in south Florida's Big Cypress country, *Storm Front* (New York: Bantam-Doubleday, 1992). She has also written two romances, using the pseudonym **Megan Ashe**: *A Mountain Man* (1983) and *The Lightning Touch* (1984).

Edgar W. Hirshberg, recently retired but still active in literary pursuits, has written two critical biographies: *George Henry Lewes* (1970) and *John D. MacDonald* (Boston: Twayne, 1985). He has also been publisher and editor of The *JDM Bibliophile* since 1978, a journal about John D. MacDonald and related subjects, under the auspices of the English department. He was co-founder of the Florida Suncoast Writers' Conference with adjunct professor **Doris Enholm** and St. Petersburg publisher **Marjorie Schuck** and has been its director or co-director since its inception in 1973.

Hans Juergensen of the humanities department is a distinguished poet and teacher. Born in Upper Silesia, Germany, in 1919, he came to Tampa in 1961 after beginning his academic career in New England, subsequent to his eventful stint in the U.S. armed forces during World War II following his escape from the Nazis. He has lectured and read widely and is the recipient of many honors and awards. His books include *I Feed You From My Cup* (1958), *In Need For Names* (1961), *Existential Canon and other Poems* (1965), *Florida Montage* (Fort Smith, AR: South and West, 1966), *Sermons From the Ammunition Hatch of the Ship of Fools* (1968), *From the Divide* (1970, 1972, 1973), *Hebraic Modes* (1972), *Journey Toward the Roots* (1976), *Major General George Henry Thomas, A Summary in Perspective* (1980), and *The Record of a Green Planet* (1982). Other works and collections include a translation of **Heinrich Kleist**'s blank-verse drama, *The Broken Jug* (1977), published along with Juergensen's long narrative poem, *The Autobiography of a Pretender*; *California Frescoes* (1980), a collection of poems with drawings; *Roma* (1986), seven poems and drawings about Rome; *Fire Tested* (1983), poems about the Old Testament prophets; *Beach Heads and Mountains* (1984), poems and drawings about World War II.

Ilse Juergensen, who was born in Frankfurt, Germany, came to Tampa in 1961 with her author-husband, Hans Juergensen. Her writings include *Confessions and Experiments* (1960), *The Second Time* (1972), *I Don't Want a Thunderbird Anymore* (1977), and *Thunderbird and New Poems* (1980). She has published poems in many magazines and has won several first prizes in Florida writing competitions and in national contests.

Robert Pawlowski, a professor of English, was chosen last year by poet/critic/translator John Ashbery as one of three Florida artists for a one-month residency at La Napoule Foundation in France, sponsored by a full scholarship from the Atlantic Center for the Arts. His latest collection is entitled *Gulf Coast* (1989), a selection of his poems about Florida. He has written two other chapbooks, *Ceremonies for Today* (1972) and *The Seven Sacraments* (1982).

Willie Duane Reader is a distinguished and prolific poet whose works have appeared in such periodicals as The *Nation*, The *Canadian Forum*, The *Madison Review*, The *Mississippi Review*, *Negative Capability*, *Poet Lore*, *Epos*, *Webster Review*, *Sparrow*, *Bitterroot*, *White Mule*, and many others.

Rick Wilber is director of student publications and a member of the mass communications department. He has published over a thousand newspaper and magazine articles and dozens of poems and short stories, both in this country and abroad. He edits *Fiction Quarterly*, the *Tampa Tribune*'s literary supplement, which has been a good market for area fiction writers. He is particularly interested in science-fiction and was co-editor with **Richard Mathews** of the University of Tampa of *Subtropical Speculations* (Sarasota: Pineapple Press, 1991), an anthology of Florida-themed science-fiction.

Other Tampa authors include **Hampton Dunn** (1916-), a highly respected authority on Florida history and president of the prestigious Florida Historical Society. Although he has never taken a college degree, he has honorary Ph.D.'s from the University of Tampa and Tampa College. Born in rural Floral City in nearby Citrus County, he started his career in journalism in high school and never stopped. After a stint as a public-relations officer during World War II, he returned to the *Tampa Times*, where he was a roving reporter and became managing editor. He worked for a time as a Miami TV commentator but returned to his beloved Tampa to become public-relations director of the Peninsula AAA, now the AAA Auto Club South, where he rose to senior

Hampton Dunn

vice president and editor of the *Florida Explorer* magazine. Meanwhile he wrote well over a dozen books about Florida's history and folklore, beginning with *Re-discover Florida* (Miami: Hurricane House, 1969). He wrote several richly illustrated histories of Florida's cities, including *Yesterday's Tampa* (1972), *Yesterday's St. Petersburg* (1973), *Yesterday's Clearwater* (1973), and *Yesterday's Tallahassee* (1974), all published by E.A. Seemann Publishing Company of Miami. His *Yesterday's Lakeland* was published by the city of Lakeland in 1976. Some of his other books are *Florida Sketches* (Miami: Seemann Publishing Co., 1974); *Wish you Were Here: A Grand Tour of Early Florida Via Old Post Cards* (St. Petersburg: Byron Kennedy & Co., 1981); *Florida: A Pictorial History* (Norfolk, VA: Donning Co., 1988); and *Florida Courthouses* (Norfolk, VA: Donning Co., 1991). Dunn is well known as a speaker throughout Florida and as a generous giver of his time and expertise. The list of his honors and awards in recognition of his services and activities runs a full column in *Who's Who in America,* and his contributions to the interest and excitement in the study of Florida history are beyond measure.

Silvia Curbelo is a young poet who has received fellowships from the National Education Association, Florida Arts Council, and the Cintas Foundation. Her poetry and short prose have been published in such magazines as *Shenandoah, Indiana Review, Southern Poetry Review, Exquisite Corpse,* and others. Her poetry collection, *The Geography of Leaving* (1991), won the 1990 Gerald Cable Chapbook Competition.

Dionisio D. Martinez has written numerous poems concerning Florida and many other places in his two collections, *Dancing at the Chelsea* (1992), winner of the 1991 State Street Press Chapbook Award, and *History As A Second Language* (1992), winner of the Ohio State University Press/*The Journal* Award in poetry. He has published poems in such periodicals as *Kenyon Review, American Poetry Review,* and *Iowa Review.*

James E. Tockley, Sr., has written an epic poem about the history of Tampa and Hillsborough County entitled *Espiritu Santo.* It begins with an account of Estevenico, a black man who accompanied the explorer Narvaez when he set foot in Tampa in 1528, and traces the area's history to the present. It was buried in a time capsule on the occasion of Tampa's centennial celebration. Tockley's *O St. Regent* (1982) is a collection of his poems about life in Tampa, with emphasis on the black community.

John R. Feegel, born in Middletown, Connecticut, in 1932, has degrees in both law and medicine and has had a career in forensic pathology. He was chief medical examiner for Hillsborough County in the 1970s and a professor of pathology at the University of South Florida. His first novel, *Autopsy* (New York: Avon, 1975), won the Mystery Writers of America Edgar Award for the best mystery paperback of 1975 and sold over 600,000 copies. His next, *Death Sails the Bay* (New York: Avon, 1978), concerned a series of murders that occurred on the seemingly peaceful shores of Tampa Bay in southern Hillsborough County. *Malpractice* (1981),and *The Dance Card* (1981) move into rural Georgia and Atlanta for more heroics by forensic pathologists in their efforts to discover the truth about how people are murdered. Feegel's most recent novel, *Not a Stranger* (New York: New American Library, 1982), tells the story of a sexual psychopath who has homosexual liaisons with small black boys and eventually kills them, under circumstances similar to those prevailing in Atlanta, where Feegel was assistant chief medical examiner. He is now practicing law in Tampa and working on another novel in his spare time.

Aubrey Hampton, cosmetic chemist and herbalist, is founder and publisher of *Organica Quarterly*, a highly regarded magazine of arts and activism with a circulation of over 200,000. His biographical drama about Bernard Shaw, *GBS & Company* (1989), was nominated for the Barnard Hewitt Theater Award and the George Freedley Memorial Award in 1990. His second book, *Wolf Trilogy* (1991), includes a preface on wolves and interviews with people at Wolf Park in Indiana. His *Mixed Blood*, a play about the AIDS virus, has been produced in Tampa and Portland, Oregon; Hampton has written and/or directed several other dramas.

Elaine Fantle Shimberg has published numerous articles and several books in the field of health, medicine, and the art and business of being a writer. Her books include *How To Be A Successful Housewife/Writer* (1979); *Two for the Money: A Woman's Guide to a Double-Career Marriage* (1981), with **Dore Beach**; *Coping with Kids and Vacation* (1983), with **Linda Albert**; *Relief from I.B.S.: Irritable Bowel Syndrome* (1988); *Strokes; What Families Should Know* (1990); and *Depression: What Families Should Know* (1992).

Though not a native of Florida, the eminent African-American educator and civil rights leader, **Benjamin Elijah Mays** (1895-1984), spent critical years in Tampa from 1926 to 1928. As executive director of the Tampa Urban League, he battled daily with a city reluctant to face the consequences of its racism. He designed and wrote one of the earliest black self-studies of urban living conditions, a mimeographed monograph that was never officially published, entitled *A Study of Negro Life in Tampa* (1927). Frequently cited by historians, the work examines the many aspects of black life, such as available jobs and housing conditions, that contributed to the second-class quality of black existence in the city. His autobiography, *Born to Rebel* (New York: Scribner's, 1971), is an excellent example of a rags-to-riches story in the tradition of Ben Franklin, combined with the tale of harsh, racially created obstacles to overcome, similar to autobiographical works by Frederick Douglass, W.E.B. DuBois, and Booker T. Washington. The story of his Tampa years is especially poignant, a frightening narrative of life in a racist southern city. Mays was a gentle but firm teacher, a former president of Morehouse College in Atlanta, and a mentor to Dr. Martin Luther King, Jr. He was critical both of whites who held or wished to impose racist beliefs on minorities and of black extremists who, he felt, also espoused racist beliefs.

English novelist **Alec Waugh** (1898-1981), who is best-known for *Hot Countries* (1930), *Island in the Sun* (1955), and *A Family of Islands* (1964), lived at 717 Bungalow Terrace from 1980 until he died at Tampa General Hospital on September 3, 1981.

Among the novels set in Tampa are **Vincent H. Aguero**'s *Two Promises To Keep* (New York: Exposition Press, 1965); **William Ard**'s *Mr. Trouble* (New York: Rinehart, 1955); **George Ryland Bailey**'s *Tampa Boy* (Chicago: Apsley House,

1971) about the city between 1912 and 1916; **Carol Balizet's** *The Seven Last Years* (Lincoln, VA: Chosen Books, 1978); **T. Ernesto Bethancourt's** *New York City Too Far From Tampa Blues* (New York: Holiday House, 1975); **Wyatt Blassingame's** *The Golden Geyser* (New York: Doubleday, 1961) about the development of Davis Island; **Gil Brewer's** *The Three Way Split* (Greenwich, CT: Fawcett, 1960); **Hugh Cleverley's** *Reunion in Florida* (New York: Penguin, 1955) under the pseudonym **Tod Claymore; Mignon Eberhart's** *Another Man's Murder* (New York: Random House, 1957); **Jesse Hill Ford's** *The Feast of St. Barnabas* (Boston: Little, Brown, 1969), where Ormond City may be a disguised Tampa; **James Noble Gifford's** *Two in Tampa* (1954) and *Let's Sit in the Sun* (1955), both under the pseudonym **Carol Holliston**, and *Winter Sun* (1956), under the pseudonym **Gay Rutherford**, all published by New York's Arcadia House; **Freida Greene's** *Within These Walls* (New York: Exposition Press, 1956); **Irene Hunt's** *The Lottery Rose* (New York: Scribner's Sons, 1976); **Patricia Matthews'** *Flames of Glory* (New York: Bantam, 1982); **Thomas Patrick McMahon's** *Jink* (New York: Simon & Schuster, 1971); **May McNeer's** *Bloomsday For Maggie* (Boston: Houghton, Mifflin, 1976); **Stephen Ransome's** *I'll Die For You* (Garden City, NY: Doubleday, 1959); **Margaret Reynolds's** *Wintergreen* (New York: Vantage, 1970); **Mary Stolz's** *Go and Catch a Flying Fish* (New York: Harper & Row, 1979); **Donald Tracy's** *The Big Blackout* (New York: Detective Book Club, 1959); **Anthony C. West's** *The Trend Is Up* (New York: Random House, 1960), where Tampa is disguised as a city called Maramee; and **Kathy Willis's** *Tropical Thunder* (New York: Kensington Publishing Corp., 1992). The last writer, Kathy Willis, is quoted as saying something that many writers have felt: "Florida has everything in its past. Pirates. Indians. Swashbuckling explorers. Why are historical romances never written about Florida?"

Finally, the well-known Georgia poet, **Sidney Lanier** (1842-1881), stayed at the Orange Grove Hotel at 806 Madison Street when he came to town in 1877 to try to regain his failing health; his poem, "Tampa Robins," which probably symbolized what Florida meant to many, especially those from the cold North, began with lines contrasting the two climates: "The robin laughed in the orange-tree:/'Ho, windy North, a fig for thee.'"

For a history of the city see *Tampa, Yesterday, Today, & Tomorrow* (Tampa: Mishler and King, 1981) by **Michael Bane** and **Mary Ellen Moore;** *Tampa* (St. Petersburg: St. Petersburg Printing Co., 1950) by **Karl H. Grismer;** *Tampa: The Treasure City* (Tulsa, OK: Continental Heritage Press, 1983) by **Gary R. Mormino** and **Anthony P. Pizzo;** *Tampa Town, 1824-1886: The Cracker Village with a Latin Accent* (Miami: Hurricane House, 1968) by **Anthony P. Pizzo;** and *Tampa That Was* (Boynton Beach, FL: Star Publishing Co., 1973) by **Evanell Klintworth Powell.** *Urban Vigilantes in the New South: Tampa, 1882-1936* (Knoxville, TN: University of Tennessee Press, 1988) by **Robert P. Ingalls** deals with the city's political and labor history. For more personal recollections of the city see *The Tampa of My Childhood, 1897-1907* (Tampa: Sylvia Dean Harbert, 1966) by **Susie Kelly Dean.** For some fine photographs of the older city see **Hampton Dunn's** *Yesterday's Tampa* (Miami: Seemann Publishing Co., 1977) and *Tampa: A Pictorial History* (Norfolk, VA: Donning Co., 1985). **Robert**

E. Snyder and Jack B. Moore's *Pioneer Commercial Photography* (Gainesville: University Press of Florida, 1992) is about Tampa's famous Burgert Brothers and their photography studio. Dunn's *WDAE - Florida's Pioneer Radio Station* (Tampa: Fort Brooke Press, 1972) is about an early Tampa radio station, the first one in Florida to begin broadcasting, having been licensed in 1922. For a description and history of the Hillsborough River and its importance to Tampa see *River of the Golden Ibis* (New York: Holt, Rinehart and Winston, 1973) by Gloria Jahoda.

Among other bookish footnotes in Tampa, a short documentary entitled *U.S. Cavalry Supplies Unloading at Tampa, Florida* (1898) was the first action-picture known to have been filmed on location in Florida.

The Tampa Writers Alliance is a "self-help, educational support group for aspiring and published writers" numbering over 100 members. Monthly meetings take place on the first Wednesday at 7:00 p.m. in the auditorium of the main branch of the Tampa Public Library downtown on Ashley Street.

Randall W. Polk, 9808 North Fifty-fourth Street, Temple Terrace, FL 33617, publishes a newsletter for area writers called *Plexus*, which sponsors a "Struggling Screenwriter" contest with a $50 prize to the winner.

Clearwater

The probable explanation of the derivation of the city's name is the fact that Clearwater's wells produced clear, pure water rather than the usual smelly sulphur water characteristic of many other areas in the vicinity.

Author Natalie Savage Carlson (1906-) was born in Winchester, Virginia, but has lived in Clearwater since 1972. She began writing professionally as a reporter for California's *Long Beach Morning Sun* (1927-1929), is the author of over 30 children's books, has won two awards in The *New York Herald Tribune* Children's Spring Book Festivals for *The Talking Cat* (1952) and *Alphonse, That Bearded One* (1954), has won Honor Book Awards for *Wings against the Wind* (1955) and *Hortense: The Cow for a Queen* (1957), was named the runner-up for the prestigious Newbery medal in 1959 for *The Family under the Bridge*, and was nominated as the U.S. candidate for the International Hans Christian Andersen Award in 1966. Since her move to Florida she has written *Marie Louise and Christophe* (1974), *Marie Louise's Heyday* (1975), *Runaway Marie Louise* (1977), *Jaky or Dodo?* (1978), *Time for the White Egret* (1978), and *King of the Cats and Other Tales* (1980).

Fiction set in Clearwater includes Jean Detra's *A Happy Ending* (New York: Simon & Schuster, 1967); Bill Granger's *Schism* (New York: Crown, 1981); Michael Largo's *Southern Comfort* (New York: New Earth Books, 1977); John D. MacDonald's *One More Sunday* (New York: Knopf, 1984); Myra Porter Phillips's *Bubble Eyes* (Rockford, IL: Bellevue Books, 1953); and Stephen Ransome's *Alias His Wife* (New York: Dodd, Mead, 1965). Hampton Dunn's *Yesterday's Clearwater* (Miami: Seemann Publishing Co., 1973) has photographs and text about the history of the town. Jon Atack's *A Piece of Blue Sky* (New York: Carol Publishing Group, 1990) is about the Church of Scientology, which established a base in Clearwater.

SCIENCE FICTION IN FLORIDA

RICK WILBER and RICHARD MATHEWS

Piers Anthony, Ben Bova, Martin Caidin, Joe Haldeman, Damon Knight, Walter M. Miller, Andre Norton, Kate Wilhelm. This brief litany of science fiction and fantasy superstars is a short list of some of the field's major contemporary authors who have lived and written in Florida. While the Sunshine State has been undeniably blessed with bounteous gifts of climate and nature, it has also basked in a constant glow from the abundant riches of the speculative literary imaginations of its distinguished authors. And not only have an impressive number of science fiction's literary lights chosen Florida as their home, they have also chosen to write about many aspects of the state in their fiction. Two of the most dramatic examples are Piers Anthony and Joe Haldeman. Anthony's Xanth series, one of the most popular fantasy series of all time, locates its fantastic geography on a map based on the state. Anthony, who delights in puns, includes such landmarks as Lake Ogre-chobee and Lake Wails. Anthony has further cemented his link to the state by recently placing a large collection of his drafts and manuscripts in the Special Collections Library at the University of South Florida in Tampa.

Haldeman has celebrated the state in his Hugo Award novella *The Hemingway Hoax* as well as other novels, short stories and poems. *The Hemingway Hoax* is double-fun in a sense, since it not only is set in Florida, but also celebrates another of Florida's most famous literary residents, Ernest Hemingway, who lived part of his life in Key West.

These are merely two of the most conspicuous examples, but there are literally hundreds. While editing our anthology of Florida science fiction, *Subtropical Speculations* (Pineapple Press, 1991) we read dozens of stories before selecting 16 of the ones we liked best which featured Florida settings. All of the submissions were written by authors who have lived and written in the state, and we barely scratched the surface.

In fact, there seems to be something irresistible about the state which has appealed to science fiction writers almost from the beginning of the genre. Jules Verne, the prolific and popular French author who helped establish the shape and the market for science fiction with classics including *20,000 Leagues under the Sea* and *Around the World in 80 Days*, launched one of his most famous science-fiction novels, *From the Earth to the Moon*, from Florida.

The lush, mysterious, subtropical setting combined with the newness of the state to make it a place ripe with possibility, a future state. These elements appealed to Verne, and have struck a similar responsive chord for contemporary writers. Florida is a land of contradictions and conflicts, a place filled with natural appeal to writers who are, of course, interested in conflict and in the resolution of conflict. In the Florida of Verne's day, settlers and New World explorers were pushing into a frontier Florida where fiercely independent Seminoles lurked in swampy jungles and where one might encounter that primitive descendent of the dinosaur, the Florida alligator. Today the old and new continue to contribute to the state's unique identity. Florida is the site of the nation's oldest city of St. Augustine, and the place from which the nation's latest new world city, the space station, will be launched. It is a place where teeming, ancient swamps bump up against glistening new condominiums, and where nature and technology teeter in delicate balance. Florida is a bellwether for many of the global threats: overpopulation, endangered species, threatened water supply, global warming (Florida will likely be one of the first places under water, since so much of the state is at or below sea level.)

Science fiction writers, we think, have found the state interesting because its very diversity mirrors the diversity of imagination among the writers themselves. Some are writing hard, extrapolative science-fiction, and find the Kennedy Space Center and the NASA programs a natural focus for their interests. Some are writing wide-open fantasy, and for these Florida offers its own array of images as a fantasy playground, from theme parks to sunshine-and-beach daydreams. The state provides a wide array of memorable settings as well as a wonderful place to live and work.

It's no wonder then that so many writers concerned with vision and the future should have taken root in Florida's soil. This state of contrasts and conflicts affords contact with both a primordial past and the cutting-edge perspectives of future possibilities. Life at the edge has a special excitement and delight with a universal human appeal, and here in Florida the cutting edges are everywhere to be found. Science has found great interest in the point where sea meets land, a critical edge where life made an evolutionary leap from sea to land and began the march toward human being. Florida's long coastline has extended an open invitation to the human imagination to take another leap forward and outward through the fecund literary imaginations of the great science fiction and fantasy writers who have called the state their home.

Rick Wilber is a journalism professor at the University of South Florida in Tampa who has had dozens of science-fiction short stories published in the genre's top magazines and anthologies. He also edits Fiction Quarterly, the Tampa Tribune's *short-story and poetry supplement.*

Richard Mathews is chair of the Department of English and Writing at the University of Tampa and is a noted science fiction critic and biographer and the author of several critical books on the field. His science fiction and experimental poetry appear widely in magazines, including Star*Line.

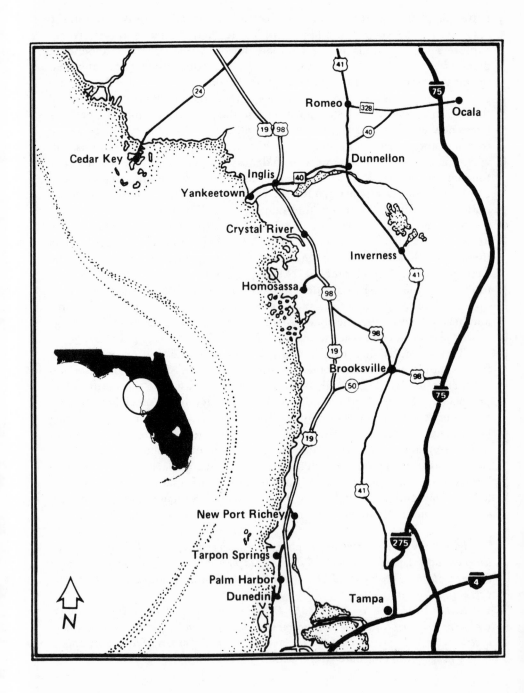

(Map for northern portion of this section on p. 365)

350

9 DUNEDIN TO PANACEA

KEVIN M. McCARTHY

DUNEDIN TO CEDAR KEY

Dunedin

Like many Florida cities, Dunedin offers the visitor the unexpected: from its name, which is Gaelic for Edinburgh, Scotland, the name bestowed on it by two Scotsmen in the late nineteenth century, to the fact that this city was the site of the first development of concentrated orange juice. Part of a fast-growing area of Florida, Dunedin and other towns stretching up toward Cedar Key offer a nearness to the Gulf of Mexico, temperate climate, less congestion and crime than south Florida, and access to huge tracts of protected wilderness. Among the growing number of settlers have been some distinguished writers.

Erskine Caldwell (1903-1987), author of *Tobacco Road* (1932) and *God's Little Acre* (1933), lived in Dunedin from 1968 to 1977. He was born in Moreland, Georgia, and worked at various odd jobs ranging from soda jerk to gunrunner; he was also a scriptwriter in Hollywood and reported from Mexico, Spain, Czechoslovakia, Russia, and China as a correspondent for the *Atlanta Journal*. While living in Florida, he wrote *Summertime Island* (1968), *The Weather Shelter* (1969), *The Earnshaw Neighborhood* (1972), *Annette* (1973), and *Afternoons in Mid-America* (1976). Caldwell, who lived at 1831 Oak Creek Drive in the Spanish Oaks subdivision, described in his autobiography how he enjoyed his Florida home, although he had difficulty adjusting to the rapidly growing foliage on his land: "All summer long I was constantly trimming and pruning the viburnum, often on a stepladder and sometimes wearing a raincoat during the afternoon thunderstorms, in an effort to keep the overnight growth from shooting higher than my head."

Caldwell is one of many scribes who, while not really Florida authors since they don't write much about their adopted state, find conditions here conducive to their writing. He once noted in an interview, "I'm not exactly a Southerner or I'm not a Floridian; I'm not a Georgian; I'm not anything you can name or pin down because I have lived everywhere and I like everywhere I've lived." In 1982, he enjoyed a resurgence of interest in his works when New American Library marked the fiftieth anniversary of *Tobacco Road* by issuing its paperback revision along with *God's Little Acre*. After leaving Florida, he and his wife moved to Arizona, where he died in 1987.

351

Two other Dunedin residents deserve mention. Jazz pianist Ivory "Dwike" Mitchell Jr. (1930-), who went on to team up with horn player Willie Henry Ruff, Jr. of Sheffield, Alabama, to form an acclaimed popular jazz duo, grew up in Dunedin, as recounted in a profile by **William Zinsser**. Mitchell's father, a garbage-truck driver for the city, found a discarded piano, brought it home, and set it up for his little boy to play with. Little Dwike went on to become one of this century's most acclaimed jazz pianists and a member of "the oldest continuous group in jazz without personnel changes." He spent many a Sunday playing piano in the Shiloh Missionary Baptist Church in Dunedin right across from the Chase Memorial School, which he attended as a child. He later attended Pinellas High School at 1220 Palmetto Street in Clearwater before joining the army and beginning his successful career. The other resident, Dr. **Willis Stanley Blatchley**, who moved to Dunedin in 1913 and had a home on the northwest corner of Bayshore Drive and Lee Street, built a platform in a huge live-oak tree on his property and wrote *My Nature Nook, or Notes on the Natural History of the Vicinity of Dunedin, Florida* (Indianapolis: Nature Publishing Co., 1931). For a history of the town see **W. Lovett Douglas**'s *History of Dunedin* (St. Petersburg, FL: Great Outdoors Publishing Co., 1965).

Palm Harbor

Just north of Dunedin is the site of a would-be-novel-in-search-of-an-author. Near the little town of Ozona (a name that replaced Yellow Bluff because the latter seemed too close to Yellow Fever and because Ozona has the connotation of healthy, gulf breezes) is the town of Palm Harbor. Its original name, Sutherland, honored the late-nineteenth-century Duke of Sutherland and was given to the town in 1888 by real estate developers who had hopes of a large financial investment from the duke. When he did not come through with the money, the promoters changed the name to the more Florida-sounding Palm Harbor. The duke was a nobleman who had abandoned his family in England, migrated to Florida, built a little house on 30 acres overlooking a lake near Tarpon Springs, and lived there with the woman he loved, a commoner from London. They were married in the small Episcopal church in Dunedin around 1888 soon after his wife died in England. The small body of water nearby, Sutherland Bayou, honors them to this day.

Tarpon Springs

Just west of U.S. 19 seven miles north of Dunedin is a little bit of Greece, or at least what we imagine a Greek town to be like. Tarpon Springs is named for the tarpon found in Florida waters. One of the points that **Beth Dunlop** makes in her *Florida's Vanishing Architecture* (Sarasota: Pineapple Press, 1987) is that fishing villages like Tarpon Springs have transformed themselves into tacky re-creations of what they used to be — all for the tourist dollar. Of more creative interest than the Greek restaurants and sponge shops is the Universalist Church on Grand Boulevard, which displays paintings by George Inness, Jr. (1854-1926), who worshiped in the church and painted many of his famous works in Tarpon Springs from 1897 to 1926; he was the son of George Inness, the famous American landscape artist.

Another church in town is St. Nicholas Greek Orthodox Cathedral at 30 North Pinellas Avenue, which has many Greek features; its painting, "Halo of St. Nicholas," has attracted many visitors because it seems to shed tears. The church sponsors the annual Greek Cross Ceremony on January 6, the feast of Epiphany; a Greek Orthodox priest throws a golden cross into the waters, and many of the children dive for it and for the momentary fame and good luck the retriever may earn. **Kathryn Vinson**'s *The Luck of the Golden Cross* (Philadelphia: Lippincott, 1960) is a novel about that ceremony and about sponging in the gulf.

Lois Lenski

Children's book author **Lois Lenski** (1893-1974) was born in Springfield, Ohio, and lived many winters in Tarpon Springs at 201 Roosevelt Avenue where she died on September 11, 1974. The author and illustrator of almost 100 of her own books and illustrator of more than 50 books by other writers, she won several awards, including the 1946 Newbery Medal for most distinguished contribution to literature for American children for *Strawberry Girl* (Philadelphia: Lippincott, 1945), a novel set on a strawberry farm in rural Florida. *Florida, My Florida* (Tallahassee: Friends of the Library, Florida State University, 1971) contains some of the poems she wrote about her adopted state. Other works by Lenski include *Bayou Suzette* (1943), *Judy's Journey* (1947), *Houseboat Girl* (1957), *Coal Camp Girl* (1959), *The Life I Live: Collected Poems* (1965), and *We Live in the North* (1965). She pointed out in her writing that an outsider to a region, as she was to Florida, had the advantage of being objective and aware of the idiosyncracies (whether in speech or action) of local residents.

For more about the town see **Gertrude Stoughton's** *Tarpon Springs, Florida, The Early Years* (New Port Richey, FL: Tri-Arts Studio, 1975); **Michel G. Emmanuel's** *Tarpon Springs Sketch Book* (Tampa: Book One, 1974); **Eileen** and **Lou Rozee's** *Sponge Docks, Tarpon Springs, Florida: "America's Sponge Diving Birthplace"* (Tarpon Springs, FL: Rozee, 1973); **R.F. Pent's** *History of Tarpon Springs* (St. Petersburg: Great Outdoors Publishing Co., 1964); and **George Theodore Frantzis's** *Strangers at Ithaca, The Story of the Spongers of Tarpon Springs* (St. Petersburg: Great Outdoors Publishing Co., 1962). **William E.D. Scott's** *The Story of a Bird Lover* (New York: Outlook Co., 1903) contains a vivid description of the slaughter of plumed birds south of Tarpon Springs, as well as an excellent account of Florida bird life from 1875 to 1895 by the curator of ornithology at Princeton University.

Among the novels set in this area are **Joseph Auslander** and **Audrey Wurdemann's** *The Islanders* (New York: Longmans, Green, 1951), describing the conflicts between the old Greek culture and the American system; **Charles M. Blackford's** *Deep Treasure* (Philadelphia: Winston, 1954), recounting the first use of a diving suit to collect sponges; **Peggy Gaddis's** *Nurse With a Dream* (New York: Arcadia House, 1963); **Elia Kazan's** *Acts of Love* (New York: Knopf, 1978), portraying a woman who disrupts the lives of a Greek family; **Alistair MacLean's** *Fear Is the Key* (Garden City, NY: Doubleday, 1961), based on an elaborate plot to use a bathyscaphe to recover treasure from a downed plane; **Don Tracy's** *Bazzaris* (New York: Ravenna Books/Trident Press, 1965), about the failing sponge industry, and his *Honk If You've Found Jesus* (New York: Putnam, 1974), concerning land development; and **Mildred Woodall's** *Sally Sponge and Sammy Seahorse* (New York: Greenwich, 1955) and *Susie Starfish and Peter Porpoise* (New York: Greenwich, 1955), two children's books.

Edwin Granberry, whose novel *The Erl King* (New York: Macaulay, 1930) tells about a young man who grows up at nearby Anclote, wrote a short story, "A Trip to Czardis," that takes place in a Florida Greek town similar to Tarpon Springs; originally published in 1932, it won the O. Henry Memorial Prize and is in such collections as *Florida Stories* (Gainesville: University of Florida Press, 1989) edited by **Kevin McCarthy**. It prompted so much interest among readers over time that 34 years later Granberry wrote a novel of the same name (New York: Trident Press, 1966) that explained why the protagonist in the short story was about to be executed. A full-length movie about spongers at Tarpon Springs was *16 Fathoms Deep* (1948).

One final anecdote about the town that shows the ingenuity of Tarponites: In 1910, the waterworks director cleaned out the city's drains by sending an alligator through the drain pipes. Attached to the gator's neck was a chain with a brush at one end; when the gator reached the end of the drain pipe, his handler pulled him back out, and the drain was cleaned.

New Port Richey

Originally settled by sea captain Aaron Richey, who gave his name to the site, this town's Chasco Fiesta each spring honors the Calusa Indians who once lived in the area. The Calusa play a part in *Their Number Become Thinned* by **Henry F. Dobyns** (Knoxville, TN: University of Tennessee, 1983), a work that describes the Florida Indian population just before the Europeans arrived to begin the long, systematic dispersal/extinction of the natives.

Among the writers attracted to this area and instrumental in letting others know about its climate and facilities were Irvin S. Cobb, Hal Lanigan, Ring Lardner, and Grantland Rice. Those writers' works attracted movie stars like Mary Pickford, Gloria Swanson, and Ed Wynn. For a description of early Pasco County and its settlers see *Tales of West Pasco* by **Ralph Bellwood** (Hudson, FL: Albert J. Makovec, Printer, 1962). *West Pasco's Heritage* compiled by the West Pasco Historical Society (New Port Richey, FL: Lisa Printing, 1974) is a history that involves interviews with longtime residents. This area is the setting for the fictional town of Evergreen in **Rex Beach's** *The Mating Call* (New York: London, Harper & Brothers, 1927), the story of a World War I soldier who returns to find that his marriage has been annulled. New Port Richey is featured in *The Suncoast Past* edited by **Glen Dill** (New Port Richey, FL: Tri-Arts Studio, 1986?); this work is a collection of newspaper articles that Dill wrote for the *Suncoast News* and the *New Port Richey Chronicle* about the history of the area.

Novelist **Frank E. Smith** (1919-1984) moved to Florida from New York City in 1959 and lived in New Port Richey at 5566 Shady Acres Boulevard until his death. In his early career he worked in the Pentagon as head research analyst for the U.S. Navy, for the Joint Chiefs of Staff during World War II, and as an adviser to President Truman at the 1945 Potsdam Conference. When he started writing, he used the pseudonyms **Jonathan Craig** and **Jennifer Hale** to produce more than 100 mystery and western books and 300 short stories. Several of his novels, all gothics published under the name Jennifer Hale, have a Florida setting: *Stormhaven* (New York: Lancer Books, 1970); *House of Strangers* (New York: Prestige Books, 1972); *The House on Key Diablo* (New York: Ballantine, 1974); *Portrait of Evil* (New York: Ballantine, 1975); and *Beyond the Dark* (New York: Berkley Publishing Group, 1978).

Highway U.S. 19 has rightfully garnered its share of bad press. One author noted that on U.S. 19 "north of New Port Richey it is possible to see what Florida is becoming everywhere — an incessant cacophony of strip shopping centers and signs, bowling alleys, supermarkets, drug stores, discount stores all sitting behind vast asphalt parking lots." Bumper stickers proclaiming "I drove on U.S. 19 — and lived" attest to the feelings of many local residents.

The highway runs along the coast, joining towns that continue to attract newcomers, and parallels one of the earliest European paths in *La Florida*: that of Spanish explorer Pánfilo de Narváez. In 1528, Narváez (1480-1528) landed with soldiers and colonists at present-day Tampa Bay and marched north to a place called Apalachen, where, according to some local Indians, lay much gold and "everything that we at all cared for." Two months later, after losing over 200 men on the trip, Narváez reached Apalachen near present-day Tallahassee but found only hostile Indians. The survivors of the march abandoned the land and set out to sea on makeshift rafts, but only 15 made it to the Texas coast.

After more years of wandering throughout the Southwest, covering some 3,000 miles, five survivors straggled into Mexico and eventually returned to Spain. One of the five, **Álvar Núñez Cabeza de Vaca** (1490-1560), wrote a narrative of his adventures that inspired others to migrate to Florida. Two novels about him in Florida are **Jeannette Mirsky**'s *The Gentle Conquistadors* (New York: Pantheon, 1969) and **Frank Slaughter**'s *Apalachee Gold* (New York: Ace, 1954). Nonfiction works about him are **Jose B. Fernandez**'s *Álvar Núñez Cabeza de Vaca, The Forgotten Chronicler* (Miami: Ediciones Universal, 1975) and **Cleve Hallenbeck**'s *Álvar Núñez Cabeza de Vaca: The Journey and Route of the First European to Cross the Continent of North America, 1534-1536* (Glendale, CA: Arthur H. Clark Company, 1940), which contains a paraphrase in English of Cabeza de Vaca's work, first published in Spanish in 1542.

Another Spanish explorer, Hernando de Soto (1496?-1542), landed in Florida in 1538 and followed a path similar to that of Narváez ten years earlier. De Soto also searched for gold and silver in north Florida, but found none. He eventually headed west to the Mississippi River and Louisiana, died in 1542, and was interred in the Mississippi. On his trek through Florida his troops happened upon a brown, tattooed man who moved like an Indian but turned out to be a Spanish Christian captured by the Indians several years before:

> When Baltasar de Gallegos came into the open field, he discovered ten or eleven Indians, among whom was a Christian, naked and sun-burnt, his arms tattooed after their manner, and he in no respect differing from them. As soon as the horsemen came in sight, they ran upon the Indians, who fled, hiding themselves in a thicket, though not before two or three of them were overtaken and wounded. The Christian, seeing a horseman coming upon him with a lance, began to cry out: "Do not kill me, cavalier; I am a Christian! Do not slay these people; they have given me my life!"

The true story of that Christian, Juan Ortiz of Seville, is remarkable. He had been in a Spanish party sent out in 1528 to look for Pánfilo de Narváez when the latter did not return to Havana in the expected time. When Ortiz's Spanish party approached the shore, he and another crew member went by boat to see what they could find on the beach. Suddenly an Indian raiding party attacked them, killed Ortiz's companion, and took Ortiz to their camp, where they planned to kill him. The chief's daughter saved him from a cruel death, and he spent the next ten years working for the Indians as a menial laborer, learning their language and customs, and becoming familiar with the Tampa area. When de Soto rescued him in 1538, Ortiz joined the Spanish forces and acted as an interpreter on the trip north, but eventually died before returning to Spain. Ortiz's story is similar to that of Captain John Smith, whom Pocahontas supposedly rescued many years later in Virginia. Some, like Florida author Marjory Stoneman Douglas, have speculated that John Smith incorporated this Florida story into his own narrative.

While writer **Andrew Lytle** taught at the University of Florida (1948-61), he wrote "Ortiz's Mass" collected in *Florida Stories* edited by **Kevin McCarthy**

Andrew Lytle

(Gainesville: University of Florida Press, 1989). The short story emphasizes the drama and suspense of the Spaniard's adjustment to Indian ways and his later rescue by de Soto. Lytle's longer novel about de Soto is *At the Moon's Inn* (Indianapolis: Bobbs-Merrill, 1941; reprinted University of Alabama, 1990). **William O. Steele**'s *De Soto, Child of the Sun* (New York: Alladin Books, 1956) is another novel about Ortiz. Also see **Ignacio Avellaneda**'s *Los Sobrevivientes de la Florida: The Survivors of the De Soto Expedition* (Gainesville: P.K. Yonge Library of Florida History, 1990). For more about Ponce de León, Pánfilo de Narváez, and Hernando de Soto see **Lindsey Wilger Williams**'s *Boldly Onward* (Charlotte Harbor, FL: Precision Publishing Co., 1986).

Hernando County takes its name from Hernando de Soto, and for a while the county seat was De Soto, thus honoring both of his names. Naming a place after a person's first name is unusual in this country, although *America* is one of those exceptions. Another Florida county received the name De Soto in 1887, honoring the great explorer with two counties.

Brooksville

Brooksville, northeast of New Port Richey, is today the county seat of Hernando County and was named for Congressman Preston Brooks of South Carolina who during the 1856 Congressional debate on the Kansas-Nebraska Bill used his cane to strike a senator who had verbally attacked Brooks's uncle. For more about Brooksville and Hernando County see **Alfred A. McKethan**'s *Hernando County: Our Story* (Brooksville, FL: McKethan, 1989) and **Richard J. Stanaback**'s *A History of Hernando County, 1840-1976* (Brooksville, FL: Action '76 Steering Committee, 1976).

Local author **Keith Laumer** (1925-) was born in Syracuse, New York; educated at the universities of Indiana, Stockholm, and Illinois; served in the U.S. Army and Air Force; was in the Foreign Service as Vice-Consul and Third Secretary in Rangoon; and has lived in Brooksville for many years. He is the author of over 40 novels and 19 collections of short stories, mostly science fiction, including *Worlds of the Imperium* (1962), *Retief's War* (1966), *Galactic Odyssey* (1967), *Assignment in Nowhere* (1968), *Dinosaur Beach* (1971), *The Breaking Earth* (1981), and *Reward for Retief* (1989). His work, *The Monitors* (1966), was made into a 1969 movie of the same name starring Guy Stockwell and Susan Oliver, and his murder-mystery, *Dead Fall* (1971), was made into a 1975 movie, *Peeper*, starring Natalie Wood and Michael Caine. He once commented: "I have been asked if my work is 'relevant,' i.e., political propaganda. It is not. I prefer to treat themes that have been important to man ever since he became man, and will continue to be important as long as humanity remains: strength and courage, truth and beauty, loyalty and justice, ethics and integrity, kindness and gentleness, and many others."

Homosassa

The little town of Homosassa west of U.S. 98/19 takes its name, which may mean *a place where wild pepper grows*, from an old Seminole settlement there. Yulee Sugar Mill Ruins State Historic Site is on a 3,000-acre sugar plantation once owned by David Yulee (1810-1886), Florida's first U.S. Senator. The site is marked with interpretive signs that explain how workers manufactured sugarcane products for Southern troops during the Civil War. (Daily; 904/795-3817) David Yulee, or *Levy* as he was called for the first 35 years of his life, was the grandson of the Grand Vizier at Morocco and the son of Moses Levy, an early immigrant to Florida. Yulee built the Florida railroad between Fernandina on the Atlantic coast and Cedar Key on the Gulf of Mexico, a railroad that he finished in 1861 shortly before Union troops destroyed it. The nearby Homosassa Springs at the juncture of U.S. 19 and State Road 490 has boat trips, alligators, manatees, and an underwater observatory where freshwater and saltwater fish swim together. (Daily 9:30 a.m. to 5:30 p.m.; 904/628-2311) **W. Horace Carter** has a long description of the site in his *Nature's Masterpiece at Homosassa* (Tabor City, NC: Atlantic Publishing Co., 1981). A made-for-TV movie, *The Wilds of 10,000 Islands*, was filmed there in 1977. American artist Winslow Homer (1836-1910), who is best known for his paintings of the sea and the Civil War, visited Florida several times to fish and paint, especially around Key West, the St. Johns River, and Homosassa Springs. He visited the Homosassa area in 1904 and painted such works as "Channel Bass," "Palm Trees, Florida," "In the Jungle, Florida," "The Turkey Buzzard," "The Shell Heap," and "Homosassa Jungle in Florida." For more about him see *Winslow Homer in the Tropics* by **Patti Hannaway** (Richmond, VA: Westover Publishing, 1973).

This is a good place to mention one of Florida's most unusual and best-loved animals, the manatee. These lumbering giants of the underwater, which are actually more closely related to the aardvark and elephant than to the sea lion and walrus, may eventually become extinct because of their inability to escape the path of speedboats. **James Merrill** wrote a poem, "Developers at Crystal River," about the fact that many a "Prince of Whales" becomes scarred "By the propellers, gaffs and garden tools/The boatmen use on them for fun." For more about these gentle giants see **Margaret Goff Clark's** *The Vanishing Manatee* (New York: Cobblehill Books, 1990); **John E. Reynolds III** and **Daniel K. Odell's** *Manatees and Dugongs* (New York: Facts on File, 1991); **Mary Unterbrink's** *Manatees: Gentle Giants in Peril* (St. Petersburg: Great Outdoors Publishing Co., 1984) and **Warren Zeiller's** *Introducing the Manatee* (Gainesville: University Press of Florida, 1992).

Inverness

East of Homosassa Springs on State Road 44, Inverness was named after Inverness, Scotland, by an early Scottish settler. A number of active and retired authors have made it their home, including **Charles Minor Blackford** (*Deep Treasure, Torpedoboat Sailor*); **Valera Grapp Blair** (*The Cook's Idea Book* and *Cook's Idea Book*); **Marie Hall Ets** (*Another Day, Gilberto and the Wind, In the Forest, Jay Bird, Just Me, Play With Me*, and *Talking Without Words*); and **Albert Jensen** (*The Cod* and *Wildlife of the Oceans*). Science-fiction writer **Piers Anthony** (1934-), who has had more than 60 books published, including *Faith of Tarot* (1980), *The Magic of Xanth* (1981), *Ghost* (1986), and his autobiographical *Biography of an Ogre* (1988), also lives in Inverness; his novel, *Tatham Mound* (New York: Morrow, 1991), is about Native Americans in Florida before and during the Spanish exploration.

A novel that takes place on the gulf is **Peggy Dern's** *Love Is Enough* (New York: Arcadia House, 1959). For a history of surrounding Citrus County see **Hampton Dunn's** *Back Home: A History of Citrus County, Florida* (Inverness, FL: Citrus County Bicentennial Steering Committee, 1977). Dunn, who was born in nearby Floral City in 1916, also wrote *Re-Discover Florida* (Miami: Hurricane House, 1969); *Yesterday's Tampa* (Miami: Seemann Publishing Co., 1972); *Yesterday's St. Petersburg* (Miami: Seemann Publishing Co., 1973); *Yesterday's Clearwater* (Miami: Seemann Publishing Co., 1973); *Yesterday's Tallahassee* (Miami: Seemann Publishing Co., 1974); *Florida Sketches* (Miami: Seemann Publishing Co., 1974); *Wish You Were Here* (St. Petersburg: Byron Kennedy, 1981); and *Florida: A Pictorial History* (Norfolk, VA: Donning Co., 1988). Now a resident of Tampa, Dunn has made thousands of Floridians more aware of the state's history through his popular books, newspaper columns, TV spots, and his duties as president of the Florida Historical Society in 1990.

Crystal River

Just north of Crystal River on U.S. 19 is the turn to an impressive pre-Columbian Indian site, the Crystal River State Archaeological Site. The museum exhibits describe the Indian tribes that lived there from 100 B.C. to A.D. 1400 and show various mounds in which the Indians were buried. An examination of such sites is in **Jerald T. Milanich** and **Charles H. Fairbanks's** *Florida Archaeology* (New York: Academic Press, 1980). Other relevant books are **Brent Richards Weisman's** *Like Beads on a String: A Culture History of the Seminole Indians of Northern Peninsular Florida* (Tuscaloosa, AL: University of Alabama Press, 1989), which traces the emergence of the Seminole Indians from the late prehistoric period in the Southeast; **Edith Ridenour Lawson's** *Florida Indians* (St. Petersburg: Valkyrie Press, 1977); **Charles Hudson's** *The Southeastern Indians* (Knoxville, TN: University of Tennessee Press, 1976); and **Thelma H. Bull's** *Anthropological Bibliography of Aboriginal Florida* (Clearwater, FL: Interprint, 1976).

Margaret Z. Searcy's *Ikwa of the Mound-Builder Indians* (Gretna, LA: Pelican Publishing Co., 1989) gives a fictional account of Indians who built large earthen mounds on which they put a temple. **Zoe A. Tilghman's** *Katska of the Seminoles* (Oklahoma City: Harlow, 1954) is a novel about the Second Seminole War. A juvenile book about two boys' search for treasure in Tampa Bay and the Crystal River is **Robert F. Burgess's** *The Mystery of Mound Key* (Cleveland, OH: World Publishing Co., 1966).

The Crystal and Withlacoochee rivers area is featured in local tales gathered and retold in **David M. Newell's** *If Nothin' Don't Happen* (New York: Knopf, 1976) and *The Trouble of It Is* (New York: Knopf, 1978); Newell, who has lived in Leesburg, Florida, for some 62 years, was editor-in-chief of *Field and Stream*, roving editor of *Sports Afield*, and a special correspondent for the *New York Times*. **Ray Washington's** *Cracker Florida, Some Lives and Times* (Miami: Banyan Books, 1983) also describes Florida's much-denigrated Cracker, while **Grady McWhiney's** *Cracker Culture: Celtic Ways in the Old South* (University, AL: University of Alabama Press, 1988) shows how the Civil War was a battle of competing cultures.

Many readers first became familiar with Florida Crackers in the 1940s, when the Federal Writers Project, which contracted with unemployed writers from 1935 to 1943, produced long, detailed descriptions of the states, including Florida. The Federal Writers Project described the Cracker in stark terms:

> The cracker, a pioneer backwoods settler of Georgia and Florida, has come to be known as a gaunt, shiftless person, but originally the term meant simply a native, regardless of his circumstances. Belief that the name may have been shortened from "corn cracker'" is given credence in Georgia, but in Florida it derives from the cracking of a whip. It is a name honorably earned by those who made bold talk with their lengthy, rawhide bullwhips in the days when timber and turpentine were the State's chief industries. Those enterprises involved heavy-haul jobs, with oxen the motive power, bullwhips to keep them moving, and the pistol-shot crack of these whips to signal the wearisome progress of the haul through the woods.

Marjorie Kinnan Rawlings (1896-1953) featured the Florida Cracker in such novels as *South Moon Under* (New York: Scribner's, 1933) and *The Yearling*

(New York: Scribner's, 1938), not in a condescending way, but rather as a testimony to their adaptability and determination to survive. The Cracker is just one of many different peoples that make up Florida's cultural and ethnic diversity. Along with Indians, African-Americans, and European descendants (Greeks, Italians, Germans, and Czechs) the Cracker has found a place in Florida's regional literature. Today one can visit a reconstructed Cracker turpentine still in St. Andrews State Recreation Area three miles east of Panama City Beach in the Panhandle and a typical Cracker homestead at Forest Capital State Museum in Perry.

Inglis

North on U.S. 19, near the town of Inglis, a name that honored an early Scotsman who piloted a ship in the area, a bridge crosses the remains of the controversial Cross-Florida Barge Canal, what had been intended as a waterway to reduce the distance from the Atlantic Ocean to the Gulf of Mexico. Various threats to gulf traffic like nineteenth-century pirates and twentieth-century German submarines, as well as the dangerous reef along the Florida Keys, encouraged canal advocates, but environmentalists opposed it because it would seriously damage the waters south of there, and construction was stopped in the late 1970s. For more about the much-argued-about Cross-Florida Barge Canal and for a history of water management in Florida see *Land Into Water—Water Into Land* (Tallahassee: University Presses of Florida, 1980) by **Nelson M. Blake**; it deals in a very readable way with the canal, swampland drainage, and the many problems associated with one of our state's most precious resources — water.

Yankeetown

This town, named by local inhabitants in derision of northern visitors in the early twentieth century, was the site of some of the filming of the 1962 Elvis Presley movie, *Follow That Dream*, which was based on *Pioneer, Go Home* (New York: Scribner, 1959) by **Richard Powell** of Fort Myers; the courtroom scene was filmed in Inverness and the bank scene in Ocala, where the producers had the world premier of the film. For a history of the town read **Tom Knotts's** *See Yankeetown: History and Reminiscences* (Yankeetown, FL: Withlacoochee Press, 1970).

Dunnellon

Northeast on State Road 40, Dunnellon, named for railroad promoter John F. Dunn, was the site of the discovery of hard rock phosphate in 1889, which made the settlement a boom town. Hordes of miners flocked to the town; some of them became very wealthy, like the man who flaunted his riches by driving a team of pure white horses, all harnessed in silver and gold trim. The town lies at the point where the Withlacoochee and Rainbow rivers converge, the latter carrying 500 million gallons of fresh water each day from

Rainbow Springs into the Gulf of Mexico. Novelist **Theresa Di Benedetto, of** Hallandale, Florida, wrote *Silver Mist* (New York: Berkley Publishing Group, 1990) about the discovery of phosphate that transformed Dunnellon into a booming mining camp. For a history of this town and nearby Rainbow Springs see **J. Lester Dinkins's** *Dunnellon, Boomtown of the 1890's* (St. Petersburg: Great Outdoors Publishing, 1969).

Romeo

North on U.S. 41 is the small town of Romeo, and nearby is Juliette, both named after the Romeo and Juliet of Shakespeare's play. Local lore insists there was a boy in one town and his girlfriend in the other, and that, as in literature, their families were enemies and so the youngsters died tragic deaths.

Cedar Key

Near the Gulf of Mexico on State Road 24 is Cedar Key, named for the area's cedar trees; the island, which is part of a group called Cedar Keys, was once the western terminus of David Yulee's railroad from Fernandina on the east coast. Local cedar was used in the manufacture of pencils, and during the Civil War salt was produced near Cedar Key.

In 1875, poet **Sidney Lanier** described this area in glowing terms:

> At Cedar Keys, and from there on in an increasing degree to the southward as one reaches the places herein after named, one finds that one has come into a country differing in many particulars from any part of Florida yet mentioned — a country of cedars, of sponges, of corals, of strange fish, of shells multitudinous in shape and tint, of hundreds of quiet bays whose circular waters lie embraced in the curves of their white beaches as the old moon in the cusps of the new. There is a certain large blandness in the atmosphere, a sense of far-awayness in the wide water-stretches, an indefinable feeling of withdrawal from harsh life, that give to this suave region, as compared with others, the proportion which mild dreams bear to realities. It is a sort of Arabian Nights vaguely diffused and beaten out into long, glittering, sleepy expanses, and the waters presently cease to be waters and seem only great level enchantments-that-shine.

For more about Lanier's visit to the area see **Charles C. Fishburne, Jr.**'s *Sidney Lanier, Poet of the Marshes, Visits Cedar Keys, 1875* (Cedar Key, FL: Sea Hawk Publications, 1986).

A nineteenth-century traveler who helped make this town famous was **John Muir**, who, at the age of 29 in 1867, walked a thousand miles — from Louisville, Kentucky, to Cedar Key — in just two months' time. During a convalescence in the small town, he wrote about the view from Cedar Key: "One day in January I climbed to the housetop to get a view of another of the fine sunsets of this land of flowers. The landscape was a strip of clear Gulf water, a strip of

John Muir

sylvan coast, a tranquil company of shell and coral keys, and a gloriously colored sky without a threatening cloud. All the winds were hushed and the calm of the heavens was as profound as that of the palmy islands and their encircling waters." His book, *A Thousand-Mile Walk to the Gulf* (Dunwoody, GA: N.S. Borg, 1969), describes the journey; for photographs of what he might have seen refer to **John Earl**'s *John Muir's Longest Walk* (Garden City, NY: Doubleday, 1975). **Linnie Marsh Wolfe's** *Son of the Wilderness: The Life of John Muir* (New York: Knopf, 1945) won the Pulitzer Prize for biography in 1946.

Cedar Key is a town that missed out on several opportunities to become a major port on Florida's gulf coast. When the first cross-Florida railroad joined Fernandina on the Atlantic with Cedar Key on the gulf, some promoters envisioned Cedar Key's becoming a major port, but the Civil War put an end to that as Union soldiers tore up the railroad. In the 1880s Henry Plant considered building his railroad line to Cedar Key, but, when the town refused to sell him the dock, he took his line to Tampa and made it the major port on Florida's west coast. Overcutting destroyed the timber industry around Cedar Key. In 1896 fire, wind, and a tidal wave destroyed much of the town. One scholar noted that when Cedar Keyites rebuffed Mormon missionaries, the latter left the town, dusted their feet, and "cursed the town," a biblical action that may have caused its problems. The changes that this former fishing village has made in order to attract more tourists come under fire in **Beth Dunlop**'s *Florida's Vanishing Architecture* (Sarasota: Pineapple Press, 1987), a work that deplores the depletion of our natural beauty in the name of progress.

Several fictional works are set near Cedar Key: **Jack Beater**'s *True Tales of the Florida West Coast* (Fort Myers, FL: Beater, 1959) includes some stories about Cedar Key; **John D. MacDonald**'s *The Empty Copper Sea* (Philadelphia: Lippincott, 1978) is a Travis McGee mystery about the apparent drowning of a rich local man; and **Harrison** and **Mathilda Reed's** *The Talbot Boys* (Maplewood, NJ: C.S. Hammond, 1961) has five stories about two Cedar Key teenagers. For some folklore of the area see **Sally Tileston** and **Dottie Comfort's** *Cedar Key Legends* (Cedar Key: no publisher, 1967). The history of Cedar Key is recorded in several places, including *Search For Yesterday: A History of Levy County, Florida* (Bronson, FL: Levy County Archives Committee, 1977). The town's **Charles C. Fishburne, Jr.** has written *Of Chiefs and Generals: A History of the Cedar Keys to the End of the Second Seminole War* (Cedar Key, FL: Sea Hawk Publications, 1982); **Jesse Walter Dees, Jr.** and **Vivian Flannery Dees** wrote *"Off the Beaten Path": The History of Cedar Key, Florida, 1843-1990* (Chiefland, FL: Rife Publishing, 1990). Also see **Harriet Smith's** *The Naturalist's Guide to Cedar Key, Florida* (Cedar Key, FL: H. Smith, 1987). Two museums in town give much of its history and highlights: the Cedar Key State Museum on Museum Drive (904/543-5350) and the Cedar Key Historical Society Museum on the corner of Second and D streets. A novel about the coastal Big Bend area north of Cedar Key is **Teresa Holloway's** *The Nurse on Dark Island* (New York: Ace, 1969).

Chiefland

Northeast of Cedar Key on U.S. 19/98, Chiefland was named after a nineteenth-century Creek Indian chief who settled there with some of his followers. A novel set near Chiefland is **Mary F. Rosborough's** *Don't You Cry For Me* (Chicago: Peoples Book Club, 1954). **Ruth Verrill's** *Romantic and Historic Levy County* (Gainesville: Storter, 1976) has many stories about the area.

TRILBY TO PANACEA

Trilby

The second part of this chapter begins southeast of Brooksville, in Trilby, a small town whose literary link comes from having been named after George Du Maurier's popular 1894 novel, *Trilby*. The townspeople also named their Svengali Square and Little Billee Street after characters in the novel.

To the east near Clermont is Lake Minnehaha honoring the heroine of Longfellow's *Hiawatha*. Several miles to the north is the town of Plymouth, founded by English immigrants and named after the British town.

Bushnell

Named for the chief engineer who helped survey the railroad right-of-way in 1884, Bushnell is two miles north of the Dade Battlefield State Historic Site off U.S. 301. The museum and the battlefield plaques describe how Seminole Indians killed Major Francis Dade and 107 soldiers on December 28, 1835, in a massacre that started the bloody Second Seminole War (1835-1842), considered the most brutal and most expensive American Indian war.

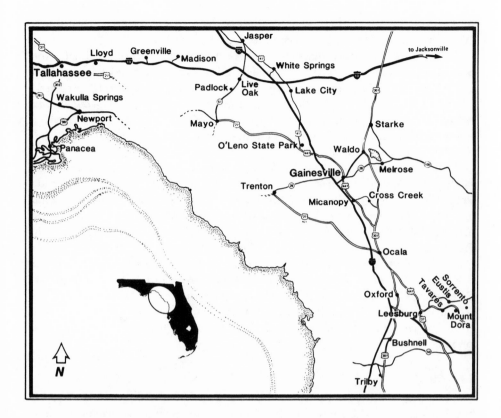

In the end, the U.S. government waged three wars against the Seminoles and succeeded in removing most of the surviving Indians to the western Indian territory. The relentless pursuit of the Indians by federal forces is one of the darkest chapters in Florida's history. It includes the capture of a band of Seminoles under a white flag of truce, the cutting off of Osceola's head after he had died, the pillaging of Indian villages to force them to leave the territory, etc. While most authors recount the tragic episodes in novels or nonfiction histories, one author, who probably never came to Florida, chose poetry to express his outrage at what happened to the Seminoles.

Albery Allson Whitman (1851-1901), a black born into a slave family in Kentucky, wrote a 95-page indictment of the United States: *The Rape of Florida* (1884 — republished in 1885 as *Twasinta's Seminoles*). Whitman's theme, the destruction of Edenic Florida by the white man in the name of progress, is one that continues to find its voice in the works of environmentalists. Whitman's poem ends as the Seminoles are transported west: "The chieftain speaks no more, but still doth gaze/Till Florida is gone and all is sea." Ironically, Whitman was born in the same year that **Harriet Beecher Stowe**'s *Uncle Tom's Cabin* was published (1851). While Stowe, who was writing her enthusiastic *Palmetto Leaves* (1873; Gainesville: University of Florida Press, 1968) about the glories of Florida, was encouraging more people to visit the Land of Sunshine, Whitman was seeing a different side to the state's history.

Novels depicting the massacre and the plight of the Indians during the Second Seminole War are **Henry Carlisle's** *The Land Where the Sun Dies* (New York: Putnam, 1975); **Betty Sue Cummings's** *Say These Names (Remember Them)* (Sarasota: Pineapple Press, 1984); and **James L. Donaldson's** *Sergeant Atkins, A Tale of Adventure* (Philadelphia: Lippincott, 1871). "The Dade Massacre," a poem by Florida balladeer **Will McLean**, describes how "Major Dade, he fell first/With a deep, mortal wound."

The definitive works about the Second Seminole War are **John K. Mahon's** *History of the Second Seminole War, 1835-1842* (Gainesville: University of Florida Press, 1967; revised 1985) and **John Bemrose's** *Reminiscences of the Second Seminole War* (Gainesville: University of Florida Press, 1966); others include **Milton Meltzer's** *Hunted Like a Wolf: The Story of the Seminole War* (New York: Farrar, Straus and Giroux, 1972) and **George Walton's** *Fearless and Free: The Seminole Indian War, 1835-1842* (Indianapolis: Bobbs-Merrill, 1977). *Africans and Seminoles: From Removal to Emancipation* by **Daniel F. Littlefield, Jr.** (Westport, CT: Greenwood Press, 1977) is a history of the African-Americans who lived with the Seminoles. A nearby town changed its name from Massacre to the more pleasant-sounding St. Catherine, probably to assuage the towns-people.

Leesburg

Leesburg, which lies to the northeast of Bushnell and was named after the two Lee brothers who founded it in 1853, charmed a famous traveler, **George Barbour**, who in 1882 described it and its one lawyer:

> Leesburg, the county-seat of Sumter County, the home of about two hundred people, is a quiet, contented, easy-going, rather old-fashioned sort of a place, all the business houses being low, plain, wooden buildings, mostly of one story, ranged along one wide, sandy street. A good winter hotel is badly needed, and would probably be a profitable investment. The town lies in the midst of a rather flat pine and hammock country, the soil of which is nearly all very rich. It has a good school and church, and an orderly society, which includes only one lawyer, who does not make a very large income, although they boast that he can earn double fees by arguing for both parties in the same case.

Author **Baynard Kendrick** (1894-1977), who lived at 120 Palmora Boule-vard in Leesburg and who sometimes wrote under the name of **Richard Hayward**, was the literary creator of both Miles Standish Rice and Captain Duncan Maclain, a blind detective, who became Mike Longstreet in a 1970 ABC television series. Born in Philadelphia, Pennsylvania, Kendrick served in England, France, and Salonica during World War I and organized the Blinded Veterans Association and the Mystery Writers of America, Inc.; he based Duncan Maclain on a wartime friend blinded in battle. Some of Kendrick's books have become films: *The Last Express* (1937) became a movie with the same title in 1938; *The Odor of Violets* (1941) became *Eyes in the Night* (1942); and *Lights Out* (1945) reached the silver screen as *Bright Victory* (1951).

Kendrick served as director of the Florida Historical Society and was the recipient of the first Florida Writer's Recognition Award for his 1964 book, *Florida Trails to Turnpikes, 1914-1964* (Gainesville: University of Florida Press, 1964). He had over a dozen short stories published, three nonfiction books, and 24 novels, including Florida-set novels like *The Iron Spiders* (New York: Greenberg, 1936) and *The Flames of Time* (New York: C. Scribner's Sons, 1948).

Tavares

This town, east of Leesburg on U.S. 441, was named after a Portuguese ancestor of the founder. The area around Tavares is the setting for **Donn Pearce's** *Cool Hand Luke* (New York: Scribner, 1965), a story about a prison chain gang and the exploits of one prisoner who escaped several times. The story is reminiscent of "Florida Road Workers," a poem by **Langston Hughes** in which a laborer proudly points to his work: "I'm makin' a road/For the cars to fly by on." The surrounding Lake County is chronicled in **William T. Kennedy's** *History of Lake County, Florida* (1929: Tavares, FL: reprinted by the Lake County Historical Society, 1988).

West of Tavares on the west bank of Lake Harris lies Eldorado, a place with a name rich in literary tradition. In Voltaire's *Candide* Eldorado was a fabulous city of gold and jewels, and in South America it was a treasure city with many legends. Eldorado is a fitting name for the area's wealth: the gold of oranges has brought prosperity.

Mount Dora

This town, east of Tavares, was named for a nearby lake, which a surveying team had named after a local woman, Dora Ann Drawdy, who had shown them kindness and hospitality. Its previous name, Royellou, derived from the names of three children (Roy, Ella, and Louis) of one of the original residents. The town is 266 feet above sea level — thus the name Mount. For more about the town see **Rupert Longstreet's** *The Story of Mount Dora, Florida* (Mount Dora: Mount Dora Historical Society, 1960). During the filming of the 1981 film *Honky Tonk Freeway*, much of the town was painted pink.

Author **Todhunter Ballard** (1903-), who has written over 90 books, mainly westerns, lives in Mount Dora. He has published under pseudonyms like Brian Agar, P. D. Ballard, Parker Bonner, Sam Bowie, Nick Carter, Hunter D'Allard, Brian Fox, Harrison Hunt, John Hunter, Neil MacNeil, Clint Reno, John Shepherd, Jack Slade, and Clay Turner. He also wrote some 50 motion-picture and television scripts and over 1,000 short stories for magazines. For more about Ballard see *Hollywood Troubleshooter: W.T. Ballard's Bill Lennox Stories* edited by **James L. Traylor** (Bowling Green, OH: Bowling Green University Popular Press, 1985).

Sorrento

East of Mount Dora is the town of Sorrento, named after a popular Italian novel of the 1870s, *Agnes of Sorrento*, which was a fitting name since the Italian city of Sorrento was famous for its oranges. The Florida town name was pulled by a blindfolded person from a hat full of suggestions.

Eustis

Northwest of Mount Dora is the town of Eustis, named for a soldier by that name. **Anne Stewart**'s novel, *Regatta Moon* (New York: Phoenix, 1937), concerns an evil Eustis moneylender, while **Sam A. Hamilton**'s book, *The Vengeance of the Mob, A Tale of the Florida Pines* (New York: Abbey, 1900), tells of the lynching in Eustis of an innocent man. Among the Eustis writers is poet **Robert Hazel** (1921-), author of three novels (*Early Spring*, *A Field Full of People*, and *The Lost Year*) and four books of poetry (*Soft Coal*; *Who Touches This*; *Poems*; *1951/1961*; and *Clock of Clay*).

Umatilla

Northeast of Eustis is Umatilla, whose name comes from an Indian word meaning "water rippling over sand." The town is home to **Jonathan Harrington**, who has edited — with Omar S. Castaneda and Christine Blackwell — *New Visions: Fiction by Florida Writers* (Orlando, FL: Arbiter Press, 1989) and has written *Tropical Son: Essays on the Nature of Florida* (Winter Park, FL: NewTech Publications, 1992).

Oxford

The little town of Oxford, while seemingly referring to the English university town, may have gotten its name, which replaced the less glamorous Sandspur, because the originator of the name wanted to join the other American Oxfords in 1879. Or the name may come from the fact that a pond just south of the town would bog down the oxen pulling heavy carts — thus Ox-ford.

Northeast of Oxford and near Ocklawaha is the site of a 1935 gun battle between the FBI and two of Ma Barker's gang, a group of dangerous bank robbers and kidnappers. Ma Barker and her son Fred were killed in the five-hour gun battle, but another member of the gang was spared: the infamous Alvin Karpis who had left for Miami the day before. The 1970 movie *Bloody Mama*, starring Shelley Winters, retells the death of Ma Barker. **Alvin Karpis's** book, *On The Rock* (New York: Beaufort Books, 1980), mentions the shoot-out and Karpis's subsequent capture in New Orleans. The actual house, now a private residence not open to the public, is to the west of the United Methodist Church on Alternate 441 and Alternate 27. For more about Ma Barker see **Gene M. Burnett**'s *Florida's Past: People and Events That Shaped the State* (Sarasota, FL: Pineapple Press, 1986+), a collection of essays in several volumes.

Ocala

The name of this city is surely Indian, but its meaning has been lost. Ocala is the former site of Fort King, where the Seminole wars began when the Indian leader Osceola killed General Thompson, an agent of the federal government. "Osceola afterward selected ten of his boldest warriors, which were to wreak vengeance on General Thompson. The General was then camping at Fort King, little dreaming that the hour of his dissolution was so near, or that Osceola was lying in wait to murder him." **Steve Glassman's** *Blood on the Moon, A Novel of Old Florida* (Brooklyn, OH: Quality Publications, 1990) also deals with Osceola and his exploits. **Dorothy M. Dunsing's** *War Chant* (New York: Longmans, Green, 1954) is a novel about the Second Seminole War around Fort King (Ocala). Other novels about Osceola are **Electa Clark's** *Osceola, Young Seminole Indian* (Indianapolis: Bobbs-Merrill, 1965); **Marion E. Gridley's**

Osceola (New York: Putnam, 1972); and **Rubylea Hall's** *Flamingo Prince* (New York: Duell, Sloan & Pearce, 1954). A modern biography of Osceola is **Patricia R. Wickman's** *Osceola's Legacy* (Tuscaloosa, AL: University of Alabama, 1991). A novel about Osceola's friend Coacoochee is **Electa Clark's** *Wildcat the Seminole* (New York: Alladin Books, 1956).

The Ocklawaha River to the east of Ocala is a 79-mile-long tributary of the St. Johns River and a part of what was to have become the Cross-Florida Barge Canal. The name of the river comes from a Creek Indian word meaning *muddy*. After the Civil War and up to the 1920s, the trip from Palatka to Silver Springs by way of the Ocklawaha was very popular, especially for northerners seeking respite from the cold and bleakness. **Harriet Beecher Stowe**, who had moved to Mandarin with her husband in 1868, wrote glowingly of the sights along the way and did much to attract countless visitors to Florida. Georgia poet **Sidney Lanier**, who had been sent to Florida by a railroad company to write a promotional piece about the beauty of Florida, in 1876 described the Ocklawaha as

Osceola

the sweetest water-lane in the world, a lane which runs for more than a hundred and fifty miles of pure delight betwixt hedgerows of oaks and cypresses and palms and bays and magnolias and mosses and manifold vinegrowths, a lane clean to travel along for there is never a speck of dust in it save the blue dust and gold dust which the wind blows out of the flags and lilies, a lane which is as if a typical woods-stroll had taken shape and as if God had turned into water and trees the recollection of some meditative ramble through the lonely seclusions of His own soul.

Like so many writers before and since, Lanier was captivated by the pristine beauty of much of the state, as well as its curative powers for consumptives and those suffering from such diseases as tuberculosis, as he himself was a year later.

At least four novels address the Ocklawaha: **May Y. McNeer's** *Up a Crooked River* (New York: Viking, 1952) is an adolescent book about a trip up the river in 1876; **Marjorie Kinnan Rawlings's** *South Moon Under* (New York: C. Scribner's Sons, 1933) tells of people living near the river in the first quarter of this century; **Frank R. Stockton's** *Captain Chap* (Philadelphia: Lippincott, 1891) is the story of two boys on the river; and **William T. Adams's** *Down South* (Boston: Lothrop, Lee and Shepard, 1908; published under the pseudonym **Oliver Optic**) is the story of a man sailing on this and other Florida rivers. **Edward A. Mueller's** *Ocklawaha River Steamboats* (Jacksonville: Mueller, 1983) is a well-illustrated book about an important form of river transportation. Perhaps the most controversial aspect of the river is the spelling of its name — *Oklawaha* or *Ocklawaha*? Residents are embroiled in a long-running dispute. In 1991, the Marion County commissioners voted unanimously for *Ocklawaha*, but many locals refused to recognize the spelling.

Ocala, a fast-growing city well-known for its horse farms, is set midway between the Atlantic Ocean and the Gulf of Mexico and is bordered on the east by the 350,000-acre Ocala National Forest, the southernmost national forest in the continental United States. Springs throughout the forest such as Alexander Springs, Juniper Springs, Salt Springs, and Silver Glen Springs offer facilities for swimming, canoeing, camping, and boating. The Ocala National Forest is the site of **Marjory Bartlett Sanger's** *Forest in the Sand* (New York: Atheneum, 1983), which recounts the history, Indian lore, and natural resources of the Big Scrub area of the forest. At one point in the 1890s, soon after phosphate was discovered in surrounding Marion County, local entrepreneurs promoted the town's central location in Florida as a reason for making it the state capital and even went so far as to publish a newspaper, *New Capitol*, from 1890 to 1897, at which time Tallahassee's claim as the capital was firmly established.

Silver Springs, with an average daily output of 800 million gallons of fresh water, is the world's largest limestone artesian spring formation. Glass-bottom boats, a petting zoo, car display, and animal demonstrations attract thousands of visitors each year (Daily 9 a.m. to 5 p.m.; 904/236-2121). A history of Silver

Springs, **Richard Martin**'s *Eternal Spring* (St. Petersburg: Great Outdoors Publishing Co., 1966), describes some of the movies shot there, e.g. *The Yearling* (1946) with Gregory Peck; *The Barefoot Mailman* (1951) with Bob Cummings and Terry Moore; *Distant Drums* (1953) with Gary Cooper; *Creature From the Black Lagoon* (1954); *Revenge of the Creature* (1955); *Jupiter's Darling* (1955) with Esther Williams and Howard Keel; and six Tarzan films. Among literature set there is **Maley B. Crist**'s short story, "The Bridal Chamber of Florida's Silver Springs," in her *Patchwork* (Atlanta: Martin & Hoyt, 1898); it features a young man and woman who could find peace and happiness together only in the deep waters of Silver Springs, where they drowned embracing each other.

Among the local authors is **Ray Cunningham**, who wrote *Old Timey Southern Talk* (Detroit: Harlo, 1987) about the southern dialect and *Simpler Times* (Ocala, FL: Cunningham, 1992) about rural living in the South during the 1920s and 1930s.

Several novels use the Ocala area for a setting: **Broome Stringfellow**'s *Trek to Florida* (St. Petersburg: Great Outdoors Publishing Co., 1972) describes a family that moves from South Carolina to Ocala in the mid-1800s; **Denton Whitson**'s *Savage Heart* (Philadelphia: Chilton Co., Book Division, 1959) is the story of Osceola, the Seminole Indian; and **James M. Thompson**'s *The Ocala Boy* (Boston: Lothrop, 1895) tells of boys visiting in Ocala. For a history of the area read **Eloise R. Ott** and **Louis H. Chazal**'s *Ocali Country* (Ocklawaha, FL: Marion Publishers, 1966) and **Eloise Knight Jones**'s *Ocala Cavalcade* (Ocala, FL: Stephen F. McCready, 1946). **Broward Lovell**'s *Gone With the Hickory Stick* (Ocala, FL: Green, 1975) gives a history of education in the county from 1845 to 1960, including the 1853 establishment of the East Florida Seminary, which developed into the University of Florida in Gainesville. **Jane Quinn**'s *Catholics of Marion County* (Ocala, FL: Mission Press, 1978) is about the oldest Catholic community in central Florida. **Faye Perry Melton**'s *Pine Needles, The Story of Pine, Florida and its People* (Pine, FL: F.P. Melton, 1984) gives the history of another small Marion County town.

Cross Creek

North of Ocala off U.S. 301 or 441 and on State Road 325 between Lochloosa and Orange lakes (thus the name, Cross Creek) is the former home of Florida's famous author, **Marjorie Kinnan Rawlings** (1896-1953). She was born in Washington, D.C., completed her A.B. degree at the University of Wisconsin in 1918, and worked as a journalist for about ten years. She moved with her husband, Charles Rawlings, to Cross Creek in 1928 and bought a farmhouse and a citrus grove. She wrote the following about this place: "When I came to the Creek, and knew the old grove and farmhouse at once as home, there was some terror, such as one feels in the first recognition of a human love, for the joining of persons to place, as of person to person, is a commitment to shared sorrow, even as to shared joy."

She soon abandoned her predilection for writing harlequin novels in favor of stories about the people she was meeting around her; she also collected local

Marjorie Kinnan Rawlings

recipes for her *Cross Creek Cookery* (New York: C. Scribner's Sons, 1942). Her stories, some of which appear in *When the Whippoorwill* (New York: Scribner, 1940), have rich dialogue and vivid scenes of a part of America known to very few at the time. One story, "Gal Young 'Un," which won the O. Henry Memorial Prize in 1933, has been made into a short movie, which won for its director, Victor Nunez, the Best First Feature Award at the Chicago International Film Festival. Her most famous work, *The Yearling* (New York: C. Scribner's Sons, 1938), which won the 1939 Pulitzer Prize, portrays a young boy growing up in the nearby scrub, now the Ocala National Forest. The movie of the same name, which starred Gregory Peck and Claude Jarman, Jr., was filmed in the area. Her other novels include *South Moon Under* (New York: C. Scribner's Sons, 1933) about a family growing up in the scrub country of central Florida; *Golden Apples* (New York: Scribner, 1935) about a young Englishman and two Cracker-Floridians; and *The Sojourner* (New York: Scribner, 1953) about midwestern farm life after the Civil War. Island Grove appeared as the town of Purley in her novel *Golden Apples*; nearby Orange Lake became Sawgrass Lake. Some real places, like Lake Lochloosa and the mythologically named River Styx, are also in the novel.

Her nonfiction work, *Cross Creek* (New York: Scribner, 1942), which described the people and customs of the village, ended up causing her much trouble. One woman featured in the book, Zelma Cason, was so offended by a sentence in Chapter 5 that implied she liked to curse that she sued Rawlings for $100,000 and, in a long, bitter trial in Gainesville, eventually received one dollar "for anguish suffered"; **Patricia Nassif Acton** describes the trial in *Invasion of Privacy: The Cross Creek Trial of Marjorie Kinnan Rawlings* (Gainesville: University Presses of Florida, 1988). Court fees and lawyers' bills cost Rawlings $32,000 and the peace of mind she had found in Cross Creek; she moved to St. Augustine with her husband and never again produced any important writing. Time eventually healed the rift between the two women, and, "though she was never completely happy with her portrayal in *Cross Creek*, Zelma found it in her heart to forgive Marjorie for the real or imagined injuries she had caused her."

Marjorie Rawlings, who died at the age of 57, is buried in Island Grove's Antioch Cemetery, a place she had not chosen as her resting place. Several years before her death, she and her second husband, Norton Baskin, attended the funeral of a friend in a cemetery Marjorie found tranquil. She told Baskin she believed she could find peace in that setting. Right after her death, when Baskin telephoned the funeral director with final instructions, he told him to bury Rawlings in the cemetery near Cross Creek, not realizing there were two such cemeteries. By the time the funeral proces-

Marjorie Kinnan Rawlings's home in Cross Creek

sion reached Antioch Cemetery, Baskin realized it was too late to have the cortege go to the other cemetery. He consoled himself by pointing out that the Antioch Cemetery "was closer to Cross Creek and most of her Cross Creek friends were there." To reach Antioch Cemetery, 7.4 miles from the Rawlings house, take State Road 325 from the house to U.S. 301; cross 301 and continue for 1.6 miles to Southeast 3C Road, a wide, graded road; turn left and proceed

1.8 miles to the cemetery. Her gravestone reads "Marjorie Kinnan Rawlings. 1896-1953. Wife of Norton Baskin. Through her writings she endeared herself to the people of the world." About 75 feet away is the gravesite of Zelma Cason, the woman who had sued Rawlings.

Cross Creek's accessibility by roads to nearby towns belies the fact that when Rawlings lived there the village was four miles from any paved road. For more about Rawlings's life see **Elizabeth Silverthorne**'s *Marjorie Kinnan Rawlings* (Woodstock, NY: Overlook Press, 1988), *Selected Letters of Marjorie Kinnan Rawlings* edited by **Gordon E. Bigelow** and **Laura V. Monti** (Gainesville: University of Florida Press, 1983), **Samuel I. Bellman**'s *Marjorie Kinnan Rawlings* (New York: Twayne, 1974), and **Gordon E. Bigelow**'s *Frontier Eden: The Literary Career of Marjorie Kinnan Rawlings* (Gainesville, University of Florida Press, 1966). *The Marjorie Rawlings Reader* (New York: Scribner, 1956) edited by **Julia Scribner Bigham** has selections from her works. *Cross Creek Kitchens* by **Sally Morrison** (1983) has recipes associated with Rawlings, as well as with Idella Parker, who lived with her for 13 years as her cook and maid. Ms. **Parker** with **Mary Keating** wrote *Idella: Marjorie Rawlings' "Perfect Maid"* (Gainesville: University Press of Florida, 1992), a frank story about working for Ms. Rawlings. **W. Horace Carter**, the Pulitzer Prize-winning North Carolina journalist, has collected stories and anecdotes about the area in his *Return to Cross Creek* (Tabor City, NC: Atlantic Publishing Co., 1985).

Among the Rawlings works that became movies were *The Yearling* (1946) and *Cross Creek* (1983), the latter starring Mary Steenburgen as Rawlings. Producer Robert Radnitz filmed it near Orange Lake in Alachua County about 2.5 miles from the Rawlings house. He used the town of Micanopy to represent Island Grove and had Norton Baskin, Rawlings's second husband, play a small part in the movie. The movie received acclaim at the 1983 Cannes Film Festival but poor commercial success in this country. During the first year after its release, 83,000 people visited the Rawlings House, so many in fact that park personnel there have had to limit visitors to 30,000 a year in order to preserve the Cracker-style house for future generations (Daily except Tuesday and Wednesday; tours from 10 to 11:30 and from 1 to 4:30 p.m. on the half hour, with each tour limited to ten persons; no reservations needed; 904/466-3672). The Marjorie Kinnan Rawlings Society, founded in 1987 and headquartered at the English Department, University of Florida, Gainesville, holds an annual spring conference and produces a quarterly newsletter and *The Journal of Florida Literature* devoted to articles about Rawlings and other Florida authors; the first volume of the journal has *A Tea With Zora and Marjorie*, a play by **Barbara Speisman** about the friendship between Rawlings and Zora Neale Hurston.

Cross Creek has managed to resist much of the commercial development that has occurred in other Florida towns, and that would no doubt have pleased Marjorie Kinnan Rawlings. She ended *Cross Creek* by asking: "Who owns Cross Creek?"

Houses are individual and can be owned, like nests, and fought for. But what of the land? It seems to me that the earth may be borrowed but not bought. It may be used, but not owned. It gives itself in response to love and tending, offers its seasonal flowering and fruiting. But we are tenants and not possessors, lovers and not masters. Cross Creek belongs to the wind and the rain, to the sun and the seasons, to the cosmic secrecy of seed, and beyond all, to time.

After she died, she willed her house to the University of Florida so that creative-writing students could live there. Among those to take advantage of that opportunity was novelist **Jesse Hill Ford** (1928-), who attended the University of Florida in 1955 and produced *Mountains of Giliad* (1961), *The Liberation of Lord Byron Jones* (1965), and *The Feast of St. Barnabas* (1969). He now lives in Tennessee.

Micanopy

North on U.S. 441 is Micanopy ("MICK-a-no-pee"), named after an Indian chief. An historic plaque in the center of town commemorates the travels of famed naturalist **William Bartram** (1739-1823). His book, *Travels Through North & South Carolina, Georgia, East & West Florida* (1791; Savannah: Beehive Press, 1973), described his 1773-1776 trip to the Southeast and detailed the hitherto unseen-by-many flora and fauna in the region. For more about the town see *The Story of Historic Micanopy* by **Caroline B. Watkins** (Gainesville: Alachua County Historical Commission, 1976). *Voices From the Countryside* by local resident **Guy Miles** (Miami: Banyan, 1977) contains a number of interviews with Alachua County residents who talk about tobacco barns, tractors, and moonshine. **John Paul Jones, Jr.**'s *Cold Before Morning* (Tallahassee: Father & Son Publishing, 1992) is a novel

William Bartram

about a Scottish family's settling down in Micanopy between 1854 and 1913.

North on U.S. 441 is the 18,000-acre Payne's Prairie named after King Payne, a local nineteenth-century Seminole chief who is portrayed in an early Florida novel: *Left-Handed Pete, The Double Knife* by **Joseph E. Badger, Jr.** (New York: Beadle & Adams, 1876). All of this area was a lake from 1871 until 1891, when in a single day the water drained out through a sinkhole. The home of many Indians from 9,000 B.C. to about 1820, it is now a wildlife preserve and the home of eagles, ospreys, hawks, Florida sandhill cranes, bobcats, raccoons, turkeys, and alligators. William Bartram described the area in 1774 in terms that are still appropriate:

> The extensive Alachua savanna is a level green plain, above fifteen miles over, fifty miles in circumference, and scarcely a tree or bush of any kind to be seen on it. It is encircled with high, sloping hills, covered with waving forests and fragrant Orange groves, rising from an exuberantly fertile soil. The towering magnolia grandiflora and transcendent Palm, stand conspicuous amongst them. At the same time are seen innumerable droves of cattle; the lordly bull, lowing cow, and sleek capricious heifer. The hills and groves re-echo their cheerful, social voices. Herds of sprightly deer, squadrons of the beautiful fleet Siminole [sic] horse, flocks of turkeys, civilized communities of the sonorous watchful crane, mix together, appearing happy and contented in the enjoyment of peace, till disturbed and affrighted by the warrior man.

More recently, local writer **Harry Crews** (1935-) in *The Hawk Is Dying*, about the raising of a hawk found on Payne's Prairie, contrasted the primitive beauty of the vast marsh with the modern superhighway nearby: "A heavy mist lay over the land and from this distance they could barely make out the swift gray cars flying over the Interstate." Payne's Prairie State Preserve with its entrance 1.5 miles north of Micanopy on U.S. 441 has a visitors' center with exhibits tracing Indian artifacts to 7,000 B.C. and an observation tower that provides a panoramic view of the land (904/466-3397).

Gainesville

Named after General Edmund Gaines, an Indian fighter, Gainesville used to be near a settlement called Hogtown. Located midway between Pensacola and Miami and between the Gulf of Mexico and the Atlantic Ocean, it is home to the University of Florida (UF), the state's major university and a place where many writers have studied over the years, often in the beginning stages of their careers. Former UF students include authors **William Golding** (*Lord of the Flies, Pincher Martin,* and *The Scorpion God*) and **Shere Hite** (*The Hite Report, Women and Love*), and former publisher of the *Washington Post,* **Philip Graham.** For more information about the published work of the graduates of UF's creative-writing program see **Margaret C. Patterson,** *Creative Writers Bibliography, 1949-1972, University of Florida* (Gainesville: University of Florida, 1973).

Harry Crews

University of Florida

Its most famous local author, **Harry Crews** (1935-), once wrote that "Living here in Gainesville seems to give me a kind of geographic and emotional distance I need to write." One can understand his need to be physically removed from south Georgia, where he grew up, after reading the traumatic story of his youth, *A Childhood: The Biography of a Place* (New York: Harper & Row, 1978), and understanding the first words of his first published novel: "Enigma, Georgia, was a dead end." His Florida novels deal with an abandoned phosphate mine southwest of Orlando (*Naked in Garden Hills* [New York: Morrow, 1969]); a beauty contest in Fort Lauderdale (*Karate Is a Thing of the Spirit* [New York: Morrow, 1971]); a man who eats cars in Jacksonville (*Car* [New York: Morrow, 1972]); falconry in Gainesville (*The Hawk Is Dying* [New York: Knopf, 1973]); a gym in Clearwater (*The Gypsy's Curse* [New York: Knopf, 1974]); lawyers experimenting with drugs (*All We Need of Hell* [New York: Harper & Row, 1987]); women bodybuilding in Miami Beach (*Body* [New York: Poseidon Press, 1990]); and people dealing with visible and interior scars (*Scar Lover* [New York:

Poseidon Press, 1992]). Crews's collections of essays are titled *Blood and Grits* (New York: Harper & Row, 1979) and *Florida Frenzy* (Gainesville: University Presses of Florida, 1982).

In addition to Crews, the department of English at the University of Florida, is the home base of poets **Donald Justice** (*The Summer Anniversaries, Night Light, Departures, Selected Poems, Platonic Scripts, The Sunset Maker, A Donald Justice Reader,* and *The Death of Lincoln*); **William Logan** (*Sad-Faced Men, Difficulty,* and *Sullen Weedy Lakes*); and **Debora Greger** (*Cartography, Movable Islands, And,* and *The 1002nd Night*); fiction writers **Padgett Powell** (*Edisto, A Woman Named Drown,* and *Typical*) and **Marjorie Sandor** (*A Night of Music*); biographer **Jim Haskins**, author of some 95 books, including biographies of Kareem Abdul Jabbar, Ralph Bunche, Adam Clayton Powell, Shirley Chisholm, Julius Erving, Stevie Wonder, and Langston Hughes; and writer/editor **Kevin M. McCarthy** (*The History of Gilchrist County, Florida Stories, Nine Florida Stories of Marjory Stoneman Douglas, Florida Lighthouses,* and *Thirty Florida Shipwrecks*). Elsewhere at the university are short-story writer **Janos Shoemyen** (pseudonym **Lawrence Dorr**: *A Slow, Soft River* and *A Slight Momentary Affliction*) and poet **Lola Haskins** (*Planting the Children, Castings, Across Her Broad Lap Something Wonderful,* and *Four-four Ambitions for the Piano*).

Another literary center of the university is the library, a two-building complex that contains 2,000,000 volumes. Its Rare Book Room contains the John D. MacDonald Collection, the Marjorie Kinnan Rawlings Collection, and the papers of Zora Neale Hurston. The Poetry Archives has tapes of Florida poets, and the Belknap Collection for the Performing Arts has materials dealing with the performing and recorded arts. The P.K. Yonge Library of Florida History has over 20,000 books and 185 periodicals dealing with all aspects of Florida history. For a pictorial history of the university see *Gator History* by **Samuel Proctor** and **Wright Langley** (Gainesville, FL: South Star, 1986). Among the student-produced literary journals at the university are *The Mangrove Review* and *Departure: GNV.*

Books about Gator sports include **Ruth H. Alexander** and **Paula D. Welch**'s *Lady Gators* (Gainesville: Klane Publications, 1991), **Tom McEwen's** *The Gators* (Huntsville, AL: Strode Publishers, 1974), **Julian Derieux Clarkson**'s *Let No Man Put Asunder* (Fort Myers, FL: Clarkson, 1968), and **Arthur Cobb's** *Go Gators!* (Pensacola, FL: Sunshine Publishing Company, 1967).

Professors in other departments who write about Florida include **Arch Fredric Blakey** (*The Florida Phosphate Industry* [Cambridge, MA: Wertheim Committee, Harvard University, 1973] and *Parade of Memories: A History of Clay County, Florida* [Green Cove Springs, FL: Clay County Bicentennial Committee, 1976]), **David R. Colburn** (*Florida Gubernatorial Politics in the Twentieth Century* — with **Richard K. Scher** [Gainesville: University Presses of Florida, 1980] and *Racial Change and Community Crisis: St. Augustine, Florida, 1877-1980* [Gainesville: University of Florida Press, 1991]), Merlin G. Cox (*Florida: From Secession to Space Age* — with **J.E. Dovell** [St. Petersburg, FL: Great Outdoors Pub. Co., 1974] and *History of Gainesville, Florida, 1854-1979* — with **Charles H. Hildreth** [Gainesville: Alachua County Historical Society, 1981]), **Kathleen**

A. Deagen (*Spanish St. Augustine* [New York: Academic Press, 1983]), **Herbert J. Doherty** (*The Whigs of Florida, 1845-1854* [Gainesville: University of Florida Press, 1959] and *Richard Keith Call, Southern Unionist* [Gainesville: University of Florida Press, 1961]), **Michael Gannon** (*Rebel Bishop: The Life and Era of Augustin Verot* [Milwaukee: Bruce Pub. Co., 1964], *The Cross in the Sand: The Early Catholic Church in Florida, 1513-1870* [Gainesville: University of Florida Press, 1965], *Operation Drumbeat: The Dramatic True Story of Germany's First U-boat Attacks Along the American Coast in World War II* [New York: Harper & Row, 1990]), **John K. Mahon** (*History of the Second Seminole War, 1835-1842* [Gainesville: University Presses of Florida, 1985]), **Jerald T. Milanich** (*Francisco Pareja's 1613 Confessionario* — edited with **William C. Sturtevant** [Tallahassee: Florida Division of Archives, History, and Records Management, 1973], *Life in a 9th Century Indian Household* [Tallahassee: Florida Division of Archives, History, and Records Management, 1974], *Tacachale: Essays on the Indians of Florida and Southeastern Georgia During the Historic Period* — edited with **Samuel Proctor** [Gainesville: University Presses of Florida, 1978], *Florida Archaeology* — with **Charles H. Fairbanks** [New York: Academic Press, 1980], *First Encounters: Spanish Explorations in the Caribbean and the United States, 1492-1570* — edited with **Susan Milbrath** [Gainesville: University of Florida Press, 1989], *Earliest Hispanic/Native American Interactions in the American Southeast* [New York: Garland Pub., 1991], and *The Hernando de Soto Expedition* [New York: Garland Pub., 1991]), **George E. Pozzetta** (*The Immigrant World of Ybor City* — with **Gary R. Mormino** [Urbana: University of Illinois Press, 1987] and *Shades of the Sunbelt: Essays on Ethnicity, Race, and the Urban South* — edited with **Randall M. Miller** [New York: Greenwood Press, 1988]), **Samuel Proctor** (*Napoleon Bonaparte Broward, Florida's Fighting Democrat* [Gainesville: University of Florida Press, 1950], *Eighteenth-century Florida and Its Borderlands* [Gainesville: University Presses of Florida, 1975], *Eighteenth-century Florida and the Caribbean* [Gainesville: University Presses of Florida, 1976], *Eighteenth-century Florida: Life on the Frontier* [Gainesville: University Presses of Florida, 1976], *Eighteenth-century Florida and the Revolutionary South* [Gainesville: University Presses of Florida, 1978], *Eighteenth-century Florida: The Impact of the American Revolution* [Gainesville: University Presses of Florida, 1978], *Jews of the South* — co-edited with **Louis Schmier** and **Malcolm Stern** [Macon, GA: Mercer University Press, 1984], and *Gator History: A Pictorial History of the University of Florida* — with **Wright Langley** [Gainesville: South Star Pub. Co., 1986]), and **S. David Webb** (*Pleistocene Mammals of Florida* [Gainesville: University Presses of Florida, 1974]).

Among the places in Gainesville associated with writers was the home of author **Barbara Joy Anderson** (1928-) at 3702 Northwest Sixth Street; a former teacher of creative writing at the university, she has published three novels for young people: *Hippolyte—Crab King* (1956), *The Pai Pai Pig* (1967), and *Hai Yin the Dragon Girl* (1970). **Andrew Lytle** (1902-), the first director of the English department's creative-writing division (1948-61), lived at 1822 Northwest Eighth Avenue; one of the 12 Agrarians who prepared *I'll Take My Stand* (1930) and who emphasized the benefits of the southern rural lifestyle in contrast to urban society, he published one major Florida work in 1941: *At the Moon's Inn* (Tuscaloosa, AL: University of Alabama Press, 1990). **Alton Morris**, former chair of the UF English department, lived at 1227 Northwest Fourth Avenue, edited *Folksongs of Florida* (Gainesville: University of Florida Press, 1990), and co-authored *Places in the Sun* (Gainesville: University Presses of Florida, 1978).

Among the creative writers with two or more published books who have lived in Gainesville are **Herbert Bevis, Martin Caidin, Jack Haldeman, Joe Haldeman, Patience Mason, Robert Mason, John Frederick Nims, Meredith Pierce, Enid Shomer, Barry Spacks,** and **Chick Wallace.** The local newspaper, *The Gainesville Sun,* has had two Pulitzer prizes for editorial writing: **John R. Harrison** in 1965 and **Horance G. Davis, Jr.** in 1971. **Robert Frost** (1874-1963) first came to Gainesville in 1937 and lived with his wife at the Brown Cottage behind the Thomas Hotel at 302 Northeast Sixth Avenue (see the plaque at the south entrance to the building). The death of his wife in Gainesville the following year grieved him so much that he left the town and moved north. In the 1940s and 1950s he spent part of almost every spring in Gainesville on his way north from his five-acre winter home in south Miami. He frequently gave poetry readings at the university and became a good friend of Marjorie Kinnan Rawlings.

Among the novels set in Gainesville are **Sterling Watson's** *The Calling* (Atlanta, GA: Peachtree Publishers, 1986) about a creative-writing professor; **Jennifer Hale's** *Beyond the Dark* (New York: Berkley Publishing Group, 1978) about a dispute over a will; **John L. Parker, Jr.'s** *Once a Runner* (Cedar Mountain, NC: Cedarwinds Publishing Co., 1978) about long-distance runners in a fictional town resembling Gainesville; **John Miglis's** *Not a Bad Man* (New York: Morrow, 1977) about an English professor at the University of Florida; **Jack Flam's** *Bread and Butter* (New York: Viking, 1977) about drug traffic; **Leah Ross's** *Dark Roads* (New York: Harcourt Brace Jovanovich, 1975) about the civil rights struggle; **Martin Dibner's** *Sleeping Giant* (Garden City, NY: Doubleday, 1960) about a law professor's fight against corruption; **William DuBois'** *A Season To Beware* (New York: Putnam, 1956) about a middle-aged man who tries to change the course of his life; and **Robert Wilder's** *Autumn Thunder* (New York: G.P. Putnam's, 1952) about a football player who cannot face reality. For a history of the area see **Charles H. Hildreth** and **Merlin G. Cox's** *History of Gainesville, Florida, 1854-1979* (Gainesville: Alachua County Historical Society, 1981); **John B. Opdyke's** *Alachua County: A Sesquicentennial Tribute* (Gainesville: Alachua County Historical Commission, 1974); **Jess G. Davis's** *History of Alachua County, 1824-1969* (Gainesville: no publisher, 1970); **F.W. Buchholz's** *History of Alachua County, Florida* (St. Augustine: The Record Co., 1929); and **Ben Pickard's** *Historic Gainesville, A Tour Guide to the Past* (Gainesville: Historic Gainesville, 1990). *Museums & More!* by **Doris Bardon** and **Murray D. Laurie** (Gainesville: Maupin House, 1991) has descriptions of local and state-wide museums, as well as cultural and heritage attractions.

Trenton

The county seat of Gilchrist County, Trenton, which a young man in the late-nineteenth century named after his hometown of Trenton, Tennessee, is the site of **Marjorie Kinnan Rawlings**'s short story, "Lord Bill of the Suwannee River," about William E. Bell, called Bill Boyle in her story. After she heard about William Bell in 1930, 11 years after he had died, she went to Trenton and interviewed his acquaintances. Her story begins, "Over in the Suwannee River country of Florida, men read little history and no mythology. They talk instead of big Bill Boyle. The children listen to stories about him." Rawlings's *Jacob's Ladder* (Coral Gables, FL: University of Miami Press, 1950) also takes place in the area.

Melrose

Twenty-five miles east of Gainesville is the little town of Melrose, which was named after Melrose, Scotland, and which replaced the name Shakerag (after the white cloth used to start local pony races). Local authors include **Al Burt** (*Becalmed in the Mullet Latitudes* [Port Salerno, FL: Florida Classics Library, 1983] and *Florida: A Place in the Sun* [Richmond: Dietz Press, 1974]) and **Zonira Hunter Tolles** (*Shadows on the Sand* [Keystone Heights, FL: Tolles, 1976] and *Bonnie Melrose: The Early History of Melrose, Florida* [Keystone Heights, FL: Tolles, 1982]). **Kennie L. Howard**'s *Yesterday in Florida* (New York: Carlton, 1970) is also about Melrose.

Waldo

This little town north of Gainesville, named after a local doctor and legislator, used to be the home of Robertson and Garth Wilkinson James, the younger brothers of novelist Henry James and philosopher William James; the young men had come to Florida right after the Civil War to establish a large plantation with freed black labor, but had to give up when the project failed. For more about the town see *East Side of Eden, A History of the Waldo Area* by **Bettee V. DeSha** (Gainesville: Arbuck Publishing, 1976). A novel set in north Florida is **Dorothy Whitney Ball**'s *Hurricane!* (Indianapolis: Bobbs-Merrill, 1965).

O'Leno State Park

About 40 miles to the east of Mayo and 20 miles south of Lake City off U.S. 41 is O'Leno State Park. The name goes back to Old Leno, which was changed from Keno, the name of a lotto gambling game; ministers and businessmen apparently had the name changed to Leno in 1876 to give the place (now a ghost town) a better image. Of particular significance in the park is the fact that the Santa Fe River "disappears" underground for several miles, a phenomenon that naturalist William Bartram noted in the late 1700s and which British poet **Samuel Taylor Coleridge** included in his poem *Kubla Khan*: "Where Alph, the sacred river, ran/Through caverns measureless to

Richard Eberhart

man/Down to a sunless sea." The park, which offers many amenities for the visitor or camper, has sinkholes, hardwood hammocks, and swamp foliage that indicate what Florida must have looked like for several thousand years (904/454-1853).

Farther west and four miles northwest of Fort White off State Road 47 and County Road 238, the Itchetucknee River and the Itchetucknee Springs State Park offer visitors an unspoiled view of life along a clear, steadily moving river (904/497-2511). Novelist **Richard Adams** (*Watership Down* and *Shardik*), who taught briefly at the University of Florida in the mid-1970s, wrote about tubing down the Itchetucknee: "A few hundred yards below its source the little stream joins another, flowing down from the Jug Spring, to form the Itchetucknee River. Reaching this confluence, we entered broader, deeper water and began swimming in earnest, borne on a faster current. It was wild country — what we could see of it for the close vegetation. There were no clearly defined banks to the river, which simply disappeared on either side into reeds, swamp and trees." Poet **Richard Eberhart**, who taught at the University of Florida from 1974 until 1990, also wrote about the river: "As the water blooms upward to become a petaled river/Each grain of sand below is visible as in air."

Branford

The little town of Branford to the west of the Itchetucknee was named by railroad developer Henry Plant after Branford, Connecticut, where he had lived. **Del** and **Martha "Marty" Marth**, who live 14 miles southeast of Branford near the Suwannee, are journalists whose news or feature stories have appeared in most major newspapers in the U.S. Before moving to this area, Del was senior editor of *Nations's Business* magazine in Washington, D.C., and

Martha was a press aide/speechwriter on Capitol Hill. He has written *Yesterday's Sarasota, Including Sarasota County* (Miami: Seemann Publishing Co., 1973) and *St. Petersburg: Once Upon a Time* (St. Petersburg: The City of St. Petersburg Bicentennial Committee, 1976); she has written *Florida Horse Owner's Field Guide* (Sarasota: Pineapple Press, 1987) and *Florida Dog Owner's Handbook* (Sarasota: Pineapple Press, 1990). Together they have edited *The Rivers of Florida* (Sarasota: Pineapple Press, 1990) and the biennial *Florida Almanac* (Gretna, LA: Pelican), an almost-500-page reference book about the state and one that Del created and produced in 1972 when he was an editor at the *St. Petersburg Times*. They also publish *Florida News Media & Valuable Sources Guide*, which they began in 1991.

Lake City

This town near the intersection of I-10 and I-75 has a name that refers to the many lakes in the area; the town used to be called Alligator after an Indian chief whose name meant "alligator warrior." Among the local writers is **Yvonne Sapia** (1946-), a teacher and the resident poet at Lake City Community College. Her publications include *The Fertile Crescent and Other Poems* (1976), which won the Poetry Chapbook Award from Florida State University; a collection of poetry, *Valentino's Hair* (1987), which won the Samuel French Morse Poetry Prize from Northeastern University Press; and a novel, *Valentino's Hair* (1991), which won the 1991 Charles H. and N. Mildred Nilon Excellence in Minority Fiction Award. For a history of the town see *A Century in the Sun: The Record of a Florida City, Lake City, Florida* (Lake City: Lake City Centennial Celebration, Inc., 1959). For a history of the county see **Edward F. Keuchel's** *A History of Columbia County, Florida* (Tallahassee, FL: Sentry Press, 1981).

White Springs

This town, which acquired its name, White Sulphur Springs, from the famous health spa frequented by thousands of visitors, is the site of the Stephen Foster Memorial, a 243-acre park featuring exhibits about the composer of Florida's state song, "Old Folks at Home" or "Suwannee River." A 200-foot-high carillon tower presents daily concerts, and the visitor can find an antebellum mansion, dioramas of Foster's songs, old musical instruments, a historical doll collection, a steamboat replica, and many exhibits about Stephen Foster (1826-1864) and his works (904/397-2733). There one can learn that in 1851 Foster was writing a new song about the South for Christy's Minstrels to sing. His first draft of "Old Folks at Home" had "Way down upon de Pedee ribber" after a South Carolina river. Dissatisfied with the choice of river, he asked his brother, Morrison Foster, for help in choosing a new name. Stephen rejected Morrison's suggestion of Mississippi's Yazoo River as unpoetic. The brothers then consulted an atlas and looked for a southern river with a musical name. When Morrison found Suwannee River, Stephen enthusiastically adopted it, shortening it to "Swanee":

Way down upon de Swanee ribber,
Far, far away,
Dere's wha my heart is turning ebber,
Dere's wha de old folks stay.
All up and down de whole creation,
Sadly I roam,
Still longing for de old plantation,
And for de old folks at home.

Stephen Foster

In literature the Suwannee is the main setting for several older books: *Suwannee Valley* by **Bernard Borchardt** and **Eugene Sears** (New York: Harbinger House, 1940) describing this area in the 1880s; *Black Wench* by **Isaac H. Trabue (General Puntagord)** (Punta Gorda, FL: Isaac Trabue, 1900), an antislavery novel set in the first half of the nineteenth century; **Opie P. Read's** *On the Suwannee River, A Romance* (Chicago: Laird & Lee, 1895) telling of a preacher and his girlfriend; **Edwin L. Bynner's** *Zachary Phips* (Boston: Houghton, Mifflin, 1892), a novel of the First Seminole War; and **Captain (Thomas) Mayne Reid's** *Osceola the Seminole* (New York: Robert N. DeWitt, 1858) depicting a white man who falls in love with Osceola's sister. A short piece, "Steamboat Whistles on the Suwannee," is in a collection of Florida tales entitled *Flickering Lights, A Treasure Chest of Floridiana* by **Virgil E. Strickland** (New York: Exposition Press, 1959). A modern novel about life along the Suwannee in the first half of the twentieth century is **Joyce Hart's** *The Last Cracker* (Lawrenceville, VA: Brunswick Publishing Co., 1986). **Cecil Hulse Matschat's** *Suwannee River: Strange Green Land* (Athens, GA: University of Georgia Press, 1980) was originally published in 1938 in the Rivers of America series; it describes the river from its headwaters in the Okefenokee Swamp in southeast Georgia to the gulf near Cedar Key. **Clyde C. Council's** *Suwannee Country* (Sarasota, FL: Council Co., 1976) is a guide to the canoeing, boating, and recreational facilities along the river. Also *Fifty Years Down the Suwannee River* by **L.L. Barnett** (Branford, FL: Barnett, 1979) and *The Suwannee* by **Dorothy Kaucher** (Lake Wales, FL: Kaucher, 1972) retell the legends, history, and personalities associated with the river.

Live Oak

Live Oak was named after a large local oak tree. Live oaks were once used in the construction of wooden clipper ships, one of which was the *Constitution*, whose nickname, Old Ironsides, attested to the durability of the wood. A *Dictionary of Historical Allusions* by **Thomas Benfield Harbottle** (London: Swan Sonnenschein, 1904; reprinted in 1968 by Gale Research Co.) referred to Florida as the Live Oak State, indicating just how important this wood was to our nation. For more about the wood itself see *Live Oaking, Southern Timber for Tall Ships* by **Virginia S. Wood** (Boston: Northeastern University Press, 1981). The town is featured in *The Best Small Towns Under the Sun* by **Robert J. Howard** (McLean, VA: EPM Publications, 1989). A description of the Indians who used to live in the area is found in *McKeithen Weeden Island: The Culture of Northern Florida, AD 200-900* by **Jerald T. Milanich, Ann S. Cordell, Vernon J. Knight, Jr., Timothy A. Kohler**, and **Brenda J. Sigler-Lavelle** (Orlando: Academic Press, 1984).

Live Oak also played an important part in **Zora Neale Hurston's** novel *Seraph on the Suwannee* (New York: Scribner's, 1948), which is partly about the turpentine industry in this area. A nonfiction work is *Ruby McCollum, Woman in the Suwannee Jail* by **William Bradford Huie** (New York: New American Library, 1964) about a wealthy black woman who killed a respected white doctor in Live Oak in 1952. Zora Neale Hurston attended McCollum's trial and wrote about it for the *Pittsburgh Courier* newspaper, including a day-by-day account of the trial and a biography of McCollum, a sad story that ended: "Whatever her final destiny may be, she has not come to the bar craven and whimpering. She has been sturdy and strong...a woman who ruled the lives and fate of two strong men, one white, the other colored. She had dared defy the proud tradition of the Old South openly and she awaits her fate with courage and dignity." **Don Tracy's** novel entitled *The Hated One* (New York: Simon and Schuster, 1963), which takes place in a north Florida fictional town, is also about a black woman accused of murdering a popular white man in town.

Live Oak was the home of Lewis Powell, alias Lewis Payne, a young man whom John Wilkes Booth recruited in an assassination conspiracy to kill President Lincoln and several of his top aides in Washington, D.C. On April 14, 1865, while Booth fatally shot the President, Payne entered the home of Secretary of State William Seward, attacked Seward and his attendants, and escaped in the night to try to meet up with Booth, but was eventually captured. Although Seward lived, Payne was executed with three others on July 7, 1865.

Lewis Payne

His family left **Live** Oak in great sadness and humiliation to settle at Lake Jesup near Orlando—there to establish several Baptist churches and try to distance themselves from what their son had done in Washington. A novel about Payne is *A Court for Owls* by **Richard Adicks** (Sarasota, FL: Pineapple Press, 1989), a more sympathetic view of the man than **Leon O. Prior** produced in "Lewis Payne, Pawn of John Wilkes Booth," *Florida Historical Quarterly* (July 1964), pp. 1-20. Another novel about Live Oak is **Jo Ann Lordahl's** *Those Subtle Weeds* (New York: Ace Books, 1974).

The county comes off very well in the history of the National Guard in Florida and is singled out for special mention: "Suwannee County's record of service with the Militia and National Guard of Florida has been equalled by few and excelled by none. If this tradition of service is to survive the stresses and demands of the modern world, it will do so in local communities. If the experience of Suwannee County is any indication, the National Guard will survive."

Padlock

Padlock, southeast of Live Oak about one mile east of State Road 249, takes its name from the padlocking of prisoners there in the last century by a contractor who hired them from the state for his own work. **Wyatt Blassingame's** *Halo of Spears* (Garden City, NY: Doubleday, 1962) is a novel about a chain gang in the Suwannee River area. For a description of the leasing of convicts in Florida to private employers see the 1976 facsimile reproduction of the 1891 edition of **John C. Powell's** *The American Siberia* (Gainesville:

University Presses of Florida, 1976). The descriptions in these works accurately portray what happened to prisoners in Florida. One prisoner, Martin Tabert of North Dakota, came to Florida in the first part of the twentieth century, was picked up by the police for vagabonding and beaten to death. **Marjory Stoneman Douglas**, south Florida's environmentalist, was working as a reporter for the *Miami Herald* when she heard of Tabert's fate. His death moved her so deeply that she wrote a poem beginning "Martin Tabert of North Dakota is walking Florida now./O children, hark to his footsteps coming, for he's walking soft and slow." The poem aroused the public to write to the legislature, which finally passed laws that stopped the beating of prisoners in the work camps. Douglas, whose 1947 book, *The Everglades: River of Grass*, helped save the Everglades, wrote that the stoppage of the prisoner beatings was the single most outstanding accomplishment that came from her writing. A novel set in the area is **Nell Cotten's** *Piney Woods* (New York: Vanguard, 1962).

Mayo

Mayo was named after a Colonel Mayo. At the corner of Clark and Bloxham streets Northwest, three blocks east of the water tower and one block north of U.S. 27, is the First Apostolic Church, a house modeled after the one Nathaniel Hawthorne wrote about in *The House of the Seven Gables* (1851). It has an octagonal-shaped main section with seven free-standing gables. A town like Mayo is the setting for **Dorothy W. Ball's** novel entitled *Hurricane: The Story of a Friendship* (Indianapolis: Bobbs-Merrill, 1965) concerning interracial

First Apostolic Church

friendships and living on a north Florida farm. For more about the area see **Holmes Melton**'s *Lafayette County History and Heritage* (Mayo, FL: Mayo Rotary Club, 1976).

Jasper

North of Live Oak on State Road 129, Jasper was named in honor of Sergeant William Jasper, a Revolutionary War hero who rescued the American flag when the British were attacking a South Carolina fort. The post office at 105 Southeast First Street has two murals done by artist Pietro Lazzari in 1942 as part of the federal government's program to use artists during the Depression; entitled "News From Afar" and "Harvest At Home," they hang on each end wall of the post office lobby. For more about the murals in Florida post offices see **Karal Ann Marling**'s *Wall-to-Wall America* (Minneapolis: University of Minnesota Press, 1982) and **Sue Bridwell Beckham**'s *Depression Post Office Murals and Southern Culture* (Baton Rouge: Louisiana State University Press, 1989). For more about the area see *Early History of Hamilton County, Florida*, compiled by **Cora Hinton** (Jasper, FL: Jasper News, 1976) and *Hamilton County* by **MacKinlay Kantor** and **Tim Kantor** (New York: Macmillan, 1970).

Author **Lillian Smith** (1897-1966) was born in Jasper and educated at Piedmont College, Baltimore's Peabody Conservatory of Music, and Columbia University's Teachers College. She taught music for three years at a Methodist mission school in China; worked as a secretary to her brother Austin, the city manager of Fort Pierce, Florida; directed a girls camp for 25 years in Georgia; and published an anti-segregationist magazine titled successively *Pseudopodia, North Georgia Review*, and *South Today*. Her first published novel, *Strange Fruit* (1944), which dealt with an interracial love affair and segregation in Georgia, sold over three million copies, was translated into 16 languages, and was dramatized on Broadway. Other works included *Killers of the Dream* (1949—revised 1963), *The Journey* (1954), *Now Is the Time* (1955), *One Hour* (1959), *Memory of a Large Christmas* (1962), *Our Faces, Our Words* (1964), and *The Journey* (1965). Smith's manuscripts are housed in the University of Florida library in Gainesville. She once wrote about advantages of living in north Florida, how topographic phenomena could be symbols of a profound experience, how Florida's contradictions and anomalies offer symbols for the creative writer:

> I was born on the rim of that mysterious terrain which spills over from Georgia's Okefenokee Swamp into Florida. As a child, I walked on earth that trembled.... There were other fabulous things: a river that, now and then, disappeared into the earth and came up thirty miles away. Suddenly it happened: the fish were feeling secure and comfortable, then *whsst!* there they were, left wriggling on white hot sand with no water within miles. I learned early not to stake much on security; if fish didn't have it, why should I? And there were the sinks: a piece of land, ordinary land, was there today,

with perhaps a house on it; tomorrow, sunk into the earth forty feet down. Today, solid fact; tomorrow, emptiness. I learned my lessons early, those the existentialists have been reminding us of in recent decades.... I think what impressed me most was this: On that trembling earth of the Great Swamp, although a child could scarcely walk on it, heavy trees and jungled growth were supported by it. Is it not a superb image of civilization: all that men have dreamed and created, springing out of and supported by massive uncertainties? In this mythic and surreal place I lived as a child. In a world full of not only spiritual but physical ambiguities, each casting a shadow on the other.

Her reference to "earth that trembled" reflects the fact that the Okefenokee Swamp, a 435,000-acre swamp in southeast Georgia and northeast Florida near Jasper, takes its Indian name, which means *land of trembling earth*, from floating islands there which "tremble" when stepped on. The river that "disappeared into the earth and came up thirty miles away" refers to the north Florida rivers like the Santa Fe that go underground for miles and then reemerge on the surface. The "sinks" are the sinkholes that occasionally open up in Florida and swallow houses and cars. For a recent biography of Smith see **Anne C. Loveland's** *Lillian Smith: A Southerner Confronting the South, A Biography* (Baton Rouge: Louisiana State University Press, 1986).

Several novels are set in the Okefenokee: **Vereen Bell's** *Swamp Water* (Athens, GA: University of Georgia Press, 1981); **Linda Cline's** *Weakfoot* (New York: Lothrop & Lee, 1974); **Cecile H. Matschat's** *Ladd of the Big Swamp* (Philadelphia: Winston, 1954); and **Marjorie A. Zaff's** *The Mystery of the Great Swamp* (New York: Atheneum, 1967). **Nixon Smiley's** fictional *Crowder Tales* (Miami: Seemann Publishing Co., 1973) has stories about a town near the Florida-Georgia line. For a description of the area see **Franklin Russell's** *The Okefenokee Swamp* (New York: Time-Life Books, 1973) and **A.S. McQueen** and **Hamp Mizell's** *History of Okefenokee Swamp* (Clinton, SC: Press of Jacobs and Co., 1926).

Madison

Thirty miles west of Jasper is Madison, named after President James Madison and the home of Captain Colin P. Kelly, Jr. (1915-41), the first American hero of World War II. Two days after the Japanese attack on Pearl Harbor, he and his B-17 bomber crew shot up a Japanese warship but were in turn attacked by the enemy. He died when his plane crashed. He is buried at the north end in the Madison Oak Ridge Cemetery, 601 Northwest Washington Street. In the city park on U.S. 90 the Four Freedoms Monument, commemorating President Franklin D. Roosevelt's 1941 speech to Congress, is dedicated to the memory of Captain Kelly.

In the lobby of the main post office at 200 East Pinckney Street is a mural done by artist George Snow Hill in 1940 as part of the federal government's program to employ artists during the Depression; entitled "Long Staple Cotton

Gin," the mural depicts a scene in the manufacture of the city's most important industry, the growing of Sea Island cotton.

A novel set in Madison and in Lakeland in the late 1800s is **Lillian B. McCall**'s *The Unconquerable, A Florida Historical Novel* (New York: Exposition Press, 1958). Author **Joe A. Akerman, Jr.**, who wrote *Florida Cowman, A History of Florida Cattle Raising* (Kissimmee: Florida Cattlemen's Association, 1976) and *American Brahman: A History of the American Brahman* (Houston: American Brahman Breeders Association, 1982), taught at Madison's North Florida Junior College. Madison is the eastern terminus of **Clifton Paisley's** *The Red Hills of Florida, 1528-1865* (Tuscaloosa, AL: University of Alabama Press, 1989), a work that describes the people, agriculture, and history of the land between Madison and Marianna, Florida. For another book about the area see **Joseph Kitchens's** *Quail Plantations of South Georgia and North Florida* (Athens: University of Georgia Press, 1991). For more about the surrounding county see **Elizabeth H. Sims's** *A History of Madison County, Florida* (Madison: Madison County Historical Society, 1986).

Greenville

About 11 miles west of Madison is Greenville. Named after Greenville, South Carolina, the Florida town was the early home of entertainer Ray Charles (1930-), who moved here with his family soon after his birth in Albany, Georgia. When he began to go blind at age seven, he was sent to the State School for the Blind in St. Augustine, and there he learned how to play the piano. He returned in the summers to Greenville, where he attended the Shiloh Baptist Church, or to Tallahassee, where he played the piano with such people as Cannonball Adderley. At 15, he went to Jacksonville (where he stayed with friends at 752 West Church Street) and then on to Orlando (where he almost starved to death) and Tampa (where he began wearing dark glasses), and finally on to fame and fortune as a singer-pianist. For more about him see **Ray Charles** and **David Ritz's** *Brother Ray, Ray Charles' Own Story* (New York: Dial, 1978).

Monticello

This town north of I-10 on U.S. 19, which was named for Thomas Jefferson's Virginia home, has a courthouse modeled on that home and serves as the county seat of Jefferson County. For more about the area see **Jerrell H. Shofner's** *History of Jefferson County* (Tallahassee: Sentry Press, 1976). A novel about the town is **Ann O'Connell Rust's** *Monticello* (Orange Park, FL: Amaro Books, 1991).

Lloyd

Twenty-two miles west of Greenville is the town of Lloyd, birthplace of novelist **Mary Edwards Bryan** (1838-1913). After a childhood spent on her parents' plantation and an elopement at about age 15, she became editor of the *Georgia Literary and Temperance Crusader, Sunny South, Fireside Companion,* and *Fashion Bazaar,* the latter two out of New York City. She had at least nine novels published, including *Manch* (1880), *Wild Work* (1881), and *The Ghost of the Hurricane Hills, or, A Florida Girl* (1891). She died in Clarkston, Georgia. Although not a great novelist, she did distinguish herself as a professional writer and well-paid editor at a time when women were often discouraged from pursuing careers of their own.

Tallahassee

By 1821, the only large towns in Florida were St. Augustine in the east and Pensacola in the west, separated by 400 miles of inhospitable land where some Indians and a few white settlers lived. The two towns balanced each other in terms of historicity and potential for future development, forcing the legislature to recognize the importance of each. The legislative council, in fact, met in each of the two towns, first in Pensacola in 1822 and then in St. Augustine in 1823, but finally decided to establish a permanent capital midway between the two rivals at a place named Tallahassee, partly because of the difficulty of traveling the width of the state in those days and partly because of the desire for a compromise between the competing towns. The name of Tallahassee comes from a Creek Indian word meaning *old town.*

The center of Tallahassee, a city that calls itself "FloridaWith a Southern Accent," is the Capitol, where the Legislature meets and where — on the 22nd floor — the Florida Artists Hall of Fame honors such writers as Ernest Hemingway, Marjorie Kinnan Rawlings, and Tennessee Williams. Other sites in the city that need to be mentioned in this Guide include "The Grove" next to the Governor's mansion and the setting of the city's most famous novel, **Maurice Thompson's** *A Tallahassee Girl* (Boston: Houghton, 1881) about the post-Civil War town. The Knott House Museum, which is also called "The House That Rhymes" at 301 E. Park Avenue, has poems attached to furniture and fixtures throughout, for example "I'm just an old, old house/Holding within my walls/Strange tales of life and love and strife/Which no one else recalls." Also, the Museum of History & Natural Science has popular exhibits like the Discovery Center and Princess Catherine Murat's plantation home, Bellevue.

Florida State University (FSU) was founded in 1857 as the Seminary West of the Suwannee River. It became the Florida State College and then a women's college in 1905 and finally Florida State University in 1947. It now has an enrollment of about 28,000 students. Among its many outstanding features is the Robert Manning Strozier Library in the center of the campus. The library has over 1,800,000 books and periodicals, over 155,000 maps, and over 595,000 government documents. The special collections division, in addition to manuscripts and rare books, includes the Florida Collection, the Shaw Collection of "Childhood in Poetry," the Carothers Memorial Collection of Bibles and Rare Books, the McGregor Collection of early Americana, the Lois Lenski Collection of books for children, the Scottish Collection, and the Kelmscott Press

Books. For more about the university see **Doak S. Campbell**'s *A University in Transition* (Tallahassee: Florida State University Press, 1964) and **Martee Wills** and **Joan Perry Morris**'s *Seminole History* (Jacksonville: South Star Publishing Co., 1987).

For more about the school's great football team see **Ben Brown's** *Saint Bobby and the Barbarians* (New York: Doubleday, 1992); *FSU Football, An Inside Look* (Tallahassee: Tallahassee Democrat, 1992); **Bill McGrotha's** *Seminoles! The First Forty Years* (Tallahassee: Tallahassee Democrat, 1987); two books by **James Pickett Jones**: *F.S.U. One Time!: The Bowden Years* (1983) and *F.S.U. One Time! A History of Seminole Football* (1973), both published by Tallahassee's Sentry Press; and **Julian Derieux Clarkson**'s *Let No Man Put Asunder* (Fort Myers, FL: Clarkson, 1968) about the rivalry with the University of Florida.

Among writers at FSU whom we should mention here are the following: **Van(dall) K(line) Brock** (1932-) spent his early years near Moultrie, Georgia, and later earned a B.A. from Emory University, and M.A., M.F.A., and Ph.D. degrees from the University of Iowa. Since 1970, he has taught writing and literature at FSU and founded/coordinated for some time the Apalachee Poetry Center, the Anhinga Press, a Florida Poets-in-the-Prisons program, and the Tallahassee Poets-in-the-Schools program. His books of poetry include *Final Belief* (1972), *Weighing the Penalties* (1977), and *The Hard Essential Landscape* (1979). He has also edited books of poems by children (*Lime Tree Prism* [1972] and *A Spot of Purple Is Deaf* [1974]) and by prisoners (*The Space Behind the Clock* [1975]). In 1977, he was one of two featured poets in the journal *Poets in the South*, in which he was the subject of a 40-page critical feature. His poems, five of them winning prestigious prizes, have appeared in numerous periodicals and anthologies.

Janet Burroway (1936-), who was born in Tucson, Arizona, is a professor of English at FSU, where she has been teaching since 1971. Her published poetry includes *But to the Season* (1961), *Material Goods* (1980), and selections in *The Guinness Book of Poetry* (1961) and *Sound and Sense* (1973). Her plays have been produced at Barnard College (*Garden Party*, 1958), the Yale School of Drama (*The Fantasy Level*, 1961), and on TV (*Hoddinott Veiling*, 1970, and *Due Care and Attention*, 1973). Her novels include *Descend Again* (1960), *Eyes* (1966), *The Dancer from the Dance* (1968), *The Buzzards* (1969 — which was nominated for the Pulitzer Prize), *Raw Silk* (1977), *Opening Nights* (1985), and *Cutting Stone* (1992). Her *Writing Fiction* (1982) is a guide to the narrative craft.

Gloria Jahoda (1926-1980), who lived in Tallahassee from 1963 until her death, wrote novels such as *Annie* (1960; republished in 1973 as *The House of Bickley*) and *Delilah's Mountain*, and five nonfiction books: *The Other Florida* (New York: Scribner, 1967) about north Florida; *The Road to Samarkand: Frederick Delius and His Music* (New York: Scribner's, 1969) about the composer who lived near Jacksonville; *River of the Golden Ibis* (New York: Holt, 1973) about the Hillsborough River near Tampa; *The Trail of Tears* (New York: Holt, 1975); and *Florida, A Bicentennial History* (New York: Norton, 1976).

David Kirby (1944-), who has taught at FSU since 1969, has written works on American literature, as well as authoring books of poetry: *The Opera Lover* (1977); *Sarah Bernhardt's Leg* (1983); *Diving for Poems* (1985); and *Saving the Young Men of Vienna* (1987), the winner of the 1987 Brittingham Prize of Poetry.

Anne Rowe (1945-) has published two significant books that deal, in whole or in part, with Florida: *The Enchanted Country: Northern Writers in the South, 1865-1910* (Baton Rouge: Louisiana State University Press, 1978) and *The Idea of Florida in the American Literary Imagination* (Baton Rouge: Louisiana State University Press, 1986).

Michael Shaara (1929-1988) was born in Jersey City, New Jersey, and earned a B.A. from Rutgers University. He worked as a paratrooper, sailor, police officer, professional boxer, and educator before becoming a writer and working at FSU from 1961 until 1973. He published four novels: *The Broken Place* (1968); *The Killer Angels* (1974),which won the Pulitzer Prize for fiction; *The Herald* (1981); and — posthumously — *For Love of the Game* (1991). Simon & Schuster published his *Collected Short Stories* in 1981. Concerning his work he said:

> I have written almost every known type of writing, from science fiction through history, through medical journalism and *Playboy* stories, always because I wrote only what came to mind, with no goal and little income, always for the joy of it, and it has been a great joy. The only trouble comes from the "market mind" of the editor when the work is done. I have traveled over most of the world, lived three years in South Africa, two years in Italy, speak some foreign languages, and love airplanes, almost as much as women. I enjoyed teaching, because it taught me a lot.

John Mackay Shaw (1897-1984) was born in Glasgow, Scotland, came to the United States in 1911, and became a U.S. citizen in 1922. He spent a good part of his career in business and did not enter the academic community until he was 63, but he was determined to inculcate in American students a love of poetry. He collected thousands of poetry books and eventually donated what came to be called the Shaw "Childhood in Poetry" Collection to Florida State University; he then worked as a voluntary curator of the collection (1960-1984) and was responsible for acquiring over 26,000 poetry books and manuscripts for FSU. He published a multi-volume index of the collection entitled *Childhood in Poetry* (1967-1980) and wrote several books of poetry for his own children, including *The Things I Want* (1967) and *Zumpin* (1969). He continued addressing students about poetry, even in his eighty-seventh year, and did much to fulfill his goal of passing on his love of poetry to countless students.

Sheila Taylor wrote novels that include *Faultline* (1982), *Spring Forward/Fall Back* (1985), and *Southbound* (1990) and poetry that includes *Slow Dancing at Miss Polly's* (1989).

Professors in other departments who write about Florida include **Roberto G. Fernández** (see Chapter Five), **James P. Jones** (*F.S.U. One Time! A History of Seminole Football* [Tallahassee: Sentry Press, 1973] and *F.S.U. One Time! The Bowden Years* [Tallahassee: Sentry Press, 1983]), **Joe M. Richardson** (*The Negro in the Reconstruction of Florida, 1865-1877* [Tallahassee: Florida State University, 1965]), and **William Warren Rogers** (*Outposts on the Gulf: Saint George Island and Apalachicola From Early Exploration to World War II* [Pensacola: University of West Florida Press, 1986], *Tallahassee & Leon County* — with **Mary Louise Ellis** [Tallahassee: Historic Tallahassee Preservation Board, 1986], and *Favored Land: A History of Tallahassee and Leon County* — with **Mary Louise Ellis** and **Joan Morris** [Norfolk: Donning, 1988]).

Other Tallahassee authors we should mention include the legendary radio broadcaster **Red Barber**, whose books include *The Rhubarb Patch* (1954), *Rhubarb in the Catbird Seat* with **Robert Creamer** (1968), and *Walk in the Spirit* (1969); **Ben Green** (*Finest Kind: A Celebration of a Florida Fishing Village* [Macon, GA: Mercer University Press, 1985] and *The Soldier of Fortune Murders: A True Story of Obsessive Love and Murder-for-Hire* [New York: Delacorte, 1992]); **Barbara Hamby**, the editor of the Apalachee Press and the *Apalachee Quarterly* and author of a poetry collection: *Eating Bees* (1992); **Tom Hillstrom** (*Coal* [1980] and *Riddle* [1987] — novels); **Allen Morris**, the distinguished clerk emeritus of the Florida House of Representatives, House historian, the first full-time political correspondent in Tallahassee, the compiler for many years of the *Florida Handbook*, and the author of *Florida Place Names* (Coral Gables, FL: University of Miami Press, 1974); **Joan Perry Morris**, the archivist of the state's collection of photographs, the photo editor for *Favored Land* (mentioned earlier), the editor — with **Lee H. Warner** — of *The Photographs of Alvan S. Harper, Tallahassee, 1885-1910* (Tallahassee: University Presses of Florida, 1983) and co-author of *Seminole History* (mentioned above); **John Parker** editor of Cedarwinds Publishing Company and author of the novel *Once a Runner* (1978) and essay collections that include *Runners and Other Dreamers* (1983) and *Aerobic Chic and Other Delusions* (1983) and *The Frank Shorter Story* (1972); **Bob Shacochis**, author of the short story collections *Easy in the Islands* — an American Book Award Winner (1985) and *The Next New World* (1989); and **Robert Sherrill**, author of many books, including *The Accidental President* (1967), *The Drugstore Liberal* — with **Harry W. Ernst** (1968), and *Gothic Politics in the Deep South* (1968); and **Charlotte Allen Williams** (*Florida Quilts* [Gainesville: University Press of Florida, 1992]).

FSU's English department has two literary magazines (*The Kudzu Review* and *Sundog: The Southeast Review*) and sponsors the World's Best Short Short Story contest, which attracts thousands of entries from around the world. The creative-writing division, under the guidance of **Jerome Stern** (*Making Shapely Fiction*, 1991), continues to attract first-rate students. Among the presses in Tallahassee are Apalachee Press, publisher of *The Apalachee Quarterly* and collections by Florida poets, for example **Christy Sheffield**

Sanford's *Only the Nude Can Redeem the Landscape* and **Sandra Castillo's** *Red Letters*; Naiad Press, which was founded in 1973 and has over 130 titles in print, especially feminist and lesbian fiction, including mysteries, science-fiction, and westerns; and Ridgefield Press, edited by Richard Milazzo and Tricia Collins and the producer of an anthology: *Fiction South/Fiction North* (1992).

When Florida Agricultural and Mechanical University (FAMU) was founded in 1887 as the first state-supported black institution of public higher education in Florida, it had 15 students, two instructors, and one building. Today it has over 5,000 students, 600 employees, and 70 buildings, and is part of the nine-university public education system in the state. Its more than 20,000 alumni are living throughout the world.

The Carnegie Library, which is the oldest standing building at the university, was the first Carnegie Library to be established on the campus of a black, land-grant college; it has housed the Florida Black Archives Research Center and Museum, which collects and preserves source material on or about African-American history and culture.

Leedell W. Neyland and **John W. Riley**'s *The History of Florida Agricultural and Mechanical University* (Gainesville: University of Florida Press, 1963) gives a good description of the school. **Wyatt Blassingame**'s *Jake Gaither: Winning Coach* (Champaign, IL: Garrard Publishing Co., 1969) is a biography of one of the school's famous football coaches. For more about many of the distinguished African-Americans in Florida see **Leedell W. Neyland**'s *Twelve Black Floridians* (Tallahassee: Florida Agricultural and Mechanical University Foundation, 1970) and **J. Irving E. Scott**'s *The Education of Black People in Florida* (Philadelphia: Dorrance, 1974). For a history of the 1956 Tallahassee bus boycott and other moves to desegregate facilities see **Charles U. Smith**'s *The Civil Rights Movement in Florida and the United States* (Tallahassee: Father and Son Publishing, 1989).

Among the novels set in Tallahassee are **Brett Halliday**'s *Lady Be Bad* (New York: Dell, 1969), **Nanci Kincaid**'s *Crossing Blood* (New York: Putnam, 1992), **Lillian B. McCall**'s *The Unconquerables* (New York: Exposition Press, 1958), **May Nickerson Wallace**'s *Challenge to Babs* (New York: Abelard, 1952), **Mary Elizabeth Witherspoon**'s *Somebody Speak For Katy* (New York: Dodd, Mead, 1950), and **Robert Wudtke**'s *The Bridge* (Lantana, FL: Literature Press, 1961).

For a history of Tallahassee and the area see **Mary Louise Ellis** and **William Warren Rogers**'s *Favored Land: Tallahassee: A History of Tallahassee and Leon County* (Norfolk, VA: Donning, 1988) and the same authors' *Tallahassee & Leon County: A History and Bibliography* (Tallahassee: Florida Department of State, 1986). Also see **Hampton Dunn**'s *Yesterday's Tallahassee* (Miami: Seemann Publishing Co., 1974) and **Bertram H. Groene**'s *Ante-Bellum Tallahassee* (Tallahassee: Florida Heritage Foundation, 1971). **Eleanor Ketchum**'s *Tales of Tallahassee* (Tallahassee: Jerry Dye and Associates, Inc., 1976) has vignettes about the people and places of the city, for example the Prince and Princess Murat. (For more about them see Chapter Two of this *Guide* and **Alfred**

Jackson Hanna's *A Prince in Their Midst* [Norman, OK: University of Oklahoma Press, 1946]).

Wakulla Springs

Ten miles south of Tallahasee on S.R. 61 is the site of these springs, which are the world's largest and deepest at 185 feet. The mouth of the spring is 100 feet wide and gushes forth about 180 million gallons of water a day. In the late 1950s divers discovered at the bottom skeletons of mammoths, mastodons, giant ground sloths, bear, deer, and camels. The site features glass-bottom boats and wildlife in their natural habitat. Over 20 movies, such as *Creature From the Black Lagoon* (1954), *Airport 77* (1976), and *Joe Panther* (1976), were filmed in the clear springs here. **Kirk Munroe**'s novel *Wakulla, A Story of Adventure in Florida* (1901) is an adolescent book about a family here in the 1880s. **Reinette Gamble Long**'s long poem *Osola, An Epic Poem: The Legend of the Mysterious Smoke of Wakulla* (1922) tells of a young Indian who kept a fire burning for many years by the spring in order to help his chief find the way back from Pensacola.

Newport

South of Tallahassee on U.S. 98 is the town of Newport, so named because it was a new port, having taken the place of storm-devastated Port Leon to the south. One of its former residents was the Reverend Charles Beecher, brother of author **Harriet Beecher Stowe** and state superintendent of education from 1871 to 1873. Although he was part of the post-Civil War carpetbag government of Florida, he used his influence to have Tallahassee hold a public reception for his sister, who was best known (and hated) for her *Uncle Tom's Cabin* (1852), but who did much to entice tourists to Florida with her popular *Palmetto Leaves* (1873).

A nineteenth-century businessman in Newport who opposed Florida's secession in the Civil War was Daniel Ladd. He helped establish the town on the St. Marks River and prospered in river transport and real estate before the Civil War crippled the area. **Jerrell H. Shofner**'s *Daniel Ladd: Merchant Prince of Frontier Florida* (Gainesville: University Presses of Florida, 1978) is a biography of this active entrepreneur.

Panacea

West and south on U.S. 98 is Panacea, a town whose nearby springs inspired developers to name it after the Greek goddess of healing. One of the authors who has made Panacea his home is poet **Francis Poole** (1947-). Born in Vermont, he came to Florida in 1951 and lived in places like Miami, Naples, Orlando, Fort Pierce, Boca Raton, and Tallahassee. He has published five chapbooks of poetry: *Red Motion Rose Ocean* (1973), *Zero Zero* (1974), *Garbo* (1975), *Dogfeast* (1976), and *Gestures* (1979). He has edited three anthologies of children's poetry: *Lime Tree Prism* (1972), *A Spot of Purple Is Deaf* (1974), and

Oh See Can We Say (1975); and he helped found Anhinga Press, which has published books of poetry over the years.

Jutting out into the Gulf of Mexico is one of the best-known docks along the coast, made famous by one of Florida's most important environmental writers, **Jack Rudloe** (1943-), who wrote the following:

> When you go out onto a dock you leave the problems of land behind you, yet you are not involved with the problems of the sea. You don't have to worry about boats breaking down or whether you're going to run out of fuel or whether your dock is going to spring a leak. If the weather is bad, you just turn around and go back to shore. Somehow, just standing there looking down into the water makes trouble fade off into the background. All your problems are left on the dry land while you have almost all the security of land beneath your feet and all the openness of the sea before you.

Rudloe's books include *The Sea Brings Forth* (New York: Knopf, 1968); *The Erotic Ocean* (New York: Crowell, 1971); *The Living Dock at Panacea* (New York: Knopf, 1977 — revised in 1988 as *The Living Dock*); *Time of the Turtle*

(New York: Knopf, 1979); and *The Wilderness Coast: Adventures of a Gulf Coast Naturalist* (New York: Dutton, 1988). One of the chapters in *The Wilderness Coast*, which was first printed in *Audubon* and then later reprinted in *Reader's Digest*, is a true story of how Rudloe unsuccessfully fought an alligator underwater to save Rudloe's dog, which the alligator had grabbed. This self-taught biologist and his wife, Anne (who has a Ph.D. in biology), own Gulf Specimen Marine Laboratories, Inc., which supplies living marine creatures to scientists

Jack Rudloe

around the world engaged in research. Through his writing and speeches he has made thousands of Floridians and non-Floridians aware of how fragile the Gulf coast is.

THE LITERARY MAGAZINES OF FLORIDA

JEROME STERN

Literary magazines come about when a community of writers reaches a critical mass. The resulting soup generates enough heat to create an organized life force. This life force, called an editor, swirls about, cajoling writings, gathering manuscripts, designing pages, talking to printers, convincing booksellers, and finally producing an offspring — The Literary Magazine.

Some literary magazines appear so quietly and vanish so quickly that they leave almost no imprint on the culture. Others explode on the scene, proclaiming new principles of writing while sending the old out to pasture. Some devote themselves to perpetuating tradition, proclaiming themselves bastions of civilization in an age of galloping degeneration. Some are only open to members of an organization, inhabitants of a particular region, or adherents of a certain aesthetic.

The magazines last one issue, or three, or twelve, but usually not very many. The editor runs out of money. The literary group has a falling out. People go on to other things. It's the nature of the beast. The magazines are not failures for being short-lived. They have served their purpose, expressing the writing and art of the moment, however long that moment is. And some of them have pretty long moments — decades, like *Poetry: A Magazine of Verse* founded in 1912 in Chicago and still running strong.

Florida's literary magazines have had similar histories. Inspired individuals, writing communitites, and cultural institutions have all engendered journals.

What occurred, however, is pretty hard to find. Collections by state and institutional libraries are miscellaneous, scant, or nonexistent. Not only is no one tracking literary periodicals produced throughout the state, but college and university libraries frequently don't even have complete files of their own publications. Independent literary magazines, even when produced right in town by local writers, are rarely found in their county libraries. The cultural loss is incalculable. If literary journals don't get saved in permanent collections they have no life after life.

According to the noted Florida bibliographer Jim Servies, "the medium for literary expression in early Florida was the newspaper. Some newspapers were so individual they almost constitute their own literature." In the twentieth century newspapers continued to print poetry and fiction, but the custom largely faded except in county papers. The *Tampa Tribune*, however, continues to publish stories in its "Fiction Quarterly." Unfortunately nearly all of Florida's early newspaper heritage has disappeared.

Jacksonville should be recognized for its pioneering launching of two ambitious literary ventures, *Florida Magazine* in 1900 and *Florida Review* in 1909. Although neither lasted very long they reflected a faith that Jacksonville was developing a metropolitan culture capable of supporting such enterprises.

The first literary magazine from an institution of higher learning appears to be Florida State College for Women's *The Talisman* in 1906. Fiction, poetry, and essays were mixed with light campus gossip and accounts of social and academic activities. College and university publications evolved differently on various campuses. Some only printed student work. Many included faculty or alumni. As major literary magazines became established in American life, Florida university publications echoed their policies by soliciting contributions from well-known writers and welcoming submissions nationally.

Magazines from community colleges tend to be primarily student work, but Florida Community College's *Kalliope* built its reputation by its focus on women in the arts. As the decades pass, community college magazines will become progressively more valuable records of their cultural period.

The long-running *Literary Florida* is somewhat deceptively titled. It turns out to be not very literary at all — devoting itself mainly to cheerful features on the delights of Florida's towns and beaches or anecdotes from Florida history.

Directly and indirectly Florida colleges and universities have provided stability by sponsoring some of the longest-lived and most successful publications. Rollins College, for example, produced its *Flamingo* for 41 years. Many independent magazines have developed from university communities; faculty and students became the source of editors, writers, and audience. The longest-running independent magazine I found was *Epos*. Tallahassee's *Apalachee Quarterly* is almost 20 years old.

Another group of magazines are identified with writer's groups and associations. Usually devoted to poetry, they tend to favor traditional verse, serious or light, often inviting widespread participation through contests recognizing a variety of forms. The *Miami Daily News* for many years included a Sunday poetry feature "Miami Muse." An annual anthology drawn from "Florida Poets and Poets Visiting Florida" was published from 1930 to 1941.

Many titles probably exist uncatalogued. Private collections, local public libraries, and community college libraries will help to make the following list more complete. A date followed by a hyphen means I am reasonably sure of the year of the first issue though the termination date is not established. A date without a hyphen means the magazine was in existence at that time; it's not clear when it started or ceased publication. No date means it exists or existed but I'm not sure when.

What follows is a step toward the recognition of Florida's literary heritage as expressed in its own journals. My hope is that this foray precipitates more awareness of their importance in the literary history of Florida.

Albatross. Anabiosis Press, Englewood, 1986-.
Almanack. Central Florida Community College, Ocala, 1990.

Ampersand: The South Florida Review. University of South Florida, Tampa, 1973-. Continues: *South Florida Review.*

Apalachee Quarterly. Tallahassee, 1973-.

Apocalypse. St. Petersburg, 1976.

Argot. Gulf Coast Community College, Panama City, 1990.

Black Mullet Review, Tampa, 1987.

Both Sides Now. Jacksonville, 1969-1973.

Brochure of the Poetry Society of Florida. Winter Park, 1928-1929.

Brushing. Rollins College, Winter Park, Spring 1971-.

Calli's Tales. Palmetto, 1982.

Caribbean Review. Florida International University, Miami, 1969-.

Cathartic. Fort Lauderdale, 1974-.

Chimera Connections. Gainesville, 1986-.

Cycle. Lily Lawrence Bow, Homestead, March 1935-March 1943.

Devil's Millhopper. LaCrosse, 1978-.

DIS. Kim MacQueen, Tallahassee 1991-.

Distaff: Spinner of Yarns. Florida State College For Women: Tallahassee 1926-1947. Title changes: 1934 *The Distaff Quarterly*; 1935-1947 *The Distaff: A Critical Literary Quarterly.*

Dragon-Fly. DeLand, Oct. 15, 1935-May 15, 1936.

Dramatika. Tarpon Springs, 1980.

Earthwise, also, *Earthwise Review.* Miami, 1978-.

Emerald Coast Review. West Florida Literary Federation, Pensacola, 1988-.

EPOS. Will Tullos and Evelyn Thorne, Crescent City, 1948-1978. Subtitled "The Work of American and British Poets," the journal was independent until Tullos' retirement. Rollins College became publisher with the Winter 1973 issue.

Escapist. St. Augustine, 1990-.

Experience. Florida Community College, Jacksonville, 1990.

Eyrie. Tallahassee Community College, Tallahassee. Winter 1982-.

Flamingo. Rollins College, Winter Park, 1927-1968.

Florida Journal of Verse. Homestead, 1935-1943.

Florida Magazine: History, Science, Health, Fiction, Recreation, Fashion, Music Review. Jacksonville, January 1900-September 1903. This lively and ambitious attempt at a general periodical with a strong cultural interest lasted a few years before merging with the Atlanta journal, *Alkahest.*

Florida Magazine of Verse. Winter Park, 1940-.

Florida Quarterly. University of Florida, Gainesville, 1967-1976.

Florida Review. Gerard Estelle Muriel, Jacksonville, 1909-1911.

Florida Review: A Magazine of Student Opinion. University of Florida, Gainesville, Dec 15, 1927-March 1928.

Florida Review. University of Florida, Gainesville, 1957-1958. *Florida Review.* University of Central Florida, Orlando, 1972-.

Florida State Literary Anthology. Florida State University, Tallahassee ,1958-1960.

Frozen Waffles. Bradenton, 1980.

Gulf Stream Magazine. Florida International University, North Miami, 1984-.

Half Tones to Jubilee. Pensacola Junior College, Pensacola, 1985-.

Human Voice Quarterly. Olivant Press, Homestead, 1965-, also known as *HVQ* was continued as *Human Voice*, then as *Weid.*

Intercom. Ridge Manor, 1980.

Isis. Polk Community College, Winter Haven, 1990.

It's. Broward Community College, Pembroke Pines, 1990.

Jacksonville Poetry Quarterly. Jacksonville, 1978.

Journey. Seminole Community College, Sanford, 1990.

Kalliope: A Journal of Women's Art. Florida Community College at Jacksonville, Jacksonville, 1978-.

Key West Journal of the Arts. Pocket Poetry Press, 1976.

Key West Review. Key West, 1988-.

Konglomerati. Gulfport, 1972-.

Kudzu Review. Florida State University, Tallahassee 1990-.

Legend. Florida State University, Tallahassee. 1961-1970.

Literary Florida. Tampa, 1944-1958.

Local Muse. Gainesville, June 1976-May 1977. Continued as *Devil's Millhopper.*

Mangrove. University of Florida, Gainesville, Spring 1982-Winter 1984; continued as *Mangrove Review*, 1984-1985; title then returns to *Mangrove.*

Middle Eastern Dancer. Casselberry, 1979.

Naiad & Odyssey. Lake Sumter Community College, Leesburg, 1990.

New Collage Magazine. Sarasota, 1970-. Title changed to *New Collage* with 1975/76 issue.

No Idea Magazine. Gainesville, 1985-.

Nomad. Tallahassee, 1991.

Obelisk. St. Petersburg Community College, St Petersburg, 1990.

Ochlockonee Review. Tallahassee, 1980.

Onionhead. Lakeland, 1989-.

Organica Quarterly. Tampa, 1991.

The Palmetto Review. Miami Springs, 1983-.

Pandora. Tampa, 1982.

Panhandler. University of West Florida, Pensacola, 1976-.

Panhandler Chapbook. University of West Florida, Pensacola.

Pentangle. Manatee Community College, Bradenton, 1990.

Pocket Poetry. Richard Marsh, Key West, 1973-. Title at first was *Pocket Poetry Monthly.*

Poetry Caravan. Lakeland, 1936-1939. Superseded by *Poetry Caravan* and *Silhouette.*

Poetry Florida And . . . [The three periods are part of the title]. Deland, 1967-, ed. William E. Taylor, Professor of English at Stetson University.

Poetry Review. Duane Locke, University of Tampa, Tampa. 1964-.

Poetry Venture. St.Petersburg, Jane McClellan, ed. 1968-1973. Continued by: *PV. Poetry Venture* "An international poetry magazine." 1973-.

Poets in the South. University of South Florida, Tampa, 1977-1982.

Proteus. Brevard Community College, Melbourne, 1990.

Purple Pegasus. Port St. Joe High School, Port St. Joe, 1982-.

Red Bass, Tallahassee, 1987.

Resonance. Sumterville, 1987.

Reverse. Miami Shores, 1988-.

Riverside Quarterly. Gainesville, 1978.

Rollins Animated Magazine. Rollins College, Winter Park, 1927-.

Ruby's Pearls. Callahan, 1991-.

Scholia Satyrica. University of South Florida, Tampa, 1975-.

Silver Fires. Coral Gables, 1935.

Silver Web. Tallahassee, 1989-. Formerly *Sterling Web*.

Smoke Signals. Florida State University, Spring 1951-1970. A satiric-comic magazine.

Sole Proprietor. Miami, 1976.

South. Stetson University, DeLand 1969-1973.

South Florida Poetry Journal. University of South Florida, Tampa, 1968-.

South Florida Poetry Review. South Florida Poetry Institute, Fort Lauderdale, 1982-.

South Florida Review. University of South Florida, Tampa, 1967-1972. Continued by *Ampersand*.

Sporan. Daytona Beach Community College, Daytona Beach, 1990.

Sun Dog: The Southeast Review. Florida State University, Tallahassee 1979-.

Swallow's Tale. Tallahassee, 1984.

Swampfire: A Literary Journal. Port St. Joe, 1982.

Talaria: A Critical-Literary Quarterly. Florida State University, Tallahassee, Fall 1947-Winter 1951. Continues *Distaff: A Critical-Literary Quarterly*.

Talisman. Florida State College for Women, Tallahassee, April 1906-May 1914.

Tampa Review. University of Tampa, Tampa, 1988-.

Tempest: Avant-Garde Poetry. Miami, 1980.

Tendril. Key West, 1987.

Thematic Poetry Quarterly. Marianna, 1987.

Tiotis Poetry News. Fort Myers, 1980.

Triad, Galleria. Hillsborough Community College, Tampa, 1990.

UT: A Magazine of Immanentist and Other Poetries. Duane Locke, University of Tampa, Tampa, 1974.

Valencian. Valencia Community College, Orlando, 1990.

Viking Horn. St. John's Community College, Palatka, 1990.

Weid; the Sensibility Revue. Olivant Press, Homestead, 1965-. See *Human Voice*.

White Mule. Thomas Abrams, Tampa, 1975-.

Woodrider. Lake City Community College, Lake City, 1990.

Yesterday's Magazette. Sarasota, 1979-.

Zelo. Winter Park, 1985-1989.

Jerome Stern is a professor of English at Florida State University in Tallahassee.

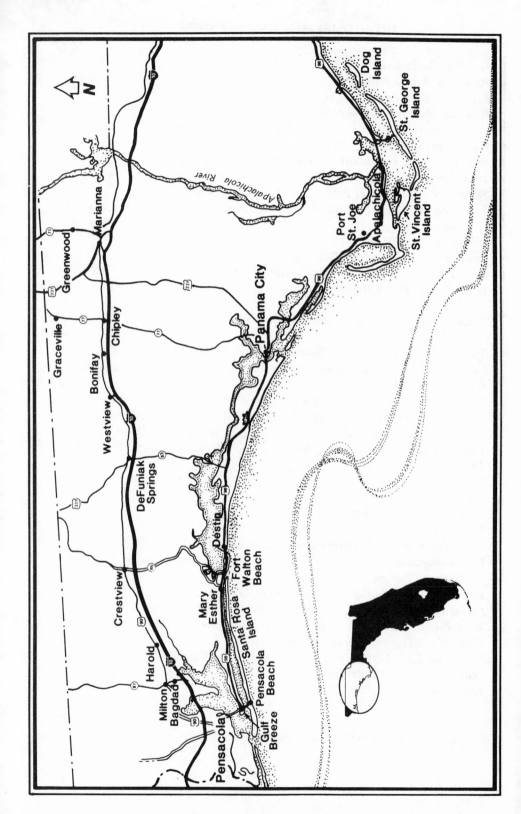

10 THE FLORIDA PANHANDLE

DEAN DEBOLT

Apalachicola River Valley

Driving west on Interstate 10, today's travelers cross the Apalachicola River and immediately adjust their watches. This river marks a time-zone boundary placing much of Florida in the eastern time zone and the Florida Panhandle in the central time zone. Yet this river and the Apalachicola River Valley have played a strategic part in Florida history. De Soto's men crossed the river on their trek into the interior, and Spanish, British, and Indian residents placed great importance on the resources of the valley.

For the Indians, the valley surrounded by fertile lands and lush forest provided food, trade goods (fur pelts), and security. During the Seminole Indian wars, the Indians used the Apalachicola River valley to evade army regulars who found the junglelike terrain nearly impassable. **Robert Wilder's** *Bright Feather* (New York: Putnam's, 1948) provides a fictional account of life in this region during the Second Seminole War.

In the 1840s, with the growth of King Cotton as the predominant southern commodity, the valley took on new importance. The Apalachicola River valley provided a transportation conduit from the interior of Alabama and Georgia to the Gulf of Mexico. A thriving movement of crops, passengers, and commerce opened up between Columbus, Georgia, the northern terminus of the Apalachicola River, and Apalachicola, Florida, 300 miles south on the Gulf of Mexico.

When the Civil War broke out, the Confederacy established the Confederate Navy Yard at Columbus, and many of the South's gunboats and ironclads were constructed by shipyards along the river. At the southern terminus, Apalachicola had an extensive salt-making operation to provide provisions for Confederate military forces. **Maxine Turner** has documented the Civil War history of the valley in *Navy Gray: A Story of the Confederate Navy on the Chattahoochee and Apalachicola Rivers* (Tuscaloosa, AL: University of Alabama Press, 1988). Dr. **Frank Slaughter**, a prolific Florida author, used the valley as a setting for his fiction about Dr. Kit Clark in *Storm Haven* (Garden City, NY: Doubleday, 1953), which is set in 1863. **Cora Mitchel's** *Reminiscences of the Civil War* (Providence, RI: Snow & Farnham Co., 1916) offers first-hand testimony of life in Columbus and Apalachicola up through the Civil War by the daughter of Thomas Leeds Mitchel, a cotton merchant from Connecticut.

The Apalachicola River winds its way south, cutting through the Panhandle and broadening out into Apalachicola Bay before meeting the Gulf of Mexico. In 1832, the county of Fayette was created between the Apalachicola River and the Chipola River, with a northern boundary of the Alabama state line. Just as quickly, in 1834, Fayette was abolished and became the only Florida county to pass out of existence; other counties have either been renamed or recarved from other counties. **Rubylea Hall**'s *God Has a Sense of Humor* (New York: Duell, Sloan, 1960) is centered on the Apalachicola River country, including Calhoun County and Wewahitchka.

Apalachicola

Located on U.S. 98 on the western edge of Apalachicola Bay, Apalachicola, a once-thriving port city, is today home to Florida's oyster industry. The name of this beautiful little town comes from an Indian word meaning *the people on the other side*, referring to the term used by one Indian tribe for another, or from an Indian word meaning *allies*. Known for its Apalachicola Bay oysters, the town was one of the most important commercial centers of Florida in the third and fourth decades of the nineteenth century because of its location southwest of Tallahassee and near the Gulf of Mexico. After its founding in 1831, Apalachicola quickly became the third-largest cotton-shipping port on the gulf. It grew even more when the city of St. Joseph (located 25 miles west on St. Joseph's Bay) was abandoned during a yellow-fever epidemic in 1841 and its population moved to Apalachicola. The booming port period is

City of Apalachicola, 1837

chronicled by **Alexander Key** (1904-) in his novel *The Wrath and the Wind* (Indianapolis: Bobbs-Merrill, 1949) about the fictitious adventures of Maury St. John, a slave-trader in Apalachicola, and the destruction of St. Joseph by yellow fever and a hurricane. It acquired its first newspaper, the *Advertiser*, in 1833, to be followed three years later by the *Apalachicola Gazette*, a newspaper whose main function was to attack the nearby town of St. Joseph. It became Florida's first daily newspaper and lasted from 1839 to 1840.

Alexander Key also used Apalachicola as a setting for another novel, *Island Light* (Indianapolis: Bobbs-Merrill, 1950), which traces the escape of Maximilian Ewing, a Confederate prisoner, from Fort Jefferson near Key West to St. George Lighthouse on Apalachicola Bay. Key is perhaps better known for illustrating other novels and for his fantasy novel *Escape to Witch Mountain* (1968), which was made into a Walt Disney film in 1975. Apalachicola is also the setting for intrigue, an inherited house, and a counterfeiting ring in **Dorothy Worley's** *Enchanted Harbor* (New York: Avalon, 1956). The surrounding area is also the setting for *The Varmints* (New York: Knopf, 1946) by **Peggy Bennett** (1925-), an Apalachicola writer; the plot centers on three orphans growing up in the late 1930s and emphasizes psychological interaction among the characters.

Apalachicola was also the home of Dr. John Gorrie, who arrived in 1833 to practice medicine. The 1843 yellow-fever epidemic led him to speculate on the fact that yellow fever does not seem to exist in dry or cold climates. In 1844 he developed a device to circulate ice-cooled air throughout a room to reduce the probability of yellow fever; chaffing at the lack of ice, he patented an artificial ice-making machine in 1850. Today visitors can learn more about his work at the Gorrie State Museum (904/653-9347). See **Raymond B. Becker's** *John Gorrie, M.D.* (New York: Carlton, 1972) and **V.M. (Vivian M.) Sherlock's** *The Fever Man* (Tallahassee: Medallion Press, 1982) for more about this Floridian whose statue is in Statuary Hall at the U.S. Capitol in Washington, D.C.

Life in Apalachicola from 1900 to 1917 is recalled in *A Florida Sandpiper, Or A Fool Rushed In Where Angels Fear to Tread* (Gainesville: Storter Printing Company, 1982), the autobiography of agricultural teacher **George Norton Wakefield** (1899-). Wakefield describes life in Apalachicola, the influence of the Episcopal Church, and the islands (St. Vincent, St. George, and Dog Island) as well as his later years at the University of Florida and as an agriculture teacher in other parts of Florida.

Several significant authors have lived in Apalachicola. **Alvan Wentworth Chapman** (1809-1899), who lived in the Chapman House on the corner of Broad Street and Chestnut Avenue, wrote *Flora of the Southern United States* (1883), an important early botanical work about Florida. **Teresa Holloway** (1906-), who was born in Apalachicola, graduated from the Florida State College for Women (1925) — later Florida State University — and worked as manager of the town's chamber of commerce (1947-1950); she later moved to Jacksonville, where she worked as an author and television documentary writer. She has published 39 novels under her own name and the pseudonyms

Elizabeth Beatty and **Margaret Vail McLeod**. Some of her novels are set in Florida, for example *Government Girl* (New York: Bouregy, 1957); *River in the Sun* by Elizabeth Beatty (New York: Bouregy, 1958); *The Nurse on Dark Island* (New York: Ace, 1969); and *A Nurse for the Fishermen* (New York: Bouregy, 1974). Her *Heart's Haven* (New York: Avalon, 1955) is set specifically in Apalachicola.

St. Vincent, St. George, and Dog Island

To the south of Apalachicola and across Apalachicola Bay lie a small chain of barrier islands: St. Vincent, St. George, and Dog Island. Only in recent years has attention been drawn to preserving these islands as unspoiled natural vegetation and animal habitats. St. Vincent Island has had a long reputation for its beauty and wildlife; **William Temple Hornaday** (1854-1937) published *A Mon-o-graph on St. Vincent's Game Preserve* (Buffalo, NY: 1909) based on his story in the *Buffalo Express* on May 30, 1909; Hornaday told of the development of the game preserve by Dr. Ray V. Pierce. In recent years, the St. Vincent National Wildlife Refuge has been established to protect the island, which is still accessible to visitors but only by boat and under controlled conditions. **Jack Rudloe** (1943-) of Panacea has done much to encourage the protection of these areas; his descriptions of Apalachicola and Choctawhatchee Bay were published in his *The Wilderness Coast: Adventures of a Gulf Coast Naturalist* (New York: Dutton, 1988).

Dog Island has a somewhat more lurid history, beginning when a ship, *Le Tigre*, foundered on a reef near the island in 1766 and 15 survivors made it to Dog Island, where Indians found them. The Indians took six survivors to another island where they robbed and abandoned them. These six were the captain of *Le Tigre*, his wife and son, together with Viaud, his black slave, and a business partner (Desclau). Captain La Couture and Desclau drowned while paddling a rotten canoe. The other four made a raft to travel to the mainland, but young La Couture was sick and had to be left behind. Four days later, Viaud and the widow, who were starving, killed the slave and ate him. A party of soldiers from St. Marks Fort at Apalache discovered the pair after another ten days and then rescued young La Couture.

In 1768, the French book *Naufrage et aventures de M. Pierre Viaud, natif de Bordeaux, capitaine de navire* was published, telling the tale of three survivors of this shipwreck: young Viaud, the newly widowed captain's wife, and the black slave. The book scandalized Europe with its gruesome tale of starvation, cannibalism, and more than a hint of sex. For several centuries, it was considered fiction until Auburn University professor **Robin Fabel** stumbled across documents which lent veracity to the story. His discovery and an English translation were published as *Shipwreck and Adventures of Monsieur Pierre Viaud* (Pensacola: University of West Florida Press, 1990).

The history of St. George Island and Apalachicola appears in *Outposts on the Gulf: Saint George Island and Apalachicola* (Pensacola: University of West

Florida Press, 1986) by **William Warren Rogers**. The first of two planned volumes, it covers from early exploration of the area to World War II.

St. Joseph

To the west of Apalachicola, along St. Joseph's Bay, is the site of Old St. Joseph, a town whose history is entwined with Apalachicola. In 1838, St. Joseph was the largest town in Florida with 8,000 inhabitants. Its location on the Gulf of Mexico made it a booming port and, some say, the richest and wickedest city in the Southeast. When yellow fever arrived aboard a South American ship in the early 1840s, panic ensued; many abandoned the city and moved to nearby Apalachicola. The port closed, ships avoided the site, and an 1844 hurricane finished off the destruction of the town. This Sodom and Gomorrah history has inspired a number of writers. **Alexander Key** wrote *The Wrath and the Wind*, mentioned earlier, and **Rubylea Hall**, *The Great Tide* (New York: Duell, Sloan, & Pearce, 1947), which chronicles life in St. Joseph in the mid-1830s through the adventures of Caline Cohran.

Port St. Joe

With the boom in naval stores in the early twentieth century, the area around Old St. Joseph saw the emergence of manufacturing plants for fish oil and fertilizers. A town and port facilities grew up around these companies, and this area, five miles north of Old St. Joseph, became known as Port St. Joe. In 1938, the Port St. Joe Paper Mill opened and became one of the largest paper mills in Florida to manufacture kraft paper. Today, over 4,000 people live in Port St. Joe.

Panama City

Panama City, on St. Andrews Bay, 67 miles west of Apalachicola on U.S. 98, is the county seat of Bay County (named for St. Andrews Bay), created in 1913. The western portion of Panama City, originally the town of St. Andrews, was promoted and laid out by the St. Andrews Bay Land and Lumber Company in the late 1880s. Three miles east of St. Andrews, the town of Panama City was developed in 1905 and possibly was named for being north of Panama City, Panama. Other small towns along this stretch included Millville, Lynn Haven, and Springfield, but a 1925 legislative act merged all of them into Panama City.

The St. Andrews Bay area has long been a major lumbering and naval-stores region. The Confederate Salt Works was established nearby to supply the military and was one of the largest such operations in the South. During the Civil War, St. Andrews Bay was an important part of the Union blockade of the South, especially with frequent federal raids on the salt works. See *Stand By the Union* (Boston: Lee and Shepard, 1892) by **Oliver Optic**, a pseudonym for **William Taylor Adams** (1822-1897). The story, part of the Blue and Gray series, tells the story of Christy Passford, a young commander in the Union blockade of St. Andrews Bay and Pensacola Bay who thwarts the plans of his Confederate cousin to take over his ship.

Newspaper editor **George Mortimer West** (1845-1926) frequently wrote about the history of the area; his columns have been collected and published in a number of books including *Gems Gleaned from the Pages of the* Panama City Pilot (Panama City, FL: Panama City Publishing Co., 1960) and *St. Andrews, Florida; historical notes...* (Panama City, FL: Panama City Publishing Co., 1922). His wife, **Lillian C. West**, became renowned as a manager or editor of three Bay County newspapers: *Panama City Pilot, St. Andrews Bay News,* and *Lynn Haven Free Press.*

Other reminiscences of the area include *Two Yankee Coastal Traders, A West Florida Diary, 1882* (Tampa: 1971) by **Francis Hand Ware** (1857-1942) comprising Ware's diary of life in the area; *Scars of Civilization* (Montgomery, AL: The Paragon Press, 1957) by **Toni Veverka**, the fictionalized story of Walter Colquitt Sherman, real-estate investor and founder of the St. Andrews Bay Land and Lumber Company; **Harold W. Bell's** *Glimpses of the Panhandle* (Chicago: Adams Press, 1961) and *Your 50 Golden Years in Bay County, Florida* (Panama City, FL: Boyd Brothers, 1967) emphasizing Panama City and other Emerald Coast areas; *On Saint Andrews Bay, 1911-1917; A Sequel to the Tampa of my Childhood* (Tampa: S. K. Dean, 1969), an autobiography by **Susie Kelly Dean**; and **Elsie Lillian Surber's** *A Study of the History and Folklore of the St. Andrews Bay Region* (Gainesville: University of Florida Press, 1950). Biographies of Bay County residents appear in *Some Who Passed This Way* (Panama City, FL: 1972) by **Ira Augustus Hutchison** (1879-1973), while poetry and essays about the area have appeared in *Bay Lines: a Bay County Anthology* (Panama City, FL: Bay Humanities Council, 1981). **James K. Cazalas's** newspaper columns covering 1981-1982 are reprinted in his *Call Me Caz* (Panama City, FL: Panama City News-Herald, 1982). The development of nearby Tyndall Air Force Base is reflected in *Yardbird* (New York: Vantage, 1958), an autobiography of **William M. Grout**, a soldier in World War II. A different perspective is provided by former University of Florida professor **Angus McKenzie Laird**, who tells of his early years in Panama City and academic life in the Florida university system in *Like I Saw It* (Tallahassee: St. Andrews Press, 1981).

A major Panama City writer has been **William Thomas Person** (1900-), many of whose books are written especially for young adults. Among his works are *Abner Jarvis: A Novel* (1943) about a poor farm boy who works his way through a southern agricultural college; *No Land Is Free* (1946) about a small-town hardware clerk who turns to farming in the Arkansas swamp country; *Bar-face* (1953) which follows a boy and his pet raccoon in the Louisiana Bayou country; *The Land and the Water* (1953) which tells the tribulations of a displaced Latvian family on a Mississippi cotton plantation; *Trouble on the Trace* (1953), an adventure of the hardships and perils of pioneer families on the Natchez Trail; *New Dreams for Old* (1957) which chronicles a high school dropout who tries to be self-sufficient in the Big Swamp; *The Rebellion of Ran Chatham* (1957) about a budding romance between a boy and girl brought home from college by the financial difficulties on their Mississippi delta farms; and *Sedge-Hill Setter* (1960), a tale of a boy and his setter pup, set "East of Memphis and South a little."

Clarence Earl Gideon of Panama City, Florida, has been immortalized in **Anthony Lewis's** *Gideon's Trumpet* (New York: Random House, 1964) and his *Clarence Earl Gideon and the Supreme Court* (New York: Random House, 1972) which recounts Gideon's application to the United States Supreme Court in the case of Gideon vs. Wainright. The case established the right of a defendant to legal counsel, a landmark decision in the legal profession.

At least one ghost story set in Panama City and around the bay has been published. **Howard Rigsby's** humorous "I'll Be Glad When You're Dead," which originally appeared in *Argosy* magazine in 1938, has been reprinted in *Dixie Ghosts* (Nashville, TN: Rutledge Hill Press, 1988). Rigsby is better known for his western novels and his scripts for the *Rawhide* TV series. Ironically, Rigsby in 1943 co-authored a dramatic Broadway play, *South Pacific*, which folded after five performances. Five years later, a musical play of the same name by Rodgers and Hammerstein, based on **James Michener's** *Tales of the South Pacific*, opened to rave reviews, and both play and book went on to win Pulitzer prizes. Recent fiction with a partial setting in a Panama City Beach locale is **John Grisham's** *The Firm* (New York: Island Books, 1991).

The Emerald Coast

For 60 miles west from Panama City, U.S. 98 parallels a strip of the most beautiful white beaches in Florida, an area referred to as the Emerald Coast because of the turquoise green of the waters. Numerous beach villages and communities dot the coast, including Seaside, a unique architecturally inspired small town, designed to bring classic Main Street to a resort setting; the town includes an amphitheater for community concerts, carefully laid-out shopping districts, and boardwalks to encourage strolling and reduce automobile traffic.

Destin

At the entrance to Choctawhatchee Bay, 50 miles west of Panama City and nestled on a narrow strip of land between Choctawhatchee Bay and the Gulf of Mexico, lies the town of Destin. Fifty years ago a fishing resort with a population of 25, today it has over 7,000 residents primarily due to the development of Sandestin, a conglomerate of condominium and hotel villages offering year-round vacation, boating, golfing, and recreational adventure. The community takes its name from Captain Len Destin, an early settler and ship pilot who is mentioned in **Nathaniel Holmes Bishop's** *Four Months in a Sneak-box: A Boat Voyage of 2600 Miles down the Ohio and Mississippi Rivers, and along the Gulf of Mexico* (Boston: Lee and Shepard, 1879). The early history of the area and its families have been collected in **Vivian Foster Mettee's** *And the Roots Run Deep* (Destin, FL: Distributed by Old Destin Post Office Museum, 1983). The resort setting of the town is captured in **Anne Rice's** *The Witching Hour* (New York: Knopf, 1990), which describes a New Orleans couple traveling along this area on a honeymoon trip in the 1980s.

Nearby Choctawhatchee Bay is bordered by white sand beaches and long stretches of shallow water lending themselves to wading, shell collecting, and water activities. This area has always been known for its beauty. An early visitor, **R.C. Irwin** wrote *Life and Scenes of the Beautiful Choctawhatchee* (Pensacola, 1900), a collection of poems and small photographs taken with a Kodak box camera. **Nell K. Walker** used the area for some of her fictional *Open Vistas* (New York: Vantage, 1951). More recently, the Northwest Florida Water Management District has collected oral history interviews and recollections, published as *Historical Remembrances of Choctawhatchee Bay* (Havana, FL, 1985) edited by **James H. Cason**.

Fort Walton Beach

At the western end of the Emerald Coast, where Choctawhatchee Bay meets Santa Rosa Sound (seven miles west of Destin and 60 miles west of Panama City) is the city of Fort Walton Beach. Originally a summer resort known as Camp Walton, the town was renamed in 1932 to honor the old Seminole War fort at this site. As beach tourism swelled in the 1950s, Fort Walton became Fort Walton Beach. From a population of just 100 in 1939, Fort Walton Beach has grown into a major metropolis, providing support services to service personnel and families at nearby Eglin Air Force Base and tourist facilities for thousands of snowbirds: northerners who winter under the warm Florida sun. Recollections of the history of this area, including folklore, have been published as *Camp Walton to Fort Walton Beach* (Fort Walton Beach, FL: The Service League, 1987). For a study of the area's native plants and wildflowers see **Fanny-Fern Davis**'s *Nature's Seasonal Splendor* (Valparaiso, FL: Florida Federation of Garden Clubs, 1988).

Mary Esther

On the western edge of Fort Walton Beach is the town of Mary Esther. After the Civil War, Presbyterian minister John Newton settled here with his family, naming the area for his wife, or perhaps his daughters, Mary and Esther. Newton was one of the earliest educators in Florida, teaching at Knox Hill Academy in Walton County in the 1840s; for his learning and scholarship, he is one of only four Floridians in the nineteenth century to be named to the American Academy of Science.

Gulf Breeze Peninsula

Continuing westward from Fort Walton Beach on U.S. 98, the highway traverses a large peninsula of land which extends westward from Santa Rosa County. This region known as Gulf Breeze peninsula is bordered on the north by East Bay and on the south by Santa Rosa Sound, the waterway between the mainland and Santa Rosa Island. Just before Gulf Breeze, the road enters a section of the Gulf Islands National Seashore known as the Naval Live Oaks Reservation. **Henry Marie Brackenridge** (1786-1821), a Pennsylvanian who arrived in Pensacola as a confidant of and diplomatic officer for Andrew Jackson in 1821, had already achieved notoriety as a writer; his *History of the Late War, Between the United States and Great Britain...* (1817) on the War of 1812, subsequently was translated into French and Italian. His *Views of Louisiana, together with a Journal of a Voyage up the Missouri River in 1811* (1814) was one of the first narratives to describe the eastern fringe of the Louisiana Purchase and was noteworthy for its description of the Indian mounds at Cahokia, Illinois, across the Mississippi from St. Louis. In 1820, he told of his diplomatic mission to South America in *Voyage to Buenos Ayres Performed in the Years 1817 and 1818, by Order of the American Government* (1820).

Brackenridge became interested in the preservation of live-oak trees to provide a source of timber for the U.S. Navy. In the 1820s, American ships could require upwards of 2,000 pounds of live-oak timber for a ship; live oak was preferred as it grew slowly and was very dense and heavy. This wood caused cannonballs to bounce off American ships and gave rise to the name Ironsides. Brackenridge purchased a large tract of the peninsula land, most of which was covered by live-oak forest, and built a plantation, adding lemon, orange, and peach trees. The plantation did not do well and, in 1827, he decided to sell his land to the federal government. The land was purchased and has remained in federal hands since 1828. His "Letter on the Culture of Live Oak," written from St. Rosa (Gulf Breeze peninsula) to Secretary of Navy Southard is the first documentation in American history of forest conservation. He urged purchase of the land to provide the government with a supply of wood and farming techniques to ensure replanting and new growth for reprovisioning. Brackenridge's "Live Oak" letter was published in his *Speeches on the Jew Bill, in the House of Delegates of Maryland...* (1829), a collection of his speeches and writings. Ironically, the forest was never needed; steel soon replaced wood in American vessels, and the Naval Live Oaks Reservation remained untouched and preserved, one of the first wilderness areas set aside for conservation in America.

Gulf Breeze

At the western terminus of Gulf Breeze peninsula lies Gulf Breeze, a town bounded on three sides by water (Pensacola Bay to the north and west, Santa Rosa Sound to the south); the eastern boundary is the Live Oaks Reservation. For many years, this area was simply a pass-through point for people traveling from Pensacola to the white-sand beaches of Santa Rosa Island. It also marked the end of the old St. Augustine-to-Pensacola trail established in the nineteenth century. From this point, boats or ferries would take travelers across Pensacola Bay to Pensacola. In 1931, a three-mile, two-lane bridge was constructed across Pensacola Bay, but Gulf Breeze was not developed until the late 1950s, when retirees and vacation-home seekers discovered its access to waterfront property.

Today Gulf Breeze is a mix of retirees and commuting Pensacolians who take advantage of being close to an urban sprawl yet near the water and beaches for relaxation. A number of writers have made Gulf Breeze their home. **Jim McDade**, former editor of the *Gulf Breeze Sentinel*, has published several compilations of his newspaper columns: *My Lawn Mower Died and Other Stories* (Gulf Breeze, FL: Sandspur Press, 1984) and *More of the Stuff I Wrote Before I Got Famous* (Gulf Breeze, FL: Sandspur Press, 1988). Other area writers who regularly contribute columns to local publications like the *Gulf Breeze Sentinel*, *Pensacola Magazine*, and other works include **Donna Freckmann** and **Doug Adams**. Playwright **Grace Thompson** has authored plays centering on historical personalities such as Louisa May Alcott (*The March Sisters of Concord*, 1978) and Andrew Jackson. In recent years, Gulf Breeze has seen numerous sightings of unidentified flying objects, prompting a rash of media reports and studies. **Ed Walters's** recollections of his experiences in 1987 and 1988 have been published as *The Gulf Breeze Sightings* (New York: William Morrow, 1990).

Santa Rosa Island/Pensacola Beach

South of Gulf Breeze, across the Bob Sikes Bridge, lies the barrier island of Santa Rosa. The eastern part of the island is part of Eglin Air Force Base and contains radar facilities scanning the gulf and the Caribbean, and the western part (between Navarre and Pensacola Bay) is part of the Gulf Islands National Seashore. Santa Rosa Island extends 60 miles eastward from Pensacola Bay to Fort Walton Beach and is noted for its sugary white sands and pristine beaches. **Pierre Francois Xavier de Charlevoix** (1682-1761) described a visit to the Island (and Pensacola and St. Joseph) in *Journal of a Voyage to North-America* (London: Printed for R. and J. Dodsley, 1761). American painter **George Catlin** (1796-1872) in his *Letters and Notes on the Manners, Customs and Condition of the North American Indians* (London: Tosswill and Myers, 1841) commented on the island with sands "as white as the drifted snow" in his Letter No. 36. His painting "Seminole drying fish, Santa Rosa Island" appears in Volume 2 of the *Letters*.

Richard Henry Wilde (1789-1847), a member of the U.S. House of Representatives from Georgia and an Italian scholar, wrote an epic poem on the theme *America* which was posthumously published in his book *Hesperia* (Boston: Ticknor and Fields, 1867). Canto I is titled "Florida" and contains references to Santa Rosa Island, Escambia Bay, and elsewhere. He, too, was captivated by the beauty of the island, the soft waves, and shimmering sand. Today these same scenes are enjoyed by thousands of Florida tourists and retirees.

The settlement of Pensacola was originally located on the island and named Santa Rosa Punta de Siguenza. A 1743 drawing by Dom Serres, resident and agent for the Havana Company, was published in *An Account of the First Discovery and Natural History of Florida* by **William Roberts** (London: Printed for T. Jefferys, 1763) and titled "A North View of Pensacola on the Island of Santa Rosa." It shows a number of buildings and a small fort. After a 1752 hurricane, the settlement and fort relocated to the mainland. The Dom Serres

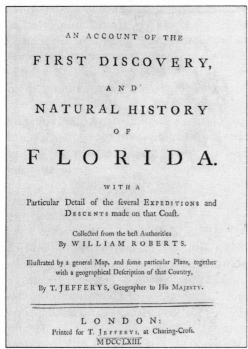

AN ACCOUNT OF THE

FIRST DISCOVERY,

A N D'

NATURAL HISTORY

O F

F L O R I D A.

W I T H A

Particular Detail of the several EXPEDITIONS and
DESCENTS made on that Coast.

Collected from the best Authorities
By W I L L I A M R O B E R T S.

Illustrated by a general Map, and some particular Plans, together
with a geographical Description of that Country,

By T. JEFFERYS, Geographer to His MAJESTY.

L O N D O N:
Printed for T. JEFFERYS, at Charing-Cross.
M DCC LXIII.

Title page of William Roberts' 1763 natural history of Florida

drawing was used as the basis for a short-lived reconstructed Spanish village on the island during the Florida quadricentennial in 1959.

Santa Rosa Island remained abandoned until 1826, when the U.S. Army began construction of Fort Pickens on the western edge of the island to guard the entrance to Pensacola Bay. After the victory at Fort McHenry in 1814, the United States recognized the usefulness of a strong system of forts guarding the entrance to each port along the Atlantic and gulf shores. Fort Pickens, along with sister forts McRee (to the west of Pickens, on the opposite side of Pensacola Pass) and Barrancas (to the northwest of Pickens, on the mainland) provided three fortifications to guard the entrance to the largest deep-water harbor in North America. The history of these forts can be found in **James C.** and **Irene S. Coleman**'s *Guardians on the Gulf: Pensacola Fortifications, 1698-1980* (Pensacola: Pensacola Historical Society, 1982). Construction of Pickens began in 1826 and was completed in 1839; its garrison was approximately 60 men, and by 1854, it mounted 179 guns.

Although in run-down condition, Fort Pickens took on strategic importance in 1861 when Florida seceded to join the Confederate States of America. While Fort McRee and Fort Barrancas fell to Confederate hands, Fort Pickens remained in Union control throughout the war, preventing the Confederacy from using Pensacola as a blockade-running base. Most of what we know of the Civil War period in Pensacola comes to us from the numerous observers sent to cover Fort Pickens for the emerging American news media. **William Howard Russell** (1820-1907), a newspaper correspondent for the *London Times* who visited the fort and other areas in Pensacola and the South in 1861, published his *Pictures of Southern Life, social, political, and military* (New York: J.G. Gregory, 1861).

To avoid another Fort Sumter, federal troops rushed to reinforce Fort Pickens in 1861 and were supplemented by additional men throughout the duration of the war. Blue wool-clad New Englanders wrote numerous regimental histories and reminiscences about life on Santa Rosa Island, tales, folklore, and reflections on southern climate. Among these are **Henry Augustus Shorey**'s *The Story of the Maine Fifteenth...* (Bridgton, ME: Press of the Bridgton

News, 1890) and **William C. Holbrook**'s *A Narrative of the Services of the Officers ... 7th Regiment of Vermont Volunteers...* (New York: American Bank Note Co., 1882), and **William Lawrence Haskin**'s *The History of the First Regiment of artillery* ... (Portland, Maine, 1878). Haskin's regiment was originally ordered to Fort Pickens in October 1845 during the Mexican War and also served during the Civil War; his book provides a longer perspective of military life on the island.

Life was not dull at Fort Pickens. Among the arriving troops were the infamous Captain Billy Wilson's Zouaves (Sixth New York Regiment), a unit known for its devilment, drinking, and mischief. Most all regimental histories about Pensacola touch on the activities of this outfit, but perhaps none match the breadth of a series of letters of the Jesuit priest, **Michael Nash**, chaplain to the Zouaves. His 11 letters from Santa Rosa Island to fellow Jesuits and friends in New York were published in the *Woodstock Letters* (1887-1890), a private Jesuit historical journal. Another source is *Recollections of a Checkered Life by a Good Templar* (Napanee, Ontario: 1868). Although the author is unidentified, it is generally accepted to be **S.T. Hammond**, a Scotsman who emigrated to New York in 1850 and enlisted in Captain Billy Wilson's Zouaves. The book is mainly a temperance account of Hammond's battle with "demon rum" but has some good accounts of life in the Zouaves on Santa Rosa Island and later the Pensacola mainland when the federals captured the city. The major account of the unit remains **Gouverneur Morris**'s *The History of a Volunteer Regiment...Known as Wilson's Zouaves* ... (New York: Veteran Volunteer Publishing Company, 1891) and touches on the theatrical programs performed by members of the company while in Pensacola.

Many narrative reports and drawings of Santa Rosa Island, Pensacola Harbor, and Fort Pickens appeared in *Harper's Weekly* newspaper during 1861 and 1862, especially the unsuccessful Confederate attempt to capture the fort in November 1862. **Benjamin LaBree**'s *Pictorial Battles of the Civil War* (New York: Sherman Publishing Co., 1884) includes an illustration titled "Pensacola Harbor at Night" by Thomas Nast, who in later years became world-famous for his depictions of corrupt Tammany Hall and the development of the iconography of Santa Claus. The Fort Pickens setting was used in *The Boy Spy* (Chicago: M. A. Donohue & Co., 1890), a cheap paperback-thriller by **Joseph Orton Kerbey**, who details his adventures as a messenger to Fort Pickens. Given Kerbey's Civil War service, the book may not be entirely fictional.

After the Civil War, Fort Pickens reverted to minimal activity. In the late 1880s, it became a prison for Apache Indians, including Chief Geronimo; see **Woodward B. "Woody" Skinner**'s *The Apache Rock Crumbles: The Captivity of Geronimo's People* (Pensacola: Skinner Publications, 1987). The fictional story of Massai, one of Geronimo's warriors, his capture, imprisonment at Fort Pickens, and subsequent escape and revenge are told in **Paul I. Wellman's** *Broncho Apache* (Garden City, NY: Macmillan, 1936). Fort Pickens was reinforced and upgraded with new armament and earthworks during World War I and II for a threat that never came. The age of jets and rockets made the fort obsolete; it became a state park in 1949 and is today administered by the National Park Service as part of the Gulf Islands National Seashore.

Pensacola

Possibly the oldest European fiction story concerning West Florida is the Welsh legend of Prince Madog ub Gwennyd. According to claims of **Richard Hakluyt** (*Principall Navigations...* London, 1589), based on Welsh bardic poems of Meredith ap Rhys (circa 1477), Madog or Madoc sailed west to the New World, traveled along the gulf coast, and finally settled on Mobile Bay. Numerous scholars, including Thomas Stephens, Robert Rea, and Dean DeBolt, have debunked the legend, but it makes for an exciting tale. See **Joan Dane**'s *Prince Madog, Discoverer of America* (Boston, MA: Everett Publishing Co., 1901-1916) and **Ellen Pugh**'s *Brave His Soul* (New York: Dodd, Mead, 1970) about Madoc's exploits.

Nevertheless, Pensacola can claim to be the oldest European city in the United States because Tristan de Luna brought 1,500 colonists into Pensacola Bay in 1559. The settlement lasted only two years and Pensacola was not resettled until the 1690s. Pensacolians continually assail St. Augustine's claim to be the oldest city by appending the term *permanent*. St. Augustine was settled in 1564, five years after Pensacola, but the former settlement persevered, making St. Augustine the oldest *permanent* European city in the United States.

De Luna's attempt failed because a hurricane destroyed his ships and Indians refused to help the inhabitants secure food and information. **Agustin Davila Padilla** (1562-1604), archbishop of Santo Domingo, wrote the history of the de Luna expedition in his *Historia de la fundacion y discurso de la prouincia de Santiago de Mexico...* (Madrid, 1596). It is more fantasy than reality, as it speaks of the angering of the wind gods, miracles, and presence of evil spirits determined to harm de Luna's goals. De Luna's own letters to Spain were compiled by **Herbert Ingram Priestley** in *The Luna Papers* (1928; reprinted Freeport, NY: Books for Libraries Press, 1971). A fictional account of the de Luna expedition is **John Appleyard**'s *De Luna: Founder of North America's First Colony* (Pensacola: Appleyard Agency, 1977).

In 1698, the Spanish returned to Pensacola under the command of Andres de Arriola, who began construction of Fort San Carlos de Austria at the present-day site of Fort Barrancas. Though never completed, Fort San Carlos, from the entrance to the bay, looked imposing, and when the French arrived two months later, they were surprised to see a formidable Spanish outpost guarding the harbor. The French commander, Pierre le Moyne de Iberville, thus took his fleet westward to settle Biloxi. Caught in the fortunes of European war, Pensacola was captured by the French in 1719; see **Michael Leigh**'s *Warrior's Trail* (London: Heinemann, 1955) for a fictional account of 1719-1722 Pensacola through the experiences of John Cotton, an Irish soldier in the service of King George I. **Sheppard Stevens**'s *The Sword of Justice* (Boston: Little, Brown, 1899) also touches on life in Florida during the conflict between Spain and France, while **Harris Dickson**'s *The Black Wolf's Breed* (Indianapolis:

Bowen-Merrill Co., 1899) is a fictional account of French activities in the settlement of Biloxi and capture of Pensacola. Spain recaptured Pensacola in 1722 and finally relinquished the region to England in 1763. See also **William Edward Dunn**'s *Spanish and French Rivalry in the Gulf Region of the United States, 1678-1702* (1917; reprinted Freeport, NY: Books for Libraries Press, 1971).

With this new territory, King George III established the royal colony of British West Florida, England's first colony west of the Appalachians. With its capital at Pensacola, the colony included the lands of southeastern Louisiana, the lower half of present-day Mississippi and Alabama, and Florida to the Apalachicola River.

Interest in the new "fourteenth" colony was met by scattered efforts of British writers to incorporate West Florida history, geography, botany, and folklore into something akin to travel guides. London magazines contained articles such as "Some Account of the Government of East and West Florida..." in *Gentleman's Magazine* (November 1763); "Florida Being Now in Our Possession..." in *Universal Magazine* (January 1764); and "Florida, being divided into two governments..." in *London Magazine* (March 1765). Among the finest natural-history documentation for this period is **William Roberts's** *An Account of the First Discovery and Natural History of Florida...* (London: T. Jefferys, 1763), which includes a number of Thomas Jefferys' maps of Pensacola, St. Joseph Bay, and Pensacola Harbor. In addition, **Jean Barnard Bossu** (1720-1792) completed his *Travels through that part of North America formerly called Louisiana* (London, 1771), which contained letters of the author from Pensacola and a catalog of plants, shrubs, and trees. Another hallmark work was **Bernard Romans**'s (1720-1784) *A Concise Natural History of East and West Florida...* (New York: Bernard Romans, 1775); Romans, a Dutch civil engineer and naturalist, covered the 1772 hurricane, the activities of Pompey (a free black man and "curious herbalist" of Pensacola), plants of the region, and topographical descriptions. Many of these guides, while extremely valuable first-hand accounts, are often compilations of personal correspondence, journals, diaries, and other writings.

The first appointed English governor of West Florida, George Johnstone, arrived in Pensacola in October 1764. Accompanying him was **James Macpherson** (1736-1796), a poet and compiler of ancient Scottish poems, whose writings caused much controversy at the time in England. In 1760, Macpherson published *Fragments of Ancient Poetry Collected in the Highlands of Scotland*, to be followed by *Fingal* (1762) and *Temora* (1763), works that the author claimed to be translations of epic poems of the third-century Gaelic poet Ossian. The well-known Samuel Johnson doubted the authenticity of the works and did much to besmirch the name of Macpherson, but the latter helped the romantic literary movement become established in Europe. When George Johnstone became governor of the western part of Florida in 1763, Macpherson joined him in Pensacola and became his secretary and surveyor-general of the province. But instead of spending much time in Florida and possibly writing some important works, Macpherson quarreled with his superior and left the state to travel to other places.

Another companion of Johnstone was **Archibald Campbell** (1726?-1780). The son of a Scottish minister, Campbell spent most of his life at sea as a purser on His Majesty's ships. Nicknamed "Horrible" because of "the malignancy of his heart [and] terrific countenance," Campbell claimed he "had the happiness to live with" Johnstone in Pensacola where he also became familiar with Macpherson. In their debates about Macpherson's poems, Campbell wrote that Johnstone extolled them "more than he might really think they deserve, and I depreciating them as much." While in Pensacola, Campbell wrote two manuscripts. In *Lexiphanes*, the bored sailor attacked the currently fashionable writing style. In the satire *The Sale of Authors*, he railed against such authors as Samuel Johnson. Campbell later published these books in London, and his *Sale of Authors* (London: 1767) is dedicated to Johnstone and was probably written in Pensacola between 1764 and 1765. West Florida, because it did not have a printing press, possibly missed out on the opportunity of printing those two early works. For more about Johnstone see **Robin F.A. Fabel's** *Bombast and Broadsides: The Lives of George Johnstone* (Tuscaloosa, AL: University of Alabama Press, 1987).

Scientific interest in the new British colony encouraged visits by and publications of cartographers including George Gauld, Thomas Hutchins, William De Brahm, and Bernard Romans. Gauld (1732-1782), upon his return to England, published a print "A View of Pensacola in West Florida" (London, 1765), a rare illustration of Pensacola as seen from the deck of a ship. The maps of Gauld, Hutchins, DeBrahm, and Romans appear in numerous atlases and gazetteers. Scientific organizations in Europe and America solicited specimens of plant and animal life from the new colony as well. Gauld's biography is told in **John D. Ware's** *George Gauld, Surveyor and Cartographer of the Gulf Coast* (Tampa: University of South Florida Press, 1982). **William Bartram's** *Travels through North and South Carolina, Georgia, East & West Florida* (Philadelphia: James & Johnson, 1791) detailed the botanical wonders of the region. John Ellis, the king's agent for West Florida, and a member of the Royal Society of London, encouraged scientific inquiry, assisted by Dr. John Lorimer, a resident surgeon. For their efforts, five men associated with West Florida — Lorimer, Gauld, Hutchins, Romans, and Ellis — earned memberships in the prestigious American Philosophical Society.

When the American Revolution broke out, Pensacola became a safe haven for Englishmen and British sympathizers (Tories) fleeing the colonies. See **Frank Slaughter's** *Flight from Natchez* (Garden City, NY: Doubleday, 1955) for a fictional account of Dr. John Powers, a Natchez Loyalist. In 1779, Spain declared war on England, and Pensacola was recaptured by Spanish forces in 1781 under the command of General **Bernardo de Galvez**. Galvez's account, *Diario de las operaciones de la expedicion contra la Plaza de Panzacola* (Habana?, 1781) is a zestful battlefield journal of the siege of Pensacola. Also see *Anglo-Spanish Confrontation on the Gulf Coast During the American Revolution* edited by **William S. Coker** and **Robert R. Rea** (Pensacola: Gulf Coast History and Humanities Conference, 1982). The British forces at Pensacola had one warship, the H.M.S. *Mentor*, which was stripped and burned to prevent capture.

The logbook of this ship has survived (in the University of West Florida library) and has been published as *The Log of H.M.S. Mentor, 1780-1781* (Pensacola: University Presses of Florida, 1982) edited by **James A. Servies**. The ship's captain, Robert Deans, apparently took the log back to England with him, for it appears to have been used as Mrs. Deans' recipe book after 1781. Another book about this period is **N. Orwin Rush**'s *Spain's Final Triumph Over Great Britain in the Gulf of Mexico* (Tallahassee: Florida State University Press, 1966).

Other sources for the Revolutionary War period in West Florida include *The Siege of Mobile, 1780* (Pensacola: Perdido Bay Press, 1982) and *The Siege of Pensacola, 1781* (Pensacola: Perdido Bay Press, 1981) by University of West Florida professor **William S. Coker**; *Siege!* (Pensacola: Pensacola Historical Society, 1981), a collection of historical essays edited by **Virginia S. Parks**; *Colonial Pensacola* (Hattiesburg, MS: University of Southern Mississippi Press, 1972) edited by University of West Florida professor **James R. McGovern** concerning the British West Florida period; **Robin F.A. Fabel**'s *The Economy of British West Florida, 1763-1783* (Tuscaloosa, AL: University of Alabama Press, 1988); and *Philipp Waldeck's Diary of the American Revolution* (Philadelphia: Americana Germanica Press, 1907), an English translation of Chaplain Waldeck's diary. The Third Waldeck Regiment, a group of Hessian soldiers, was sent to Pensacola in the British service, 1779-1780. A book about this period for younger readers is **Robert James Green**'s *Patriot Silver* (New York: St. Martin's; 1961), a history of the Revolutionary War in the Floridas. **Michael Leigh**'s *Warrior's Trail* (London: Heinemann, 1955) is the fictional account of Captain John Cotton, an Irishman who along with his English friends is washed ashore in Pensacola during the Revolutionary period.

Between 1781 and 1821, Pensacola remained under Spanish control, and the Spanish authorities encouraged the English inhabitants to remain, even supporting the efforts of British firms such as the Panton, Leslie and Company trading empire. This company became the largest trading concern in the southeastern United States, owning vast tracts of present-day Alabama, Mississippi, and Florida through its trade with the Indians. The extraordinary history of the company has been documented in **William S. Coker**'s *Historical Sketches of Panton, Leslie and Company* (Pensacola: University of West Florida Press, 1976) and **William S. Coker** and **Thomas D. Watson**'s *Indian Traders of the Southeastern Spanish Borderlands: Panton, Leslie & Company and John Forbes & Company, 1783-1847* (Pensacola: University of West Florida Press, 1986). The company dealt extensively with British, Spanish, and Indian representatives, including Alexander McGillivray of the Creeks. During this period (1781-1821), the Southeast remained embroiled in the intrigue and suspicion of rival factions (the French, English, Spanish, Americans, and Indians). **Robert P. "Bobby" Dews**'s *Mobile East* (Edison, GA: Rebel Books, 1972) offers a fictional perspective of the company based on the diary of Rebecca Sherwood Panton (1776-1852), the adopted daughter of William Panton.

Welbourn Kelley's fictional *Alabama Empire* (New York: Rinehart, 1957) tells the exploits of Dr. John Adam Fyfe, McGillivray's physician, and the Creek country in 1789-1793. A frequent Pensacola visitor and general agent for the

Creeks was William Augustus Bowles, whose flamboyant visit to London in 1791 electrified Londoners. His self-aggrandizing memoirs, *Authentic Memoirs of William Augustus Bowles* (London: R. Faulder, 1791) by **Benjamin Baynton**, were rushed into print to take advantage of English curiosity; a novel about him is **Joseph Millard's** *The Incredible William Bowles* (Philadelphia: Chilton Books, 1966).

The story of an American privateer in waters off Spanish-held Pensacola is told in **Albert W. Aiken's** (1846-1894) *The Winged Whale; or, Red Rupert of the Gulf* (New York: Beadle and Adams, 1876), one of the many dime novels of the 1870s. Aiken wrote over 125 books for Beadle & Adams, some under other names.

Another novel about the southwestern frontier (1790-1815) is **Odell Shepard** and **Willard Shepard's** *Holdfast Gaines* (New York: Macmillan, 1946). **James Howell Street** (1903-1954), a journalist and clergyman who served a reportorial stint with the *Pensacola Journal* in 1926, wrote *Oh, Promised Land* (New York: Dial Press, 1940). Street's book details the adventures of the Dabney family in the southwestern frontier of West Florida; later exploits about the family included *Tomorrow We Reap* (New York: Dial Press, 1949) with **James Childers** and *Mingo Dabney* (New York: Dial Press, 1950). Other fiction covering this period includes **Eugenia Price's** *Maria* (Philadelphia: Lippincott, 1977) which offers a woman's perspective, and *Zachary Phips* (Boston: Houghton, Mifflin, 1892) by **Edwin Lassetter Bynner** (1842-1893); Bynner's novel is set in the Florida Panhandle from the Suwannee to Pensacola and details the adventures of a young boy who falls into the company of Aaron Burr and later Andrew Jackson and others on the Florida frontier. **David Hart White's** *Vicente Folch, Governor in Spanish Florida — 1787-1811* (Washington, DC: University Press of America, 1981) is also about this era.

Spanish influence in West Florida continued to dwindle. American forces under General Andrew Jackson attacked Pensacola in 1814 during the War of 1812 and again in 1818 as part of an American military expedition against the Seminoles who had been attacking settlers along the southeastern frontiers. The 1814 incursions are covered in *Historical Memoir of the War in West Florida...* (Philadelphia: John Conrad & Co., 1816) by **Arsene L. Latour**, Napoleon's agent in Louisiana and Jackson's chief engineer, and in **John Henry Eaton's** *Life of Andrew Jackson* (Philadelphia: M. Carey, 1817). The fictional *The Lost Virgin of the South: A Tale of Truth Connected with the History of the Indian War of the South...* (Tallahassee: n.p., 1831) is perhaps one of the earliest Florida-published fictions about the Creek Indians of this period. A viewpoint of the Choctaws who accompanied Jackson is given in **Horace G. Ridaught's** *Hell's Branch Office* (Citra, FL: Florida's Choctaw Indians, 1957).

Another unique perspective is provided by one of Jackson's Tennesseans, **Davy Crockett**, whose biography *A Narrative of the Life of David Crockett of the State of Tennessee* (Philadelphia: E.L. Carey and A. Hart, 1834) tells of Pensacola, life along the "Scamby" (Escambia) River, and tracking Creeks in the Panhandle. University of West Florida professor **Richard Hauck** (*Crockett: A Bio-Bibliography* [Westport, CT: Greenwood Press, 1982]) calls the book Crockett's contribution to American comic literature. The West Florida setting was used in Walt Disney's *Davy Crockett* TV series in the 1950s and remembered for the resulting coonskin-cap fad.

The life of the soldiers in Jackson's army in 1817-1818 is recounted in **Joel P. Walker's** *A Pioneer of Pioneers* (Los Angeles, CA: Alen Dawson, 1953), his memoirs dictated in 1878, and *Diary of John Banks* (1936), those of a Georgian volunteer angered over repeated Indian depredations. The third edition of **John Henry Eaton's** *The Life of Major General Andrew Jackson...* (Philadelphia: McCarty & David, 1828) is the only one to include a special addendum on the history of the Seminole War and "Cession and Government of Florida" on the second Jackson invasion in 1818. A fictional account of Florida's annexation to the United States appears in **Baynard H. Kendrick's** *Flames of Time* (New York: Scribner, 1948). A fictional account of a company of boys in Andrew Jackson's army in 1814 is told in *Captain Sam; or, The Boy Scouts of 1814* (New York: Putnam's, 1876) by **George Cary Eggleston** (1839-1911). A similar juvenile adventure is *The Land Hero of 1812; or, Campaigning with General Jackson* (Philadelphia: David McKay, 1904) by **Chauncey Crafts Hotchkiss** (1852-1920). A different narrative told from a multi-generational Creek Indian family perspective is **David P. Mason's** *Five Dollars A Scalp: The Last Mighty War Whoop of the Creek Indians* (Huntsville, AL: Strode Publishers, 1975).

The Adams-Onis Treaty of 1819 transferred both East and West Florida to the United States, and in 1821 Jackson was appointed governor of the new provisional territory of Florida. Rachel Jackson accompanied her husband to Pensacola in 1821; her distress about the local customs are preserved in her letters which appeared in **James Parton's** three-volume *Life of Andrew Jackson* (New York: Mason Brothers, 1860) and fictionally in **Irving Stone's** *The President's Lady* (Garden City, NY: Doubleday, 1951). Homesick for Tennessee, the Jacksons left Pensacola after only three months. *Andrew Jackson and Pensacola* (Pensacola: Department of History, University of West Florida, 1974) edited by **James R. McGovern** provides a good overview of the Jackson period from 1814 through 1821. Glimpses of Pensacola life during the military occupation can be found in **John Lee Williams's** *A View of West Florida* (Philadelphia: H.S. Tanner, 1827) and in *Travels through North America during the years 1825 and 1826* (Philadelphia: Carey, Lea & Carey, 1828) by **Karl Bernard,** duke of Saxe-Weimar-Eisenach.

Compilations of folklore and tales of this period are *Where Romance Flowered: Stories of Old Pensacola* (Pensacola: Pensacola Printing Co., 1947) and *Jackson and the Enchanted City: Stories of Old Pensacola* (Pensacola: Pensacola Printing Co., 1949) by Pensacola society columnist **Celia Myrover Robinson.** These provide factual and apocryphal stories about Pensacola places and community leaders such as the Jacksons, William Panton, Alexander McGillivray, and others. A companion volume is her *The Crown Jewel: Fabulous Families of Old Pensacola* (Pensacola: Pensacola Printing Co., 1948) with family histories and genealogies of Spanish families that settled in Pensacola just prior to and during the Jackson period. Some of these legends and stories also appear along with modern addenda in *Ghosts, Legends and Folklore of Old*

Pensacola (Pensacola: Pensacola Historical Society, 1990) compiled by **Sandra Johnson** and **Leora Sutton**. Finally, **Henry M. Brackenridge's** *A Topographical Description of Pensacola and Vicinity in 1821* edited by **Brian R. Rucker** (Badgad, FL: Patagonia Press, 1991) gives a good view of the area.

For most of the eighteenth century, Pensacola remained a small town, more a frontier village than an urban destination. John James Audubon visited Pensacola in 1837, observed the brown ibis, and wrote that the town "is a small place at present; principally inhabited by Creole Spaniards of the lowest class, and some few amiable and talented families of Scotch; and Americans." Traders, frontiersmen, and Indians traveled through the area constantly. Alexander McGillivray, chief of the Creeks and a frequent Pensacola visitor, traveled to Washington in 1791 to negotiate a treaty with President George Washington. His likeness was captured by artist John Trumbull. Other portraits of West Florida Indians were published in **Thomas L. McKenney** and **James Hall's** *History of the Indian Tribes of North America*, (1836-1844) reprinted as *The Indian Tribes of North America* (Totowa, NJ: Rowman and Littlefield, 1972) and preserved in paintings of George Washington Sully, a Pensacola artist in the mid-1830s.

Contacts with southeastern Indians greatly diminished after their defeat in the Second Seminole War in the late 1830s. Fiction about this period, covering Pensacola and the Panhandle, include **Frank G. Slaughter's** *The Warrior* (Garden City, NY: Doubleday, 1956); **Robert Wilder's** *Bright Feather* (New York: Putnam's, 1948); *The Red Eagle: A Poem of the South* (New York: Appleton, 1855), an epic poem about the Creek Indian chief Weatherford and the war, by **Alexander Beaufort Meek** (1814- 1865); and **Peter Hansen's** *Creek Rifles* (New York: Dell, 1982), a historical adventure. The forced removal of the Creek Indians and other West Florida tribes is covered in **Gloria Jahoda's** *The Trail of Tears* (New York: Holt, 1975) and in **Luke Wallin's** *In the Shadow of the Wind* (New York: Bradbury Press, 1984) about a Creek Indian village in Florida/Alabama.

With congressional approval of the new territory of Florida in 1822, American troops were sent to Pensacola to assist in guarding the port and providing protection against Indians. One of the new West Point graduates assigned to Pensacola, **George A. McCall** (1802-1868), wrote a number of letters to his family in Philadelphia describing Pensacola. These appear in his *Letters From the Frontiers* (1868; facsimile reprint Gainesville: University Presses of Florida, 1974). Pensacola was also the childhood home of **Octavia Walton Le Vert** (1810?-1877); her later move to Mobile and world travels are recounted in two volumes of her *Souvenirs of Travel* (Mobile, AL: S.H. Goetzel, 1857), and her Pensacola years are told in **Frances Gibson Satterfield's** *Madame Le Vert* (Edisto Island, SC: Edisto Press, 1987). For the most part, Pensacola in the antebellum period was a small port city. Rogue **Joseph T. Hare** stated in his autobiography, *The Life of the Celebrated Mail-Robber and Daring Highwayman...* (Philadelphia: J.B. Perry, 1844), that the gains of his crimes on the road between Baton Rouge and Pensacola were spent in Pensacola on balls and Spanish ladies.

Octavia Walton Le Vert

Other forms of entertainment included the theater. An 1832 anecdotal theatrical journey through the Creek Nation is recorded by **Solomon Franklin Smith** (1801-1869), a stage-company manager, in his autobiography, *Theatrical Management in the West and South for Thirty Years* (1868; New York: B. Blom, 1968). Smith was instrumental in the development of theaters in the southeastern frontier including Mobile, Natchez, St. Louis, and other cities. A companion view is provided by **Noah Miller Ludlow** (1795-1886), a former business partner of Smith, in his *Dramatic Life As I Found It* (1880; Bronx, NY: B. Blom, 1966), considered one of the best stage histories ever written and a major source for a social history of the Old Southwest. Ludlow, influential in the Mobile, Alabama, theater, considered Pensacola to be the El Dorado of the South.

Pensacola's rough reputation and predominantly Catholic population were a natural magnet for religious missionaries. **Sara Jenkins's** *Saddlebag Parson* (New York: Crowell, 1956) tells the story of the fictional Jared Crittenden, newly converted to Methodism, and his difficulties as the first Methodist circuit rider in west Florida in the 1830s. Nevertheless, Pensacola remains home to one of the oldest Catholic churches in Florida whose story is told in **Mary Merritt Dawkins's** *The Parish of Saint Michael, the Archangel: The First Hundred Years, 1781-1881* (Pensacola: University of West Florida, 1991).

While the population was small, there was increasing demand for labor — on the docks, at the Pensacola Navy Yard, and in the new brickyards along Escambia Bay. Slave-owning residents often earned income renting their slaves to the navy or local businesses. Thus, abolitionists, like Captain **Jonathan Walker** of Massachusetts, who lived in Pensacola from 1837 to 1843, were considered a threat to economic livelihood. In 1844, he returned to Pensacola and on June 22, 1844, sailed from the harbor, carrying seven black slaves. He attempted to reach the Bahamas, but suffered a sunstroke, and his boat was seized and returned to Pensacola. He was charged with stealing slaves, narrowly avoided being lynched, was placed in a pillory and pelted with rotten eggs, and given a jail sentence and fine. His case was closely chronicled in the northern abolitionist press including William Lloyd Garrison's *The Liberator* and *The Emancipator*. Possibly his worst punishment was to be branded on the hand with the letters *SS* for slave stealer.

Finally freed, Walker returned to New England and wrote his *Trial and Imprisonment of Jonathan Walker, at Pensacola, Florida, for Aiding Slaves to Escape from Bondage* (1845; reprinted Gainesville: University Presses of Florida, 1974). Walker's ill treatment in Pensacola and horrifying disfigurement shocked many northerners. **John Greenleaf Whittier** composed a popular poem, "The Branded Hand," which appears in the second edition of Walker's book (1846). Walker himself joined the abolitionist lecture circuit, displaying his branded hand and inciting abolitionist emotion. He allowed his hand to be photographed by the daguerreotype firm of Southworth and Hawes, providing one of the earliest conceptual portraits to show a part of the human body; see **Robert A. Sobieszek** and **Odette M. Appel**'s *The Spirit of Fact* (Boston: Godine, 1976). **Philip Van Doren Stern** wrote a fictional account of this episode in his *The Drums of Morning* (Garden City, NY: Doubleday, Doran, 1942) about Jonathan Bradford, an abolitionist leader in the period, 1837-1860.

Walker was not the only northerner to call attention to the slavery issue in Pensacola. A brickmaker, **John Williamson Crary, Sr.** (1814-1897), came to Pensacola in 1857 to the firm of Bacon and Abercrombie. The firm held a contract to provide millions of bricks for Fort Jefferson near Key West and other government construction projects but could not produce quality bricks rapidly enough. Crary invented a brick-making machine which appeared on the cover of *Scientific American*, January 5, 1861. Crary's manuscript memoirs, written in the 1890s, have been published as *Reminiscences of the Old South from 1834 to 1866* (Pensacola: Perdido Bay Press, 1984) and equally detail his concern over the plight of the slaves in the South.

With the election of President Lincoln in late 1860, Florida joined the new Confederate States of America. Pensacola promised to become a major port for the new government and thousands of troops were rushed to the city to secure its facilities. Fort Pickens, guarding the entrance to Pensacola harbor, remained securely in Union hands, and after an unsuccessful attempt to capture the fort in 1862, Confederate forces abandoned the area. Federal forces continually occupied the nearly deserted city until the war's end in 1865. One interesting literary product of this period is *Adrift on the Black Wild Tide* (Philadelphia: Lippincott, 1879) by **James Johnson Kane** (1837-1921). It purports to be a vision of a soul's journey to heaven experienced by Kane while ill with yellow fever in Pensacola in 1863. An 1896 reprint alluded to this experience as a nautical version of *Pilgrim's Progress*. Kane claimed his experience inspired him to preach about it on 20 different occasions and a version was published in the *New York Herald* in March 1874. The Union blockade of Pensacola harbor is recounted in **Oliver Optic**'s *Stand By the Union* (Boston: Lee and Shepard, 1892). Recollections of a Pensacola-born soldier, beginning with his service in Pensacola, are told in **Henry H. Baker**'s two-volume *A Reminiscent Story of the Great Civil War* (New Orleans: The Ruskin Press, 1911).

Pensacola author **Frasier Franklin Bingham** wrote *Ashore at Maiden's Walk* (New York: Broadway Publishing Co., 1913) about the fictitional adventures of a Pensacola blockade-runner and its return to Pensacola harbor in 1865. **Ernest F. Dibble**'s *Ante-bellum Pensacola and the Military Presence* (Pensacola: University of West Florida Press, 1974) is about the area before the Civil War.

Between 1865 and 1920, Pensacola grew from a small town into an urban sprawl. The trans-Panhandle railroad was completed in 1882, linking the city with Jacksonville and establishing a dozen new cities in west Florida. See *Iron Horse in the Pinelands* (Pensacola: Pensacola Historical Society, 1982) for the full history of this effort. The railroad brought travelers to Pensacola, and shipments of gold, money, and goods became the target of outlaws. See the autobiography *The Life of John Wesley Hardin* (Seguin, TX: Smith & Moore, 1896) and *They Died With Their Boots On* (New York: Doubleday, 1935) by **Thomas Ripley** (1895-) for the story of outlaw John Wesley Hardin, whose gang was captured in Pensacola in 1877.

The railroad made possible the development of lumber companies by providing a means to get timber to ships in Pensacola harbor; the Pensacola waterfront boomed with shipping companies, passenger lines, telegraph facilities, foreign consulates, and businesses. Along the waterfront were places of entertainment: bars, saloons, and houses of ill repute. A young piano player at one such establishment, **Danton Walker**, who went on to become a respected columnist for the *New York Daily News*, recounted his life in Pensacola in 1910-1920 in his *Danton's Inferno* (New York: Hastings House, 1955). **J.C. Powell**, an overseer in one of north Florida's prison camps, wrote of the "wildest sort of debauchery along the harbor front" in reference to Pensacola in his autobiography, *The American Siberia; or, Fourteen Years' Experience in a Southern Convict Camp* (Chicago: H.J. Smith & Co., 1891). Powell tells of Pensacola life and his exploits in west Florida with moonshiners, Ku Klux Klan members, and county sheriffs, from a lawman's perspective of crime and violence. Another gripping memoir of crime and lawlessness is **Jeff M. Herrington**'s *When Crime Pays Off* (Mobile, AL: Press of Heiter-Starke, 1937) about his service on the Pensacola police force between 1907 and 1936.

As America moved into the 1880s, interest in health and leisure led to the development of resorts, the concept of vacations, and the quest for scenic and invigorating climates. Literature promoting Florida and Pensacola began to appear in such publications as **Ellen Call Long**'s *Florida Breezes* (Jacksonville: Ashmead Bros., 1882); **Benjamin Robinson**'s *An Historical Sketch of Pensacola, Florida...* (Pensacola: Advance-Gazette, 1882); and **Silvia Sunshine**'s *Petals Plucked from Sunny Climes* (Nashville: Southern Methodist Publishing House, 1880). Famed American poet and musician **Sidney Lanier** (1842-1881) came to Florida to try to revive his failing health; his *Florida: Its Scenery, Climate, and History* (Philadelphia: Lippincott, 1875) became one of the earliest Florida guidebooks, and he took note of the lumber and shipping industry in Pensacola and its navy yard.

Pensacolian **William Dudley Chipley** (1840-1897) praised the climate and promoted west Florida in his *Pensacola, the Naples of America* (Louisville, KY:

Courier-Journal Press, 1877) and *Facts About Florida* (New York: New York Economical Printing Co., 1885). Readers of fine print could spot Chipley's title as manager for land sales for the Louisville and Nashville Railroad. His biography is told in **Lillian D. Champion's** *Giant Tracking* (Pine Mountain, GA: L.D. Champion, 1985). **Charles Henry Bliss** (1860-1907), one-time mayor of Pensacola, began publishing *Bliss' Quarterly*, a magazine of literature, but full of historical and promotional pieces about Pensacola's natural resources and business opportunities. Pensacola in 1880 is reflected in *One of the Duanes* (Philadelphia: Lippincott, 1885), a novel about a northern girl's search for romance.

Progressivism found a natural outlet in journalism. More Pensacola newspapers were established in the 1880s and 1890s than in any period before or since. Inventor **John Williamson Crary** (1814-1897), at various times on the editorial staff of three different Pensacola papers, used the columns to discuss commercial tariffs, the circulation of money, the eight-hour workday, and other progressive ideals. His *Sixty Years a Brick Maker: A Practical Treatise...* (Indianapolis: T.A. Randall & Co., 1890) brought him national renown in the brick-making industry and as an expert in the firing of clay. Another printer and former ship-loader, **Don McLellan**, recalled his work with various Pensacola newspapers and used salty comments on their owners and editors in *Fifty Years in Pensacola: Personal Reminiscences and Anecdotes* (Pensacola: Mayes Printing Co., 1944).

As Pensacola moved into the twentieth century, it changed from a small port city to a major urban center. This change is the theme of **James R. McGovern's** *The Emergence of a City in the Modern South: Pensacola, 1900-1945* (DeLeon Springs, FL: E.O. Painter, 1976). A good view of the city's history is **Norman Simons** and **James R. McGovern's** *Pensacola in Pictures and Prints* (Pensacola: Pensacola-Escambia County Development Commission, 1974). The history of the county with emphasis on the development of schools and growth in government is recounted in *History of Escambia County, Florida* (St. Augustine: The Record Company, 1930) by **Henry Clay Armstrong** (1870-1950), headmaster of the Pensacola Classical School and a mayor of Pensacola. **Booker T. Washington** (1856-1915), visiting Pensacola, commented on the progress of the African-American business community in his *The Negro in Business* (Boston: Hertel, Jenkins & Co., 1907); included in this community was a major Florida African-American newspaper, The *Florida Sentinel*, under the leadership of **M.M. Lewey**. Eventually this paper moved to Jacksonville, Florida. Dramatic changes for Pensacola took place with the founding of the Pensacola Naval Air Station in 1911 and an increased military presence after World War II. **Pete Hamill** (1935-) set down a fictionalized autobiography of his days at Ellyson Field, Pensacola, 1952-1954, in *Loving Women: A Novel of the Fifties* (New York: Random House, 1989); his novel interpolates vignettes of the 1950s in contrast with a return trip to Pensacola in 1987. As an occasional columnist for *Esquire*, Hamill incorporates Pensacola themes as appropriate; see his "America's Holy War" about the bombing of the Pensacola abortion clinics in the November 1989 issue. His columns for the *New York Post* and *The*

Daily News were published as an anthology in *The Invisible City: A New York Sketchbook* (1980). A good history of the city is **Lucius** and **Linda Ellsworth's** *Pensacola: The Deep Water City* (Tulsa, OK: Continental Heritage Press, 1982).

Pensacola writers include **Evelyn Dahl**, whose *Belle of Destiny* (New York: Greenberg, 1958) is a fictionalized account of the life of Octavia Walton Le Vert. **Florence Glass Palmer**'s, *Life and Miss Celeste* (Indianapolis: Bobbs-Merrill, 1937) is about two spinsters who maintain their independence and interest in life despite their poverty during the Great Depression; her *Spring Will Come Again* (Indianapolis: Bobbs-Merrill, 1940) tells of life in the Alabama cotton-growing black-belt during the Reconstruction. **Elna Stone**'s gothic romances include *The Secret of the Willows* (1970); *Dark Masquerade* (1973); *Whisper of Fear* (1973); and *The Visions of Esmaree* (1976).

Compilations of newspaper columns by Pensacola journalists writing about Pensacola, politics, and other area topics include humorist **Mark O'Brien**'s *Sand in My Shoes: A Former Bostonian's Reflections about Life along the West Florida and South Alabama Gulf Coast* (Pensacola: Pensacola News-Journal, 1984) and *Pensacola on My Mind* (Pensacola: Pensacola News-Journal, 1987); also **Dot Brown**'s *A Cracker Crumb Trail: Lake Okeechobee to Soldier Creek* (Pensacola: Pensacola Press Club, 1986), an anthology of her wit and humor. Pensacola physician and world-traveler **Arthur J. Butt**'s columns have been collected in his *The Best of A-OK Butt* (Pensacola: Pfeiffer Printing, 1975). Another newspaperman, **Arthur E. Cobb**, a managing editor of the *Pensacola Journal*, authored *Go Gators!* (Pensacola: Sunshine Publishing Company, 1966), the official history of University of Florida football, 1889-1966.

Newspaper editor **Jesse Earle Bowden** (1928-) has authored a number of west Florida books including *Always the Rivers Flow; Deliberately a Memoir* (Pensacola: University of West Florida Foundation, 1979), a collection of essays about west Florida supplemented by editorial cartoons drawn by Bowden and taken from the pages of the *Pensacola News-Journal*. His *The Write Way: Editor's Guidebook for Students of Writing* (1990) grew out of his journalism instruction at the University of West Florida. Bowden has also written for the Pensacola Historical Society, including the text of its recent photographic history *Pensacola: Florida's First Place City* (Norfolk, VA: Donning Co., 1989).

Michael Leigh (1912-), a native of Ireland, came to Pensacola as a *Pensacola News-Journal* columnist in 1948. His books have included *Cross of Fire* (1949), a fictional retelling of the conquest of Zululand; *Rogue Errant* (1951), an adventure set against the romantic background of seventeenth-century Ireland; and *He Couldn't Say Amen* (1951), an adventurous prose version of Shakespeare's *Macbeth*.

Biographical writings by Pensacolians include **Thomas Jefferson Thompson**'s *The Thrilling Adventures of Thomas Jefferson Thompson* (1922) which tells of his life in the frontier West (Arizona, Colorado, and South Dakota) during the period 1880-1910; *The Fourth Quarter* (Tallahassee: 1976) by **Alto Lee Adams** (1899-) is an autobiography by a former justice of the Florida Supreme Court chronicling his early career in Pensacola and legal personalities and cases of the area in the 1920s; the humorous memoirs of an Escambia

County deputy sheriff are recalled in **Don Parker**'s collected stories, *You're Under Arrest, I'm Not Kidding* (Pensacola: Caroldon Books, 1988) and *Officer Needs Assistance: Again* (Pensacola: Caroldon Books, 1990); the biography of **Trader Jon** (**Martin Weissman**) and his famous "aviator watering-hole" is told in *Trader Jon* (Memphis, TN: Castle Books, 1986) by **Fred Brown**.

White Wings in Bamboo Land (Emmitsburg, MD: St. Joseph's Provincial House Press, 1973) covers the experiences in China, 1925-1945, of Pensacola author **Clara Groell** (1882-1980), a member of the Daughters of Charity of St. Vincent de Paul; **James R. McGovern**'s *Black Eagle, General Daniel "Chappie" James, Jr.* (University, AL: University of Alabama Press, 1985) tells the life of a black Pensacolian who becomes a four-star general. A more chilling autobiography is *Kill the Messenger: One Man's Fight against Bigotry and Greed* (Atlanta: Peachtree Publishers, 1989) by **Ken H. Fortenberry**, managing editor of the *Pensacola News-Journal*; Fortenberry tells the story of corruption in politics in McCormick, South Carolina, and his fight for freedom of the press that led to his interview on CBS-TV's *60 Minutes* in 1987.

Juvenile fiction by Pensacola authors includes **Celia Myrover Robinson**'s *Rowena's Happy Summer* (Chicago: Rand McNally, 1912); **Gene S. Stuart**'s *Three Little Indians* (Washington, DC: National Geographic Society, 1974) describing life for children in Cheyenne, Creek, and Nootka Indian tribes; University of West Florida graduate **E. Paul Braxton**'s *The Bubble and Burp Machine* (Marianna, FL: Hermit Press, 1986); McMillan schoolteacher **Dorothy Cawthon**'s *Pedro the Pig* (New York: Exposition Press, 1960); and **Cynthia Brosnaham Richardson**'s *Susie Cucumber; She Writes Letters* (New York: S. Gabriel Sons, 1944) about the letter-writing campaign of a little dog — the book was so popular that numerous letters were sent to Richardson over the years simply addressed to Susie Cucumber.

Works set in and around Pensacola include **Anna Cosulich**'s *The Belle of Pensacola* (Cincinnati: Editor Publishing Co., 1898), a fictional account of life in the city in 1895; Pensacola in the 1940s during World War II is revealed in *Repent in Haste* (Boston: Little, Brown, 1945) by **John Phillips Marquand** (1893-1960); *Midnight Water* (New York: E.P. Dutton, 1983) by **Geoffrey Norman** is a fictional account of a drug-smuggling ring in the Florida Panhandle; **Suzannah Davis**'s *Flight of Desire* (New York: Dell, 1987), is a "candlelight ecstasy romance" set in Seville Square of Pensacola. **James P. Hogan**'s *The Mirror Maze* (New York: Bantam Books, 1989) is an espionage-thriller about two former University of West Florida students; the story deals with a contemporary social issue of the 1980s in Pensacola: the problems of nude dancing in bars. Poetry about the area includes **Maude Haynes Hollowell**'s *These Little Things* (New York: Vantage, 1979).

Juvenile fiction with a Pensacola-area setting includes **Wesley Ford Davis**'s *The Time of the Panther* (New York: Harper, 1958) about a 14-year-old's coming of age in a west Florida lumber camp; **Borden Deal**'s *A Long Way To Go* (New York: Doubleday, 1965) about three children who, when their parents fail to return from Gulf Beach, begin walking up the west Florida coast to Alabama; and **Rubylea Hall**'s *Davey* (New York: Duell, Sloan, 1951) about a west Florida schoolboy growing up on a sharecropper's farm in the 1920s. An eight-year-old orphan's arrival in the fictional town of Bishop in West Florida is the theme of **Mary N. Dolim**'s *The Bishop Pattern* (New York: William Morrow, 1962); **Wylly Folk St. John**'s *The Mystery of the Other Girl* (New York: Viking Press, 1971) is a novel for young people based on scenes and activities in Pensacola, including the Night in Old Seville (Square) Festival; sunken treasure is the theme of **Ann Waldron**'s *The Luckie Star* (E.P. Dutton, 1977). North Florida locales are also the setting for **Cora Cheney**'s books, *Fortune Hill* (New York: Henry Holt, 1956) and *The Rocking Chair Buck* (New York: Henry Holt, 1956); and **Layne Shroder**'s *The Four of Them* (Boston: Houghton, Mifflin, 1957) is a psychological novel of four young artists at a resort town on the Florida gulf coast.

Other less-definable but Pensacola-influenced books include **Mickey Friedman**'s *Hurricane Season* (New York: Dutton, 1983) and **Michael McDowell**'s *Blackwater* (New York: Avon Books, 1983), originally published as six suspense paperbacks about a family and a town situated between the Perdido and Blackwater rivers, somewhere a little west of Pensacola.

Pensacola religious literary expression includes **David Shepherd Rose**'s *Lord, Make Everything All Right* (Sewanee, TN: The University Press, 1982), an autobiography of a Pensacola Episcopal clergyman; Rabbi **Julius A. Leibert**'s *The Lawgiver: A Novel About Moses* (New York: Exposition Press, 1953); Methodist minister **Charles C. Ellis**'s *Power of Prayer* (New York: Vantage Press, 1976); **John William Frazer**'s *The Untried Civilization* (Nashville, TN: Parthenon Press, 1921), a book of essays published to celebrate the centennial of Methodism in Pensacola; and **Grace Dorothy Bell**'s *From Stage to Pulpit* (Cross City, FL: Dixie County Advocate, 1935), the autobiography of a Pensacola evangelist with a meandering account of her battles with the devil.

Pensacola's setting on the water has been the theme of a number of novels narrating life on the water and sailing the bay. One of the earliest is *Four Months in a Sneak-Box: A Boat Voyage of 2600 Miles down the Ohio and Mississippi Rivers, and along the Gulf of Mexico* (Boston: Lee and Shepard, 1879) by **Nathaniel Holmes Bishop** (1837-1902); it details a voyage in a home-like boat with descriptions of Santa Rosa Island, Fort Pickens, Choctawhatchee Bay, St. Joseph and other points, and stories of local personalities such as Captain Len Destin. **Prentiss Ingraham**'s *The Wild Yachtsman; Or, The Cruise of the War Cloud* (New York: Beadle & Adams, 1885) is a novel about a ship and its participation in the Cuban revolution and its cruise in Pensacola Bay. Pensacola's red-snapper industry is recalled in "Snapper Fishermen of the Gulf" about Pensacola's red-snapper fishing fleet in *Tales of Old Florida* (New Jersey: Castle Books, 1987) edited by **Frank Oppel**. A cruise near Pensacola in 1900 is recounted in "A Florida Outing" in *'Neath Sunny Souther Skies* (New Orleans: Press of Palfrey-Rodd-Pursell, 1908) by **Clara Marion Williamson**.

Yacht trips of the F.F. Bingham family throughout west Florida are humorously recounted in *Log of the Peep O' Day: Summer Cruises in West Florida Waters, 1912-1915* (Bagdad, FL: Patagonia Press, 1991) edited by **Brian R. Rucker** and **Nathan Woolsey** and compiled from the original Sunday newspaper columns written by Bingham. These excursions on Pensacola waters probably led composers **Frank E. Ormsbee** and **Perry W. Reed** to write their songs "Down Pensacola Way" (1923) and "In a Florida Houseboat" (1924). Other west Florida trips are recalled in **William C. Anderson**'s *The Headstrong Houseboat; or, Barnacles are Better than Blowouts but Beware of a Leaky Basement* (New York: Crown, 1972); Lady **Peg Wilks**'s *Skippy Rides through Florida: A Dog's Eye View of the Sunshine State* (New York: Vantage Press, 1959), where Skippy, a Boston terrier, narrates her travels through Panama City and Pensacola. A cruise of a different sort is given by **Jay Norwood Darling** (1876-1962), a popular cartoonist in the 1930s, in *The Cruise of the Bouncing Betsy; A Trailer Travelogue* (New York: Stokes, 1937); a portion covers his gulf-coast exploits from Gulfport, Mississippi, to Pensacola illustrated by "Ding" himself.

As Pensacola's quadricentennial approached in 1959, the city felt a renewed interest in local history. The Pensacola Historical Society, located in Old Christ Church in Seville Square, preserves unpublished and published materials about city history as well as artifact collections to support its museum. Its publishing program has included quarterly journals (*Pensacola Historical Quarterly*, *The Echo*, *Pensacola History Illustrated*) as well as monographs by local historians including Norman Simons, Leora Sutton, Woody Skinner, Virginia Parks, and Jesse Earle Bowden. **John Appleyard** has published a number of histories of agencies including the United Way, Baptist Hospital, the school district, and city government. These efforts have been complemented by regional publications of University of West Florida faculty.

The West Florida Literary Federation, founded in 1985, oversees the publishing of works of several local writers. It has awarded the title of poet laureate of the Panhandle to such writers as **Adelia Rosasco-Soule** and **Leonard Temme**. In 1988, the federation began publishing an annual *Emerald Coast Review*, which is an anthology showcasing dozens of authors, works including poetry, drawings, stories, and essays. The federation also provides support and encouragement for writers, including high school students.

Pensacola schools also foster literary production: among their efforts are Washington High School's *Flashback* of literary efforts and oral histories collected by English classes; Escambia High School's *Rebel Writer* of 1964 and 1965, an anthology of student writings; Woodham High School's *Woes: Works of Erudite Students* (1985) and *Works of Erudite Students Too* (1986), collections of student prose and poetry, under the leadership of teacher Betty Martin; and Warrington Middle School's *Arts, Etc.*, creative-writing anthologies.

Poetry, the music of literary expression, has been alive since **Richard Henry Wilde** composed his *Hesperia* in 1867. Other nineteenth century poets writing of Pensacola included **Richard Henry Brownell**'s *War Ly-rics* (Boston: Ticknor and Fields, 1866) with Civil War odes mentioning Pensacola and Mobile; **Laura Hinsdale**'s *Legends and Lyrics of the Gulf Coast* (Biloxi, MS: Herald Press, 1896), an anthology of her local newspaper and magazine pieces.

Samuel L. Robertson's *Gulf Songs* (Birmingham, AL: Roberts & Son, 1908) is an epic poem (200 p.!) with references to Pensacola and other Gulf Coast cities and areas. An unusual compilation is *The Barefoot Barber: original Negro folklore poems and other compositions* (Pensacola, FL: 1922?) by Ed. **St. Clare Thomas** of poetry and prose heard in Pensacola and written in the Negro dialect. Father **Malachi E. Kitrick** (?-1939), pastor of St. Michael's Church, Pensacola, frequently published poetry in area newspapers and magazines under the name "**Gus Blunt.**" These were collected and published by his brother in *A book of verse* (Latrobe, PA: P.J. Kitrick, 1939). The work of another minister, Charles Haddon Nabers, was collected in *Viewpoints: sketches [and poems]* (Pensacola: Burrows Press, 1926).

Other Pensacola poets whose work has been published publicly and privately include **Ruth Welles Langford, Eunice Geiger, Louise M. Porter, Walt Aymond** (whose Alphonse Alligator is a poem told in Cajun dialect), **Zoli B. Engel, William Tyler, Clarice Burrell,** and **Adelia Rosasco-Soule.** Continuing support of poet writers comes from the Backdoor Poets, a support group promoting oral presentations and readings, and the West Florida Literary Federation which has published **Leonard Temme's** *Songs of Passion: Selected Poems, 1985-1989* (Pensacola, FL: 1990).

Southwest of Pensacola lies the Pensacola Naval Air Station (NAS), formerly the Pensacola Navy Yard. The Pensacola Navy Yard was begun in 1826 to serve as a naval supply base for the gulf coast and to provide naval back-up to the military forces at Fort Pickens and Fort Barrancas. The navy yard achieved strategic importance during the Civil War when it fell to the Confederates, but proved unusable since Union forces controlled Fort Pickens and the entrance pass into the Gulf of Mexico. After the Civil War, the yard deteriorated and contained minimal staffing until the turn of the century. The history of this era is told in **George F. Pearce's** *The U.S. Navy in Pensacola; From Sailing Ships to Naval Aviation (1825-1930)* (Pensacola: University of West Florida Press, 1980). The *Memorial of Henry Sanford Gansevoort* (Boston: Franklin Press, 1875) edited by **John Chipman Hoadley** details the career of Captain Gansevoort, Commander of Pensacola Harbor and Fort Barrancas in 1868; it includes a long series of letters written to his sister in Boston detailing life at the navy yard and Barrancas, the yellow-fever epidemic in 1867, and the quarantine station at Fort Pickens, illustrated with photographs. The memoirs of a surgeon-general of the U.S. Army at the Pensacola Navy Yard in 1872-1875 including observations of the yellow-fever epidemics are told in **Martha L. Sternberg's** *George Miller Sternberg, A Biography* (Chicago: American Medical Association, 1920).

In 1914, the navy yard was reclaimed as a training site for naval aviators, which became more important during World War I and World War II. The military build-up during the Cold War along with frosty Cuban relations has made the Pensacola Naval Air Station (NAS) into a major military center for naval and aerospace support. With the development of aircraft carriers, the U.S.S. *Lexington* was assigned to Pensacola for use in training; the history of this ship is given in *Taraway to Tokyo, 1943-1946* covering its building, the disastrous Japanese kamikaze attacks in World War II, and the end of the war.

The U.S.S. *Lexington* was decommissioned in 1991 and transferred to Corpus Christi, Texas, and is to be replaced by the U.S.S. *Forrestal*.

Barrett Studley's *Learning to Fly for the Navy* (New York: Macmillan, 1931) is a description of early aviator training in Pensacola. Fictional accounts of life at NAS include **Harold Blaine Miller**'s *Bob Wakefield, Naval Aviator* (New York: Dodd, Mead, 1936); **Cameron Rogers**'s *Flight Surgeon* (New York: Duell, Sloan, 1940) and *Aviation Cadet; Dick Hilton Wins His Wings at Pensacola...* (New York: Macmillan, 1941). Development and history of the NAS are given in *Naval Aviation, 1911-1986* (Pensacola: Southern Publishing Co., 1986) and in *The Cradle* (Pensacola: Southern Publishing Co., 1989), the latter titled to reflect Pensacola as the "cradle" of naval aviation. A Matt Helm adventure novel, *The Shadowers* (Greenwich, CT: Fawcett, 1964) by **Donald Hamilton**, is set in the Pensacola Navy Yard, with the cornering of the villain in an abandoned Santa Rosa Island fort.

Pensacola has always been positive in supporting the presence of the navy, although, as with all seaport cities, there is some parental concern about young women and sailors. The song "Peggy, the Pearl of Pensacola," in *62 Outrageous Songs* (New York: Oak Publications, 1966), is reminiscent of this feeling, with Peggy wasting her days, singing sad songs, and waiting for the return of her sailor from the sea.

Memoirs of Pensacola authors and NAS aviators include **Richard Evelyn Byrd**'s *Skyward* (New York: Putnam's, 1928), an account of his training at Pensacola, 1917-1918; *A Landlubber at Sea* (Ames, IA: Powers Press, 1930) by **John Leslie Powers** about his trip aboard the U.S.S. *Langley* aircraft carrier on its trip to Pensacola from Guantanamo (the *Langley* was one of the first ships used for naval aviation); *Believed to be Alive* (Middlebury, VT: Eriksson, 1981) by **John W. Thornton** (1922-) about the experiences of a helicopter pilot captured in Korea in 1951-1953; **George C. Kenney**'s *The Saga of Pappy Gunn* (New York: Duell, Sloan, 1959), a biography of Colonel Paul Irving Gunn, who trained and was stationed at Pensacola from 1917 to 1928; **James Roberts Nix**'s *Shadows of the Past of Pensacola Navy Yard* (Pensacola: 1966); and *Baa Baa Black Sheep* (New York: Putnam, 1958), the memoirs of Gregory "Pappy" Boyington and his Black Sheep Squadron. Though briefly mentioned, Boyington was an instructor at Pensacola NAS before leaving for the warfront. See also *The Heart has its Reasons; The Memoirs of the Duchess of Windsor* (New York: D. McKay, 1956) for the autobiography of **Wallis Warfield Simpson Spencer**, her account of life in Pensacola, marriage to Lieutenant Earl Winfield Spencer, and life at the navy yard in 1916. Chaplain **Raymond W. Johnson**'s *Postmark: Mekong Delta* (Westwood, NJ: Revell, 1968) tells the reminiscences of a Pensacolian in the Vietnamese conflict in 1961.

Eleven miles north of Pensacola is the campus of the University of West Florida. Founded as an upper-level university in 1965, the university today has over 6,000 students and 250 faculty members on its 1,000-acre campus. The John C. Pace Library with over 500,000 volumes includes the special collections department, which collects, preserves, and makes available primary and secondary materials documenting the history and development of west Florida's ten-county Panhandle. The 600,000 items in the collections include rare books, manuscripts, maps, photographs, newspapers, and related materials, making it one of the largest research collections in Florida. The published and unpublished literary manuscripts and papers of such west Florida writers as E.W. Carswell, John Diamond, Odell Griffith, William S. Rosasco III, Adelia Rosasco-Soule, and others are housed here, as well as a large Florida-author book collection. A unique collection is the West Florida Cookbook Collection of hundreds of culinary compilations from cooks, churches, and Florida organizations. These include Pensacola chef **Earl Peyroux**'s multi-volume *Gourmet Cooking* (Pensacola: Pensacola Junior College, 1983-) taken from his PBS-TV series on WSRE-TV, Pensacola.

The library is also home to the Bibliography of West Florida project, an ongoing bibliographic indexing program to locate and annotate every major item published in and about west Florida regardless of subject. Arranged by publication date and comprehensively indexed, four volumes (1535-1981) were published by library director **James A. Servies** in 1981; continuing under **Dean DeBolt**, four additional volumes have been compiled, bringing the coverage up through 1992. The library has also issued a number of special library publications for Friends; among these are **James A. Servies**'s *The Siege of Pensacola, 1781: A Bibliography* (Pensacola: John C. Pace Library, 1981); *H.L. Mencken on Pants-pressers, Publishers & Editors* (Pensacola: John C. Pace Library, 1980) on Mencken's remarks at the National Conference of Editorial Writers in 1947, taken from a manuscript in special collections; and **John Updike's** poem *The Angels* (Pensacola: King & Queen Press, 1968), a private press printing by James A. Servies.

The university faculty have contributed immensely to the literature of the Panhandle with articles, books, and college textbooks. It is impossible to list but only a few. The history department continues to sponsor the biannual Gulf Coast History and Humanities Conference; the 20 volumes of the published *Proceedings* of the conference include hundreds of scholarly articles and papers on west Florida history and culture. History department faculty **William S. Coker, James McGovern**, and **George Pearce** are widely known for their books and publications on west Florida — many already cited in these pages. **Wiley Lee Umplett** has written a number of books on sports culture, including a recent history of the Heisman Trophy. Psychologist **William Mikulas** has seen his books on metaphysics reprinted and translated into several foreign languages. Spanish culture and thought are reflected in **Allen Josephs's** *White Wall of Spain: The Mysteries of Andalusian Culture* (Ames, IA: Iowa State University, 1983), and his studies on Hemingway have made the university the home of the *Hemingway Review*. One of the more interesting sociological studies based on Pensacola life is **Ray Oldenburg's** *The Great Good Place: Cafes, coffee shops, community centers, beauty parlors, general stores, bars, hangouts and how they get you through the day* (New York: Paragon House, 1989).

The English department has published the *Panhandler* since 1976; the twice-a-year literary magazine of essays and poems features the work of writers from around the United States as well as local authors. This is supplemented by the *Panhandler Chapbook Series*, an annual which features longer manuscripts.

Milton

Milton is located on U.S. 90, 20 miles east of Pensacola. Situated on the Blackwater River, Milton is the seat of Santa Rosa County and in the nineteenth century was a major shipping port for goods sent by water to nearby Pensacola. The town became the center for a manufacturing complex of shipyards, lumber companies, and naval-stores operations. The history of the town and county is recounted in **Brian Rucker's** *Blackwater and Yellow Pine: The Development of Santa Rosa County* (Tallahassee: Florida State University, 1990) as well as **M. Luther King's** *History of Santa Rosa County* (Milton, FL: 1972). Other historical sources include **Linda Lasure's** columns in the *Santa Rosa Free Press* and **Brian Rucker's** *Jackson Morton: West Florida's Soldier, Senator, and Secessionist* (Milton, FL: Patagonia Press, 1990), a biography of this Milton citizen and United States senator (1849-1855). These histories are complemented by personal reminiscences of area writers like William S. Rosasco III, Adelia Rosasco-Soule, and William Wells.

William S. Rosasco III (1929-) is a local businessman active in real-estate development; his columns from the *Milton Press-Gazette* newspaper were compiled into *Musings: In God We Trust* (Pensacola: University of West Florida Press, 1980). **Adelia Rosasco-Soule** (1901-) immigrated to Milton in 1903 from Genoa, Italy, to join her father, Peter S. Rosasco, and his two brothers, who founded a thriving lumber business in Santa Rosa County. The genealogy of the Rosasco family has been traced in **Jane E. Richards's** *Born to Serve: the Rosasco Story* (Pensacola, FL: 1976). Adelia Rosasco-Soule's memories of life in the county, at Bay Point and the Bay Point Lumber Company, and travels as a military wife and mother are recounted in the delightful *Panhandle Memories* (Pensacola: West Florida Literary Federation, 1987). Her other writings include short stories and poems which have appeared in numerous national and regional publications and three published books of poetry: *The Thinking Chair* (1979), *Listen, Pilgrim* (1980), and *A Bird with a Broken Wing* (1982). In 1986, she was named the first poet laureate of the Panhandle by the West Florida Literary Federation. **William James Wells** has written on the families of south Santa Rosa County in *Pioneering in the Panhandle* (Fort Walton Beach, FL: Melvin Business Services, 1976) and in a personal memoir on growing up in Santa Rosa County in *Eighty-seven Years in Dixie* (Foley, AL: Metropolis Printing, 1986).

Celestine Sibley, journalist and writer, grew up in East Bay in Santa Rosa County and became a newspaper reporter for the *Mobile* (Alabama) *Register* under editor Marion Toulmin Gaines (later with the Pensacola newspaper). Sibley's memoirs *Turned Funny* (New York: Harper and Row, 1988) include her remembrances of life at East Bay and in Pensacola (1936-1939), as well as stories about the Colley, Broxson, and Lovett families of Santa Rosa County.

She frequently mentions her mother, who lived in Alford, Florida, north of Tallahassee, in her stories and in her *Mothers Are Always Special* (1970).

Creative writing by young people is fostered by the National Journalism Honor Society at Milton High School. Since 1982 they have annually published a literary magazine known under the title *Reflections* and later *Rhapsody*. And at the Milton campus of Pensacola Junior College (PJC), the Santa Rosa Center for the Literary Arts has produced an annual *Santa Rosa Review* of prose and poetry by students of PJC, under the direction of Donald Mangum.

Bagdad

One mile south of Milton on Highway 89, just north of Interstate 10, lies the village of Bagdad. In the 1830s, this region became one of the first major manufacturing areas of Florida. It began with John Hunt's brickyard, and lumber companies and a shipyard soon followed. At nearby Arcadia, one of the first cotton mills in Florida opened, its machinery powered by water. Many of these companies were destroyed during the Civil War, but in the 1880s, lumbering returned to the region to satisfy the demand of Victorian America and Europe for southern pine-wood products. An eyewitness account of the lumber industry and the area is provided by **Emory Fiske Skinner's** *Reminiscences* (Chicago: Vestal Printing Co., 1908); Skinner came to Bagdad and Pensacola in 1874 after running a sawmill in Nevada. The presence of the Bagdad Sash Company and the later Bagdad Land and Lumber Company influenced the growth of a small company-town of early twentieth-century pine cottages, churches, and company stores. The Bagdad Land and Lumber

Pages from Anna Cosulich's *The Belle of Pensacola* and Emory Skinner's *Reminiscences*

Company closed in 1939, and today most residents commute to work in nearby Milton and Pensacola.

In recent years, the new Bagdad Village Preservation Association has led a renaissance to create a historic district, preserve the company-town, and restore several donated buildings. **Brian R. Rucker**, an instructor at Pensacola Junior College, has written *A Bagdad Christmas* (Milton, FL: Patagonia Press, 1990) and documented the early manufacturing history of the Bagdad region, known as Black Water, in his Ph.D. thesis: *Blackwater and Yellow Pine: The Development of Santa Rosa County, 1821-1865* (Tallahassee, 1990). Famous aviator **Jacqueline Cochran** grew up near Bagdad and recorded her early experiences in her autobiographies: *The Stars at Noon* (Boston: Little, Brown, 1954) and *Jackie Cochran: An Autobiography* (New York: Bantam, 1987).

Another Bagdad native was **Leon Odell Griffith** (1921-1984). Griffith, though born in Crestview, grew up in Bagdad, the son of a Methodist minister. His journalistic career included stints with newspapers in Pensacola, Fort Walton Beach, and Jacksonville, and he returned to Pensacola in 1954 to found a public-relations agency. His novel *A Long Time Since Morning* (New York: Random House, 1954) is set in a northern Florida community somewhere between Pensacola and Jacksonville and tells of life in a small southern town with Deep South characters and smoldering conflicts. Certainly the book has some Bagdad, Milton, and Pensacola in it, especially since the fictional town is named Creighton, possibly from Creighton Avenue, a major thoroughfare in Pensacola. Griffith followed up with *Seed in the Wind* (New York: Random House, 1960), a novel about integration in a small southern town. Griffith's focus on racial intolerance may have sprung from his World War II experience. After serving with an integrated military, he recalled his experiences in a story for *Negro Digest* in 1946 titled "Back home in Dixie: A Southern White Veteran Comes Home to Get a New View on Race Prejudice."

Griffith also wrote two major nonfiction Florida works: *John H. Perry, Florida Press Lord* (Tampa: Trend Publications, 1974) about the man who acquired the *Pensacola News* and *Pensacola Journal* newspapers in 1924; and *Ed Ball: Confusion to the Enemy* (Tampa: Trend Publications, 1975), a biography of an influential Florida developer and heir to the DuPont interests. Griffith's poetry was published as *Ampersand* (Pensacola: Fiesta Press, 1977); his wife, **Mary C. Griffith**, wrote a biographical anthology, *Pensacola Women* (Pensacola: Griffith Agency, 1978). Until his death in 1984, Pensacolians were frequently treated to Griffith's opinions about politics, business, and Escambia County history in his newspaper, The *West Florida Official*.

Floridale and Harold

Proceeding eastward from Milton, following the railroad along U.S. 90, are the towns of Harold, Holt, and Milligan. Harold, originally known as Good Range, was one of the first stops for the Louisville and Nashville Railroad when it began service in 1883. Sometime in the 1890s, Senator Ebenezer Porter of Kansas visited the area and purchased the land around Good Range and around Holt, the next eastward stop of the train. He attempted to rename the two towns for his sons, but only Good Range was replatted as the Harold E.F. Porter subdivision.

In the ten-mile stretch between Milton and Harold, U.S. 90 also passes by a now-invisible site originally known as Floridale. The Floridale Townsite Corporation in 1926 acquired 50,000 acres and began construction of a 150-room, Spanish-style hotel. Partners in the corporation were architect W.L. White and Richard T. Ringling, of the Ringling Brothers, Barnum and Bailey Circus. The lavish hotel was white with red tiles and constructed in the best style of the day with hot and cold running water, an ice plant, a powerhouse, billiard room, and a tower which could be seen for several miles. The tower housed the power plant and provided a panoramic view of the town and graded (but unpaved) streets which had been laid out around the hotel. Plans called for sales of five- and ten-acre lots, a golf course, shopping center, and orchards, and the site would be the winter quarters for the Ringling Brothers, Barnum and Bailey circus. Construction on the project halted in mid-1928 and never resumed, doomed by the Great Depression. The deteriorating hotel and tower were eventually demolished, and little remains of this dream today. Histories of the area have been collected and written by **Audrey A. Stabler** in *Memories Coming Home* (Harold, 1985) and in **Max Cooper**'s *History of Holt, Florida* (Pensacola: University of West Florida Press, 1969).

Crestview

Located 40 miles east of Pensacola on U.S. 90, Crestview sits on a peak of a range of hills and boasts the second-highest altitude in Florida at 345 feet above sea level. A post office was established here in 1883, and the town owes its founding to the construction of the Louisville and Nashville Railroad. It became the county seat of the newly formed Okaloosa County in 1916, which took on more prominence when Eglin Air Force Base was established in 1944. Crestview is the home of **Robert Lee Fulton Sikes**, United States congressman in the House of Representatives from 1940 to 1979. His papers and office are in the Sikes Public Library in Crestview, and his autobiography *He-coon: The Bob Sikes Story* (Pensacola: Perdido Bay Press, 1984) documents his congressional career and impact on Crestview, Okaloosa County, and Eglin Air Force Base.

A charming folktale set in this area and written in black dialect is "De Snow White Buck o' Okaloosa" by **Susan W. Partridge**. Published in the short-lived *Outdoor Florida* in 1936, it tells the adventures of two little black children who become frightened at the appearance of the ghost in the nighttime forest. The works of Okaloosa poets appear in *Poems of Okaloosa* (Crestview: Webb's County Museum, 1973).

Eglin Air Force Base, the largest in the world, came into existence primarily as a bombing test center for World War II. Since that time it has been home to thousands of aviators and Special Forces units and a major facility for Star

Wars research. One biography set at the base is **Lloyd Mallan's** *A Day in the Life of a Supersonic Project Officer* (New York: D. McKay Company, 1958).

DeFuniak Springs

In May 1881, the survey party for the Pensacola and Atlantic Railroad (later Louisville and Nashville) was riding eastward about 90 miles from Pensacola when they came out of a forest to find themselves on the shores of a round lake. Entranced with the beauty of the spot, Colonel William Dudley Chipley ordered the building of a railroad way station (supply stop), and they named the site Lake de Funiak in honor of Fred R. de Funiak, general manager of the L&N line. By 1883, there was a small village at this site, which quickly grew when the Florida Chautauqua was established in 1885. For a history of the Chautauqua and town, see **Dean DeBolt's** "The Florida Chautauqua: An Overview of Its History" in *Threads of Tradition and Culture along the Gulf Coast* (Pensacola: Gulf Coast History and Humanities Conference, 1986) and his "The Florida Chautauqua" in *Florida Endowment for the Humanities Forum* (Fall 1990), pp. 6-10. Some of the lecturers at the first Florida Chautauqua discovered the lake was not a lake but a spring, and the town name was changed to DeFuniak Springs in 1885.

The Florida Chautauqua had a major impact on the city and the region. Today one original building still stands, the Hall of Brotherhood, built in 1909, surrounded by dozens of Victorian cottages and homes erected by visitors and Chautauqua entrepreneurs. The Chautauqua presence led to the creation of the coeducational Florida State Normal University in DeFuniak Springs, Florida's first public teachers' college. In 1905, it was moved to Tallahassee and became part of the Florida State College for Women, which later became Florida State University (FSU). In 1886, the Florida Chautauqua hosted the first State Teachers Institute in DeFuniak Springs; two organizations were created during this institute: the Escambia County Teachers Association (Escambia Education Association) and the Florida Education Association United, both organizations still active today.

A frequent Chautauqua speaker, **Wallace Bruce** (1844-1914) of Poughkeepsie, New York, eventually became president of the Florida Chautauqua and settled in DeFuniak Springs. His *In Clover and Heather* (1890) and *Forget-me-nots* (1898) contain poems written and read at DeFuniak Springs and used for Florida Chautauqua events. From his stint as U.S. Consul to Edinburgh, Scotland, he wrote a number of books, including *Here's a Hand* (1893), a biography of Robert Burns, and *Scottish Poems* (1907). He lectured about the Hudson Valley and Yosemite, writing about these places in *Along the Hudson with Washington Irving* (1913), *From Grant's Tomb to Mt. MacGregor: Patriotic Poems and Addresses along the Hudson* (1897), *The Hudson* (1881), *The Hudson River by Daylight* (1873), and *The Yosemite* (1880), this latter being poems about Yosemite's grandeur. He composed other books of poetry including *Old Homestead Poems* (1888), *Leaves of Gold* (1907), and *Wayside Poems* (1895). Wallace's son, **Kenneth**, wrote a novel about the American Revolution, *The*

Return of the Half Moon (1909), which was published under the pseudonym of **Diedrick Crayon, Jr.**

When the Walton County Courthouse burned at Eucheeanna in 1885, DeFuniak Springs, located on the railroad, became the new county seat. **John L. McKinnon**'s *History of Walton County* (Atlanta: Byrd Printing Co., 1911), the only county history so far published, is actually more of a memoir than an accurate retelling of the area's history. It is, however, a splendid account of the immigration of and settlement by Scotch Presbyterians in the region.

Westville

Eleven miles east of DeFuniak Springs is the small town of Westville in Holmes County. During 1890-1892, **Laura Ingalls Wilder** (1867-1957), author of the *Little House on the Prairie* books, lived here with Peter Ingalls and his family before returning to South Dakota. Information collected from Ingalls' descendants was published by **Alene M. Warnock** in *Laura Ingalls Wilder: The Westville, Florida Years* (Mansfield, MO: The Laura Ingalls Wilder Home Association, 1979).

Bonifay

Bonifay, county seat of Holmes County, is another in the string of west Florida towns which owes its existence to the Pensacola and Atlantic, later Louisville and Nashville, Railroad. As the railroad moved eastward from Pensacola in 1882, railroad camps were established and named for individuals associated with the railroad. Towns were laid out around these camps and lots sold by the railroad. Bonifay was named for Frank Bonifay, a Pensacola judge and railroad official; a post office was established in 1883. *Iron Horse in the Pinelands, Building West Florida's Railroad: 1881-1883* (Pensacola: Pensacola Historical Society, 1982) edited by **Virginia Parks** is a centennial history of the area.

The history of the town and county along with folklore and customs is covered in two books: **Anna Paget Wells**'s *Heart and History of Holmes County* (1980), which delves heavily into family history and genealogy, and **E.W. Carswell**'s *Holmesteading* (Chipley, FL: E.W. Carswell, 1986). The county itself was carved from three surrounding counties in 1848, possibly because of distance and perhaps because of the presence of the wilderness along the Choctawhatchee River, which meanders through the county. Music seems to be inspired by this area; Bonifay teacher Maymie Oriska Adams Griffen composed "Feeling Lonesome and Blue" (New York, 1934), and Pensacolian Margaret Axelson published "Where the Choctawhatchee Flows" (Cincinnati, 1924), an oft-requested song.

Life along the river is documented through oral history collected in *Historical Remembrances of Choctawhatchee River* (Havana, FL: Northwest Florida Water Management District, 1989).

Chipley

Chipley is another of the Pensacola and Atlantic railroad camps which became a town. It was named for Colonel William Dudley Chipley, who came to Pensacola in 1881 to be President of the P&A Railroad. The county seat of Washington County, it is centered in a predominantly agricultural region. Children's writer and illustrator **Ray Prather** used this agricultural setting for *Anthony and Sabrina* (New York: Macmillan, 1973) about two children visiting their grandmother's farm in Chipley. Chipley is also home to one of Florida's most prolific and honored writers, **Elba Wilson Carswell** (1916-). For many

years, Judge Carswell was the west Florida bureau chief, writer, and reporter for the *Pensacola News-Journal*. Along the way, he came to know the history, people, politics, and folklore of the Panhandle heartland better than any other person. In addition to news writing, his weekly newspaper columns covered such subjects as folklore, food, biographies, reminiscences, history, and a myriad of other west Florida topics.

Carswell has collated and reprinted these columns into books around central themes. These have included *Commotion in the Magnolia Tree: Commentary and Recollections about Country Living* (Bonifay, FL: Taylor Publications, 1981) about Washington County; *A Grateful Note to Gracie Ashmore* (Bonifay, FL: Taylor Publications, 1982), a collection of biographical columns of people in the Panhandle and Florida; *He Sold No 'Shine Before its Time: More Commentary and Recollections about Country Living* (Bonifay, FL: Taylor Publications, 1981); *Remembering World War II before Kilroy* (Bonifay, FL: Taylor Publications, 1982) on recollections of the war; and *Tales of Grandpa and Cousin Fitzhugh* (Bonifay, FL: Taylor Publications, 1982). A lifelong interest (inquisitory and culinary) in possums led to *Possum Cookbook: America's Amazing Marsupials and Dozens of Ways to Cook Them* (Chipley, FL: Carswell Foundation Press, 1975) and more compilations about cooking and folktales titled *A Possum in Every Pot (A Slogan for our Next Election): All You Ever Wanted to Know About Possums, But Were Afraid*

E.W. Carswell

to Ask, (1991 — enlarged and revised as *A Possum in Every Pot* (Tallahassee: Rose Printing Co., 1991) edited by **Sue Riddle Cronkite**.

Carswell's interest in history led him to write *Tempestuous Triangle: Historical Notes on Washington County, Florida* (Chipley, FL: Washington County School Board, 1974) which he revised and enlarged with *Washington: Florida's Twelfth County* (Chipley, FL: Carswell, 1991). The history of nearby Holmes County was covered in *Holmesteading: The History of Holmes County, Florida* (Chipley, FL: Carswell, 1986). Judge Carswell has been honored by the Florida Folklore Council for his contributions to preserving the history and folklore of the Panhandle, and his work has established him as a major Florida author.

Other tales and histories of the Chipley area have been collected and published by **Joan P. Chance** in her *Through the Years* (Chipley, FL: Panhandle Area Educational Cooperative, 1986) and *Reflections* (Chipley, FL: Panhandle Area Educational Cooperative, 1983), anthologies of writings about area businesses, families, and folk stories. **Sam Shuemake** has written *Peace at Sundown: True Life Story of the Trials and Tribulations of one West Florida Pioneer* (Opp, AL: 1974), fictional reminiscences of the author's grandfather, a Chipley clergyman in the early twentieth century. Civil War reminiscences predating the creation of Washington County are found in **Henry W. Reddick's** *Seventy-seven years in Dixie* (Freeport, FL: Observer job print, 1910) including his service in the Walton Guards and Confederate Army. An appendix contains poetry by Reddick and others. **George C. Cates's** religious revival in 1916 is recounted in his *Cates Union Revival, Chipley, Florida* (Louisville, KY: Pentecostal Publishing Co., 1917).

Chipley has another claim to fame. In 1902, Chipley resident C.E. Pleas, a Quaker horticulturist and naturalist, obtained some cuttings of a small plant which the Japanese had shown at the 1876 Centennial Exposition in Philadelphia. He found the plant more of a nuisance than a benefit, but it did thrive in sandy soil and on very little water. Eventually he developed a nursery, sold cuttings all over the South, and widely promoted the vine as a food for cattle. Because of its prolificity, the vine soon outgrew domestication and is today known as kudzu or, as some say, the "cuss-you" vine. Pleas was one of the first photographers to study nature photography, producing some of the earliest and finest nature photographs in Florida. These are still preserved in the C.E. Pleas Collection at the University of West Florida.

Chipley was also the home of **Will McLean**, Florida balladeer and author. His works include *Florida Sand: Original Songs and Stories of Florida* (Earleton, FL: Lake & Emerald Publications, 1977) and *'Cross the Shadows of My Face* (Seattle, WA: Typographics/Seattle, 1980).

Graceville

Thirteen miles north of Chipley is Graceville, which sits almost astride the state line between Florida and Georgia. The feverish minor-league baseball activities here are chronicled in **Robert P. Dews's** *GA-FLA League (1935-1953)* (Edison, GA: Rebel Books, 1985). **Paul Hemphill** recounted his 1954

Graceville adventure of playing Class D baseball in "I Gotta Let the Kid Go" in *Life* (September, 1972), which was reprinted in his anthology *The Good Old Boys* (New York: Simon and Schuster, 1974); the story was expanded into the book-length *Long Gone* (New York: Viking, 1979) about the Graceville Oilers and turned into the 1987 movie of the same name but with a team called the Tampico Stogies.

A companion tome to the Dews book is **Ken Brooks's** *The Last Rebel Yell: The Zany but True Misadventures of Baseball's Forgotten Alabama-Florida League* (Lynn Haven, FL: Seneca Park Publishing, 1986).

Marianna

Twenty miles east of Chipley on U.S. 90 is Marianna, the seat of Jackson County. Founded in 1829, the town was named for Mary and Anne, two daughters of a pioneer merchant. Today Marianna is known for its architecture and mansions, having escaped destruction during the Civil War. For the history and folklore of the county see **J. Randall Stanley's** *History of Jackson County* (Marianna, FL: Jackson County Historical Society, 1950) and also **Jerrell H. Shofner's** *Jackson County, Florida: A History* (Marianna, FL: Jackson County Heritage Association, 1985). A collection of family stories, poems, and historical sketches is **Janie Smith Rhyne's** *Our Yesterdays* (Marianna, FL: Jackson County Floridan Press, 1968), taken from her writings in the newspaper. Rhyne has also published a collection of poems, *Salt Wind* (1945). Rhyne's daughter, **Mary Elizabeth Witherspoon** (1919-), has written *Somebody Speak for Katy* (New York: Dodd, Mead, 1950) about a 17-year-old girl who goes off to Florida State College for Women and then to a career in social services in New York City and *The Morning Cool* (New York: Macmillan, 1972); both are fiction dealing with social issues. Northern Jackson County is the setting for **Iris Tracy Comfort's** *Echoes of Evil* (New York: Doubleday, 1977), a fictional account of a psychic investigator.

Another Marianna writer is **Wilma Russ**, whose *Quivering Earth: A Novel of the Everglades* (New York: David McKay, 1952) tells of life in the Everglades at the turn of the century. A brief mention of Marianna is afforded in **Melvin Reeves's** *Marianna, Catherine and I* (New York: Pageant Press, 1957) about a honeymoon trip through the area in 1937.

Marianna is also the home of Governor John Milton of Florida. His son, Jeff Davis Milton (1861-1847), grew up in Marianna, moved to Texas, and had an illustrious career as a Texas ranger; see his biography, *Jeff Milton, A Good Man With A Gun* (Norman, OK: University of Oklahoma Press, 1948) by **James Evetts Haley.** Marianna's **Rita Dickens**, a great granddaughter of Governor Milton, has written *Marse Ned: The Story of an Old Southern Family* (New York: Exposition Press, 1959) based on the Miltons and dealing with southern white folks and their relationships with black families before and after the Civil War.

The Reconstruction era was difficult for the area. A Freedman's Bureau was established, and its work, coupled with local animosity toward carpetbaggers, provided for unrest in race relations. The lynching of Claude Neal at

Marianna in 1934 was investigated by the National Association for the Advancement of Colored People and is recounted in **James R. McGovern's** *Anatomy of a Lynching* (Baton Rouge: Louisiana State University Press, 1982). **J. Russell Reaver's** compilation of *Florida Folktales* (Gainesville: University Presses of Florida, 1988) includes a tale about carpetbaggers in Jackson County (Tale 20).

A major African-American writer from Marianna is **Timothy Thomas Fortune** (1856-1928), who was born a slave in Marianna and attended a Freedman's school in Tallahassee and Howard University in Washington, D.C. He moved to New York City in 1879 and in 1884 began publishing a black newspaper, the *New York Freedman*, which became the *New York Age*. At the turn of the century, he was probably the best-known, most-militant, and most-articulate race spokesman in the North. His books, *Black and White; Land, Labor, and Politics in the South* (1884) and *The Negro in Politics: Some Pertinent Reflections on the Past and Present Political Status of the Afro-American...* (1885), reflect his severe views of race relations. He is also one of the earliest Florida African-American poets to publish a poetry anthology: *Dreams of Life* (1905). For biographical information, see **Emma Lou Thornbrough's** *T. Thomas Fortune, Militant Journalist* (Chicago: University of Chicago Press, 1972).

Caroline Lee Whiting Hentz

Ironically, Marianna was the final home of another writer who achieved literary stardom over the issue of race relations — **Caroline Lee Whiting Hentz** (1800-1856). A major novelist, Hentz was one of the best-selling fiction writers in antebellum America, with her well-written books about domestic life and rebellious women protagonists. A Massachusetts native, Hentz followed her husband through six southern and western states. After he fell ill in 1849, it was her writing which supported the family until her death in Marianna. Her books include *Lovell's Folly* (1833); *De Lara: or, The Moorish Bride: A Tragedy in Five Acts* (1843); *Aunt Patty's Scrap-Bag* (1846); *Linda; or, The Young Pilot of Belle Creole* (1850); *The Mob Cap; and Other Tales* (1850); *Rena, or The Snow Bird* (1851); *Eoline; or, Magnolia Vale* (1852); *Marcus Warland; or, The Long Moss Spring, a Tale of the South* (1852); *Helen and Arthur; or, Miss Thusa's Spinning Wheel* (1853); *Wild Jack; or, The Stolen Child and Other Stories* (1853); *The Planter's Northern Bride* (1854; reprinted Chapel Hill, NC: University of North Carolina Press, 1970); *Robert Graham* (1855); *Courtship and Marriage; or, The Joys and Sorrows of*

American Life (1856); *Ernest Linwood* (1856); and *Love After Marriage; and Other Stories of the Heart* (1857). Some of these works were published with different titles as well.

Hentz's most important work is *The Planter's Northern Bride*, written as a southern answer to Harriet Beecher Stowe's *Uncle Tom's Cabin*. Some critics castigated *Bride* for its too-rosy view of southern life. As with most popular fiction, it is hard to place Hentz's books in a specific geographical setting, but *Marcus Warland* appears to be set in St. Andrews Bay, Florida. Hentz is almost forgotten today, but she was one of the most prolific writers of popular literature in the antebellum South.

Greenwood

Settlers from South Carolina changed the name of this town from Panhandle to Greenwood to honor their former home. **Rubylea Hall** (1910-1973) was born in Greenwood, Florida, and went on to earn a degree at Florida State University. She taught in Florida public schools (1927-32), worked with the Federal Emergency Relief Administration (1932-33) and at Camp Blanding in Florida (1943-44) and in the chemistry-pharmacy library at the University of Florida (1944-49), and then became director of customer services for Q-Tips, Inc. in New York (1959+).

She wrote three significant Florida novels. *The Great Tide* (New York: Duell, Sloan & Pearce, 1947), which won the Bohnenberger Award of the Southeastern Conference of Libraries for the best novel of the South, 1947-48, was about the doomed Florida town of St. Joseph during the 1830s and 1840s; it was the town where Florida's first constitution was written (1838-39) and the place known as the wickedest city in the Southeast; it was devastated by a yellow-fever epidemic, a hurricane, and a tidal wave. Her *Flamingo Prince* (New York: Duell, Sloan and Pearce, 1954) was about the great Seminole leader, Osceola. Her *God Has a Sense of Humor* (New York: Duell, Sloan and Pearce, 1960) was about two sides of a family growing up in the Florida Panhandle around 1900.

Clifton Paisley's *The Red Hills of Florida, 1528-1865* (Tuscaloosa, AL: University of Alabama Press, 1989) gives the history of the surrounding area, especially the counties of Leon, Gadsden, Jackson, Jefferson, and Madison. For more personal recollections of the area see *On St. Andrews Bay, 1911-1917* (Tampa: Sylvia Dean Harbert, 1969) by **Susie Kelly Dean**.

SPIRALS IN THE SEA

JACK RUDLOE

The north wind gusted over the choppy waters of Alligator Harbor in the Florida panhandle, where I was on a quest for left-handed whelks for the University of Michigan. For more than a quarter century now, I had trod those same flats, bringing back striped sea cucumbers, tunicates, crabs, and mollusks for Gulf Specimen Marine Laboratory, our small biological supply house in Panacea, Florida. Sometimes the sea was bountiful, and I brought back an abundance of creatures. Other times, it was fickle, and there were lean pickings.

It was my forty-ninth birthday. I stood on the edge of the all-too-familiar tide flats, watching the winds pushing water off the flats, exposing a vast panorama of oyster bars, mud flats and grass beds, painfully feeling the cold penetrate into my slightly aching bones, wondering what I was doing here and why after all these years, I didn't have a secure office job, why I had chosen this bizarre lifestyle without a speck of security.

At first life was a series of exciting and intriguing quests, searching for red-footed sea cucumbers, shipping live sharks and electric rays to laboratories and aquariums, hauling up bucket dredges of *Amphioxus*. There had been travel, adventure, and quests that I enjoyed so much. I had to share them with others by describing them in books, articles, and films. But in the past few years it was harder to get up at two o'clock in the morning and pick up horseshoe crabs on the high tide, and when I did, the buckets seemed heavier than they used to.

I stood there, watching the sand dollars making semi-circular trails in the sand, enjoying a mid-life crisis. The green had turned to gray. The sense of discovery, of finding a moon snail tunneling beneath the substrate and making a furrowed trail, had long since passed. Sometimes it came back vicariously when I took a group of students out and saw that glowing look of wonder and excitement in their eyes, when I showed them a snake eel worming its way through the sand or picked up a sea hare and showed them how it exuded bright purple ink.

But now I was questing for something else. And whatever it was, I knew I would find it here and not in the world of office buildings, publishers, universities, or television studios. I glanced down at the holes made by acorn worms that bubbled from deep in their burrows, as their kin had done for the past billion years. They weren't worried about mortality, fame, fortune, or the future, so then why should I?

Then my eyes came upon a gray starfish that was crawling over the ridged sand; the tiny number of invertebrate zoologists who study them call them *Luidia clathrata*. Automatically I scarfed it up and put it in my bucket and went on; it was worth five dollars, and we could use it for inventory in our aquariums. Sometimes gray starfish were abundant; thousands were heaped up on the deck of our boat when we emptied the trawls. Lately they were scarce, and I found a few individuals out on the flats, prowling about feasting on snails.

Soon I came to another one, but something stopped me from collecting it. It was so alive, it seemed imbued with its own power. Fascinated, I watched it travel with its lead arm extended, its multitudes of centipedelike feet gliding over the bottom in an inch of water. I started to pick it up, but I couldn't. Suddenly I felt like an intruder. What right did I have to confine this starfish to a bucket? To take it from its world, where it was minding its own business, and ship it away to a laboratory where it would be gawked at, dissected and probed.

I walked on, leaving this invertebrate being, this soul manifested in the form of a starfish, and, as I distanced myself, I asked the wind, the sea, the sky and myself aloud, "What *is* this all about?"

"None of your business," returned a familiar flippant voice from deep in my inner psyche, in a particularly rude and snobby tone. At first I was shocked, and walked on in silence. Then I returned angrily, "If it's none of my business, then what *is* my business?"

It chose not to answer. I up-ended my bucket and dumped the first starfish out to go free. "I came here for left-handed whelks, and not gray sand stars!" And then moving on admonished, "Very good! Keep going like that, throwing away money and how are you going to pay the bills?"

Ahead were oyster bars, where the whelks buried down in the mud. I found a few actively feeding, their large black feet plastered over rugged, gray shells of the oysters, relentlessly smothering them until the valves opened slightly. Then the whelk inserted its proboscis, and with a complex moving set of zipperlike teeth sheered away the soft flesh, until only an empty shell was left behind. It was all done in snail and oyster time, slowly, ruthlessly, efficiently. That is the way it is done in the sea; everything munches on everything else.

I wrenched several out of the mud and tore them off their prey. I was another predator in the food chain. Man has foraged along the edge of the sea since the beginning.

Not far from there, there were shell middens filled with left-handed whelks, dating back thousands of years. Similar kitchen middens were found all along the coast of Florida, covering numerous occupational periods. The Indians cracked the whelks open and systematically hewed them out of their shells in a characteristic way to extract the tough, tasty flesh.

But the whelks were more than food. They were ceremonial objects, traded wide and far. Archaeologists have found them hundreds of miles from the sea, as far north as Ohio. They were sacred to the American Indian. Horse conchs, the "great white sharks" of the snail world that devour the left-handed whelks, became musical instruments. The Indians made a hole in the apex and blew through it, cupping the opening with their hand to modulate the notes. No doubt the sound of conch shells could be heard, blaring out across the landscape, summoning the people to religious meetings. I remembered the Reverend Thurlow Weed at the Episcopal Church in Key West, who used to play hymns on the conch shell for his congregations. If he found God in a shell, why not me?

I picked up another conch and beheld its spiraling body. Somehow it was telling me something about myself, how my life had been an endless spiral, going round and round, but never making the same loop twice. It represented two infinities, forever expanding outward and yet contracting inward. Early mankind venerated that symbol, and repeated it on their pottery, in petroglyphs and ancient cave paintings. Archaeologists say that spirals in pre-Columbian art were water signs, but they could just as easily have represented the soaring flight patterns of eagles, hawks, and vultures. Or the way branches spiraled up a tree. Or when a lightning bolt hits a pine, how it spirals down the trunk, making a furrow.

Looking at the sturdy tan whelks with their thick coiling shells in my bucket, I thought about all the other spirals I'd seen in nature. There were the coiled tails of big green chameleons with popping eyes in Madagascar, the trunks of elephants, the prehensile tails of sea horses, the horns of mountain sheep. There were pea vines that coiled and the fiddleheads of ferns. I watched moths spiraling around light bulbs and saw garden peas corkscrewing their way up sticks. I created whirlpools by jabbing my canoe paddle into the water, pulling back and creating a vortex — a three-dimensional spiral. The waves spiraled at my feet; all about me were *Terebra* snails that looked like small gray ice cream cones — another vortex. Satellite photos from space show the ocean to be one vast mosaic of interconnecting gyres that reach from the arctic to the tropics. And miles offshore was the Gulf Loop current, a giant eddy that swirled around the center of the Gulf of Mexico before streaming past Cuba, up the continental shelf of the United States, and then over to Europe and Africa as part of the Gulf Stream.

Without telescopes and satellites, the Indians could not have known that there are spiraling gas clouds on Jupiter, or that we are part of a vast universe of spiraled galaxies. The ancient Celts, who etched interconnecting spirals into granite, knew nothing of DNA molecules that make up the fabric of life, or that they're shaped into double helixes. But all the ancients knew the spiral as the symbol of life and death itself.

The Mayan glyph for "birth" depicts a reptilian head — perhaps a turtle's, hatching out of the sand — with a swirl by its mouth. It reminds me of the moment when Sky, my son, was born. When I saw his head emerging from his mother's womb, his hair plastered to his head made a perfect spiral — it was beautiful.

I felt the icy winds. I was excited, as I stood holding my bucket of left-handed whelks, watching them slowly pulling their meaty body back into their shells, spurting out water. They closed their doors, so no one could get in, sealing their shells tight with their operculums the way I found myself doing to new ideas. But not today. I saw these lowly gastropods, not as ten-dollar bills, but as the bearer of the mystical symbol of life.

My mind continued racing dizzily on spirals, and how they went the other way on the other side of the equator. It was called the Coreolis Force. And suddenly I thought about the Tibetan monk who happened through Panacea years ago and told me that one of his dreams was to find a left-handed snail, because they were so rare and were considered sacred in the temples of Tibet. Nothing could be easier. I showed him all the whelks in our tanks, and the empty shells we'd collected, and he left loaded down and more overjoyed than if he'd won the lottery.

Why, I wondered, was there such a paucity of left-handedness in nature? Logically the ratio of left- to right-handedness should be fifty-fifty, but it isn't. As rare as left-handed people, only a small number of snail species turn counterclockwise. Sometimes it is only a single species of mollusk among a large genus. Most left-handed snails are small and relatively rare. But not so *Busycon contrarium*, which abounds on the sandy bottoms. Why should the Gulf of Mexico have cooked up such an abundant non-conforming whelk as that? Was there something about the energies of the currents or the shape of the land that made it flow the other way? Across the isthmus of Florida, out in the Atlantic, the closely related channel whelk, which looked almost identical and spiraled to the right, was so common that it was fished commercially for food.

Maybe there was a connection between left-handed whelks and my living on the shores of the Gulf in isolation and doing the things I did. I lifted out of my body, in my mind, and soared above the ocean and shoreline and looked down at myself, alone out on the tide flats with the north wind howling and my nose running in the cold. I looked at all the other humans, in their homes, in their offices, in their secure jobs, and somehow I understood that was the way it was. Maybe it was wisdom, or enlightenment, or something.

Then another spiral flashed into my mind. Some American Indians said "shaman" in sign language by pointing their forefingers at their temples and spiraling it around and around. Somehow the gesture became corrupted in our culture to mean "crazy" or "touched in the head."

I couldn't say which one I was, but the tide was coming in, the water was covering the oyster bars and gushing around my feet, and it was time to go. I took my captive whelks, with their counterclockwise shells, and headed for my car. I had come for the snails and ended up with an idea.

It was a good day.

Jack Rudloe, who is mentioned at the end of Chapter Nine, is the author of five books, including The Living Dock at Panacea *(1977) and* The Wilderness Coast *(1988).*

PHOTO CREDITS

Pages 15 and 19, Florida State Archives; page 25, E. L. Konigsburg; pages 29, 31, 32 and 35, Florida State Archives; page 36, Kevin M. McCarthy; pages 43, 48, 51, 56 and 57, Florida State Archives; pages 67 and 68, David Nolan; page 70, Sudie Nolan; page 82, Hamilton Nolan; page 92, Sudie Nolan; page 103, David Nolan; page 104, Hamilton Nolan; pages 115 and 120, Sudie Nolan; pages 127 and 130, David Nolan; page 136, Stetson University Archives; page 142, University of Florida Libraries, Rare Books and Manuscripts; page 145, Rollins College Archives; page 149, Kevin M. McCarthy; page 151, George Garrett; page 152, University of Central Florida Public Affairs; page 153, Kevin M. McCarthy; page 161, Rollins College Archives; page 172, NASA; page 176, Stuart McIver; page 184, Joan Leonard; pages 187 and 188, Historical Society Palm Beach County; page 190, Helmut Koller; page 191, Ballantine Books; page 195, Stuart McIver; pages 202 and 203, Bahia Mar Resort; page 205, Kevin M. McCarthy; page 220, James Hall; page 222, Jerry Bauer; page 227, Brandon Kerchner; page 234, Coconut Grove Playhouse; page 236, Florida State Archives; page 242, Kevin M. McCarthy; page 243, Florida State Archives; page 245, Rafael Llerena; page 248, Felix Morisseau-Leroy; pages 260, 261 and 273, Florida State Archives; page 274, Jeffry Cardenas; page 276, Florida State Archives; page 286, Nancy Crampton; page 287, Florida State Archives; page 296, Richard W. Brown; page 300, Kevin M. McCarthy; page 302, Walter Farley; page 313, Steinmetz; page 327, Timothy Meinke; page 328, Eckerd College; page 334, Marjorie E. Schuck; page 335, Frank C. Strunk; page 336, Florida Department of Commerce; pages 337, 338, 340 and 343, Hampton Dunn; page 353, Florida State Archives; page 357, Kevin M. McCarthy; pages 363 and 369, Dictionary of American Portraits, Dover Publications, Inc., 1967; page 372, Florida State Archives; page 373, Darcy Meeker; page 375, Dictionary of American Portraits; page 377 (top), Kevin M. McCarthy; page 377 (bottom), Herb Press; page 382, Kevin M. McCarthy; pages 384 and 386, Dictionary of American Portraits; page 387, Kevin M. McCarthy; page 397, Mona Lisa Abbott; page 406, Mariner's Museum, Newport News, VA; pages 415, 424 and 436, University of West Florida Library, Special Collections; page 441, Kevin M. McCarthy; page 444, University of West Florida Library, Special Collections.

BIOGRAPHIES OF CONTRIBUTING WRITERS

Richard Adicks, a sixth-generation Floridian, was born in Lake City. He earned his B.A. and M.A. degrees at the University of Florida and the Ph.D. from Tulane University. He taught in Florida high schools, at Rollins College, and at Georgia Tech before joining the charter faculty of the University of Central Florida, where he is professor of English. Besides a novel, *A Court for Owls,* he has written on local history and on English and American literature.

Gisela Casines was born in Havana, Cuba, and left the country for political reasons in 1961. Since that time she has lived in Dade County and thus considers herself almost a native of the county. She has been at Florida International University since 1981 and is now Associate Professor and Head Advisor. Although her research specialty is Restoration and 18th-century and Spanish Golden Age drama, she has always been interested in the Miami literary scene; to that end she is on the advisory board of The Writer's Voice.

Dean DeBolt is a University Librarian at the John C. Pace Library, University of West Florida. He oversees the Special Collections Department or West Florida Archives, one of the largest research collections in Florida about the Panhandle and Gulf Coast. He is a frequent lecturer on history and genealogy, and his writings have appeared in a number of professional journals and publications. He is currently completing a book on the history of the Florida Chautauqua at DeFuniak Springs.

Gary L. Harmon is Professor of Literature and English at the University of North Florida, which he helped found in 1971-72 and where he teaches and writes about American culture and literature, film, and criticism. From 1977 to 1980, he conducted the Florida Authors Project, to profile the novelists, poets, and dramatists who wrote or are writing in Florida. In 1979, with Kevin McCarthy, who researched literature featuring Florida, the two collaborated for a statewide meeting of English professors to focus attention on "Literature in Florida/Florida in Literature," leading to the idea for this book. Professor Harmon's fourth book, due for publication next year, is *Film and Gender: Myth, Power, and Change*; his essays explore meaning and importance in such symbols and myths as tycoons, saviors, and mythic heroes and heroines as cultural mediators.

THE BOOK LOVER'S GUIDE TO FLORIDA

Edgar W. Hirshberg was a member of the charter faculty at the University of South Florida, joining the English Department in 1960, the first year of the University's operation. He is a specialist in 19th-century literature and received degrees from Harvard and Cambridge before earning his Ph.D. from Yale, all in English. He has published two books and numerous scholarly and critical articles. His interest in Popular Culture led him to specialize in John D. MacDonald, a personal friend, and he has been editor and publisher of *The JDM Bibliophile* and directed four conferences concerning MacDonald's work. Since 1972 he has also directed or co-directed the Florida Suncoast Writers' Conference. Though retired, he is still teaching part-time at USF. His Twayne book on John D. MacDonald is still in print.

Kevin McCarthy, professor of English at the University of Florida, has an M.A. in American literature and a Ph.D. in linguistics, both from the University of North Carolina. He has taught in Turkey for two years as a Peace Corps Volunteer and in Lebanon for one year and Saudi Arabia for two years as a Fulbright Professor. He has published books on English grammar, Saudi Arabia, Florida lighthouses, shipwrecks, and Florida stories.

Stuart McIver, the author of seven books on South Florida history, lives in Lighthouse Point, Broward County, with his journalist wife, Joan. The writer of an award-winning series of historical stories in the Fort Lauderdale Sun-Sentinel's Sunshine Magazine, he also serves as editor of the South Florida History Magazine, published by the Historical Association of Southern Florida. He is a director of the Florida Historical Society and a former two-term president of the Book Group of South Florida, an organization of authors, writers and publishers. A 30-year resident of Florida, he is a graduate of the University of North Carolina. Among the honors won by documentary films he has written and produced are two CINE Golden Eagles and a Silver Medal at the Venice (Italy) Film Festival.

David Nolan is the author of *Fifty Feet in Paradise: The Booming of Florida* (Harcourt Brace Jovanovich, 1984). He is a trustee of the Marjorie Kinnan Rawlings Society and the Council for Florida Libraries. He is writing a book about the adventures of famous authors in Florida. The father of two children, he makes his home in St. Augustine.

David Warner lives in Sarasota and Lochloosa, Florida, and has been a contributing editor for *Sarasota* and *Gulfshore Life* magazines. He has published over 50 stories and articles in literary, national, state, and local magazines. In 1986, he was awarded a Certificate of Merit by the Florida Magazine Association. Recently, he has co-authored an introduction for a re-release of Sarasota novelist Bordon Deal's *The Least One* by the University of Alabama Press. Warner has also written and co-produced two TV documentaries about Bimini and northern New Mexico and is currently working on a documentary about soul singer Otis Redding.

QUOTATION SOURCES

Chapter 1

P. 9. "...we landed on the main." William Bartram, *Travels Through North & South Carolina, Georgia, East & West Florida, The Cherokee Country, the Extensive Territories of the Muscogulges, or Creek Confederacy, and the Country of the Chactaws* (1791; New York: Viking Penguin Inc., 1988), p. 80.

P. 10. For further information about Muir and his idea to save humans for the wilderness and humans for the wilderness, see Stephen Fox, *John Muir and His Legacy* (New York: Little, Brown, Publishers, 1981).

P. 10. "On the north-western side of the city..." Ledyard Bill, *A Winter in Florida* (New York: Wood and Holbrook, 1867), as quoted in Mackle Elliott James Jr., *The Eden of the South: Florida's Image in American Travel Literature and Painting 1865-1900* (1977: Emory University; reproduced by UMI Dissertation Information Service, 1990), p. 61.

P. 15. "under a just and prudent system..." Zephaniah Kingsley, *A Treatise on the Patriarchal System of Society* (1829; Freeport, NY: Books for Libraries Press, 1970), p. 8.

P. 16. "whereas I have an African wife..." Zephaniah Kingsley, his will, quoted in Stetson Kennedy, *Palmetto Country* (1942; reprinted by Florida A & M University Press, 1989), p. 80.

P. 17. "Each story speaks... " Charles Bennett, *Twelve on the St. Johns* (Jacksonville: University of North Florida Press, 1989), p. vii.

P. 18. "the morning brought them..." Robert Wilder, *God Has a Long Face* (New York: Bantam, 1952), pp. 14-15.

P. 20. "cradle of United States history..." See T. Frederick Davis, *History of Jacksonville, Florida, and Vicinity, 1513 to 1924* (1925; reprinted by University of Florida Press, 1964).

P. 20. "Lib, the girl with the most beautiful legs in Florida." From the dust jacket of *Alas, Babylon.*

P. 22. "...My subject/has always been..." William Slaughter, *Untold Stories* (Port Washington, WA: Empty Bowl, 1990), p. 89.

P. 24. "...have been accused of grossness and viciousness." David L. Vanderwerken, *Modern Fiction Studies*, spring, 1987.

P. 26. "to draw and paint and..." From author profile, "Forty Percent More Than Everything You Wanted to Know About E. L. Konigsburg," Atheneum Publishers, 1974 and 1991.

P. 26. "The town was old..." Blaine Stevens, *The Outlanders* (New York: Jove Books, 1979), p. 48.

P. 27. "There was a brawling vigor..." Robert Wilder, Ibid., p.15.

P. 27. "I was ... able..." Henry James, *The American Notebooks* (Bloomington, IN: Indiana University Press, 1968), pp. 433-434.

P. 28. "...largest blaze in American history..." and "...2361 buildings..." H. L. Mencken, *Newspaper Days 1899-1906* (New York: Alfred A. Knopf, 1941), p. 94.

P. 28. "I found, as I expected, that the fire..." Mencken, Ibid., p. 105.

P. 29. "one of the highlights..." Will McLean, *Florida Sand, New Enlarged Edition (Earleton, FL: Lake and Emerald Publications, 1977), from the introduction (unpaginated).*

P. 31. "The streets are remarkably wide..." George M. Barbour, *Florida For Tourists, Invalids, and Settlers* (1882; reprinted Gainesville: University of Florida Press, 1964), p. 10.

P. 34. "In my mind..." From conversation with Gary L. Harmon, June, 1992.

P. 34. "We were quartered in..." Ann Hyman, *Chaos Clear as Glass: A Memoir* (Atlanta, GA: Longstreet Press, 1991), p. 39.

P. 36. "Lift ev'ry voice and sing..." James Weldon Johnson, "Lift Ev'ry Voice and Sing" (The Edward B. Marks Music Corporation and the heirs of Edward B. Marks, 1900).

P. 37. "And God stepped out on space..." James Weldon Johnson, *God's Trombones, Seven Negro Sermons in Verse* (New York: Viking Press, Inc. 1927, copyright renewed 1955 by Grace Nail Johnson), p. 17.

P. 37. "In large measure the race question..." From James Weldon Johnson, *Along This Way: The Autobiography of James Weldon Johnson* (New York: Viking Press, Inc. 1933, copyright renewed 1961 by Grace Nail Johnson).

P. 39. "Now, them Johnson gals is mighty fine gals..." Stetson Kennedy, *Palmetto Country* (1942; Boca Raton: reprinted by Florida A & M University Press, 1988), p. 240. Stetson Kennedy personally gave the version printed here to Gary Harmon in June 1992.

P. 39. "the nation's economic problem..." (p. 289); "$1,000 per pound ..." (p. 284); and "the single most important ..." (p. 289), Wyn Craig Wade, The Fiery Cross: The Ku Klux Klan in America (New York: Simon and Schuster, 1987).

P. 40. "...to infiltrate the hooded order..."; Stetson Kennedy to Gary Harmon, personal interview.

P. 40. "Beluthahatchee Bill, old Beluthahatchee Bill..." Stetson Kennedy, Ibid., pp. 271-272.

P.42. "I wrote a poem called..." From an interview with Charles Brock, "Pulitzer Winner's Roots Extend into Jacksonville," *The Florida Times-Union*, April 20, 1977.

P. 43. "I love living in Florida..." From a letter to Gary L. Harmon from Mary Freels Rosborough, April 2, 1977.

P. 43. "...interest in what may best be called the cultural side of medicine..." and "stored away deep in my mind..." Frank G. Slaughter, MD, "When the

Scalpel Sharpens the Pen," *The Journal of The American Medical Association*, Vol. 200, April 3, 1967, p. 19.

P. 44. "...historical events exactly as..." Frank G. Slaughter, Ibid., p. 21.

P. 45. "When I turned from medicine..." Frank G. Slaughteer, Ibid., p. 22.

P. 45. "My grandmother..." From a letter to Gary L. Harmon from O.Z. Tyler, July 2, 1977.

P. 47. "Even in its current degraded..." From Robert C. Broward, *The Architecture of John Henry Klutho: The Prairie School in Jacksonville* (Jacksonville: University of North Florida Press, 1983), p. 93.

P. 50. "For ourselves, we are getting reconciled..." Harriet Beecher Stowe, *Palmetto Leaves* (1873; reprinted Gainesville: University of Florida Press, 1968), p. 36.

P. 52. "...received not even an incivility..." From a letter to the *New York Tribune*, February 8, 1877, quoted in Mary B. Graff, *Mandarin on the St. Johns* (1953; reprinted Gainesville: University of Florida Press, 1963), p. 63.

P. 52. "...misguided by the feeling..." Mary B. Graff, Ibid., pp. 80-81.

P. 54. "When I was a child..." From Florida Pier Scott-Maxwell, *The Measure of My Days* (1979).

P. 55. "...my mother's family arrived in Florida..." and other Madeleine L'Engle quotations are from an April 6, 1977, letter to Gary L. Harmon.

P. 56. "At this time there was one road..." Margaret Seton Fleming Biddle, *Hibernia: The Unreturning Tide* (New York: Vantage Press, 1974), p. 32.

P. 57. "My novels are about me in one way or another..." and other James McLendon quotations come from a July 13, 1977, letter to Gary L. Harmon. Other McLendon information comes from "A Mountain Idyll," *Gold Coast of Florida* (June, 1977), pp. 34-35.

Chapter 2

P. 63. "First, we went to St. George Street..." Ring Lardner, *Gullible's Travels* (1917; reprint, University of Chicago Press, 1965), p. 65.

P. 64. "second home." Eugenia Price, "The St. Augustine Historical Society Library — My Second Home," *El Escribano* 14 (1977), pp. 39-43.

P. 65. "endeavoring to become..." *The Tatler*, February 18, 1905, p. 8.

P. 65. "an hotel..." Henry James, *The American Scene* (Bloomington, IN: Indiana University Press, 1968), p. 459.

P. 66. "so we had to stand..." *The Ring Lardner Reader*, ed. by Maxwell Geismar (New York: Scribner's, 1963), p. 48.

P. 66. "our greatest humorist..." Stanley J. Kunitz and Howard Haycraft, *Twentieth Century Authors* (New York: H.W. Wilson Co., 1942), p. 406.

P. 69. The "small house..." A.J. Hanna, *A Prince in Their Midst* (Norman, OK: University of Oklahoma Press, 1946), p. 72.

P. 69. "every dispute..." Ibid., p. 87.

P. 74. "after that other writers..." *The Van Wyck Brooks-Lewis Mumford Letters*, ed. by Robert Spiller (New York: Dutton, 1970), pp. 90-92.

P. 74. "I will unblushingly record..." Branch Cabell, *The First Gentleman of America: A Comedy of Conquest* (New York: Farrar & Rinehart, 1942), pp. 297-298.

P. 75. "But there is iron..." *The American Guide*, ed. by Henry G. Alsberg and others (New York: Hastings House, 1949), p. 866.

P. 77. "a thrilling story..." Review in *New York Times* (November 11, 1951), p. 14.

P. 77. "St. Johns County famous jail..." Paul Good, *The Trouble I've Seen* (Washington: Howard University Press, 1975), p. 78.

P. 80. "What I particularly like..." *The Letters of James Branch Cabell*, ed. by Edward Wagenknecht (Norman, OK: University of Oklahoma Press 1975), pp. 158-9.

P. 80. "One walk is good for a page..." Jane Quinn, "Wilder Walks, Writes at St. Augustine Beach," *St. Augustine Record* (May 16, 1940), pp. 1, 3.

P. 80. "St. Augustine Beach has been ideal..." Jane Quinn, *Minorcans in Florida: Their History and Heritage* (St. Augustine: Mission Press, 1975), p. 132.

P. 81. "the lack of simple courtesy..." *St. Augustine Record* (April 15, 1953), p. 2.

P. 81. "The nicest people..." *Atlanta Journal and Constitution* (September 11, 1977), p. 14.

P. 85. "he was quite young..." John Bemrose, *Reminiscences of the Second Seminole War* (Gainesville: University of Florida Press, 1966), p. 12.

P. 85. "It is surprising..." J.B. Priestley, *Trumpets Over the Sea* (London: Heinemann, 1968), p. 76.

P. 88. "The elder John D...." *The Autobiography of Will Rogers*, ed. by Donald Day (Boston: Houghton Mifflin, 1949), p. 178.

P. 88. "wandering off..." C.D.B. Bryan, *The National Geographic Society* (New York: Abrams, 1987), p. 121.

P. 89. "I'm so glad to meet you..." Edith Wharton, *A Backward Glance* (New York: Appleton-Century, 1934), pp. 110-111.

P. 90. "the most heroic act..." John F. Kennedy, *Profiles in Courage* (New York: Harper, 1961), p. 126.

P. 90. "historian with a paintbrush." Carleton I. Calkin, "James Calvert Smith: Historian With a Paintbrush," *El Escribano* 16 (1979), pp. 33-42.

P. 91. "claims power to heal..." *The New York Times* (October 6, 1901), p. 1.

P. 92. "The lighthouse of Mosquito Inlet..." Stephen Crane, *The Red Badge of Courage and Other Stories* (New York: Dodd, Mead, 1957), p. 107.

P. 92. "the best experience..." Ibid., p. 76.

P. 95. "Fans invented..." Gorton Carruth, ed., *The Encyclopedia of American Facts and Dates* (New York: Crowell, 1956), p. 415.

P. 95. "Jesus, I'm killed!" Robert W. Creamer, *Stengel: His Life and Times* (New York: Simon and Schuster, 1984), p. 87.

P. 96. "I don't know why..." *Daytona Beach News-Journal* (April 25, 1961).

P. 96. "We turned on a shower..." J.B. Priestley, *Trumpets Over the Sea* (London: Heinemann, 1968), pp. 1-3.

P. 97. "all the other boat owners..." Robert E. Hemenway, *Zora Neale Hurston: A Literary Biography* (Urbana, IL: University of Illinois Press, 1977), p. 296.

P. 99. "All this ridge..." William Bartram, *Travels of William Bartram* (New York: Dover, 1955), p. 134.

P. 100. "This was the spot..." Jacob Rhett Motte. *Journey Into Wilderness* (Gainesville: University of Florida Press, 1953), p. 152.

P. 100. "At New Smyrna..." John M. Schofield, *Forty-Six Years in the Army* (New York: Century, 1897), p. 19.

P. 101. "The son, Charles..." John McPhee, *Oranges* (New York: Farrar, Straus and Giroux, 1967), p. 95.

P. 101. "The waters..." Sidney Lanier, *Florida* (Gainesville: University of Florida Press, 1973), p. 135.

P. 102. "It is said that Mrs. Connor..." The *New York Times (June 11, 1927), p. 19.*

P. 102. "They live..." J.M. Hawks, "Volusia County Family Register," manuscript at Edgewater Public Library.

P. 103. "*A Canticle for Leibowitz...*" *Christian Century* (May 25, 1960), p. 640.

P. 103. "A remarkable..." *San Francisco Chronicle* (March 8, 1960), p. 27.

P. 103. "A member of..." *New York Times* (April 10, 1937), p. 19.

P. 107. My piece of land..." Stetson Kennedy, *The Klan Unmasked* (Boca Raton, FL: Florida Atlantic University Press, 1990), pp. 219, 267, 271, 272.

P. 108. "Poor Billy Bartram..." Francis D. West, "John Bartram and Slavery," *South Carolina Historical Magazine* 56 (1955), p. 116.

P. 109. "His mind retained its vigor..." Daniel G. Brinton, *Notes on the Floridian Peninsula* (Phildelphia: Joseph Sabin, 1859), pp. 71-72.

P. 109. "It is a very beautiful spot..." M.A. DeWolfe Howe, ed., *Home Letters of General Sherman* (New York: Scribners, 1909), pp. 17-18.

P. 110. "he showed us the spot..." William Cullen Bryant, *Letters of a Traveler* (New York: Putnam, 1850), p. 100.

P. 110. "very demurely walked up..." Lester B. Shippee, *Bishop Whipple's Southern Diary 1843-1844* (Minneapolis: University of Minnesota Press, 1937), pp. 69-70.

P. 110. "A more disgraceful..." George Ward Nichols, "Six Weeks in Florida" reprinted in Frank Oppel and Tony Meisel, eds., *Tales of Old Florida* (Secaucus, NJ: Castle, 1987), p. 95.

P. 111. "Good-by, and God bless you..." George Ward Nichols, Ibid.

P. 111. "a place formerly of some importance..." Sidney Lanier, *Florida* (Gainesville: University of Florida Press, 1973), p. 126.

P. 111. "state of complete mental demoralization..." Sir Thomas Beecham, *Frederick Delius* (New York: Knopf, 1960), p. 33.

P. 111. "it was then and there..." Gloria Jahoda, *The Other Florida* (New York: Scribner's 1967), p. 252.

P. 111. "it was there he found his soul." Clare Delius, *Frederick Delius: Memories of My Brother* (London: Ivor Nicholson & Watson, 1935), p. 83.

P. 112. "to an unknown splendor..." Glorida Jahoda, op cit., pp. 262-263.

P. 113. "Quite true, sir,..." Greville Bathe, *The St. Johns Railroad 1858-1895* (St. Augustine, 1958), p. 9.

P. 113. "the prototype..." Jackson J. Benson, *The True Adventures of John Steinbeck, Writer* (New York: Penguin Books, 1990), pp. 14-15.

P. 115. "War is hell." John Bartlett, *Familiar Quotations*, 15th ed. (Boston: Little, Brown, 1980), p. 579.

P. 116. "full of persons..." Patricia Clark, "A Tale to Tell From Paradise Itself," *Florida Historical Quarterly* 48 (January 1970), p. 273.

P. 116. "Florida's first serious historian..." George R. Fairbanks, *History and Antiquities of the City of St. Augustine, Florida* (1858, reprinted Gainesville: University Presses of Florida, 1975), p. lix.

P. 116. "One of the advantages..." A.J. Hanna, *Recommended Readings on Florida* (Winter Park, FL: Union Catalog of Floridiana, 1945), p. 23.

P. 116. "To the memory..." George R. Fairbanks, *History of Florida* (Philadelphia: Lippincott, 1871), p. v.

P. 116. "It was a pleasure..." Henry Benjamin Whipple, *Lights and Shadows of a Long Episcopate* (New York: Macmillan, 1899), pp. 15-16.

P. 117. "was perhaps, in all naval record..." Branch Cabell and A.J. Hanna, *The St. Johns: A Parade of Diversities* (New York: Farrar & Rinehart, 1943), p. 214.

P. 118. "an unusually pretty..." Harriet Beecher Stowe, *Palmetto Leaves* (1873; facsimile reprint, Gainesville: University of Florida Press, 1968), p. 265.

P. 118. "To see Palatka..." Wanton S. Webb, *Webb's Jacksonville and Consolidated Directory of the Representative Cities of East and South Florida 1886* (Jacksonville and New York: n.p., 1886), p. 336.

P. 118. "the Florida world..." Sidney Lanier, op. cit., pp. 127-128.

P. 119. "The wheel that squeaks the loudest..." John Bartlett, *Familiar Quotations*, 12th ed. (Boston: Little, Brown, 1950), p. 518.

P. 119. "When he heard..." David Nolan, *Fifty Feet in Paradise: The Booming of Florida* (San Diego: Harcourt Brace Jovanovich, 1984), p. 102.

P. 119. "A person's political preferences..." *St. Augustine Weekly News* (December 5, 1889), p. 8.

P. 121. "talked to me earnestly..." Leola Smith Young, *The Peniel Lighthouse: History of the Peniel Baptist Church (Peniel), Palatka, Florida 1852-1982* (published by the author, 1982), pp. 41-42.

P. 121. "The main industry..." *The Compass* (St. Augustine Record) (March 1, 1985), p. 3.

P. 122. "the most comprehensive and pungent indictment..." *Nation* (May 29, 1948), p. 608.

P. 122. "there has never been any memoir..." *Saturday Review of Literature* (May 29, 1948), p. 8.

P. 123. "Palatka was a suffocating place..." Pat Jordan, *A False Spring* (New York: Dodd, Mead, 1975), p. 264.

P. 124. "After I saw him..." David L. Porter, ed., *Biographical Dictionary of American Sports: Baseball* (New York: Greenwood Press, 1987), p. 334.

P. 125. "But it seems..." Mark Van Doren. ed., *Travels of William Bartram* (New York: Dover Publications, 1955), p. 97.

P. 126. "At Rollestown..." Mrs. Henry Ward Beecher, *Letters From Florida* (New York: Appleton, 1879), p. 76.

Chapter 3

P. 138. "Everybody should..." Rosemary Banks Harris, "Poet Lets Glory Take Its Time," *Orlando Sentinel* (December 5, 1989), pp. E3, 4.

P. 138. "the most important..." Joseph A. Fry, *Henry S. Sanford* (Reno, NV: University of Nevada Press, 1982), p. 174.

P. 139. "I was working..." Red Barber, *The Broadcasters* (New York: Dial, 1970), p. 57.

P. 141. "Author of 55 books..." From a publicity leaflet by Robert Newton Peck.

P. 142. "I was born..." Zora Neale Hurston, *Dust Tracks on a Road* (Philadelphia: Lippincott, 1971), p. 3.

P. 143. "They lived..." Anna Lillios, "Excursions into Zora Neale Hurston's Eatonville," in *Zora in Florida*, ed. by Steve Glassman and Kathryn Lee Seidel (Orlando: University of Central Florida Press, 1991), p. 14.

P. 143. "used to take a seat..." Hurston, op. cit., p. 45.

P. 146. "Associated with the literary life..." Noella LaChance Schenck, *Winter Park's Old Alabama Hotel* (Winter Park, FL: Anna Publishing, 1982), p.32.

P. 147. "the brightest..." Edwin Granberry, untitled and unpublished manuscript, "Granberry, Edwin," Rollins College Archives vertical file.

P. 147. "I went there..." Rex Beach, *Personal Exposures* (New York: Harper, 1940), p. 18.

P. 147. "faculty and students..." Ibid., p. 19.

P. 147. "Rollins College played a large part..." Hurston, op. cit. and also Maurice J. O'Sullivan, Jr., and Jack C. Lane, "Zora Neale Hurston at Rollins College," in *Zora in Florida*, ed. by Steve Glassman and Kathryn Lee Seidel (Orlando: University of Central Florida Press, 1991), pp. 130-145.

P. 148. "Some folks say..." Wilbur Dorsett, *A Song for Rollins*, unpublished manuscript, Rollins College Archives vertical file, "Dorsett."

P. 148. "I can never be drawn..." Robert Frost to Hamilton Holt, February 6, 1936. Letter in Rollins Archives.

P. 150. "For reading..." George Garrett, "My Two One-Eyed Coaches," in *The Best American Essays 1988*, ed. by Annie Dillard (New York: Ticknor and Fields, 1988), p. 143.

P. 150. "Garrett's father..." Ibid., p. 144.

P. 154. "Once a distinct town..." William Fremont Blackman, *History of Orange County, Florida*, reprint of 1927 edition (Chuluota, FL: Mickler House, 1973), pp. 186-187.

P. 158. "We would rather..." From an untitled publisher's brochure for Bill and Vera Cleaver.

P. 159. "The Singing Tower..." Don Blanding, *Floridays* (New York: Dodd, Mead, 1945), p. 99.

P. 160. "Florida is..." Maxwell H. Forrest, "Florida Sole Remaining Center of Sanity and Tolerance," *Tampa Sunday Telegraph* (January 31, 1926), p. 30.

Chapter 4

P. 169. "It is this 'streak of silver...'" C. Vickerstaff Hine, *On the Indian River* (Chicago: Charles H. Sergel, 1891), pp. 58-59.

P. 169. "...is not really a river..." Walter R. Hellier, *Indian River—Florida's Treasure Coast* (Coconut Grove, FL: Hurricane House, 1965), p. 1.

P. 178. "The Miami paper said..." Robert E. Hemenway, *Zora Neale Hurston — A Literary Biography* (Chicago: University of Illinois Press: 1977), p. 348.

P. 179. "We are a people..." Alice Walker, *In Search of Our Mother's Garden* (San Diego: Harcourt Brace Jovanovich, 1988), p. 92.

P. 179. "Fort Pierce was a little cracker town..." Jim Bishop, *A Bishop's Confession* (Boston: Little, Brown, 1981), p. 348.

P. 180. "Called out loudly..." Janet Hutchinson, *History of Martin County* (Hutchinson Island, FL: Martin County Historical Society, 1975), p. 199.

P. 180. "Their jungle scenery of cabbage palms..." Ernest Lyons, *My Florida* (Cranbury, NJ: A.S. Barnes, 1969), p. 93.

P. 186. "The Royal Poinciana Hotel..." Theodore Pratt, *That Was Palm Beach* (St. Petersburg: Great Outdoors Publishing Co., 1968) p. 19.

P. 187. "From one end of it to the other..." Ring Lardner, *The Ring Lardner Reader* (New York: Charles Scribner's Sons, 1963), p. 53.

P. 187. "There as nowhere else..." Henry James, *The American Scene* (Bloomington, IN: Indiana University Press, 1968), p. 449.

P. 190. "Architecturally..." Arthur Maling, *Loophole* (New York: Harper & Row, 1971), p. 55.

P. 193. "To Janie's strange eyes..." Zora Neale Hurston, *Their Eyes Were Watching God* (Urbana, IL: University of Illinois Press, 1979), p. 193.

P. 193. "It woke up old Okechobee [sic]..." Ibid., p. 234.

P. 194. "You either hate this swamp..." John Dufresne, *The Way That Water Enters Stone* (New York: Norton, 1991), p. 109.

P. 200. "Some bugs ate 'em." Elmore Leonard, *Cat Chaser* (New York: Arbor House, 1982), p. 10.

P. 201. "...a knight in slightly tarnished armor..." Linda Robertson and Joan McIver, *Miami Herald*, February 22, 1987, p. 1 BR.

P. 202. "Somebody came burbling..." John D. MacDonald, *The Lonely Silver Rain* (New York: Knopf, 1985), pp. 131-132.

P. 204. "It was a hard-metal trinity..." Cherokee Paul McDonald, *Blue Truth* (New York: Donald I. Fine, 1991), p. 1.

P. 208. "Someone has caught a hideous fish..." Edmund Skellings, *Showing My Age* (Gainesville: University Presses of Florida, 1978), p. 44.

Chapter 5

P. 222. "You used to..." Edna Buchanan, *Nobody Lives Forever* (New York: Random House, 1990), p. 124.

P. 222. "was struck by..." Asher Z. Milbauer, *Transcending Exile: Conrad, Nabokov, I. B. Singer* (Miami: Florida International University Press, 1985), p. 105.

P. 222. "despite his pessimistic..." Ibid., p. 106.

P. 223. "It is a wild..." Edna Buchanan, *The Corpse Had a Familiar Face: Covering Miami, America's Hottest Beat* (New York: Random House, 1987), p. 43.

P. 226. "to turn Florida sand into..." Helen Muir, *Miami, U.S.A.*, 2nd ed. (Miami: Pickering Press, 1990), p. 131.

P. 233. "he can afford a little culture..." *Antioch Review*, 46 (1988), p. 247.

P. 236. "There, on a writer's..." Marjory Stoneman Douglas with John Rothchild, *Marjory Stoneman Douglas: Voice of the River* (Sarasota: Pineapple Press, 1987), p. 190.

P. 237. "wasn't very good" and "was a terrible struggle..." Ibid., p. 202.

P. 239. "to give..." Howard T. Young, *Juan Ramón Jiménez* (New York: Columbia University Press, 1967), p. 5.

P. 239. "the fact..." Ibid., p. 41.

P. 240. "to attract..." Muir, op. cit., pp. 136-137.

P. 244. "in a clearing..." Lawrance Thompson and R.H. Vinnick, *Robert Frost, A Biography* (New York: Holt, Rinehart, and Winston, 1981), p. 490.

P. 244. "New England..." Reprinted in *Interviews with Robert Frost*, ed. by Connery Lathem (New York: Holt, Rinehart, and Winston, 1966), pp. 272, 274.

P. 244. "I am farming..." in *Robert Frost: Life and Talks-Walking* (Norman, OK: University of Oklahoma Press, 1965), pp. 311-312.

Chapter 6

P. 257. "Since the major part..." John Huston, *An Open Book* (New York: Knopf, 1980), p. 151.

P. 259. "I thought of finding..." *Something About the Author*, vol. 30 (Detroit: Gale Research Company, 1983), p. 225.

P. 261. "Perhaps no single piece..." James R. Warnke, *The Ghost Towns and Side Roads of Florida* (Boynton Beach, FL: Roving, 1978), p. 40.

P. 262. "We were the first..." *Ernest Hemingway Selected Letters 1917-1961*, ed. by Carlos Baker (New York: Scribner's, 1981), p. 421.

P. 262. "I would like..." Ernest Hemingway, "Who Murdered the Vets?" in *New Masses: An Anthology of the Rebel Thirties*, ed. by Joseph North (New York: International Publishers, 1969), p. 185.

P. 263. "It is sad to think..." Zane Grey, Foreword to *Salt Water Fishing* by Van Campen Heilner (New York: Knopf, 1943), p. 7.

P. 263. "This is one of the choicest places..." *Letters of Wallace Stevens*, ed. by Holly Stevens (New York: Knopf, 1970), pp. 224-225.

P. 263. "The railroad had folded..." John Dos Passos, *The Best Times* (New York: New American Library, 1966), p. 210.

P. 264. "I doubt..." Rachel Carson, *The Edge of the Sea* (Boston: Houghton Mifflin, 1955), p. 191.

P. 265. "In the first place..." *By-Line: Ernest Hemingway*, ed. by William White (New York: Scribner's Sons, 1967), pp. 237-238.

P. 268. "He was the biggest tourist attraction..." Dakin Williams and Shepherd Mead, *Tennessee Williams: An Intimate Biography* (New York: Arbor House, 1983), p. 321.

P. 272. "There is no sanitation." *The Letters of Robert Frost to Louis Untermeyer* (New York: Holt, Rinehart and Winston, 1963), p. 250.

P. 273. "To discourage visitors..." *By-Line: Ernest Hemingway*, op cit., p. 192.

P. 277. "Waldo [Pierce] set up his easel..." John Dos Passos, *The Best Times* (New York: New American Library, 1966), p. 216.

Chapter 7

P. 284. "Here is a unique..." John Kunkel Small, *From Eden to Sahara* (Lancaster, PA: Science Press, 1929), p. 114.

P. 285. "Mystery hovered..." Zane Grey, *Tales of Southern Rivers* (New York: Grosset & Dunlap, 1924), p. 47.

P. 286. "1. Suspect every man..." Stuart McIver, *Glimpses of South Florida History* (Miami: Florida Flair Books, 1988), p. 138.

P. 288. "The Barron River..." John Rothchild, *Up for Grabs* (New York: Viking Press, 1985), p. 23.

P. 288. "a dowager..." Ibid., p. 24.

P. 289. "Within a half-hour..." Alistair Cooke, *One Man's America* (New York: Knopf, 1952), p. 117.

P. 293. "A science fiction story..." Ron Marr, "Today's Tomorrow Is Yesterday," *Gulfshore Life* (Summer 1991), pp. 60-61.

P. 293. "Part of my motivation..." Janis Lyn Johnson, "Cooking Up Thrillers," *Gulfshore Life* (January 1989), pp. 143-144.

P. 294. "I write every day..." Lori Capulla, "Master of the Pine" *Gulfshore Life* (March 1989), p. 143.

P. 297. "One gets the sense of life..." Anne Morrow Lindbergh, *War Within and Without* (New York: Harcourt Brace Jovanovich, 1980), pp. 77-79.

P. 299. "sail away from the..." Harry T. Moore, *The Priest of Love* (New York: Farrar, Straus and Giroux, 1962), p. 213.

P. 299. "a small world..." Ibid, p. 230.

P. 304 "Thus was born my Hiawatha..." *The Poetical Works of Henry Wadsworth Longfellow* (London: George Routledge and Sons, 1869), p. 330.

P. 305. "...wild-looking individuals..." Frederic Remington, "Cracker Cowboys of Florida" in *Crooked Trails* by Frederic Remington (New York: Harper, 1898; reprinted as a facsimile by Bonanza Books, 1974), pp. 116-117.

P. 305. "The saloons outnumbered..." James R. Warnke, *Ghost Towns of Florida* (Boynton Beach, FL: Star Publishing Co., 1971), p. 54.

P. 308. "dreaded the thought..." Dick Glendinning, *A Host of Fridays* (unpublished pamphlet), pp. 15-17.

P. 308. "He was grand guru..." David Warner, "A Club For Liars," *Gulfshore Life* (March 1988), p. 55.

P. 310. "The Congo is not more different..." Carl Carmer, *Stars Fell on Alabama* (New York: Farrar & Rinehart, 1934), p. xiv.

P. 311. "about fifteen miles..." David Warner, "Borden Deal," *Cimarron Review* (January 1984), p. 58.

P. 313. "In his presence..." Glendinning, op. cit., p. 55.

P. 315. "Jolson didn't have..." Ian Hamilton, *Writers in Hollywood, 1915-1951* (London: Heinemann, 1990), pp. 38-39.

P. 317. "Willie loved living..." Joy Williams, *Breaking and Entering* (New York: Vintage Books, 1981), p. 8.

Chapter 8

P. 323. "The trend, in uncertain times,..." See the entry for Joseph Hayes. *Contemporary Authors* New Revision Series (Detroit: Gale Research Inc., 1990), Vol. 30, p. 188.

P. 324. "Cortez is a community..." Ben Green, *Finest Kind: A Celebration of a Florida Fishing Village* (Macon, GA: Mercer University Press, 1985), pp. 2-3.

P 329. "The Don Ce-sar..." F. Scott Fitzgerald, *The Crack-Up* (New York: New Directions, 1945), pp. 54-55.

P. 346. "Florida has everything..." *Tampa Tribune*, March 25, 1992, Baylife, p. 1.

P. 346. "The robin laughed..." *Poems of Sidney Lanier*, ed. by his wife (New York: Scribner's, 1915), p. 28.

Chapter 9

P. 351. "All summer long..." Erskine Caldwell, *With All My Might: An Autobiography* (Atlanta: Peachtree Publishers, 1987), p. 288. Other references to his Florida home are in *Conversations with Erskine Caldwell*, ed. by Edwin T. Arnold (Jackson, MS: University Press of Mississippi, 1988), especially John Dorschner, "Caldwell's Little Acre," pp. 148-154.

P. 351. "I'm not exactly a Southerner..." "An Interview in Florida with Erskine Caldwell," *Studies in the Novel*, vol. 3, no. 3 (Fall 1971), p. 331.

P. 352. "'the oldest continuous...'" William Zinsser, *Willie and Dwike: An American Profile* (Philadelphia: Harper & Row, 1984), p. 8; in that book see Chapter 2, "Dunedin," for more about Dwike's youth.

P. 354. About the drain-cleaning gator see Roger Racine, "Remember When an Alligator Cleaned Drains?" *100 Years and Growing*, Supplement to the *Tarpon-Palm Harbor Leader* (June 27, 1987), pp. 3-4.

P. 355. "north of New Port Richey..." Beth Dunlop, *Florida's Vanishing Architecture* (Sarasota: Pineapple Press, 1987), p. 85; reprinted in *The Florida Reader: Visions of Paradise From 1530 to the Present*, ed. by Maurice O'Sullivan, Jr. and Jack C. Lane (Sarasota: Pineapple Press, 1991), p. 246.

P. 355. "everything that we..." Alvar Núñez Cabeza de Vaca, *The Narrative of Cabeza de Vaca*, ed. by Frederick W. Hodge. In *Spanish Explorers in the Southern United States* (New York: Scribner's Sons, 1907); partly reprinted in *The Florida Reader*, pp. 25-28.

P. 356. "When Baltasar de Gallegos..." The Gentleman of Elvas, *The Narrative of the Expedition of Hernando de Soto,* ed. by Theodore H. Lewis; in *Spanish Explorers in the Southern United States* (New York: Scribner's Sons, 1907); partly reprinted in *The Florida Reader,* p. 31. See also Marjory Stoneman Douglas, "An Earlier Pocahontas," *The Reader's Digest,* November 1947, pp. 17-20.

P. 356. For "Ortiz's Mass" see Andrew Lytle, *A Novel, A Novella and Four Stories* (New York: McDowell, Obolensky, 1958); it was reprinted in *Florida Stories,* ed. by Kevin McCarthy (Gainesville: University of Florida Press, 1989), pp. 187-214.

P. 358. "I have been asked..." *Twentieth-Century Science-Fiction Writers,* ed. by Curtis C. Smith (New York: St. Martin's Press, 1981), p. 320.

P. 359. "By the propellers..." James Merrill, "Developers at Crystal River," in *Anthology of Magazine Verse,* ed. by Alan F. Pater (Beverly Hills: Monitor Book Company, 1981), p. 295.

P. 360. "The cracker..." *Florida: A Guide to the Southernmost State* (New York: Oxford University Press, 1939), p. 128.

P. 362. "At Cedar Keys..." Sidney Lanier, *Florida: Its Scenery, Climate, and History,* a facsimile reprint of the 1875 edition (Gainesville: University of Florida Press, 1973), pp. 98-99.

P. 362. "One day in January..." John Muir, *A Thousand-Mile Walk to the Gulf* (Boston: Houghton Mifflin, 1916), p. 143.

P. 363. "cursed the town..." Roger M. Thompson, "The Decline of Cedar Key: Mormon Lore in North Florida and Its Social Function," *Southern Folklore Quarterly* 39 (1975), p. 40.

P. 365. "The chieftain speaks..." Albery Whitman, *Twasinta's Seminoles* (1885; reprinted Upper Saddle River, NY: Literature House/Gregg Press, 1970), p. 83.

P. 366. "Major Dade..." Will McLean, "The Dade Massacre," *Florida Sand* (Earleton, FL: Lake & Emerald Productions, 1977), p. 64.

P. 366. "Leesburg, the county-seat..." George Barbour, *Florida For Tourists, Invalids, and Settlers* (New York: Appleton, 1882), pp. 49-50.

P. 367. "I'm makin' a road..." Langston Hughes, "Florida Road Workers," in Langston Hughes, *One-Way Ticket* (New York: Knopf, 1949), pp. 91-92.

P. 369. "Osceola afterward selected ten..." Sylvia Sunshine [Abbie M. Brooks], *Petals Plucked from Sunny Climes,* a facsimile reprint of the 1880 edition (Gainesville: University Presses of Florida, 1976), p. 98.

P. 370. The Ocklawaha is "the sweetest..." Sidney Lanier, *Florida: Its Scenery, Climate, and History* (Philadelphia: Lippincott, 1876), p. 20.

P. 371. "When I came to the Creek..." Marjorie Kinnan Rawlings, *Cross Creek* (New York: Scribner's Sons, 1942), p. 9.

P. 373. "though she was never completely happy..." Patricia Nassif Acton, *Invasion of Privacy: The Cross Creek Trial of Marjorie Kinnan Rawlings* (Gainesville: University of Florida Press, 1988), p. 144. The illustrator of the book is J. T. Glisson, who had been Rawlings's neighbor in Cross Creek.

P. 373. "'was closer to Cross Creek...'" Elizabeth Silverthorne, *Marjorie Kinnan Rawlings: Sojourner at Cross Creek* (Woodstock, NY: Overlook Press, 1988), p. 8.

P. 375. "Houses are individual..." Rawlings, op. cit., p. 368.

P. 376. "The extensive Alachua savanna..." *Travels of William Bartram*, ed. by Mark Van Doren (New York: Dover, 1955) p. 165.

P. 376. "A heavy mist..." Harry Crews, *The Hawk Is Dying* (London: Secker & Warburg, 1974), p. 33.

P. 377. "Living here in Gainesville..." Harry Crews, "Why I Live Where I Live," *Esquire* (September 1980), p. 47.

P. 377. "Enigma, Georgia..." Harry Crews, *The Gospel Singer* (New York: Morrow, 1968), p. 9.

P. 381. "Over in the Suwannee River country..." It is printed in its entirety in *The History of Gilchrist County* by Kevin M. McCarthy (Trenton: Historical Committee of the Trenton Women's Club, 1986), pp. 219-232.

P. 381. "Where Alph..." Samuel Taylor Coleridge, *Kubla Khan*, in *The Complete Poetical Works of Samuel Taylor Coleridge*, ed. by Ernest Hartley Coleridge (Oxford: Clarendon Press, 1912), p. 297.

P. 382. "A few hundred yards..." Richard Adams, *The Girl in a Swing* (New York: Knopf, 1980), p. 143.

P. 382. "As the water blooms..." Richard Eberhart, "Ichetucknee," in Richard Eberhart, *Florida Poems* (Gulfport, FL: Konglomerati Press, 1981), p. 26.

P. 385. "Whatever her final destiny..." Zora Neale Hurston, "The Life Story of Mrs. Ruby J. McCollum!" *Pittsburgh Courier* (May 2, 1953), p. 2. The ten-part series began in the Feb. 28, 1953 issue and continued in the March 3, March 14, March 21, March 28, April 4, April 11, April 18, April 25, and May 2 issues.

P. 386. "Suwannee County's record..." Robert Hawk, *Florida's Army: Militia, State Troops, National Guard, 1565-1985* (Sarasota: Pineapple Press, 1986), p. xxiv.

P. 387. "Martin Tabert of North Dakota..." Marjory Stoneman Douglas, *Voice of the River* (Sarasota: Pineapple Press, 1987), p. 135.

P. 388. "I was born on the rim..." Lillian Smith, "The Mob and the Ghost," *The Progressive* (December 1962), pp. 29-30.

P. 393. "I have written almost every known type..." Interview with Michael Shaara, *Contemporary Authors* (Detroit: Gale Research Co., 1981) vol. 102, p. 464.

P. 397. "When you go out onto a dock..." Jack Rudloe, *The Living Dock at Panacea* (New York: Knopf, 1977), pp. 11-12.

Chapter 10

P. 419. "more than he might..." Lucius and Linda Ellsworth, *Pensacola, the Deep Water City* (Tulsa, OK: Continental Heritage Press, 1982), p. 24.

P. 423. "is a small place..." Ellsworth, *Pensacola, the Deep Water City*, p. 42.

APPENDIX:
BOOKSTORES IN FLORIDA

Altamonte Springs

B & L Books
990 N. Highway 434

B Dalton Bookseller
451 E. Altamonte Drive

Battaglia's Books & Cards
995 N. Highway 434

Bookstop
303 E. Altamonte Dr.,

Cornerstone Institute
400 Maitland Ave.

Family Bookstores
451 E. Altamonte Dr.

Hammett's Learning World
303 E. Altamonte Dr.

Kingdom Connection
851 W. St. Rd. 436, # 1029

Reader's Market, K Mart
945 W. Hwy 436

The Source
110 N. Longwood Ave.

Waldenbooks
Altamonte Mall, Hwy. 434

Apopka

Battaglia's Books & Cards
2183 E. Semoran Blvd.

Love Gospel Christian Books
813 S. OrangeBlossom Trl

Stuff For Kids
522 S. Hunt Club Blvd.

Arcadia

Bomar N' Things
133 S. Desoto Ave.

T.L. McDonald Used Books
Hwy. 70, W.

Astor

Imagination Store
23835 SR 40

Atlantic Beach

Book Mark
299 Atlantic Blvd

Dragon's Tale
28 Seminole Rd.

Living Word Book Shop
469 Atlantic Blvd.

Tappin Book Mine
705 Atlantic Blvd

White's Books & Gifts
989 Atlantic Blvd. #B

Avon Park

Avon Park Book Exchange
22 E. Main St.

S. Fla. Comm. College
600 W. College Dr. Ext.

Babson Park

Webber College Cubbyhole
Alt. 27 S.

Bal Harbour

Doubleday Book Shop
9700 Collins Ave., #153

FAO Schwarz Book Dept.
9700 Collins Ave.

Kenneth R. Lawrence Gal.
1007 Kane Concourse

Williams Sonoma
9700 Collins Ave., #157

Bartow

Bartow Christian Books &
Gifts
326 E. Main St.

Booktraders Exchange
140 S. Wilson Dr.

Whatley's Pipe & Page
365 E. Main St.

Belleview

Book Warehouse
2109 SW Highway 484

In Goode Company, Inc.
5701 SE Abshier Blvd.

Nevers Martin J
5310 S. Pine Ave.

Rainbow Bible & Book Store

5906 SE Abshier Blvd.

Reader's Market, K Mart
10301 SE US Hwy. 44

Big Pine Key

Edie's Hallmark Shop
Big Pine Plaza

Boca Raton

B Dalton Bookseller
244 Town Center Mall

Better Bear
7050 W. Palmetto Prk Rd., #45

Book Store
21222 St. Andrews Blvd.

Bookstop
8903 Glades Rd. #15

Brentano's
402 Town Center Mall

Christian Supply Centre
4701 N. Federal Hwy

Chrysallis Connection
48 NE 1st Ave.

Dee's Candy 'n News
23014 Sandrift Plaza Dr.

HB Books at Crocker Ctr
5250 Town Center Cir

It's Academic
668 Glades Rd.

Learn, Inc.
9863 Glades Rd.

Liberties Fine Books
& Music
309 Plaza Real

Morning Star Christian
Supply
370 SW 3rd St.

New Beginnings in Christ
Delmar Shopping Vlg.

New Shack
1375 W. Palmetto Park Rd.

Storylines, Inc.
658 Glades Rd.

Bonita Springs
Book Emporium
4415 Bonita Beach Rd.

Newsboy Bookstore
3300 Bonita Beach Rd.

Reader's Market, K-Mart
3470 Bonita Bch. Rd.

Boynton Beach
Amity Bookstore
4747 N Congress

B. Dalton Bookseller
901 Congress Ave.

Boynton Book Exchange
1403 W Boynton Beach Blvd.

Reader's Market, K Mart
1606 S. Federal Hwy

Reader's Market, K Mart
9903 Military Trail

Vincentian Book Mart
10701 Military Trail

Waldenbooks
901 Congress Ave.

Bradenton
A Real Bookstore
6733 Manatee Ave., W.

Ace Book Exchange
4307 26th St., W

Amanda's Create-A-Book
3624 Lorraine Rd.

B Dalton Bookseller
Desoto Square Mall

Bookworm
2225 14th St., W

C&J Book Mart
4949 14th St., W

Club Video/Book World
3929 Manatee Ave., W

Desoto Nat. Mem. Bkst.
PO Box 15390

Garms Grady, Jr.
302 Old Main St.

Little Professor Book Center
4657 Cortez Rd., W

Love Works
Desoto Square Mall #939

Manatee Comm. College.
  Lancer Shop
5840 26th St., W

One Books
302 Old Main St.

Reader's Market, K Mart,
4124 14th St., W

Reader's Market, K Mart
7412 Manatee Ave., W.

Religious Book & Supply
  Center
5203 Cortez Rd., W

School Days
3213 Manatee Ave., W

Second Reading
5227 14th St., W

Socolof Enterprises Book
  Dept.
PO Box 1987

Time Machine II
5748 14th St., W

Unity Church in Manatee
5700 Manatee Ave, W

Vineyard Book Store
Upper Manatee River Rd.

Vogt's Bible Book Store
4230 26th St., W

Waldenbooks
Desoto Square Mall

Brandon
All About Antiques
113 Brandon Blvd., E #G

Ave Maria Religious Supplies
815 E. Brandon Blvd.

Book Corner
113 E. Brandon Blvd.

Book Stall
606 Oakfield Dr.

Brandon Bookworld
1957 Lumsden Rd., W

Brandon Christ. Supply
322 W. Robertson St.

Brandon Comic Shoppe
107 Beverly Blvd.

Hillsboro Comm. College
  Bookstore
1404 Tech Blvd.

Little Professor Book Center
869 E. Bloomingdale Ave.

New Life Books & Gifts
401 S. Parsons Ave., #G

New Life Books & Gifts
401 Parsons Ave., S

Reader's Market, K Mart
1602 W. Brandon Blvd.

Scriptura Inspirational
2020 W. Brandon Blvd.,

Brooksville
C & C Christian Supply Center
12995 Cortez Blvd.

North Campus Bkst.
11415 Ponce DeLeon Blvd.

Reader's Market
K Mart, 920 S. Sq. SR 577

Bushnell
Disciple Christian Book Store
221 N. Florida St.

Callaway
Reader's Market
K Mart, 225 S. Tyndall

Cape Canaveral
Mary-Dee's Books
8040 N. Atlantic Ave.

Cape Coral
Audio Library
1112 Cape Coral Pky, E.

Book Nook
909 Miramar St., #C

Book Store
2301 Del Prado Blvd., S.

The Canticle
4419 Del Prado Blvd., S

Cape Coral Book & Bible
1322 Cape Coral Pky, E

Christ Centered Book & Music
1119 Del Prado Blvd.

Dave Mattson Nautical Books
PO Box 803

Reader's Market
K Mart, Del Prado Blvd.

Rip-Lin Paperback
  Exchange
2942 Del Prado Blvd., S.

Cassadaga
Cassadaga Spiritualist Camp
1112 Stevens St.

Purple Rose Trading Co.
1097 Stevens St.

Universal Centre of
Cassadaga
460 Cassadaga Rd.

Casselberry
Book & Bible Shop
5600 S. US Hwy 17

Bookstop
Hwy 436

Encyclopedia Britannica
853 Semoran Blvd. #115

Harbar Book Exchange
916 E. Semoran Blvd.

Charlotte Harbor
Reader's Market, K Mart
4265A Tamiami Tr.

Chiefland
Artifacts
708 N. Main St.

Chipley
Main Street Christian
Depot
104 N 6th St.

Christmas
Brocket Books, Inc.
Box 164

Chuluota
Mickler's Antiquarian Books
Box 38

Clearwater
A Blue Moon Books
& Records
1415 Cleveland St.

Adult Book Store
6555 142nd Ave., N

B Dalton Bookseller
111 Countryside Mall

B Dalton Bookseller
20505 US Hwy 19 #257

Book Case
4900 E Bay Dr., #A

Book Cellar
16100 Fairchild Dr.

Book Fair
2570 Sunset Point Rd.

Bookland Outlet
15525 US 19, S.

Bookstop, Inc.
2541 Countryside Blvd, #5

Camelot Books & Games

2907 State Rd. 590 #5

Clearwater Christian
College Bkst.
3400 Gulf to Bay Blvd.

Cokesbury Books & Church
2781 Gulf to Bay Blvd.

D & S Publishers
2030 Calumet St.

D D's Book Nook
1479 Belcher Rd., S

Downtown Newsstand
522 Cleveland St.

Flightshops
St. Pete/Clearwater Airport

Follett's St. Pete Book Store
2465 Drew St.

Hammett's Learning World
15579 US Hwy 19 N

Jacobsen Stores, Inc.
2522 McMullen Booth Rd.

Love Shop
Countryside Mall

The Midnight Bookman
2908 Seagull Dr.

Paperback Palace Book Outlets
26948 US Hwy 19, N

Paperback Palace, Inc.
1293 S. Missouri Ave.

Reader's Market, K Mart
136 Clearwater Mall

Reader's Market, K Mart
2130 Gulf to Bay Blvd.

Sandy's Bookmart
1000 Cleveland St.

Selective Books, Inc.
Box 1140

Sphinx Law Book Shop
1725 Clearwater Largo Rd.,

St. Pete Jr. Coll. Campus
Bookstore
2465 Drew St.

Tampa Christian Supply
1414 Missouri Ave., S

Thinking Cap
2601 US Hwy 19, N #819

Trinity Book Store
2235 NE Coachman Rd.

Unity Bookstore
2465 Nursery Rd.

Waldenbooks
Clearwater Mall

Waldenbooks
Countryside Mall #307

Waldenbooks
49 Sunshine Mall

Wilhite Collectibles
425 Cleveland St.

World Book-Childcraft
2271 Habersham Dr.

Clermont
Reader's Market
K Mart, 684 E. Hwy 50

Clewiston
Evangel Christian Book Store
350 S. Berner Rd.

Reader's Market, K Mart
955 Sugarland Hwy.

Cocoa
Barnes & Noble Bookstores
1517 Clearlake Rd.

Brevard Comm. Coll. Bkst.
1517 Clearlake Rd.

Little Professor Book
Center
1137 Byrd Plaza Mall

Real Unique Place
Collectors
226 King St.

Three Mystics Book Shoppe
216 Brevard Ave.

Cocoa Beach
Beach Cinema
150 E. Cocoa Beach Cswy

Book Nook
17 N. Orlando Ave.

Innervision Metaphysical
1980 N. Atlantic Ave.

Little Professor Book
Center
2041 N. Atlantic Ave.

Luke Four Eighteen
Christian
159 Minuteman Causeway

Rainbow New Age Books
275 E. Cocoa Beach Cswy

Rainbow New Age Books & Gifts
275 W Cocoa Beach Cswy

Surf Is Up Books & News
285 W. Columbia Ln

Coconut Creek
Athene, Inc.
2996 McFarlane Rd.

The Grove Bookworm
3025 Fuller St.

Waldenbooks
3399 Virginia St.

Coral Gables
Adolph's Readers World
166 Alhambra Cir

Agartha Secret City
1618 Ponce DeLeon Blvd.

Americana Bookshop & Gallery
175 Navarre Ave.

Books & Books Inc.
296 Aragon Ave.

Books & Records Plus
1815 Ponce DeLeon Blvd.

Gables Booksellers
222 Andalusia Ave.

La Moderna Poesia
5246 SW 8th St.

Softhouse, Inc.
1934 Ponce DeLeon Blvd.

Coral Springs
Belmore, Timothy & Nora
2365 NW 20th Ln.

Book Rack
9876 W Sample Rd.

Hammett's Learning World
9601 W. Atlantic Blvd.

Jacob's Ladder Christian
8249 W. Atlantic Blvd.

Lowe Art Music Shop
1301 Stanford Dr.

Parent Teacher Store
2067 University Dr.

University of Miami Bkst.
PO Box 148086

Waldenbooks
Coral Square

Crestview

Charlie's
101 Duggan Ave.

Crystal River
Book Nook
437 NE 1st Ter.

Cookin' Emporium
Crystal River Mall #557

Fisherman Bible Book Store
1151 NW Hwy 19

Reader's Market, K Mart
1801 NW Hwy 19

Tomorrow's Treasures
650 N Citrus Ave

Dade City
Book Shack
306 S 7th St.

Bread of Life Book Store
103 N 7th St.

Pasco Hernando Comm. College
E. Campus Bookstore
2401 County Rd. 41, N.

Dania
Dania News & Books
310 E. Danie Beach Blvd

Davie
Barrister's Books
4400 SW 95th Ave.

Davie Bookstore
4693 S University Dr

Encyclopedia Britannica
4801 S University Dr #5S

Gibson's Book Store South
3728 SW 64th Ave

I Am Books & Things
4290 S. University Dr.

Nova Books, Inc.
6508 SW 39 St.

Reading Tree
3514 S University Dr

Daytona Beach

Aero Supply, Inc.
1624 Aviation Center Pky

Angels and Dolphins Book Store
524 N Grandview Ave.

Atlantic News
2663 N. Atlantic

B Dalton Bookseller
Volusia Mall

Bethune Cookman College Bookstore
640 Second Ave.

BW Video News
308 Madison Ave.

Book Barn
2289 S Ridgewood Ave.

Book Rack
1132 Beville Rd., #C

Bookland of Daytona
2679 N. Atlantic Ave.

Bookland Outlet
2396 S. Ridgewood Ave.

Campus Stores-Florida
640 2nd Ave.

Christian Book & Gift Shop
2753 S. Ridgewood Ave.

Christian Book Nook
146 S. Beach St.

Daytona Beach Community Book
1200 Volusia Ave.

Embry Riddle Aeronautical Univ. Bkst.
600 S. Clyde Morris Blvd.

Mandala Books
204 Volusia Ave.

Reader's Market, K Mart
1300 Volusia Ave.

602 N Ridgewood Ave.
32114

Waldenbooks
Volusia Mall 32114

World of Books
5606 S. Ridgewood ave.

DeBary
Bible Book Center
78 S. US Hwy 17

Deerfield Beach
A New Choice Books & Gifts
601 S. Federal Hwy

The Book Rack
620 S. Federal Hwy

CLF Bookstore
747 S. Federal Hwy

Reader's Market, K Mart

3597 W. Hillsboro Blvd.

Robert Richshafer
Americana
1500 SE 3rd Ct., Ste 105

DeFuniak Springs
Book Store
102 E. Baldwin Ave.

DeLand
Atlantic News
101 N. Woodland Blvd.

Bread Basket
218 N. Woodland Blvd.

Family Book Shop
1301 N. Woodland Blvd.

Helikon Books, Inc.
112 S. Woodland Blvd.

Jabberwocky
113 W. Rich Ave.

Muse Bookshop
112 S. Woodland Blvd.

Reader's Market, K Mart
1201 S. Woodland Blvd.

Stetson University Bkst.
Box 8259

Delray Beach
Bushey's Religious Store
2401 N. Federal Hwy

Christian Supply Centre
328 E. Atlantic Ave.

Delray Mall Bookstore
1660 S. Federal Hwy.

Hand's Office Supply, Inc.
325 E. Atlantic Ave.

Pell's Books
2275 S. Federal Hwy #340

Postmark Pack & Ship Service
1336 N. Federal Hwy.

Reader's Market, K Mart
14539 Military Trail

Silver Cloud Antiques
840 E Atlantic Ave.

Deltona
Cornerstone Bibles & Books
2071 Saxon Blvd.

Jody's Shepherd Shoppe
2922 Howland Blvd.

Paperback Trader
1255 Providence Blvd.

Destin
Armchair Sailor Books &
Charts
546 Hwy. 98 E.

Bookland
4091 H Emerald Coast Pkwy

Jan's Book Nook East
Shores Shopping Center

Reader's Market, K Mart
761 E. Hwy 98

Dunedin
Abba Religious Specs, Inc.
1380 Pinehurst Rd.

Book Rack of Dunedin
2676 Bayshore Blvd.

Book Swap
2246 Main St.

The Learning Scene
1276 County Rd. 1

Oarhouse Marine Antiques
733 Edgewater

Sparky's Newsstand
1363 Main St.

Dunnellon
Book Depot
308 E. Pennsylvania Ave

Englewood
Barb's Book Stop
117 S. Indiana Ave.

Book Mark
560 Palm Plaza

Butterflies Christian Book
362 W. Dearborn St.

Dearborn Books Exchange
457 W. Dearborn St.

Eustis
Raintree Books
432 N. Eustis St.

Fern Park
The Book Scout
Box 300583

Intergalactic Comics
6205 S. US Hwy 17/92 #92

Reader's Market, K Mart
6735 S. US Hwy 17/92

Fernandina Beach
Alexanders
4850 First Coast Hwy

Book Loft
214 Centre St.

Harbour Lights
31 N 3rd St.

Mitchell's Books 'n Things
215 Centre St.

Reader's Market, K Mart
1525 Sadler Rd.

Fort Lauderdale
All Books & Records
420 E. Oakland Park Blvd.

All Books & Records
917 N. Federal Hwy.

All Kids Bookstore, Etc.
1947 N. Pine Island Rd.

Anonymously Yours
1940 E. Sunrise Blvd.

Arnold Hecht Book Store
1971 S. State Rd. 7

B Dalton Bookseller
2514 E. Sunrise Blvd. #K8

Bahia Mar Marine Store
801 Seabreeze Blvd.

Baptist Book Store
8219 W. Sunrise Blvd.

Bluewater Books & Charts
1481 SE 17th St.

Bob's News & Book Store
1515 S. Andrews Ave.

Book Emporium
52 W. Oakland Park Blvd.

Book Explosion Discount
2039 Wilton Dr.

Book Rack
1374 SE 17th St.

Book Rack
2703 E. Commercial Blvd.

Book Warehouse
12801 W. Sunrise Blvd., #331

Bookland-Inverrary
5535 W. Oakland Park Blvd.

Bookland-Southland
957 W. State Rd. 84

Books II
4238 N SR 7

Books Unlimited
8966 W. State Rd. 84

Bookstop
5975 N. Federal Hwy.

Broward Adult Bookstore
3419 W. Broward Blvd.

Broward Comm. Coll. Bkst.
3501 SW Davie Rd.

C R Book Nook, Inc.
3928 Davie Blvd.

Christian Book Store
1933 NE 4th Ave.

Christian Books & Gifts
4318 N. Federal Hwy.

Christian Family Book Store
3421 Davie Blvd.

Clark's Out of Town News
303 S. Andrews Ave.

Comic & Gaming Exchange
8432 W. Oakland Park Blvd.

Cornerstone Christian Gift
2452 Griffin Rd.

D M Burch Co.
2881 W. Sunrise Blvd.

Dangerous Ideas
2416 Wilton Dr.

Dragon's Lair Games
5108 S. State Rd. 7

Encyclopedia World Book
1392 N. University Dr.

Family Book Center
409 E. Broward Blvd.

First Baptist Church
301 E. Broward Blvd.

First Page Book Store & Gifts
2219 Wilton Dr.

Flightshops Aviation Books
2233 S. Federal Hwy.

Florida Atlantic Univ. Bookst.
Univ. Twr. 22d SE 2nd Ave.

Ft. Lauderale Coll. Bkst.
1040 Bayview Dr.

Glad Tidings Book Store
201 SW 38th Ave.

Medical Shop
7155 W. Oakland Park Blvd.

Museum of Art
One E. Las Olas Blvd.

The Nature Co.

2392 E. Sunrise Blvd.

New Age Books & Things,
4401 N. Federal Hwy.

North Terminal Book Shop
100 Terminal Dr., N.

Nova Law School Bkst.
3100 SW 9th Ave.

Omni Adult Bookstore
3224 W. Broward Blvd.

P F Collier, Inc.
2455 E. Sunrise Blvd.

Prospect News & Books
55 NE 44th St.

Pyramid Treasures
920 E. Las Olas Blvd.

Robert A Hittel Bookseller
3020 N. Federal Hwy. #6

Saint Michael & Santa
   Barbara
1609 N. State Rd. 7

Spanish Evangelical
   Literature
3585 NW 54th St.

Stellink Enterprises
4119 N. State Rd. 7

Sunny Side Up
2510 NE 15th Ave.

Trade-N-Save
The Bazaar

Waldenbooks
Broward Mall #816

Waldenbooks
2380 E. Sunrise Blvd.

Waldenbooks & More
3396 N. University Dr.

Western Union
8260 Sunset Strip

Williams Sonoma
2392A E. Sunrise Blvd.

Fort Myers

Armchair Sailor
13451-3 McGregor Blvd., SW

Audubon Nature Store
13499 US Hwy 41, S.

Bargain Books
2155 Andrea Ln.

Book Buffet

4901 Palm Beach Blvd.

Book Den South
2249 E. 1st St.

Book Rack
1704 Colonial Blvd.

Book Rack
5662 Bayshore Rd., #18

Book Trader
11601-4 S. Cleveland Ave.

Book Warehouse
2855 Colonial Blvd. #216

Bookstore at Cypress Lake
7101 Cypress Lake Dr.,

Campus Stores of Florida
8099 College Pky.

Christ Centered Book & Music
4650 S. Cleveland Ave.

Cover to Cover
16450 S. Tamiami Trl #6

Cypress Paperback Book
   Exch.
9541 Cypress Lake Dr., #5

Davis Neu, Inc.
5285 Summerlin Rd.

Downtown Bookshoppe
2218 First St.

Gilded Quill Bookshoppe
2219 Main St.

Gulfbreeze Bookstore
13499 S. Cleveland Ave.

Gulfshore Delights Cook-
   book
6296 Corporate Ct.

Ives Book Shop
Edison Mall Center

Jacobson Stores, Inc.
13499 US 41, SE

Kid's Connection
12995 S. Cleveland Ave.

Little Professor Book Center
15600-13 San Carlos Bl

The Parable, Inc.
5100 Cleveland Ave.

Planet Earth Book Center
1720 Colonial Blvd.

Publisher's Book Outlet
Metro Mall

Reader's Market, K Mart
3853 Cleveland Ave., S.

Reader's Market, K Mart
15271 33 McGregor Blvd.

Record Trader 1
3291 Cleveland Ave.

School Stuff
8595 College Pky.

Shakespeare, Beethoven &
Co.
1400 Colonial Blvd.

USF at Fort Myers
Edison Comm. College Bkst.
St. No. 171, PO Box 6210

Waldenbooks
4125 S. Cleveland Ave.

Fort Myers Beach

Beach Book Nook
7205 Estero Blvd.

MacIntosh Book Shop
17105 San Carlos Blvd.

Fort Pierce

B Dalton Bookseller
46 Orange Blossom Mall

Book Rack
2579 S. US Hwy. 1

Book Warehouse
2711 Peters Rd.

Christian World
2407 Okeechobee Rd.

Faith Baptist Church Book
Store
3607 Oleander Ave.

Indian River Comm. Coll.
Bookstore
3209 Virginia Ave.

Learning Center
2505 S. US Hwy. 1

Paperback Shack
800 Virginia Ave. #17

Reader's Market, K Mart
2111 S. Federal Hwy.

Wings of Joy
2407 Okeechobee Rd.

Fort Walton Beach

B Dalton Bookseller
300 Mary Esther Cutoff, NW

Book Harbour
246B N. Eglin Pky.

The Bookmaster
20 Oak

Book Nook & Hallmark Card
Shop
99 Eglin Pky, NE

Book Rack
29 Miracle Strip Pky, SW

Emmanuel Christian Books
126 Miracle Strip Pky, SE

Family Book Pack
22 Walter Martin Rd., NE

Gospel Lighthouse Center
62 Beal Pkwy., N.

K P M Publishing
318 Cloverdale Blvd.

Maison Le Cel, Inc.
176 Eglin Pkwy., NE

Playground Religious Center
109 Racetrack Rd., NE #G

Reader's Market, K Mart
201 Irwin, NE

Sword of the Spirit
511 N. Eglin Pky.

T B S Comics
550 Mary Esther Cutoff

Frostproof

Cole's Book Exchange
29 S. Scenic Hwy

Gainesville

B Dalton Bookseller
6275 W. Newberry Rd.,

Book Gallery, Inc.
1206 N. Main St.

Book Gallery West
4121 NW 16th Blvd.

Book Rack
1169 NW 78th Blvd.

Book Warehouse
2603 NW 13th St.

Book Warehouse
7205 NW 4th Blvd.

Bookland, Inc.
2540 NW 13th St.

Books
114 NW 13th St.

Builder's Bookstore
680 NE 23rd Ave.

Comics Plus
1117 W. University Ave.

Construction Bookstore,
1830 NE 2nd St.

Crossroads Bookstore
2720 SW 2nd Ave.

Displays for Schools, Inc.
PO Box 163

Eagle Books
2446 NW 13th Place

Flora & Fauna Books
PO Box 15718

Florida Book Store
1614 W. University Ave.

Florida School of Massage
5408 SW 13th St.

Gainesville Medical Books
2614 SW 34th St.

Goerings' Book Center
1310 W. University Ave.

Learning Path
2020 NW 6th St.

The Little Bookworm
244-19 NW 43rd St.

Love & Learn
6325 W. Newberry Rd.

Love Shop
6321 W. Newberry Rd.

Mike's Bookstore & Tobacco
116 SE 1st St.

Novel Ideas
3206 SW 35th Blvd.

Novel Ideas
804 W. University Ave.

Omni Books
99 SW 34th St.

Original Book Gallery
1206 N. Main St.

Philosophy Store
3460 W. University Ave.

Ray The Trader's 3 for Dollar
1710 SW 13th St.

Reader's Market, K Mart
2400 N. Main

Reader's Market, K Mart
900 NW 76 Blvd.

Unity of Gainesville

4451 NW 19th St.

UF Medical Bookstore
PO Box J263

UF Div. Continuing Ed. Bkst.
1223 NW 22nd Ave.

UF Gift Shop
J Wayne Reitz Union,
  Campus

University Book & Supply
1227 W. University Ave.

University Book & Supply
3700 NW 91st St.

Waldenbooks
6465 W. Newberry Rd.

Graceville

Florida Baptist Theo. Coll.
  Bookstore
1306 College Dr.

Gulf Breeze

Gospel Lighthouse Bible
  Book
3066 Gulf Breeze Pky.

Gulf Island Natl. Seashore
  Bookstore
1801 Gulf Breeze Pkwy

Herron-King Bookstore
913 Gulf Breeze Pky., #30

The New Age Shop
19 Harbourtown Shoppe
  Village

Reader's Market, K Mart,
3371 Gulf Breeze Pkwy.

World Book-Childcraft
Pensacola Beach Blvd.

Haines City

Landmark's KJV Bible
  Bookstore
2222 E. Hinson Ave.

Hallandale

Reader's Market, K Mart
1425 E. Hallandale Bch.

Z Z's Nespaper & Books
117 E. Hallandale Beach
  Blvd.

Hernando

Sue's Book Mart
2780 N. Florida Ave., #18

Hialeah

Bethany Bookstore
4200 W. 12th Ave.

Cervantes Bookstore
4008 W. 12th Ave.

Charlie's Comics & Games
1255 W 16th St.

Drago, Newton School
  Equip.
8205 W 20th Ave.

Fla. Adventist Bk. Ctr.
740 E. 25th St.

Libreria Betania
4200 W. 12th Ave.

New Perceptions
1460 W. 5th Ct.

Reader's Market, K Mart
1460 W. 49th St.

Waldenbooks
1625 W. 49th St.

Hialeah Gardens

Mi-World Supplies
9808 NW 80th Ave.

Hobe Sound

Florida Classics Library Book
12010 SE Dixie Hwy.

Hobe Sound Bible Coll. Bkst.
11305 SE Gomez Ave.

Holly Hill

Angels & Dolphins Book
  Store
1501 Ridgewood Ave.

Book Rack
1678 Ridgewood Ave.

University Bookstore
908 Ridgewood Ave.
Hollywood

Advantage Resources
1450 Sheridan St., #10

A/R G Shoppe, Inc.
2411 Johnson St.

Book Fair
5650 Stirling Rd.

Broward Comm. Coll. Bkst.
7200 Pines Blvd.

Christian Book Nook
1926 Tyler St.

Crystal Vision
5937 SW 21st St.

Florida Exam Bookstore
6750 Pembroke Rd.

Hollywood Book & Video
1235 S. State Rd. 7

Magical Forest, Inc.
5725 Hollywood Blvd.

Metaphysical Bookstore
2336 Hollywood Blvd.

Pete's Book Shelf
7140 Stirling Rd.

Reader's Market, K Mart
651 S. 60th Ave.

Trader John's Paperback
  Exch
2418 1/2 Hollywood Blvd.

Waldenbooks
Hollywood Fashion Ctr.

Waldenbooks
220 Hollywood Mall

Holmes Beach

Wm. W. Gaunt & Sons, Inc.
3011 Gulf Dr.

Homestead

Delk's Homestead
  Stationers
322 Washington Ave.

Fla. Nat. Parks and
  Monuments.
PO Box 279

Homestead Adult Book &
  Video
29005 S. Dixie Hwy.

Living Way Bible Book Store
442 Washington Ave.

Paperbacks Ink
27435 S. Dixie Hwy.

St. Leo College Ctr.
Bldg. 670 31st Mssq MSE,

Hudson

Books 'n Stuff
6924 Southwind Dr.

Reader's Market, K Mart
12412 US 19

Word of Life
PO Box 7345

Immokalee

Revelations Bookstore, Inc.
1402 New Market Rd.

Indialantic

Bud's Used Paperback
142 5th Ave.

Indian Harbor Beach

Reader's Market, K Mart
1942 Hwy A1A

Village Book Shoppe
250 E. Eaugally Blvd.

Indian Rocks Beach

Crystal Connection
1401 Gulf Blvd.

Inverness

Cornerstone Christian
Supply
440 Hwy. 41, S.

Jim & Mary's Out of Print Bks.
231 N. Robin Hood Rd.

Lena's Book Barn
105 W. Dampier St.

Paperback Paradise
1221 N US Hwy 41

Reader's Market, K Mart
1660 Hwy 41 N

The Top Shelf, Inc.
2617 E. Gulf to Lake Hwy

Islamorada

A to Z Beauty/Nutrition
81913 Overseas Hwy.

Four Winds
US Hwy 1 Mile Marker 82-1/2

Graton & Graton
PO Box 889

Jacksonville

Agape Christian Book Store
926-6 Dunn Ave.

Agape Christian Book Store
10601 San Jose Blvd. #206

Agape Christian Book Store
1066 Arlington Rd.

All College Book Rack
11292 Beach Blvd.

Archway Christian
Bookstore
1265 Penman Rd.

Audio Bookworm
3837 Southside Blvd. #8

Awareness Center
1003 Park St.

B Dalton Bookseller
Jacksonville Lndg.

B Dalton Bookseller
9501 Arlington Expy #169

Baptist Book Store
1320 Hendricks Ave.

Bill's Bookstore, Inc.
107 S. Copeland St.

Bolles School Student Store
7400 San Jose Blvd.

Book Bin
629 Cassat Ave.

Book Co.
10601-5 San Jose Blvd.

Book Mark
299 Atlantic Blvd.

Book Nook
4345 University Blvd., S.

Book Port, Inc.
14286-20 Beach Blvd.

Book Rack
1680 Dunn Ave.

Book Rack
3568 University Blvd., W.

Book Warehouse
3637 Philips Hwy #182

Bookland
Pablo Plaza

Bookland Gateway
4515 Roosevelt Blvd.

Bookland, Inc.
64 Regency Sq.

Bookland Stores, Inc.
12200 San Jose Blvd. #14

Bookland Stores, Inc.
1954 3rd St., S.

Books & Comics Unlimited
8713 S. Old Kings Rd.

Bookworld
7900 103rd St., #27

Chamblin Bookmine
4304 Herschel St.

Child Evangelism Fellowship
6316 San Juan Ave.

Christian Book & Supply
5020 Normandy Blvd.

Christian Teacher Visuals
6132 Merrill Rd., #8

Cummer Gallery Shop

829 Riverside Ave.

Duval News Management
5638 Commonwealth Ave.

Edward Waters College Bkst.
1658 King's Road

Episcopal H. S. Book Store
4455 Atlantic Blvd.

Family Bookstores
The Avenues

First Baptist Church
525 N. Laura St.

FL Comm. College at Jax
Bookstore
101 W. State St.

FL Comm. Coll. Kent
Campus Bookstore
3939 Roosevelt

FL Comm. Coll. No. Campus
Bookstore
4501 Capper Rd.

FL Comm. Coll. So. Campus
Bookstore
11901 Beach Blvd.

FL State Univ. Bookstore
Student Union Bldg. R127

Follett Corp.
101 W. State St., #1142

Ft. Caroline Nat. Mem. Bkst.
12713 Ft. CAroline Rd.

Gateway Books
4515 Roosevelt Blvd.

Gospel World, Inc.
2236 Soutel Dr.

Jacksonville Art Museum,
4160 Blvd. Center Dr.

Jacobson Stores, Inc.
9911 Bay Meadows

Jerry's Bookshop
917 N. University Blvd.

Jones College Bkst.
5353 Arlington Expwy

Ju Bil Books
1521 Atlantic Blvd.

Kemet House
4315 Brentwood Ave.

Little Professor Book Center
11250 St. Augustine Rd.

Master Sermon Library

7207 Sandy Bluff Dr.

McQuarry Orchid Books
5700 W. Salemo Rd.

The Nature Co.
10300 Southside Blvd.

Nefertiti Books & Gifts
5133 Soutel Dr.

New Covenant Ministry Bkst.
2361 Cortez Rd.

No. Jacksonville Christ. Bkst.
174 E. 43rd St.

Northside Christian Book
2938 Leonid Rd.

Old Book Shop
3142 Beach Blvd.

Paper Back Trade Mart
10578 St. Augustine Rd.

Parramore's, Inc.
3548 St. John's Ave.

Paxon Discount Christian
  Books
7010 Normandy Blvd.

Peb's Paperback Book
  Exchange
1537 Cesery Blvd.

Positive Living Book Ctr.
8820 Arlington Expy.

Progressive Baptist Bkst.
2003 W. Beaver St.

Reader's Market, K Mart
9600 San Jose Blvd.

Reader's Market, K Mart
3790 S. Third St.

Reader's Market, K Mart
7890 Normandy Blvd.

Reader's Market, K Mart
9824 Atlantic Blvd.

Reader's Market, K Mart
3435 Univ. Blvd., N.

Reader's Market, K Mart
4645 Blanding Blvd.

Reader's Market, K Mart
9459 Lem Turner Rd.

Reader's Market, K Mart,
5751 Beach Blvd.

Reddi Arts
2285 Kingsley

Reddi Arts
1037 Hendricks Ave.

St. Marks Bkst.
4129 Oxford Ave.

San Marco Bkst.
1971 San Marco Blvd.

Seminole News
3111 Mayhan Dr.

Seniors & Juniors, Inc.
11700-21 San Jose Blvd.

SHVH Psychic Book Shop
4154 Herschel St.

Tappan Book Mind, Inc.
705 Atlantic Blvd.

Tots to Teens Book Cellar
10950 San Jose Blvd. #40

Twice Loved Tales
6630 Beach Blvd.

US Govt. Prtg. Ofc. & Bkst.
Fed. Bldg., Rm 158
400 W. Bay St.

Univ. of North Florida Bkst.
4567 St. Johns Bluff Rd., S.

Waldenbooks
The Avenues

Waldenbooks & More
Regency Park

White's Books Cards & Gifts
1992 San Marco Blvd.

White's Books Cards & Gifts
4000 St. Johns Ave., #4

White's Books Cards & Gifts
9978 Baymeadows Rd., #3

Xeno's
103rd St. Walmart Plz.

Xeno's
39 University Blvd., N.

Jacksonville Beach
Light House
215 S. 4th Ave.

Jenson Beach
Aspirations
2003 NE Dixie Hwy.

B Dalton Bookseller
Treasure Coast Sq.

For Heaven's Sake Christian
1834 NE Jenson Beach Blvd.

Jensen Book Exchange
1880 NE Dixie Hwy.

New Creation's Christian
  Child
1333 NE Jensen Beach Blvd.

Waldenbooks
3152 NW Federal Hwy.

Juno Beach
Reader's Club of America
1223 US Hwy 1

Jupiter
ALM Associates
3264 Cove Rd.

Annie's Book Stop
6671 W. Indiantown Rd.,

Bodhi Books & Gifts
4050 US Hwy 1S, #314

Gideon's International
4546 County Line Rd.

Marks Used Books
6390 W. Indiantown Rd.

Teach of Jupiter, Inc.
1695 W. Indiantown Rd.

Key Largo
Book Nook
99603 Overseas Hwy.

Flamingo Books, Inc.
Mile Marker 99-5

Reader's Market, K Mart
101495 Overseas Hwy.

Key West
Alligator Adult Books
533 Duval St.

Book Rack
1114 Truman Ave., #A

Duval Books
817 Duval St.

Faith Baptist Church
255 Mars Ln.

Fla. Keys Comm. Coll. Bkst.
5901 W. College Rd.

Key West Classics Booksellers
PO Box 1368

Key West Island Bkst.
513 Fleming St.

Key West Video Connection
528 Duval St.

L Valladares & Son
1200 Duval St.

Lay Witness Bookstore
3708 N. Roosevelt Blvd.

Waldenbooks
Searstown Shopping Ctr.

Waldenbooks
2212 N. Roosevelt Blvd.

Kissimmee

Book Warehouse
2523 Old Vineland Rd.

Comic Books & Collectibles
615 N Main St.

Cornerstone
1700 N. Main St.

Fla. Bible Coll. Bkst.
1701 Poinciana Blvd.

Fla. Christ. Coll. Bkst.
1011 Osceola Blvd.

Old Town Carousel Books
Ste. 411 Old Town

Reader's Market, K Mart
2211 W. Irlo Bronson Hwy

Reader's Market, K Mart
2220 Irlo Bronson Hwy.

Universal Books, Inc.
1102 N. Bermuda Ave.

Waldenbooks
Dyer Square

La Belle

The Place
340 N. Bridge St.

Lake Buena Vista

White's of Lake Buena Vista
PO Box 22828

Lake City

Books Galore 'n' More
417 N. Marion St.

Lake City Comm. Coll. Bkst.
Rt. 3, Box 7

Lighthouse Christian Bkstr.
2717 W. US Hwy. 90

Reader's Market, K Mart
Rt 13, US 90, W.

Rowand's
315 N. Marion St.

Lake Mary

Reader's Market, K Mart

3639 Lake Emma Rd.

Lake Park

Garage Sale-Antiques
720 Park Ave.

Reader's Market, K Mart
1220 N. Lake Blvd.

Revelations - A New
Beginning
905 N. Federal Hwy.

Second Chapter Bkst.
1433 10th Street

Lake Placid

Book Exchange
206B Interlake Blvd.

Du Bey's Books Cards & Gifts
S Highlands Shpg. Ctr.

Emmanuel Bible Book Shop
125 US Hwy. 27, S.

Previously Owned Books
12 S. Main St.

Lake Wales

Christian Book Store
218 E. Park Ave.

Reader's Market, K Mart
201 W. Central Ave.

Warner Southern Coll. Bkst.
5301 Hwy. 27, S.

Lake Worth

Alla T. Ford Rare Books
114 S. Palmway Ave.

Amity Christian Bkst.
4745 N. Congress Ave.

Best Life Press
4281 10th Ave., N.

Book Rack
7328 Lake Worth Rd.

The Bookworm
4111 Lake Worth Rd.

Comics, USA
5883 Lake Worth Rd.

Happily Ever After
805 Lake Ave.

Harold's Adult Book Store
4266 Lake Worth Rd.

Jeani's Secrets New Age
Bkstr.
4469 S. Congress Ave.

Little Professor Book
Center
7151 Lake Worth Rd.

Main Street News
608 Lake Ave.

Martin B. Raskin Medical
Books
4349 Trevi Ct.

Narrative Enterprise
3939 S. Congress Ave., #106

Palm Beach Comm. Coll.
Bookstore
4200 Congress Ave.

Teach of Palm Beach County
3915 Jog Rd.

Trinity Christian Bkst.
7255 S. Military Trail

Two on a Shelf Book Shop
2521 N. Dixie Hwy.

Lakeland

Abacus Coin & Comic World
2088 E. Edgewood Dr.

B Dalton Bookseller
Lakeland Square Mall

Book Bazaar
2120 S. Combee Rd.

Bookmart-Lake Miriam
4740 S. Florida Ave.

Carpenter's Shop Bkst.
777 Carpenters Way

Chamberlin Natural Foods
98 S. Grove Park Center

Cornerstone Christian
Bookstr
1288 E. Memorial Blvd.

Family Bookstores
3800 US Hwy. 98, N.

First Church Religious
Science
2821 E. Skyview Dr.

Fla. Southern Coll. Bkst.
Columbia Way

Gospel Inn
4245 S. Florida Ave.

Lake Miriam Bookmart
4740 S. Florida Ave.

Lakeland Christian Supply
221 N. Kentucky Ave.

LVS Church Supplies
119 Allamanda Dr.

McKay Bay Adult Entrtn.
1071 US Hwy. 92, E.

Reader's Market
K Mart, 4275 US 98, N.

Remarkable Bookshop
1535 US Hwy. 98, S.

Schoolhouse, Inc.
2438 Azalea Park Rd.

Southeastern Coll.
  Assemblies
1000 Longfellow Blvd.

Southern Secrets
741 N. Wabash Ave.

Waldenbooks
3800 US Hwy. 98, N.

Land O' Lakes

One Stop Reading Center
21609 Vlg. Lakes Shpg Ctr Dr

Reader's Market, K Mart
SR 54, Collier Pkwy.

Lantana

Dawn's Daily Report
121 S. Third St.

Little Professor Bookstore
1593 W. Lantana Rd.

Past Present Future Comics
6186 S. Congress Ave.

Reader's Market, K Mart
1201 S. Dixie

Largo

Bee's Paperbacks
871 W. Bay Dr.

Books 'N Stuff
Largo Mall

Bookworm Store
2575 E. Bay Dr., #2

Charis Christian Book Store
12156 Ulmerton Rd., W

Comic Cave & Book
  Emporium
1610 Missouri Ave., N

Geppi's Comic World,
2200 E. Bay Dr., #203

Incredible Journey
12499 Seminole Blvd.

Lamp Ministries, Inc.

12546 Starkey Rd.

Learning Encounters, Too
7740 Starkey Rd.

Martha's Book Vineyard
12005 Indian Rocks Rd., S.

Merlin's Books
2200 E. Bay Dr., #203

Paperback Palace Book Outlets
12987 Walsingham Rd.

Pussy Cat Adult Bookstore
14100 66th St., N.

Reader's Market, K Mart
1000 Missouri Ave.

Reader's Market, K Mart
13100 66th St., N.

Lauderhill

Bookland Inverrary
5535 W. Oakland Park Blvd.

Under the Stars
1760 NW 38th Ave.

Reader's Market, K Mart
1010 NW 40th Ave.

Leesburg

Church Supply Center
606 W. Main St.

Lake Region Bible
  Book Store
900 North Blvd., W.

Lake Sumter Comm. Coll.
  Bookstore
5900 S. US Hwy 441

Reader's Market, K Mart
1715 N. Citrus Blvd.

Robinson Books & Clothing
  Outlet
1410 W. Griffin Rd.

Solar South
705 N. Blvd., W.

Waldenbooks
10401 US Hwy 441, S.

Lehigh Acres

Reader's Market
1209 W. Homestead Rd.

Lighthouse Point

Bookshelf, Inc.
2424 N. Federal Hwy #A

Lighthouse Pt. Bookstore
3650 N. Federal Hwy.

Live Oak

Reader's Market, K Mart
1522 S. Ohio Ave.

Longwood

Book Gallery
Longwood Village Shpg. Ctr.

Intergalactic Trading Co.
PO Box 1516

Jacobson Stores, Inc.
1855 St. Rd. 434

Legible Leftovers
706 N US Hwy 17/92 #92

Longwood Better Books &
  Gifts
909 E. Church Ave.

Spiritual Advisory Council
2965 SR 434, W., #300

Lynn Haven

Bread Basket Christian Books
1812 S. Hwy 77 #118

MacDill AFB

St. Leo College Center
PO Box 6063

Madeira Beach

Book Nook of Madeira
15029 Madeira Way

Books to the Ceiling
15170 Municipal Dr.

Madison

North FL Jr. College Bkst.
Turner Davis Dr.

Old Bookstore
112 W. Pinckney St.

Malabar

Warrior Books, Inc.
2005 Township Ave.

Marathon

Book Key Paperbacks
11300 Overseas Hwy

Food for Thought Bookstr.
5800 Overseas Hwy #23

Mid Keys Mar Spl.
  Marathon Co.
2055 Overseas Hwy

Reader's Market, K Mart
5561 Overseas Hwy

Marco

Book End
1000 N. Collier Blvd. #14

Create A Book
1415 Delbrook Way

Mark Hanks Bookseller
190 N. Collier Blvd.

Margate

Abundant Life Christian
  Bookstore
1490 Banks Rd.

Margate Card & Book Shop
5869 Margate Blvd.

Reader's Market, K Mart
560 SR 7

Marianna

Basford Christian Supply
642 E. Lafayette St.

Chipola Jr. Coll. Bkst.
3094 Indian Cir.

Old & Rare Book Shop
Hwy 90, E.

Southern Solutions
602 E. Lafayette St.

Reader's Market, K Mart
Rt. 5, Box 26, US 90

Mary Esther

B Dalton Bookseller
300 Mary Esther Cutoff

Black Perspectives Book
  Bazaar
217 Page Bacon Rd.

Bookland, Inc.
300 Mary Esther Cutoff

Crystal Center
251 Mary Esther Cutoff

Waldenbooks
251 Mary Esther Cutoff

Melbourne

Annie's Books
971 E. Eau Gallie Blvd.

B Dalton Bookseller
Melbourne Square Mall

Book Harbor
940 Pinetree Dr.

Bookery, Inc.
2045 S. Babcock St.

Books, Etc.
806 W. New Haven Ave.

Books-A-Plenty
1878 N. Wickham Rd.

Bookstop
1135 W. NW Haven Ave.

Brevard Art Ctr. Music Shop
1463 Highland Ave.

Brevard Community College
  Book
3865 N. Wickham Rd.

Chapter 1 Book Store
795 S. Wickham Rd.

City News & Books
901 E. New Haven Ave.

Cobweb Corner
323 N. Babcock St.

Family Bookstores
Melbourne Square Mall

FL Inst. Tech. Bkst.
Country Club Rd.

Health Nut Antiquarian Book
1916 Waverly Pl.

High Tide Books & News
3288 W. New Haven Ave.

Mustard Seed Christian
  Supply
1381 S. Babcock St.

Mustard Seed Kids
1381 S. Babcock St.

Paperbacks Galore
1702 N. Wickham Rd.

Reader's Market, K Mart
850 Apollo Blvd.

Shelf Bookstore
824 E. New Haven Ave.

Space Coast Science Center
PO Box 361816

St. Jos. Crafts
422 S. Babcock St.

Sun Rose Gift Shop
265 E. Eau Gallie Blvd

Waldenbooks
Melbourne Square Mall

Merritt Island

Big Boys' R C & Hobbies
45 E. Merritt Ave.

Bookland, Inc.
777 E. Merritt Island Cswy

Christian Book Store &
  Supply
405 S. Courtenay Pky.

R & D Smoke Shop
326 W. Merritt Island Cswy.

Reader's Market, K Mart
750 E. Merritt Is. Cwsy.

Shorin-RYU Karate USA
1755 S. Tropical Trl.

Waldenbooks
Merritt Square Mall

Waldensoftware
777 E. Merritt Island Cswy

Miami

A Kid's Book Shoppe
1849 NE Miami Gardens Dr.

Afro-In Books & Things
5575 NW 7th Ave.

Al's Newsstand
8219 SW 124th St.

All Books Unlimited
12133 S. Dixie Hwy

All the Write Stuff, Inc.
111 NW 1st St., #142

Almar Books
1672 NE Miami Gardens Dr.

Alms Book Store
13981 Biscayne Blvd.

Alpha Libreria
2710 SW 8th St

American Institute of Con-
  sumer
7326 SW 48th St.

American Mktg & Advg. Grp.
7326 SW 48th St.

Athene
2996 McFarland Rd.

Athene
6851 Bird Rd.

B Dalton Bookseller
Bayside Market

B Dalton Bookseller
Cutler Ridge Mall

B Dalton Bookseller
Omni International

B Dalton Bookseller
The Mall at 163rd St.

B Dalton Bookseller
1455 NW 107th Ave.

B Dalton Bookseller

19575 Biscayne Blvd.

B Dalton Bookseller
3015 Grand Ave.

B Dalton Bookseller
7525 N. Kendall Dr.

Bayside News
401 Biscayne Blvd.

Bible Bookstores, Inc.
662 NE 125th St.

Bible Center
9350 Miller Rd.

Book and Art Prints
4329 SW 8th St.

Book Barn Book Exchange
10597 SW 40th St.

Book Collection
7795 W. Flagler St.

Book Horizons
1110 S. Dixie Hwy.

Book Outlet
12155 Biscayne Blvd.

Book Review
1553 Sunset Dr., #J

Bookarama, Inc.
20279 Old Cutler Rd.

Book of Paige's
420 NE 125th St.

Books & Art Prints Store
4329 SW 8th St.

Books for Less
12558 N. Kendall Dr.

Books for Less
5753 SW 40th St.

Bookstop, Inc.
7710 N. Kendall Dr.

Bookworks, Inc.
6935 S. Red Rd.

Brandeis Used Book Store
850 Ives Dairy Rd.

Brentano's
Miracle Ctr.

Center Art Store
101 W. Flagler

Cervantes Bookstore
1891 SW 8th St.

Cervantes Libreria
1126 W. Flagler St.

Child Read
13619 S. Dixie Hwy. #129

Chosen Gift & Bookstore
7146 SW 117th Ave.

Common Market, Inc.
8400 SW 146th St.

Computer & Tech Books, Inc.
3900 NW 79th Ave.

Coral Comics
6791 S. Red Rd.

Cruising Books & Charts
2751 NE 2nd Ave.

Downtown Book Center
215 NE 2nd Ave.

Downtown Book Center
247 SE 1st St.

Durenda Koenig Bookseller
PO Box 248051

Educating Hands Bkst.
261 SW 8th St.

El Haitiano
7220 SW 8th St.

Encylcopedia Britannica
5805 Blue Lagoon Dr.

Fairchild Tropical Gdn.
  Bookshop
10901 Old Cutler Rd.

FL Intl. Univ. Bkst.
11000 SW 8th St.

AL Mem. Coll. Bkst.
15800 NW 42nd Ave.

Frank's Comic Book & Card
2678 SW 87th Ave.

Get Smart, Inc.
13724 SW 84th St.

Gordon's Books & Records
1815 Ponce DeLeon Blvd.

Grove Antiquarian
3318 Virginia St.

Grove Bookworm
3025 Fuller St.

Happy Adult Books
9514 S. Dixie Hwy.

Helen's Books
16640 NE 2nd Ave.

I Love Books, Inc.
4018 Royal Palm Ave.

It's Academic at Miami
1415 SW 107th Ave.

J & R Book & Video
7455 SW 40th St.

Jesus Fellowship
9775 SW 87th Ave.

Jim's Books & News
9364 SW 58th St.

Joe's News, Inc.
1549 Sunset Dr.

Jorey Sujam Enterprises
12174 SW 131st Ave.

Judaica Enterprises Gifts
1125 NE 163rd St.

Kendale Corp.
13351 SW 102nd St.

Keystone Book Center
12559 1/2 Biscayne Blvd.

Lambda Passages Bookstore
7545 Biscayne Blvd.

Land of the Brave Home of
  Free
19501 NW 2nd Ave.

Le Jeune Road Bookstore
928 SW LeJeune Rd.

Les Cousins Book & Record
  Shop
7858 NE 2nd Ave.

Libraria Alpha
2710 SW 8th St.

Libreri Mapou
5927 NE 2nd Ave.

Libreria Distribuidora
3090 SW 8th St.

Libreria Horeb
4750 NW 7th St.

Libreria Interamericana
2155 W. Flagler St.

Libreria Religiosa Distr.
21 SW 13th Ave.

Lisa Book & Video
14817 W. Dixie Hwy.

Little Haiti Books
113 NE 54th St.

Miami Christian College
  Bookstore
500 NE 1st Ave.

Miami Dade Comm. Coll.
  Bookstore
101 NE 4th St.

Miami Dade Comm. Coll.
  Bookstore
950 NW 20th St.

Miami Dade Comm. Coll
  Bookstore
11011 SW 104th St.

Miami Dade Comm. Coll.
  Bookstore
11380 NW 27th Ave.

Militant Labor Forum
137 NE 54th St.

Museum of Science Store
3280 S. Miami Ave.

New Testament Baptist
Church Christian Bkst.
6601 NW 167th St.

Omni Intl.
1601 Biscayne Blvd.

Open Books & Records
44 NW 167th St.

Palace Videos
190 NE 187th St.

Perrine Book & Video
18093 S. Dixie Hwy

Pot Pourri-Athene
13609 S. Dixie Hwy #152

Publications Exchange,
8306 Mills Dr., Ste. 241

Reader's Market, K Mart
8400 Coral Way 24, SW

Reader's Market, K Mart
Kendale Lk Shop Ctr.

Reader's Market, K Mart
750 Ives Dairy Rd.

Reader's Market, K Mart
3825 NW 7th St.

Reader's Market, K Mart
7900 SW 104th St.

Reader's Market, K Mart
11905 SW 152nd St.

Reader's Market, K Mart
19191 S. Dixie Hwy

Rex Art
2263 SW 37th Ave.

Rich Adult Book Store

180 NE 79th St.

Saeta Ediciones
310 Fontainebleau Blvd.

Science of Mind Garden
  Bookshop
7800 Sw 56th St.

South Dade Religious Str
17011 S. Dixie Hwy

Spiritual Center-Health
103 SW 17th Ave.

St. Paul Bk. Media Ctr.
145 SW 107th Ave.

St. Thom. Villanova U Bkstr
15400 NW 32nd Ave.

Sunshine Comics & Games II
18721 S. Dixie Hwy

Sunshine Comics & Games
7921 SW 40th St.

Trinity Cathedral Book Store
464 NE 16th St.

Tropic Comics South
742 NE 167th St.

UM Medical Bookstore
901 NW 17th St.

Unity on the Bay Bkst
411 NE 21st St.

Waldenbooks
Dadeland Mall

Waldenbooks
Omni International Mall

Waldenbooks
1648 NE 163rd St.

Waldenbooks
19575 Biscayne Blvd.

Waldenbooks
20505 S. Dixie Hwy

Waldenbooks
304 Miami Int.l Mall

Waldenbooks
3399 Virginia St.

Waldenbooks
8888 SW 136th St.

Waldenbooks & More
11190 N. Kendall Dr.

Walter Mercado Offices
7934 SW 8th St.

Westchester News

8859 SW 22nd Ave.

Whispers an Inner Journey,
2018 NE 184th St.

World Book Encyclopedia
420 S. Dixie Hwy

World Transport Press
1224 NW 72nd Ave.

Zenobia
1737 Coral Way

11711 Adult Book & Video
  Store
11711 Biscayne Blvd.

187 St. XXX Book & Video
14 NE 167th St.

6833 Bird Road Adult Book
6833 SW 40th St.

72nd St. Adult Book & Video
10494 SW 72nd St.

8080 Office Center, Inc.
8080 S. Flagler St.

Miami Beach
A Book A Brac Shop
6760 Collins Ave.

Bass Museum of Art Gift
  Shop
2121 Park Ave.

Books & Books, Inc.
933 Lincoln Rd.

Nat'l Hebrew Israel Gift Ctr.
7364 1st St.

Regency Book Svc.
337 Lincoln Rd.

Torah Treasures Dept. Str.
1309 Washington Ave.

The Tree of Life Books
1500 Bay Rd., Ste. 770

Miami Shores
Colossal Book Mart
9070 Biscayne Blvd.

Miami Springs
Aviation International
5555 NW 36th St.

The Olive Branch Bkst.,
270 Westward Dr.

Micanopy
O. X. Brisky Books
Chokalocka Blvd.

Milton

The Booklet
793 Hwy 90 E#A

Gospel Lighthouse Bible
Book
616 Hwy 90 W

PJC Bookstore
Hwy. 90

Reader's Market, K Mart
424 Caroline, SW

Miramar

Donna's Discount Books
6331 Miramar Pky.

Mt. Dora

Christian Book Inn
101 S. Highland St.

Reader's Market, K Mart
3100 New US Hwy 441, W

Southeast Bkst.
1755 New Hwy 441, Ste. 1

Way of Life Book Store
127 W. 5th Ave.

Naples

A Book Swap
4754 Golden Gate Pkg

Annie's Book Stop
3741 Tamiami Trl, E.

Aquarian Center Mind &
Body
5600 Tamiami Trl, N.

B Dalton Bookseller
1920 9th St., N

Book Exchange
2371 Davis Blvd.

Book Nook
824 5th Ave., S

Book Trader
170 10th St., N

Bookstore at the Pavilion
857 Vanderbilt Beach Rd.

Christ Centered Book & Music
2795 Davis Blvd.

Comic Warehouse
1029 Airport Rd., N #6

Edison Comm. Coll. Bkst.
7107 Lely Cultural Pkwy

Mycophile Books
PO Box 93

Mycophile Books
1800 Tiller Terrace

Reader's Market, K Mart
3701 Tamiami Tr., E.

Reader's Market, K Mart
4384 N. Tamiami Tr.

Song & Story Shop
659 5th Ave., S

Village Bookstore
4350 Gulf Shore Blvd., N.

Village Bookstore, Inc.
11196 Tamiami Tr., N.

Vineyard Book Store
4365 Tamiami Trl, N.

Waldenbooks
Coastland Ctr.

Wise Old Owl
854 Neapolitan Way

Your Local Bookie
4139 Tamiami Trl, N.

Your Local Bookie
4864 Davis Blvd.

Naranja

Reader's Market, K Mart
27455 S. Federal Hwy.

Neptune Beach

Reader's Market, K Mart
500 Atlantic Blvd.

New Port Richey

Annie's Book Stop
5620 Trouble Creek Rd.

Comics & Games
6320 Bank St.

Nu 2U Books & Puzzles
4924 US Hwy 19

Pasco Hernando Com. Clg.
Bkst.
7025 Moon Lake Rd. 587

Reader's Market, K Mart
5725 US 19

Reader's Market, K Mart
4134 Ltl. Rd.

Sandy's Books
7270 SR 54

Tampa Christian Supply
5748 Main St., E.

Village Book Exchange
4928 State Rd. 54

World Wide Gifts
6041 SR 54

New Smyrna Beach

Behren's Book Store
512 Canal St.

Bookland, Inc.
1944 St. Rd. 44

Christian's Book Store
91 N. Causeway

Irene's
1125 N Dixie Hwy

Reader's Market, K Mart
1724 St. Rd. 44

Sea Side Books
715 E. 3rd Ave.

Niceville

Bayou Book Co. Hallmark
1114 E. John C. Sims Pky

Okaloosa Walton Com.
College Bookstore
100 College Blvd.

Reader's Market , K Mart
1140 E. John Sims Pkwy.

Rocky Bayou Christian
Bookstr
2101 N. Partin Dr.

North Fort Myers

Book Trader
1846 N. Tamiami Trl.

The Bookworm
1027 N. Tamiami Trl.

North Lauderdale

Waldenbooks
1319 S. SR 7

North Miami

ABC Distribution
14445 NE 20th Lane

Arts & Sciences Bookstore
841 NE 125th St.

Bible Book Store
662 NE 125th St.

The Book Outlet, Inc.
12155 Biscayne Blvd.

Books for All Interests
841 NE 125th St.

Books of Paige's
420 NE 125th St.

Brandeis Book Store
850 Ives Dairy Rd.

Fla. Intl. Univ. Bookstore
NE 151 St. & Biscayne Blvd.

Reader's Market, K Mart
10700 Biscayne Blvd.

The Unicorn Village
Boutique
3575 NE 207th St

North Miami Beach
A Kid's Book Shoppe, Inc.
1849 NE Gardens Dr.

Almer Books
1672 NE Gardens Dr.

Family Educational Ctr.
1897 NE 164th St.

St. Bernard Gift Shop
16711 W. Dixie Hwy

Superheros Unlimited
1788 NE 163rd St.

Waldenbooks & More
1648 NE 163rd St.

World Wide News
1699 NE 163rd St.

North Palm Beach
Book Exchange
623 Northlake Blvd.

Brentanos
3101 PGA Blvd.

Catholic Store
8929 N. Military Trail

Jacobson Stores, Inc.
11700 US Hwy 1

Waldenbooks
Oakbrook Square

Oak Hill
Richard G. Uhl
PO Box 439

Oakland Park
Reader's Market , K Mart
670 E. Oakland Pk. Blvd.

Sonshine Books, Inc.
4861 N Dixie Hwy

Ocala
Book Nook
3221 NE Silver Springs Blvd.

Book Rack
3233 SE Moore Camp Rd.

Bookland of Paddock Mall
3100 SW College Rd.,

Central Florida Comm.
College
3001 SW College Rd.

Cosmic Connection
833 E. Silver Springs Blvd.

Crystal Beginnings
3820 E. Silver Spgs. Blvd.

Dayspring Christian Sply.
4901 E. Silver Springs Blvd.

Learning Wheel
2400 SW College Rd.,

Ocala Christian Supply
3131 SW College Rd.

Ray The Traders
121 NE 13th Ave.

Reader's Market, K Mart
3711 E. Silver Spgs Bl

Reader's Market, K Mart
2403 SW 27th Ave.

Waldenbooks
3100 SW College Rd.

White's Books Cards & Gifts
1915 E. Silver Springs Blvd.

White's Books Cards & Gifts
3444 NE Silver Springs Blvd.

World Book Childcraft
2014 SE 3rd Pl.

Ocoee
Duga's Books
610 Aldama Ct.

Okeechobee
Abba Christian Spl.
105 NE 4th St.

Conrad's Christian Supply
105 NE 4th St.

Elliott's
419 W. South Park St.,

Once Upon A Time Bkst.
1210 SW 2nd Ave.

Plaza Book Mark
3264 Hwy 441, S.

Reader's Market, K Mart
2780 Hwy 441, S.

Oldsmar
Reader's Market, K Mart
3140 Tampa Rd.

Opa Locka
Follet's St. Thomas Bkst

16400 NW 32nd Ave.

Hangar One Bookstore
15001 NW 42nd Ave.

Orange City
Patty's Paperbacks
238 E. Graves Ave.

Reader's Market, K Mart
810 Saxon Blvd.

The Right Way Family Bkst.
172 N. Industrial Dr.

Orange Park
Agape Christian Bkst.
700 Blanding Blvd.

B Dalton Bookseller
1910 Wells Rd.

Book Bin
2177 Kingsley Ave.

Book Rack
524 Kingsley Ave.

Christian Renewal Bkst.
2285 Kingsley Ave.

Dot's Used Book Store
731 Washington Ave.

Final Frontier Comics
418 Blanding Blvd.

For Heaven's Sake
Orange Park Mall

Heritage Book & Gift Shoppe
4325 Hwy. 17

Reader's Market, K Mart
380 Blanding Blvd.

St. Johns River Comm. Coll.
283 College Drive

Waldenbooks
44 Wells Rd.

Xenos
868 Blanding Blvd., S.

Orlando
Abbey Catholic Books & Gifts
2300 E. Robinson St.

Acorn Books
7230 W. Colonial Dr.

An Adv. In Novel Ideas
8445 S. Intl. Dr., #114

B Dalton Bookseller
268 Florida Mall Ave.

B Dalton Bookseller

3424 E. Colonial Dr.

Baptist Book Store
3208 E. Colonial Dr., #A

Benjamin Books
9328 Airport Blvd.

Book Gallery-Comics
6910 Silver Star Rd.

Book Nook
7627 S. Orange Blossom Trl.

Book Rack
6012 S. Orange Ave.

Book Warehouse
5281 W. Oak Ridge Rd.

The Bookery
1723 W Oak Ridge Rd.

Bookland Outlet
5401 W. Oak Ridge Rd.

Bookstop, Inc.
4924 E. Colonial Dr.

Canterbury Books
8001 N. Orange Blossom Trl.

Car Craft Gifts & Novelty
534 W. Church St.

Cartoon Museum
4300 S. Semoran Blvd.

Cathedral Bkst. & Gift
130 N. Magnolia Ave.

Christian Supplies, Inc.
3107 W. Colonial Dr.

Coliseum of Comics
4103 S. Orange Blossom Trl.

College Park Books
711 W. Smith St.

Cristo La Roca
955 W. Lancaster Rd. #3

Enterprise 1701
2814 Corrine Dr.

Family Bookstores
730 Sand Lake Rd.

FL Adventist Book Ctr.
PO Box 1313

Hiawassee Christian Bkstr.
2523 N. Hiawassee Rd.

Interprise 1701
2841 Corrine Dr.

It's Academic
12299 University Blvd.

Keane's Books
1233 W. Fairbanks Ave.

Logue Bible Bookstore
888 N. Orange Ave.

Long's Christian Bkst.
2322 Edgewater Dr.

Mid FL Tech. Inst. Bkst.
2900 W. Oak Ridge Rd.

Montsho Books, Etc.
2009 W. Central Blvd.

Murmur, Inc.
709 W. Smith St.

New Beginnings Christian
Bookstore
19 S. Semoran Blvd.

Orange Avenue News &
Tobacco
64 N. Orange Ave.

Orlando College Bkst.
5500-5800 Diplomat Cir.

Orlando Christian Center
Books
7601 Forest City Rd.

Orlando Mus. of Art,
Museum Shop
2416 N. Mills Ave.

Pine Hills Bible & Bkst.
6415 W. Colonial Dr.

Plaza News, Inc.
16 Colonial Plaza Mall

Read It Again Book Store
2749 N Hiawassee Rd.

Reader's Market, K Mart
2620 N. Hiawassee Rd.

Reader's Market, K Mart
1801 S. Semoran Blvd.

Reader's Market, K Mart
3228 E. Colonial Dr.

Reader's Market, K Mart
7602 Turkey Lake Rd.

Reader's Market, K Mart
7825 S. Orange Blossom Trl.

Reader's Market, K Mart
12151 E. Colonial Dr.

Sam Flax, Inc.
1401 E. Colonial Dr.

Shirley's Bible & Bkst.
329 E. Michigan St.

Spiral Circle, Inc.
750 N. Thornton Ave.

Troll Book Fairs
9777 Satellite Blvd.

Universal Books, Inc.
1712 Woolco Way

Universal Books, Inc.
2374 W. Oak Ridge Rd.

Universal Books-Plaza News
2650 E. Colonial Dr.

Univ. Cen. FL Bookstore
Box 25001

Valencia Comm. Coll. Bkst.
1800 S. Kirkman Rd.

Waldenbooks
Colonial Plaza Mall

Waldenbooks
3205 E. Colonial Dr.

Waldenbooks
3481 E. Colonial Dr.

Waldenbooks
8001 N. Orange Blossom Trl.

White's Book Store
12542 SR 535

Word of Life Christian Supls.
927 S. Goldwyn Ave., #1

Ormond Beach
Atlantic News
2663 N. Atlantic

Books & Comics
429 S. Nova Rd.

Cloak & Dagger Comics
154 W. Granada Blvd.

For Heaven's Sake
15 N. Ridgewood Ave.

Gladstar Bookshop
158 Cone Rd.

Osprey
Jacobson Stores, Inc.
1350 S. Tamiami Tr.

Oviedo
The Episcopal Book Shoppe
1601 Alafaya Tr.

Palatka
Andrea's Book Store
308 S. Hwy 19

Guide Post
117 N. 2nd St.

Joy Shop
104 N. 189h St.

Lori's
2401 Crill Ave.

Putnam Hobbies & Books
218 St. Johns Ave.

Reader's Market, K Mart
111 Town Country Dr.

St. Johns River Com. Coll.
  Bookstore
5001 St. Johns Ave.

Waldenbooks
400 N. US Hwy 19

Palm Bay
The Bookmark
4651 Babcock St., NE

Reader's Market, K Mart
160 Malabar Rd., SW,

Reader's Market, K Mart
4711 Babcock St., NE

Palm Beach
B Dalton Bookseller
150 Worth Ave.

Classic Bookshop
310 S. country Rd.

Doubleday Book Shop
228 Worth Ave.

FAO Schwarz Book Dept.
318 Worth Ave.

Main Street News
255 Royal Poinciana Way

Williams Sonoma
3101 PGA Blvd., #Q217

Palm Beach Gardens
The Nature Co.
3101 PGA Blvd.

Noah's Ark
3826 Northlake Blvd.

Past, Present, Future
  Comics
4270 Northlake Blvd.

Palm Harbor
Annie's Book Stop/West
  Union
35200 US Hwy 19, N

The Book Swap, Inc.
32840 US Hwy 19

Follett's St. Pete Bkst.
600 Klosterman Rd.

Haynes Better Books, Inc.
37748 US Hwy 19, N.

N. St. Pete Jr. College Bkst.
600 E. Klosterman

Paperback Trader
36271 US Hwy 19, N

Panama City
Ageless Book Shoppe
1090 Florida Ave.

B Dalton Bookseller
2202 N Cover Blvd.

Bahama Book & Pawn
13498 Front Beach Rd.

Bo Suns Gear
1006 Beck Ave.

Book Bin
1415 Gulf Ave.

Book Bin
5428 E. 15th St.

Book Nook II
109 Harrison Ave.

Book Warehouse
6646 W Hwy 98

Christian Book Store
1704 1/2 W. 23rd St.

Christian Book Store
233 N. Tyndall Pky

Cooper's News
474 Harrison Ave.

Family Bookstores
2246 N Cove Blvd.

Florida Health Foods Ctr.
886 W 11th St.

Friends Cnty Libraries
25 W. Government St.

Gospel Book & Gift Shop
2508 E. 5th St.

Gulf Coast Comm. Coll. Bkst.
5230 Hwy 98, W

Haney VoTech Ctr. Bkst.
3016 Hwy 77

Jack L. Wheeler Books
609 Granada Cir.

Money Haven, Inc.
11th St. Shopping Ctr.

Reader's Market, K Mart
7100 W. Hwy 89

Reader's Market, K Mart
1329 W. 15th St.

Waldenbooks
Panama City Mall

Pembroke Pines
Bible Book Shoppe
8383 Pines Blvd.

Goods News Variety Store
1740 N. University Dr.

St. Boniface Book/Gift
8330 Johnson St.

Volume One Books
158 N University Dr.

Pensacola
B Dalton Bookseller
5100 N 9th St.

B Dalton Bookseller
7171 N Davis Hwy

Bible Baptist Bookstore
1173 Jojo Rd.

Bobbee's Books
4807 Huron Dr.

Book Rack
324 S. Mini Mall

Book Rack
6927 N. 9th Ave.

The Bookrack
324 S Navy Blvd.

The Bookrack
6927 N 9th Ave.

The Bookstore
125 St. John St.

The Bookworm
509 E. Fairfield Dr.

Civil War Soldier's
  Museum
108 Palafox Pl.

Everyman Natural Foods
  Books
1200 N. 9th Ave.

Fairfield Christian Bkst.
4901 W. Fairfield Dr.

Family Bookstores
5100 N 9th Ave.

Farley's Old & Rare Books
5855 Tippin Ave.

Fiddlestix
4400 Bayos Blvd

Gospel Lighthouse Bible Book
1132 Creighton Rd.

Gospel Lighthouse Bible Book
310 N Navy Blvd.

Hammett's Learning World
8084 N. Davis Hwy

Hawsey's Book Index
803 N Navy Blvd.

King & Queen Books
PO Box 15062

Lemox Book Company
1014 Underwood Ave.

Liberty Christian Bkst.
8600 W US Hwy 98

Living Word
15 S. Palafox Pl.

Metaphysical Unity Bkst.
716 N 9th Ave.

My Bookstore
1200 N. Baylen St.

Nat. Mus. Nav. Aviation Flightdeck Mus. Shop
NAS Pensacola

Page & Palette Inc.
14110 Perdido Key Dr.

Pensacola Jr. College Bookstore
1000 College Blvd. #12

Pensacola Christian Campus
118 St. Johns St.

Quayside Thieves Market
712 S. Palafax St.

Reader's Market, K Mart
1650 Airport Blvd.

Reader's Market, K Mart
235 E. Nine Mile Rd.

Reader's Market, K Mart
4211 Mobile Hwy

Secondhand Prose Bkst.
1241 W Nine Mile Rd.

Seville Book Store
660 E. Government St.

Sincere Comics, Inc.
PO Box 8273

Some Like It South

3298 Summitt Blvd. #44

Sovereign Grace Christian Book
1220 E. Blount St.

Tree of Life Christian Bookshop
2 E. Nine Mile Rd.

Univ. West FL Bkst.
11000 Univ. Pkwy

Waldenbooks
7171 N Davis Hwy

Perry

Book Mart
Taylor Square Shpg. Ctr.

Country Christian Bkst.
2052 S. Jefferson St.

Reader's Market , K Mart
1057 S. Byron Butler Pkwy

Pinellas Park

B Dalton Bookseller
472 Pinellas Square Mall

Book Lover's
5915 Park Blvd.

Family Bookstores
402 Pinellas Square Mall

Health Sciences Bkst.
7200 66th St.

Quill & Clef Books
7301 55th St., N.

United in Spirit
4640 Park Blvd.

Uncle Al's United in Spirit
4640 Park Blvd., N.

Waldenbooks
Pinellas Square

Wolf's Newsstand
7620 49th St., N

Plant City

Christian Book Store
109 E. Reynolds St.

Dick & Jane Book Sellers
2214 J L Redman Pky

Hillsborough Comm. Coll. Bkst.
1206 N. Park Rd.

Thy Word and Music
1844 J L Redman Pky

Plantation

A B C Educational Sply.
1255 S SR 7

B Dalton Bookseller
321 N University Dr., #N6

Book Boutique
6945 W. Broward Blvd.

Bookstop
801 S. University Dr.

Brentano's
321 N. University Dr.

Child Read
801 S. University Dr.

Comics n' Stuff
6949 1/2 W Broward Blvd.

Historical Bookshelf, Ltd.
4210 SW 3rd St.

Tropic Comics, Inc.
313 S. SR 7

Tuck's Nutrition Shop
6921 W Broward Blvd.

Waldenbooks
816 Broward Mall

Williams Sonoma
321 N. Univ. Dr.

Plymouth

International Seminary Bkst.
PO Box 1208

Point Washington

Sundog Books
Seaside Ave.

Pomona Park

Carling's of Florida
PO Drawer 580

Pompano Beach

Adult Books
1700 N. Federal Hwy.

Adult Novelties
2500 N. Powerline Rd.

B Dalton Bookseller
Coral Square Mall

B Dalton Bookseller
Pompano Fashion Square

Book Market
1213 S. Ocean Blvd.

Broward Comm. Coll. Bkst.
1000 Coconut Creek Blvd.

Christian Way Book Store
251 SW 6th St.

Coral Springs Christian School
2251 N. Riverside Dr.

Divinity Religious Shop
230 S. Cypress Rd.

Giant Book Warehouse
1020 E. Sample Rd.

Hammett's Learning World
Beachway Shopping Ctr.

Jacob's Ladder Christian Ctr
8249 W Atlantic Blvd.

Parent-Teacher Store Division
2067 N University Dr.

Reader's Market, K Mart
2421 N. Federal Hwy.

Sonshine Books
2800 Gateway Dr.

Swinger Boutique
35 N Federal Hwy

Waldenbooks
Coral Square Mall

Waldenbooks
N. Fed. Hwy & Atlantic Blvd.

Waldenbooks
Pompano Fashion Square

Ponte Vedra Beach

Cookbook Center 870
Sawgrass Village

Mr. B's
880 A1A Hwy N

Port Charlotte

Book Trader Paperback Exchange
Charlotte Square

Gospel Gifts Christian Book
3786 Tamiami Trl.

Little Professor Book Center
Promenades Shopping Ctr.

Paper Pad
2811 Tamiami Tr.

Waldenbooks
1441 Tamiami Tr.

Waldman's
3642A Tamiami Tr.

Port Richey

Book Rack
6610 Ridge Rd.

Book Store at Jasmine Ctr.
10622 Devco Dr.

Bookland, Inc.
9409 US Hwy 19, N

Dial American Mktg.
6450 Ridge Road

Learning Station
10451 US Hwy 19

Paperback Exchange
8121 US Hwy 19

Waldenbooks
119 Gulf View Square Mall

Port St. Lucie

Bookstyles
9120 S. Federal Hwy

P S L Book Trader
6837 S Federal Hwy

Reader's Market
K Mart, 9022 S. US Hwy 1

Reader's Market
K Mart, 9500 S. US Hwy 1

Treasured Books
3227 SW Port St. Lucie Blvd.

Port Salerno

Florida Classic Lib. Bkst.
PO Box 1657

Punta Gorda

B Dalton Bookseller
1441 Tamiami Tr.

Bookshelf
1200 W Retta Esplanade

Charlotte Paperback
115 Tamiami Tr.

Esquire Videos & Books
1825 Tamiami Tr.

Waldenbooks
Port Charlotte Town Ctr

Reddick

Discovery Books
7350 NW 118th St., Rd

Rockledge

Reader's Market, K Mart
1501 US Hwy 1

Royal Palm Beach

Reader's Market, K Mart

10101 Southern Ave.

Ruskin

Ken & Sharon's Books
3026 SR 674

Safety Harbor

NTL Bookstore
105 N. Bayshore Dr.

Sanford

Kathy's Books & Baby Shop
211 E. 1st St.

Osborn's Book & Bible Store
2599 S Sanford Ave.

Reader's Market, K Mart
3101 Orlando Dr.

Seminole Comm. Coll. Bkst.
100 Weldon Blvd.

Sanibel

Island Book Nook
2330 Palm Ridge Rd.

MacIntosh Book Shop
1021 Periwinkle Way

Sanibel Island Bookshop
955 Rabbit Rd.

Sarasota

A. Parker's Books
1488 Main St.

Amen Corner Gospel Record
1864 Martin Luther King Way

Bargain Bookcase
6555 Gateway Ave.

Bee Ridge Books
4104 Bee Ridge Rd.

Book Bazaar
1532 Main St.

Book Nook
3650 Webber St., #A

Books Unlimited
5433 Fruitville Rd.

Books Unlimited
6260 N Lockwood Ridge Rd.

Books 4 Less
4880 S. Tamiami Trl

Brant's Used Books
3913 Brown Ave.

Campus Bookshop
6301 Tamiami Trl, N

Charlie's News
1341 Main St.

Christine's Books
1962 Main St., 3rd Fl.

Classic Books
107 Crossroads Shopping Plz

Daystar
2345 Bee Ridge Rd

Etc Old Book Shop
2250 Aspinwall St.

Ethnic Emporium
5637 Forest Lakes Dr.

Expressions of Love
3604 Webber St.

Gulf Gate Bookshop, Inc.
2222 Gulf Gate Dr.

Hadassah Resale Shop
3737 Bahia Vista St.

Helen's Bookstore
1531 Main St.

Hermit's Hearth Crystals
5212 Ocean Blvd.

Jacobson's Stores, Inc.
443 St. Armand's Cir.

Kingsley's Book Emporium
24 N Blvd of Presidents

Learning Depot
560 Town N Country Plz

Little Professor Book Ctr.
3466 Clark Rd.

Main Bookshop
1962 Main St.

New Life Ministries
2881 Clark Rd.

Osprey Books
3546 S Osprey Ave.

Our Lady's Garden
4930 Fruitville Rd.

Paperback Booksmith
Sarasota Square Mall

Pathways Unlimited
2041 Bahia Via

Patty's Paperback Bk
 Exchange
7509 S. Tamiami Trl.

Publishers Book Outlet
180 Gulf Gate Mall

Read All Over
1819 Main St., #107

Read All Over
2245 Bee Ridge Rd.

Reader's Market, K Mart
8191 S. Tamiami Tr.

Reader's Market, K Mart
3535 Fruitville Rd.

Reader's Market, K Mart
3941 Cattleman Rd.

Religious Book & Sply.
3123 S. Gate Cir.

South Trail Book Store
7338 S. Tamiami Tr.

Street Level Books
1668 Main St.

Tropicat
5023 Ocean Blvd.

Unity Church of Sarasota
800 Cocoanut Ave.

Waldenbooks
Southgate Plz

Waldenbooks
8201 S. Tamiami Tr.

Satellite Beach

Little Professor Book
 Center
1040 Atlantic Plz Shpg Ctr

Living Light ministries
1127 S Patrick Dr

Space Age Adult Books
63 Ocean Blvd

Sebastian

Discovery Book Store
16600 US Highway

Vita Village Natural Foods
8530 US Highway 1

Sebring

Bookland
901 Us Hwy 27

Center Book Exchange
113 S Ridgewood Dr

Dove Christian Book Ctr.
2183 US Hwy 27 N

Du Bey's Books Cards & Gifts
Southgate Shpg Ctr

Lighthouse Christian Book
 Store
Southgate Shpg Ctr

Reader's Market, K Mart

928S E. Lakeview Dr.

Seffner

Donna's Books
129 SR 574

Seminole

Book Emporium
7898 Seminole Mall

Brasser's Books
8701 Seminole Blvd

Gateway Books & Gifts
7879 Seminole Mall

Reader's Market, K Mart
7351 Seminole Blvd.

Shalimar

Bard's Tales Book Shoppe
1020 N. Eglin Pky

South Daytona

The Book Barn
2289 S. Ridgewood Ave.

Bookland Book Outlet
Daytona Outlet Mall

Christian Book & Gift Shop
2753 S. Ridgewood Ave.

South Miami Beach

A & M Comics & Books
6650 SW 40th St.

A Likely Story
5740 Sunset Dr.

South Pasadena

Reader's Market, K Mart
950 Pasadena Ave., S.

Trade A Book
6800 Gulfport Blvd.

Spring Hill

Book Fair
1225 Kasa Cir

Christian Book & Music Ctr
5135 Commercial Way

Reader's Market, K Mart
2468 Coml. Way

St. Augustine

All Books & Comics
1395 US Hwy 1, S

All Things Are Possible
212 SR 312

B Dalton Bookseller
1700 Volusia Ave.

Bettye's Baubles & Books

60 Cuna St.

Book Tank
3683 US Hwy A1A, S

Book Warehouse
2700 SR 16

Book Warehouse
51 Cordova St.

Booksmith
8 Cathedral Pl

Booktown
4085 Hwy A1A, S

Cathedral Bell Tower
  Religious
35 Treasury St.

Dream Street
64 Hypolita St.

Flagler College Book Store
31 Cordova St.

Ft. Matanzas Nat.
  Monument Bkst.
8635 A1A, S

Lighthouse Christian
  Outreach
900 Anastasia Blvd

Ray the Traders
Hwy 207, I95

Reader's Market, K Mart,
1777 US 1, S.

St. Augustine Historical
  Society
271 Charlotte St.

St. Aug. Paperback Book
  Exchange
224 San Marco Ave.

St. Johns River Com. Coll.
  Bkst
10 Hildreth Dr.

Waldenbooks
Ponce De Leon Mall

Wolf's Head Books
48 San Marco Ave.

St. Cloud
Book Nook
1118 New York Ave.

Harmony Video
2432 13th St.

St. Leo
St. Leo Coll. Bkst.
PO Box 2096

St. Petersburg
A-1 New & Used Bkst.
4733 66th St., N

Attic Bookshop
6601 1st Ave., S

B & L Books
4201 4th St., N

B Dalton Bookseller
Tyrone Square

Bay Campus Bkst.
140 7th Ave., S., COQ 101

Bayboro Books
121 7th Ave., S

Berean Christian Store
3993 Tyrone Blvd, N #402

The Book Rack
7127 Gulf Blvd.

Book Villa
6042 Haines Rd., N

Brigit Books
3434 4th St., N #5

Cathedral Book Store
355 2nd Ave., N

Central Ave. Adult Bkst.
1622 Central Ave.

Eckerd Coll. Bkst.
4200 54th Ave., S

Follett Regional Buyer
6700 7th Av.e, N

Fourth Street Book Store
6620 4th St., N

Gateway Books & Gifts
7991 Gateway Mall

Haslam's Book Store, Inc.
2025 Central Ave.

Interfaith Metaphysical Bkstr
1950 2nd Ave., N

Key Books
PO Box 21342

Lighthouse Books
1735 1st Ave., N

N. St. Pete Jr. Coll. Bkst
6700 7th Ave.

The Oriental Book Shelf
6940 9th St., S.

P.S. I Love You Personalized
800 2nd Ave., NE

Paper Palace of St. Pete
Disston Plaza

Paperback Palace Book
  Outlets
1159 82nd Ave. N

Paperback Palace Book
  Outlets
3725 49th St., N

Rae's Book Store
7110 5th Ave., N

Reader's Market, K Mart
2900 34th St.

Reader's Market, K Mart
3951 34th St.

Reader's Market, K Mart
4501 66th St.

Reader's Market, K Mart
9500 Ninth St.

Salvador Dali Foundation,
1000 Third St., S.

Dorothy Sullivan Books
PO Box 7045

Sunshine Book & Video
280 37th Ave., N

Tampa Christian Supply
1941 34th St., N

Temple of the Living God
  Bkst.
255 Beh Dr., NE

Tradeabook
6800 Gulfport Blvd. S #D

Unity Center of St.
  Petersburg
6168 1st Ave., N

Waldenbooks
Tyrone Square

Wilson's Book Store
2394 9th St., N

Wings of Light, Inc.
9629 Bay Pines Blvd

4th Street Adult Book Mart
1427 4th St., S

St. Petersburg Beach
Dolphin Book Nook
4667 Gulf Blvd.

Stuart
Arcade Book Nook, Inc.
23 SW Osceola St.

Book Rack
2293 SE Federal Hwy

Christian Book Store
816 S Dixie Hwy

Jolie's Books
1998 SE Federal Hwy

Leonardo & Co.
65 SW Flagler Ave.

Reader's Market, K Mart
5803 SE Federal Hwy

Reader's Market, K Mart
2160 SE Federal Hwy

Stuart Stitchery
2155 SE Ocean Blvd.

Unity Metaphysical Bkst.
658 SE Monterey Rd.

Waldenbooks
Martin Square Mall

Summerfield
Spiritual Advisory Council
14345 SE 103rd Terrace

Sunrise
Reader's Market, K Mart
8050 W. Oakland Pk. Bl

Sunny's at Sunset, Inc.
8260 Sunset Strip

Waldenbooks
3396 N. University Dr.

Tallahassee
Amen-Ra's Bookshop
1326 S Adams St.

B Dalton Bookseller
Governor's Square Mall

Bill's Bookstore Art City
107 S. Copeland St.

Books a Million
Parkway Center

Bookshelf
1303 S. Monroe St.

Christian Book Store
1834 Thomasville Rd.

Cosmic Cat
1907 W Pensacola St.

Cosmic Cat
220 W Tharpe St.

Du Bey's Books Cards & Gifts
1715 Apalachee Pky

Du Bey's Bookstore
2020 W Pensacola St.

Du Bey's News Center
115 S Monroe St.

Family Bookstores
1500 Apalachee Pky

FSU Bookstore
Stu. Un. Bldg. R127

FSU College Textbooks
FSU Box 66577

FL A&M Univ. Bkst.
Union Bldg.

Gateway Book Store
2415 N Monroe St.

Get Smart, Inc.
2030 Thomasville Rd., #5

House of Books
833 W Tharpe St.

It's Just a Matter of Crime
200 John Knox Rd.

Paperback Rack
2037 W Pensacola St.

Reader's Market, K Mart
1701 Apalachee Pkwy.

Reader's Market, K Mart
1700 N. Monroe

Reader's Market, K Mart
3521 Thomasville Rd.

Rubyfruit Books
666 W Tennessee St., #4

Seminole News & Books
3111 Mahan Dr. #15

Seminole News & Books
3491 Thomasville Rd.

Tallahassee Comm. Coll. Bkst.
446 Appleyard Dr.

Tallahassee Museum of Natural History
3945 Museum Dr.

Unity of Tallahassee
1630 Crowder Rd.

Waldenbooks
1500 Apalachee Pkwy

Waldenbooks
2415 506 N. Monroe St.

Tampa
Adult Book Store
4132 S 50th St.

All American
2411 E. Diana St.

B Dalton Bookseller
2009 Tampa Bay Ctr.

B Dalton Bookseller
2112 Univ. Square Mall

Baptist Book Store
14366 Dale Mabry Hwy N

Book Mart
3308 S Westshore Blvd.

Book Rack
5101 E Busch Blvd

Book Swap of Carrollwood
13020 N Dale Mabry Hwy

Book Warehouse
10019 N Dale Mabry Hwy

Bookland
6302 E. Buffalo Ave.

Books & More
4625 N. Lois Ave.

Bookstop
1251 B Fowler Ave.

The Bookworm
4556 S. Manhattan Ave.

Builders & Contractors Books
7207 N Nebraska Ave.

Christian Armory
15213 Dale Mabry Hwy N

Christian Armory
4812 E Busch Blvd #B

Comic Book Cafe, Inc.
6755 N. Armenia Ave.

Cosmic Book Center
9919 N US Hwy 301

Doubleday Book Shop
1604 W Snow Ave.

Encyclopedia Britannica
13540 N Florida Ave.

Extra Extra Newsstand
8436 W Hillsborough Ave.

Front Page Newsstand
11733 N Dale Mabry Hwy

Good News Bookstore

8620 Temple Terrace Hwy

Gratitudes, Inc.
1420 Waters Ave., W

Green Shift Discount
5226 N. Nebraska Ave.

Heart of the Rose
1955 W. M. L. King Jr. Blvd.

Heartsong Crystals, Inc.
3318 W Bay to Bay Blvd.

Hillsborough Adult Center
5421 W. Hillsborough Ave.

Hills. Comm. Coll. Bkst.
PO Box 30030

Hills. Comm. Coll. Bkst.
15th & Palm Ave.

Hometown Newsstand
1441 E. Fletcher Ave.,

Host Intl., Inc.
Tampa Int. Airport,

Hyde Park Book Shop
1109 W. Swann Ave.

Inwood Books
216 S. Armenia

Jacobson Stores, Inc.
1510 W. Swann Ave.

Just Books
2002 E. Fletcher Ave.

Barbara J. Kuchau, Bookseller
3405 W. Fielder St.

Leon's Books & Things
3803 N 29th St.

Little Professor Book Center
15203 Dale Mabry Hwy N

Little Professor Book Center
3667 W Waters Ave.

Love Shop
3302 W. Buffalo Ave.

Maida's Book Store
8204 W. Waters Ave.

Mary's Book Exchange
2507 W. Hillsborough Ave.

McFarland Books
112 N. Gilchrist Ave.

Merlin's Books
2307 S Dale Mabry Hwy

Merlin's Books
2568 Fowler Ave., E

Microcomputer Systems,
316 W. Cypress

Metaphysical Academy,
4112 W. Linebaugh Ave.

Metaphysical Academy,
5537 Sheldon Rd.

Monocle Book Shop
Tampa Intl. Airport

Monocle Book Shop
15744 N Dale Mabry Hwy

Palma Ceia News Stand
1155 S Dale Mabry Hwy

Paperback Shop
1824 W Waters Ave.

Pirate's Toy Chest
1914 S Dale Mabry Hwy

Publisher's Book outlet
Belz Factory Outlet

Ray's Lock & Key
5522 Hanley Rd., #112

Reader's Market, K Mart
2915 N. Dale Mabry Hwy

Reader's Market, K Mart
5400 E. Busch Blvd.

Reader's Market, K Mart
6714 Mem. Hwy

Reader's Market
8245 N. Florida Ave.

Reader's Market, K Mart
11311 N. Nebraska Ave.

Reader's Market, K Mart
12701 N. Dale Mabry Hwy

Reading Room
2106 Busch Blvd., W

Red Horse at Ybor Square
1901 N. 13th St.

Rhema Books & Gifts
2115 Univ. Square Mall

James Shelton Bookseller
2201 Dekle Ave.

St. Michael's Catholic Store
320 W Waters Ave.

Sign of the Fish
1728 S Dale Mabry Hwy

Tampa Antiquarian Books
6310 N Armenia Ave.

Tampa Christian Supply

2908 W Hillsborough Ave.

Tampa Libros
3608 N Armenia Ave.

Tampa Museum Store
601 Doyle Carlton Dr.

Three Birds Bookstore & Coffee
1518 E 7th Ave.

Tomes & Treasures
202 1/2 S. Howard Ave.

Univ. of Tampa Campus Bkst.
UT 616W N "B" St.

USF Bookstore
4202 E. Fowler Ave.,

U S F Medical Clinic
12901 Bruce B Downs Blvd, E

USF Tampa Book Center
4015 E. Fowler Ave.

University Book & Supply,
USF
4015 Fowler Ave., E

Waldenbooks
Eastlake Square Mall

Waldenbooks
Tampa Bay Center Mall

Waldenbooks
1475 E. Lake Square Mall

Waldenbooks
2262 Univ. Square Mall

Waldenbooks
254 Westshore Plz

Waldenbooks & More
13101 N Dale Mabry Hwy

Wise Book Swap
12937 N. Florida Ave.

Young Editions Bookstore
14308 N Dale Mabry Hwy

Your Book Nook Newsstand
3942 Britton Plz #B

Zack Street News
410 E. Zack St.

Tarpon Springs

First Amendment Adult Ctr
1342 Alt 19 N

Pussycat II
39468 US Hwy 19N

Reader's Market, K Mart
41232 US Hwy 19

Sandy's Bookmart
40964 US Hwy 19N

Tavares

Cornerstone Publications
389 W Alfred St.

Temple Terrace

Florida College Bookstore
119 N Glen Arven Ave.

Tequesta

Book Center & Art Center
171 N US Hwy 1

Book Nook
383B Tequesta Dr.

Jacob's Ladder
150 N US Hwy 1

My Book Place
124 Bridge Rd.

Nutrition World
150 N US Hwy 1 #23

Reader's Market, K Mart
500 US Hwy. 1, N.

Video Suite
133 N US Hwy 1

Titusville

Bookworm
333 S Washington Ave.

Brevard Comm. Coll. Bkst.
1111 N. US1

King's Christian Bookstore
3558 S. Hopkins

Merritt Is. Nat. Wldlf
  Refuge
Canaveral Natl. Seashore
2532 Garden St.

Reader's Market, K Mart
810 Cheney Hwy

Sunshine Health Foods
300 N US 1

Waldenbooks
2500 S. Washington Ave.

Warehouse Books
3405 S Washington Ave.

Valparaiso

American Opinion Bkst.
19 John C. Sims Pky

Bookshelf Discount Books
141 W John C Sims Pky

TBS Comics
481 E John C Sims Pky

Venice

Anderson's Paperback Book
2005 Tamiami Trl, S

The Bookshop
241 W Venice Ave.

Books Et Cetera
4145 Tamiami Trl, S

F D L Book Sale
101 Venice Ave., W

Good Stuff Antiques
223 Miami Ave., W #A

Moon Shadows
601 Cypress Ave.

Reader's Market, K Mart
1687 S. Bypass

Religious Book & Supply
1225 US Hwy 41, Byp S

Unity Church of Venice
125 N Jackson Rd.

Vernon

Inspiration Gospel Music
Star Rt., Box 113A

Vero Beach

B Dalton Bookseller
Vero Mall

Bakker For The Home
2855 Ocean Dr.

Foggy Notion Books
600 6th Ave.

Good Book & Religious Sply.
1705 20th St.

Paperback Place
1911 14th Ave.

Psychic Bookstore/Learning
Ctr
2237 14th Ave.

Reader's Market, K Mart
1501 US 1

Tropic Comics
1018 21st St.

Vero Beach Book Center
2145 Indian River Blvd.

Wings of Joy Book & Gift
Shop
1185 Old Dixie Hwy #A

Wauchula

With Love Christian Book
Store

113 N 7th Ave.

Wellington

Books of Wellington, Ltd.
12794 Forest Hill Blvd.

West Palm Beach

Art Mart
419 Clematis St.

Atlantic College Bkst.
PO Box 24708

Book Depot
1244 Royal Palm Beach Blvd.

Book Warehouse
5700 Okeechobee Blvd.

Brentano's
3101 P G A Blvd

Christian Bookstore
883 S Military Trl.

Cloud Lake Adult Books
1320 Southern Blvd.

Construction Bookstore
1800 Forest Hill Blvd.

Florida Exam Book Store
2424 N Congress Ave., #A

Golden Rule Christian Sply.
518 Northwood Rd.

Great American Book Co.
4356 Okeechobee Blvd.

Halsey & Griffith, Inc.
313 Datura St.

Howell's Religious Book &
  Gift
5909 S Dixie Hwy

Inspiration House Christian
4358 Okeechobee Blvd.

The Learning Plant, Inc.
PO Box 17233

Metaphysical Book Store
1957 S Flagler Dr.

Nature Company
3101 P G A Blvd

Nautical Booksellers, Inc.
295 Sixth St.

Ner Tamid Book Dist.
104 Lake Paula Dr.

Norton Gallery Store
1451 S. Olive Ave.

Past Present, Future Comics

4270 Northlake Blvd.

Rainbow Bridge
131 Clematis St.

Reader's Market
4346 Okeechobee Blvd.

Rubenfine, Joseph
505 S. Flagler Dr.

Shamballa
1195 N Military Tr.

Waldenbooks
1801 Palm Beach Lake S.
  Blvd.

Waldenbooks
2625 S Military Tr.

Waldenbooks
3101 P G A Blvd

Waldensoftware
1801 Palm Beach Lakes Blvd.

World Book-Childcraft
8895 N. Military Tr.

World of Paperbacks
1318 N Military Trl

45th St. Adult Book Store
5665 N Military Trl

Westville
Alec Allenson, Inc.
Rt. 1, Box 464

Wildwood
Green Parrot
200 N Main St.

Wilton Manors
Clergy Apparel & Supply,
2242 Wilton Dr.

Winter Garden
Country Boy's Motorcycles

900 Vineland Rd.
Reader's Market, K Mart
555 E. SR 50

Winter Haven
AAB Comics
Po Box 1996

Book Traders, Inc.
301 W. Central Ave.

The Bookworm
1080 Havendale Blvd. NW

Campus Stores of Florida
999 Avenue H, NE

Charlie's at the Mall
701 Winter Haven Mall

Charlie's News & Tobacco
8 4th St., NW

Christian Book Store
331 3rd St., NW

Du Bey's Books Cards & Gifts
1391 6th st., NE

King's Korners
323 1st St., S

Polk Comm.Coll. Bkst.
999 Ave. H, NE

Reader's Market, K Mart
2008 8th St.

Shangri-La Book Shop
100 Orchid Springs Dr.

Waldenbooks
Winter Haven Mall

Winter Park
Brandywine Books
114 E. Park Ave., S

Calvary Book Store
1199 Clay St.

Charles Billings' Books
200 St. Andrews Bl.

Downes T. Orvis Sporting
538 Park Ave., S.

Jacobson Stores, Inc.
339 Park Ave.

Living Word Ministry Bkst.
1316 Lindenwood Ln.

One On Earth
339 Park Ave., S

Park Books
342 Park Ave., S.

Pauline's Paperbacks
6728 Aloma Ave.

Pooh's Corner, Inc.
324 N. Park Ave.

Rainbow's Promise
2385 Aloma Ave.

Reader's Market, K Mart
501 N. Orlando Ave.

Reader's Market, K Mart
4000 Goldenrod Rd.

Rollins College Bkst.
PO Box 2739

Waldenbooks
Winter Park Mall

Waldenbooks
591 S. Semoran St.

Winter Springs
Reader's Market, K Mart
1425 Tuskawilla Rd.

Zephyrhills
Reader's Market, K Mart
7422 Gall Rd.

INDEX TO AUTHORS
AND PLACES